THE INDIVIDUAL IN HISTORY

The publication of this Festschrift
in honor of Jehuda Reinharz
has been made possible by the generosity of
Lester Crown, Martin Gross, Stephen A. Levin,
and Michael Steinhardt

THE
INDIVIDUAL
IN
HISTORY

Essays in Honor of Jehuda Reinharz

ChaeRan Y. Freeze, Sylvia Fuks Fried,
and Eugene R. Sheppard, editors

BRANDEIS UNIVERSITY PRESS | WALTHAM, MASSACHUSETTS

Brandeis University Press
An imprint of University Press of New England
www.upne.com
© 2015 Brandeis University
All rights reserved

Manufactured in the United States of America
Designed by April Leidig
Typeset in Warnock Pro by Passumpsic Publishing

For permission to reproduce any of the material in this book,
contact Permissions, University Press of New England, One Court Street,
Suite 250, Lebanon NH 03766; or visit www.upne.com

Frontispiece: Julian Brown, photographer, 1994.
End-of-book photo: Michael Lovett, photographer, 2007.

Library of Congress Cataloging-in-Publication Data
The individual in history: essays in honor of Jehuda Reinharz /
ChaeRan Y. Freeze, Sylvia Fuks Fried, and Eugene R. Sheppard, editors.
pages cm. — (Tauber Institute series for the study of European Jewry)
ISBN 978-1-61168-732-3 (cloth: alk. paper) —
ISBN 978-1-61168-733-0 (ebook)
1. Jewish leadership — History. 2. Jews — Politics and government.
3. Zionism — History. 4. Judaism. 5. Ideology. 6. Antisemitism.
I. Reinharz, Jehuda. II. Freeze, ChaeRan Y., editor.
III. Fried, Sylvia Fuks, editor. IV. Sheppard, Eugene R., editor.
BM729.L43I53   2015
296.6'109 — dc23   2014042798

5 4 3 2 1

CONTENTS

Part II. Statecraft

Part III. Intellectual, Social, and Cultural Spheres

Part V. In the Academy

THE INDIVIDUAL IN HISTORY

Introduction

❋

A solitary youth with dark wavy hair gazed out at the sea of curious faces in the auditorium of the Essen-Werden Gymnasium. Originally a Catholic school for training priests in the sixteenth century with its roots going back to the medieval monastery of St. Liudger, the institution came under the supervision of the Prussian state in 1803 and was designated a "higher Catholic rector's school." In 1906 it was converted into a city school and eventually became a regular gymnasium with a proud history of its illustrious past. It was at this historic school that sixteen-year-old Jehuda Reinharz, clutching a painstakingly researched paper, began to refute his history teacher's claim that the imputed criminality of the Nazis was overblown, for, after all, "only three and a half million Jews" died during World War II.

How a young Jewish teenager ended up delivering his first public speech before an entire German gymnasium still surprises Reinharz as he reflects back on his life. In many respects, that speech symbolized a turning point in a momentous life journey—one that took him from a carefree childhood in Israel to the strict gymnasia of Germany, where he first experienced the insidious sting of antisemitism and urgent beckoning of Zionism.[1] It marked a moment when Reinharz began to develop the personal qualities that would make him a future leader—some of the many traits he would come to identify in Chaim Weizmann, whose biography he undertook decades later: "stamina and tenacity, grasp of original ideas, clarity of thinking, adaptability to political situations, organizational abilities, [and] a penchant for synthesizing difficult and disparate concepts."[2] These formative years in Israel, Germany, and later America would shape the future of a prolific scholar who would devote his life to the study of German Jewry, Zionism, and antisemitism.

Jehuda Reinharz was born on August 1, 1944, in Haifa to German Jewish parents who had immigrated in the 1930s to Palestine with their respective families. His mother, Anita Weigler, grew up in a wealthy Orthodox Zionist family in Leipzig, a city that had prohibited Jewish settlement until the early nineteenth century, although Jewish merchants visited its major fairs regularly, contributing to its economic growth. This belated establishment of the community left an indelible mark on its character. According to one study, "the Israelitische Religionsgemeinde of Leipzig was a child of emancipation; it established itself from the outset as a distinctly liberal community and was administered in this spirit for decades by its German members."[3] The small minority of German Jewish residents initially maintained control over the Israelitische Religionsgemeinde, shunning the *Ostjuden*, who arrived in droves, initially as visitors to the fairs and later as refugees fleeing pogroms and wars; the latter had no right to vote in the community until 1923. Reinharz's grandfather Hermann Weigler was one of the impoverished Polish Jews in this stream of migration. Being religiously observant, he must have welcomed the appointment of Leipzig's first Orthodox rabbi Ephraim Carlebach (1879–1936) in 1924, which followed a lift on the ban on kosher slaughter in 1911 and the creation of a ritual bath just before World War I.[4] By the time the Third Reich came to power in 1933, approximately twelve thousand Jews were residing in Leipzig—a diverse and fractious population divided by class, religious denomination, and political affiliation.[5]

Reinharz recollects that his grandfather, who had become a successful businessman in Leipzig by the 1930s, crossed these rigid boundary lines: he was both a devout Orthodox Jew and a Zionist—"a rare combination in Germany" for the times. Reinharz's grandmother Leena Weigler had already traveled to Palestine with an entourage of domestic servants. After an exhilarating trip to Mount Carmel, which she described as the most beautiful place in the world, Leena impulsively purchased a house in the Haifa suburb of Kiryat Bialik, desiring to own a piece of the land. That decision would serve as their "exit visa" after Hermann lost his soda factory during the Nazification of Leipzig. The couple gained legal entry into Palestine by claiming truthfully at the British consulate in Berlin that they owned property in Haifa. Five of their children also settled in Palestine. Like other Jewish families during this chaotic period, the Weiglers experienced the trauma of separation from familiar surroundings in Germany.[6]

In contrast to Anita Weigler, his father, Fritz (Fred) Reinharz experienced a more acculturated upbringing: he attended the prestigious Humboldt Gymnasium in Essen, which was established as a city school in 1864. Essen, in contrast to Leipzig, began as a small agrarian town and developed into "an industrial city of coal and steel." The small Jewish community increased from 832 residents in the 1870s to 2,839 by 1912.[7] Like its Jews, the Essen synagogue, designed by local architect Edmund Körner in 1913, blended into "its surroundings rather than dominating them," despite its imposing and monumental size. An architectural critic praised the artifice for "not being too Jewish" in contrast to other synagogues that intruded into the "German skies."[8]

When the Nazis took over Essen in 1933, approximately forty-five hundred Jews were residing there. Despite his father's reticence about his past, Reinharz learned that he fled three years later, crossing illegally into Holland. A black-and-white photograph that Reinharz later discovered in a cabinet following his father's death showed a young gentleman dressed in an impeccable suit, illicitly crossing the border with a group of other (presumably Jewish) men. In Holland he forged connections with the Zionist movement, joining a *hakhshara* group and studying carpentry. He finally made his way to Palestine via Paris and Trieste.

The Reinharz home on Bezalel Street in Haifa was reminiscent of the Old World with its distinct European habitus: the family spoke German, read German books, and socialized with other German Jewish émigrés. Every day, after his father set off for work, Reinharz recalled racing to his grandparents' apartment across the street. He was especially attached to his grandfather, who was the solid anchor of the family: "Every Friday I would come to them for an early dinner. I would sit and talk with my grandfather. He spoke German, Polish, passable Hebrew, good Yiddish, and most important, he knew how to listen. You could tell him everything."[9] Outside their German Jewish home lay a different world, where the children romped freely in the beauty of nature. At the end of the street lay an expansive field, where they listened to the cadence of the Arab farmers walking with their donkeys. This carefree existence contrasted sharply with the strict discipline of the Alliance Israélite Universelle School in Haifa, where Reinharz received his early education.

Life in Israel proved to be arduous for the Reinharz family: Fritz, the gymnasium graduate, was forced to open a small one-truck delivery business to support his family. As Reinharz reminisced: "Both he and his brother stood day after day with their trucks in a small street between Hehalutz and Herzl Streets. During the 1950s and 1960s, the brothers had a small area among all the taxicabs, and whoever needed to deliver something came to the Reinharz brothers. [My father] also had other jobs and probably borrowed money from my grandfather in order to buy the small truck. To make a long story short: we hardly got by. There was never enough money in the house." To his family's dismay, the grueling hours and drudgery of work drove Reinharz's father to silence: "Every day the same thing, not talking, like some kind of suffering animal."[10] Frustrated with his menial, low-paying job and mounting bills, Fritz and Anita decided that their future lay elsewhere.

When efforts to immigrate to the United States failed, the family moved back to Germany in 1958 — back to his father's hometown of Essen. It was at the Humboldt Gymnasium (his father's alma mater), which was now located in a new building constructed by the architects Rolf Allerkamp and Wilhelm Eggeling on Steeler Straße, that the young Reinharz first experienced the sharp sting of antisemitism. Upon their introduction, the principal grimaced at the sound of his Jewish name and proposed that he adopt a more German-sounding name like Johann. "After all, you will be living in Germany," he reminded the new student. Undeterred by his father's pleas, Reinharz stubbornly insisted: "My name is Jehuda and that's it."[11] The situation deteriorated after his Latin class when a large boy blurted out: *"Du Judeschwein!"* (You Jewish swine!). Instinctively, Reinharz kicked the offender without considering the consequences, especially how his respectable father might respond. "Germany is a state of law," his principal reprimanded him severely. "Here no one takes the law into his own hands." The intransigent boy stood his ground, declaring boldly that he would respond exactly the same way if someone insulted him again. "In that case, you are suspended from school for two weeks," responded the principal, but Reinharz already had decided never to return.

That indignant teenager probably never imagined that at the turn of the twenty-first century the city of Essen would initiate a campaign to rename the school after a Jewish resident who was deported to a Riga concentration camp, where she perished during World War II. In 2001 the Humboldt Gymnasium had a new name — the Frida Levy Gesamtschule (comprehensive school), which promised to be a "school without racism, a school of courage." Its namesake Frida Levy (neé) Stern (b. 1881) was an ardent feminist who dedicated her life to the rights of working-class women, female suffrage, and pacifism through her participation in the International Women's Association for Peace and Freedom after World War I.[12]

Transferring to different schools brought no relief for the lone Jewish student in postwar German gymnasia in Essen. A watershed experience occurred at the Essen-Werden Gymnasium, when an anemic-faced history teacher claimed that the Nazis had not committed such terrible atrocities, especially with the death of *only* 3.5 million Jews. Unable to contain his outrage, Reinharz challenged this presentation of the war, violating all the etiquettes of proper German student-teacher relations. Untroubled, the teacher merely asked the agitated student to present a research paper in front of the class to support his claims, perhaps thinking this would intimidate the boy. Reinharz agreed to present his findings on the condition that he be allowed to do so in front of the entire gymnasium, which is where he found himself that morning.

Documenting the Holocaust proved to be both an academic and political challenge. As Reinharz undertook this serious research project in the late 1950s, he immediately confronted the paucity of sources; the cornucopia of Holocaust scholarship had not yet come into existence. Desperate, he turned to Dr. Hans Lamm, the cultural advisor to the Central Council of Jews in Germany (Zentralrat der Juden in Deutschland), who had received his doctorate from the University of Erlangen in 1951 based on his dissertation "On the Internal and External Development of German Jewry, 1933–45." This influential scholar, who later became the head of the Jewish community of Munich, not only assisted Reinharz by sending him pamphlets and brochures, but also referred him to the work of a number of scholars in Israel.

The challenge also propelled Reinharz to participate more actively in the Zionist youth movement in Germany. To be sure, Reinharz, who had imbibed his early Zionism from his grandparents, had been a member of the Zionist youth group Tsofim in Israel before he moved to Germany. His activities now took on a more urgent and intense character, however. He was one of a few teenagers who participated in early organizational efforts to create what became the Zionistische Jugend in Deutschland (ZJD), which was formally created in May 1960. From the start, Reinharz served as a counselor in the summer and winter camps in Germany, Austria, and Switzerland, honing his leadership skills. He also participated in writing articles for the movement's magazine, a task that sharpened his perspective on Zionism and Jewish history.

In 1961 the peripatetic Reinharz family moved to the United States and settled in Newark, New Jersey, where the high school senior met his future wife Shulamit Reinharz, who was born in Amsterdam. Her parents, who were also from Germany, had survived World War II in hiding in Holland. Upon graduating from high school, Reinharz studied Jewish and European history at the Jewish Theological Seminary of America, where he earned his BRE, and Columbia University, where he earned his BS. "I was on scholarship the whole time, every cent," he recalled, "but I also worked at various jobs, one of which was in a supermarket. To this day, I am a member of the Meat Cutters Union of America."[13] The recipient of the prestigious Five-Year Ford Fellowship, Reinharz completed his MA in medieval Jewish history at Harvard University in 1968.

The decision to pursue his doctorate at Brandeis University was influenced by the eminent scholars who dominated the Near Eastern and Judaic studies department, especially Benjamin Halpern, Alexander Altmann, and Nahum Glatzer, who would become his lifelong mentors, as well as Walter Laqueur, who taught in the Department of the History of Ideas. In 1970–71 Reinharz received the Woodrow Wilson Fellowship to conduct research for his dissertation in Germany and Israel. From the start, his scholarship on German Jewish emancipation, antisemitism, and Zionism gravitated toward iconoclastic young leaders and groups who exerted ideological, cultural, and even institutional influence far beyond their numbers in moments of crisis and transformation.

In his dissertation, which was revised and published as *Fatherland or Promised Land: The Dilemma of the German Jew, 1893–1914* (1975), Reinharz provided an account of how German Jewry grappled with antisemitism, postemancipation aspirations for integration, and nationalism (both German and Jewish). The lineage of fin de siècle responses to these challenges could be ascertained only by first tracking how organized German Jewish groups and representatives abysmally failed to defend their constituents. He vividly described the ominous mood of the mid-

1870s when radicalized conservative figures expressed deep criticisms of Bismarck's misbegotten liberalizing program in the wake of the Second Reich's recent victory over France, unification, and emancipation for all Jews in the empire. The Jews increasingly became a favorite scapegoat for the misfortunes of Germany. Thunderous accounts of the malevolent specter of Jewish domination emerged among populists, politicos, and renowned academics as well. The public landscape became permeated with not only virulent racial conspiracies offered by Adolf Stöcker and Wilhelm Marr (the founder of the Antisemitic League), but also academic writings in a more sophisticated guise by renowned historians such as Heinrich von Treitschke at the University of Berlin. Reinharz sought to understand how the dominant Jewish organizations in Germany were positioned to respond to this new threat. Based on extensive research, he found that protests articulated by liberal philosophers Moritz Lazarus (Berlin University) and Hermann Cohen (Marburg University) and the Jewish nationalist historian Heinrich Graetz were quite exceptional; for their part, the Jewish leadership offered only mild apologetics and simple defensiveness. To be sure, he argued, Theodor Mommsen and Johann Gustav Droysen garnered several signatories to condemn the antisemites, but the silence of the leadership left most German Jews completely disoriented and somewhat dumbfounded by the frequency and intensity of the assaults. Reinharz contended that the efforts of German Jews to "eradicate distinctions between themselves and their Christian fellow citizens had [paradoxically] reduced the Jewish community to a religious and social welfare-driven institution." So fearful were they of condemnations about separatism that the Jewish leadership was "reluctant to organize for any but philanthropic purposes, and as a result they had no effective organization of defense against the antisemites."[14]

Reinharz posited that in contrast to the established Jewish leadership, Jewish student organizations were crucial for forging an independent political path of defense. German student societies and fraternities (*Burschenschaften*) proved to be the inspiration for the greatest ferment of Jewish nationalist agitation starting in the 1880s, precisely at a moment when German and especially Russian Jews found themselves excluded from their ranks. The fledgling Eastern European Hibbat Zion movement began to interest some students in Germany, and in 1886, for example, a group of Jewish students in Breslau founded the Freie Verbindungen Viadrina, an unapologetic and independent organization devoted to the affirmation of both national belonging and Jewish distinctiveness. Several student groups joined in 1896 to form the Kartell Convent deutscher Studenten jüdischen Glaubens, whose primary task was to combat antisemitism among German students. According to Reinharz, this marked a new response to antisemitism, one that was met largely with disapproval by established Jewish organizations.

After receiving his doctorate from Brandeis, Reinharz continued to explore these new political responses to the failures of emancipation and growing antisemitism in Germany, especially in his groundbreaking research on Zionism. Much of his early research concentrated on Central European Zionist efforts in the realm of diplomacy to secure a Jewish homeland à la Herzl as well as efforts to combat antisemitism in Europe. He illustrated how the Zionist ideology of national Jewish awakening provided a viable alternative to the liberal bourgeois aspirations of civic and social integration within Germany. Indefatigable, iconoclastic, but principled leadership, according to Reinharz, distinguished all the major organizations such as the Zionistische Vereinigung für Deutschland (Zionist Federation of Germany, ZVfD) and the post–World War I student Zionist federation, the KJV (Kartell Jüdischer Verbindungen). Even after the World Zionist Organization (WZO) moved its headquarters to London, the leadership was still dominated by figures educated in Germany and German-speaking lands.

Reinharz's interest in the role of personality and leadership during crisis developed further while he was editing a volume of Chaim Weizmann's letters. In the first two volumes of his magisterial biography of Weizmann, Reinharz sought to interrogate the relationship between "the individual or hero and his era." On the one hand, he considered the historiographical position of the Russian Marxist leader Georgi Plekhanov that "influential individuals can change the individual features of events and some of their peculiar consequences but they cannot change the general trend which is determined by other forces." On the other, Reinharz registered Sidney Hook's view that "the actions of the leader are independent of his or her generation's socio-economic conditions." As his nuanced biography showed, he refused to accept such "clear-cut" binaries but rather sought to grapple with Weizmann's own writings about himself as well as the perceptions of others, exposing some of the myths that had developed around this larger-than-life Zionist statesman.

Not only did Reinharz focus on illustrious figures such as Weizmann (thus contributing significantly to the history of the Zionist movement and the State of Israel), but also on a seemingly marginal and untethered youth movement in the 1930s—Hashomer Hatzair in Germany. He revealed how this group, which had its origins in the German youth movement and developed a happenstance ideological embrace of Marxism, nevertheless developed a reputation for embodying the vanguard of Zionism. Reinharz revealed how such an unlikely youth movement infiltrated and peeled away support from larger and more established competing groups.

The zealous youth who delivered his first speech in the auditorium of the Essen-Werden Gymnasium in postwar Germany could hardly have predicted his future in the world of Jewish studies. A couple of decades later, Reinharz became the first professor of Jewish history at the University of Michigan, where he established the school's first Judaic studies program. In 1982 he returned to Brandeis University, where he was appointed the Richard Koret Professor of Modern Jewish History in the Department of Near Eastern and Judaic Studies. To promote scholarship on European Jewry, Reinharz took over at the helm of the Tauber Institute for the Study of European Jewry in 1984 and later founded the Jacob and Libby Goodman Institute for the Study of Zionism and Israel. From 1991 to 1994 Reinharz served the administration as the provost and senior vice president for academic affairs, and in 1994 became the seventh president of Brandeis University. During his seventeen-year tenure as president, he advanced the field of Jewish studies by initiating and supporting the establishment of numerous chairs, centers, and institutes devoted to Sephardi studies, Holocaust studies, Israel studies, Jewish women's and gender studies, Jewish education, and Jewish social and demographic studies, while strengthening the humanities through the creation of the Mandel Center and affirming the university's commitment to the sciences, the arts, social justice, and global engagement.

The key themes of Jewish emancipation, antisemitism, and Zionism have served as the cornerstones of Reinharz's prodigious scholarship, as evident in the lengthy bibliography at the end of this volume. He continued to publish throughout the years of his presidency, including critically acclaimed studies of the Jewish love-hate relationship with Europe, European Jewry on the eve of World War II, popular antisemitism in contemporary Germany, and Israeli historiography, as well as a third revised and expanded edition of the now standard textbook in the field of Jewish history, *The Jew in the Modern World*. For Reinharz, the transformation of Jewish life in the modern age—from the "ghettoes of Europe" to the establishment of the State of Israel—has led him to ask not only "where they [the Jews] have been but what it means to be a Jew in today's world."[15] The essays in this volume, written in Jehuda Reinharz's honor, reflect his wide-ranging scholarly interests, institutional leadership, and deep concerns about the Jewish past, present, and future.

NOTES

1. Jehuda Reinharz, interview by authors, June 2, 2013.

2. Jehuda Reinharz, *Chaim Weizmann: The Making of a Statesman* (Oxford: Oxford University Press, 1993), 393.

3. Fred Grubel and Frank Mecklenburg, "Leipzig: Profile of a Jewish Community during the First Years of Nazi Germany," *Leo Baeck Institute Yearbook* 42 (1997): 159.

4. Ibid., 160.

5. Ibid.

6. Benny Landau, "Tracking Truth's Innermost Parts," *Haaretz*, April 12, 2002.

7. Michael Meng, *Shattered Spaces: Encountering Jewish Ruins in Postwar Germany and Poland* (Cambridge: Harvard University Press, 2011).

8. Ibid.

9. Landau, "Tracking Truth's Innermost Parts."

10. Ibid.

11. Ibid.

12. Frida-Levy-Gesamtschule, "Frida Levy." http://www.frida-levy-gesamtschule.de/frida-levy/.

13. Landau, "Tracking Truth's Innermost Parts."

14. Jehuda Reinharz, *Fatherland or Promised Land: The Dilemma of the German Jew, 1893–1914* (Ann Arbor: University of Michigan Press, 1975), 23.

15. Paul Mendes-Flohr and Jehuda Reinharz, *The Jew in the Modern World: A Documentary Reader*, 3rd ed. (Oxford: Oxford University Press, 2010).

PART I

Ideology and Politics

1

Theodor Herzl

Charisma and Leadership

DEREK J. PENSLAR

The authority of leaders derives from the trust, admiration, and even ex-altation that they inspire in their followers. All the more so for political leaders upon whom people project deep-seated, unfulfilled longings, as is the case for leaders of movements for national liberation. The early Zionist movement was particularly dependent on charismatic leader-ship because it was so small, weak, and scattered, lacking mechanisms of patronage or means of coercion. Theodor Herzl had nothing to offer his followers but hope and nothing to maintain their support other than trust. For all that has been written on Herzl's charisma, his prepossessing persona and appearance, there has been little consideration of the cul-tural specificity of charisma. Had Herzl been dropped into a different era or continent he might not have been charismatic or prepossessing at all. Under different circumstances, Herzl might have been nothing more than a manic demi-intellectual, whiling away his days in cafés, scribbling fever-ishly in a diary that no one would ever read. To understand the secrets of Herzl's charisma we must look as closely at his *Sitz im Leben* as at his soul.

A recent scholarly article characterizes a certain nineteenth-century, Central European celebrity by his "dandyism, upscale hobnobbing, chi-valric gestures, royal insignia, and physiognomic distinction." This char-ismatic figure, possessed of mesmerizing good looks and stylistic genius, was both flamboyant and aloof, media savvy yet aristocratic, and he exuded qualities of "natural leadership."[1] The individual in question was not Theodor Herzl, but rather Herzl's fellow Hungarian, the composer and pianist Franz Liszt. Liszt entered the world a half century before Herzl and departed it when Herzl was only twenty. Biographies of Herzl routinely have placed him within the context of fin de siècle antisemitism, and the highly influential work of Carl Schorske presented Herzl as the child of fin de siècle Vienna's illiberal and aestheticized politics. Yet Herzl was the product of something much broader and deeper than this particular place and moment. He lived in a time of rapid advances in newspaper and photographic technology that made it possible for information and images to be disseminated more widely than ever before in human history. It was easier than ever to be widely recognized, admired, even adored—in sum, to be famous. Liszt was one of modernity's first celebrities; he carefully promoted his media image as a pseudoaristocrat to whom the public had virtual access through his dramatic musical performances. Like Liszt, Herzl was a nineteenth-century virtuoso, but he was a political, not artistic, figure, and so the effects of his charisma were transformative rather than merely performative.

In popular parlance, "charisma" is associated with charm, magnetism, and sex appeal, but according to Max Weber, who created the modern meaning of the term, true charismatics are by definition political or religious leaders, not performers, and they attract followers, not fans. According to Weber, charisma is an ineffable characteristic of mysterious origin, related to the New Testament concept of *charis*, or divine grace, itself the Greek translation of the Hebrew *chen*. Weber defines charisma as "a certain quality of individual personality by virtue of which he is considered extraordinary and treated as endowed with supernatural, superhuman, or at least specifically exceptional powers or qualities."[2] Charismatic authority asserts itself only in times of collective distress and in environments where traditional or bureaucratic-statist power structures are weak or nonexistent. The charismatic can be a revolutionary or stabilizing force, what Weber, employing his celebrated ideal-types, calls a "prophet" or a "magician." (The magician solves specific problems while maintaining stability, while the prophet calls forth a new order.) In either case, the charismatic's authority is as fragile as it is dazzling, for if the leader fails to resolve the crisis that brought him to power, he will quickly be cast aside.

Weber's concept of charisma is associated most often with antiquity and the non-Western world, and with types whom Weber called the prophet, shaman, and "berserker" given to fits of manic passion and "epileptoid seizures."[3] Such leaders do not occupy themselves with humdrum administrative matters such as securing predictable sources of revenue or constructing bureaucratic institutions. The charismatic may appoint a successor or leave behind a void. Although this description is far removed from Weber's own society, Weber believed that charisma played a vital role in modern parliamentary politics. In his lecture "Politics as a Vocation" (1919), Weber presented political parties as dependent on charismatic leaders both to inspire cadres of activists and to bring practical benefit to the party by delivering votes and dispensing patronage. Weber related modern charismatic authority to the extension of the franchise, drawing on examples from England and the United States. Weber saw William Gladstone as a master of "grand demagogy," which won the masses' belief in "the ethical substance of his policy and, above all, . . . the ethical character of his personality."[4] Theodore Roosevelt was another charismatic politician whose individual aura was inseparable from his party's machine.

The charismatic authority establishes a bond with his following, and although Weber himself emphasized the charismatic's generation of authority over his followers, over the past half-century scholars increasingly have stressed the interactive quality by which charisma is constructed and perceived. Following Weber's contemporary Emil Durkheim, Bryan Wilson writes of the "charismatic demand" made by followers to turn to one potential leader after another before finding the right match. Marcel Mauss, Pierre Bourdieu, Charles Lindholm, and Roy Wallis all have depicted charisma as a projection and social construction, specifying the conditions under which an individual chooses to represent himself and perform as a charismatic. Psychosocial approaches seek a middle ground between essentialist and contextualist approaches to charisma, presenting the individual personality as a dependent yet crucial variable in any equation of power relations. The charismatic personality is prone to narcissism and grandiosity yet also has an insatiable hunger for love and approval. Such an individual, if possessed of ambition, intelligence, charm, audacity, and no small amount of good luck, may not simply respond to people's expectations but elevate them, inspiring them to hope for what they had considered impossible. In Freudian language, people who cannot fulfill the universal needs of the id (sexuality and aggression), superego (social solidarity), ego (physical and psychic security), and ego ideal (self-esteem) need someone who can do it for them. The charismatic allays their anxiety, raises the self-worth of the oppressed, and channels their rage into purposeful, goal-oriented collective activity.[5]

In most respects, Herzl fits well into the Weberian ideal-type of the modern charismatic leader. The Zionist movement arose at a time when traditional, that is, rabbinic, authority was in crisis, and the law of the modern state failed to protect the physical security and psychological well-being of great swathes of European Jewry. Herzl emerged from outside of the traditional centers of Jewish power, the rabbinate and the Jewish financial elite. He claimed authority to act as the agent (*gestor*) on behalf of the entire Jewish people and created the Zionist Organization (ZO) with himself as its self-appointed head, not subject to recall. He not only captured and represented human longing but realized those desires and thereby transformed the world. Herzl exemplified Isaiah Berlin's definition of the great leader whose goal is "antecedently improbable," as there was no political goal in modern history more improbable than that of Zionism.[6]

Yet Berlin also observed that Herzl "understood issues but not human beings," that he lacked Chaim Weizmann's ability to connect with the masses. Similarly, Hedva Ben-Israel notes that Herzl was admired for his oratory and prose but lacked the populist touch and warmth of other great leaders of stateless peoples such as Charles Stewart Parnell, Jan Masaryk, Edvard Benes, or Josef Piłsudski.[7] In this sense Herzl differed as well from Joseph Chamberlain, William Gladstone, Theodore Roosevelt, and other party politicians, whom Weber identified as the modern carriers of political charisma.

What is more, unlike the charismatic prophet of antiquity, who had no need of fixed institutions, or the charismatic party politician of Weber's day, who was as much the party's implement as he was its leader, Herzl created the ZO, its congress and executive, authorized the formation of parliamentary factions (the "Democratic Faction," Mizrahi), and either single-handedly or cooperatively developed institutions that acted independently of his own authority (the Jewish Colonial Trust, Anglo-Palestine Bank, Jewish National Fund). Like the ideal-typical charismatic figure who does not care for his personal enrichment, Herzl doggedly spent down his fortunes as well as that of his father and wife on his Zionist endeavors. He also established the shekel as the Zionist Organization's primary source of revenue as well as a symbol of belonging to a common political enterprise.

Herzl's close relationship with David Wolfssohn, who succeeded Herzl as the Zionist Organization's president after Herzl's untimely death, is typical of that between a charismatic leader and his epigone. But Herzl prepared far more diligently for a Zionist world without him than the Weberian stereotype would predict. Weber writes of the routinization (*Veralltäglichung*) of charisma as occurring primarily after the leader has passed from the scene, yet Herzl undertook a systematic process of self-routinization. Although he expected unreserved support for his diplomatic activities, and was enraged when it was not forthcoming, Herzl had no choice but to be pushed in directions that he himself did not favor. Herzl resisted the "practical" Zionists' call for immediate settlement activity prior to the attainment of a charter from the Ottoman sultan or the establishment of a Great Power protectorate over Palestine, but he acknowledged the strength of the pro-settlement contingent by endorsing the establishment of the Jewish National Fund and bringing the economist Franz Oppenheimer into the Zionist movement as an expert on cooperative agricultural settlements.

Herzl encountered stiff opposition on the issue of voting rights for women in the movement. At the First Congress, Herzl paternalistically said of the twenty-two women present, "The ladies are, of course, very distinguished guests, but they do not participate in voting." According to one of Herzl's first biographers, Reuven Brainin, "The women, some of them writers and intellectuals, accepted [Herzl's ruling] quietly, but with broken hearts. Then one of the men participants remarked, 'If the women have no rights, we have not gained anything!'" One female attendee, Marie Reinus, insisted on speaking and voting. In the preparations for the Second Congress a year later, women who paid the shekel were accorded the right to vote for congressional delegates, and women delegates were allowed to vote and address the floor. The most likely reason for the change in policy and for Herzl's acquiescence was that enfranchising women would boost the fledgling movement's membership.[8]

Aside from indicating challenges to Herzl's authority and his negotiations with those challenges, this incident also epitomizes Herzl's stiffly bourgeois mores, which extended from gender relations to politics and the arts. (Herzl's aesthetics were solidly middlebrow; he had a journalistic gift for narrative description, but his plays were painfully conventional and pedestrian.) Despite his progressive social views, Herzl was fearful of radicalism. In Weber's typology of charismatics, he was a magician, not a prophet. His political legerdemain would rid Europe of its Jews but would otherwise leave the social order as it was, like the tablecloth trick in which the cloth is deftly removed while leaving a mass of dishes and cutlery undisturbed.

The most poignant indication of the limits of Herzl's authority was the Uganda controversy of 1903. Technically, the Sixth Congress of that year accepted Herzl's proposal that the ZO seriously investigate the possibility of Jewish settlement in British East Africa along the Uganda railroad. But before the congress even started, the Russian caucus had voted to reject the proposal. Three months after the congress, Russian members of the Zionist Executive met in Kharkov and threatened to secede from the ZO if Herzl did not take the Uganda proposal off the table. Deeply embittered, Herzl made empty threats to "mobilize the lower masses against these inciters to rebellion,"[9] and at the last meeting of the Zionist Executive before his death, Herzl continued to assert his authority over the recalcitrant Russians. But Herzl already had prepared for his defeat by publicly welcoming the British offer so long as the territory proved to be habitable and would be met with enthusiasm on the part of "our own people." Tellingly, in his final confrontation with the obdurate Russian Zionist leader Menachem Ussishkin, Herzl spoke not only of his own authority but also that of the congress as the instrument of the nation. Max Nordau passionately depicted the congress as "the autonomous parliament of the Jewish Risorgimento," "the authorized, legitimate, representative of the Jewish people."[10] Herzl was, true to his Hebrew name (Binyamin Zev), a lone wolf, a man without a party. He was a dazzling presence, described by David Vital as "the pre-eminent national figure in contemporary Jewry . . . upon whom [the hopes of Eastern European Jewry] were placed."[11] Yet his greatest legacy was a national parliament and a host of protogovernmental institutions.

Herzl's personal charisma was, then, a means to an end. It manifested itself in his carriage, his voice, and most important, his face. In an essay of 1937 titled "What Did Herzl Look Like?," Samuel Bettelheim describes Herzl's visage as combining aspects of an English lord and Eastern European rabbi "in his Jerusalemite glory." The First Zionist Congress, writes Bettelheim, could have had little more import than the 1884 Katowice conference of the Hovevei Zion had there not sat in the congress president's chair "a miracle. . . . as if King Solomon had arisen from his grave, because he could no longer bear the suffering of his people and its humiliation."[12] Many an observer was fascinated by Herzl's "Assyrian" beard, which bestowed upon him the look of ancient Semitic royalty. The artist Ephraim Lilien depicted Herzl as Moses, that prince of Egypt who rejoined and redeemed his people, and also as the biblical figures Jacob, Aaron, Joshua, David, Solomon, and Hezekiah. But Bettelheim, like most who recorded their impressions of Herzl, was drawn most of all to Herzl's eyes: "large and circular," darkly tinted yet possessed of a "mysterious light" that captivated world leaders and common folk alike. "Herzl's eyes were of enormous expressive power. Often in speech he lost himself in infinite distance, as if he saw things that were insensible to us, and in the next moment fixed his forceful gaze upon his interlocutor." It was a gaze filled with "nobility, power, spirit, genius, and goodness. He never displayed indecisiveness or resignation: the greater the obstacle or danger, the sharper was his eagle's gaze."[13]

Herzl's comportment connoted the impression of great stature. Observers frequently represented Herzl as tall, particularly at moments of great consequence. For example, the Mizrahi activist Mordekhai Nurock, recalling the tumultuous Sixth Zionist Congress's debate about Uganda, reports that Herzl "rose to his full historic stature" before reciting Psalm 137 ("If I forget thee, O Jerusalem").[14] Bettelheim, however, acknowledges that "Herzl was tall yet seemed taller than he really was, for, as is not really mentioned anywhere, he was strikingly slim, even thin."[15] What is more, according to Herzl's military examination papers from Vienna in 1880, Herzl was of "medium" height, and the French police prefecture, with which Herzl was required to register upon moving to Paris as *Die Neue Freie Presse*'s correspondent, recorded him as five foot eight. This was about three inches taller than average for a man born in western or

Central Europe in 1860.[16] Relative to the five-foot-nine average height of an American middle-aged male in our own day, Herzl would be about six feet tall—an attractive but by no means exceptional height. But what do a few inches matter when one is face to face with a latter-day Moses, or perhaps the Messiah himself?

The cultural specificity of Herzl's charisma is indicated clearly by the reactions of Jews who perceived Herzl as a redeemer figure from within the Jewish religious tradition. At the First Zionist Congress's opening session, Herzl's approach unleashed a storm of applause, foot stomping, and the waving of handkerchiefs. Many men grasped and some kissed his hands. Amid the commotion, which lasted for a full quarter of an hour, the Russian Zionist journalist Mordechai Ben Ami wrote, "That is no longer the elegant Dr. Herzl of Vienna, it is a royal descendant of David risen from the grave who appears before us in the grandeur and beauty with which legend surrounded him. Everyone is gripped as if a historical miracle had occurred . . . it was as if the Messiah, the son of David, stood before us." Ben Ami could not prevent himself from shouting "*yehi hamelekh* [long live the king]!" and others soon joined in.[17]

Herzl the leader was the creation of his followers; as Berthold Feiwel put it, "In our earliest youth he [Herzl] signified all beauty and greatness. We, the young, had been yearning for a prophet, a leader. We created him with our longing."[18] His position as a secular, assimilated, Western Jew, alien to the world of traditional Jewish practice and culture, enhanced his charismatic appeal to Eastern European Jews who never could have accepted one of their own, as he would have been so utterly familiar. Isaac Breuer of the Agudat Israel fiercely opposed secular Zionism yet venerated Herzl for his dedication, purity of motive, and self-sacrifice. Only someone removed from the Jewish tradition, reasoned Breuer, could act so boldly and speak so baldly, daring to parlay with world leaders as equals and demand that they restore to the Jews their ancient homeland.[19]

Menachem Ussishkin expressed a similar sentiment in a far less charitable fashion: "[Herzl's] greatest deficiency will be his most useful asset. He does not know the first thing about Jews. Therefore he believes there are only external obstacles to Zionism, no internal ones. We should not open his eyes to the facts of life, so that his faith remains potent."[20] Ussishkin's snide opinion was shared by many of his colleagues who had founded the

Hovevei Zion movement in Eastern Europe. They were passionate, ambitious, vain, difficult, deeply intelligent, and articulate men who viewed Herzl with a mixture of veneration, envy, suspicion, and even derision. Within the Zionist Organization they formed a loyal but rancorous opposition, accusing Herzl of high-handedness, failure to delegate authority, and even dictatorial behavior. Yet it was Herzl, not they, who captured the attention of the masses, dazzled them with his very strangeness, and replenished their self-esteem.

The Galician Zionist Nathan Birnbaum is a case study of a failed leader who could educate the masses but not inspire them. A fluid writer and intense, engaging orator, Birnbaum was a prominent Zionist activist in Vienna already in the early 1890s. For a brief period at the end of the century, Birnbaum was Herzl's deputy, but he resented as much as he admired Herzl's charisma, graceful prose style, and position of influence in the world of European journalism. Because of a combination of personal pique and ideological disagreements, Birnbaum abandoned Zionism for other causes—first Diaspora nationalism, then ultra-Orthodoxy—but his personal and intellectual idiosyncrasies ensured that he would remain a would-be leader in search of a following.[21]

Did Herzl exert the same magnetic spell on gentiles that he did on Jews? Did his charisma transcend religious and cultural barriers? Herzlian Zionism attracted a motley yet influential crew of Christian admirers, ranging from restorationist visionaries (or cranks) such as William Hechler, chaplain to the British embassy in Vienna, to the Orientalist Carl Heman, the radical writer Hermann Bahr, and Baroness Bertha von Suttner, an Austrian noblewoman whose causes in addition to Zionism included disarmament, feminism, and animal rights. All of these figures were predisposed to philosemitism, but Herzl's charisma was often a key factor in attracting them to Zionism.[22]

The prominent German Orientalist Johannes Lepsius attended the First Congress, and his impressions, published a few months after the congress's conclusion, indicated how deeply he shared the Zionists' enthusiasm:

Whoever experienced the fanatical, enthusiastic applause with which Dr. Herzl was greeted at the Basel Congress must have the impres-

sion that here is not only a party leader in the midst of his supporters, but rather a great lord in the midst of his retinue. A tall, manly
appearance, of a classical, semitic type, he would have done no dis-
honor to his forefathers had he sat on the "throne of the governor
of the province beyond the River [Euphrates]" in Ephraim's Gate in
Jerusalem, which was once held by Zerubavel. But also the tranquil
harmony of a commanding spirit and the moral solemnity, which sat-
urates the greatness of the project, appear to be rooted within him.
When in his opening address he said, "The matter is so great that
one must speak of it only in the simplest of words," so he remained,
throughout leading the congress's proceedings, true to this sincere
and modest tone, scorning any pose or empty words and showing
himself to have grown into his task in every way.[23]

Later in his essay, Lepsius explicitly calls Herzl the new Zerubavel and the
congress the new Sanhedrin. Lepsius notes that the congress presented
itself as "an entirely political movement" and strove to avoid messianic
imagery, "yet here and there a religious undercurrent came to the surface."
"The messianic hope, the dream of the re-establishment of the Davidic
kingdom on the ruins of Jerusalem, has remained, despite talmudism, the
authentic religion of the Jews."[24] For a Christian Zionist such as Lepsius,
Herzl was even more purely a messianic figure than for the Jewish Zionist
faithful whose enthusiasm for Herzl was frequently tempered by reservations about his diplomatic approach, secularism, and indifference to
Hebraic culture.

   Christians did not have to be pious restorationists or even philosemites
to be captivated by Herzl's charisma. The British journalist Sidney Whitman, who was the *New York Herald*'s correspondent in Constantinople
in the mid-1890s, was struck by Herzl's appearance—"I never saw a man,
whose role was so inscribed upon his body," he wrote[25]—but his positive impression may have been enhanced by the services Herzl promised
to fulfill for the Ottoman sultan, with whom Whitman sympathized in
his reportage on the Armenian massacres of 1894–1896. Herzl could also
find favor with antisemites for reasons that overlapped with his successes
with philosemites. Individuals predisposed to cherish and loathe Jews
alike were captivated by Herzl's ancient semitic appearance and nobility

of manner. The latter, though, were wont to distinguish the new prince of the Jews from what they saw as the unsavory lot of avaricious peddlers and financiers whom Herzl promised to whisk out of Europe. In this spirit, Count Phillip zu Eulenberg, the German ambassador to Vienna, called Herzl "undeniably one of the most interesting personalities I ever met. . . . the prototype of a militant Jewish leader from the age of the Jewish kings, without a particle of the type we call 'trading Jew.' My association with this high-minded, *selfless*, distinguished man will remain in my memory forever."[26] Even the German kaiser, who did not shy away from calling Jews Christ killers and moneybags, viewed Herzl favorably, although the kaiser's flirtation with Herzl was brief and ended abruptly when the kaiser was made aware that the Ottoman sultan's opposition to Zionism was unshakable.

At the end of the nineteenth century, the Jewish Question loomed large in public consciousness in the Western world, and for many people, Jews and Christians alike, Herzl was the hero whom the needs of the moment had created. Still, one must not exaggerate the extent of Herzl's appeal. During Herzl's lifetime the vast majority of world Jewry was anti- or a-Zionist. Christian observers were as likely to view Herzl with skepticism as with adulation. The Zionist press (and Herzl himself) claimed massive public interest in the early Zionist movement, and existing Zionist historiography has tended to accept those claims at face value. True, in the United Kingdom Herzlian Zionism received attention in the major dailies and reviews, but it ranged from positive to cautious to negative, and the First Congress left few positive impressions. Only twenty-six journalists attended the First Zionist Congress, and between eight and twelve of them represented the Jewish press. Virtually all of the journalists for the world press were freelancers who submitted terse, purely descriptive reports for multiple newspapers or wire services. The only major non-Jewish newspaper with a dedicated correspondent was London's *Pall Mall Gazette*.[27] Prior to the congress the paper's Vienna correspondent, I. W. Bouthon Willy, published an interview with Herzl that described him as "tall, handsome and courteous" yet "disappointingly phlegmatic" when discussing anything other than his pet project. The first descriptions of Herzl in the *New York Times* were deceptively straightforward and even a bit puckish: "Whatever the merits of this undertaking, the doctor brings to its execution the vigor of maturity and a large amount of varied experience, for he has been in turn a lawyer and a playwright, and is now a journalist and bicycle rider. . . . As detailed to his English interviewer, Dr. Herzl's scheme is entirely practical — whatever may be the case as to its practicability."[28] The placement of this story is telling: it was put in the "Topics of the Times" column, which was filled with droll tidbits about subjects such as tax dodging by the assessors of Lewiston, Maine; efforts by Prince Ferdinand of Bulgaria and the Ottoman sultan to recruit competent assassins; and an unusual friendship in a local menagerie between a rhinoceros and a cat.

After 1897 the number of journalists attending the Zionist congresses steadily multiplied, yet for the most part their reports remained brief, and Herzl did not figure prominently in them. In London, there were two turning points: the Fourth Congress, held in that city in 1900, and Herzl's testimony before the Royal Commission on Alien Immigration in 1902. The British press gave the congress wide coverage, and Herzl enjoyed epithets such as the "New Moses," "Modern Moses," and "Uncrowned King of the Jews."[29] In his testimony of 1902, Herzl's lapidary presentation of Zionism as the only effective solution to the immigration problem made him known to the United Kingdom's governing circles and to the *Times*, which gave Herzl's testimony far more extensive treatment than it had devoted to any of the Zionist congresses to date. Whereas until then the *Times* had made do with reports from the congresses by Reuters' journalists, in 1903 it sent its own correspondent to cover the Sixth Congress in Vienna. By then, scores of international newspapers were following the Zionist movement closely. It took years of dogged diplomatic activity and institutional development on Herzl's part to reach this stage. And even then the center of attention was not Herzl himself but rather the cause for which he stood and the movement that he had transformed from a congeries of scattered activists into a government in exile.

Herzl was aware of his charismatic powers. In a celebrated diary entry of July 15, 1896, following a mass meeting in London's East End, Herzl wrote of how he saw "my legend is being born. The people are sentimental; the masses do not see clearly. I believe that even now they no longer have a clear image of me. A light fog is beginning to rise around me, and it may perhaps be the cloud in which I shall walk."[30] Herzl did not create the mist; he was encapsulated by the affective field created by his followers. Herzl himself was as likely to be derided as adored: "King of the Jews" could be a term of adulation at a Zionist congress or a scornful epithet when hurled by scoffers when Herzl entered the Vienna opera house. The troubled relationship between performance and messianism crops up in Herzl's novel *Altneuland*, where the opera in Palestine's utopian New Society is performing a work about the notorious messianic pretender Shabbetai Zvi. In *Altneuland*, this symbol of premodern Jews' superstitious longings for divine salvation has been replaced by a rational striving for self-improvement.

Herzl said of himself that unlike Shabbetai Zvi, who elevated himself to appear alongside the great of the earth, Herzl "finds the great small, as small as myself."[31] This statement is somewhat disingenuous, as Herzl venerated, even idolized, most of the world leaders with whom he dealt, and he sensed a chasm between himself and his followers, whom he called "the little people." But Herzl's self-assessment was accurate in that he considered himself to be a conduit for a political project of immeasurably greater importance than the fame he had pursued prior to his Zionist conversion. Herzl was well aware that self-styled political and religious leaders can turn out to be charlatans and that his followers "would probably show the same affection to some clever deceiver and imposter as they do to me, in whom they are not deceived."[32] Herzl's politics were suffused with a stringent ethics: he was given to fantasies but not willful fabrication, and he seldom descended into demagoguery. A man without a party, emerging from the interstices between traditional and bureaucratic power, Herzl was typical of his generation's leaders of stateless and colonized peoples, whose need for a charismatic leader was far more acute than that of the great nations whose political systems formed the basis for Weber's own research.

NOTES

1. Dana Gooley, "From the Top: Liszt's Aristocratic Airs," in *Constructing Charisma. Celebrity, Fame and Power in Nineteenth-Century Europe*, ed. Edward Berenson and Eva Giloi (New York: Berghahn, 2010), 83.

2. Max Weber, *Economy and Society*, ed. Guenther Roth and Claus Wittich, vol. 1 (Berkeley: University of California Press, 1967), 241.

3. Max Weber, "The Nature of Charismatic Authority and Its Routinization," in *Max Weber on Charisma and Institution Building*, ed. S. N. Eisenstadt (Chicago: University of Chicago Press, 1968), 48–65.

4. Max Weber, "Politics as a Vocation," accessed September 3, 2013, http://www.sscnet.ucla.edu/polisci/ethos/Weber-vocation.pdf.

5. For up-to-date analyses of Weber's concept of charisma and its modification by subsequent generations of scholars, see the Introduction to Berenson and Giloi, *Constructing Charisma*; Edward Berenson's contribution to that volume ("Charisma and the Making of Imperial Heroes in Britain and France, 1880–1914," 21–40); and John Potts, *A History of Charisma* (London: Palgrave, Macmillan, 2009), 106–36.

6. Isaiah Berlin, *Personal Impressions* (New York: Viking, 1980), 32–34, 39, 44.

7. Hedva Ben-Israel, "Herzl's Leadership in Comparative Perspective," in *Theodor Herzl: Visionary of the Jewish State*, ed. Gideon Shimoni and Robert S. Wistrich (Jerusalem: Magnes, 1999), 155.

8. Joseph Frankel, "The History of the Shekel" (1952, 1956), accessed April 26, 2013, http://begedivri.com/ZionistShekel/History.htm; Hayim Orlan, "The Participants in the First Zionist Congress," *Herzl Year Book*, vol. 6 (New York: Herzl Press, 1964–65), 135; Alison Rose, *Jewish Women in Fin-de-Siècle Vienna* (Austin: University of Texas Press, 2008), 130–31. At that time, only Australia, New Zealand, and a few US states had female suffrage, and female members of Parliament did not address the UK's House of Commons until the end of the First World War.

9. Cited in David Vital, *Zionism: The Formative Years* (Oxford: Oxford University Press, 1982), 320.

10. Ibid., 290.

11. Ibid., 131.

12. Samuel Bettelheim, "Wie hat Herzl ausgesehen?," *Theodor Herzl Jahrbuch*, ed. Tulo Nussenblatt (Vienna: Heinrich Glanz Verlag, 1937), 337.

13. Ibid.

14. Cited in Joseph Adler, "Religion and Herzl: Fact and Fable," *Herzl Year Book*, vol. 4 (New York: Herzl Press, 1961), 295.

15. Bettelheim, "Wie hat Herzl ausgesehen?," 337.

16. Amos Elon, *Herzl* (New York: Holt, Rinehart and Winston, 1975), 9; Timothy J. Hatton and Bernice E. Bray, "Long-Run Trends in the Heights of European Men, 19th-20th Centuries," *Economics and Human Biology* 8, no. 3 (2010): 405–13.

17. Cited in Robert S. Wistrich, "In the Footsteps of the Messiah," in *Theodor Herzl: Visionary of the Jewish State*, ed. Gideon Shimoni and Robert S. Wistrich (Jerusalem: Magnes, 1999), 321.

18. Ibid., 331.

19. Mordechai Breuer, "Four Eulogies Written by an Opponent," in Shimoni and Wistrich, *Theodor Herzl*, 308–20.

20. Cited in Elon, *Herzl*, 186.

21. Jess Olsen, *Nathan Birnbaum and Jewish Modernity* (Stanford: Stanford University Press, 2013).

22. Alan Levenson, "Gentile Reception of Herzlian Zionism: A Reconsideration." *Jewish History* 16, no. 2 (2002): 187–211. On support for early Zionism in the American missionary press, see Milron Plesure, "Zionism in the General Press, 1897–1914: From Basel to Sarajevo," *Herzl Year Book*, vol. 5 (New York: Herzl Press, 1963), 127–45.

23. Johannes Lepsius, "Der Zionisten-Congress," *Der Christliche Orient* 1, no. 10 (October 1897): 434.

24. Ibid., 435, 443.

25. Bettelheim, "Wie hat Herzl ausgesehen?," 336.

26. Cited in Vital, *Origins*, 81.

27. Bettelheim, "Wie hat Herzl ausgesehen?," 216; Orlan, "The Participants in the First Zionist Congress."

28. *New York Times*, August 11, 1897.

29. Benjamin Jaffe, "The British Press and Zionism in Herzl's Time (1895–1904)," *Transactions of the Jewish Historical Society of England* 24 (1975): 89–100.

30. Theodor Herzl, entry of March 15, 1896, in *The Complete Diaries of Theodor Herzl*, ed. Raphael Patai, vol. 1 (New York: Herzl Press, 1960), 421.

31. Theodor Herzl, entry of June 11, 1900, in *The Complete Diaries of Theodor Herzl*, ed. Raphael Patai, vol. 3 (New York: Herzl Press, 1960), 960.

32. Herzl, continuation of entry of March 15, 1896, *The Complete Diaries of Theodor Herzl*.

2

The President before Weizmann

David Littwak and the Politics of "Old New Land"

MICHAEL BRENNER

Chaim Weizmann, whose biography was written so eloquently by Jehuda Reinharz, was the first president of the State of Israel. And yet, in a certain way, he had a predecessor. David Littwak was elected for a seven-year period shortly after Passover of 1923 by an overwhelming majority of 363 out of 395 delegates of the congress. He succeeded the late Dr. Eichenstamm, who had passed away a week before. Littwak was a compromise candidate, after the established political figures—Joe Levy, general manager of the New Society, and Dr. Marcus, president of its academy—had both withdrawn their candidacies. Littwak was only thirty years old at the time of his election. This son of poor Eastern European immigrants to Vienna was a Zionist since childhood and settled in Palestine together with his parents.

David Littwak was, of course, elected not by the Knesset but by the congress of the New Society. Just like Eichenstamm, Levy, and Marcus, he too was the brainchild of Theodor Herzl and the hero of the utopian novel *Altneuland* (Old New Land), which Herzl had completed two years before his death. Even though Littwak was a fictional character, historians should not simply disregard him. In many ways he embodies Herzl's ideals of politics in the Jewish state.

Old New Land's Politics

In the six years that passed between the publication of Theodor Herzl's political tractate *Der Judenstaat* (1896) and that of his utopian novel *Alt-*

neuland (1902), he had created a political mass movement, achieved diplomatic success, and witnessed the organized Jewish immigration to the
Land of Israel. *The Jews' State* and *Old New Land* envision similar but
not identical societies. This can be only partly ascribed to the different
genres of literature. One has to take into account that Herzl's views did
not remain static over the course of these six years. He had given up his
original preference for Argentina, which he had mentioned in his early
diary entries. While his *Old New Land* was now set in Palestine, it was
not a Jewish state. In fact, it was neither Jewish nor was it a state. As
many critics have noticed, there was very little that was Jewish in *Old
New Land*. Moreover, not all Jews living in Palestine belonged to the New
Society, and at the same time it was open to non-Jews. Herzl makes clear
in his novel that the New Society is a *Genossenschaft*, a society or commonwealth rather than a state. "We have no state like the Europeans of
your time. We are merely a society (*Genossenschaft*) of citizens seeking to
enjoy life through work and culture."[1]

In Amos Elon's words, Herzl "devised an original kind of polity, based
on syndicalist ideals and derived in part from French anarchist thinking.
There was little or no striking coercion and almost none of the forms
of sovereignty associated with the European nation-state."[2] All land was
publicly owned, and the industries, as well as newspapers, theaters, and
banks, were cooperatives owned by workers and consumers. No one was
excluded and no particular language was spoken. It was a highly pluralist
and tolerant society.[3]

Modern interpreters often have gone to one of two extremes, either
considering Herzl's novel irrelevant to his political thought or taking it at
face value. This essay treats the novel as a literary expression of the political attitudes of the late Herzl. He worked for three years on this novel,
considered it one of his masterpieces, and was soon to realize that this was
indeed his final word on how the Jewish society would look. His biographer
Ernst Pawel was right when he observed that "in terms of political theory,
Altneuland may have marked a significant advance over *Der Judenstaat*."
He also was right when he observed: "Within the Zionist movement, however, the book was for the most part greeted with consternation."[4]

Old New Land starts out with a brief visit of two friends, the Prussian
nobleman Kingscourt and the Viennese Jew Friedrich Löwenberg (Herzl's

alter ego), to Palestine in 1903, on their way to a Pacific island, as far as possible from Europe. Disappointed in the appalling condition of the soil and of the people, of the economic situation, and of the social problems in Palestine, they continue on their journey to their Pacific island. Before they return to Europe for a visit in 1923, they stop again in Palestine. To their utter surprise they witness a dramatic change. Since European Jews established there what Herzl calls the "New Society," they do not recognize the land and the people anymore. In the rest of the novel Herzl draws a highly idealistic portrait of this society, emphasizing not so much its Jewishness (its name is not Israel or anything reminiscent of Jewish history but "New Society") but rather its general social achievements.

Herzl described a peaceful society with Jews and Arabs living side by side, with no army and almost no political conflicts, a society that took the best from all European countries, among them English boarding schools and Austrian coffeehouses. There were German, French, English, Spanish, and Italian theaters, and the opera performed *Sabbatai Zvi*. The Russian Zionist thinker Ahad Ha'am, Herzl's most pronounced opponent from within the Zionist camp, argued correctly that Herzl's vision was not that of a Jewish state but one of an asylum for persecuted Jews who imitated their version of Europe in the Near East: the society that Herzl foresaw would be a new and better society with revolutionary aspects but with no elements of a renewal of Judaism. This aspect in particular served as a point of criticism for the Russian Zionists, whose main interest was precisely that. All one finds here "is a monkey's imitation without any integral national character, reeking of the spirit of 'slavery within freedom,' a daughter of Western exile," claimed Ahad Ha'am in his devastating review of the book.[5]

Herzl never denied that he had in mind to create a universalist society that would serve as a model state. Perhaps the most symbolic suggestion of Herzl's New Society was his design of its flag. It should have seven stars, one for every hour of the working day. Herzl deemed this characteristic so important that he frequently referred to the "New Society" simply as the "Seven-Hour-Land." But there were many other indications that Herzl's "Old New Land" was a society that would stand not only for the progress of the Jews but also for humankind as a whole. Herzl made clear that this was "an experiment for the good of humanity."[6] In *Altneuland* women enjoy equal rights, including active and passive voting rights, which they were not yet granted in Europe at that time.

Jewish traditions are, of course, not entirely absent. Thus the soil of Palestine is not only recultivated by new technologies but also by old traditions. Modern collectivism is combined with biblical commands by having the land held on a jubilee leasehold. Every fifty years it reverts to collective ownership. Doctors in "Old New Land" work to find a cure for malaria, while engineers construct a channel from the Dead Sea to the Red Sea to solve the water problems in the whole region. Other revolutionary inventions were related to Herzl's enthusiasm for electricity, such as the monorail in Haifa and the electric train systems throughout the country, telephone newspapers (with spoken advertisements), and street lights, hanging from palm trees like big fruits of glass. Here again, Herzl's conviction that the Jewish state would be a model for a better world society was clearly visible. "I believe," he writes, "that electric light was not to enable a few snobs to illuminate their fancy palaces, but to help mankind solve its problems. One of them is the Jewish question. By solving it we don't act just for ourselves but also for many others filled with sorrow and pain." Herzl simply could not imagine that the native Arab population would oppose a society politically and socially so perfect.[7]

In his attempt to build a model society in which all social problems would be resolved, Herzl also dedicated some effort to turn his readers' attention to the problem of other oppressed people: "There is still one problem of racial misfortune unsolved. The depths of that problem, in all its horror, only a Jew can fathom. I mean the Negro problem. . . . I am not ashamed to say, though I be thought ridiculous, now that I have lived to see the restoration of the Jews I should like to pave the way for the restoration of the Negroes."[8]

Herzl leaves no doubt: "Yes, we are strong enough to form a state, and, indeed, a model state."[9] It seems clear that toward the end of his life, Herzl's ideas became increasingly universalistic and less particularistic. The New Society should guarantee a safe haven for all persecuted Jews, but more than that: it was to be a model society for all nations, religions, and races. The Jewish state became for him more and more a means to achieve a much more ambitious goal: a better society for mankind.

As for its political system, "Old New Land" is no monarchy like most

European states, but at the time also no clear-cut democracy. There is a congress that elects delegates, but it is in session for only a short period during the year; and it seems that important questions, such as the election of its president, are decided by gentleman's agreement rather than by fierce party infighting. "We are not a state. . . . We are simply a large co-operative composed of affiliated co-operatives. And this, our congress, is really nothing more than the general assembly of the co-operative association which is called the New Society."[10]

There are different parties, and one of them is characterized in extremely negative terms. Its leader is a rabbi called Dr. Geyer, and the main characteristic of his political party is its demand for an exclusivist Jewish state. The other party, which rallies the clear majority behind it, propagates an inclusive multinational and multireligious society, even though Jews constitute a majority. When the old president Eichenstamm wants to transmit his legacy to David Littwak (during an opera performance of *Sabbatai Zvi*) he chooses the following: "My last word to the Jews will be: The stranger must be made to feel at home in our midst."[11]

The central political divide in the New Society is thus the question of inclusiveness versus exclusiveness. Should the New Society be open only for Jews or also for others? Herzl's answer is unequivocal. When the Prussian nobleman Kingscourt doubts whether he would be able to become a member of the New Society, David Littwak proclaims: "Let me tell you, then, that my associates and I make no distinctions between one person (*Mensch*) and another. We do not ask to what race or religion a person belongs. If he is a person, that is enough for us."[12] Herzl includes the Arab Reshid Bey and the Prussian Kingscourt in the New Society and has Littwak proclaim, "You must hold fast to the things that have made us great: to liberality, tolerance, love of mankind. Only then is Zion truly Zion!"[13]

The only ones who have no place in the New Society are those who deny non-Jews equal rights. Herzl's poignant opposition to Geyer's intolerance is uttered over and over again in *Altneuland*. He has the respected architect Steineck become enraged when he speaks about Geyer: "He's a cursed pope, a provocateur, a blasphemer who rolls up his eyes. He wants to bring intolerance into our country, the scamp! I am certainly a peaceful person, but I could cheerfully murder an intolerant fellow like him."[14]

Not only is Geyer an intolerant politician who opposes the inclusion of

non-Jews in the New Society, but he also is an opportunist and a hypo-
crite. As long as it was not en vogue to side with the Zionists, he was their
opponent. When they got the upper hand, he joined them. "Now he is the
patriot, the nationalist Jew. And we — we are the friends of the alien. If we
listened to him he would make us out to be bad Jews or even strangers in
Palestine," his opponents opine.[15] In the elections to the congress, Geyer's
party loses in almost all districts against the all-inclusive liberal-minded
candidates supported by Herzl's protagonists David Littwak and the architect Steineck (based on the Viennese Zionist Oscar Marmorek). There
is no doubt with which political camp the sympathies of the author lie.

David Littwak, the newly elected president of "Old New Land," person-
ifies the ideal of the successful immigrant who rises from great poverty to
wealth, from the ghetto to the Jewish homeland, from slavery to freedom.
His father was a peddler in Vienna and, after working hard, his son became a wealthy shipping company owner and lives in his Alhambra-like
mansion near Tiberias. His fairy-tale-like social rise had its origins at the
beginning of the book when Friedrich Loewenberg (the Herzl-like character in the novel) decided to give all his money to this poor Viennese
family before leaving Europe. In gratitude to his noble patron whom he
had deemed dead, David Littwak named his son Fritz and his home Fried-
richsheim. This may well be a reference to Friedrichsruh, the home and
burial place of another of Herzl's heroes, Count Bismarck.

Leadership Ideals and Realities

In many respects, Herzl shaped his hero Littwak after his closest associate in the Zionist movement (and later successor), David Wolffsohn.
Wolffsohn was actually a "Litvak," a Lithuanian Jew, and like Herzl's Littwak had grown up in a poor traditional Yiddish-speaking family. His father was a *melamed* with seven children in a small Lithuanian shtetl not
far from the Prussian border. In his own pious way he imbued his son with
a love for Zion, as did David Littwak's father in *Old New Land*. Wolffsohn
later recalled that he developed his attachment to the Land of Israel when
he saw his father crying about the destruction of Jerusalem on the 9th
of Av.[16] While the real Wolffsohn moved to Germany, Herzl situates his
Littwak in Vienna.

Just like the young David Littwak, young David Wolffsohn too first worked as a peddler selling matches. In an autobiographical sketch Wolffsohn recalled, "I sold matches and pens as a peddler early in the morning on the boats of the port; during the day I stayed at the attic of my brother's place, where I also slept at night without anyone's knowledge and read during the day."[17] In later years Wolffsohn settled in Cologne and moved up from selling matches to become a successful lumber merchant who accumulated considerable wealth.

David Wolffsohn remains to this day "one of the most underestimated and misjudged leaders of Zionism."[18] As Yvonne Meybohm's biography of Wolffsohn points out, much of Herzl's practical politics was shaped by his friend and successor, although he always remained in the background as long as Herzl was alive.[19] The two first met shortly before *Der Judenstaat* was published. Wolffsohn, who had been exposed to proto-Zionist ideas by Rabbi Isaak Rülf during his stay in Memel and by the writer A. D. Gordon when he lived with him in the town of Lyck, received the galleys of the book and immediately went to Vienna to pay tribute to Herzl. During their first encounter in 1896, Wolffsohn asked Herzl why he did not give credit to his predecessors (a criticism Rülf had mentioned to Wolffsohn) and was astonished to hear that he was unfamiliar with their writings. Herzl had read neither Moses Hess nor Leon Pinsker or Isaak Rülf.[20]

Despite frequent quarrels over practical issues, Wolffsohn continued to admire Herzl. On October 21, 1898, he wrote in his diary: "The 18th October in Constantinople was the most precious and most important day in my life. Our Herzl was received by our majesty, the German kaiser, in an hour-long audience."[21] In his Cologne mansion he kept a life-size image of Herzl by Ephraim Moses Lilien.

Wolffsohn was well aware that there was a certain paternalistic attitude in Herzl's view of Eastern European Jews, including himself. The way Wolffsohn described their first encounter underlines this. When Wolffsohn suggested to Herzl that he should rely on Russian Jews rather than on Western Jews, Herzl seemed utterly surprised. As Wolffsohn noted, "I realized that he had no idea about Russian Jews and I had to educate him about them. He was surprised to hear that I am one myself and that Russian Jew and European are no contradictions."[22] Wolffsohn regarded himself as and was often seen from the outside as a mediator between East and West European Jews, which played a significant role in his becoming Herzl's successor.

To be sure, not all of David Littwak's traits were modeled after David Wolffsohn. There also are biographical aspects of Herzl himself in the figure of Littwak. Littwak's sister, for example, resembles Herzl's sister Pauline. But the parallels between Littwak and Wolffsohn are overwhelming. They continued even after Herzl's death. Just like David Littwak in *Old New Land*, Wolffsohn initially rejected the idea that he should head the movement. He might have remembered at that moment that in the New Society it seemed to be a ritual for any future president first to reject his candidacy.

We do not know how successful Littwak was as president, as his election occurs at the very end of the novel and Herzl did not write a sequel. We do know, however, that Wolffsohn's presidency was plagued by internal strife and enjoyed only limited diplomatic success. He held fast to a political Zionism that faced growing opposition by a mainly Eastern European group of Zionists, among them Chaim Weizmann. As Jehuda Reinharz has shown, Wolffsohn and Weizmann were engaged in some serious controversies, which at times took the form of personal attacks. At the height of their infighting, in 1910, Weizmann led the attack by asking: "Who has promulgated the axiom that the Movement must be led by a businessman? . . . Businessmen are fine in their way, but they must be given ideas. And what we require of our leader is not the proper supervision of an office—we have many paid officials to do this; our leader must give us a program." Wolffsohn later retorted that "it is not written anywhere that a leader must necessarily be a Doctor of Chemistry" and insinuated that Weizmann was incompetent and not completely honorable in his financial dealings.[23]

The case of Wolffsohn shows how difficult it is for any real person to step into the role written for a character in a novel. The real David Wolffsohn, although often praised as a mediator, never was able to play the same harmonizing role of a statesman, which Theodor Herzl had envisioned for David Littwak in the New Society. Demoralized and sick, Wolffsohn decided not to seek office again in 1911 and died three years later.

Modern Interpretations

Wolffsohn's successors at the head of the World Zionist Organization and the State of Israel did not have to play a role written in Herzl's script. The universalist ideals of *Altneuland*, however, flared up occasionally among them. Nahum Goldmann, chairman of the World Zionist Organization in the post-World War II era, underlined Israel's mission at the occasion of Herzl's centenary: "Do you think that what other nations admired about Zionism was the fact that the Jews, too, wanted a state with ministers, ambassadors, cabinet crises and a flag? As if the world had not enough states. . . . In the historical perspective, what inspired the finest of the Jews with enthusiasm for Zionism was precisely its Utopian aspect." Jews, he continued, still have to cling to the great humanitarian ideals, "not the short-sighted, provincial realism of some groups in Israel."[24]

While he agreed on little else with Goldmann, Israel's first prime minister, David Ben-Gurion, shared his universalist ideal of the Jewish state. In numerous speeches he emphasized the uniqueness of the Jewish state in the family of nations, often through biblical allusions: "We are building the State with prophetic vision and messianic longings, to be an example and a guide to all men. The words of the Prophet remain true for us: 'I will give thee for a light to the Gentiles, that thou mayest be my salvation unto the end of the earth.'"[25] Like Herzl's "Old New Land," Ben-Gurion's Israel should not be just another tiny state in the family of nations but a model state: "The Messianic vision that has lighted up our path for thousands of years has prepared and fitted us to a light unto the nations. Moreover, it has imposed upon us the duty of becoming a model people and building a model state."[26] David Littwak, the hero of *Altneuland*, could have signed on to these visions by Goldmann and Ben-Gurion.

In present-day debates over Israel, however, Littwak and his positions are often deemed outdated, questionable, or simply wrong. Depending on one's political point of view, the ideals he represented are seen either as irrelevant or prophetic. The political right is troubled with the universalistic views that are such a prominent feature in *Altneuland*. In his *Jewish State* (2000) Yoram Hazony, the founder of the politically conservative Shalem Center, dismissed *Altneuland* as a utopian text not to be taken seriously: "It is a utopia, and like all utopias, this one also invited the reader to close his eyes and believe. . . . We know from Herzl's diaries and other sources that, far from trying actually to employ the utopian schemes presented in *Altneuland*, he never wavered from his original goal of seeking an independent and sovereign Jewish state, complete with an army and navy, borders and power politics." Thus Hazony questions all those "who have insisted on reading the novel literally, as though it were intended to be a practical political program."[27]

Even though *Altneuland* is clearly a different literary genre from *Der Judenstaat* and is filled with the kind of kitsch common in fin de siècle Vienna, there can be no doubt that Herzl wanted it to be taken seriously. As he emphasized in the book itself, it is up to its readers if it remains a fairy tale or if it becomes reality. The minute details in which he described its political system, its heroes, and its villains, show where his vision of a Jewish state had arrived in 1902. The Herzl of 1902 had moved far beyond the Herzl of 1896. The "Jewish Society" of *Der Judenstaat* had given way to the New Society of *Altneuland*. When he sent a copy of the novel to Lord Rothschild, Herzl wrote in an accompanying letter: "There will, of course, be stupid people who, because I have chosen the *form* of a Utopia which has been used by Plato and Thomas More, will declare the *cause* to be a Utopia. I fear no such misunderstanding in your case."[28] In another letter to Reich Chancellor von Bülow he emphasized: "I wrote the Utopia only to show that it is none."[29]

Hazony has to reconcile his particular image of Herzl with a text by the real Herzl he can hardly embrace. His way of doing so is to interpret the novel as a deception of the Ottoman authorities or to dismiss it altogether. In this respect, and only in this respect, Herzl shares the fate of another Jewish hero many centuries earlier. Just as traditional Jews embraced Maimonides' *Mishneh Torah* as part of the Jewish canon and at the same time rejected or reinterpreted his *More nevukhim*, there are plenty of voices today who love the Herzl of *Der Judenstaat* but reject, misread, or ridicule the Herzl of *Altneuland*.

Herzl's hero David Littwak probably would not be a popular candidate for the political right today. It is ironic that the political camps that are closer to *Altneuland*'s Dr. Geyer than to David Littwak invoke the memory of Herzl.

While the political right dismisses the visions Herzl laid out in *Alt-*

neuland, the political left — in Israel and beyond — embraces them whole-heartedly. In his controversial book *The Crisis of Zionism,* American-Jewish writer and political scientist Peter Beinart cites David Littwak as one of his heroes. To be sure, he criticizes Herzl's lack of foresight when it came to Arab nationalism, but unlike Hazony, who sees *Altneuland* as a pure fantasy, he calls it an "impressive place." He applauds the fact that Littwak can speak Arabic and that one of his close associates is an Arab engineer from Haifa. He quotes Littwak's call for tolerance and reminds his readers that the racist Dr. Geyer never gains control over the Jewish state.[30]

Herzl might find fault with many features of today's Israeli society. He might realize that the Geyers of his day have not disappeared but instead have strengthened their position. But he also might be pleasantly surprised to find a former president of Israel who aspired to be the David Littwak of the twenty-first century. A decade before he became president, Shimon Peres embarked on an imaginary voyage with the founder of Zionism to revisit his utopian novel. He set out by admitting that it was only late in life when he read Herzl's writings. Once he read *Altneuland,* he was so fascinated that he brought Herzl back to life to show him present-day (1998) Israel. In many ways, as he proudly states, Israel constitutes the fulfillment of Herzl's dreams. In some respects, however, it is still far from its founder's vision. Politics is one of the areas where much remains to be improved.

In this personal book written a few years after Yitzhak Rabin's assassination and his own retreat into the political opposition, Peres painfully admits that extremist voices have been on the rise during recent years. "The father of Zionism was the first to suspect that these hateful ideas, which run counter to Judaism's tradition of tolerance and sense of justice, might arise, and he denounced them with all his might."[31] After a lengthy quote from Steineck's speech against Geyer's opportunism and hypocrisy, and his exclusivist theories of the New Society, Israel's elder statesman remarks: "As I read these lines again I became fully aware of Herzl's prophetic intelligence, his love of purity, his complete embrace of the biblical injunction from Isaiah for 'perfect peace.'"[32]

In 1993, in the middle of the short-lived enthusiasm for a peaceful solution of the Israeli-Arab conflict, Peres had created his own vision of the future. In his book *The New Middle East* Peres argued against a particularistic nationalism and in favor of a new Jewish-Arab entity. Herzl's *Old New Land* was his inspiration: "At the end of the nineteenth century, it was fine to dream. At the end of the twentieth, it is time to transform the dream into reality," he writes, referring to Herzl's original ideas, and more specifically to Herzl's vision of a Red Sea–Dead Sea Canal, which Peres now sees as within reach.[33] Just as Herzl's New Society was no traditional nation-state, Peres ultimately envisions "the creation of a regional community of nations, with a common market and elected centralized borders, modeled on the European community."[34]

Twenty years later, the notion of a New Middle East survived only in literature, often in the form of satire and irony. In the vision of American Jewish intellectual Jerold Auerbach, a big sign, "Welcome to the New Middle East" greets the visitors to the airport in Lod. In an essay called "Welcome to Palisdan" and situated in the year 2023 (exactly one hundred years after Loewenberg's and Kingscourt's journey), the Wellesley historian Auerbach has his fictitious character Jacob visit the place that once used to be Israel. He arrives in a territory now called Palisdan, which includes the former Israel, the Palestinian territories, and Jordan, where most Jews are assimilated Hebrew-speaking Canaanites, and only a small Orthodox Jewish refuge remains in Hebron. Tel Aviv has become New Canaan, and Jerusalem a United Nations city.[35]

Perhaps the most fascinating modern parody of *Altneuland* is the 2011 novel *Neuland*, in which Israeli writer Eshkol Nevo reverses the journey of Loewenberg and Kingscourt. He lets an Israeli history teacher called Dori (which was Herzl's name as a child in Budapest) go on a search for a new life in South America where he meets Inbar, the producer of a radio advice show. A century after *Altneuland*, the parents of both main protagonists have gone abroad and their children follow them, at least temporarily. It is no longer clear if the dream remains to build a Jewish society in Israel or to return to the Diaspora in a literary motif first suggested by Philip Roth in his 1993 novel *Operation Shylock*. Nevo, one of the most celebrated Israeli writers whose novels have been translated into many languages, belongs to a new generation of Israelis, many of whom have found a new home in America, Europe, or Australia. His New Society, a universalistic and idealized mini-Israel, is located in Argentina. In an intelligent and at the same time disturbing twist of Herzl's own ideas, Nevo's novel reflects the search of many young secular Israelis who, a century after Herzl's protagonists, embark on the search for a new *Altneuland*.

NOTES

1. Theodor Herzl, *Old New Land/Altneuland* (Minneapolis: Filiquarian, 2007), 94.

2. Amos Elon, *Theodor Herzl* (New York: Holt, Rinehart and Winston, 1975), 348–349.

3. On the utopian aspects of *Altneuland* and its literary traditions, see: Leah Hadomi, "Jüdische Identität und der zionistische Utopieroman," in *Bulletin des Leo Baeck Instituts* 86 (1990): 30–34.

4. Ernst Pawel, *The Labyrinth of Exile: A Life of Theodor Herzl* (New York: Farrar, Straus and Giroux, 1989), 471.

5. Ahad Ha'am, "Altneuland," *Ha-shiloah* 10, no. 6 (Kislev 5663/December 1902); German translation in *Ost und West* 3, no. 4 (April 1903).

6. Theodor Herzl, *The Jewish State* (Minneapolis: Filiquarian 2006), 90.

7. Derek J. Penslar has pointed to the different political readings of Herzl and the Arabs in *Altneuland* in his article, "Historians, Herzl, and the Palestinian Arabs: Myth and Counter-myth," in *Israel in History: The Jewish State in Contemporary Perspective* (London and New York: Routledge, 2007), 51–61.

8. Herzl, *Old New Land*, 193.

9. Herzl, *Jewish State*, 24.

10. Herzl, *Old New Land*, 314.

11. Ibid., 132.

12. Ibid., 79.

13. Ibid., 161.

14. Ibid., 146.

15. Ibid., 160.

16. Yvonne Meybohm, *David Wolffsohn: Aufsteiger, Grenzgänger, Mediator: Eine biographische Annäherung an die Geschichte der frühen zionistischen Bewegung, 1904–1914* (Göttingen: Vandenhoeck and Ruprecht, 2013), 60

17. Quoted in Meybohm, *David Wolffsohn*, 23.

18. Erik Petry, "David Wolffsohn," in *Der Erste Zionistenkongress von 1897: Ursachen, Bedeutung, Aktualität*, ed. Heiko Haumann (Basel: Karger, 1997), 166.

19. Meybohm, *Wolffsohn*.

20. Emil Bernhard Cohn, *David Wolffsohn: Herzls Nachfolger* (Amsterdam: Querido, 1939), 64.

21. David Wolffsohn, "Meine erste Begegnung mit Herzl," quoted in Meybohm, *Wolffsohn*, 56.

22. Meybohm, *Wolffsohn*, 52.

23. Jehuda Reinharz, *The Making of a Zionist Leader* (New York: Oxford University Press, 1985), 335–36.

24. Nahum Goldmann, "The Road towards an Unfulfillable Ideal," *Herzl Year Book*, vol. 3 (New York: Herzl Press, 1960), 131–43, here: 141–42.

25. David Ben-Gurion, "The Call of Spirit in Israel," in *Like Stars and Dust: Essays from Israel's Government Year Book* (Sede Boqer: Ben-Gurion Research Center, 1997), 72.

26. David Ben-Gurion, "Israel in the Diaspora," in *Like Stars and Dust*, 202.

27. Yoram Hazony, *The Jewish State: The Struggle for Israel's Soul* (New York: Basic/New Republic Books, 2000), 144–45.

28. Theodor Herzl, *The Complete Diaries of Theodor Herzl*, ed. Raphael Patai, vol. 4 (New York: Herzl Press, 1960), 1357.

29. Ibid., 1358.

30. Peter Beinart, *The Crisis of Zion* (New York: Times Books/Henry Holt, 2012), 12.

31. Shimon Peres, *The Imaginary Voyage: With Theodor Herzl in Israel* (New York: Arcade 1999), 117.

32. Peres, *The Imaginary Voyage*, 119–20.

33. Shimon Peres with Aryeh Naor, *The New Middle East* (New York: Henry Holt, 1993), 141–42.

34. Peres, *The New Middle East*, 62.

35. Jerold S. Auerbach, "Welcome to Palisdan," in *Against the Grain: A Historian's Journey* (New Orleans: Quid Pro, 2012).

3

Herzl, Ahad Ha'am, and the *Altneuland* Debate

Between Utopia and Radicalism

ERAN KAPLAN

In 1923 Lewis Mumford, an urban designer and an architectural critic, who wrote expansively on technology and its social impact, penned a review of Herzl's *Altneuland*.[1] It is not accidental that Mumford decided to offer a historical assessment of Herzl's novel that year. Herzl's novel was published in 1902, but most of it takes place in 1923 — the year in which Herzl placed his depiction of a thriving Jewish society in the Land of Israel. But Mumford was not interested in evaluating the historical fate of Herzl's vision — he did not offer a checklist of just how much of Herzl's vision actually became a living reality in Palestine in 1923 (not even Herzl's harshest critics condemned him for his futuristic excesses); Mumford sought to evaluate the historical context that informed Herzl's utopian vision and to explore what it might say about the Jewish national movement.

Mumford maintained that Jews in the Diaspora were united by a kind of pragmatic utopianism that helped them sustain a community despite living under constant pressures and threats. To Mumford, Herzl's utopian vision drew its inspiration from a different source: the belief that Israel is a chosen people, the leader of all nations — a myth, which gave them a unique sense of identity. According to Mumford, Herzl combined in his utopian novel universal themes of creating a just and productive society, but unlike other utopias, Herzl's vision was not universal; ultimately it was tied to the Jewish people and its constituting myth. To Mumford, Herzl

identified the historical "fork in the road" that modern Judaism found itself at by the start of the twentieth century: on the one hand, attempting
to create a separate Jewish society, and on the other, reforming the different Jewish communities around the world according to universal values.
Mumford preferred the latter—a Jewish community that aspires to live
according to universal values among other people (to serve as a kind of
light unto the nations among the nations). As for Herzl's choice, Mumford was not optimistic: he believed that it was doomed because it lacked
universal character.

Mumford published his critique well after the publication of *Altneuland* and nineteen years after Herzl's death. But he was not *Altneuland's*
first major critic, nor nearly its fiercest. That honor belonged to Ahad
Ha'am—the pen name of Asher Ginsberg, the writer and thinker and
the leader of what was called "cultural Zionism"—who criticized Herzl's
novel shortly after its publication in very harsh terms (and whose critique clearly informed Mumford's and other critics' take on Herzl's novel).
Today we tend to think of Herzl and Ahad Ha'am as representatives of
political and cultural Zionism respectively; and certainly their different
brands of Zionism—one that emphasized the necessity of establishing
a Jewish state and one that stressed the need to revitalize Jewish culture
as a way to address the Jewish Problem in the modern world—informed
the debate over *Altneuland*. But the debate over the book exposed other
differences between the two men. The ideological gap between them had
to do with their perception of the place of the Jew in the modern world
and the relationship between the individual (Jew) and the political order.
This ideological gap could be understood in the different ways they dealt
with the idea of utopia—the genre that Herzl chose for his novel—and
what it meant for Jews in a rapidly changing world.

Altneuland (Old New Land), which Herzl published in 1902, was written in the style of political utopias. Completed less than a decade after
Herzl began to formulate his Zionist plan to solve the Jewish Problem, it
offered a detailed look at what Herzl hoped a future Jewish society in Palestine might look like. The novel tells the story of Friedrich Lowenberg,
a frustrated, assimilated middle-class Viennese Jew, who decides to join a
German-American (not Jewish) aristocrat, the eccentric Kingscourt, on a
journey to a faraway Pacific island. On the way to the island they stop in

Palestine and encounter a backward, hostile land with a small, struggling Jewish community. After spending twenty years on the island, Lowenberg and Kingscourt decide to return to civilization, and on their way to Europe they again stop in Palestine. This time, to their great surprise, they find what can be described only as a utopia. What they encounter are the marvels of modern technology and a society (the New Society that the Jews founded in Palestine) that practices the most progressive ideals of the era. The bulk of the novel is dedicated to Lowenberg's and Kingscourt's travels in Palestine, where they are hosted by David Littwak, one of the leaders of the New Society, who takes them to see various cities, agrarian communities, and even the New Society's jail, which is an open farming colony that seeks to reform rather than to punish criminals: a utopia if ever there was one.

Shortly after the novel's publication, Ahad Ha'am published a scathing account of *Altneuland*. What stood out to him were two elements in Herzl's novel that were linked: that the New Society depicted in *Altneuland* lacked any unique Jewish cultural characteristics (the residents of the book's New Society, for example, did not necessarily speak Hebrew); and Ahad Ha'am was highly critical of the fact that the New Society's political and social institutions, the political blueprint that Herzl drew upon, were borrowed from other European or North American models. Without exhibiting much intellectual or political restraint (or deference to the leader of the Zionist movement), Ahad Ha'am wrote in his review, "And so faithful was the author [Herzl] to his system, to deprive the Jews any talent for new inventions and to attribute everything to the Gentiles, that even the name of his new state — *Altneuland* — he did not want to leave for the Jews themselves, and put it first in the mouth of one of the Christian characters. . . . Here [*Altneuland*] we see monkeys imitating without any distinctive national trait, and we smell the stench of slavery within liberty, the stench of the European exile, everywhere."[2] Indeed, as Ahad Ha'am argued, several characters throughout the novel tell Lowenberg and Kingscourt that what they created in Palestine was not new — that everything they saw in Palestine, from technological innovations to social experiments, was already tried out in Europe or the United States. For example, at a political rally, David Littwak said, "The New Society, however, did not evolve all this by itself. It did not derive it either from the brains of its leaders or from the pockets of its founders alone. The New Society rests, rather, squarely on ideas which are the common stock of the whole civilized world."[3] Indeed, elsewhere in the novel, Joe Levy, one of the founding fathers of the New Society, says in a recording that Littwak plays for his visitors that, "I do not claim that we created anything new. American, English, French and German engineers had done the same things before us."[4] For Ahad Ha'am, *Altneuland*'s New Society amounted to no more than a simple imitation of non-Jewish ideas and political models. *Altneuland* was nothing more than the work of an ape imitating his masters (non-Jewish Europeans); it was the work of someone who had lost his national pride and was willing to give up on Jewish tradition and history in order to gain acceptance among the nations. Herzl's allies, quite naturally, were dismayed and offended by Ahad Ha'am's tone and style, and they offered various rebuttals of his criticism. The sternest and most personal came from Herzl's lieutenant in the Zionist movement, Max Nordau, who compared Ahad Ha'am to the rabbis who opposed the Zionist movement—he called him a *Protestrabiner*—and claimed that Ahad Ha'am should not be allowed to call himself a Zionist.[5]

In a recent study of Jewish utopian writings, Russell Jacoby[6] has distinguished between what he describes as blueprint utopias, which offer detailed prescriptions as to how people should live their lives (Herzl's *Altneuland* falls squarely within this category), and what Jacoby depicts as iconoclastic utopias, which, following the biblical prohibition on graven images, are not concerned with drawing a clear picture of how a society should look but offer a glimpse at an alternative future by promoting certain humanistic qualities (Martin Buber, as well as Ahad Ha'am, are two of Jacoby's iconoclastic heroes). Jacoby has revisited Buber's own critique of *Altneuland* that, much like Ahad Ha'am, found Herzl's novel lacking in any spiritual qualities (for Buber it was cold and mechanical).[7] To achieve a true change among the Jews (and the entire world) Buber held, a spiritual message of revival was needed—which Herzl's novel lacked. Jacoby, quite correctly, has argued that from our post-Stalin (and post-Hitler) perspective, utopias are seen as dangerous political tools that helped paved the way for the worst totalitarian regimes (after all, one aspect of utopian thinking was that their authors tried to convince people that under the right political and social conditions human beings can be radically transformed). Jacoby has tried to salvage a space for utopian thinking today, by distinguishing between the kinds of utopias that envisioned a highly controlled social order and those that had a radical, humanistic vision for society—those that defied rigid political structures (iconoclastic). In our hypertechnological world, Jacoby has sought to rediscover our humanity as an antidote to the ills of the modern age. And to him, *Altneuland* was part of the problem of the twentieth century, not part of the solution.

Neither Ahad Ha'am nor Buber (and Jacoby could be included here as well) were outlandish in branding Herzl's worldview as mechanical and technical. Herzl himself described in various places his plans for the Jewish people as mechanical in nature. In a letter to Rabbi Moritz Güdemann, for example, in which Herzl described his plan to solve the Jewish Problem, Herzl employed the following imagery: "My plan calls for the utilization of a driving force that actually exists. What is this force? The distress of the Jews! Who dares deny that this force exists? Another known quantity is the steam power which is generated by boiling water in a tea-kettle and then lifts the kettle lid. . . . Such a tea-kettle phenomenon are the Zion experiments. . . . But I say this force is strong enough to run a great machine and transport human beings."[8] Zionism was but a scientific or technical device: there exists historical pressure (antisemitism) that can be released by utilizing its own inertia. And also, we can consider here the way Herzl chose to open *Der Judenstaat* (*The Jews' State*), the pamphlet that introduced his political plan: "It is astonishing how little insight into the science of economics many of the men who move in the midst of active life possess."[9] It is almost *astonishing* that Herzl, a playwright and a famous literary critic and editor, did not look for inspiring metaphors or stirring historical images to open his political manifesto (one can conjure up here the opening lines of the *Communist Manifesto* or the *Futurist Manifesto*) and draw the attention of the masses. Instead he chose to lament the lack of scientific knowledge. In the second chapter of *The Jews' State*, Herzl analyzed the causes of antisemitism: "Antisemitism increases day by day and hour by hour among the nations; indeed, it is bound to increase, because the causes of its growth continue to exist and cannot be removed. Its remote cause is our loss of the power of assimilation during the Middle Ages; its immediate cause is our excessive production of mediocre intellects, who cannot find an outlet downwards or upwards — that is to say, no wholesome outlet in either direction. When we sink, we become a revolutionary proletariat, the subordinate officers of all revolutionary parties; and at the same time, when we rise, there rises also our terrible power of the purse." (This was precisely the cause of Lowenberg's malaise in *Altneuland*: while the previous generation of assimilated, educated Jews was able to find meaningful work, his generation faced stiffer competition as more and more members of European society entered universities in search of upper social mobility.) To Herzl, cultural and religious factors have played a minor role in explaining antisemitism — ultimately, it is the result of modern economic conditions that were brought about by modern, global capitalism. And therefore the solution to antisemitism would need to address the structural issues that underlie the problem. Cultural remedies might work in the short term. But to radically solve the Jewish Problem, the very social and political basis of Jewish life must be altered — and only a political solution can achieve that goal. *Altneuland* was an (admittedly radical) illustration of what such a solution might look like, peppered with lively descriptions of technological innovations.

But did Herzl have a cold and mechanistic view of society (as his critics charged)? Did he think that technology could simply solve social ills without appealing to spiritual sources? In 1900 Herzl wrote a short story, "Solon in Lydia," that tackled the question of the relationship between technology and society. In the story, Solon the Athenian warns Croesus, the king of Lydia, not to accept a revolutionary gift: a device that produces flour without requiring any human toil. Solon tells Croesus, "Consider the heights to which Greek culture has risen compared to older ages. This we owe to hunger, which taught us the value of work. At its highest, work is ennobled into art, just as pondering one's own advantage may be enhanced to the loftiest peaks of philosophy. . . . Do not paralyze man's vision! Perhaps, some far-off cloudless day in history, man will no longer need the goad of hunger. I cannot see that day."[10] Croesus first accepted the fantastic device and then anarchy overtook his kingdom — peace was restored only when the magical tool was destroyed.

Also throughout *Altneuland*, Herzl celebrated the virtues of labor. In keeping with the tradition that was established by earlier Zionist utopian texts (Menachem Eisler's *The Image of the Future* [1882]; Elhanan Leib

Lewinsky's *A Journey to the Land of Israel in the 800th Year of the 6th Millennium* [1902]),[11] David Littwak, for example, tells his visitors that, "Here everyone has the right to work—and therefore to bread. This also implies the duty to work. Beggary is not tolerated."[12] Utopian writers, especially since the early part of the nineteenth century, sought various technological and political solutions that would relieve people of the need to work. To these writers, labor was one of the core evils of modern industrialized society. To Herzl, however, in true Zionist fashion, labor was seen as crucial in the process of transforming Jews into modern citizens. In this regard, Herzl was much closer to A. D. Gordon and his "religion of labor" than to some futuristic writers who reimagined a society beyond labor (and its inherent divisions and conflicts).

Moreover, Herzl's ambivalent view of technology (*Altneuland* is filled with technological wonders, yet for him technology is never the solution) is tied to his very ambivalent view of utopia itself. *Altneuland* was clearly fashioned and structured as a utopian novel. It has many of the genre's core characteristics: chiefly, the depiction of a harmonious future society that is the antithesis of contemporary society. But Herzl himself was very suspicious of the utopian tradition. In the second chapter of *The Jews' State*, in his discussion of the effects of antisemitism, he claimed:

> The oppression we endure does not improve us, for we are not a whit better than ordinary people. It is true that we do not love our enemies; but he alone who can conquer himself dare reproach us with that fault . . .
>
> "No!" Some soft-hearted visionaries will say: "No, it is possible! Possible by means of the ultimate perfection of humanity."
>
> Is it necessary to point to the sentimental folly of this view? He who would found his hope for improved conditions on the ultimate perfection of humanity would indeed be relying upon a Utopia![13]

While in his diaries, in which he chronicled what he described as his Jewish adventure, he wrote, "What, then, differentiates a plan from a Utopia? I shall now tell you in precise language: the vitality which is inherent in a plan and not in a Utopia. . . . There have been plenty of Utopias before and after Thomas More, but no rational person ever thought of putting them into practice. They are entertaining, but not stirring."[14]

More interestingly, in *Altneuland* itself, David Littwak gives a lengthy speech in which he questions and criticizes the modern utopian canon:

The nineteenth century, however, was a curiously backward era. . . . Napoleon the Great did not believe that Fulton's steamboat was practical. On the other hand, the absurd Fourier won adherents for his phalansteries, which were intended to provide homes and workshops for several hundred families. Stephenson, the inventor of the railway, and Cabet, the dreamer of Icaria, were contemporaries. . . . Clouds of smoke ascended from the chimneys of that factory, and darkened the blue heavens. . . . When the wishful human beings looked up, they no longer saw the heavens, but the factory-born clouds of Utopia . . . *Freiland*, a utopian romance by the publicist Hertzka. *Freiland* is a brilliant bit of magic, which may well be compared with the juggler's inexhaustible hat. Beautiful dreams, indeed, or airships if you care to call them that — but not dirigibles. Because those noble lovers of humanity based their ingenious schemes on a false premise. . . . They used as evidence something that still had to be proven, namely, that humanity had already achieved that degree of maturity and freedom of judgment which is necessary for the establishment of a new social order. . . . We did nothing very meritorious. We achieved nothing extraordinary. We did only that which, under the given circumstances and at the given moment, was an historical necessity.[15]

This is utopian writing *against* utopia; in the book itself, a key protagonist, clearly articulating Herzl's own vision, is undermining the significance and historical relevance of the utopian tradition itself. In fact, this speech reads almost like a variation on Marx and Engels's screed against the utopian socialists in their *Communist Manifesto*. There they lampooned their socialist predecessors for relying on fantastical solutions rather than on a political analysis of social and class dynamics. To them, the utopian writers lacked a political quality — their solutions will not change society, they would only exacerbate existing conditions by diverting people from the true causes of social ills. Herzl relied on the bells and whistles of a utopian novel to draw the reader in; but as he said again and again in his Zionist writings, his solution to the Jewish Problem was a simple one: to create a politically independent Jewish society in its own land. After considering the economic and social causes of antisemitism, he came to the conclusion that only a Jewish state would relieve the Jews of their oppression: at its core, *Altneuland* is a simple story—middle-class Jews and poor Jews from the East were caught in a historical dead end, and the only way out was to take them away from Europe and its rigid social structures and create similar conditions away from Europe in which the Jews would be the masters of their historical fate. And while at the time such a solution may have seemed fantastical, to him it was the most practical remedy to what was ailing his people. It was not a utopian solution, but a revolutionary solution: he called on the people to upend the social and economic condition of the Jews.

Perhaps the reason that Herzl chose utopia as a genre to describe the future Jewish national home in Palestine is because he realized how daunting a task he and his movement were facing (this was a crucial component of Ahad Ha'am's criticism of political Zionism). In 1903, a year after *Altneuland*'s publication, the writer, playwright, and political satirist Samuel Gronenmann commented on the feud between Herzl and Ahad Ha'am over the novel, and firmly in Herzl's corner, he suggested the Zionist movement was extremely fortunate to have at its head a person who was a poet, a thinker, and a man of action.[16] Gronenmann mocked those who took issue with the details in the novel—does it matter how people dress when they attend the theater? To him, *Altneuland*'s true achievement was its poetic force—it allowed people to imagine that a future Jewish national home was possible. In Gronenmann's view, Herzl was a leader of a political movement, but the task before that movement was so difficult that only a man with the ability to inspire people and to appeal to their subjective imagination could place it on a viable path.

And wasn't this precisely the core of Ahad Ha'am's (and Buber's) criticism of Herzl's plan? To Ahad Ha'am, political Zionism was simply impractical and therefore dangerous. Palestine couldn't absorb the Jewish masses and provide for them. At the most, Palestine could become a cultural center that would help revitalize Jewish culture worldwide. In some key respects, Ahad Ha'am's critique of Herzl is Burkean to the core. Burke did not argue that the French monarchy was a good political system —he feared the outcome of the revolution, that it would undermine the basic social structures and lead to anarchy. Likewise, Ahad Ha'am did not minimize the dangers of antisemitism. He just felt that political Zionism, Herzl's Zionism, would lead to even greater turmoil. What Ahad Ha'am searched for were ways for Jews to adapt to the rapidly changing world. He sought an agile and evolving Jewish culture that would fit the times. But he did not call for a fundamental change in the political and social lives of Jews—history would take care of that. Martin Buber, in an article supporting Ahad Ha'am's criticism of *Altneuland*, summarized Ahad Ha'am's opposition to Herzl's vision as resting on two pillars: one is that the culture described in the novel was not specifically Jewish, and two, that the Jewish state described in the novel is not an entity that evolved organically but was created too hastily. To Ahad Ha'am (and his supporters), culture was where Jews could achieve real impact and change for themselves and for the world and that was the realm in which they should focus their collective efforts. The Jew was to be a citizen of modern society (wherever that may be); what would set him apart was his culture. And this, politically, is a very conservative point of view. (This is why, ultimately, Jacoby adopts Ahad Ha'am's position; he was afraid of political programs with a clear political goal.) Herzl's position, however, was fundamentally revolutionary.

Ahad Ha'am's biographer, Steven Zipperstein, has argued that Ahad Ha'am's intellectual temperament may best be described as anti-utopian.[17] In a response to those who criticized his initial review of *Altneuland*, Ahad Ha'am argued that if Herzl were to embrace the utopian spirit fully, he would have had to adopt a more radical social program for his New Society and not simply imitate existing models.[18] Ahad Ha'am maintained that since the (Western) political platforms that Herzl wanted to embrace were the ones that created the Jewish Problem in first place, simply importing them to Palestine would not solve the Jewish Problem; the same core problem simply would be imported to the Middle East. If Herzl was a true utopian, according to Ahad Ha'am, he would try to create a unique social program that would address all social ills and eventually also solve the Jewish Problem. Simply creating another state that would be like all other states would not be a sufficient solution. Ultimately for Ahad Ha'am, Herzl was not utopian enough. This was certainly a clever argument. But could Ahad Ha'am point to any actual society or state that exhibited the kind of social vision that Herzl formulated in *Altneuland*? Clearly Herzl was inspired by non-Jewish as well as Jewish Western thinkers. But as Gronenmann suggested, the real impact of Herzl's novel was not in the details of his vision of the future, but in envisioning the very possibility of a Jewish state.

To Jacoby, Ahad Ha'am, while anti-utopian in spirit, was a true iconoclastic utopist. To Jacoby, Ahad Ha'am was a truly radical visionary who could break away from restrictive political formulas and contemplate future scenarios that escape the limits of contemporary paradigms.[19] But it is worthwhile considering here that it is easy to be radical when you eschew actual political, ethnic, and class divisions. When your vision is purely cultural, conflicts are easier to resolve. Or as some of Ahad Ha'am's critics wondered: what does it mean to have a cultural center in Palestine? Will it not need people to support and sustain it? And how will these people live in Palestine, under what political framework? The writer Shmuel Rosenfeld wrote in 1903 that the main lesson to be drawn from the debate between Ahad Ha'am and Herzl is that a radical change in the economic and political life of the Jews was necessary.[20] Rosenfeld pointed to the experience of Hovevei Zion (admirers of Ahad Ha'am) during the first wave of Zionist immigration to Palestine and to their economic and social failures. To him, the lesson was that spiritual urgency was not enough. For Zionism to succeed it needed to upend the economic and social structure of Jewish life. And to him that was the real message of Herzl's novel (and overall Zionist platform). From Rosenfeld's perspective, it was in fact the cultural Zionists who imported the Diasporic way of life to Palestine, while Herzl, who in his novel was critical of Hovevei Zion (the depiction of Palestine in 1902 in the beginning of the novel was bleak to say the least) called for a radical departure from the past in a call for a revolution (and rejuvenation) in Jewish life.

In 1923 Lewis Mumford believed the Western Jews faced two social options: to create a separate Jewish society (which would be unique in the fact that it was Jewish but would be like all other societies) or to live among the nations but aspire to inspire—as a cultural community—the rest of the world by providing a universal message for humanity. Perhaps with regard to his own Jewish community in the United States Mumford was correct—that seeking to leave the United States for a Jewish state in Palestine was a bad trade-off—and the best role that Palestinian/Israeli

Jewry could perform is that of a Jewish cultural center, not a political safe haven—arguably many American Jews still view that as Israel's ultimate role. But was he correct with regard to European Jewry? Was cultural rejuvenation enough for them? It was in analyzing their social situation that Herzl called for a radical change in Jewish life: a singular state for the Jews where they could live like others.

NOTES

1. Lewis Mumford, "Herzl's Utopia," *Menorah Journal* 9 (August 1923): 155–69.

2. Ahad Ha'am, "Yalkut Katan," *Ha-Shelah* 10 (1902): 566–78 in Yossi Goldstein, ed., *Ahad Ha'am ve-Herzl: Ha-Ma'avak al Ofyah ha-Politi ve-ha-Tarbuti shel ha-Tziyonut be-Tzel Parshat Altneuland* (Jerusalem: Merkaz Dinur, Merkaz Zalman Shazar, 2012), 68.

3. Theodor Herzl, *Old New Land* (New York: Markus Wiener, 2000), 152.

4. Herzl, *Old New Land*, 205.

5. Max Nordau, "Achad ha-Am uber Altneuland," *Die Welt* 11 (March 13, 1903) in Goldstein, *Ahad Ha'am ve-Herzl*, 83.

6. Russell Jacoby, *Picture Imperfect: Utopian Thought for an Anti-Utopian Age* (New York: Columbia University Press, 2005).

7. Jacoby, *Picture Imperfect*, 89–93. See also Avi Sagi and Yedidiah Z. Stern, "Haglayat ha-Zehut: Altneuland be-Medinat ha-Yehudim," in *Herzl Az ve-ha-Yom: Yehudi Yashan, Adam Hadash?* (Tel Aviv: Shalom Hartman Institute, 2008), 269.

8. Theodor Herzl, *The Complete Diaries of Theodor Herzl*, ed. Raphael Patai, vol. 1 (New York: Herzl Press, 1960), 237.

9. Theodor Herzl, *The Jewish State*, trans. Sylvie D'Avigdor (New York: American Zionist Emergency Council, 1946). http://www.geocities.com/Vienna/6640/zion /judenstaadt.html.

10. Theodor Herzl, "Solon in Lydia," in *When the Shofar Sounds: Herzl—His Image, Achievements and Selected Writings*, ed. Rëuben R Hecht and Ohad Zemorah (Haifa: Moledeth Development, 2006), 678.

11. Rachel Elboim-Dror, *Ha-Mahar shel ha-Etmol* (Yesterday's Tomorrow), vol. 1 (Jerusalem: Yad Ben Zvi, 1993), 117.

12. Herzl, *Old New Land*, 78. Derek Penslar has argued that *Altneuland* is the embodiment of the Zionist ideal of Jewish occupational transformation. See Derek Penslar, *Zionism and Technocracy: The Engineering of Jewish Settlement in Palestine* (Bloomington, IN: Indiana University Press, 1991), 50.

13. Herzl, *The Jewish State*.

14. Herzl, *Complete Diaries of Theodor Herzl*, 236.

15. Herzl, *Old New Land*, 145–47.

16. Samuel Gronenmann, "Ost und West," *Judische Rundschau* (April 24, 1903) in Goldstein, *Ahad Ha'am ve-Herzl*, 164–65.

17. Steven J. Zipperstein, *Elusive Prophet: Ahad Ha'am and the Origins of Zionism* (Berkeley: University of California Press, 1993), xxii.

18. Ahad Ha'am, "Ha-Het ve-Onsho," *Ha-Shelah* 11 (April 1903) in Goldstein, *Ahad Ha'am ve-Herzl*, 121.

19. Jacoby, *Future Imperfect*, 91.

20. Shmuel Rosenfeld, "Michtav el-ha-Orech," *Ha-Tzfira* 66 (March 18, 1903) in Goldstein, *Ahad Ha'am ve-Herzl*, 101.

4

The Vilna Gaon and His Disciples as Precursors of Zionism
The Vicissitudes of a Myth

IMMANUEL ETKES

From 1808 to 1810, a group of Talmidei Hakhamim emigrated from White Russia and Lithuania to the Land of Israel. The group, about fifty households, headed by several disciples of the Vilna Gaon, laid the foundation for the settlement of the *perushim* in the Land of Israel. These immigrants regarded themselves as bearers of the heritage of the Vilna Gaon, and their immigration is the historical kernel around which the myth was formed, according to which the Gaon of Vilna and his disciples were precursors of Zionism. This myth underwent several metamorphoses and at certain stages had a deep influence on a particular segment of Israeli society.

I. The Myth in the Writings of the Rivlin Family

Two books by Shlomo Zalman Rivlin (1883–1962) were published in Jerusalem in 1947: *Hazon Zion* (The Vision of Zion) and *Kol Hator* (The Voice of the Turtledove). The former describes the rise of a messianic-Zionist movement centered in the city of Shklov, in White Russia, in the late eighteenth century. The founder and first leader of this movement was Rabbi Benjamin Rivlin, the patriarch of the Rivlin family, a Torah scholar and disciple of the Vilna Gaon.

According to *Hazon Zion*, in 1780 Rabbi Benjamin received a large sum of money and took it as a sign that he had been given a mission from heaven. He asked the Gaon to explain the essence of this mission, telling him that he had had a marvelous dream, in which a rabbinical saying figured: "Everyone who dwells in the Land speaks the holy tongue," as well as the verse from Psalms, "to behold the graciousness of the Lord and to visit His temple." The Gaon interpreted this dream as a sign that Rabbi Benjamin and his son Rabbi Hillel must immigrate to the Land and do everything they could for the return to Zion.

The father and son set out to publicize their plan, and their efforts gave rise to a mass movement named Hazon Zion, which sent out preachers to spread their ideas, and officials were appointed to collect money to finance the project. They also advocated the use of Hebrew as a spoken language and composed melodies for songs of Zion.

When Rabbi Benjamin grew old, the leadership of the movement passed to his son, Rabbi Hillel Rivlin, who convened and chaired a national assembly for the return to Zion. Community rabbis, philanthropists, and functionaries from all over the Russian Empire participated in this assembly, which supposedly took place in Shklov in 1806. Resolutions were passed to organize immigration to the Land and support the settlers.

Shlomo Zalman Rivlin's account of the Hazon Zion movement is actually an anachronistic projection of the Hibbat Zion movement of the late nineteenth century back to the late eighteenth century. Moreover, the national assembly was most likely an echo of the meetings of Hovevei Zion in Odessa, and perhaps of the First Zionist Congress in Basel. However, unlike the founders of Hovevei Zion, who were spurred into action by the pogroms in Russia and the inspiration of modern nationalism in Europe, the disciples of the Vilna Gaon were inspired by verses from the Bible, numerology, and a vision that came in a dream.

As for *Kol Hator*, the other book by Shlomo Zalman Rivlin, also published in 1947, it claims to present an early-nineteenth-century work in which Rabbi Hillel Rivlin supposedly recorded the Vilna Gaon's messianic-Zionist teachings: the Gaon was to fulfill the function of the Messiah, son of Joseph. As such, he was responsible for the first stage of redemption: the ingathering of the exiles and settlement of the Land. Like the events during the Second Temple period at the time of Cyrus, the actions of the Messiah, son of Joseph, are supposed to be natural. In the following stage complete redemption would come at the hands of heaven. The Gaon revealed his messianic doctrine to his disciples, and they promised him to immigrate to the Land and begin the work of ingathering the exiles.

Without doubt the manuscript from which *Kol Hator* was printed was written by Shlomo Zalman Rivlin himself, the author of *Hazon Zion*. However, the latter claims in the introduction that he received "the main points of this holy work" from Rabbi Isaac Zvi Rivlin, who was born in White Russia in 1857 and moved to the Land in 1884. He was regarded as a great Torah scholar and an expert in the writings of the Gaon. In 1903 he established the first branch of the Mizrachi movement in Jerusalem and frequently gave sermons with a religious-Zionist tone in Jerusalem synagogues.

Why must we conclude that the story that appears in *Hazon Zion* is entirely divorced from historical reality? First, it is anachronistic, a transparent effort to project the Hibbat Zion movement a century back in time. Moreover, the messianic-Zionist story is not supported by any writings of the Gaon or his disciples. In a testament that the Gaon wrote before his effort to emigrate to the Land, there is no hint of a messianic motive, nor is there any hint at a messianic narrative in what his sons and his greatest students wrote about him.[1] In the first biography of the Gaon, *'Aliyot Eliahu* (The Ascents of Elijah), published in 1856 and based on the traditions and testimony of his disciples and the members of his circle, there also is no support for the messianic story. Finally, as we shall see below, the *perushim* themselves explained the motives for their immigration and did not connect it with any messianic-Zionist vision.

The claim that the Vilna Gaon and his disciples acted in the light of a messianic-Zionist vision was meant to legitimize the Zionist project. Moreover, the myth that represents the immigration of the *perushim* as a proto-Zionist project was a protest and a provocation on the part of the descendants of the *perushim* against secular Zionism, which was contemptuous of what it called the "Old Yishuv." Finally, the myth was intended to bolster the status of the Rivlin family.

As far as we know, the publication of *Hazon Zion* and *Kol Hator* aroused little interest, and the Rivlins' myth had to wait until after the Six-Day War to garner extensive public attention.

II. *Hatequfa Hagedola* by Rabbi Menahem Kasher

In 1969 Rabbi Menaham Kasher published a book entitled *Hatequfa Hagedola* (The Great Age). The author was a learned Haredi, well known for his books on Torah. Rabbi Kasher had no doubt that the events of the Six-Day War were miracles, signs of the beginning of messianic redemption. For that reason he felt an urgent need to interpret events in the light of the sources and to present what he called a "Torah viewpoint" on their meaning. He cited many hundreds of proofs from the Bible, from rabbinical literature, and from the Zohar, as well as the writings of medieval and modern rabbis, to prove that historical events, beginning with the 1948 War of Independence and reaching their climax with the liberation of Jerusalem in the Six-Day War, were indeed clear manifestations of messianic salvation. Rabbi Kasher's book is relevant to this discussion because he published *Kol Hator* as an appendix.

In the introduction that he added to *Kol Hator*, he states that after the chapters of *Hatequfa Hagedola* already had been set in type, he happened upon *Kol Hator* and realized that this was "a great light from the Torah of our rabbi the Gaon Rabbi Eliahu of blessed memory, illuminating our eyes on the matter that stands at the height of the world of Judaism today." The reprinting of *Kol Hator*, two years after the Six-Day War, caused a stir in religious Zionist circles, especially those influenced by the messianic mood that developed under the influence of Rabbi Zvi Yehuda Kook and his disciples.

III. The Academic Stage

The next incarnation of the myth is expressed in its acceptance by academic writers. In 1978 Mordecai Eliav's book appeared: *Erets Yisrael Veyishuva Bameah Ha-19* (The Land of Israel and Its Settlement in the Nineteenth Century). The author, a professor of Jewish history at Bar-Ilan University, wrote this book with a general readership in mind. When he discusses the immigration of the *perushim*, he embraces the Rivlin myth lock, stock, and barrel. Here are his words:

> In the teachings of the Vilna Gaon, a significant place was set aside
> for reflection on imminent redemption and calculations of the end of

days, which were based on Kabbala, with which the Vilna Gaon was deeply involved. The Gaon regarded preparation for redemption as his task: before the advent of the messiah a period would come like that of the time of Cyrus . . . in which there was an ingathering of the exiles and liberation from servitude to foreign kingdoms. . . . Immigration to the Land and establishment of a settlement there were taken to be the basis for the imminent redemption. . . . Only afterward would come the spiritual redemption in miraculous fashion.

After the Vilna Gaon's death, the first practical steps were taken, and a true immigration movement came into being. Shklov, which is near Vilna, was the center of the awakening and propaganda of Hazon Zion. The leaders of the movement were close disciples of the Vilna Gaon, who held a kind of assembly in preparation for emigration in 1806.

The motivating force in this awakening was Rabbi Benjamin Rivlin, the scion of the Rivlin family, a student and relative of the Vilna Gaon, great in Torah learning and general education, and his son Rabbi Hillel, who wrote a pamphlet entitled *Kol Hator*, which deals with ways of hastening redemption in the spirit of the Gaon's teachings, and in the course of time this became the ideological platform of the *perushim*.[2]

Thus, Eliav repeats the essentials of the story in *Hazon Zion*, without its high rhetorical style and allusions to verses and numerologies, giving his account the appearance of solid, historical discussion. The willingness of a historian such as Eliav to accept the Rivlin myth, without doubting the reliability of the stories of *Hazon Zion* and *Kol Hator* and without seeking corroboration in contemporary sources, is surprising. One way to explain (but not to justify) this is Eliav's ideological and cultural connection to religious Zionism and the mood that prevailed at that time in those circles.

In 1985 Yad Yitzhak Ben Zvi published a book on this topic by Arieh Morgenstern.[3] Whereas Eliav cited the Rivlin myth in passing and devoted a page or two to it, Morgenstern devoted an entire monograph to establishing and perfecting it. He accepted the main details of the myth: that the *perushim*, led by the disciples of the Vilna Gaon, immigrated to the Land of Israel out of messianic motivations. This was a new kind of messianism, which spoke of redemption in a natural manner as a first stage, while the second stage would bring full redemption at the hands of heaven. The two actions required in the first stage of the process of redemption were settlement in the Land and building up Jerusalem. These actions were central to the project of the *perushim*. The messianic teaching that underlay their immigration derived from the Vilna Gaon himself, and in the eyes of his disciples he had a messianic mission.

Morgenstern also wrapped the Rivlin story in an ostensibly scholarly envelope. Thus, for example, he devoted an entire chapter to what he called "the background of messianic awakening in the nineteenth century."[4] In that chapter he surveyed a series of historical events, beginning with the French Revolution, the Napoleonic Wars, the emancipation of the Jews of France, the rise of the Reform movement, the Russian conscription decrees, and more. Each of these events, he claims, aroused messianic hopes. And what are his sources? He presents about ten citations from preachers who were active in various places — Germany, England, Holland, Russia, and America — and at various times, from the late eighteenth century to the mid-nineteenth century, all of whom found a sign of imminent redemption in one event or another.

How should we interpret these sources? If we accept Morgenstern's outlook, the Jews of Western, Central, and Eastern Europe all harbored intensive messianic expectations from the late eighteenth until the mid-nineteenth centuries. However, another possibility is that this was a familiar convention: for many generations authors and preachers frequently sought hints that could be used in support of hopes for redemption. In fact, Jewish historians of the modern period have seen no signs of intense messianic expectations in these places and times, indicating that if some authors expressed messianic expectations in relation to one event or another, these were episodic and minor phenomena.

One of Morgenstern's central arguments, which is an addition to the Rivlin story, relates to the cancellation of the three oaths. In the Song of Songs, the expression, "I adjure you, O daughters of Jerusalem," appears three times. This repetition was given a midrashic explanation in the Gemara: "What was the purpose of those three adjurations? — One, that Israel shall not storm the wall; the second, that whereby the Holy One, blessed be He, adjured Israel that they shall not rebel against the nations of the world; and the third is that whereby the Holy One, blessed be He, adjured the idolaters that they shall not oppress Israel too much" (BT Ketubot 111a).

According to Morgenstern, in the early nineteenth century among the disciples of the Gaon a change took place in the traditional view. This change, which can be described as having strategic significance, was based on the gentiles' failure to keep the oath that God had imposed on them: not to oppress Israel too much. This was expressed in the decrees of the cantonists in tsarist Russia, which, Morgenstern believes, threatened the very existence of the Jewish people. Hence, the disciples of the Vilna Gaon concluded that the oaths imposed on the Jewish people also were annulled. In Morgenstern's words: "Not only were the Jewish people free of the prohibition against forcing the end and storming the wall, but they were obligated to insist on their right to religious existence, to take action, and to save themselves from those who threatened to wipe them from the face of the earth. For that purpose it was permitted and even necessary to force the end."[5]

The source upon which Morgenstern bases his claim is a letter of 1830 from Rabbi Israel of Shklov to the Ten Tribes.[6] Rabbi Israel was one of the leaders of the *perushim* who immigrated to the Land, and he was the head of the community of *perushim* who settled in Safed. He entrusted the letter to the Ten Tribes to a Torah scholar named Rabbi Baruch of Pinsk, who had sought the Ten Tribes in the Middle East and Asia and ultimately in Yemen. Here is the passage of the letter on which Morgenstern bases himself: "Give many prayers and tears in your pure souls and your holy souls, dress in royal raiment and enter the inner court before the King of kings, the Holy One, blessed be He, and with their awesome meditations in the holy temples deeply within, because things have gone too far, and if He does not do it for us. . . . Let Him remember our fathers Abraham, Isaac, and Jacob, and be merciful, and gather our exiles and build the House of our sanctity and glory."[7] The argument that, in asking the Ten Tribes to pray for the redemption of the Jewish people, Rabbi Israel of Shklov was acting on the basis of the assumption that the oath not to rush the end had been annulled is simply ridiculous. After all, the daily and festival prayer books are full of prayers calling upon God to redeem the Jewish people. Moreover, nowhere in Rabbi Israel of Shklov's letter does he hint that because the gentiles were oppressing the Jewish people excessively, the oaths were annulled. On the contrary, Rabbi Israel mentions the prohibition against mass immigration to the Land: "Although permission has not been given to all or most of us to storm the wall, this was not said to individuals."[8]

The letter to the Ten Tribes is a fascinating document. Rabbi Israel makes three requests of the Ten Tribes: to pray to God to redeem the Jewish people from the yoke of exile; to send a delegation of Sages to renew rabbinical ordination, which is a precondition for redemption; to contribute money to sustain the Jews who lived in the Land. However, there is no hint of activist messianism in the letter, redemption in a natural manner, or as noted, annulment of the three oaths. This is thus a typical example of Morgenstern's way of "reading" from the sources what is not in them.

Morgenstern's book is not historical research intended to understand the immigration of the *perushim*. Rather, it is an effort to give scholarly backing to the myth created by the Rivlin family, and admittedly it succeeded to a considerable degree. The book was reprinted by Yad Yitzhak Ben Zvi at least six times, and several scholars have overlooked its true character.

IV. Responses to Morgenstern's Book

Responses of academics and public figures to Morgenstern's book varied significantly. In 1985 Yaacov Barnai, a historian of Jewish settlement in the Land of Israel, published a critical assessment of Morgenstern's book in *Davar*. He presented methodological arguments that cast doubt on Morgenstern's statements and also criticized his use of the sources. A longer and more detailed response to Morgenstern's theses by Israel Bartal appeared in *Cathedra* in 1984, following the appearance of an article by Morgenstern in that journal. In 1987 Bartal published a critique of Morgenstern's book in *Zion* and later included both articles in a book.[9] Bartal's arguments are based on expertise in the history of the Jews of Eastern Europe and of Jewish settlement in the Land. Among other things, he wrote: "The simplistic and general formulations typical of many pages in the book often involve completely erasing historical matters, if they are inconsistent with the 'correct direction' of history, as well as the distortion of other matters to make them consistent."

Bartal presented many examples of Morgenstern's manipulation of his sources. However, this criticism did not prevent Morgenstern from continuing to publish articles repeating the same theses. Evidently, Bartal's critique did not prevent readers with a national-religious outlook from using Morgenstern's book as a "scholarly" basis for a myth that suited their leanings. A typical expression of the adoption of this myth among the supporters of Gush Emunim can be found in an article by Zalman Melamed, the rabbi of the settlement of Beit El and one of the leading rabbis of Jewish settlement in "Judea and Samaria." Here are his remarks: "For several generations we have been in a process of 'the beginnings of redemption.' The Vilna Gaon prepared himself for redemption, sent his students to the Land — and, as he did, so, too, the great Hasidic leaders sent their students to the Land with the intention of beginning the process of return and construction of our Land.... Little by little this tendency expanded; the procession grew stronger, the pace increased, the steps grew longer, until, forty years ago, we reached a new stage: the rise of the State of Israel."[10] Here we have a new history of the Zionist project. Zionism is not connected to the pogroms in Russia in the 1880s, nor to the modern antisemitism in Central and Western Europe in the last decades of the nineteenth century. Nor was Zionism influenced by modern nationalism in Europe. Who ever heard of leaders such as Pinsker, Lilienblum, Rabbi Mohilever, and Ahad Ha'am? What's the meaning of Herzl, Nordau, and Jabotinsky for us? Not to mention Weizmann and Ben-Gurion. It all began with the disciples of the Ba'al Shem Tov, who moved to the Land in the late eighteenth century, and the disciples of the Vilna Gaon, who immigrated in the early nineteenth century. From the time of those immigrations, Jewish settlement in the Land of Israel gradually increased until the State of Israel was established.

In contrast, an article in *Davar* (in the same issue as Barnai's critical article) by Tsvi Shiloah, one of the founders of the Movement for the Whole Land, considered the book trustworthy research and embraced its conclusions.

Yet another manifestation of the adoption of this myth, imbued with an official aura, was expressed in the speech given by the former speaker of the Knesset and now president of Israel, Rubi Rivlin, at a conference held in Jerusalem to mark the two hundredth anniversary of the immigration of the Gaon's disciples. Here are his words:

The Rivlin family has the right to be proud of its stability and the deep roots that it struck in the Land during the past two hundred years, of being among the first immigrants, a hundred years before the Zionist movement. Our family was granted the privilege of spearheading immigration to the Land, under orders from the Vilna Gaon and his disciples. Herzl and his associates in the Zionist enterprise have much merit, but the merit of priority belongs to the parents of our parents, who changed the reality in the Land and laid the foundations of Zionism. This was truly the First Aliyah.

Their great deed refutes the theses that are heard from time to time, mainly in the Arab world, that the establishment of the state and even all of Zionism are solely a response to the Holocaust in Europe. The disciples of the Vilna Gaon did not immigrate to the Holy Land out of economic necessity or because of antisemitism. They left behind a whole world of splendid and flourishing communities. Zionism did not begin from economic distress or antisemitism, just as one cannot attribute the establishment of the State of Israel solely to the Holocaust. The Jewish people returned to its historic homeland, and the first immigrants decided to take action and no longer to be content with prayers for Jerusalem, but to renew the connection with it in a practical manner.[11]

Here the Rivlin myth takes on a new task: the immigration of the *perushim* in the early nineteenth century proves that the growth of Zionism was not connected to the persecution of the Jews in the Diaspora. Needless to say, this claim is historically unfounded.

V. The Motivations for the Immigration of the *Perushim*

The immigration of the *perushim* in the early nineteenth century as well as that of the Hasidim that preceded it must be understood as links in a larger continuum of traditional immigration to the Land that extends from the Middle Ages into the nineteenth century. The immigrants were individuals or small fellowships, mostly belonging to the spiritual and religious elite. Immigration to the Land expressed the desire for religious perfection. To live in the Land was to fulfill a commandment; only someone living in the Land can keep the commandments that depend on the Land; prayer in the Land is more influential, because the Land stands before the gate of heaven; because of its sanctity, the Land is most appropriate for those who wish to devote themselves to the study of Torah, and so on. The traditional immigrants moved to the Land with the intention of devoting all their time to the service of God and relied on contributions from the Diaspora. They expected support because they saw themselves as representatives, since no one thought that all or even most of the Jews could immigrate to the Land. Moreover, they were worthy of support because they prayed for their brethren in the Diaspora.

These were the general characteristics of the traditional immigration. As for the particular motivations behind the immigration of the *perushim*, these were stated explicitly in a letter in rhymed prose written by the leaders of the *perushim* in Safed, which they placed in the hands of Rabbi Israel of Shklov in 1810, when they sent him back to Russia to organize fund-raising there. This letter is a kind of "calling card" that presents the program of the *perushim*. Here are a few passages from it:

> The Land announces, the Land arouses, the Land, what does its tongue say? . . . In me the Torah is explained, in me fear of Him is strengthened, in me the soul is liberated from the sins engraved with an iron and lead pen. . . .
>
> Now blessed be God who has mercy on the Land, and He has visited me with the gathering of sons who are prepared for every holy matter. . . . They gather to raise the horn of Torah . . . to join the four ells of the Halakha to the four corners of the pure and holy Land. . . .
>
> In our yeshiva here, which is named after the Rabbi of the Exile, our master the true Gaon, our rabbi Eliahu the righteous man of blessed memory from Vilna, we study Gemara together with concentration and the halakhot of the *Shulhan 'Arukh* with the explanations of our rabbi the Gaon of blessed memory we explain it fully. On our days of study we wrap ourselves in prayer shawls and tefilin all day long, happy is the eye that has seen all these things.[12]

This is a ceremonious letter expressing the powerful experience of renewal and mission. The *perushim* sought to restore the status of the Land as a major center of Torah study. This entire movement was inspired by the Vilna Gaon. The House of Study was named after him. They studied the Gaon's commentary on the *Shulhan 'Arukh*, and like the Gaon, wore prayer shawls and tefilin all day long. In this context the meaning of the name *perushim* becomes clear. Both in his way of life and in his writings, the Vilna Gaon fostered an ideal of asceticism (*perishut*), the avoidance of all matters of this world for the sake of Torah study. The disciples and admirers of the Gaon strove to adopt this ideal, with his inspiration.

Conclusion

I have presented the motivations for the dissemination of the myth and the reasons for its acceptance and adoption in certain circles. The question with which I wish to conclude this discussion is: why was it so easy to adopt such a myth? The explanation is to be sought in the complex encounter between messianism and Zionism. Scholars all agree that Zionism was born from modern European nationalism and that without modern nationalism, it is impossible to imagine the growth of Zionism. An important question, one that deserves investigation on its own account, is whether and to what degree Zionism was influenced by traditional messianism. However, regardless of the answer to that question, there is no doubt that in retrospect, after the appearance of Zionism, its proponents employed messianism, both as a historical precedent and as a source of inspiration. The most famous example of historiography that enlisted messianism for the purposes of Zionism is in the writings of Ben-Zion Dinur, as is well known.

Metaphorical use of messianic symbolism is found in Herzl's *Altneuland*. Herzl calls the great synagogue in Jerusalem the Temple, which was to be built of hewn stone, and within it Herzl placed the copper altar and the basin. When the Hebrew University was founded in Jerusalem, the Zionist leaders, including Weizmann, called the university a Temple. These are only a few examples of a broader phenomenon: Zionism's use of concepts and symbols from the tradition, while secularizing them.

However, secular historians such as Dinur, who occasionally see messianism as a source of inspiration for Zionism, undoubtedly are aware of the essential difference between them, and while leaders such as Herzl and Weizmann used messianic symbols metaphorically, this is not the case regarding the leaders of religious Zionism. For them the messianic idea is a serious matter. Therefore, some of the rabbis who supported Zionism regarded it as an expression of the beginning of the process of redemption in the traditional sense. Among these were the Netsiv of Volozhin (Rabbi Naftali Zvi Yehuda Berlin) and of course Rav Avraham Isaac Kook. Two precursors of Zionism paved the way for these rabbis: Rabbi Kalischer and Rabbi Alkalai, who devised the formula to bridge traditional messianism and Zionism, stating that the first stage in redemption was to be expressed in immigration and settlement in the Land "in a natural way," whereas in the second stage, full redemption would come at the hand of heaven.

The myth about the Vilna Gaon and his disciples as precursors of Zionism is based on the anachronistic projection of this idea several decades into the past. Fostering and disseminating this myth express a desire to blur the distinction between traditional messianism and Zionism as a modern phenomenon. Whether this blurring is a result of innocence and historical ignorance or malicious distortion, its meaning is an effort to deny the origins of Zionism and its character as a modern phenomenon —with all that it implies. In some national religious circles, the view is prevalent that the settlements in the occupied territories are the legitimate heirs of Zionism. This myth of the disciples of the Gaon as precursors of Zionism enables them to appropriate the history of Zionism as well.

NOTES

1. See Immanuel Etkes, *The Gaon of Vilna: The Man and His Image* (Berkeley: University of California Press, 2002), 10–36.

2. Mordechai Eliav, *Eretz Israel in the Nineteenth Century* (Hebrew) (Jerusalem: Keter, 1978), 85–86.

3. Arieh Morgenstern, *Messianism and the Settlement of Eretz-Israel in the First Half of the Nineteenth Century* (Hebrew) (Jerusalem: Yad Ben Zvi, 1985).

4. Ibid., 13–37.

5. Ibid., 32.

6. Avraham Yaari, *Letters from the Land of Israel* (Hebrew) (Ramat Gan: Masadah, 1971), 342–57.

7. Ibid., 353. Cited by Morgenstern, *Messianism and the Settlement of Eretz-Israel*, 32.

8. Yaari, *Letters from the Land of Israel*, 354–55.

9. Israel Bartal, *Exile in the Homeland* (Hebrew) (Jerusalem: Mossad Bialik, 1994), 250–95.

10. *Nequda*, no. 119 (March 1988).

11. From the website of 'Aruts 7, October 15, 2009.

12. Yaari, *Letters from the Land of Israel*, 329–30.

5

Me'ir Ya'ari and Hashomer Hatza'ir

The Movement Is Me

AVIVA HALAMISH

For over half a century, Me'ir Ya'ari (born in 1897 in Galicia) was the undisputed leader of Hashomer Hatza'ir [hereafter: HH], a three-wing socialist-Zionist movement. Founded prior to World War I in Eastern Europe, HH was the first and largest Zionist *youth movement* between the World Wars, with approximately seventy thousand members in 1939. In 1927 graduates of HH founded a countrywide *kibbutz movement*—Hakibbutz Ha'artzi [hereafter: KA], which numbered about 6,500 members and a total population of 13,611 on the eve of Israel's independence. In 1946 the KA, which since its establishment had constituted an independent political stream in the Jewish labor movement in Palestine, merged with its urban branch the "Socialist League" (founded in 1936) to form a *political party*, Hashomer Hatza'ir, which in January 1948 joined two other socialist-Zionist parties to form a new party—Mapam (Mifleget Hapo'alim Hame'uhedet: the United Workers Party).

Though Ya'ari was the leader of HH as a whole, he was, first and foremost, the leader of the KA. In February 1987, the day after he passed away at his home in Kibbutz Merhavia, Abba Kovner, a long-time rival, wrote:

> In 1927 he was the one who stood up, as a young man, and made the decision to establish Hakibbutz Ha'artzi, and on that very day he turned a band of young dreamers into a society of builders and fighters and transformed them from rootless symbols into a movement that had an enduring imprint on the map of the Land of Israel, achieved through labor and trials.

Even had this been the only deed he performed during his richly active life, Me'ir Ya'ari should be remembered alongside the most distinguished names in the chronicle of the life of the Jewish People throughout the generations.[1]

This article aims to examine Ya'ari's decisive role in shaping the ideology and praxis of HH and in molding its structure and modus operandi, as well as his influence on the lives and fate of many of its members. The discussion will focus on his role as leader of the KA. His involvement in the youth movement was marginal; indeed, he is not once mentioned in the book by Jehuda Reinharz about HH in Germany in the 1930s.[2] Since both HH and Ya'ari's leadership underwent a substantial transformation as a result of the devastating impact of the Holocaust and the fundamental changes following the founding of Mapam and the establishment of Israel, and since Ya'ari's role as the general secretary of the political party was not the apex of his career, this article focuses on the period from the early 1920s to the first years of Israeli statehood.

The Making of an All-Encompassing Leader

Ya'ari's prolonged leadership seems, on the face of it, enigmatic: he was not one of the founders of HH; he had difficulty creating, nurturing, and preserving personal ties with his peers; his speech and ideas were difficult to follow; his health was fragile for much of his life; and he was easily angered and often hurt the feelings of his associates.[3] But from an early age, he was driven by the sense that he was born to lead. Nonetheless, his ascent to leadership began after his arrival in Palestine in 1920. In the early stages, he proved to be a charismatic leader, in accordance with Max Weber's definition of *charisma* as "a certain quality of an individual personality, by virtue of which he is set apart from ordinary people and treated as endowed with supernatural, superhuman, or at least specifically exceptional powers or qualities."[4] According to Weber, it is irrelevant whether the leader actually possesses extraordinary powers or qualities; what is important is that his followers believe that such qualities exist. Thus, Weber's definition of charisma depends more on the disciples and how they view the leader than on his actual qualities, and this was the case with Ya'ari.[5]

Ya'ari first emerged as a leader toward the end of 1920 at Bitanya Ilit, a camp overlooking the Kinneret (Sea of Galilee), among a group of about two dozen young men and a few women, HH graduates who recently had arrived in Palestine. As the eldest member of the group, he was in the right place at the right time. He shared his comrades' crisis resulting from the dramatic shift from the euphoria of the national and personal revolution inherent in the very act of 'aliyah (Jewish immigration to Eretz Israel), to the grief and hardships of "the day after the revolution": hard work, arduous physical conditions, malaria, and social isolation; and he helped them to overcome these difficulties. He responded to the spiritual and emotional needs of his comrades by holding talks that combined sincere exposure, frank discussion, and authoritative instruction. He had the gift of empathetic listening, which produced both openness and psychological dependence among members of the group, while at the same time incurring resentment in others, particularly those who were competing with him for the leadership role. The first stage of his leadership ended in a fiasco in late 1921, when he was expelled from the group after his comrades tired of his authoritative behavior and selective attitude.

Beginning with his comeback in mid-1923, he adjusted to the new conditions by aspiring to be a leader of a network of groups spread throughout the country. He did not relinquish all the features of his early leadership style, but rather modified some and added new ones. Since his charisma was most effective in small, intimate groups, in order to gain a hold over wider circles, he needed to build institutions, and these were embodied in the KA as a movement and in every member kibbutz.

The KA incorporated kibbutzim that had developed as a synthesis of the two earlier forms of the kibbutz: the small group (kvutzah), which operated as an intimate, selective, enclosed settlement, conducting its collective life with little involvement in political activity; and the large, growing, and open kibbutz, which considered itself, first and foremost, a tool for the realization of national and social aims. The kibbutz founded by graduates of HH was defined as an "organic kibbutz," large enough to be economically and socially self-sustaining and to fulfill national and social goals, but small enough to maintain close, friendly relations among its members. Its development was gradual ("organic"), absorbing groups of graduates of the HH youth movement from a common geographical area.[6]

In 1927 when the KA was established, Ya'ari was already its official recognized leader, standing shoulder to shoulder with Ya'akov Hazan (1899–1992). The two were known as the "historic leadership" of HH, with Ya'ari always the indisputable number one.[7] Ya'ari strove to be the all-encompassing leader of an exclusive and selective movement rather than a leader of limited scope in a more loosely structured organization such as a political party. And he molded the structure and the modus operandi of the movement to suit his type of leadership, by establishing each individual kibbutz as a comprehensive and total economic, social, cultural, and political entity, and the KA as an exclusive and selective organization, which opened its gates only to those who had received prior educational training, and did not aspire to integrate society as a whole. For many years he was a total leader (not to be confused with totalitarian, though there is a claim that he verged on that type of behavior), in charge of all spheres of movement activities and involved in many circles of its members' lives, from ideological matters to intimate family relations.

Ya'ari was able to control his disciples partially because, like most of the Jewish population in Mandatory Palestine, the founders of the KA and the majority of its members were newcomers. Most of them had entered the country through the quotas for working immigrants allotted by the Mandate government, without any economic means of their own. They were dependent on the movement, which had enabled them to immigrate to Palestine and then served as their absorption network.[8] The dependence of the members on their kibbutz and that of each kibbutz on the nation-wide movement reinforced the centralist control of Ya'ari (and Hazan) over the movement.

Ya'ari's way up was paved, partially, by eliminating potential rivals, thus probably depriving the movement of persons of stature. Then, with Hazan's consent and cooperation, he consistently staved off competition. The two controlled the movement assertively, expecting full obedience to all instructions coming from above. They unilaterally decided where the graduates of the youth movement would settle and which kibbutz would receive additional members. Moreover, during the first forty years, Ya'ari especially exercised control over the appointment of members to movement institutions. Actually, the selection process in the KA (and in Mapam) took the form of "democratic approval" rather than democratic elections. It was a process of consensual appointment in two stages: first, the candidate was selected, in most cases by Ya'ari, through informal procedures, and then, with no competition, the candidacy was approved by the authorized forums of the movement. In the language of the movement, the candidate "accepted the movement's ruling."[9]

Ya'ari exerted moral pressure on members to work for the movement. He would come to kibbutz assemblies in order to convince the members to release one of them for a movement mission, and it was clear that it would be hard for them to resist his personal authority. Thus he wrote to a kibbutz member: "You have to go immediately, and there is no moral justification for refusal. I am telling you wholeheartedly: it is not a tragedy if you leave a child for a month with a dedicated caretaker (*metapelet*). This is the smallest sacrifice that can be demanded of a member of the movement in an emergency."[10]

He controlled the movement's emissaries and functionaries with a strong hand, and it was well known that he was the person who determined who would take on a mission in the city and who would go overseas. He also brought about the return to their kibbutzim of officeholders who fell out of favor. This tightened his control over members of the movement at times when public office, missions, and travel abroad were almost the only escape from tedious work on the kibbutz. The option of higher education rarely was available to kibbutz members in those days.

Ideological Collectivism

"Ideological collectivism," which Ya'ari invented and strictly guarded, was designed to preserve the cohesiveness of each kibbutz and of the movement as a whole.[11] He defined "ideological collectivism" as freedom of debate; the search for a common resolution; solidarity (i.e., discipline) in action.[12] Put simply, debates and disagreements were regarded as legitimate up to the point when a decision was taken. From then on, everyone had to conform to the "movement line."

Ideological collectivism had a double meaning. One was obedience, namely, the organizational centralism discussed above: each member and each kibbutz had to comply with the decisions of the movement. The leadership subjected the kibbutzim to the authority of the movement's institutions and threatened to impose sanctions on those failing to allow their members to work for the movement, as well as on members who shirked such missions. "It is unacceptable," Ya'ari said in 1936, "that the free will of the individual or the kibbutz be the decisive factor. There is no autonomy in political action."[13] A kibbutz that did not accept the decisions of the movement's central institutions faced expulsion from the KA.

The other, and better-known, manifestation of ideological collectivism was loyalty of all members to the ideological and political line of the movement. No opposition was allowed. KA members were prohibited from joining any political framework other than the KA or its political party — Hashomer Hatza'ir (1946–1947) and Mapam after 1948—and certainly from playing an active role in any other political body. Ya'ari not only introduced the notion of ideological collectivism, he also determined its content and blocked the implementation of changes demanded by other members; however, when he deviated from the old line, the movement followed suit. The most prominent issues on which ideological collectivism was enforced were adherence to the Marxist line, hand in hand with affinity for the Soviet Union, and the stance on the Arab question, mainly promoting and supporting the binational solution for Palestine.

Revolutionary Marxism and Soviet Orientation

At the beginning of his public life, Ya'ari did not exhibit a cohesive ideological outlook. It was not until 1923 that he publicly presented his worldview, in the essay "Smalim tlushim" (rootless symbols), which reflected a kind of religious approach in the style of A. D. Gordon.[14] Within a year, however, he relinquished this outlook and adopted the revolutionary Marxist version of socialism as the guiding ideology of HH, second only to its primary ideological pillar: Zionism.[15] The shift to Marxism was made, to a great extent, out of Ya'ari's desire to distinguish HH from other political frameworks of the time and to maintain its cohesive unity and social uniqueness, with the implicit intention of safeguarding his status as leader. The movement followed his new path, though not without paying a price. Members who were stuck between their more introverted inclinations and the extroverted, hyperactive Marxist temperament and collective ideology that Ya'ari imposed on the movement were caught in a bind that could be resolved only by leaving the kibbutz, which was not always a real option, or by quiet compliance.

For many years, Ya'ari approved of the policy of the Soviet Union, identified with it, supplied justifications for its flaws, and defended it in speeches and writings. His esteem for the Soviet Union was not diminished by the purges in the Communist Party and the Red Army, the Moscow show trials (1936–1938), Stalin's totalitarianism, and even the Molotov-Ribbentrop Pact of August 1939, which he insisted on calling "the neutrality pact." His views became the official line of the movement; reservations expressed by members within the narrow scope permitted by ideological collectivism were ignored. Admiration for the Soviet Union became widespread after the Nazi invasion of the Soviet Union (June 1941), thanks to the heroic battle of Stalingrad and the asylum granted to hundreds of thousands of Jews in the central Asian republics, and later because of the role played by the Red Army in liberating concentration camps, Soviet diplomatic support for establishing a Jewish state in Palestine, and the arms supplied to Israel (via Czechoslovakia) during the War of Independence. In the late 1940s, admiring the Soviet Union was the bon ton, and Ya'ari's favorable stance in fact echoed the general consensus of the time.

After the establishment of Israel, Ya'ari idolized the Soviet Union, in keeping with prevailing winds. But his admiration persisted in spite of clear signs of a negative turn in Soviet policy toward Israel and Zionism, and the accumulating gloomy news about its attitude toward Soviet Jewry. The jewel in his ideological crown was the *étapes* (stages) theory, incorporated into the KA's ideological platform in 1927, as an intellectual effort to relieve the tension—that bordered on an internal contradiction—between the nationalist Zionist aspect that characterized HH from its inception and revolutionary Marxism, which was added later. The core of the theory was the gradual realization of socialist Zionism, in two main stages: first, the national, Zionist stage, and then the socialist revolution. Taking this theory at face value, the establishment of the State of Israel was tantamount to accomplishing the first stage, signaling that now was the time to launch the second stage. Therefore, the kibbutz, the apple of Ya'ari's eye, had completed its national role and now had to undergo a metamorphosis in order to carry out its role in the social revolution. Such a scenario posed a grave dilemma for the KA, and Ya'ari sought to postpone the shift from the first, national stage to the second, socialist one. In the interim, he tried to channel the revolutionary fervor, through a kind of sublimation, toward the country where socialism actually was being realized. In a society that was in need of ideological backing and eager for a guiding theory, at a time when Zionism had become self-evident, an almost-fulfilled mission, and people were realizing that socialism would not be quick to arrive in Israel, the Soviet orientation was intended to serve as verbal and emotional compensation for postponing the socialist revolution in the here and now.

At that juncture, Ya'ari turned to the writings of Ber Borochov in search of ideological fortification, and he integrated Borochov's doctrine as a guiding line into the ideology of HH, by modifying Borochov's original phrase, "the territorial concentration of the Jewish people in Palestine," into the most popular Israeli slogan of the time: "the ingathering of the exiles." As long as this ultimate goal was not achieved, he contended, the national stage had not been completed and the second stage, the revolutionary one, should be postponed. Borochov's theory also was intended to supply a Zionist response to the Marxism-Leninism still popular in the movement. As in 1924, when he adopted Marxism and turned it into one of the central pillars of HH ideology, so in the early 1950s he used Borochov's theory to provide an updated ideology to supplement Marxism-Leninism with elements of Zionism. He made loyalty to Borochov's theory an ideological litmus test for membership in the movement, and again, once he made the shift, the movement followed suit. In 1952 the central committee of Mapam decided to carry posters with Borochov's picture during the May Day parade alongside the four traditional ones, those of Karl Marx, Friedrich Engels, Vladimir Lenin, and Joseph Stalin. In the following years, the KA publishing house (Sifriyat po'alim) published three substantial collections of Borochov's writings.

The Rise and Fall of the Binational Idea

The binational idea had been discussed in HH deliberations ever since the establishment of the KA (1927), but only in 1937, after the Peel Commission Report recommended partitioning Palestine and establishing a Jewish state in a rather limited segment of it, did binationalism actually surface as a major issue for HH, attracting attention as well as criticism.[16] In the heated controversy generated by the Peel report in the Yishuv and in the Zionist Movement, HH objected to the partition plan, and at the vote during the Twentieth Zionist Congress (1937), HH was in the minority camp that opposed partition.

The Arab question did not rank high on Ya'ari's ideological agenda, and he did not really deal with it until late 1941, when he launched the move toward founding a full-scale political party. In order to justify turning HH into an independent political party rather than joining the hegemonic labor party Mapai, Ya'ari found it necessary to emphasize issues of disagreement with the latter, mainly the attitudes toward the Soviet Union and toward the Arab question. He elaborated on the binational issue for the first time in his book *Befetah tekufa* (At the doors of an epoch), which was published in early 1942 and served as the movement's official platform. Until he began writing the book in 1941, he never had formulated a comprehensive position regarding the Arab question; therefore, he relied on a book written a few years earlier by another member of HH, Mordechai Bentov, advocating the establishment of a binational regime in Palestine, which would be neither an Arab nor a Jewish state, but rather an Arab-Jewish state or a Palestinian state.

After 1942 HH's voice on binationalism became louder and clearer. During the deliberations of the Extraordinary Zionist Conference convened by the American Emergency Committee of Zionist Affairs at the Biltmore Hotel in New York in May 1942, HH stood alone in its abstention from voting on what would be known as the "Biltmore Program," urging that the gates of Palestine be opened to massive Jewish immigration and that Palestine be established as a Jewish commonwealth integrated into the structure of the new democratic world.[17] For the next five years, until late 1947, there were only two Zionist proposals for the future of Palestine: the Biltmore Program and the binational plan of HH, according to which the partition would not be territorial but rather in the governance—parity in the ruling institutions, regardless of the relative size of the Arab and Jewish populations. As a result, during the intensive international activity regarding the future of Palestine following World War II, the distinct ideas and plans of HH received publicity and attention far beyond the political weight of the organization presenting them.

Thus, when the Anglo-American committee of inquiry came to Palestine in 1946, HH submitted a printed memorandum in English and Hebrew, entitled *The Case for a Bi-National Palestine*,[18] proposing the establishment of a binational Arab-Jewish state in Palestine with joint sovereignty, which should be called neither Jewish nor Arab, with the ideal for the future similar to that of the Swiss Confederation. It is commonly believed that this memorandum influenced the conclusions and recommendations of the Anglo-American Committee, which vaguely proposed "that Palestine shall be neither a Jewish state nor an Arab state" but rather binational.[19]

A similar scenario took place in July 1947, during the visit of the United Nations Special Committee on Palestine (UNSCOP). Again, HH submitted and published a memorandum, *The Road to Bi-National Independence for Palestine*.[20] The memorandum's point of departure was the stipulation that there was no solution to the complex realities in Palestine other than a binational one that preserved territorial integrity; in the interim, HH insisted on unrestricted Jewish immigration and the creation of a Jewish majority in Palestine.

The binational chapter in the history of HH came to an abrupt end late in the summer of 1947. At a Zionist general council meeting in August 1947 in Zurich, Ya'ari castigated the chairperson of the Jewish Agency Executive, David Ben-Gurion, for demanding only a major part of Palestine for the Jewish state and not its entirety.[21] A few days later, right after the publication of the UNSCOP conclusions (on August 31), which essentially called for the partition of Palestine with economic unity,[22] Ya'ari dispatched a series of letters from Zurich to movement leaders and members, calling on them to recognize the reality and avoid cutting themselves off from it. He expressed the apprehension that though HH may be right, the movement would be left alone when all the others turned their backs on it. Once the UNSCOP conclusions were published, he went on to argue, HH no longer could state its position in exactly the same manner as it had before.

Ya'ari preceded his movement's institutions in shifting from a binational vision toward consent to partition. While he was still in Europe, and before his instructions and explanations reached Palestine, the executive committee of the KA expressed opposition to partition in principle. It went on to define UNSCOP's recommendations as a "poor partition" with impossible borders.[23] By force of inertia, HH maintained its previous positions and allowed no drastic changes to be made while Ya'ari still was abroad. Once his revised stance was fully explained to them, the movement's institutions adopted it with all due expedience.

When the moment of truth arrived, HH abandoned binationalism without much difficulty. Years later, Bentov, the personality in the movement most closely identified with binationalism, said that "in our movement matters moved very quickly," and since the party concluded that Zionism faced a historic opportunity and it also became clear that neither the Jews nor the Arabs wanted to work together, the obvious conclusion was that there was no choice but to partition the country. This position was accepted with virtually no anguish or sacrifice.[24] The ease with which HH shifted from its vision of a binational society throughout Palestine to reconciliation with partition and the establishment of a Jewish state in part of the country may well indicate that the movement's binationalist roots were never too deep and that replacing one plan with another did not require brute force. On the contrary, the establishment of a Jewish state responded to aspirations that had existed in HH for some time, which Ya'ari had ignored and in some instances suppressed. It is quite evident that the Soviet Union's support of partition eased the turnabout by Ya'ari and his movement regarding binationalism.

Several days after the United Nations General Assembly decided to partition Palestine into a Jewish state and an Arab state (November 29, 1947), Ya'ari said, "This day, on which independence is granted to the Jewish People in only half of the homeland, is a day that fills us with joy. . . . joy mingled with sorrow. We are happy about independence — we mourn because of partition." Despite his disappointment, he declared that HH was prepared to be "among the originators, builders and defenders of this Hebrew state."[25] This declaration embodies HH's behavior all along: an outspoken ideological and political opposition, but a loyal one and a full partner to the execution of the Zionist policy. HH, as a youth movement and as a settlement movement, took part in the Zionist struggle and activities on all fronts, far beyond its political weight. In retrospect, the actual contribution of HH to the fulfillment of the Zionist enterprise transcended its controversial positions; both should be attributed to a great extent to its leader: Me'ir Ya'ari.

Assessing Ya'ari's Role in Jewish History

The relationship between Ya'ari and HH reflects the connection between the "hero" and his era, and should also be interpreted as a variant of the interaction between a leader and his followers. An assessment of Ya'ari's role as a leader shows not only that he answered the needs and yearnings of individuals and of the collective, but in many respects, reflects the story of his time and society. It reveals not only the *zeitgeist* of the era, but also what can be termed the "movement*geist*," the unique features of HH, mainly as a kibbutz movement.

Refraining from speculations such as if and how HH could have been conceived without Ya'ari's leadership, suffice it to say that he played an indispensable role in shaping the movement into an organization and had a remarkable impact on the private lives of many of his disciples. In real time, they yearned for his advice and opinions, and in retrospect, many admitted that he had a notable influence on their lives; some view this favorably with a sense of gratitude, others with contempt, anger, and sorrow. In both instances, the fact of his imprint is evident. He, as a leader, held the conviction that "the movement is me," and for many of his disciples, he indeed personified the movement. The unique and generally accepted contribution of HH to the history of the Jewish people in the twentieth century and of Israel, in particular the involvement of its members in various manifestations of resistance and endurance during the Holocaust, and its network of kibbutzim spread throughout the country, expands Ya'ari's historical significance as the leader of that movement far beyond its modest numerical size.

NOTES

1. Abba Kovner, "Ne'esaf el amav," *'Al hamishmar*, February 22, 1987.
2. Jehuda Reinharz, *Toldot hashomer hatsa'ir begermania, 1931–1939* (Tel Aviv: Sifriyat Po'alim, 1989).
3. Ya'ari's ascent to leadership is more fully discussed in Aviva Halamish, "Manhig mehapes tzibur: Darko shel Me'ir Ya'ari lehanhagat hashomer hatza'ir, 1918–1927," *'Iyunim Bitkumat Israel* 12 (2002): 99–121; his prolonged leadership is analyzed in Aviva Halamish, "The Historic Leadership of Hakibbutz Ha'artzi: The Power of Charisma, Organization and Ideology," *Journal of Israeli History* 31, no. 1 (March 2012): 45–66.

4. Max Weber, *The Theory of Social and Economic Organization*, trans. A. M. Henderson and Talcott Parsons (New York: Columbia University Press, 1947), 359.

5. Ibid., 358.

6. For the history of the various kibbutz movements and the differences between them, see Henry Near, *The Kibbutz Movement: A History*, 2 vols. (Oxford: Oxford University Press, 1992–97).

7. For Hazan's role in the historic leadership of HH, see Ze'ev Tzahor, *Hazan—tnu'at hayim: Hashomer hatza'ir, hakibbutz ha'artzi, mapam* (Jerusalem: Yad Ben Zvi, 1997).

8. For a general survey of the immigration issue in Mandatory Palestine, see Aviva Halamish, "The *Yishuv*: The Jewish Community in Mandatory Palestine," sect. 6: "Major Spheres of *Yishuv* Activity," in Jewish Virtual Library Publications. http://www.jewishvirtuallibrary.org/jsource/isdf/text/halamish.html.

9. See Natan Yanai, "He'arot letipus manhiguto shel Me'ir Ya'ari," in *Haguto umanhiguto shel Me'ir Ya'ari z"l: Shanah lemoto*, ed. Moshe Tchijik (Haifa: Haifa University, 1988), 27–36.

10. Ya'ari to Avraham Yaffe, July 5, 1939, Hashomer Hatza'ir Archive, Giv'at Haviva (hereafter HHA), 95–7.8(10).

11. For further discussion and references, see Halamish, "The Historic Leadership of Hakibbutz ha'artzi."

12. Ya'ari, "Zichronot," October 21 [year missing], Kibbutz Merhavia Archive, Me'ir Ya'ari Files, 8 (3).

13. Meeting of Hakibbutz ha'artzi Executive Committee (Hava'ad hapo'el), December 22, 1936, HHA, 5–10.1(13).

14. Me'ir Ya'ari, "Smalim tlushim," *Hedim: Kovetz lesifrut* 2 (1923): 93–106. See also Aviva Halamish, "Hashpa'ato hadi'alektit shel A. D. Gordon 'al hashomer hatza'ir," *Cathedra* 114 (December 2004): 99–120.

15. For further discussion and references, see Aviva Halamish, *Me'ir Ya'ari, biografiyah kibutzit: Hamishim hashanim harishonot, 1897–1947* (Tel Aviv: Am Oved, 2009), 256–73; Aviva Halamish, *Me'ir Ya'ari: Ha'admor mimerhavia, shnot hamedina* (Tel Aviv: Am Oved, 2013), 46–98.

16. For further discussion and references, see Aviva Halamish, "Bi-Nationalism in Mandatory Palestine: The Case of ha-Shomer ha-Tza'ir," in *The Nation State and Religion*, vol. 1: *Nationalism and Binationalism: The Perils of Perfect Structures*, ed. Anita Shapira, Yedidya Z. Stern, and Alexander Yakobson (Brighton, UK: Sussex Academic Press, 2013), 89–120.

17. "Declaration Adopted by the Extraordinary Zionist Conference, Biltmore Hotel," New York City, May 11, 1942; Walter Laqueur, ed., *The Israel-Arab Reader: A Documented History of the Middle East Conflict*, 3rd ed. (New York: Penguin Books, 1976), 79.

18. *Executive Committee of Hashomer Hatza'ir Workers' Party, The Case for a Bi-National Palestine* (Tel Aviv: Executive Committee of Hashomer Hatza'ir Workers' Party, 1946).

19. For the Commission's full report, see http://avalon.law.yale.edu/subject_

menus/angtoc.asp, and for its conclusions see http://avalon.law.yale.edu/20th_
century/angcho1.asp.

20. *The Road to Bi-National Independence for Palestine: Memorandum of the Hashomer Hatza'ir Workers' Party of Palestine* (Tel Aviv: Executive Committee of Hashomer Hatza'ir Workers' Party, 1947).

21. Central Zionist Archives, Jerusalem, S5/320.

22. United Nations Special Committee on Palestine, *Report to the General Assembly*, 4 vols. (Geneva: United Nations Publications, August 31, 1947).

23. Kibbutz Artzi Executive Committee, September 4, 1947, HHA, 90.19 (3).

24. Mordechai Bentov, *Yamim mesaprim: Zichronot mehatekufa hamachra'at* (Tel Aviv: Sifriyat Po'alim, 1984), 91.

25. Ya'ari, meeting of the Histadrut Executive Committee, December 3, 1947, Labor Archive, Tel Aviv.

6

"The Wise Woman of Givat Brenner"

Jessie Sampter on Kibbutz, War, and Peace, 1934–1938

MEIR CHAZAN

Jessie Sampter came from New York to Palestine on September 22, 1919, and a few months later she decided to settle there. At first she lived in Jerusalem, and later in the town of Rehovot. In 1934 she moved to the nearby kibbutz, Givat Brenner. Sampter died on November 25, 1938, at the age of fifty-five. This essay deals with the last years of her life, when she was a member of the kibbutz, and it is based mainly on summaries of dozens of diverse articles, which she published in the newsletter of Givat Brenner.[1]

In the gallery of women from the American Zionist movement who settled in Palestine, we can identify a few unique and extraordinary figures. Among them were Golda Meir, Henrietta Szold, and Irma Lindheim. Unlike them, throughout her life Sampter stayed away from organizational and political activity. Her influence on Zionist life and on the consolidation of kibbutz life in the 1930s was manifested mainly in the intellectual sphere.

Kibbutz Givat Brenner, named after the writer Yosef Haim Brenner, who was murdered in May 1921, was founded in 1928 and belonged to the Hakibbutz Hameuhad Movement. Six years later, in February 1934, the kibbutz started publishing a newsletter, which at first was posted every few days on the bulletin board in the common dining room, and later was distributed to the members. The need for the newsletter stemmed from the accelerated expansion of the local population, a result of the Fifth Aliyah, which brought many new immigrants from Germany to the kibbutz. The newsletter had two purposes: first, to distribute to the members information about what was going on at Givat Brenner with regard to social, economic, educational, and cultural issues, in order to mediate between the collective administrative institutions and the regular members, and assist in exposing and correcting problems of everyday life. Second, it was to serve as an ideological and intellectual forum for the exchange of ideas and for presenting dilemmas that were on the public agenda—on the local level, on the movement-kibbutz level, and on the Yishuv-Zionist level (Yishuv—the Jewish population of Palestine before 1948). Thus the newsletter was meant to reinforce the bonds of human and social solidarity between Jews who identified with the realization of the socialist-Zionist vision, but who nevertheless had come from diverse backgrounds and from different countries in Europe.

In those very days when the newsletter of Givat Brenner began to appear, Sampter became a regular member of the kibbutz. She came to live there with her friend Leah Berlin, in order to establish on the kibbutz a vegetarian convalescent home, which was opened in 1935 and after she died was named "Beit Yesha" ("Jessie's Home"). Thirty years later in the gallery of extraordinary types, which characterized Givat Brenner from its inception, Eliezer Regev described Sampter as the most original.[2] When she arrived at Givat Brenner, she had already had a rich career in the area of educational-ideological writing about Zionist topics, both as part of her educational activity at the Hadassah Organization, under the guidance of Henrietta Szold, during World War I and following it, and as a gifted writer and poet, seeking to bring the events in Palestine to the attention of Jewish public opinion in the United States.[3]

Sampter was not a typical kibbutz member. Her experience of kibbutz life was mediated by her focus on the ideological discourse that was constantly bustling in it and random scholarly conversations she conducted with members who liked and appreciated her. But as a close friend of hers on Givat Brenner, Ruth Cohen, noted, "Jesse never knew kibbutz life in its entirety, in its simple reality. She was not really familiar with that hard life movement which turns quite a few among us into cogs in the machine."[4] Through the thin veil of bitterness revealed in Cohen's grim description of the reality of the kibbutz, we can discern Sampter's skill in weaving, out of the ideals and values as she conceived them, a sublime human fabric, which should guide the realization, "here, on the face of the earth" (in the words of the poet Rahel) of the kibbutz.

In March 1934, while the ideological-political confrontation in the Yishuv between the Labor movement and the Revisionist movement over the hegemony in the Zionist movement intensified, following the murder of the head of the political department of the Jewish Agency, Haim Arlosoroff, Sampter wrote for the first time for the Givat Brenner newsletter. A few days earlier, the members of the kibbutz participated in a violent confrontation with the Revisionists, after a conflict about the allotment of working positions in a building in Rehovot. Contrary to the prevailing approach on her kibbutz, Sampter stood up and refused to back the supporters of the struggle between Jews and other Jews seeking to justify their ideological view. She determined that "from the murder of Abel (by Cain) until the murder of Arlosoroff, war between brothers had fed on defending prestige, self-righteousness and the pursuit of honor. But we are one, we are brothers. No one is guilty and no one is right. There is a past, there is a legacy, there is education and there are different conditions, and we should therefore be careful that our position is one of protecting life only." These words introduced a poem she wrote, entitled "War between Brothers": "I hit you my brother, with my hand, with my fist, I hit you my brother. / I killed you my brother, with my sword, with my gun, I killed you my brother. / Why did I kill my beloved brother? For what? For whom? / To protect another opinion, to show that I was right, I killed my own brother."[5] Eight months after it was published in the kibbutz newsletter, Sampter's poem also appeared in *Davar*, the newspaper of the Histadrut (Labor Federation). The opinion she expressed was adopted by the leaders of Mapai, David Ben-Gurion and Berl Katznelson (the editor of *Davar*), who tried to promote reaching an agreement with the Revisionist movement, despite the bitter opposition of a considerable number of the members of their own party.[6]

Sampter often expressed herself on the pages of the newsletter on prosaic matters, concerning everyday life on Givat Brenner. One of these opportunities presented itself following the theft of a lamp from the tent of a member of the kibbutz by three youngsters from the Hanoar Ha'oved youth movement, who lived for a while on Givat Brenner. In the internal kibbutz jargon, such an act usually was referred to as "filching" and dismissed with a chuckle. On the pages of the newsletter, the victimized member reported that he had located his lamp in the closet in the tent of Hanoar Ha'oved group members, retrieved his stolen property, appropriated their lamp as a punishment, and handed it over to the central storehouse of the kibbutz. Through the newsletter, he demanded that the institutions of the kibbutz see to it that the offenders be punished, that the common tendency on the kibbutz to dismiss such cases with the lenient term "filching" be stopped, and that this behavior be severely reprimanded and clearly defined as "stealing." Sampter, in her didactic way, commented that in a socialist society it was not acceptable to call youngsters "thieves" only "because of minor filching." She preached that in a "free society" individuals had no right to look for missing items in the closets of others or to punish them at their own discretion. They always had the possibility and the right to summon those who they felt had wronged them to a public hearing. "Actions of filching," she clarified, were not an appropriate social-cultural phenomenon, and we should educate ourselves, including the youth, to avoid them. "But we cannot educate our members by curses and abuse, and not in this way will we show our ability to educate." After all, she concluded, "there was filching here before these youths came. Who instructed them in this craft?"[7]

Around that time, in the organ of the Hakibbutz Hameuhad movement, *Mibifnim*, Sampter protested the discrimination against members of the Hanoar Ha'oved movement, in comparison with the Jewish youths arriving in Palestine at that time from Germany, through Youth Aliyah. While the youths from Germany received financial support from the Jewish agency for their absorption on the kibbutz and had concrete buildings built for them with these funds, Sampter said sharply, the local youths absorbed on the kibbutz had to make do with temporary housing and live in tents or shacks. "The youths from Germany enjoy decent housing conditions, they are well-dressed, they work only five hours a day and study during the rest of the day." At the same time, the Jewish youths from Palestine lived in harsh housing conditions; in most cases, they had not brought adequate clothing with them from their parents' homes, because of their low standards of living; they worked for many hours in the fields and workshops and had only a little time for studying. Where were the principles of equality that were the ideal in a socialist society? Sampter protested the discrimination against the youths from Palestine as "inappropriate phenomena, smacking of philanthropy." Although, she admitted, the youths coming from Germany did have to study the language, the local youths also needed a variety of studies in order to acquire minimal general knowledge, and the question, therefore, was: "Can we accept among us a reality of privileged youth, with special rights, next to disadvantaged youth? Is it possible to buy extra rights on the kibbutz with money?" Although the enterprise of Youth Aliyah, headed by her friend Henrietta Szold, was perceived at that time as one of the clear manifestations of solidarity in Jewish life, in light of the Nürenberg Laws and the harassment of the Jews in Germany by the Nazi regime, the American Sampter came out for the locally born youths and demanded, with the kind of audacity that deviated from what seemed reasonable and acceptable in public discourse: "Let us not complacently tolerate within our camp, the camp of the dreamers of equality, the insult inflicted on some of our children."[8]

Time and again Sampter extended the boundaries of public discourse and allowed herself to say outright what, presumably, others thought and believed but could not openly express, because of their social status or other personal and public commitments. This pattern was a common characteristic of her conduct in the various debates on the issues that were on the agenda in the last years of her life. Her choice to opine frequently on controversial topics, free from accepted conventions or struggles over ideological or political positions, influence, and prestige, gave her the status of an intellectual who sought to challenge the prevalent thinking and behavior. Sampter behaved in this way in a society in which collectivist thinking, perceived as desirable, dictated to a considerable extent what was worthy and correct to think, and set the limits of expression in the ideological arena. Sampter made good use of her status as a person who was accountable only to herself and to the truth in which she believed.

A year later Sampter returned to the issue of stealing in kibbutz society, this time in the context of the disappearance of various books, which belonged to her and had been placed on a bookcase in the hall of the guest house for the benefit of the guests. Among the missing books, in addition to a volume of poetry by Rahel and issues of the journal *Asia*, was a collection of German poems, with an elegant, leather, gold-embossed binding, which she had received as a childhood present from one of her teachers. The book went missing and then suddenly reappeared, about half a year later, on the bookcase in the convalescent home. Sampter described her losses in the kibbutz newsletter and consoled herself with a socialist saying to the effect that "property is theft," noting that this referred to general property which was needed by others, and not to property someone was using. "Any speck of property which I don't need and others do is theft in my hands," she determined in this spirit, but, she warned, it was forbidden to touch what a person was using. How good it would be if the lost things were returned, Sampter wrote, but if that did not happen, "we would not consider such wantonness bad intention. We would make do with what is left and be sorry" that we couldn't leave all the books out for the benefit of everyone. "There is no reason for despair," she concluded. "After all, the person is more valuable to me than the book."[9]

On December 23, 1936, the five hundredth issue of the Givat Brenner newsletter appeared. Selecting Sampter to write the lead article of this festive issue testified to the kibbutz's high value of her opinions. At the beginning of her article, Sampter, who often used conversations with members whom she encountered at the guest house to express her opinions on kibbutz life, related a question by a veteran of the Labor movement, who had visited Givat Brenner: Why was the kibbutz investing so much effort and money to produce the newsletter? "As simple workers, fighting the tough war of survival," he argued, "you should not indulge in such luxuries. If you don't have butter for the bread, or a room to sleep in, why you need a daily newsletter?" We already have mentioned Sampter's sensitivity to the issue of the housing conditions of the youth movement members who were being educated on the kibbutz. Still, she rejected the complaint, saying that the newsletter "is more important for us than butter for the bread, or maybe even a room." And since Givat Brenner was growing exponentially, because of the absorption of the Fifth Aliyah from Central European countries, which within a short time turned it into a kibbutz numbering more than six hundred inhabitants, Sampter thought that the newsletter played a crucial role. It constituted "an adhesive for a new, weak society. Especially here, where difficult social problems inevitably arise, due to the speedy absorption from different countries, the word that unites is necessary, and it touches every heart." She further attested that writing for the newsletter helped her improve and enhance her Hebrew.[10]

The newsletter was published more frequently in times of crisis, and such days were numerous in the months following the outbreak of the Arab Revolt in April 1936. Sampter was an arrant pacifist and even in the hard days of the Arab Revolt upheld the vision of a joint existence with the Arabs, like the best-known member of Givat Brenner, Enzo Sereni. After the first month of the hostilities, Sampter clarified, in the newsletter, that her opposition to war in all forms was still in force, and in 1918 she mentioned her objection to the Jewish Legion, even though "self-defense, protecting one's life from the attacker, is the first duty of human beings. Without it they cannot exist." Sampter shared with the new immigrants, who swelled the ranks in Givat Brenner and who were in the country only a few years or even months, her experiences and travails from the bloody incidents with the Arabs in the early 1920s and in 1929. She related how, during the riots in Jerusalem in April 1920, one of her friends asked her if she would not want to keep a revolver in her home, and in reply, she showed him a large kitchen knife, hidden in her room, for any eventuality. She recalled that during the riots, in August 1929, she lived with her young daughter in an isolated neighborhood in Tel Aviv, near Jaffa. A friend of hers, who lived nearby, walked every day to Tel Aviv to take part in guard duty. One evening, "he returned in horrible grief, threw his pistol down, and said he would never go back to this job." He then reported to her that in response to the murder of a Jewish youth, Jews broke into a home full of women and children in an Arab neighborhood, and "shot and killed! This disaster is more terrible than all the others! How could the Haganah defend such Jews! How could it be responsible for order if there's no discipline?" The lesson of these two anecdotes was, from Sampter's point of view, that the "Jewish defense" created in Palestine had to have unique qualities that combined the preservation of life and readiness for self-defense with a morality of forbearance and restraint. In this respect, the kibbutz was for her also a shelter and refuge of sorts. "It is good to be at Givat Brenner on these hard days," she confessed, "rather than among the masses in the city. I fear only weakness and the possibility of an attempt for revenge. . . . It is good to stay in a home guarded by our watchmen."[11]

On August 17, Sampter finished an article bearing the self-explanatory title "Watchwoman," which later appeared in the US labor movement's monthly magazine *Jewish Frontier*. In light of the circumstances of August 1936, Sampter acknowledged the necessity for defense. In the article, she reviewed, extensively and with deep empathy, the history of the struggle of women to play an active role in the realization of Zionism. The article opened with a description of the efforts of Manya Shochat and her female comrades, whom Sampter described as "armed Amazons," endowed with a "quality as of bronze," to take an active part in defense during the time of the Hashomer organization (1909–1920), and it ended with a series of rhetorical questions that bothered women at that time: "Shall half of the community protect the other half? Shall half lie on the floor while the other half is facing the shots? What will our children say? What will our daughters say when they grow up and are differentiated from the little boys with whom until now they shared everything? Will a mother send her fifteen year old boy to go on guard while she hides in the concentration room?"[12] Addressing her readers, especially the female ones, among the American Jews, the well-liked poet promised and pledged:

> The pioneer Jewish woman must stand by her man at this hour in defense, and at a later hour attain in the work of cooperation and peaceful upbuilding. The little girls who came from Germany last year are already bronzed by the sun; they have the same color and speak the same Hebrew as the little girls born in Jerusalem or Warsaw. There stands one on the hillock, against the rising sun, a white kerchief on her head, wearing a deep blue sleeveless blouse, short black bloomers, over sandalled feet. She is brown and straight as a young tree, a lonely tree, standing guard on a hillock. The wind blows her brown curls and her hand shades her eyes against the rising sun.[13]

During 1936 and early 1937, Sampter continuously justified the policy of restraint. Tactical arguments from the military field were outside her range of expertise, and therefore she focused on raising practical reasons from the moral domain, trying to extract them from the abstract, theoretical sphere and endow them with a concrete dimension. In this context, she claimed that acts of retaliation "will reduce us to the same level as the base terrorists," and that such actions "will prove to the world at large that we are also aggressors who deserve punishment." She sought to counter those who maintained that "we should educate ourselves to overcome our nausea regarding war" through lessons from history: "The goal of the French Revolution was to free human beings. It had wonderful slogans and enthusiastic fighters. Did it achieve its aim? It was also said about the World War [I] that it would bring an end to all wars. It was said that it would save democracy. But it brought the opposite, because love cannot come out of hate, or an improved society out of blood and fire. It is superstitious to believe that justice can grow out of killing, and that the benevolence of the next world can bloom out of the consuming fire. This is what the perpetrators of the Inquisition believed."[14] Sampter openly explained her reasons for taking the risk of being called naïve and out of touch with reality even at times of blood and fire, despair and hopelessness: "We should take pains to acquire wisdom, because we also have to educate others, younger than ourselves, and their future is in our hands."[15] The educational calling was for her a sacred tenet and an independent goal, although she had never been a public leader, never worked as a teacher in Palestine, and never had a group of staunch, attentive adherents.

In May 1938, while she was in and out of the hospital because of her frail medical condition, Sampter chose to discuss two of the most sensitive topics on the agenda of the kibbutz in the newsletter of Givat Brenner: the place of religion in the explicitly secular collective life and the unification of the kibbutz movements. From her point of view, the link between these issues stemmed from the following thesis: "I differentiate between religion and ideology, on the one hand, and faith and folk customs, on the other. The former are indications of petrifaction, while the latter are signs of life." On the basis of this critical distinction, Sampter called for the design of one Passover Haggadah, which would be read on all kibbutzim and give expression to the values of communality and equality. She urged the members of Givat Brenner not to shy away from holding public ceremonies to welcome the Sabbath, including customs such as lighting candles and singing traditional songs. For her, there was a basic difference between what "father had done" in the past "because of religion" (i.e., law), since "he was associated with a petrified ideology," and the free search for faith and folk customs, which could lead, out of choice rather than fear and coercion, to the adoption of nice customs that had been followed "in our parents' home." Sampter clarified that "when we choose the parts of the literary tradition which are suitable for us today, we should take great care not to introduce into our customs anything which contradicts our outlook." She emphasized, however, that any person who recognized the existence of "an occult life force, which is differently revealed to each one of us," recognized God too, and therefore she suggested: "Let us vote whether we should accept the God of Israel among us, into our society."[16]

According to Sampter, the same basic principle that separated religion and ideology from belief and folk life applied to the unification of the three kibbutz movements: Hakibbutz Hameuhad, Hever Hakvutzot (Kvutza), and Hakibbutz Haartzi (Hashomer Hatzair). Those movements had developed separately and were grappling with the question of forming one organization despite their ideological differences. She thought that the differences between them were manifested in certain "charming words" versus other "charming words," while in everyday life there was much in common between the various movements.[17] She expressed her opinion in an article that was first published in *Davar La'ole*, the section of the *Davar* newspaper geared to new immigrants, and later selected by Berl Katznelson to conclude the book he edited about the Kibbutz movement (note that the following is a direct quotation with the errors intact):

> Something happened! There came immigrants; and we had no room, not in barracks nor tents. So what did we do? We saw it through: We emptied out the library, and made of it a dormitory. We formed a ring and sing and dance, because we welcomed immigrants, who fled to take their stand here in the Holy Land.
>
> Where did this occur? In the *Kibbutz Hameuhad*, in the *Kvutza*, and in the *Shomer Hatzair*.
>
> Something happened. Hundreds of chicks burst from the incubator; and we were in a fix, for their houses will not be finished till later. So what did we do? Our reading room new, and clean and fine, and spick and span, we cleared for them and there they ran. We formed a ring and dance and sing, in joy for what the seasons bring.
>
> Where did this occur? In the *Kibbutz Hameuhad*, in the *Kvutza*, and in the *Shomer Hatzair*.
>
> Something happened. A great storm mowed down the tents, es-

pecially those with holes and rents. So, what did we do? In the rooms
for two, the man and wife made extra place, so girls soaked through
could rest a space, a month or two till Winter's through. And we
shiver and are glad for making good what was so bad!

Where did this occur? In the *Kibbutz Hameuhad*, in the *Kvutza*,
and in the *Shomer Hatzair*.

Something happened. Oh, so sad! Death took from us a little lad;
one of our flowers, a child of ours. What did we do? What could we
do? We wept and wept and were not done; all of us, we wept as one.
And then we gathered, sad and still, to bury him on the green hill,
weeping still.

Where did this occur? In the *Kibbutz Hameuhad*, in the *Kvutza*,
and in the *Shomer Hatzair*.

Something happened. Shots were poured, from ambush, on our
men on guard. A comrade fell before our eyes, bathed in his blood,
who shall not rise. What did we do? We saw it through. Silently we
veiled his face; with broken hearts, we kept our place. We stood on
guard and so shall stand till peace and freedom bless our land.

Where did this occur? In the *Kibbutz Hameuhad*, in the *Kvutza*,
and in the *Shomer Hatzair*.[18]

It took the leaders and members of the kibbutz movements sixty-one
years, during which time the kibbutz suffered countless travails and sustained a dramatic attrition in its status and in that of the values it represented and symbolized in Israeli society, to adopt the spirit of Sampter's
insights and wisdom.

The same basic qualities of Sampter's personality and worldview—innocence, rejection of helplessness, a sense of mission, optimism, and the
awareness that taking a stand in the public sphere was pointless unless it
was accompanied by a personal commitment—also appeared in her last
poem published during her lifetime in September 1938, in the thousandth
issue of the Givat Brenner newsletter. Entitled "Le'an?" ("Where to?"), a
word that was repeated throughout the poem, she poignantly related the
fate of the Jews, condemned by their Jewishness, in Europe of those days:

> "Away, Jew, away!
> Hit the road, do not stay!

Aliens have no business here!"
Where to?

"Hell, inferno — that's your place!
Don't defile the superior race!
From Berlin to devil's care!"
Where to?

In Switzerland we will find shelter.
There we can rest till things get better.
"These are our mountains! Who is there?"
Where to?

In Italy we will abide.
"For Jews entry is denied!
Strangers are not welcome here!"
Where to?

"To the sea, to the abyss!
But in Rome there is no place!
Do not plead, since we don't care!"
Where to?

To America we'll flee,
To shelter in the land of the free.
"We have no room!" Yes, even there.
Where to?

To the river, to the sea!
There's no place for us to be!
Balak here and Haman there . . .
Where to?

To our land, to our nest.
With our brothers we'll find rest.
But it's closed and there's no key
For the refugee.

"Nonetheless, there is a choice.
We'll open the gates and raise our voice!"

Who is singing for me there?
Where to?

"Listen, brothers, thus we say:
We'll not retreat, here we shall stay.
From Beer Sheba to Dan, it is clear —
We are here."[19]

In this poem, published about two-and-a-half months before her death, Sampter reflected on the plight of the Jews and offered what she viewed as the only solution—the realization of Zionism in Palestine. We can understand what the word "realization" symbolized for her from her attempt to explain why the daily newsletter of Givat Brenner was so meager and prosaic. Her answer was that the newsletter also was a kind of "realization." The descendant of the most prosperous Jewish Diaspora in the first half of the twentieth century glorified, on the pages of the newsletter of Givat Brenner, what had been perceived in the labor settlement movement as the key for understanding the message of Zionism for Jewish life.

I have long ago come to believe that each people, like each person, has its own unique qualities. The People of Israel has been endowed with the quality of realization. Not realism, mind you, but the realization of thought in action. The history of our persistence as a living people, and that of our religion, which realized in everyday life, minute by minute, the thoughts and belief of our people, attests to the ongoing realization of unifying spirit and action. We are faithful children of our ancestors when we realize our faith in the life of a collective society. To realize a desire in sublime moments is a splendid and wonderful thing, but to do it every day, in cold and heat, in times of enthusiasm and in times of despair, is, sometimes, boring and prosaic.[20]

No wonder that in the eulogy dedicated to her upon her death Sampter was called "the wise woman of Givat Brenner."[21]

NOTES

1. Bertha Badt-Strauss, *White Fire: The Life and Works of Jessie Sampter* (New York: Reconstructionist Press, 1956); Susan Blanshay, "Jessie Sampter: A Pioneer

Feminist in American Zionism" (master's thesis, McGill University, Montreal, Québec, 1995); Rebecca Boim Wolf, "Jessie Sampter School of Zionism," in *The Women Who Reconstructed American Jewish Education, 1910–1965*, HBI Series on Jewish Women, ed. Carol K. Ingall (Waltham, MA: Brandeis University Press, 2010), 46–62.

2. Eliezer Regev, "Haesha halevana," in *Beit Yesha: 30 shanah* (Givat Brenner, 1965), 1.

3. See, for example, Jessie E. Sampter, *A Course in Zionism* (New York: Federation of American Zionists, 1915); Jessie E. Sampter, *Around the Year in Rhymes for the Jewish Child* (New York, 1920); Jessie E. Sampter, *The Emek* (New York: Bloch Publishing, 1927).

4. Ruth Cohen, "Yesha Sampter," in *Yesha Sampter: leyom hashloshim* (Kibbutz Givat Brenner, 1939), 31.

5. Yesha [Sampter], "Milkhmet ahim," *Alon Givat Brenner*, March 23, 1934.

6. Yesha [Sampter], "Milkhmet ahim," *Davar*, November 16, 1934.

7. Yesha [Sampter], "Hevra sotsialistit vegnevot . . . ," *Alon Givat Brenner*, March 4, 1936; Yosef H., "Gneva o ma'se yaldut," *Alon Givat Brenner*, March 2, 1936.

8. Yesha [Sampter], "Eifa ve'eifa," *Mibifnim*, April 1936.

9. Yesha [Sampter], "Hirhurim," *Alon Givat Brenner*, March 12, 1937.

10. Yesha [Sampter], "Leyom hahamesh meot," *Alon Givat Brenner*, December 23, 1936.

11. Yesha [Sampter], "Tkhunat hahaganah haivrit," *Alon Givat Brenner*, May 22, 1936.

12. Jessie Sampter, "Watchwomen," *Jewish Frontier*, November 1936.

13. Ibid.

14. Yesha [Sampter], "Al hahavlaga," *Alon Givat Brenner*, August 31, 1936; Yesha [Sampter], "Hirhurim," *Alon Givat Brenner*, December 11, 1936.

15. Ibid.

16. Yesha [Sampter], "Hihurim," *Alon Givat Brenner*, May 27, 1938, June 10, 1938; Yesha [Sampter], "Leyom hahamesh meot," *Alon Givat Brenner*, December 23, 1936.

17. Yesha [Sampter], "Hihurim," *Alon Givat Brenner*, May 27, 1938.

18. Jessie Sampter, "Something Happened," *Palestine Post*, May 31, 1938 (emphasis in the original); Jessie Sampter, "Kara davar," *Davar*, May 23, 1938 (original in Hebrew, trans. Jessie Sampter, *Palestine Post*).

19. Yesha [Sampter], "Le'an," *Alon Givat Brenner*, September 9, 1938.

20. Yesha [Sampter], "Leyom hahamesh meot," *Alon Givat Brenner*, December 23, 1936.

21. Haim Ben-Asher, "Hahakhama miGiv'at Brener," *Davar*, December 27, 1938.

7

Robert Briscoe, Jewish Lord Mayor of Dublin

Revisiting the Irish-Jewish Connection

FRANCES MALINO

On Tuesday, September 30, 1958, Robert Briscoe, former lord mayor of Dublin and member of the Irish Dáil (parliament), was the guest of honor at a luncheon in Boston, Massachusetts. The invitees included the presidents of the Combined Jewish Appeal and the Associated Jewish Philanthropies as well as the president of the Eire Society of Boston and the vice consul for Ireland. The occasion for this interfaith gathering was the launching of Briscoe's warm, witty, anecdote-filled memoir (*For the Life of Me*) in which he recounts his fight for "Irish freedom" and the "creation of a homeland for the Jewish people."[1]

Briscoe's first trip to the United States had been as a twenty-year-old intent on making his fortune. Only three years later, however, in 1917, his seething homeland beckoned him. After the war ended, he left Ireland once again, this time for Germany to gather arms, ammunitions, and explosives for the Irish Brigades. When he returned to the States in 1922, it was with orders from the Irish Republican Army to take over the New York consular offices, then in the hands of the Free State Government. Although he failed in this, he managed to earn a reputation as Éamon de Valera's leading gunman. Numerous invitations to speak followed. "I am not of your faith," he told a tumultuous crowd in Boston's Faneuil Hall in 1922. "I am, as you well know, of a particular faith of which I am probably the only member of this great hall."[2]

Briscoe was in the States once again in 1939, as a member both of the Irish Dáil—from which he had taken a six-months leave of absence—and of the New Zionist Organization (founded in 1935 by Ze'ev Vladimir Jabotinsky as an alternative to the "official" Zionist movement). His mission, applauded by many of his Irish American friends, was to garner American public and government support for urging Britain to bring one million Eastern European Jews to Palestine. He met with Justice Felix Frankfurter, Stephen S. Wise (whom he had publicly heckled in 1922 when Wise spoke in favor of the "first partition" of Palestine), and Justice Louis Brandeis.

> Justice Brandeis was as delicate as Frankfurter had said, but his mind had lost none of its penetration. He questioned me acutely on the physical force movement of Irgun, and the illegal shipping of human beings to Palestine. I told him of my fears for European Jewry and my hopes of influencing President Roosevelt to pressure England.
>
> When I had finished, Mr. Brandeis said, "I am sorry but I cannot go along with you. I do not agree with your ideas, nor can I approve of the things you are doing."
>
> It was a great blow to me that I had made no impression on this wonderful old gentleman. He must have seen the distress and sorrow in my face for he said very kindly, "Anyway, let's have a cup of tea."
>
> Mrs. Brandeis brought the tea and we chatted for perhaps half an hour more. He told her some of the things I had said, restating my arguments in a brilliant and accurate summation. When the time came for me to leave, he said, "I am against you because I am an old man and have seen too much of bloodshed and violence, and fair hopes befouled by the fog of war. But if I were a young man like you, I would be with you, talking as you have talked, doing exactly what you are trying to do."
>
> "Will you then wish me luck?" I asked.
>
> And he answered emotionally, "I wish you luck."[3]

Briscoe would not return to the States again until eighteen years later— just one year before the publication of his memoir. Recently elected lord mayor of Dublin (a tie had required the victor's name to be pulled from a dirty "slouch hat" evocative of a scene from Harry Potter), he viewed his three-month tour, subsidized by the United Jewish Appeal (UJA), as a triumph. He raised $30 million for the UJA, proudly led the Saint Patrick's Day parades in New York City and in Boston (one of the city's newspapers greeted him with a green headline saying, "AARON GO BRAGH" in both English and Yiddish characters), and presented President Eisenhower with a hand-loomed rug, the arms of the four provinces of Ireland defiantly woven into it. "When I gave it to the President," he recalled with typical pride and amusement, "I got in my sly little bit of propaganda. I stood on the rug covering the Red Hand of Ulster and said, 'Mr. President, may I call your attention to how it unbalances the design when one of the four provinces is taken away.'"[4]

Surprisingly, few today have heard of Robert Briscoe. There is no entry for him in the *Encyclopedia of Zionism and Israel*; in the standard biographies of Irish leaders with whom he was associated, such as Éamon de Valera and Michael Collins; or in the general histories of modern Ireland. Modern Jewish historians have tended to ignore him as well.[5] The explanation for his being overlooked may be quite simple: Irish republican–Jewish nationalist connections are just not "in."

Nevertheless, a century and more of dialogue between Irish Catholics and Jews, Irish nationalism and Zionism, during which slogans were borrowed, leaders emulated, persecutions compared and empathized with, and political and military strategies shared, should neither be overlooked nor underestimated. Indeed, the ease with which Robert Briscoe navigated his political and personal commitments as an observant Jew and a Jewish and Irish nationalist (were his Jewish contemporaries outside of Ireland so seamlessly identified?) testifies to these connections just as his subsequent obscurity both signifies and contributes to their fading from collective memory.

On July 12, 1690, on the banks of the Boyne, William of Orange's army defeated King James's force of 25,000 Irish Catholics. The victorious Protestants sought to secure their position in Ireland by the imposition of a code—the penal laws—that imposed crippling restrictions on Catholics. Already living in a land they no longer owned (by 1703 they owned only 15 percent of Irish soil), Irish Catholics were deprived of the right to bear arms and of the franchise, debarred from practicing the professions, and prohibited from keeping a school, carrying arms without a license, or owning a horse worth five pounds. The purpose of these laws was neither to destroy Irish Catholicism nor to bring about conversions. Rather, they were instruments of terror comparable to restrictions on Jews in the ghettoes of Europe's cities or in the Pale of Settlement. As such they reinforced a religious identity that was both the basis for discrimination and the principal source of consolation and recreation.

The eighteenth century saw the abolition of many of the disabilities Irish Catholics suffered, first as a result of the parliamentary autonomy enjoyed by Anglo-Irish patriots after the withdrawal of British troops during the American Revolution and subsequently by the British decision —in the face of the French Revolution—to "buy" Catholic loyalty. But these reforms were far less than the democratic republic and universal suffrage advocated by the United Irishmen and their Protestant leader Theobold Wolfe Tone.

Tone was in Paris when the National Assembly debated extending full rights to Protestants and Jews. Echoes of these debates as well as the rationale for inclusion of the Jews appear in his "Argument on Behalf of the Catholics of Ireland" published in August 1791, a month before the French "emancipation" of the Jews: "We plunge them by law, and continue them by statute, in gross ignorance, and then we make the incapacity we have created an argument for their exclusion from the common rights of man! We plead our crime in justification of itself. If ignorance be their condemnation, what has made them ignorant? . . . It is the iniquitous and cruel injustice of Protestant bigotry."[6] Tone's rhetoric brings to mind the arguments found in Christian Wilhelm Dohm's *De la réforme politique des Juifs*, published in Berlin in 1781 and translated into French the following year: "We ourselves are guilty of the crimes we accuse him of; and the moral depravity into which this unfortunate nation has now fallen as a result of a mistaken policy cannot be a just reason to continue that policy."[7]

In October 1798, after failing in an attempt—with French support—to invade Ireland, Tone committed suicide in a Dublin cell. To Irish Catholics, who ignored his rejection of sectarianism and his rather patronizing attitude toward them, Tone became and remains a martyr. And to Robert Briscoe's Lithuanian-born father Abraham, Wolfe Tone Briscoe became a fitting name for his younger son.

Not until 1829 with the Catholic Relief Act were Catholics in the United Kingdom of England and Ireland "emancipated," thus bequeathing a terminology for the decrees that also would offer political rights to the Jews of Europe.[8] For both the Jews of France and the Catholics in the United Kingdom, however, emancipation came only with humiliating strings attached.

Once Daniel O'Connell, whose Catholic Association had spearheaded the struggle for emancipation, finally was permitted to take his place as a member of the British Parliament, he immediately extended his support to the Jews of England and Ireland. "You will find me," he wrote in 1829 to Isaac Lyon Goldsmid, financier and leading figure in the struggle for Jewish emancipation in England, "the constant and active friend to every measure which tends to give the Jews an equality of civil rights with all the other King's subjects, a perfect unconditional equality. . . . Allow me at once to commence my office of your advocate and to begin by giving you advice. It is: not to postpone your claim of right beyond the second day of the ensuing session. Do not listen to those over cautious persons who may recommend postponement. Believe an agitator of some experience that nothing was ever obtained by delay."[9] More than a century later, in January 1941, Rabbi Abba Hillel Silver ended his fiery speech in New York City advocating the large-scale settlement of displaced Jews in Palestine with Daniel O'Connell's well-known advice: "Agitate! Agitate! Agitate!"[10]

The legal process of emancipation, for both Irish Catholics and Jews, would prove inadequate. In contrast to the Irish, however, whose response to the 1829 Roman Catholic Relief Act was to demand home rule, the majority of Jews in Western and Central Europe eschewed the idea of establishing a homeland. When Theodor Herzl founded political Zionism more than a half century later, however, Ireland became his model. "I shall be the Parnell of the Jews," he confided in his diary entry of October 20, 1895.[11] Although he undoubtedly had Charles Stuart Parnell's success as a nationalist leader in mind, Herzl could not have been more prescient in seeing in the "un-crowned King of Ireland" a reflection of himself.

Both Herzl and Parnell were outsiders, Parnell as a Protestant, Herzl as an assimilated Central European Jew. Charismatic and worshipped as a modern Moses by their followers, neither really had great respect for the "rabble" they led.[12] Both were aristocratic by temperament; both adopted the tactics and dress of the non-Irish, non-Jewish elite. They died in their prime at the same age, leaving behind movements on the brink of disarray, the one because of a long-standing relationship with a married woman, the other for contemplating a homeland other than the Land of Israel. Both became martyrs, more powerful in death than in life.

"Ireland has claims on your ancient race," O'Connell had written Goldsmid in 1829, "as it is the only Christian community that I know of unsullied by any one act of persecution of the Jews."[13] A century later this was no longer true. In 1904 the local population of Limerick—incited by Father John Creagh (he denounced the Jews as bloodsuckers and crucifiers) and by influential republican leader Arthur Griffith—struck out against its tiny community of Jews. Economic boycotts and physical attacks followed. Although there were no deaths, the incident remained significant in Ireland's collective memory.[14]

Griffith had fought with the Boers in 1899. He publicized their prejudices against Jews and blacks both in his pioneering newspaper *The United Irishmen* ("I have in former years often declared that the Three Evil influences of the century were the Pirate, the Freemason and the Jew. . . . United they stand in Europe against France. United they stand in Africa against the Transvaal Republic") and in the Sinn Féin movement he founded in 1906.[15] Inexplicably, Briscoe's father Abraham spoke of Griffith as a "friend" with whom he often played chess at the Dublin Bread Company tearoom.[16] Equally inexplicably, Robert Briscoe referred to the president of the Dáil Eireann—who, in contrast to so many others during the civil war, died of natural causes—as "poor, gentle Arthur Griffith who hated the idea of fighting even foreign foes, let alone fellow Irishmen."[17] Although antisemitism in Ireland would never develop into a mass movement, it was present, albeit at times rather silent, through World War II and into the postwar era.[18]

Michael Davitt stands in sharp contrast to Griffith. Secretary of the National Land League of Ireland under Parnell and a member of Parliament —he left in protest against the Second Boer War—Davitt stood almost alone in publicly condemning the antisemitism of Father Creagh. A year prior to the Limerick persecutions, at the behest of William R. Hearst's American papers (Davitt supported himself with writing and lectures and as a journalist), he traveled to Bessarabia to investigate the Kishinev pogroms. The dispatches he sent to America were included in his book

Within the Pale: The True Story of Anti-Semitic Persecutions in Russia, published both in New York and London in 1903.[19]

"It is deemed necessary," Davitt writes in the preface, "for the twofold aim of this book, — to arouse public feeling against a murder-making legend [ritual murder] and to put forward a plea for the objects of the Zionist movement, — to tell the story of the Russian Jew, apropos of recent massacres."[20] Davitt's journalistic skills served him well. In clear yet elegant prose, he provided the reader with a history of the Jews of Russia and the scurrilous charges against them. "As a friend of Polish freedom remarked to the writer in Warsaw in the spring of 1903, 'the nobles cultivated their pride, rack-rented their tenants, and lost their independence.' And, with this fall of the one Christian nation in Europe, which had fairly ruled and humanely treated the hunted Hebrew up to the eighteenth century, the era of systematic persecution began for the Polish Jew when a cruel fate compelled him to become a Russian subject."[21]

Davitt took photos (unfortunately not included in his book) and interviewed rabbis, leaders of the Jewish community, and Russian political dignitaries, including the mayor of Kishinev. He personalized the pogroms with stories of the victims — women, children, and men — and provided a list of names of all those killed and how they were killed, including those who subsequently died from their wounds in the hospital.

> There ought to be a truly Christian crusade waged against this infamous product of ancient, insensate, sectarian hate. It was the inspiration of the most horrible of the Kishineff murders: the driving of nails through the eyes of a woman, the cutting out of the tongue of a two-year-old child, and of nameless sexual mutilations. Thousands of innocent people have been done to death in the centuries through which these crimes have been the bloody fruit of a monstrous invention, born of a spirit of superstitious savagery, which no age has yet made any honest civilized endeavor to exorcise out of ignorant and fanatical Christian minds.[22]

Although Davitt explicitly referred to Ireland only once at the very end when he compared the "ordinary" Russian policeman to the "average member" of the Royal Irish Constabulary, every page of *Within the*

Pale suggests an empathy with the situation of the Jews born of his Irish experience.[23]

> This is the conclusion to which one is irresistibly driven by a full survey of the cruelly anomalous position occupied by the Jew in relation to all the dominant factors of Russian life and government. He is under the obligations of citizenship, military and otherwise without its privileges or full protection. Special taxes are imposed upon him. He is confined by law within a kind of economic concentration camp. The legal difficulties put in the way of the full exercise of his industrial capacities are both the source of his poverty and of his oppression. He cannot own land, within the Pale, or work it. . . . His faith is assailed by almost every form of human temptation, including the terrorism of such periodical crimes as those perpetrated a few weeks ago. And the very fidelity which enables him to resist both the powers of proselytism and of persecution, only adds one more prejudiced ground to the many which appeal against him to the religious side of an autocratic régime which decrees that an invulnerable heterodoxy is one of the worst of crimes in Russia.[24]

Davitt's travel to the Russian Empire overlapped with that of Theodor Herzl. It is unlikely, however, that they met, for certainly Davitt would have mentioned it. Yet by the time Davitt left, he was "a convinced believer in the remedy of Zionism" and an ardent advocate for eliciting the financial cooperation of wealthy Jews, a guarantee of protection from the Turkish government, and the moral help of the great powers.[25]

Not until 1955 would another Irishman's "conversion" to Zionism gain such public attention. In this instance, however, it was a fictional conversion poignantly portrayed in Israel's first full-length feature film, "Hill 24 Doesn't Answer."[26] On July 18, 1948 (four hours before a ceasefire), an Irishman named James Finnegan is sent to secure a peak overlooking the road to Jerusalem. A sergeant in the British Army during the mandate, Finnegan had returned to fight for the new state and to marry his sweetheart (Miriam Mizrahi). Needless to say, in the cinema of the 1950s, controversial topics such as intermarriage were best dealt with by avoidance. Although Finnegan dies taking Hill 24, as do the three Jewish volunteers, this Irishman's participation served both to legitimize the struggle for a Jewish homeland and to universalize the Zionist narrative.[27]

Briscoe's embrace of Zionism (triggered by his personal experience of Nazism in Germany and a meeting with Ze'ev Vladimir Jabotinsky) was not so different in origin from that of Michael Davitt a few decades earlier, for it, too—indeed, perhaps even more so—drew upon and never failed to reflect a commitment to Irish nationalism. Briscoe first encountered Jabotinsky when the latter came to Ireland. "Since I was, perhaps, the only Jew in the I.R.A.," Briscoe writes, "he was naturally directed to me. Though I say it myself, he could not have come to a better man. I taught Jabotinsky how we had secretly trained our Fianna Eireann boys in the time of peace; and the methods we had found most effective in the guerrilla war. I explained British military weaknesses and where their strength lay; and how to profit by the first and combat—or evade—the second."[28] Briscoe arranged a meeting between Jabotinsky and de Valera (he would come close to deifying both of these men). Subsequently, after having sold his interest in the Roscrea Meat Company to pay his debts, he devoted much of his time to Jabotinsky and organizing the Irgun. "You must understand," Briscoe consoled him after the first time a young member of the Irgun was executed by the British for carrying arms, "that in Ireland we never accomplished anything until we showed that we were willing to shed our blood for our cause."[29]

The first and only time Briscoe suggests he thought "as a Jew" in connection with his country was during the Irish Civil War (1922–23).[30] Should he, he asked himself, and did he have the right to at a time of looming violence between Irishmen, choose sides? The Irish Civil War was also the "saddest" and "most trying time" of his life.[31] There was more, of course, to Briscoe's failure to come to terms with this war. He had experienced its toll and could neither justify the cost nor make full peace with his own contribution (he had brought the last big shipment of arms into Ireland through the British blockade). "Civil war in any country," he muses at the very end of his memoir, "is a most horrible tragedy and something that should be avoided at almost any cost."[32]

Fear of civil war in the newly proclaimed Jewish state led Briscoe to request a meeting with Irgun leader Menachem Begin. If the chronology in his account is correct (hindsight in a memoir is alas all too easy to adjust), it was soon after the Altalena affair (June 20, 1948) when under orders from David Ben-Gurion, the newly formed Israel Defense Forces sank a ship in the Tel Aviv harbor (there were sixteen casualties) which had been sent by the Irgun from France and loaded with fighters, arms, and ammunition.

"At the touch of a match you could have civil war in Israel," Briscoe warned Begin at a meeting in Paris. "You are in the same position that we were. For God's sake benefit by my knowledge of the disaster which overtook us." Briscoe advised Begin to do as the Irish republicans had finally done and convert the Irgun into a constitutional party. "I think it had some effect, perhaps it was even decisive."[33]

If Briscoe's engagement in the Irish Civil War was the "saddest" period in his political life, his accompanying de Valera and his two sons to Israel in 1950 was certainly among the happiest. Since de Valera had ceased to be head of government in 1948 (he would return in 1951–54 and 1957–59 and then remain as president until 1973), he was free of official responsibilities. This would be Briscoe's first trip to Israel (given his standing with the British, he would have risked imprisonment had he gone to Palestine), and his excitement was apparent, from the confusion on his arrival at the "Lidda Airport" (the Israelis mistook Briscoe for de Valera, thus allowing him to sneak in a case of Irish whisky without duty for his "old friend," Chief Rabbi Herzog, who he knew loved a drop of the "Irish") to the lively dinner — mathematics and classical Greece were discussed — held at Herzog's home.

Yitzhak HaLevi Herzog had served previously as chief rabbi of Ireland from 1922 to 1936 and had close ties with de Valera as well as Briscoe. Indeed de Valera may well have taken refuge in the chief rabbi's home during the Irish War of Independence. Their friendship had survived these many years despite de Valera's failure to respond adequately to Herzog's tireless appeals during World War II.[34]

> Rabbi Herzog had invited illustrious guests to honor Dev. Prime Minister and Mrs. Ben-Gurion were there, Minister for Finance and Industry Don Josef and several other members of the Cabinet. We sat down at the dinner table and the Chief Rabbi prepared to say

grace. As he looked around the table he could see that every head was covered except only the great fuzzy white locks of Ben Gurion, who prided himself on being most unorthodox. As the Chief Rabbi hesitated for an instant, the Prime Minister sheepishly held out his hand for a yarmulke and clapped it on that ocean of hair. Herzog smiled in his whimsical way and proceeded to say grace.

We had our meal. Then pressmen and photographers were allowed in. The big news in the papers next morning was that Mr. Ben-Gurion had worn a yarmulke and it had taken the example of de Valera to bring that revolutionary act about.[35]

Briscoe believed that as a result of their trip to Israel, de Valera had gained new understanding of the problems and aspirations of the Jewish people. And that he had come to see the "remarkable likeness" between Israel and Ireland.[36] Perhaps. Often, however, and certainly in his memoir, Briscoe relegates unpleasant or conflicting facts to the sidelines. He overlooks Griffith's antisemitism, for example, downplays the controversial neutrality of Ireland during World War II—referred to by some critics of de Valera as a "principle of moral bankruptcy"—and overlooks altogether the visit by de Valera to the German ambassador in 1945 to express his condolences on the death of Hitler. Hero worship came easily to Briscoe —witness his adoration of both de Valera and Jabotinsky—as did a casual attitude to chronology and historical details (Briscoe suggests that the Battle of the Boyne in 1690 was between King William's Orangemen and Prince Charles Stuart). Nevertheless, recent scholarship confirms, at least in part, Briscoe's assessment of de Valera as a friend of the Jews and Israel.[37]

Abram Sachar, president of Brandeis University, who shared Briscoe's admiration for de Valera, planned to interview him as part of the Living Biographies program he had established at Brandeis. "If only," Sachar explained, "such a technique [adding the visual dimension of the camera to oral history] had been perfected and available for interviews with Woodrow Wilson, Lloyd George, Mahatma Gandhi, Chaim Weizmann, or Justice Brandeis. How much clearer our insights would be in appraising and understanding temperament and motivation."[38] The interview was to be taped in Dublin. De Valera was nearing ninety, and by the time Sachar arrived, the Irish president had succumbed to an attack of bronchitis that led his physician to request elimination of the television aspect of the interview. The oral interview, however, took place, Sachar tells us, and it was "memorable."

> De Valera expressed wistful envy of his much-admired friend, David Ben-Gurion, "who knew so much about philosophy, including the wisdom of the Orient." He declared that he regarded Ben-Gurion [as] one of the most remarkable of the world's contemporary statesmen. "Think of the achievement," he said. "Into his newly created state poured the Jewish immigrants from seventy nations, all with different languages. Ben-Gurion knew well that there never could be a visceral national consciousness unless a common language united such diverse components. And it had to be Hebrew, not just classical Biblical Hebrew, but the colloquial language of daily life. . . . We failed to accomplish this in Ireland. . . . We are obliged to communicate in English, the language of our oppressors!"[39]

Sachar's portrayal of de Valera, like that of Briscoe (they also shared the same Boston publisher), reflects a particular moment in time. More-recent works feature a young and martyred Michael Collins on center stage. As for the Irish republican/Jewish nationalist dialogue, it is all but ignored. In so doing, however, historians risk shaping a collective memory that obliterates that rich and complex dialogue altogether. For this reason, if none other, Robert Briscoe and *For the Life of Me* merit revisiting.

NOTES

1. Robert Briscoe, *For the Life of Me* (Boston: Little, Brown, 1958). Photos of Briscoe and publicity from the publisher, Little, Brown and Company, are located in the archives of the American Jewish Historical Society. I would like to thank archivist Judith Garner for calling my attention to this material and Anne Wasserman at Wellesley College for the documents she brought to my attention.

2. Ibid., 205.

3. Ibid., 274.

4. Ibid., 326.

5. There are two excellent recent exceptions: Shulamit Eliash, *The Harp and the*

Shield of David: Ireland, Zionism and the State of Israel (London and New York: Routledge, 2007) and George Bornstein, *The Colors of Zion Blacks, Jews, and Irish from 1845 to 1945* (Cambridge: Harvard University Press, 2011).

6. Theobold Wolfe Tone, *An Argument on Behalf of the Catholics of Ireland* (Belfast: Society of United Irishmen of Belfast, August 1, 1791), 355.

7. Christian Wilhelm Dohm, *De la réforme politique des Juifs*, with preface and notes by Dominique Bourel (Paris: Stock, 1984), 51

8. Wolfe Tone's pamphlet and the "emancipation" of the Jews in France complicates Jacob Katz's German-centric exploration of the term *emancipation* and its applicability to the situation of European Jews and Irish Catholics. Katz argues that the term first appeared in 1828 long after it had lost its real meaning (Katz minimizes the disabilities Catholics in Ireland still suffered) and that it subsequently "gained currency" in the struggle for political equality for Europe's Jews (Katz overlooks France, its Jews, and the Revolution). Jacob Katz, "The Term Jewish Emancipation," in *Studies in Nineteenth-Century Jewish Intellectual History*, ed. Alexander Altmann (Cambridge: Harvard University Press, 1964), 1–25.

9. *Correspondence of Daniel O'Connell*, vol. 4: 1929–31, ed. Maurice R. O'Connell, Irish Manuscripts Commission, Dublin, 1977, 95–97.

10. Walter Laqueur, *A History of Zionism* (New York: Schocken, 1989), 550.

11. Eliash, *The Harp and the Shield*, 6.

12. In his diary Herzl referred to his having made a people out of a "decadent rabble." Shlomo Avineri, "Theodor Herzl's Diaries," *Jewish Social Studies* (fall 1999): 434.

13. *Correspondence of Daniel O'Connell*, 95.

14. Eliash, *The Harp and the Shield*, 54.

15. Cited in Manus O'Riordan, "Anti-Semitism in Irish Politics," *The Irish Jewish Year Book* 34 (1985): 17.

16. Briscoe, *For the Life of Me*, 50. Abraham told Robert that Griffith was a "loyal Irishman who did not advocate violence, but believed that Irish freedom could be secured by peaceful means."

17. Ibid., 179.

18. Manus O'Riordan suggests that it was "the small size of the Jewish community which militated against the development of a mass antisemitic movement, rather than any innate virtues of Irish society during the 1930s and 40s." O'Riordan, "Anti-Semitism in Irish Politics," 23.

19. My citations are from the London edition republished by Arno Press in 1975. In both the American and London editions, there is a list of Davitt's books under his name. In the London edition, however, *The Boer Fight for Freedom* is omitted.

20. Davitt, *Within the Pale*, v.

21. Ibid., 7.

22. Ibid., 52–53.

23. Ibid., 233–34 and 82.

24. Ibid., 66–67.

25. Ibid., 86–87.

26. Thorold Dickinson directed the film; he also directed *Gaslight*.

27. When one of the Israelis asks Finnegan whether Ireland is in England, another responds: "Where's Israel? In Egypt?" Esther, of Yemenite background, who joins the three men in securing the peak, is delighted to discover how similar Finnegan's quotation "My house has many mansions" is to the phrase in Isaiah: "For my house shall be called a house of prayer for all people" (Isaiah 56:7).

28. Briscoe, *For the Life of Me*, 264. Unfortunately, Briscoe gives no dates for his encounters with Jabotinsky.

29. Ibid., 266.

30. Ibid., 150.

31. Ibid., 334.

32. Ibid., 335.

33. Ibid., 300. Briscoe's physical description of Begin ("He was clearly in the final stages of a fatal illness, burning up with the intensity of his attempt to pit effort against time") would lead one to assume Begin died soon thereafter, rather than more than thirty years later.

34. Eliash, *The Harp and the Shield*, 50.

35. Briscoe, *For the Life of Me*, 304–305.

36. Ibid., 307.

37. Eliash, *The Harp and the Shield*, provides a sophisticated and nuanced assessment of de Valera's attitude toward the Zionist movement.

38. Abraham Leon Sachar, *Brandeis University: A Host at Last* (Boston: Little, Brown, 1976), 316.

39. Sachar, *Brandeis University*, 317–18.

8

The Zionist Leadership
of Louis D. Brandeis

EVYATAR FRIESEL

Louis D. Brandeis (1856–1941) left an enduring impression both on American public memory as on the Zionist movement, and scholarly attention to the man and his life continues to this day.[1] The present essay concentrates mainly on Brandeis's active Zionist period, from 1914 to 1921. One is soon drawn to an elusive issue: the characteristics of leadership and the interdependence between a strong leader and his social environment.[2] The power of Brandeis's personality deeply affected people who came in contact with him. Julius Simon, a distinguished European Zionist of the post–World War I period and a man known as clearheaded and independent-minded, met Brandeis in the United States in 1920. Back in London, he told Chaim Weizmann, his friend of many years and the emerging leader of the Zionist movement: "Chaim, you have rendered an immortal service to the cause of Zionism. Now I ask you to crown your work by offering [the] leadership to Brandeis."[3] At that point, Brandeis had been an active Zionist for only a few years.

Brandeis's turn to Zionist activity happened in mid-1914. By then already fifty-seven years old, he was an established Boston lawyer, in his views and behavior a typical American of the New England type. Thus far Brandeis had shown little interest in matters Jewish and had almost no ties with the Jewish community or to Jewish traditions. Also, after turning to Zionism he remained unconnected to Jewish beliefs or affairs. He identified with the ways of the Bostonian Brahmins and admired their qualities: "In many ways you are a better example of New England virtues than the natives," opined Samuel Warren, an old Bostonian himself and Brandeis's friend since their days at Harvard.[4] Louis Lipsky, both collaborator and adversary on the Zionist scene, described Brandeis years later: "He was a Puritan in spirit and conduct. . . . He was thoroughly American, feeling himself a product of his history, grateful to its great men, and endeavored at all times to measure up to the obligations of American democracy."[5]

Brandeis's legal activities and civil interests also had brought him into the public realm. He became known for his critiques of and battles against influential American financial groups whose activities he considered detrimental to the public good. His pursuits begot as many admirers as detractors. By 1910 he was gravitating toward direct political action and became an important presence in the Progressive movement headed by Robert LaFollette, who in 1912 sought the American presidency. When the LaFollette campaign collapsed, Brandeis gave his support to the Democratic candidate, Woodrow Wilson, and soon became one of his close advisors. Early in 1913, when President-elect Wilson was forming his cabinet, Brandeis was considered for a position, but fierce political opposition brought the idea to naught.[6] His turn to Zionist activity happened shortly afterward, in the middle of 1914.

How and why Brandeis became a Zionist remains an open question. Alon Gal, Ben Halpern, and others have meticulously catalogued Brandeis's pre-1914 pro-Zionist steps and utterances, aiming to show a gradual opening and interest for Zionist ideas. By contrast, Yonathan Shapiro stresses that weaknesses in Brandeis's standing in the American public arena led him to search for supportive social backing, which was provided by the Zionist movement.[7] Both explanations are interesting; neither is entirely satisfactory. Did anti-Jewish prejudice play a role in Brandeis's turn to Zionism? The matter demands caution, not the least because American attitudes toward Jews had characteristics different from the European experience.[8] In American WASP society of that time a reticence reigned with regard to "outsiders" in general and apparently even more so if they were Jews, expressed by subtle (or unsubtle) social discrimination. Brandeis himself never referred to it, but here and there are indications he cannot have ignored. For instance, when Samuel Warren, his law firm partner and closest friend in Boston, scion of an old New England family, married in 1883 (his bride was from an established

Philadelphia WASP family), Brandeis was not invited, and later no social relations developed between the two families.[9] Afterward, Brandeis's legal activities against financial interests involving members of the New England aristocracy did little to strengthen his social standing in town.

Brandeis practically was "declared" head of a new Zionist framework, the Provisional Zionist Executive Committee (PZEC), founded in New York at the end of August 1914.[10] The World Zionist Organization (WZO) had been thrown into disarray by the outbreak of the war, and it was thought necessary to create an emergency body in a neutral country, with the rather far-reaching aim to act instead of the Berlin-based headquarters of the WZO. However, some weeks later new organizational arrangements were decided by the international Zionist leadership. The tasks of the PZEC became limited to the United States, and the new body acted in parallel to the existing Federation of American Zionists (FAZ). That organizational abnormality came to an end in mid-1918, at the Pittsburgh Zionist convention, when the FAZ and the Provisional Zionist Committee merged to form the Zionist Organization of America.

Undeterred by these initial hiccups, Brandeis went on with his new Zionist endeavors. He soon formed around him a circle of gifted and devoted high-level collaborators, such as Julian W. Mack, Jacob de Haas, Felix Frankfurter, Stephen S. Wise, Robert Szold, Bernard Flexner, and several more, among them the young Benjamin V. Cohen. Most were American born or American educated, many of them lawyers. Brandeis's Zionist activities did not cease with his nomination to the Supreme Court of the United States in April 1916. Although critiques against his participation in internal Jewish affairs brought Brandeis to resign from his official Zionist position by July 1916, he continued to lead the American movement from behind the scenes as fully and effectively as before. Indeed, in the years from 1918 to 1921 his Zionist activity reached new heights, now also on the international scene. In 1919 he went to Palestine, his first and only visit there. On the way, in London he met several European Zionist leaders, foremost among them Chaim Weizmann. His first encounter with the European Zionists was not auspicious and presaged the misunderstandings that were to ensue.

A year later, during the London Zionist Conference in July 1920, severe disagreements surfaced between the American and the European Zionists.

The conference itself, the first international meeting of the movement in the completely altered circumstances of the postwar era, was a chaotic affair. Each side presented different views about the desirable line of development of the Jewish National Home in Palestine, while ideological differences and divergent concepts about how to lead the movement and how to administer the Zionist finances loomed large. In Brandeis's words, the conference was little more than a "talkfest."[11] At a crucial moment in mid-July 1920, when Brandeis had to decide between full participation in Zionist international activity and his American commitments, his decision fell to the American side. In the following months, the unfolding crisis between what at the time was called the "Brandeis Group" and the European heads of the movement led to a dramatic outcome: at the Cleveland Conference of the Zionist Organization of America in June 1921, the rank-and-file of the American movement sided with the European leadership, headed by Chaim Weizmann. Brandeis and his associates resigned from their Zionist positions.[12] They continued to be active in initiatives related to the economic development of the Jewish National Home; but only in 1930, in changed circumstances, did members of the Brandeis circle return to the formal leadership of the American movement. All in all, the years 1914–1921 were the main Zionist period in Brandeis's life.

Brandeis's Zionist Position

Brandeis's Zionist views were presented mostly in lectures given between 1915 and 1918. Very representative was an address from June 1915, "The Jewish Problem: How to Solve It."[13]

Zionism seeks to establish in Palestine, for such Jews as choose to go and remain there, and for their descendants, a legally secured home, where they may live together and lead a Jewish life, where they may expect ultimately to constitute a majority of the population, and may look forward to what we should call home rule. The Zionists seek to establish this home in Palestine because they are convinced that the undying longing of Jews for Palestine is a fact of deepest significance ... and that it is not a right merely but a duty of the Jewish nationality to survive and to develop.

Brandeis stressed the difference between nation and nationality: *nation* was described as a political frame, related to the state; *nationality* meant the cultural characteristics of a people, preserved and developed through history. In that sense, the Jews were not a nation, but a nationality, with its own religion, traditions, and customs: "Standing against this broad foundation of nationality, Zionism aims to give it full development," Brandeis stated. Since the destruction of the Jerusalem temple nearly two thousand years ago, "The longing for Palestine has been ever present with the Jew." Only in Palestine could the Jewish nationality be protected from the forces of disintegration that threatened it presently, and "there alone can the Jewish spirit reach its full and natural development; and by securing for those Jews who wish to settle there the opportunity to do so, not only those Jews, but all other Jews will be benefited."[14]

An echo of cultural Zionism is discernible in Brandeis's utterances. There are no indications that Brandeis was influenced directly by Ahad Ha'am, but since the early years of the twentieth century, an American version of the cultural approach had been formulated in the leadership of American Zionism (but less so in the rank-and-file of the American movement), expressed in the writings of Israel Friedlaender, Judah L. Magnes, and others.[15] Later, during the Brandeis years, a younger generation of American Zionists, such as Horace M. Kallen and Mordecai M. Kaplan, further developed the Americanized cultural approach.[16] As Ben Halpern has pointed out, Brandeis's own position, while running parallel to past ideological elaborations in American Zionism, was very much bound to his American progressivism and signified no conversion to new beliefs not attuned to his American intellectual self-definition: "His reverence . . . attached itself in lifelong piety to the Pilgrim Fathers, his adopted patrimony."[17] A central point of his position was the connection between Zionism and "Americanism": "Let no American imagine that Zionism is inconsistent with [American] Patriotism. Multiple loyalties are objectionable only if they are inconsistent"; and further on: "There is no inconsistency between loyalty to America and loyalty to Jewry. The Jewish spirit, the product of our religion and experiences, is essentially modern and essentially American. Not since the destruction of the Temple have the Jews in spirit and in ideals been so fully in harmony with the noblest aspirations of the country in which they lived." The consequence was that "every

American Jew who aids in advancing the Jewish settlement in Palestine, though he feels that neither he nor his descendants will ever live there, will likewise be a better man and a better American for doing so." Here Brandeis went a step further: "Indeed, loyalty to America demands rather that each American Jew become a Zionist"[18] — a far-reaching conclusion, which may have irritated the many American Jews who did not adhere to the Zionist position.

Furthermore, in the brand of Zionism embraced by the Brandeis circle, Brandeis's own position had a personal dimension: he was insistently pragmatic and quite indifferent to the ideological aspects of a given Zionist situation or problem. Indeed, when differences and tensions arose between Brandeis and the European Zionists, especially from 1919 to 1921, one reason the Europeans had trouble coping with Brandeis's proposals was because he always stressed the pragmatic side of the matter and was consistently indifferent to its ideological aspects, which for the European Zionists were important and frequently even decisive. One of Brandeis's close associates, Julian W. Mack, compared the positions of the Brandeis circle, both in the positive and in the negative sense, to the concepts dominant in European Zionism. This happened first during the intensive discussions with the banker Jacob H. Schiff, seen by many as the leading figure in American Jewry. Having opposed Zionism for many years, by 1917 Schiff changed his views and sought an ideological formulation that might allow him to enter the Zionist movement. Mack fulfilled a leading role in the ensuing negotiations in which other persons also took part, among them Louis Marshall, the president of the American Jewish Committee. The participants sought to define in what sense are the Jews a people and what exactly was meant by "nation" and "nationalism" in an American-Jewish context. As for Brandeis, the harmonic relationship between Americanism and Zionism was the centerpiece of Mack's position, although more generally formulated. In the end, Schiff did not join the Zionist movement, but for mainly personal reasons.[19] Brandeis did not participate openly in the interchange, a rule he had established since his nomination to the US Supreme Court, but he directed the contacts behind the scenes.

Modern research has shown how the formulations current in the diverse branches of the Zionist movement also were influenced by in-

tellectual trends dominant in the non-Jewish environment.[20] These include not only factors such as nationalism and antisemitism, but also
—and Brandeis's Zionist approach was an excellent example—the general ideological background of modern societies in whose midst Jews
lived. Accordingly, there were certain similarities between the views of
Brandeis and his associates and those expressed in other sectors of the
Zionist movement, such as the "post-assimilatory" approach formulated
in German Zionism by Kurt Blumenfeld,[21] an example of a Jew who was
highly integrated in the German cultural realm and who became a Zionist. The turn to Zionism was related to many reasons, among them
a reawakening of Jewish consciousness, or problems in the relationship
with the non-Jewish environment, or both. Such "new" Zionists (the "old"
ones being Eastern European Jews or Jews in Muslim lands) explained
their positions in terms that bore the imprint of their non-Jewish cultural
milieu, whose ideas they had absorbed. In the case of the German Zionists, they justified their views with arguments from German or European
thought and political ideas.[22] Brandeis and his associates, for their part,
were immersed deeply in the concepts of American society. For Brandeis,
the Jewish pioneers in Palestine were "our Jewish Pilgrim Fathers."[23] Very
few of these post-assimilatory Zionists in Europe or in America (and
certainly not Brandeis himself) quoted from Jewish classical sources to
explain their Zionism.

If the sociological profile of these new Zionist trends was similar, their
ideological paths pointed in different directions. Blumenfeld and his colleagues stressed that the full integration of the Jews in German society had
failed. Brandeis built on the presumption of a positive social and cultural
integration of the Jews in the American environment. Zionism was a sup-
plementation, even an enrichment, to the integration of the Jews in American life. In their case, the national issue served as an ideological dividing
line, as became clear during the meetings and clashes with the European
Zionists from 1919 to 1921. For the Americans, the national component
of the Zionist idea was limited strictly to the cultural realm. As Brandeis
explained it to Kurt Blumenfeld in 1920, ties should be built—obviously,
spiritual ones—between Jerusalem and the diverse Jewish centers of the
Diaspora, but not between the centers themselves.[24] Again, it was Julian
W. Mack who fully explained the implicit differences: "Ussishkin and the

others [Eastern European Zionists] wish to emphasize that the Jews form a part of the world[-wide Jewish] nation. I agree with this view, but only insofar as the [term] world nation is used in the cultural and not in the political sense. We freely admit the necessity for claiming not only the cultural, but also the political rights of national minority for the Jews in the East of Europe . . . but it seems unthinkable for the Jews scattered all over the world at present to present a united political front."[25] Many European Zionists saw such a position as ideologically shallow: "The leaders of American Zionism are not nationalist Jews," Weizmann wrote to Herbert Samuel in August 1920. "To them Zionism is not a movement which gives them a definite view point of the world, which gives them a definite outlook on Jewish life. . . . They have further not the slightest understanding for all those questions in Zionism which have contributed so much towards the real life of the movement, like the Hebrew revival, like the desire of the Zionists to 'Judaize' the Jewish communities of the world, to make their consciousness to fight assimilation with all its manifestations, short for all those imponderabilia which form a national movement of which Palestine and Palestinism is merely a territorial aspect of a national-political upheaval."[26] This view expressed Weizmann's Zionist credo but did not do justice to American Zionism. There was a strong Jewish-ethnic dimension in the position of the American Zionists that bore the marks of their American background, but which did not square with European-shaped national concepts.

The national issue was intrinsically bound to another central tenet in Zionist ideology, the notion of *galut*: European Zionism defined the condition of Jewry in terms of classical Jewish thought, namely, as "exile," exile from the Land of Israel. Weizmann (and Blumenfeld) endorsed the idea of *sh'lilat hagalut*, the negation of the Diaspora. Brandeis and his associates hardly dealt with that issue, but implicitly rejected it. The despair regarding life in *galut* did not apply to American Jewry, Judah L. Magnes, a leading American Zionist, wrote to Weizmann in 1914.[27] For Brandeis and his associates, it was the relationship between Zionism and "Americanism" that was key and a major trope in most of their pronouncements. Last, it is worthwhile to note that antisemitism did not become a factor in their conception of American Zionism.

However we might interpret Brandeis's Zionist ideas, there can be no doubt regarding his utmost conviction and sincerity. There was a pathos in Brandeis's Zionism that rubbed off on his associates and enthralled them. Hence, Stephen S. Wise, a devout Brandeis follower but a famously independent soul, described a meeting of the Brandeis circle during the struggle with Weizmann in 1921: "I have never seen or heard him when he made the impression upon a group of men that he did yesterday. He took the meeting in the hollow of his hand and lifted it up enabling all of us to see the thing anew, steadily, and whole! I shall never forget his words: 'Our aim is the kingdom of heaven, paraphrasing Cromwell. We take Palestine by the way. But we must take it with clean hands; we must take it in such a way as to ennoble the Jewish people. Otherwise it will not be worth having.'"[28]

Organization

The relatively short period of Brandeis's active Zionist leadership saw him for the first (and only) time in his life in an executive role, openly so until mid-1916 and later on behind the scenes.

The organizational situation of American Zionism was a constant concern. All Zionists, in America or Europe, recognized the great promise imbued in the huge American branch, in its numbers, its wealth, its latent influence on the local and international scene. At the same time, everybody bemoaned the fact that this potential remained unrealized, that American Zionism was feeble and chaotic. For years a debate went on among the American activists between two possible approaches to improve the organization of the movement, the centralized and the decentralized way. In the pre-Brandeis years, the decentralized approach had become dominant: besides a number of chapters directly associated with the Federation of American Zionists, the majority of the supporters of the movement were found in a multitude of fraternal orders, *landsmanshaftn*, student groups, synagogues, and so on, all only loosely associated with the FAZ. In addition, there were the Zionist parties, such as Mizrachi, Poale Zion, or the semi-independent Hadassah.[29]

European Zionist activists who came in contact with the American movement remained unimpressed by the explanations and proposals they heard, and their tendency was to suggest extreme measures. "The convention was quite relaxed, the attendance was good, the functions were nice indeed," wrote Shmaryahu Levin, member of the central committee of the World Zionist Organization, after participating in the yearly convention of the Federation of American Zionists early in July 1914, "but one thing is clear for me: if also now we do not intervene *radically* everything will remain as it was, and Zionism [in America] will also in the future drag on its wretched existence." About fifteen years later in 1929, Chaim Arlosoroff, then the rising star in the Zionist international leadership, recollected a period of eighteen months as envoy to the United States: "I suggest that American Zionism has to undergo a fundamental and comprehensive reorganization, and that this work of reconstruction will not be undertaken unless the World Zionist authorities intervene."[30]

Once Brandeis had accepted the leadership of the American movement, he concentrated on organization, with uncompromising emphasis on the centralized approach. "Men, money, and discipline" was the motto he presented and imposed on the expanding American movement. Brandeis's performance was most impressive: he had detailed knowledge of everything going on in the organization, demanded constant reports, kept a tight control over the movement, and was decisive in matters large and small. Although inexperienced in Jewish communal matters, Brandeis understood quickly enough that Zionist and Jewish leadership, especially in times of stress, were inseparable. Under his direction the American Zionists became a leading force in the most significant Jewish public initiatives in the United States, such as relief efforts for Jews in the European war zone and, especially, the creation and activities of the first American Jewish Congress.[31] The Zionist Organization of America, established in 1918, stood at the head of a centralized structure of Zionist districts to which every American Zionist was supposed to belong. The number of registered Zionists grew from about 7,400 in 1914 to 149,000 in 1919, organized in 300 Zionist districts.[32] American Zionism now became a leading force in American Jewry.

And yet the huge expansion of the American movement was a short-lived episode. Two years after its creation, the organizational structure created and controlled by Brandeis and his associates began to collapse. It has been claimed that one reason was the distance between the Brandeis circle and the rank and file of the movement. An implicit condition for stable public leadership is a level of identification between the leader and the broad mass of supporters. In Brandeis's case, there were few intellectual ties or social similarities between him and the large American Zionist public, mostly Jews of Eastern European origin. Brandeis's short appearances at American Zionist conferences never failed to arouse great enthusiasm among the participants, but there was no real contact between him and the rank and file of the organization. They were all attuned to a common ideal: the Zionist hopes with regard to Palestine. But Zionism meant one thing for Brandeis and his associates, and another for the majority of American rank and file, still bound to Zionist Eastern European values.

A more convincing explanation for the organizational breakdown is that the organizational structures of American Zionism were influenced by certain trends that only become evident in a historical perspective. In the words of Ben Halpern, American Zionists "resembled a demobilized army that could be made effective for action only by some influence that drew on their latent sentiment with compelling power."[33] Three times during the first half of the twentieth century American Zionism rallied and expanded dramatically, always in response to a Jewish crisis: during the years 1903–1904, reacting to the Kishinev massacre; in the years 1915–1919, responding to the problems and the opportunities caused by World War I; and in the years 1943–1948, the years of the Holocaust and later the creation of the Jewish state. After each of these time periods, American Zionism, following a short period of intense enthusiasm, collapsed and returned to its former relative weakness and disarray.

The Brandeis period of Zionist leadership coincided with the second of these upsurges. Undoubtedly, Brandeis's prestige, forceful personality, and firm leadership contributed to the dimensions and the intensity of the American Zionist expansion and neutralized for a time the underlying weaknesses of the American movement. At the same time, it may well be that when the tide changed, the Brandeis organizational formula of a highly centralized structure, embodied in the newly founded Zionist Organization of America, only accelerated the organization's debacle. An immigrant community in a fluid social situation apparently was not able to be organized in centralized structures. One may even ask how compatible centralized social models were with the reigning patterns of American society in general. In any event, the Zionist upsurge in America during World War I was impelled by social and ideological forces in the American Jewish community unrelated to Brandeis and beyond his control. For a short period, an army of American Zionist enthusiasts moved into high action, only to return shortly afterward to its former demobilized condition. Indeed, when in 1930 Brandeis tried to repeat his Zionist performance of the years 1914–1920, he saw soon enough that in the reigning conditions his efforts had no chance.[34]

Brandeis's Zionist performance had significant personal elements. Thrown into an administrative position of broad scope, Brandeis revealed himself as an extremely able manager, wielding tight control over the organizational structures of the American movement, extremely effective in his relationships with people; and by all accounts, he enjoyed his new role very much.[35] Hidden qualities (and some flaws) soon emerged. The Brandeis of the American public scene was an extremely reserved person who kept his emotions well hidden. In 1912–1913 when he was considered for a position in President-elect Wilson's cabinet, and again in 1916 when he was proposed for membership in the Supreme Court, Brandeis was the object of bitter campaigns of vilification, both professional and personal.[36] Nevertheless, it is almost impossible to find a comment of his with regard to his tormentors. The Zionist Brandeis was a stern figure ("an exacting master!" according to Emmanuel Neumann[37]), but still he appeared more open and outspoken, much more liberated from constraints. Occasionally, that "new" Brandeis showed some harsh facets. For instance, he was unable to make concessions: in the confrontation between him and Weizmann during the years 1919–1921, where the main issue was the organization and the policies of the Zionist movement in the post–World War I period, it is hard to find a single case in which Brandeis changed his mind. Furthermore, Brandeis was apt to wield a sharp axe against Zionist activists who crossed him. He waged an unforgiving vendetta against Louis Lipsky, a most distinguished figure in American Zionism: Lipsky was the man who had challenged him, in July 1920, to resign his position at the Supreme Court and dedicate himself fully to Zionist activity and who soon organized the resistance against the Brandeis circle in the American movement. "We should keep domestic foes on the run — and should not fool ourselves again into believing that they will aid us in carrying out the program. . . . They are definitely against us — and we should be definitely and relentlessly against them," so Brandeis opined on the opposition group in the Zionist Organization of America (ZOA), led by Lipsky, in March 1921.[38] Judah L. Magnes, who had dared to criticize him in 1916 for mixing his Zionist and Supreme Court occupations, earned a lifelong label as an unstable character. Chaim Weizmann, the president of the Zionist movement, was humiliated by Brandeis, when during their clash in 1921 Weizmann sought to reach an understanding.[39] Conversely, Brandeis had no trouble in reconciling with William Howard Taft, in the recent past one of his worst detractors, when they met by chance in December 1918.[40] Apparently, the art of compromise did not extend to the Jewish scene.

Conclusion

In spite of their disappointing end, the Zionist years of Louis D. Brandeis, from 1914 to 1921, were certainly a high point in his life, a period when he was able to give powerful expression to his manifold capacities. For a latter-day observer, the Brandeis of those years remains an intriguing phenomenon: on the one hand, the leader of American Zionism in a period of strong expansion in the United States and turbulent activity on the international scene; on the other hand, the calm participant in the highest juridical court of the United States. It is difficult to imagine a greater incongruity between two occupations, but Brandeis managed to affirm himself, and forcefully so, in both—an awesome feat!

Still, Brandeis's Zionist episode leaves questions, especially regarding the complex connection between personal charisma and social circumstances. Brandeis's Zionist leadership rode on the surging crest of a public mood in American Jewry he neither created nor could rule. His personality, organizational talent, and dedication made the most of these conditions. Nevertheless, by 1920, more than a year before the rout at the 1921 Cleveland Convention of the ZOA, the acme of Zionist fervor in American Jewry had passed and the organizational structures created by the Brandeis circle were disintegrating.

As impressive as Brandeis's Zionist leadership was, in 1921 when the rank and file of the American movement had to decide between Weizmann and Brandeis, they opted for Weizmann, to whose brand of Zionism, obviously, they felt closer. But it was Brandeis who best expressed the ideological tenor of American Zionism. In Europe, the "negation of *galut*" represented a major thrust of Zionist endeavors. America was different. The *galut* issue already had been sidelined before 1914, and among Brandeis and his associates, the matter practically went unmentioned. "Zionism and Americanism," defined in positive terms, was the leading idea for them. The question is, how much ideological fervor was such a tenet capable of generating. As it turns out, there was a built-in ideological weakness in American Zionism: American Jews were America-directed, America was not *galut*, and consequently, their commitment to Zionism had inherent limitations. American Jews could be rallied for a Jewish or a Zionist cause—for a short time. In final analysis, this may explain the ups and downs of the movement that so upset European observers. On a more personal level, when it came to the moment of decision between their American and their Zionist interests, neither Brandeis nor any of his associates opted for the Zionist alternative—which was not a matter of accident, or of personal deficiency, but the reflection of an ideological way.

Which brings one to reflect anew on the impact of Zionism, that perplexing ideal capable of taking hold, to an extent, on Jews whose connection to Judaism, to the Jewish people, or to Jewish traditions had become tenuous to the point of obliteration. At the end of the day, we are still unable to explain in common logical terms what moved Brandeis to become a Zionist. But here he was, the ultimate outsider in matters Jewish, apt to speak with the utmost sincerity and conviction about the reestablishment of a Jewish homeland in Palestine as if it were for him the most natural, the most credible of public ideas, to the point of stating that it was the duty of a good American Jew to become a Zionist. Since he was far from being the only modern Jew of his kind in America or in Europe to be drawn to the Zionist creed, one wonders if there is much that remains to be understood about the power of the Zionist idea.

As much as Brandeis, the man and his achievements, impresses the observer, does one not detect in his life a hint of unrealized potential? If one concentrates on only his Zionist episode, there is a sobering dimension, almost a lesson, in Brandeis's endeavors.[41] His extensive skills and his impressive personality became engaged in an enterprise that ended in a personal debacle for ideological and organizational reasons beyond his control and understanding. What remains is the impact of a man who seemingly had in him the stuff of still greater deeds. Brandeis's short period at the head of American Zionism hints at what he might have been capable of in a different time and in other circumstances, in the Zionist or, indeed, in the general American sphere.

NOTES

1. The prominent biographer of Brandeis is Melvin I. Urofsky, who recently published an impressive work, *Louis D. Brandeis: A Life* (New York: Pantheon, 2009); see also Melvin I. Urofsky and David W. Levy, *Letters of Louis D. Brandeis*, 5 vols. (Albany, NY: State University of New York, 1971–78) (hereafter BL); Melvin I. Urofsky and David W. Levy, *The Family Letters of Louis D. Brandeis* (Norman: University of Oklahoma Press, 2002). Among the many works on Brandeis, see the perceptive analysis of Brandeis's Zionist ideas and activities by Ben Halpern, *A Clash of Heroes: Brandeis, Weizmann, and American Zionism* (New York and Oxford: Oxford University Press, 1987), and in his essay "The Americanization of Zionism, 1880–1930," *American Jewish History* 69 (1979): 15–33; for an interesting sketch of Brandeis as Zionist, see Louis Lipsky, *Memoirs in Profile* (Philadelphia: Jewish Publication Society of America, 1975), 201–11; see also Alon Gal, *Brandeis of Boston* (Cambridge, MA and London: Harvard University Press, 1980); Jehuda Reinharz, *Chaim Weizmann: The Making of a Statesman* (New York and Oxford: Oxford University Press, 1993), esp. chaps. 8–9; Melvin I. Urofsky, *American Zionism from Herzl to the Holocaust* (Garden City, NY: Anchor Press, 1975), esp. chaps. 4–7; Evyatar Friesel, "Brandeis' Role in American Zionism Historically Reconsidered," *American Jewish History* 69 (1979): 34–59; Yonathan Shapiro, *Leadership of the American Zionist Organization 1897–1930* (Urbana/Chicago/London: University of Illinois Press, 1971), esp. chap. 3.

2. "Leadership has proved impossible to define, despite decades of research and a huge number of publications," starts a recent study of Nancy Harding et al., "Leadership and Charisma: A Desire That Cannot Speak Its Name?" *Human Relations* 6 (July 2011): 927.

3. Julius Simon, *Certain Days: Zionist Memoirs and Letters* (Jerusalem: Israel Universities Press, 1971), 100.

4. Quoted by Gal, *Brandeis of Boston*, 83.

5. Lipsky, *Memoirs in Profile*, 202.

6. See Gal, *Brandeis of Boston*, 188–201; Stuart M. Geller, "Why Did Louis D. Brandeis Choose Zionism?," *American Jewish Historical Quarterly* 62 (1973): 386–389.

7. Gal, *Brandeis of Boston*, chaps. 5–6; Halpern, *A Clash of Heroes*, 94–108; Shapiro, *Leadership of the American Zionist Organization 1897–1930*, 61–70; Shapiro's

approach is criticized by Halpern and also in Geller, "Why Did Louis D. Brandeis Choose Zionism?," 383–400; see also Urofsky, *Louis D. Brandeis*, 405–409.

8. A classical work on the theme is John Higham, *Strangers on the Land: Patterns of American Nativism, 1860–1925* (New Brunswick, NJ: Rutgers University Press, 1955); see also his "Anti-Semitism Historically Reconsidered," in *Jews in the Mind of America*, ed. Charles H. Stember (New York and London: Basic Books, 1966), 237–70.

9. Alon Gal mentions several of such discriminatory cases in Brandeis's life, including the typical case of social clubs that restricted themselves to their "own people." See Gal, *Brandeis of Boston*, 36–43, 169–73; see also Halpern, *A Clash of Heroes*, 80. Urofsky ponders (too) critically the views of Gal and Halpern, see Urofsky, *Louis D. Brandeis*, 53–54, 117, 406–407.

10. See Halpern, *A Clash of Heroes*, 109–111; Shapiro, *Leadership of the American Zionist Organization 1897–1930*, 61–76.

11. See Lipsky, *Memoirs in Profile*, 207–10; Halpern, *A Clash of Heroes*, 212–18.

12. Shapiro, *Leadership of the American Zionist Organization 1897–1930*, 167–79; Urosky, *American Zionism*, 283–98.

13. See the collection of his speeches and statements in: *Brandeis on Zionism* (Washington, DC: Zionist Organization of America, 1942), 12–35.

14. Ibid., 24–25.

15. See "The Problem of Judaism in America (1907)," as well as his preface (1919) in Israel Friedlaender, *Past and Present: A Collection of Jewish Essays* (Cincinnati: Ark Publishing, 1919); Judah L. Magnes, "The Melting Pot," *Emanu-El Pulpit* 3 (New York, 1909): 8–9; Judah L. Magnes, *What Zionism Has Given the Jews* (New York: Federation of American Zionists, 1911), 3, 6–7.

16. Shapiro, *Leadership of the American Zionist Organization 1897–1930*, 40–41, 71; Urofsky, *Louis D. Brandeis*, 410–11.

17. Halpern, *A Clash of Heroes*, 94–95, 96–108.

18. Louis D. Brandeis, *The Jewish Problem: How to Solve It* (Cleveland, OH: J. Saslaw, 1934), 28–29.

19. See Julian W. Mack, *Americanism and Zionism* (New York: Federation of American Zionists, 1918); Louis Marshall to Jacob H. Schiff, November 14, 1917, in *Louis Marshall, Champion of Liberty: Selected Papers and Addresses*, ed. Charles Reznikoff, vol. 2 (Philadelphia: Jewish Publication Society of America, 1957), 710–14; Evyatar Friesel, "Jacob H. Schiff Becomes a Zionist: A Chapter in American-Jewish Self-Definition, 1907–1917," *Studies in Zionism*, no. 5 (1982): 55–92.

20. The theme underlies the reflective work of Gideon Shimoni, *The Zionist Ideology* (Waltham, MA: Brandeis University Press, 1997).

21. See Kurt Blumenfeld, *Erlebte Judenfrage: Ein Vierteljahrhundert deutscher Zionismus* (Stuttgart: Deutsche Verlags-Anstalt, 1962). A perceptive work on the ideological trends that influenced young German Zionists is Jörg Hackeschmidt, *Von Kurt Blumenfeld zu Norbert Elias: Die Erfindung einer jüdischen Nation* (Hamburg: Europäishe Verlags-Anstalt, 1997).

22. See the letters of Norbert Elias in Hackeschmidt, *Von Kurt Blumenfeld zu Norbert Elias*, 327–42.

23. Brandeis, "The Jewish Problem," 28.

24. Kurt Blumenfeld, *Erlebte Judenfrage: Ein Vierteljahrhundert deutscher Zionismus* (Stuttgart: Deutsche Verlags-Anstalt, 1962), 124–25.

25. Minutes of meeting of the Zionist Executive Committee with representatives of the ZOA, London, May 20, 1919, Jerusalem, Central Zionist Archives (hereafter CZA), z4/302/1.s).

26. Chaim Weizmann, letter from October 8, 1920, *The Letters and Papers of Chaim Weizmann*, Series A Weizmann Letters, vol. 10 (July 1920–December 1921), 7–13.

27. Chaim Weizmann, letter from June 8, 1914, Weizmann Archives, Rehovot, Israel.

28. Chaim Weizmann to Felix Frankfurter, April 18, 1921, Wise Papers, American Jewish Archives, Cincinnati, OH.

29. See Shapiro, *Leadership of the American Zionist Organization 1897–1930*, chap. 2; Halperin, *A Clash of Heroes*, 86–90, 93–94.

30. Shmaryahu Lewin to the Small Actions Committee of the ZWO, July 4, 1914, Central Zionist Archives, Jerusalem, z3/395; Chaim Arlosoroff, *Surveying American Zionism* (New York: Zionist Labor Party "Hitachduth" of America, 1929), 32. Arlosoroff's shattering analysis of the American Zionist movement went on for thirty-five printed pages.

31. See Shapiro, *Leadership of the American Zionist Organization 1897–1930*, chap. 4; Halpern, *A Clash of Heroes*, 117–26.

32. Friesel, "Brandeis' Role," 48.

33. Halpern, *A Clash of Heroes*, 107.

34. See Urofsky, *Louis D. Brandeis*, 687–90.

35. See Urofsky, *American Zionism*, 156–60.

36. The slanderous private and probably not-so-private comments of William Howard Taft, a powerful public figure in his time (president of the United States from 1909 to 1913), are very telling of what Brandeis had to cope with in the pre-justice phase of his American public career. For passages from Taft's many utterances, see Geller, "Why Did Louis D. Brandeis Choose Zionism," 392–98. See also Urofsky, *Louis D. Brandeis*, 372–77, and esp. 433–59.

37. See Emanuel Neumann, "Justice Louis D. Brandeis' 80th Birthday," in *Palestine on Brandeis* (Jerusalem, 1937), 22–27.

38. Letter to Julian W. Mack et al, March 22, 1921, de Haas Papers, CZA. Or, even worse and completely unwarranted by facts: "But I know L.L. and his ilk. They not only have not 'performed'; they have destroyed. They gradually undermined, by self-seeking and lowered standards, the Z.O.A which was flourishing in 1920. They bankrupted it financially, morally, intellectually, and depleted its membership . . . That is the main cause of our present plight." —Brandeis to Jacob H. Gilbert, January 4, 1931, in Urofsky and Levy, *The Brandeis Family Letters*, 512. See also

Brandeis to Felix Frankfurter, October 1920, BL, 4, 490; or to Robert Szold, January 1938, BL, 5, 599.

39. Regarding Magnes, see BL, 4, 442, and Brandeis to Robert Szold, January 1930, BL, 5, 594 ("My lack of faith in Magnes' judgment continues . . ."); regarding the April 1921 Brandeis-Weizmann meeting in Washington, see Brandeis to Julian W. Mack and Jacob de Haas, April 18, 1921, de Haas Papers, CZA, mentioned also in Halpern, *A Clash of Heroes*, 332.

40. See Urofsky, *Louis D. Brandeis*, 571, ff.; Halpern, *A Clash of Heroes*, 125.

41. Admittedly, a point where I beg to differ from the conclusions of Melvin I. Urofsky—see *Louis D. Brandeis*, 754–56.

9

America's Most Memorable Zionist Leaders

JONATHAN D. SARNA

Jewish Literacy, a widely distributed volume by Joseph Telushkin that promises "the most important things to know about the Jewish religion, its people, and its history," highlights two American Zionists as worthy of being remembered by every literate Jew: Louis Brandeis and Henrietta Szold.[1] Brandeis and Szold likewise are the only two American Zionists to make Michael Shapiro's somewhat idiosyncratic list of "The Jewish 100," a ranking of the most influential Jews of all time.[2] In addition, they are the highest-ranking Zionist man and woman in the journal *American Jewish History*'s small scholarly survey of "the two greatest American Jewish leaders."[3] They have been the subject of more published biographies than any other American Zionists, and they dominate children's textbook presentations of American Zionism as well. They are, in short, the best-known American Zionists by far.

Scholars may lament that other critical figures—people such as Harry Friedenwald, Israel Friedlaender, Richard Gottheil, Hayim Greenberg, Louis Lipsky, Julian Mack, Emanuel Neumann, Alice Seligsberg, Marie Syrkin, and so many others—have not achieved immortality in this way. Stephen S. Wise, Abba Hillel Silver, and Mordecai Kaplan may have come close, but they are neither as well known as Brandeis and Szold nor as universally respected. Kaplan, moreover, is far better known as the founder of Reconstructionism. Whether others deserve greater recognition, however, is not the question to be considered here.[4] That would demand an extensive inquiry into what "greatness" in Zionism entails and how it should be measured. Instead, our question is *why* Brandeis and Szold achieved special "canonical status" among American Zionist leaders, while so many others did not.

Existing studies of American Zionist leadership fail to consider this question. Taking their cue from social scientific studies of leadership, they focus instead on the sources from which Zionist leaders drew their authority, the strategies that they pursued, and the extent to which they preserved tradition or promoted change. Yonathan Shapiro's well-known volume entitled *Leadership of the American Zionist Organization, 1897–1930* (1971), for example, follows Kurt Lewin in distinguishing between leaders from the center (such as Louis Lipsky) and leaders from the periphery (such as Louis Brandeis) and analyzes differences between the backgrounds, styles, and leadership methods of different American Zionist leaders. But questions of long-term reputation and popular memory — why, in our case, Brandeis and Szold won historical immortality while so many others were forgotten — go unanswered.

Here, I shall argue that the historical reputation of Brandeis and Szold rests upon factors that reach beyond the usual concerns of leadership studies. How they became leaders and what they accomplished during their lifetimes is certainly important, but even more important is the fact that both Brandeis and Szold became role models for American Jews: they embodied values that American Jews admired and sought to project, even if they did not always uphold them themselves. Brandeis and Szold thus came to symbolize the twentieth-century American Jewish community's ideal of what a man and a woman should be. Their enduring reputations reveal, in the final analysis, as much about American Jews as about them.

What Louis Brandeis and Henrietta Szold accomplished in their lives is, in broad outline, widely known. Brandeis (1856–1941), born in Louisville, Kentucky, attended Harvard Law School and went on to become a successful and innovative Boston lawyer, achieving fame as the "people's attorney." During these years he maintained no formal Jewish affiliations, but in midlife, for reasons historians continue to debate, he became attracted to Zionism and in 1914 assumed leadership of the American Zionist movement, transforming its image and identity. He resigned in 1921, following a dispute with Chaim Weizmann, but remained a significant behind-the-scenes player. In 1916, President Woodrow Wilson nominated

Brandeis to the United States Supreme Court, the first Jew to be so honored. He survived a bruising confirmation fight, tainted by antisemitism, and served on the Court for twenty-three years, earning a reputation for "prophetic vision, moral intensity, and [a] grasp of practical affairs."[5]

Henrietta Szold (1860–1945), born in Baltimore, Maryland, was the eldest child of Rabbi Benjamin Szold and served as his amanuensis and aide. Graduating first in her class (and as the only Jew) at Western Female High School, she became a private school teacher, founded a night school for Russian Jewish immigrants, wrote essays for the Jewish press, and then worked for twenty-three years as editor (though without that title) of the Jewish Publication Society in Philadelphia. She was one of the founders of Hadassah in 1912, as well as its first national president; she traveled to Palestine in 1920 to supervise the organization's Zionist Medical Unit; and she lived for most of her remaining years in Jerusalem, organizing social services and assuming (in her seventies) responsibility for Youth Aliyah, the immigration of Jewish refugee children to Palestine. Lauded as "Mother of Israel" for her tireless efforts on behalf of Jews in need, she believed in practical Zionism and invested every task that she undertook with a sense of spiritual purpose.[6]

All of these accomplishments surely earned Brandeis and Szold the accolades showered upon them, but they still leave open the question of why others, who also achieved a great deal, in the course of time have been totally forgotten. Why, in other words, has popular memory operated so selectively in the case of America's Zionist leadership, to the advantage of Brandeis and Szold and the disadvantage of everybody else? No definitive answer to this question is possible, but five factors stressed by the biographers of Brandeis and Szold seem particularly revealing. At the very least, they help to explain why the lives of these two Zionist leaders took on special relevance to subsequent generations of Jews.

First, Louis Brandeis and Henrietta Szold both were native-born, second-generation Americans, children of Central European Jewish immigrants. As leaders, they stood in marked contrast to the vast majority of American Jewish adults (and the even greater majority of American Zionists) who were immigrants, born in Eastern Europe. This disjunction between leaders and led was common in the early decades of the American Zionist movement. Every national president of Hadassah until 1939 was American-born, and not one of the early presidents of the Federation of American Zionists or the Zionist Organization of America was born in Eastern Europe.[7] The reason is that native-born leaders such as Brandeis and Szold helped to legitimate the Zionist movement. They understood American norms and mores, spoke English without a foreign accent, attracted other native-born Jews to join them, and made it more difficult for opponents to label Zionism "un-American." No less important, they served as living proof that those born and bred in America could, through Zionism, preserve their Jewish loyalties. The life stories of Brandeis and Szold thus offered reassurance to immigrants that their own American-born children would not necessarily assimilate and be lost to Judaism. They also reinforced one of Zionism's central claims—that it held the key to Jewish survival.

A second element stressed by biographers of Brandeis and Szold concerns the quality of their minds: their well-deserved reputation for broad learning and superior intelligence. Alfred Mason, Brandeis's first major biographer, quotes a Harvard Law School classmate who recalled that "Mr. Brandeis, although one of the youngest men" in his class, "had the keenest and most subtle mind of all." Brandeis finished first among his peers, received a special dispensation from the university allowing him to graduate at a younger age than the rules allowed, and was described as late as 1941 as "the most brilliant student ever to have attended the Harvard Law School."[8] Near the end of his life, his "outstanding qualities of great learning" were described by the *Universal Jewish Encyclopedia* in terms usually reserved for the greatest rabbis and scholars, including "keen perception, rare analytical powers, [an] orderly and constructive mind . . . and profound knowledge of the historical roots of institutions."[9]

Henrietta Szold's reputation for brilliance was similarly stellar. She graduated top of her class at Western Female High School; commanded German, French, and Hebrew; studied Judaica and the classics with her father (who considered her his "disciple"); audited classes in rabbinics at the Jewish Theological Seminary; and was an omnivorous reader. One biographer described her as "the most learned Jewess in the United States."[10] Another recalled how Szold's "probing mind" revealed facets of problems "that had occurred to no one else and plumbed depths unfathomed by the others." Even Jerusalem's doctors, we are told, "listened agape" while

Szold, who had no formal medical training, "expounded before them the interrelationships among the various fields of medicine with the clarity of one long conversant with problems of hospitalization."[11]

Even if exaggerated for effect, the reputation shared by Brandeis and Szold for wide-ranging learning and intellectual brilliance reinforced both a basic Jewish value and a long-standing tradition that rewards wisdom with status. Just as so many of the great heroes of Israel's past were renowned for their genius, so too, according to Zionism's followers, its contemporary heroes. For American Jews, the fact that Brandeis and Szold were smarter than their peers both explained their success and justified the adulation that their followers showered upon them.

One might have expected that Szold, as a woman, would have been held to a different standard. Her formal academic achievements, after all, fell well below those of Brandeis. He held a graduate degree from America's finest university; her highest earned degree was a high school diploma. Moreover, Jews traditionally considered higher education more important for men than for women. Szold herself, however, often condemned this double standard and from an early age championed women's higher education.[12] Through her writings and career, she demonstrated that women were as intellectually able as their male counterparts. Her editorial work at the Jewish Publication Society, in fact, made clear that she was actually *more* able than many of those whose books she tacitly improved.[13] The image of the brainy Miss Szold underscored this feminist lesson by showing that learning and wisdom were no less important for Jewish women than for Jewish men.

Third on the list of revealing characteristics stressed in popular presentations of the lives of Brandeis and Szold is meticulous efficiency. Both leaders, according to their biographers, hated to waste time and championed order and precision—values central to America's ethos, but not to Zionism's. Szold sought to bring efficiency to Zionism as early as 1910. Charged with the task of clearing up what she described as the "almost hopeless condition" into which the Federation of American Zionism's affairs had fallen, she labored "night and day" as "honorary secretary" and within four months was able to report that "the muddle had been cleared."[14] Brandeis, when he took over as leader of American Zionism in 1914, made a similar thrust for efficiency. He installed a time clock in the

Zionist offices, introduced a file-card system for names, and even proposed fines "for absence or tardiness."[15]

Both leaders also personally embodied the values that they preached. Szold, according to those who knew her, led a "systematic, well-ordered life." "One hesitates," one biographer writes (with obvious didactic intent), "even to hint to our somewhat careless younger generation just how meticulous Henrietta Szold really was in all things, whether great or small."[16] Brandeis, according to his biographers, was no less punctilious. Philippa Strum speaks of his "organization," "efficiency," "energy," and "concern for detail." Alfred Leif, writing a half century earlier, reported simply that "he made efficiency a household word."[17]

The meticulous efficiency that these leaders personified and preached reflected modern business values, alluring yet still somewhat foreign to immigrant Jews from Eastern Europe. Traditional rabbis may have taught the virtue of wasting as little time as possible on pursuits other than Torah, but the secular idea that time should be husbanded for productive labor was new. Benjamin Franklin popularized this idea in America, and Frederick W. Taylor transformed it into a "scientific" management technique with his time-study experiments of the 1880s and 1890s, aimed at eliminating waste and inefficiency.[18] Something of a "cult of efficiency" developed in early twentieth century America, and American Zionism's main followers, success-oriented Eastern European Jews and their children, stood among its most ardent disciples. To them, Brandeis and Szold appeared as "priests and priestesses" of this new faith, the very antithesis of "Old World" habits. In this, as in so many other ways, Brandeis and Szold served as role models, projecting a vision of Zionism fully consonant with modernity and suffused with values that followers sought to incorporate into their own lives.

Closely akin to meticulous efficiency was a fourth characteristic stressed by biographers of Brandeis and Szold: the commitment to hard work. Szold rose early—often at five and rarely after seven—and labored long into the night. In her forties, she sometimes complained about the "crazy orgy of work" to which she subjected herself.[19] Later, at Hadassah, friends recalled that "she worked harder and longer than anyone else on her staff."[20] Even when she was eighty-three, she wore out her companions. Norman Bentwich, who was twenty-three years her junior, recalled a day with her at that time as "an experience of physical and intellectual vitality." It involved meetings in different parts of Israel and lasted for seventeen hours, interrupted only by catnaps.[21] Long hours and hard work were for Szold a permissible way for her to compete successfully with her peers—male and female alike. Into old age, she delighted in her victories: her ability to outlast men and women much younger than herself.[22]

Brandeis too was known for working hard, but his secret was efficiency. He once claimed that he "could do twelve months' work in eleven months."[23] He then spent the twelfth month, usually August, on vacation. His days began early, just as Szold's did, but they generally ended at five. "He knew his health limited his work hours," Philippa Strum explains, "so he organized his time to accomplish all that he wished to do."[24] In the time allotted, he completed an astonishing amount of correspondence and legal writing and kept up with a wide array of interests. His secret, as his colleagues noted when he retired, was "vigor," "devotion," and "intensity." One biographer reports that he was happiest "working for leisure and using leisure for work."[25]

This passionate embrace of work as a calling, rather than simply as a means of earning a living, calls to mind the Protestant work ethic, as described by Max Weber, and serves as yet another reminder that this ethic scarcely was confined to Protestants alone.[26] Through their success, Brandeis and Szold demonstrated that for Jews, too, hard work pays off. Again, they served as role models that others sought to emulate.

In the narratives of Brandeis and Szold, hard work was not only rewarded, it also yielded financial independence and freedom—goals that many an American Jew fervently desired. Brandeis, we are told, had nothing but pity for the man without capital who had "to slave and toil for others to the end of his days."[27] Reputedly, he sought to avoid that sad fate himself by always living carefully and by accumulating from a young age a fortune substantial enough for him to be his own master, free to select the clients and the causes in which he believed. Henrietta Szold gained financial independence in a different way at age fifty-five when a group of wealthy admirers rewarded her with an annuity. Like Brandeis, she too was now able to devote herself fully to the causes in which she believed. Shrewdly, if all too modestly, she once credited her monthly checks with being "the whole secret" of her success in Palestine. Had she worked equally hard and not been financially independent, she recognized, her devotion would "at best" have gone "unnoted."[28] Freedom and financial independence were magical terms to hardworking, upwardly mobile American Jews of that time; they represented, for them, the essence of the American Dream. This explains, in part, the allure for Jews of occupational choices such as law, medicine, and accounting, which promised to make this dream come true faster, and was reflected too in the allure of Zion, which at least in its American version offered brawny pioneers something of this same dream on the soil of Palestine. Brandeis and Szold served, in a sense, as poster children for this dream. The freedom and financial independence that hard work brought them amply validated America's promise, and they made the Zionist promise seem that much more credible.

The value of hard work went along with the fifth characteristic pointed to by all biographers of Brandeis and Szold: their penchant for spartan living and their commitment to social justice. In an age characterized by materialism and hedonism, both leaders represented "traditional values"; they firmly opposed the conspicuous consumption so frequently witnessed in their day. Brandeis, for example, was said from a young age to have "limit[ed] his wants to the barest minimum." A biography written in his lifetime spoke of the "Stoic simplicity of his needs." He was known to abhor ostentation and personal debt and to shun the kinds of luxuries that most men of his class indulged in; his ideal instead was to be "economical."[29] His friend, the Catholic social reformer Monsignor John A. Ryan, went so far as to describe his tastes and manner of living as approaching "the standards of an ascetic." Philippa Strum reminds us that this was something of an exaggeration, for Brandeis indulged in horses, canoes, summer homes, servants, and private schooling for his daughters. The image he cultivated, however, did border on the ascetic: he never owned a car, his dinners were "spare in provision," and his office "was furnished with austerity. There was no rug or easy chair." Where others spent more than they earned, he did the opposite and donated the excess to causes such as Zionism in which he passionately believed. This was a deeply held value lived out in life and at the same time a silent polemic, an attack on the materialism of American society in general and particularly, one suspects, on the "crude, materialistic Boston Jews" of whom he was so very contemptuous.[30]

Henrietta Szold displayed similar values and ideals. "For decades she had been frugal," her biographer reports.[31] She preached simple household virtues—"economy, order and system."[32] Philanthropy was central to her life, and like Brandeis she preferred to give rather than to receive. Her own home in Jerusalem was described as "simple [and] tastefully furnished,"[33] while she herself, according to her longtime secretary Elma Ehrlich (Levinger) was "unbelievably straitlaced in all matters great or small."[34] "Scrupulous about the use of public funds," her friend Rose Zeitlin recalled, "Miss Szold rarely indulged in any but second-class travel (third when second was not available). . . . On the Palestine roads her travel was by bus and third-class rail, unless a taxi was indispensable. 'I am no more than one of the people of Israel,' she said, when found waiting for a bus on a windy corner. . . . At the hotel where she lived for years a tablemate could not help noticing that invariably she chose the least expensive foods."[35] To Szold, as to Louis Brandeis, crude materialism and conspicuous consumption were anathema. At twenty-seven she lamented the "rampant materialism" that afflicted "our co-religionists in Europe."[36] Late in life, she deprecated, in a letter to her family, "America's business greed."[37]

Jewish ideals of social justice and American Progressivism underlay many of these attitudes and life patterns. Brandeis and Szold, like other Jewish and Christian social reformers of their day, believed in a better world and conducted their lives according to *its* values, rather than those of their surroundings. For them, Zionism served as an extension of this vision. Both strongly supported the 1918 Pittsburgh Program of the Zionist Organization of America, which set forth a social justice agenda for Palestine, and both were fired up by the ideals of "Social Zionism," which in its American garb advocated the creation of "a model state in the Holy Land—freed from the economic wrongs, the social injustices and the greed of modern-day industrialism."[38] Zionism for them took on the aura of a sacred agenda, at once lofty and prophetic. Indeed, it was their semblance to the Prophets that led so many to revere them—in their own lifetimes and thereafter.

As these shared images illustrate, those who portrayed Brandeis and Szold transformed them into larger-than-life symbols embodying the values, aspirations, and ideals that American Jews cherished and hoped to pass on to their children. In their eyes, Szold and Brandeis served as living proof that those who were smart, efficient, hardworking, and righteous could rise to positions of prominence in America and still find time to improve the world—without hiding their faith or abandoning commitments to Jews in need. Through them, American Jews validated some of their fondest hopes concerning the land that they now called home. Szold and Brandeis thus came to function as beau ideals in American Jewish life, akin to venerated rabbis, scholars, and philanthropists. No wonder Jews carefully tended the memories of their two native "saints," even as they allowed the memories of so many other American Zionist leaders to fall into neglect!

Beyond serving as role models, however, Brandeis and Szold also came to symbolize future directions for American Jews in an era of changing religious identities and new communal challenges. For one thing, they validated alternative modes of Jewish identification. Brandeis was an avowedly secular Jew who displayed no interest in Jewish religious rituals and never belonged to a synagogue.[39] Szold was something of a Jewish seeker: kosher, Sabbath-observant, and deeply spiritual, yet fiercely unorthodox in many of her beliefs and practices.[40] Neither fit comfortably into the community's standard religious categories. As a result, both conveyed to American Jews the reassuringly latitudinarian message that they could find their own way in Judaism, for there were many ways to be a good Jew. In marked contrast to those who resisted religious change fearing assimilation, they extended Zionism's embrace to all who sought to join them. In so doing, they paved the way for the movement's emergence as part of the common-faith "civil religion" of American Jews,[41] and gave added legitimation to the optimistically pluralistic and broadly inclusive model of American Jewish communal life that took shape during the interwar years.

Brandeis and Szold reinforced this sense of inclusivism by showing how, in America, Jews of Central European descent could work harmoniously with their counterparts from Eastern Europe for the betterment of Jewish life. While scarcely a new message—the leadership of the Federation of American Zionists had included "uptown" and "downtown" as well as Orthodox and Reform representatives even before 1900[42]—tensions between the two communities continued to divide American Jews well into the twentieth century. Through their Zionist efforts, Brandeis and

Szold helped to bridge these divisive tensions by serving as exemplars of intracommunal cooperation. Szold felt particularly strongly about this point. Her friend Alice Seligsberg recalled that she would not permit Hadassah to have more than one chapter in a city, and "that chapter had to include rich and poor, Americanized socially elite and foreign born."[43] In this way, she worked to redirect the agenda of American Jews away from differences rooted in the Old World past and toward the common (if ultimately no less divisive) goal of shaping the Zionist future.

Finally, and perhaps most important, Brandeis and Szold symbolized and projected a message of cultural inclusiveness, personally embodying the grand synthesis—Judaism and Americanism, Hebraism plus Hellenism—that so many aspired to but so few actually achieved. Brandeis, compared in his own lifetime to both Isaiah and Lincoln, was known to be a devotee both of fifth-century Athens and of Puritan New England.[44] Szold too embraced both Jewish and secular culture. In addition to her much-celebrated Judaic learning, as a young schoolteacher in Baltimore, she taught subjects as diverse as French, Latin, mathematics, history, botany, and physiology; and throughout her life she maintained an absorbing interest in plants and nature.[45]

In an era when many doubted the ability of American Jews to negotiate both sides of their "hyphenated" identity, Szold and Brandeis served as prominent counterexamples. They provided reassuring evidence that the ideal of inclusiveness could be realized, and that Judaism, Zionism, and Americanism all could be happily synthesized.[46] For this, as much as for their more tangible organizational contributions, American Jews revered them and remembered them. Perhaps at some level they also understood that through them they saw their own aspirations and ideals reflected backward.[47]

NOTES

In honor of Jehuda Reinharz: dedicated scholar, able administrator, memorable leader, valued friend.

1. Joseph Telushkin, *Jewish Literacy* (New York: William Morrow, 1991), 410–13.

2. Michael Shapiro, ed., *The Jewish 100: A Ranking of the Most Influential Jews of All Time* (New York: Carol Publishing, 1994); the list is reprinted in Sander L.

Gilman, *Smart Jews: The Construction of the Image of Superior Jewish Intelligence* (Lincoln: University of Nebraska Press, 1996), 234.

3. *American Jewish History* 78 (December 1988): 169–200.

4. Evyatar Friesel, "Ha-manhigut Be-tenuah Ha-tsiyonut Be-artsot Ha-berit, 1900–1930," *Manhig Ve-hanhaga: Kovetz Ma'amarim* (Jerusalem, 1992), 187–202, deals in part with this question.

5. Paul A. Freund, "Louis D. Brandeis," *Dictionary of American Biography*, supp. 3 (New York: Charles Scribner, 1973), 100; standard biographies include Alpheus T. Mason, *Brandeis: A Free Man's Life* (New York: Viking Press, 1946), Philippa Strum, *Louis D. Brandeis: Justice for the People* (Cambridge: Harvard University Press, 1984), and Melvin I. Urofsky, *Louis D. Brandeis: A Life* (New York: Pantheon Books, 2009).

6. Eric L. Goldstein, "The Practical as Spiritual: Henrietta Szold's American Zionist Ideology, 1878–1920," *Daughter of Zion: Henrietta Szold and American Jewish Womanhood*, ed. Barry Kessler (Baltimore: Jewish Historical Society of Maryland, 1995), 17–33; standard biographies include Irving Fineman, *Woman of Valor: The Story of Henrietta Szold* (New York: Simon and Schuster, 1961), and Joan Dash, *Summoned to Jerusalem: The Life of Henrietta Szold* (New York: Harper and Row, 1979).

7. The early national presidents of Hadassah are conveniently listed in Marlin Levin, *Balm in Gilead: The Story of Hadassah* (New York: Schocken Books, 1973), 270; the presidents of the FAZ and ZOA are listed in the annual volumes of the *American Jewish Year Book*. For capsule biographies, see Jacob R. Marcus and Judith M. Daniels, eds., *The Concise Dictionary of American Jewish Biography* (New York: Carlson Publishing, 1994).

8. Mason, *Brandeis*, 47; Strum, *Louis D. Brandeis*, 33.

9. Seymour S. Guthman, "Brandeis, Louis, Dembitz," *Universal Jewish Encyclopedia*, vol. 2 (New York: Universal Jewish Encyclopedia, 1948), 495.

10. Elma Ehrlich Levinger, *Fighting Angel: The Story of Henrietta Szold* (New York: Behrman House, 1946), 45.

11. Rose Zeitlin, *Henrietta Szold: Record of a Life* (New York: Dial Press, 1952), 47, 64.

12. Alexander Lee Levin, *The Szolds of Lombard Street* (Philadelphia: Jewish Publication Society of America, 1960), 153–55, 257.

13. Jonathan D. Sarna, *JPS: The Americanization of Jewish Culture, 1888–1988* (Philadelphia: Jewish Publication Society of America, 1989), 47–135.

14. Marvin Lowenthal, *Henrietta Szold: Life and Letters* (New York: Viking Press, 1942), 70–74.

15. Strum, *Louis D. Brandeis*, 255.

16. Levinger, *Fighting Angel*, 103, 60.

17. Strum, *Louis D. Brandeis*, 46, 249; Alfred Lief, *Brandeis: The Personal History of an American Ideal* (New York: Stackpole, 1936), 200.

18. Richard D. Brown, *Modernization: The Transformation of American Life*

(New York: Hill and Wang, 1976); Alan Trachtenberg, *The Incorporation of America: Culture and Society in the Gilded Age* (New York: Hill and Wang, 1982), 69.

19. Sarna, *JPS*, 72.

20. Zeitlin, *Henrietta Szold*, 117.

21. Norman Bentwich, *My Seventy-Seven Years* (Philadelphia: Jewish Publication Society of America, 1961), 200.

22. See, for example, Levinger, *Fallen Angel*, 107; Zeitlin, *Henrietta Szold*, 210–11.

23. Strum, *Louis D. Brandeis*, 42.

24. Ibid., 38; Lief, *Brandeis*, 423; Mason, *Brandeis*, 77.

25. Strum, *Louis D. Brandeis*, 42; Mason, *Brandeis*, 634; Lief, *Brandeis*, 47.

26. See, on this theme, Ewa Morawska, *Insecure Prosperity: Small-Town Jews in Industrial America, 1890–1940* (Princeton: Princeton University Press, 1996), 226, n. 21, which cites all the relevant literature.

27. Mason, *Brandeis*, 77.

28. Lowenthal, *Henrietta Szold Life and Letters*, 197–98.

29. Lief, *Brandeis*, 22, 47.

30. Strum, *Louis D. Brandeis*, 47–48, 62; for other sources, see Jonathan D. Sarna, "'The Greatest Jew in the World since Jesus Christ': The Jewish Legacy of Louis D. Brandeis," *American Jewish History* 81 (Spring–Summer 1994), 350, from which portions of this paragraph are drawn.

31. Dash, *Summoned to Jerusalem*, 148.

32. Fineman, *Woman of Valor*, 359.

33. Zeitlin, *Henrietta Szold*, 70.

34. Levinger, *Fallen Angel*, 163.

35. Zeitlin, *Henrietta Szold*, 236–37.

36. Lowenthal, *Henrietta Szold Life and Letters*, 28.

37. Michael Brown, "Henrietta Szold's Progressive American Vision of the Yishuv," in *Envisioning Israel: The Changing Ideals and Images of North American Jews*, ed. Allon Gal (Detroit: Wayne State University Press, 1996), 65.

38. Bernard A Rosenblatt, *Social Zionism* (New York: Public Publishing, 1919), 10–11; Lowenthal, *Henrietta Szold Life and Letters*, 107–108, 203; Jonathan D. Sarna, "A Projection of America as It Ought to Be: Zion in the Mind's Eye of American Jews," in Gal, *Envisioning Israel*, 55.

39. Sarna, "The Greatest Jew in the World," 347–49.

40. For an unusual private expression of her religious perplexities ("What do I want?"), see Henrietta Szold to Alexander Marx, July 3, 1912, Alexander Marx Papers, Jewish Theological Seminary of America, New York.

41. Jonathan S. Woocher, *Sacred Survival: The Civil Religion of American Jews* (Bloomington: Indiana University Press, 1986), 76–80.

42. Marnin Feinstein, *American Zionism, 1884–1904* (New York: Herzl Press, 1965), esp. 134.

43. Cited in Goldstein, "The Practical as Spiritual," 30.

44. Sarna, "The Greatest Jew in the World," 346, 362–63.

45. Zeitlin, *Henrietta Szold*, 15.

46. Sylvia Barack Fishman, *Negotiating Both Sides of the Hyphen: Coalescence, Compartmentalization and American-Jewish Values*, Jacob and Jennie L. Lichter Lecture, University of Cincinnati, Cincinnati, Ohio, 1996.

47. An earlier version of this essay appeared in *Why Is America Different?*, ed. Steven T. Katz (Lanham, MD: University Press of America, 2010), 80–90.

10

The Rise of Stephen S. Wise
as a Jewish Leader

MARK A. RAIDER

Rabbi Stephen S. Wise (1874–1949) first attracted public attention at the turn of the nineteenth and twentieth centuries as the outspoken Zionist minister of New York City's venerable Bnai Jeshurun Congregation. In fact, he was barely twenty years old when in 1896 he became Bnai Jeshurun's senior rabbi, a pulpit that quite literally put him at the center of American and Jewish affairs.[1] Why then would Wise—young, ambitious, and safely ensconced in one of New York Jewry's leading congregations —go elsewhere? And yet, implausibly, that is what he did. In 1900, at the invitation of a group of elite Jewish merchants, lawyers, and politicians in the Pacific Northwest, Wise stepped down to assume the pulpit of Portland's Beth Israel Congregation.[2] His move was a chance to strike out on his own and break free of a highly competitive environment, including the creeping institutionalization of Reform, Conservative, and Orthodox Judaism—none of which suited him. It seems Wise's decision to leave Bnai Jeshurun for Beth Israel was a little impulsive but not entirely unstrategic.[3]

In Portland, Wise made common cause with local leaders of the social gospel movement, liberal Christian activists who believed, in Walter Rauschenbusch's words, "they could 'Christianize the social order' and thus save the nation."[4] Wise also continued to court and rely on Ben Selling, Solomon Hirsch, Bernard Goldsmith, Philip Wasserman, Joseph Simon, and other Jewish community leaders—powerful businessmen, landowners, railway entrepreneurs, and politicians of Central European Jewish ancestry—even as he collaborated with left-leaning religious and citizen activists who challenged the commercial-political establishment's hegemony. In the space of just a few years, he garnered a reputation as a vociferous opponent of prostitution and white slavery, a champion of women's suffrage, an advocate of child labor protections and reforming the region's juvenile punishment system, and a defender of the rights of workers (including Chinese immigrants) in the shipyard, timber, fishing, and railway industries. He also stood out as the region's most prominent Zionist spokesman.

Wise's Progressive sensibility and political talents caught the attention of Oregon's Democratic party establishment. When the left-wing Democrat Harry Lane was elected mayor of Portland, he invited Wise to serve in his city cabinet. Wise declined the offer. At the state level, Wise was pressed to run "as a reform candidate for the United States Senate against the entrenched Republican machine."[5] Again, he declined. It is uncertain if Wise entertained these possibilities seriously, though the record suggests he much preferred the role of an *engagé* minister to that of elective office.

Wise's emerging profile was brought into sharp relief in 1903 by a meeting with Theodore Roosevelt, in the midst of the president's Pacific Northwest tour. The two men met privately to discuss Jewish colonization in Palestine and the potential for US intervention on behalf of persecuted Jews in Romania.[6] The encounter marked a turning point for Wise, who thereafter leveraged his access to Roosevelt. In the wake of the Kishinev pogrom of 1903, for example, Wise aided Leo N. Levi, national president of the Independent Order of B'nai B'rith, in orchestrating a countrywide petition later presented to Roosevelt.[7] As American Secretary of State John Hay later reported, the petition did not "reach the high destination for which it was intended."[8] The net result of the B'nai B'rith campaign, however, was not insubstantial. In his 1904 State of the Union address, Roosevelt proclaimed, America "desire[s] eagerly to give expression to its horror on an occasion like that of the massacre of the Jews in Kishinev." Among the examples he used to articulate the Roosevelt Corollary to the Monroe Doctrine, i.e., "the exercise of an international police power" by the United States, the president cited the need to "secure from Russia the right for our Jewish fellow-citizens to receive passports and travel through Russian territory."[9] While the events of 1903 had yet to run their course, including the eruption in 1905 of another pogrom in Kishinev, it is interesting to note how Wise inserted himself into the mix of "pressure politics" that shaped American policy.[10]

Given Wise's overwhelming interest in the "larger sphere" of American society, it is perhaps unsurprising that his sojourn in Portland did not last.[11] In 1905 he was courted by Temple Emanu-El in New York City, home to Manhattan's elite Jews of Central European ancestry. What Emanu-El's leaders did not realize, however, was that the independent-minded Wise never would accept their terms, namely, as articulated by the influential lawyer Louis Marshall, who was the group's commanding spokesman, "The pulpit should always be subject to and under the control of the Board of Trustees."[12] Such conditions were totally inconsistent with Wise's social gospel sensibility. He defiantly characterized Marshall's demands as an attack on the "duty" and "conscience" of the American minister.[13] As the Wise-Marshall exchange ballooned into a full-blown confrontation, major newspapers across the country reported on Wise's "plea for pulpit freedom."[14] "As a Jewish minister," Wise argued, "I claim the right to follow the example of the Hebrew Prophets, and stand and battle in New York, as I have stood and battled in Portland, for civic righteousness."[15] In response, the New York Times (whose publisher Adolph S. Ochs was an Emanu-El trustee) upbraided Wise in an editorial: "Clergymen who are by temperament incapable of forming and maintaining [relationships with their congregations] . . . are not necessarily martyrs to the cause of freedom of speech."[16] In fact, the Times' rebuke was grist for Wise's mill. It also gave his views a full public hearing and threw a spotlight in his direction.

Pulpit and Politics

Wise returned to New York in the fall of 1906 hoping to advance his social and political agenda. With the support of several uptown elite Jews, he founded the "Free Synagogue" and attracted a following that included "large numbers of unaffiliated and alienated Jews" as well as "younger people" who "found Orthodoxy insufficient and preferred his combination of Reform Judaism and social liberalism."[17] Initially, the Free Synagogue held services at the Hudson Theater, then Clinton Hall, and finally

Carnegie Hall. Wise also launched a Free Synagogue movement with several branches in other metropolitan New York neighborhoods and nearby Newark, New Jersey. In addition, he threw himself into a host of ambitious public undertakings: organizing interfaith forums, cementing relations with the Yiddish-speaking immigrant community, championing the rights of labor, fighting for women's suffrage and civil rights, and spearheading the battle against corrupt and dishonorable New York politicians.

Nowhere was Wise more visible on the New York scene than in his confrontation with Tammany Hall. Shortly after his arrival, Wise, together with John Haynes Holmes, the prominent Unitarian minister of the Church of the Messiah (and later the Community Church of New York), entered the political fray. When, for example, disgraced former Tammany boss Richard Croker, who had relocated to Ireland with a considerable fortune, paid a triumphant return visit to New York City on the eve of the 1908 municipal elections, an outraged Wise addressed the Ethical Social League proclaiming a gala dinner honoring Croker "a night of shame for the city." The presence of the state's legal stewards, he declared, "consorting with the former Tammany leader," would "serve to crystallize the rising revolt of all that is decent and clean in New York citizenship against the threatened renewal of the reign of Crokerism." "It is true . . . that many of our Judges are the creatures of the political bosses," he said. "Under the Penal Code limitations are operative . . . but the moral code knows no limitations." He decried "the spectacle of New York's judiciary . . . uniting to do honor to one who for many years was the leader of Tammany Hall at its worst."[18] The *New York Times* carried front-page coverage of Wise's attack. In response, Croker evinced incredulity. Calling Wise a "Republican buffer," Croker added, "I am told that this proclivity of Dr. Wise to use the pulpit to exploit his political views caused him (and I think justly) to lose a place in a prominent Jewish pulpit in New York which he was very anxious to secure. The American people do not want to see their churches and synagogues desecrated in exploiting any man's political bias."[19] Such was the heated New York political climate into which Wise plunged with "Rooseveltian gusto."[20] Though Tammany's cronyism and corruption remained entrenched until the early 1930s, Wise was among the handful of outspoken figures who fought tirelessly to achieve a measure of justice in the near term.

Wise's activism also is evident in his defense of the "rights of labor" as a "basic structure of democracy" and his advocacy on behalf of the Jewish labor movement.[21] Consider, for example, his involvement in the 1909 eleven-week general strike of the New York shirtwaist makers known as the "Uprising of the 20,000." Led by radical female activists, including Rose Schneiderman, Clara Lemlich (Shavelson), and Pauline Newman, the strike against three of the city's largest manufacturers of shirtwaists —the Leiserson Company, the Rosen Brothers, and the Triangle Shirtwaist Company—was made up largely of Yiddish-speaking immigrant women. At one point, a parade of protesting strikers marched to City Hall to petition Mayor George B. McClellan for his help and call attention to the "insults, intimidations, and to the abuses" as well as the "flagrant discrimination of the Police Department in favor of the employers, who are using every method to incite violence." McClellan's tepid response was to suggest he would "look into the matter."[22] In the weeks and months that followed, New York uptown patrician Jewish leaders displayed sympathy for the striking workers. Some, such as Louis Marshall and Judah L. Magnes, rabbi of Temple Emanu-El and head of the New York Kehillah, a new citywide organization of Jewish life, enjoyed access to both sides of the divide. They believed they could help bridge the gap through arbitration and open up a new possibility for "bypassing ideological rifts and establishing a viable, if limited, relationship" with Yiddish-speaking labor leadership.[23] In contrast, Stephen Wise, who derided the "small coterie of men" running the Kehillah "according to their own sweet will," emphasized his allegiance to the striking workers.[24] "The synagogue may hope to speak *to* the workingman only if it first speak *for* the workingman," Wise declared. Rather than "waging fictitious warfare about the question of the closed shop with labor organizations," he called for "an honest and serious attempt to bring about an understanding between capital and labor" and a recognition of "the right of trade unionism."[25]

The historian Moses Rischin has described Wise as a neophyte "glorying in his tactlessness."[26] To be sure, by conviction and temperament Wise exhibited the traits of a crusader eager for frontline duty, and his outsized "personality was an indispensable ingredient" to his ministry. Yet it is also hard to imagine how a young man, who for all practical purposes lacked financial resources and political backing—but understood the value of skillful oratory—might otherwise have inserted himself into the rough and tumble of New York's political arena. An attractive personality whose "fire and conviction" electrified the atmosphere of many a crowded hall, Wise shrewdly blended his social gospel worldview with a strategic commitment to effecting this-worldly change.[27] "Religion is a vision or ideal of life," he was fond of saying. "Politics is a method, or modus vivendi."[28] In other words, it is helpful to understand Wise's posture as, in part, a strategy for exploiting his marginalization by the Jewish community's dominant leaders and the hostility of city officials. By burnishing his left-leaning and fierce antiestablishment credentials, Wise reinforced his growing reputation as a champion of values embraced by New York's middle-class and immigrant Jewish quarters as well as the city's liberal Protestant community. In this way, unlike Magnes, who enjoyed the high standing of a well-connected insider (and the backing of his brother-in-law, Louis Marshall), Wise positioned himself as the "People's Rabbi."[29]

Like the New York Kehillah leaders, Wise aimed to use his talents to facilitate conciliation between Jewish employers and workers. In general, however, he insisted, "When I speak to capitalists I speak for labor . . . pointing out their duty as I [see] it."[30] That Wise remained unperturbed about offending public opinion, even as he reached new heights of recognition, is exemplified by his 1911 address to the annual banquet of the New York Chamber of Commerce. Seated at the dais with Thomas Edison, Bishop David H. Greer, J. P. Morgan, Andrew Carnegie, New York's governor John A. Dix and mayor William J. Gaynor, and other dignitaries, Wise rose to lecture the "captains of industry and commerce" on their "high and solemn duty" in the midst of ongoing labor unrest and in the aftermath of the Triangle fire, which caused the deaths of 146 female wage workers.[31] "No business order is just nor can it long endure," he intoned, "if it be bound up with the evil of unemployment on the one hand and over-employment on the other, the evil of man's underwage and a child's toil. . . . The conscience of the nation is not real unless the nation safeguard the workingman. . . . The conscience of the nation is not vital unless we protect women and children in industry."[32] Interestingly, some of Wise's harshest criticism in the aftermath of the Triangle fire was directed at American religious leaders, including those responsible for the Jewish community's congregations and institutions. "If the church and synagogue were forces of righteousness in the world instead of being the farces of respectability and convention," he asserted at a mass protest meeting, "this thing need not have been. If it be the shame and humiliation of the whole community, *it is doubly the humiliation of the synagogue and of the church* which have suffered it to come to pass."[33]

Wise appreciated the preacher-politician's task of straddling the twin aims of moral uplift and theatricality. He also cared deeply about specific goals and policies—from social services for immigrants, to legal protections for women and children, to blunting the influence of Jim Crow and the Klan, to strengthening the hand of American labor—and he worked vigorously to promote them. As with his popular rival Judah L. Magnes, the *New York Evening World*, the *New York Tribune*, and the *New York Times* frequently reprinted Wise's sermons, addresses, and public utterances.[34] Wise capitalized on such publicity as a fulcrum for action. Of course, not everyone favored Wise's tactics. The Free Synagogue, one critic sneered, was little more than "a hall with an orator, an audience, and a pitcher of ice water."[35] In fact, however, the synagogue's success enabled Wise to carry his claim that "the rabbi speaks not *for* but *to* the congregation" into the public square.[36] In 1910 he elaborated on this theme before the People's Institute, an offshoot of the Cooper Union Mechanics School, on the eve of the US midterm elections.

Not despite the fact that I am a minister of religion, but because I am a minister of religion, I accepted the invitation . . . to speak upon this platform tonight. If I had to give up the privilege of speaking because I wear the cloth, the cloth would have to go and I would just remain a citizen of New York (applause). . . . In the main, political questions are moral questions. . . . For my part I am free to admit that . . . I am a Roosevelt Republican [and] I am a Grover Cleveland Democrat. . . . It is not Tammany Hall in New York which we are preparing to engage in battle with. . . . In Philadelphia, in Chicago, the dominant parties indeed are Republican, but Tammany by any other name would smell as foul and putrid. . . . There are going to be two votes cast in the coming election . . . one will be for New York and the other will be against New York. . . . I want to tell Tammany not to be deluded into the nominating of a Jew for any office, in the hope that the Jewish candidate can deliver the Jewish vote (applause) for there is no Jew-ish vote (applause). And a Jew who accepts a Tammany nomination in order to win for Tammany Hall the so-called Jewish vote, that Jew is a perfidious betrayer of his people (applause)."

As the foregoing illustrates, Wise was prepared, even at considerable personal risk, to challenge Charles F. Murphy, the powerful Tammany boss who dominated New York politics from 1902 to 1924 and stood atop a vast system of patronage that benefited, among others, the Lower East Side Jewish immigrant community.[37] The latter, of course, were the rank and file on whom much of Wise's developing political clout depended. But Wise made clear he was not beholden to any political camp nor would he hesitate to speak truth to power. He believed in the special obligation of clergy to dignify those elements in American politics that were honest, decent, and trustworthy, and to hold elected officials accountable — no less than business and religious leaders — for promoting social and eco-nomic justice in all areas of local, state, and federal government activity.

How are we to understand Wise's denial of the existence of a "Jewish vote"? What may appear to be a disingenuous assertion in fact reflects the prevailing American Jewish sensibility of the day. The doctrine of "political neutrality," Naomi W. Cohen observes, was a theme commonly sounded by prominent American Jewish figures including the elite New York circle grouped around Jacob Schiff, Oscar Straus, Louis Marshall, and Mayer Sulzberger. It antedated the American Civil War and lasted into the twentieth century.[38] "Jewish group interests, if indeed there were any," this view held, "had no place under that name in any politi-cal forum."[39] Meanwhile, as David Dalin has shown, "the ideal of Jewish political neutrality was much greater in theory than in practice." Indeed, irrespective of statements by Marshall, Wise, and others, Progressives, Democrats, and Republicans alike recognized "the power of Jewish vot-ers, especially in New York State," and they did not hesitate to make "eth-nic appeals aimed at Jewish voters."[40] The growing political strength of New York City's Jewish population, numbering approximately 1.2 million out of a total of 2.2 million Jews in the United States, including roughly nine hundred thousand Yiddish-speaking immigrants, proved irresistible to American politicians.[41] For their part, as the tide of Eastern European

Jewish immigration in this period surged, New York's newly enfranchised Jewish citizens acclimated to their political environment and rallied to politicians who favored their communal and ethnic interests. "If Jews had not rewarded their friends with votes," historian Lawrence H. Fuchs notes, "they would certainly [have been] different from any other group which ever crossed the American political scene."[42]

Wise's political behavior may thus be understood, first, as a reflection of what Jonathan D. Sarna calls the "cult of synthesis": an ongoing effort by American Jews "to interweave their 'Judaism' with their 'Americanism'" and to "fashion for themselves some unified synthetic whole."[43] Second, the fact that Wise championed Americanism while zealously guarding Jewish interests reflected the political landscape of early twentieth-century America—a reality fueled by the competing forces of, on the one hand, optimism and Progressivism and, on the other, xenophobia and racism. After all, it was Theodore Roosevelt who famously declaimed, "There is no room in this country for hyphenated Americans."[44] Navigating the poles of Americanism and nativism, Wise recognized the pitfalls of the Jewish community's emerging ethnic power in an era fraught with antisemitism and antipathy to immigrants. His idealistic declaration that Jews would place "Americanism" ahead of tribalism was a shrewd way of laying claim to America's inclusive social contract. Jews from all walks of life, he argued, would be drawn naturally to parties across the political spectrum that espoused "the practical use of government power" to ensure social and economic justice.[45]

Wise also was keenly aware that ethnic political power held the key to his intracommunal agenda. He undoubtedly was sincere in his belief that the Free Synagogue and the metropolitan region's Free Synagogue movement would serve as models for a renewed and fully Americanized brand of non-Orthodox Judaism. It also is useful to note that Wise's efforts were part of a broader trend in American Jewish life. Consider, for example, the aforementioned New York Kehillah and the parallel strivings of Mordecai M. Kaplan, who sought to redefine Conservative Judaism in this period and, with the help of Judah L. Magnes, launched the Society for Jewish Renascence—a precursor to Reconstructionist Judaism's Society for the Advancement of Judaism.[46] To be sure, a great deal of foresight, talent, and pluck energized Wise as he developed and cultivated an entirely new base of support on the eastern seaboard. It was at this juncture that he seems to have realized his larger objectives required a much grander platform. His next move, ostensibly a brazen attempt to reorder the whole of Reform Judaism, was also a bid to increase his own authority.

In 1911 Wise issued an invitation to a sizable cohort of colleagues and called into being the Eastern Council of Liberal Rabbis (later renamed the Eastern Council of Reform Rabbis). Note the new group's name closely approximated that of the Central Conference of American Rabbis (CCAR), Reform Judaism's venerable rabbinic association. Given Wise's track record, it was not unreasonable to suspect he might seek to outflank the New York Kehillah and challenge Reform Judaism's dominant Cincinnati leadership. Indeed, news of the Eastern Council generated considerable controversy. The Jewish press, Wise complained to Rabbi Emil G. Hirsch of Chicago's Temple Sinai, wasted no time in lining up with the Jewish establishment. The Reform-sponsored *American Israelite*, he noted, "naturally was shocked" while the *American Hebrew* "took it upon itself to defend the character of the [CCAR] as against the innovating founders of the Eastern Council." He also pointed out that the CCAR leadership was pressuring the "*bachurim* of Wise" (i.e., the former students of Rabbi Isaac M. Wise, the American movement's founder) to withdraw from the group and requested that "the title 'New York and Vicinity' should be used instead of 'Eastern.'" "It is a sorry piece of business, but what is now to be done?" he lamented. "Having taken the first step, I must go on and do what I can, if anything can be done, to save the situation. . . . There are so few men, alas, upon whom one can really count. Even Moses, I am sorry to say, is virtually within the corral of the Cincinnatians."[47]

Tension mounted as the CCAR leadership demanded the Eastern Council "disband" or else it "would not be recognized" and the group's renegade members would become *personae non gratae*.[48] Undeterred, the Eastern Council responded publicly, asserting that contrary to the CCAR's "dogmatic statement," it "was formed to deal with pressing local Jewish problems peculiar to the East. . . . The [Eastern Council] has been called into being not for destructive, but for constructive work . . . [and] to reach our young people who are drifting away from the synagogue and from all religious moorings."[49] In short order, both sides backed away from a full-blown confrontation, and the dispute settled into an uneasy equilibrium.

The Eastern Council now accepted some restraints imposed by the CCAR. However, Wise and his colleagues pressed forward with plans to grow their ranks, create a monthly publication, and organize a high-profile lecture series.[50] "I refuse to pay any attention to the action of the Central Conference," Wise commented. "It is too trivial and puerile. The Eastern Council is to fight for principles and not to exhibit its power in fussing with pygmies."[51] Cyrus Adler, a confidant of Louis Marshall and president of the Philadelphia Jewish Community, a counterpart to the New York Kehillah, kept a close watch on the Eastern Council's progress. "In my opinion, there is at present going on a great struggle for dominance in the Reform party," Adler wrote to Solomon Schechter, president of the Conservative movement's Jewish Theological Seminary. The campaign to upend the CCAR, he asserted, was "being engineered" by Hirsch of Chicago—"the real brains of the affair"—with Wise as his "principal lieutenant." "I have no doubt that if the movement succeeds," he added, Wise "would be treacherous to his chief."[52]

Adler and others grouped around the American Jewish Committee viewed Wise as reckless, opportunistic, and unscrupulous. Yet Wise's maverick determination endeared him in middle-class and immigrant Jewish quarters. He insisted on using the Eastern Council to showcase controversial topics and themes that resonated among liberal and left-leaning circles. One particularly important instance in this regard was Louis D. Brandeis's speech on "The Jewish Problem: How to Solve It." Delivered before the group in June 1915, Brandeis's dictum was to become a hallmark of American Zionism: "Let no American imagine that Zionism is inconsistent with patriotism. Multiple loyalties are objectionable only if they are inconsistent."[53] Two years later, Wise again provoked considerable controversy by proposing that the Eastern Council "pledge itself to the support of the suffrage referendum" under consideration in New York State. Rabbi Joseph Silverman of Manhattan's Temple Emanu-El denounced Wise's proposal and sought to foreclose any such discussion, prompting Wise to threaten resigning from the group. "I will not allow Dr. Wise or anyone else to inject Zionism, women's suffrage, or any other political question into this meeting," declared Silverman. "It is not in our province, even though by a play of sophistry, the woman suffrage question may become twisted into a moral issue."[54] When it became clear that a majority favored Wise's proposal, Silverman relented and the group adopted a resolution supporting women's suffrage.

Wilson, War, and Realpolitik

In 1911 Henry Morgenthau Sr., long a booster of Woodrow Wilson, arranged a private meeting for Wise with the New Jersey governor. The two men developed a warm rapport, and Wilson accepted an invitation from Wise to speak at the Free Synagogue later that spring. This was the first of many instances when Wise provided Wilson with a platform to reach a broad constituency of liberal-minded Jews. Some months later, after Wilson had emerged as the Democratic party's standard bearer, Wilson addressed an overflowing Free Synagogue audience at Carnegie Hall on "The Rights of the Jews." Explicitly denouncing tsarist policy as backward and obscurantist, he decried the regime's mistreatment of American Jews traveling in Russia and reiterated his assertion that "no divergence [existed] among patriotic Americans on [the] passport question."[55] In amplifying his support for the abrogation of the Russo-American Treaty of 1832, then under consideration by the US Congress, Wilson won over many native-born and immigrant Jews who were suspicious of President William Howard Taft and the Republican party's reluctance to confront Russia.

The ensuing presidential election of 1912 ushered in a sea change in American politics. The rare four-way contest featured William Howard Taft, the sitting Republican president; Theodore Roosevelt, a former Republican president and now founder of the Progressive ("Bull Moose") party; Woodrow Wilson, the Democratic nominee; and Eugene V. Debs, the Socialist party candidate. In addition to Wilson's sympathetic stance on the passport issue, Wise was attracted by the New Jersey governor's "New Freedom" platform, a Progressive agenda largely crafted by Louis D. Brandeis.[56] Brandeis, the "People's Lawyer" from Boston, attained heroic status in working-class circles after helping to negotiate the "Protocol of Peace," the pathbreaking agreement that ended the Great Revolt of 1910. For his part, Wilson also recognized the considerable importance of recent immigrants from Eastern Europe, including the Yiddish-speaking masses "who had already attached themselves to local Democratic machines" and a variety of left-leaning and radical labor groups, trade unions, cultural and fraternal associations, and political organizations.[57] Enamored of Wilson's New Freedom agenda and cheered by his legislative priorities, Wise emerged from the election as one of Wilson's most visible champions and a Brandeis confidant. He thereafter enjoyed substantial access to the new president and his administration.

Wilson's first term as president coincided with a period of significant upheaval and transformation in American life as well as the outbreak of World War I.[58] In 1915 Wise found himself at odds with Wilson as the president edged away from a policy of noninterventionism and announced plans for "preparedness" and enlarging the American military.[59] While Wise believed the Allied "cause to be just," he was torn by the plight of Jews living under the tsarist regime "who cannot hope that the victory of Russia will redound either to the advantage of civilization or to the betterment of the Jewish status."[60] As the European conflict unfolded and expanded, Wise participated actively in the fund-raising and relief efforts of the Provisional Executive Committee for General Zionist Affairs—together with the People's Relief Committee (organized by Yiddish-speaking immigrant groups), the Central Relief Committee (organized by Orthodox groups), and the American Jewish Relief Committee (a coalition of forty national groups organized by the American Jewish Committee)—to assist Jews trapped in the eastern war zone. In time, Wise—and American Jewry generally—steadily drifted with American opinion toward support of Wilson's preparedness program and pro-Allied policies. For Wise, the decisive "moment" came in early 1917 when he abandoned his stance as a "lifelong anti-militarist" and emerged as "an inflexible supporter" of Wilson. This transformation, he explained at the time, reflected an unavoidable global political reality that undermined the peace camp's raison d'être.

They who cry out that we at last yielded to the war-impulse and the war-hysteria forget or will to ignore the three years of unexampled patience on the part of the American people and our leader, and that we have not so much gone to war as set out to stay the fury of a desolating forest fire, its murderous flames fed of human will and purpose. If in the process we . . . must put our hands to weapons of force and fury, the fault before God lies not in ourselves but in those creatures of blood and iron. . . . This is to be our last war that it may never again become possible to renew [Germany's] criminal aggressions. . . . Grimly mocking paradox though it be, we have taken up the burden of war not for the war's sake but for the sake of peace.[61]

Wise's change of heart on the matter was not simply a matter of expediency. It was part of a larger social and political process that crystallized in a "pro-Ally tide that engulfed the Jewish middle class, lower middle class, and parts of the working class."[62] Of course, some of Wise's contemporaries, including John Haynes Holmes and Judah L. Magnes, remained steadfast pacifists. This principled stance, particularly in Magnes's case, undercut their authority as religious and communal spokesmen. Even if we assume Wise's transformation was fueled, in part, by political ambition, it would be wrong to overlook the groundswell of pro-war sentiment that unified an array of "Progressive intellectuals and reformers [as well as] labor leaders and socialists." The looming probability of war, hastened by an alloy of patriotism, moralism, and romantic liberalism, appeared to Wilson's supporters as a chance "to disseminate Progressive values around the globe."[63]

Two distinct but interrelated fronts now opened up in the American Jewish war effort. On the one hand, the various relief efforts swiftly coalesced around a new umbrella organization known as the American Jewish Joint Distribution Committee (JDC), which became the chief conduit for transferring and distributing relief funds overseas. The JDC leadership worked energetically to gather Jewish support from across the country, and it received contributions from over sixteen hundred localities. When the campaign reached its goal, including the Jewish philanthropist Julius Rosenwald's contribution of $1 million, Wilson wrote a personal note of congratulations to the Chicago-based president of Sears, Roebuck and Company. In the final analysis, the partnership of radicals, Zionists, Orthodox, and elite Jews raised, transferred, and distributed roughly $38 million of overseas aid between 1914 and 1920, including a sizable allocation to the Yishuv.[64]

Parallel to the JDC's countrywide relief campaign, a tidal wave of popular support for democratization in American Jewish life surged forward in the movement for an American Jewish Congress. Initially, the American Jewish Committee and the Jewish labor movement strenuously opposed the call for an all-inclusive Jewish communal framework. Neither America's elite Jewish leaders nor the radical Jewish advocates of class warfare saw any political advantage in submitting their authority to a larger constellation of groups and parties. A three-year power struggle ensued between "plutocrats" and "democrats," *yahudim* (the Jewish elite) and *yidn* (the downtown Jews). The battle was waged in every corner of the country as well as in the Yiddish and Anglo-Jewish press. Wise frequently mounted the rostrum to make the case for the pro-congress forces. In 1916, for example, he addressed a Philadelphia meeting. "The people are resolved to be free of their masters whether these be malevolent tyrants without or benevolent despots within," he proclaimed. "Are we forever to suffer men to think and act for us, not because we have chosen and named them, but because they have decreed that we are not fit to be trusted with the power of shaping our own destiny?"[65] Wise's jeremiad, rhetorical and somewhat theatrical, was not entirely unfounded.

The critical year for European, American, and Palestinian Jewry during World War I was 1917. The overthrow of the Russian tsar, America's idealistic entry into the war, and the British conquest of Palestine, soon followed by the Balfour Declaration, which recognized Palestine as "a national home for the Jewish people," stirred a fever of enthusiasm. Approximately a quarter-million Jews served in the American military in 1917 and 1918, a majority of them young immigrants. Buoyed by the wartime context, Zionism acquired unprecedented influence in American Jewish circles and in American society. Wise, now an ardent champion of Wilson's internationalism, played an increasingly significant role in crafting and articulating a synthesis of American and Zionist wartime arguments.[66] The building of Palestine's new Jewish society-in-the-making, he asserted, was a corollary of Wilson's postwar vision of the "self-determination of nations."[67] Finally, in a widely publicized August 1918 letter to Wise, who together with Brandeis had participated behind the scenes in helping to pave the way for the Balfour Declaration, Wilson declared his satisfaction "in the progress of the Zionist movement in the United States and in the allied countries since the declaration by Mr. Balfour."[68]

When in December 1918 the American Jewish Congress finally convened, 367 delegates from 87 cities gathered for several days of impassioned public debates and stormy plenary negotiations. Wise and other leading Zionists, with the support of the Eastern European Jewish immigrant community, capitalized on this event to fundamentally alter the terms of the public debate concerning communal organization. A sparkling array of talented left-wing and radical leaders—Chaim Zhitlowsky, Nachman Syrkin, Meyer London, Joseph Barondess, Baruch Zuckerman, and others—underscored the commitment of the rank and file to democratic principles and three cardinal issues: minority rights, postwar Jewish reconstruction, and "the development of Palestine into a Jewish commonwealth."[69] The net result was a broad-based platform and a new mandate subsequently represented by a ten-person American Jewish delegation, headed by Julian W. Mack and including Louis Marshall, Stephen S. Wise, and others, which accompanied Wilson to the Versailles Peace Conference.[70] Wise thus achieved a new level of national authority with the victory of the Brandeis group and Yiddish-speaking forces over the American Jewish Committee, while Wilson's triumphant expedition to Europe situated him as a leader of international stature. In the event, it was Marshall who (despite losing the battle for the congress) emerged as American Jewry's most influential figure in Paris and won accolades for his instrumental role in drafting the conference's minority rights treaty.[71]

It is, of course, one of the more ironic twists of historical fate that Wilson's idealistic vision of a new world order collapsed with the war's end and that American society succumbed to the isolationism, racism, and xenophobia of what John Higham has termed the "tribal twenties."[72] The abrupt transformation dovetailed in the spring of 1921 with the Pyrrhic victory in the American Zionist arena of the Weizmann forces (led by Louis Lipsky) over the Brandeis group even as the extraordinary convergence of the Zionist movement and the Allied Powers at this juncture caused a tectonic shift in modern Jewish politics.[73] Wise temporarily lost his political moorings. Rather than retreat, however, he renewed his activist strategy and rallied to a variety of liberal and reform causes that punctuated American and Jewish life in the 1920s. In this period, he cemented his base by reorganizing the American Jewish Congress as an independent organization and creating the Jewish Institute of Religion, an independent liberal rabbinic seminary. In the early 1930s, when the political sands of America, Europe, and Palestine again shifted, he returned to the public arena fortified with considerable political capital. The domestic and global crises of the ensuing decade would elevate Wise to the very pinnacle of Jewish and Zionist leadership and, in the process, test the limits of his ability.

NOTES

1. In this period, American Jewry skyrocketed by 300 percent in just a couple of decades and grew to 1,777,000 (or approximately 2 percent of the US population). New York's Jewish community grew to some 417,000 strong, twice the size of Warsaw (219,128), and three and four times larger than Budapest (166,198), Vienna (146,926), Odessa (138,935), Lodz (96,671), and Berlin (92,206). Data compiled from (1) Nathan Goldberg, "The Jewish Population in the United States," *The Jewish People Past and Present*, vol. 2 (New York, 1948), 25; (2) American Jewish Committee, *American Jewish Year Book*, vol. 1 (Philadelphia: Jewish Publication Society of America, 1899), 283–84; and (3) Paul Mendes-Flohr and Jehuda Reinharz, eds., *The Jew in the Modern World: A Documentary History*, 3rd ed. (New York: Oxford University Press, 2010), 884.

2. At this time, Oregon's total Jewish population was estimated to be between 4500 and 5000 (out of a total of some 70,000 inhabitants), while Portland itself was home to approximately 500 Jews. Data compiled from (1) "Three Cities in One," *New York Times*, June 14, 1891, 12; (2) "Statistical Summary by States," *American Jewish Year Book*, ed. Cyrus Adler (Philadelphia: Jewish Publication Society of America, 1901), 147; and (3) "Table 2. Jewish Population of Selected Western Towns, 1880" in Ellen Eisenberg, Ava F. Kahn, and William Toll, *Jews of the Pacific Coast: Reinventing Community on America's Edge* (Seattle: University of Washington Press, 2009), 59.

3. Stephen Wise, *The Personal Letters of Stephen Wise*, eds. Justine Wise Polier and James Waterman Wise (Boston: Beacon Press, 1956), 20.

4. Susan Curtis, *A Consuming Faith: The Social Gospel and Modern American Culture* (Baltimore: Johns Hopkins University Press, 1991), 130.

5. Melvin I. Urofsky, *A Voice That Spoke for Justice: The Life and Times of Stephen S. Wise* (Albany: State University of New York Press,1982), 45.

6. William Toll, *The Making of an Ethnic Middle Class: Portland Jewry over Four Generations* (Albany: State University of New York Press, 1982), 97.

7. Stephen S. Wise to Leon N. Levy [*sic*], June 27, 1903, Stephen S. Wise Papers, Oregon Jewish Historical Society, Portland, OR.

8. John Hay to Leo N. Levi, October 3, 1903, reprinted in Cyrus Adler and Aaron M. Margalith, *With Firmness in the Right: American Diplomatic Acton Affecting Jews, 1840–1945* (New York: American Jewish Committee, 1946), 270–271; Jonathan Frankel, *Prophecy and Politics: Socialism, Nationalism, and the Russian Jews, 1862–1917* (Cambridge: Cambridge University Press, 1981), 475.

9. Theodore Roosevelt, "Annual Message to Congress for 1904," House Records HR 58A-K2, Records of the US House of Representatives, Record Group 233, Center for Legislative Archives, National Archives of the United States. http://www.ourdocuments.gov/doc.php?flash=old&doc=56html.

10. Naomi W. Cohen, "The Abrogation of the Russo-American Treaty of 1832," *Jewish Social Studies* 25, no. 1 (January 1963): 3.

11. Wise, *Personal Letters of Stephen Wise*, 110.

12. Louis Marshall to Stephen S. Wise, December 1, 1905, in *Louis Marshall: Champion of Liberty. Selected Papers and Addresses*, ed. Charles Reznikoff, vol. 2 (Philadelphia: Jewish Publication Society of America, 1957), 831.

13. Stephen S. Wise to Louis Marshall, January 5, 1906, in Reznikoff, *Louis Marshall*, 833.

14. Stephen S. Wise, *Challenging Years: The Autobiography of Stephen S. Wise* (New York: Putnam and Sons, 1949), 87.

15. "Rabbi Wise on Jerome," *New York Times*, January 10, 1906, 2.

16. "Pulpit and Pews," *New York Times*, January 11, 1906, 8.

17. Michael A. Meyer, "*Kelal Yisrael*: The Jewish Institute of Religion," in *Hebrew Union College–Jewish Institute of Religion at One Hundred Years*, ed. Samuel E. Karff (Cincinnati: Hebrew Union College Press, 1976), 141; Carl Hermann Voss, *Rabbi and Minister: The Friendship of Stephen S. Wise and John Haynes Holmes*, 2nd ed. (Buffalo, NY: Prometheus Books, 1980), 79.

18. "Croker Hits Back; Meets a New Attack," *New York Times*, December 3, 1908, 1.

19. Ibid., 2.

20. Moses Rischin, *The Promised City: New York's Jews, 1870–1914* (Cambridge: Harvard University Press, 1977), 242.

21. Wise, *Challenging Years*, 81.

22. "Striking Shirtwaist Workers March on City Hall," *New York Times*, December 4, 1909, 20.

23. Arthur A. Goren, *New York Jews and the Quest for Community: The Kehillah Experiment, 1908–1922* (New York: Columbia University Press, 1970), 196.

24. Ibid., 54.

25. Wise's statement, reprinted in the *American Hebrew* of December 24, 1909, is quoted in Rischin, *Promised City*, 248.

26. Ibid., 243.

27. Voss, *Rabbi and Minister*, 82; Wise, *Challenging Years*, 120.

28. Wise, *Challenging Years*, 109.

29. Rischin, *Promised City*, 243.

30. Wise, *Personal Letters of Stephen Wise*, 96, 130–131.

31. Wise, *Challenging Years*, 60.

32. See the reprint of Wise's Chamber of Commerce address (November 16, 1911) in Wise, *Challenging Years*, 60–61; "Bryce Thinks City Is Well Governed," *New York Times*, November 17, 1911, 5.

33. See the reprint of Wise's Metropolitan Opera House address (April 22, 1911) in Wise, *Challenging Years*, 63 (emphasis added).

34. Arthur A. Goren, ed., *Dissenter in Zion: From the Writings of Judah L. Magnes* (Cambridge, MA: Harvard University Press, 1982), 16.

35. Quoted in Wise, *Challenging Years*, 95.

36. Ibid., 71.

37. Annie Polland and Daniel Soyer, *Emerging Metropolis: New York Jews in the Age of Immigration, 1840–1920* (New York: New York University Press, 2012), 178–83.

38. See Jonathan D. Sarna, *When General Grant Expelled the Jews* (New York: Schocken, 2012), 70–72.

39. Naomi W. Cohen, *Encounter with Emancipation: The German Jews in the United States, 1830–1914* (Philadelphia: Jewish Publication Society of America, 1984), 129.

40. David G. Dalin, "Louis Marshall, the Jewish Vote, and the Republican Party," *Jewish Political Studies Review* 4, no. 1 (Spring 1992): 58, 60, 77.

41. Data compiled from (1) Paul Ritterband, "Counting the Jews of New York, 1900–1991: An Essay in Substance and Method," *Jewish Population Studies (Papers in Jewish Demography)* 29 (Jerusalem: Avraham Harman Institute of Contemporary Jewry, 1997): 204–206; (2) American Jewish Committee, *American Jewish Year Book* (Philadelphia: Jewish Publication Society of America, 1912), 264–66; and (3) Mendes-Flohr and Reinharz, *The Jew in the Modern World*, 884.

42. Lawrence H. Fuchs, *The Political Behavior of American Jews* (Glencoe, IL: Free Press, 1956), 60.

43. Jonathan D. Sarna, "The Cult of Synthesis in American Jewish Culture," *Jewish Social Studies* 5, nos. 1–2 (fall 1998/winter 1999): 52–53.

44. "Roosevelt Bars the Hyphenated," *New York Times*, October 13, 1915, 1.

45. Polland and Soyer, *Emerging Metropolis*, 177.

46. Mel Scult, *Judaism Faces the Twentieth Century: A Biography of Mordecai M. Kaplan* (Detroit: Wayne State University Press, 1993), 127–29.

47. Stephen S. Wise to Emil G. Hirsch, May 17, 1912, box 1, folder 12, Stephen S. Wise Papers, MS-49, American Jewish Archives, Cincinnati, OH (hereafter AJA).

48. Solomon Foster to the Eastern Council of Reform Rabbis, June 16, 1912, AJA.

49. "Eastern Rabbis Reply," *New York Times*, June 19, 1912, 9.

50. Stephen S. Wise to Maurice Harris, July 11, 1912, AJA.

51. Stephen S. Wise to Clifton H. Levy, July 16, 1912, AJA.

52. The letter is dated October 31, 1912; Cyrus Adler, *Cyrus Adler: Selected Letters*, ed. Ira Robinson, vol. 1 (Philadelphia: Jewish Publication Society of America, 1985), 217.

53. Mendes-Flohr and Reinharz, *The Jew in the Modern World*, 555.

54. "Clash on Suffrage at Rabbis' Council," *New York Times*, April 24, 1917, 11

55. Quoted in American Jewish Committee (1912), *American Jewish Year Book*, 196.

56. Melvin I. Urofsky, *Louis D. Brandeis: A Life* (New York: Pantheon Books, 2009), 344–51.

57. Ibid., 375.

58. See Robert H. Wiebe, *The Search for Order, 1877–1920* (Westport, CT: Greenwood Press, 1980), ch. 11.

59. John Milton Cooper, *Woodrow Wilson: A Biography* (New York: Knopf, 2009), 297, 304–10.

60. Stephen S. Wise and C. H. Voss, *Stephen S. Wise: Servant of the People* (Philadelphia: JPS, 1969), 62.

61. "'What Are We Fighting For': Dr. Stephen S. Wise, Once Pacifist, Now Is Firm for War," *Sunday Oregonian*, October 21, 1917, 11. http://oregonnews.uoregon.edu /lccn/sn83045782/1917-10-21/ed-1/seq-51.pdf.

62. Morris U. Schappes, "World War I and the Jewish Masses, 1914–1917," *Jewish Life* (Febuary 1955): 19.

63. Eric Foner, *Give Me Liberty! An American History*, vol. 2 (New York: W. W. Norton, 2012), 726; Morris U. Schappes, "The Attitude of Jewish Labor to World War I, 1917–1918," *Jewish Life* (March 1955): 21–24.

64. Data in this section are drawn from Arthur A. Goren, *The Politics and Public Culture of American Jews* (Bloomington: Indiana University Press, 1999), ch. 6.

65. *American Hebrew*, March 31, 1916, 587–88.

66. Stephen S. Wise, "The Balfour Declaration: Its Significance in the U.S.A." in *The Jewish National Home: The Second November, 1917–1942*, ed. Paul Goodman (London: J. M. Dent, 1943), 41–43.

67. Wise advocated granting "home rule to the Irish people." See his April 11, 1917, letter to Woodrow Wilson in *The Papers of Woodrow Wilson*, ed. Arthur S. Link, vol. 42 (Princeton: Princeton University Press, 1983), 41–42, 44–45.

68. Quoted in "Events in 5679—United States," American Jewish Committee, *American Jewish Year Book*, vol. 21 (Philadelphia: Jewish Publication Society of America, 1919), 175–176. See Jehuda Reinharz, *Chaim Weizmann: The Making of a Statesman* (New York: Oxford University Press, 1993), 190–191, 201, 284; Frankel, *Prophecy and Politics*, 537–38.

69. Quoted in Harry Barnard, *The Forging of an American Jew: The Life and Times of Julian W. Mack* (New York, 1974), 241; Frankel, *Prophecy and Politics*, 541–46.

70. Rufus Learsi (Israel Goldberg), *The Jews in America: A History* (Cleveland, OH: World Publishing, 1954), 265.

71. Carole Fink, "Louis Marshall: An American Jewish Diplomat in Paris, 1919," *American Jewish History* 94, nos. 1–2 (March–June 2008), 21–40; M. M. Silver, *Louis Marshall and the Rise of Jewish Ethnicity in America: A Biography* (Syracuse, NY: Syracuse University Press, 2013), 250–51.

72. John Higham, *Strangers in the Land: Patterns of American Nativism, 1860– 1925* (New Brunswick, 1983), ch. 10.

73. Reinharz, *Chaim Weizmann*, ch. 8.

PART II

Statecraft

11

Weizmann and Ben-Gurion

Portraits in Contrast

ANITA SHAPIRA

When Chaim Weizmann died in 1952, he was eulogized in the Knesset by David Ben-Gurion. It was a eulogy replete with praise of the deceased, in the spirit of *de mortuis nil nisi bonum* — say nothing but good of the dead. It is difficult to find harsh words directed at Weizmann in Ben-Gurion's correspondence or diaries. He was always very courteous toward him when referring to him in writing. This was not the case with Weizmann, in whose correspondence one can find scathing criticism of his younger rival. Now, with his great adversary lying dead, Ben-Gurion allowed himself veiled criticism, a wordless comparison between him and Weizmann. After describing him as "the great man of his generation," preceded only by Edmond de Rothschild and Theodor Herzl, he spoke of the difference between those two great men and Weizmann: "He did not come from the West like them, from the assimilated and alienated Jewry. He came from within, from deep in our heartland, from the wellspring of the Jewish people's vitality, a small town in the Russian Pale of Settlement."[1] The audience grasped the subtext: Ben-Gurion's and Weizmann's common origins. After describing their similarities, he went on to speak of the basic difference between them: "As a natural scientist he did not believe in shortcuts but in gradual growth, and perhaps he was unaware of the rule that historical processes are dissimilar to natural ones, and that in nature too there are secret processes that lead to a sudden explosion." The difference between the revolutionary who exploits a historic opportunity — Ben-Gurion — and the evolutionist who strictly observes a step-by-step

approach and does not read the historical process — Weizmann — is what
Ben-Gurion was alluding to. After presenting Weizmann as a synthesis
between political and practical Zionism, he further lauded him as a leader
who understood the value of pioneering Zionism, "and there has not been
a Zionist leader who was as close to and who so well understood the spirit
of self-realizing pioneering as Weizmann." Then he quickly qualified this:
he did not belong to the pioneering camp, "and a large part of that camp
did not identify with Dr. Weizmann's political worldview." Ben-Gurion
spoke at length about the nameless pioneers who brought "the gift of
self-realization, the gift of their life and death" to the Zionist enterprise,[2]
a subject that had no place in a eulogy of Weizmann but which he used
to emphasize that Weizmann was not one of those unsung heroes but
was as close to them as an outsider could be. The advantage held by the
worker from Sejera (Ben-Gurion) over the scholar and diplomat was al-
luded to between the lines. The audience also would have noticed that
he stated that Weizmann *made possible* the establishment of the State"
(emphasis added), hence somebody else actually established it. Indeed, in
the long-standing rivalry between the two men, in the end fate smiled on
Ben-Gurion, who had the last word.

Although both men came from and grew up in the Pale of Settlement,
a chasm separated them. Weizmann was born in 1874 and Ben-Gurion in
1886, and this twelve-year difference was one of a generation. Weizmann
grew up in the liberal period of Tsar Alexander II, who allowed Jews to
acquire an education and integrate into Russian society and culture. He
enrolled in a Russian high school before the *numerus clausus* (quota)
was imposed, which made acceptance into high schools or institutions of
higher learning difficult for young Jews. Ben-Gurion grew up during the
reactionary period of Tsars Alexander III and Nicholas II. Despite his best
efforts, he was not admitted to a Jewish technical school, since acceptance
was restricted solely to gymnasium graduates, not external students such
as Ben-Gurion. The age difference between the two also affected their
political affiliation: both were dyed-in-the-wool Zionists who aspired to
the rebirth and renewal of the Jewish people. But Weizmann was a moderate, secular, liberal Zionist. The ideological disputations of the Marxist
streams did not speak to him, and he never was attracted to the turbulent
world of Russian revolutionism. His political activity was always in the

Zionist Organization framework. Ben-Gurion, however, discovered the world of politics during the First Russian Revolution, which saw the founding of the socialist-Zionist Po'alei Zion party. Ben-Gurion's Zionism was always Zionism with a hyphen. Weizmann was focused on his chemistry studies, and they were the center of his life. Ben-Gurion, from the moment he discovered political activity, was totally overwhelmed by it, and his life was given the purpose and direction it previously had lacked. Whereas throughout his life Weizmann moved along two parallel tracks—his scientific activity and his Zionist activity—and never saw himself as a "professional" politician supported by the movement, Ben-Gurion did not have a life outside politics. It was his profession, his vocation, and his future.

Motol and Plonsk were two small, poor townships, the former in Belorussia and the latter in Congress Poland. As the years went by, and particularly after the Holocaust, Ben-Gurion tended to sing the praises of his birthplace. He claimed it was the most important Zionist town in the Pale of Settlement, whose young people spoke Hebrew and from which some of the first members of the Second Aliyah had immigrated to Palestine. Weizmann left Motol when he was about twelve, with the start of his gymnasium studies in Pinsk, and later his family also moved there. Pinsk undoubtedly was more advanced than Plonsk, but when the young Weizmann returned home from Germany, he found the town contemptible, dirty and miserable, compared with splendid Berlin.

Weizmann's attitude toward East European Jews has not been comprehensively researched. Memorable is his criticism of the Fourth Aliyah immigrants, and particularly his remarks about the Dzika and the Nalevki: he turned the commercial streets in Warsaw into a symbol of what Palestine should not be. Nevertheless, Weizmann projects the image of a man closely tied to Eastern European Jewry, comforted by the warm *yiddishkeit* showered on him by the masses of Eastern European Jews. Ben-Gurion's image, however, is of a cold man who did not identify with that *yiddishkeit*, who insisted on speaking Hebrew, and to whom an insulting remark about Yiddish is attributed following Rozka Korczak's speech at the 1945 Histadrut conference. But deeper inquiry shows that Ben-Gurion was never patronizing about the town of his birth, and the more meaningful human relations he had were with fellow townsfolk. Between the two World Wars, Weizmann visited the Jewish émigré centers in Western Europe, but he visited Eastern Europe no more than once or twice, if at all. It seems that Polish Jewry was not close to his heart and Soviet Russia was closed to him. As far as we know, he did not visit the Jewish immigrant neighborhoods in London's East End, and he preferred the company of important intellectuals and affluent British Jews. In contrast, Ben-Gurion saw Poland as the heart of the Jewish people. In the election campaigns in which he took part, particularly the 1933 campaign, there was not a township that was too wretched for him to visit, deliver a speech, shake hands, and encourage the members of the Hechalutz movement who worked to increase the movement's membership. Despite the zealotry for Hebrew he had harbored since his youth, the book that made his name with American Jewry was the *yizkor* (memorial) book commemorating the fallen of Hashomer, which he published in Yiddish in the United States in 1916. He addressed town meetings in Yiddish, and even spoke Yiddish at the Zionist Congress if he felt that it suited his purpose. The Jews of America admired Weizmann, and through the good offices of Louis Lipsky, president of the Zionist Organization of America, he reached the poorer Yiddish-speaking strata of the Jewish population. But here, too, he maintained an aristocratic distance from the Jewish masses, particularly those who had not yet become Americanized. After World War II, Ben-Gurion visited the displaced persons camps in Germany, visits that were replete with emotion and tears, whereas Weizmann did not. Despite the tremendous admiration of many in the Yishuv, he scarcely visited Palestine, especially after 1939. He engaged in weapons development for the Allies, was physically weak, suffered from ophthalmic ailments, and probably found travel difficult. His grief over the loss of his son, a Royal Air Force pilot, also possibly curtailed his activities. Yet one cannot but wonder about this.

Weizmann came from a middle-class family which, although it endured hardship, was able to provide ten of its eleven children with higher education. Ben-Gurion's family found it difficult to send him to high school in Warsaw, not to mention university. While he was studying in Istanbul, his letters were filled with complaints about the late arrival of his allowance from his family. However, he never bothered to work for a living during his studies, whereas Weizmann did and even helped his siblings to acquire an education.

Weizmann's relations with his family were close and warm. When he broke off his engagement to Sophia Getzova, he feared his parents' reaction, which was important to him, but they quickly reconciled with him. He preferred the beautiful, sophisticated, and elegant Vera Chatzman, the daughter of an aristocratic Russian-Jewish family from Rostov-on-Don, who did not speak Yiddish. His choice of Vera was not only one of a better-looking woman, but also an indication of his preference for a different cultural circle, far distant from Jewish folksiness, an expression of a desire to integrate into a more aristocratic culture. Despite this, his relations with his family continued to be close and warm. In contrast, Ben-Gurion remained in the low social class of his father's family. His wife, Paula, was a nurse — a lower rank than that of Vera, who studied medicine. Paula was not an intellectual, was unsophisticated, and did not elevate Ben-Gurion's social class. Furthermore, no love was lost between her and her husband's family, and they met only on rare occasions.

Weizmann was a tall, handsome man who dressed well and had a striking appearance. Ben-Gurion was short, slim up to his forties, and from then on had a potbelly that got bigger with time. In the last decade of his life, he resembled a ball. He had a striking head with a mane of white hair that became his trademark. He paid scant attention to his outward appearance: the trends of European fashion had not reached Plonsk. In Palestine he mixed with people from the Pale of Settlement who came from a class similar to his. They espoused the untidy look, and the more threadbare the garment, the more it was considered appropriate. The European manners that Weizmann first adopted in Germany and afterward in England fitted him and Vera like a glove. In their first years in England, the Weizmanns' life was not easy, but once Weizmann made a name for himself and registered patents, and consequently had an independent income, they lived at a standard that Ben-Gurion and Paula could only dream about. Weizmann, and especially Vera, sought a standard of living similar to that of the British or Anglo-Jewish aristocracy. This was the milieu in whose drawing rooms they mingled and with whose denizens they forged friendships. Weizmann spoke and wrote perfect English. He had a faint Eastern European accent, which added to his charm in the eyes of non-Jews, while among Jews it hinted at his being "one of us." Weizmann did not attempt to shed his Jewish identity — it was an inseparable part of his attraction. He was considered an authentic, proud Jew who was also at home with British nobility He was a fine conversationalist with a sense of humor and an understanding of social situations. He charmed his British interlocutors: the mixture of the known and the dignified and the mystery of the slightly slanted eyes, the faint foreign accent, made him a sought-after guest in British drawing rooms.

Ben-Gurion remained rooted in the society he adopted from the Second Aliyah period. It was an ascetic society: making do with little was a necessity, but it became a symbol, a banner borne aloft by Ben-Gurion and his comrades. It was manifested in simple manners, directness in relations with simple folk and dignitaries alike, modest dress, few household furnishings and then only those that were absolutely necessary, and little sense of beauty and elegance. But in one thing Ben-Gurion was profligate: books, which from the early 1920s he bought obsessively. They were the only luxury he allowed himself. Compared with a day laborer, Ben-Gurion earned a handsome salary, especially after his appointment as director of the Jewish Agency Political Department in 1933. But still, the difference between the standard of the hotels at which he stayed on travel and those frequented by Vera and Chaim Weizmann was vast. But nobody remarked about the president of the Zionist Organization living at a standard inappropriate for an impoverished movement. First, he did not receive a salary from the organization and financed his standard of living out of his own pocket. Second, the Jews loved basking in the aura of royalty exuded by Weizmann's lifestyle and viewed it as a symbol of his status.

The twelve years that separated the two men created a vast gap between them. The year Herzl died, 1904, can serve as a point of comparison: at that time Weizmann was already a well-known leader in Zionist circles who headed the Democratic faction that challenged Herzl's leadership. When the great but controversial leader passed away, Weizmann was about to move from Geneva to Manchester, on his way to a decade of scientific activity. His letters reflect confusion, the Zionist movement's loss of direction, but no particular admiration of Herzl and his leadership. Although he stated that the friction between them appeared trivial in the aftermath of Herzl's death, he wrote to Vera that "he has left us a shocking inheritance,"[3] and went on to urge her, "Verochka, wear black. We are all doing so."[4] The appearance of mourning was the important thing. In contrast, Ben-Gurion was at the time an eighteen-year-old youth, still in Plonsk, and Herzl's death for him was the death of a great hope, of a once-in-a-lifetime leader, who combined all the sublime qualities of leadership and who was particularly outstanding for his willpower, that vital creative quality of the Nietzschean school. Their different attitudes toward Herzl were to symbolize the contrasts between them in the future: whereas Weizmann appreciated Herzl, he did not share Ben-Gurion's hero worship of him. Weizmann did not like the revolutionary shortcuts initiated by Herzl and viewed them as a painful delusion. He saw himself as a disciple of Ahad Ha'am, Herzl's rival, carrying the banner of Zionism as a culture. Ben-Gurion, however, admired Herzl for his daring, the courage to try to accomplish the impossible, and his attempt to change the course of history with a revolutionary step. Ben-Gurion appreciated Ahad Ha'am as a pure-hearted critic and moral guide, but did not see him as a model for a leader.

Chaim Weizmann attained leadership of the Zionist movement and the Jewish people by dint of the Balfour Declaration: a virtuosic act that combined his scientific achievements, social skills, political wisdom, and amazing talent for improvisation and persuasion, together with seizing the historic opportunity that presented itself to him and Zionism when David Lloyd George became prime minister and Arthur Balfour foreign secretary. Weizmann established himself as the leader of the Zionist movement because of the position he enjoyed among the British elite. His regal aura derived, first and foremost, from the fact that the Jewish masses saw him as the man representing them vis-à-vis Britain. His power among Jews stemmed from his influence in the British corridors of power. From this standpoint he was like Louis Brandeis, whose influence among American Jewry derived from the fact that he was a Supreme Court justice and a man who gained approbation in the non-Jewish arena. Weizmann's early activities in the Zionist sphere, his opposition to Herzl, his caprices, and his political manipulations were all forgotten in light of the great hope generated by British rule. Therefore, as the alliance between Britain and Zionism waned, Weizmann's status was diminished.

Ben-Gurion was not blessed with Weizmann's charm. He did not possess the talent for small talk, the brilliance for the richly imaginative improvisation that shone through Weizmann's speeches and conversation.

He did not have Weizmann's sense of humor or his irony. He also was incapable of casting warmth on his interlocutors as Weizmann did whenever he pleased. His road to leadership was a long and arduous one, without dramatic leaps. He acquired influence by dint of his work, perseverance, dedication, and energy. His influence was acquired in gradually expanding circles, but slowly. Until the 1930s he was thought of as a leader of the labor movement in Palestine, and no more. His attempt to gain influence outside Palestine through the Congress of Labor Palestine, which he strove to establish in the late 1920s, failed. The lever for action abroad that he hoped to create through that congress turned out to be an abortive scheme. It was then that Ben-Gurion realized that expansion of the labor movement's sphere of influence would come about only if it controlled the Zionist Organization. The 1933 election campaign leading up to the Eighteenth Zionist Congress reflected his qualities: stubbornness, resolute decision making, political intuition, and understanding the need to engage with the masses. Ben-Gurion was a party man who knew the secret of organization, who accepted the fact that in the modern era virtuosos succeed only rarely. A leader needs broad popular support. Weizmann was a leader in the Herzl mold who personally approached the foci of non-Jewish world power and hoped that by means of his persuasiveness he could move them to accept his ideas. Ben-Gurion was a man of the twentieth century, the century of the masses, of town-square politics and political organization. In the 1933 elections in Poland, he succeeded in achieving hegemony in the Zionist movement by means of propaganda and organizational skill. Now his sphere of influence extended to the Jewish masses in Eastern Europe. His figure with its mane of hair was familiar to them. But outside the circle of Hebrew and Yiddish speakers he was little known. During World War II he spent many months in the United States, attempting to break into the American corridors of power and succeeding only in reaching the president's aides. While Weizmann was invited to the White House, he was pushed into activity on solely the Jewish front. He had not yet made a name for himself outside the Jewish arena, but there he extended his sphere of influence. Until the establishment of the state he was not considered a leader of international stature. British Foreign Secretary Ernest Bevin described him as a terrorist, Hajj Amin al-Husseini's Jewish doppelgänger. Up until 1948 the British and

American *Who's Who* presented him in several short lines as a Jewish workers' leader in Palestine, and in later years added that he was chairman of the Zionist Organization. It was only after the establishment of the Jewish state and the victory in the War of Independence that he was the subject of a *Time* magazine cover story, which until then had ignored his existence. At the time he was sixty-two years old. Weizmann was forty-three when he gained world fame with the Balfour Declaration. From 1946 Weizmann did not serve in an official capacity, but President Truman received him in his office both before the establishment of the state and after it, on the latter occasion as president of the State of Israel, when he was an official guest at the White House. Ben-Gurion was not accorded that honor. He was received by President Kennedy for a talk, but was not invited for an official visit.

Weizmann realized early on that the opportune moment of the ending of World War I and the two years that followed, during which the foundations of the British Mandate were laid and the Jews were given the opportunity of establishing the national home, had passed, and thenceforth the Zionist movement would have to go on the defensive to protect its achievements and prevent Britain from reneging on its commitments. From that time he fought unceasingly and resolutely, and with considerable success—until 1938—against the increasingly anti-Zionist positions of the British government. While he truly believed in British-Zionist common interests, he was also a realist and was fully aware of the limited power of the movement he headed. All he had at his disposal were his powers of persuasion, the moral commitment of a great power, and the image of the power of the Jewish people in the world. In normal times, as in the early 1930s, they were enough to nullify the Passfield White Paper, but in the turbulent days of 1939, when a world war was imminent and the Jews' influence was at its feeblest, Weizmann's qualities or the moral commitment undertaken by Britain in happier times were not enough to annul the MacDonald White Paper. Here Weizmann's decline began. He was only sixty-five, but sick and exhausted, and mainly felt that his leverage had been taken from him. He continued to view Britain as the Zionist movement's ally, which because of the needs of the war had deviated from its path, but would return to it after the war. In his eyes the British Empire was one of the cornerstones of international order, and he could not visualize a world without it. In the course of the many years he lived in Britain, he put down roots in his adopted homeland and sought a way of striking a balance between his loyalty to it—particularly in wartime—and his first loyalty to Zionism. He opposed violent clashes with the British, and even anti-British propaganda in the United States. Like other great statesmen, he totally identified with the cause he strove for. He presented the modes of action acceptable to him as ideologically suited to the Jewish people. He repeatedly said that states are built slowly and gradually, adhering in the 1940s to the evolutionary methods that were suited to the 1920s. He rejected any use of force as irreconcilable with the moral character of the Zionist movement. His Ahad Ha'amism accorded him the ideological justification for the realism that was the guiding light of his activity between the two world wars. To this was added his belief that Britain would mend its ways and he, with the old methods in which he excelled, of one-on-one meetings with the heads of the British government, would succeed in achieving a breakthrough at the end of World War II, as he had done at the end of World War I. But he faced a different reality: Britain was no longer the leading world power, politics ceased to be the politics of the elites, and the Jewish people was not the same people. The people who survived the Holocaust were impatient and demanded an immediate national solution, and were not prepared to wait any longer. Ben-Gurion's slogan, "A State Now," won hearts and minds. Just as the alliance with Britain had elevated Weizmann to the height of power among Jews, the end of that alliance brought about his downfall.

Ben-Gurion began his journey as a utopist challenging reality, then he became a realist, and finally he reverted to the revolutionary shortcut policy of his early years. In the 1920s he admired Lenin as a leader prepared to do anything to achieve the long-awaited objective—the great revolution. When eulogizing Lenin, Uri Zvi Greenberg wrote, "In every impenetrable possibility which is like a stone wall to man, there is one wonderful moment when an aperture is opened. Then it is possible to pass through to the other side. And Lenin knew the secret as well as the *when*. He therefore looked, entered, and was not hurt."[5] Ben-Gurion always sought the aperture in the impenetrable wall. He was not prepared to accept the reality that mandated acceptance of the slow move, of step by step, acre after acre, as the balance of power in Palestine dictated.

Ben-Gurion's revolutionary zeal did not wane and would erupt at times when it seemed that his life's vocation, the Zionist enterprise, was facing disaster. Thus it happened in 1931 and again in 1939. He admired Britain, the democratic power, and the British people, who displayed spirit and resolve during World War II, but he had no illusions about a British-Jewish partnership, which he viewed as instrumental: its effectiveness had ended and so had its time. He therefore had no difficulty in altering the Zionist orientation and attempting to engage with the United States, which he viewed as a power that would be dominant in the postwar world. Ben-Gurion's unceasing efforts to find the crack in the wall through which he could pave the way to the Jewish state characterized his policy in the 1940s: the time had come for the Zionist revolution. No longer would he take cautious steps à la Ahad Ha'am, but foster breakthroughs à la Lenin, and if necessary, force reality's hand. He was prepared to use the Yishuv's military power to challenge the Mandatory government, and therefore Weizmann's preaching of Jewish morality fell on deaf ears. All the tools at the disposal of the Zionist movement must be enlisted for this historic breakthrough, which Ben-Gurion felt in his bones was possible; he was not prepared to brook any excuse for delay. The realist again made way for the revolutionary utopist, but with the experience accumulated over the years and the tools he now knew to enlist for the great breakthrough.

Weizmann was a man of Western culture. He had never shown interest in Arab or Middle Eastern culture. In 1918, when he headed the Zionist Commission to Palestine, he learned the importance of an agreement between the Zionists and the Arabs, two national movements supported by Britain. At the time, the power of the Arab national movement was in the hands of the Hashemite Emir Faisal, who sparked the Arab imagination with the revolt in the desert, aided by T. E. Lawrence's publicity and fame in Britain. Thus, the meeting in Aqaba came about, and the famous Weizmann-Faisal Agreement in which Faisal expressed his agreement with the establishment of the Jewish national home in Palestine in return for Jewish aid in attaining Arab national aims, but he added that this was conditional upon the assurance he had been given regarding the Greater Arab State. Faisal's collapse was also the collapse of the agreement with Weizmann. Weizmann understood the need to reach a dialogue with the Arabs of Palestine if only to block the British withdrawal from their commitments to the Jews. But he did not trust the Arabs, and as far as we know, he did not meet with their leaders in Palestine. He always sought the centers of power outside Palestine that might influence the Arabs of the country to accept Zionism. This resulted in his attempts at a dialogue with Iraqi Prime Minister Nuri Said, or Harry St. John Philby, a confidant of King Ibn Saud of Saudi Arabia, who toppled the Hashemite dynasty there. He was prepared to compromise on the rate of Jewish immigration in order to moderate Arab opposition. He was an enthusiastic supporter of the partition plan, which he saw as a real breakthrough toward a solution of the Arab problem and the establishment of a Jewish state. He did not toy with the binational ideas that in the 1940s spread among moderate Zionists, who feared that the establishment of a state without Arab agreement would lead to a bloody war. In a letter to Herbert Samuel, Weizmann declared, "The Arabs would offer the same resistance to a bi-national state as they do to partition, because nothing will satisfy them except domination over the whole of Palestine as a unified Arab state."[6] After the War of Independence, his attitude toward the flight or expulsion of the Arabs of Palestine was similar to that of other Israelis: happiness with "the Arabs' disappearance," and more particularly great satisfaction with the Israeli victory that surprised the Western press, especially in Britain, which had forecast a Jewish defeat—and was even looking forward to it.

Between 1906 and 1915 Ben-Gurion lived in Palestine. For him the Arab problem was not one of high policy but a day-to-day problem of encounters on the open road, Jewish watchmen being ambushed, and bloody clashes in the fields. At first, following Borochov, he thought that the Arabs of Palestine were descended from Jews who had converted to Islam, and that with the return of the Jews to their land the Arabs would assimilate among them. In the 1920s, when he became aware of the increasing power of the Arab national movement, he sought a compromise between the socialist ideology, which demanded recognition of the rights of a rival national movement and the Zionist interest. Thus was born the theory that there was nothing to talk about with the feudal leadership of Arab nationalism, but that a dialogue should be opened with the Arab worker: once they were organized and advanced with the help of the Jewish workers, they would constitute a bridge between the two national movements. These ideas, which even at the time smacked of sanctimoniousness, became irrelevant in the wake of the 1929 riots. When Ben-Gurion was appointed director of the Jewish Agency Political Department in 1933, he embarked on a series of meetings with Arab leaders in Palestine; but once he realized they were making no progress, he took Weizmann's path and tried to talk with representatives of the Arab national movement abroad. It was only after two years of such attempts that he accepted the fact that the Arabs were not prepared for a compromise which would enable the continued development of the Jewish national home, and he despaired of dialogue. In 1937 he pinned his hopes on the partition plan, but when the British reneged on their commitments to Zionism, he resigned himself to the fact that the establishment of a Jewish state would lead to war with the Arabs. In the end, like Weizmann, he viewed the establishment of a Jewish state as the supreme objective—with or without an agreement with the Arabs. But in contrast to Weizmann, who treated the Arabs with aristocratic aloofness, Ben-Gurion tried his hand at direct contact, even though wiser men such as Arthur Ruppin knew that his communications had no chance of success. After 1948 Ben-Gurion sought a partner for dialogue in the Arab states. Until his assassination, King Abdallah of Jordan seemed the most promising choice, but Ben-Gurion also was prepared to negotiate with Gamal Abdel Nasser. The Palestinian problem was no longer on his agenda.

Both Weizmann and Ben-Gurion sought to nurture intellectual life in order to benefit the Zionist experience. Weizmann was excited by the idea of a university in Palestine as a central symbol of the establishment of a "spiritual center" à la Ahad Ha'am. After World War I he wasted no time in laying the cornerstone of the Hebrew University in Jerusalem and was involved in the university's activities, but it brought him disappointment. In his mind's eye, he saw a research institute that would develop slowly and at a high standard, mainly in the sciences. Just as he thought that states must be built slowly, the same should apply to the university. The contrast between his vision of the university and the reality that was created, coupled with the fact that he was edged out of involvement in its running, frustrated him. The establishment of the Weizmann Institute of Science was some compensation for his frustration. Weizmann displayed no interest in literature, the theater, or philosophy. He did not possess the intellectual's curiosity for political theories. After the political debates of his youth with Russian students in Germany and Switzerland, he did not participate in intellectual discourse. He liked the practical approach of the British upper class, not the polemics of the Germans or the Russians.

Ben-Gurion always felt a need to complete the education he had not acquired, and he did so through incessant reading. As he grew older, he focused on philosophy, history, and Jewish studies. He loved the theater and attended plays even after his interest in literature had waned. He was keen on intellectual give and take, and liked nothing better than debating with scholars or autodidactic intellectuals. He held scientific research in high esteem and viewed it as the element that would give the Jewish state an advantage over its neighbors. Like Weizmann, his interest lay in applied, not pure, research.

Despite the difference in education, culture, and manners, the two men had much in common. They totally identified with the enterprise they headed and viewed its realization as their vocation. Since Herzl's time, Weizmann constantly was involved in political intrigue, envied the success of others, and was jealous of his status. He was easily hurt by real or imagined insults and tended toward self-pity and depression. He was quick-tempered, and when his ire rose, he cast terror on those around him. Weizmann knew his value to the movement and behaved like an autocrat not obliged to consult with anyone, and did not owe anyone explanations for his actions unless the mood took him. After his election as president of the Zionist Organization, he behaved in the same manner for which he had once criticized Herzl.

Ben-Gurion was not an easy man. When beset by tension—which was a frequent occurrence—he was given to eruptions of rage, would display impatience with his subordinates, and would assign missions whose execution sometimes was impossible. He demanded total loyalty, and for him anyone whose loyalty lay elsewhere was dismissed. He bore grudges. His adversaries in the various parliamentary oppositions liked to attribute vindictiveness to him, but their suspicions were exaggerated. In the instances in which he was suspected of vengefulness, regarding the Palmach or Herut for example, he would ascribe his behavior to practical reasons, such as striving for unity in the army or fear of the irredentism of Begin's party. He enjoyed confrontation, and once his mind was fixed on an objective, he did not flinch from any obstacle in his path. He was no less autocratic than Weizmann, but did not indulge in self-pity. Whereas Weizmann's emotions—his loves, hates, and frustrations—were out in the open, at least to his confidants, Ben-Gurion kept his feelings to himself and did not reveal them to a soul.

In 1935, when he was elected chairman of the Jewish Agency Executive, Ben-Gurion made a strategic decision to restore Weizmann—who since 1931 had been in the political wilderness—to the presidency of the Zionist Organization. He took this step because he regarded Weizmann's talents as vital for the success of Zionism. He and his Mapai leadership comrades were aware of Weizmann's shortcomings: his tendency to improvise, the fact that he did not consult anyone, his personal politics vis-à-vis the heads of the British government. But they felt that his virtues outweighed his failings and that Weizmann had learned a lesson from his four years of exile. They were both right and mistaken: Weizmann's qualities as the movement's representative vis-à-vis government authorities were indeed vital, at least until 1938. But it appeared that he had learned nothing and forgotten nothing. To put it mildly, he did not like Ben-Gurion. He liked Moshe Sharett. Apparently he did not feel threatened by Sharett, and the latter's elegant appearance was the diametrical opposite of Ben-Gurion's open-necked shirt. Weizmann's hostility toward Ben-Gurion and the disregard he displayed toward him began a short time after he was reelected president of the Zionist Organization. In 1937 he slighted Ben-Gurion when he publicly praised Sharett's speech to the Zionist Congress and did not have a word to say about the speech delivered by Ben-Gurion, his staunch ally in the fight for partition. Weizmann's slighting of Ben-Gurion was the personal side of the story. The far graver aspect was his exclusion of Ben-Gurion from the political meetings he held in Britain, and later in the United States. Weizmann was a soloist, and he was not prepared to restrict his activities by committing himself to making the chairman of the Jewish Agency a party to political meetings, with the formulation of the arguments and claims to be presented in them; and of course he did not agree to turn the one-on-one meetings, in which he excelled, into meetings at which the Zionist side would be represented by two people.

Ben-Gurion's attitude toward Weizmann was complex. It was a mixture of admiration and frustration, a willingness to acknowledge Weizmann's lofty status together with a demand that he cooperate with him. In at least two of Ben-Gurion's letters to Weizmann, he recognizes Weizmann's primacy: "You are now King of Israel," he wrote, when hopes of partition were on the horizon.[7] And on the eve of the 1946 Zionist Congress at which Weizmann was not reelected to the presidency, he writes that for him he remains "the chosen one of Jewish history who, more than any other, symbolizes Jewish suffering and genius."[8] He wanted Weizmann, but a disciplined Weizmann who accepted collegial authority, who would relinquish his sole representation of the Zionist cause in the corridors of power in London and Washington. This Weizmann was neither prepared for nor capable of doing. In his book *The Roman Revolution*, Ronald Syme describes the difference between Julius Caesar and Pompeius as follows: "Caesar would tolerate no superior, Pompeius no rival."[9] The Caesar-Ben-Gurion and Pompeius-Weizmann analogy seems fitting.

At the end of their lives, both men knew pain and the loss of rule, the loss of power and potency, and loneliness and sickness. Is this the fate of great leaders who, when their time is past, are doomed to be left out on the ice, and hope that their death will be swift and merciful? Both of them chose to be buried in their own burial plots and not in the national pantheon on Mount Herzl. They preserved their uniqueness—and their loneliness—to the grave.

Bibliographical Note

In writing this article, I was assisted by the biographies of Ben-Gurion and Weizmann written by Michael Bar-Zohar, Shabtai Teveth, and Jehuda Reinharz; by the correspondence and writings of the article's two subjects; and also by additional studies and memoirs about them. I also was helped by the copious material I read for the purpose of my past research and for the writing of my own biography of Ben-Gurion, *Ben-Gurion: Father of Modern Israel* (New Haven: Yale University Press, 2014).

NOTES

1. Prime Minister David Ben-Gurion's eulogy on the death of the president of the State of Israel, Dr. Chaim Weizmann, delivered in the Knesset plenum on November 10, 1952. Louise Fisher, ed., *Chaim Weizmann: The First President—Selected*

Documents, ed. Yemima Rosenthal (Jerusalem: Israel State Archives, 1995), 532 (Hebrew).

2. Ibid., 533–34.

3. Weizmann to Vera Chatzman, Rostov-on-Don, Geneva, July 6, 1904, in *Chaim Weizmann: The First President—Selected Documents*, ed. Yemima Rosenthal (Jerusalem: Israel State Archives, 1995), 41.

4. Ibid., 42.

5. Uri Zvi (Greenberg), *"El ever moskva"* (To Moscow), *Kuntress*, January 20, 1924.

6. Weizmann to Viscount Samuel, London and New York, April 12, 1948, in *The Letters and Papers of Chaim Weizmann*, ed. Barnet Litvinoff, ser. A, Letters, vol. 23 (New Brunswick, NJ, and Jerusalem: Transaction Books, Rutgers University, and Israel Universities Press, 1980), 102–3.

7. Ben-Gurion to Weizmann, August 22, 1937, IDF Archive, 890/73–1958.

8. Ben-Gurion to Weizmann, Paris, October 28, 1946, IDF Archive, 890/73–2002.

9. Ronald Syme, *The Roman Revolution* (London and New York: Oxford University Press, 1960), 42.

12

Role, Place, and Time

The Case of Sir
Alan Gordon Cunningham
in Palestine, 1945–1948

MOTTI GOLANI

Writing about Chaim Weizmann, Isaiah Berlin explained why he can be considered a historically "great man." In Berlin's view, contrary to the impersonal approach to history, a "great man" is one whose personal intervention effects a transformation in the various events, currents, and trends of history.[1] In what follows, I shall take Berlin's comments as my point of departure, albeit with reservations about the term "great man" —not, however, at the feasibility of such an individual existing. We have seen such figures, notably in the twentieth century, for good, for ill, and for the horrific. From Churchill or Gandhi to—at the other extreme— Stalin and Hitler. In modern Jewish/Zionist history, Herzl, Weizmann, and Ben-Gurion undoubtedly fit this category.

What I am suggesting is the possibility of a clear personal influence, even if relatively modest, on the course of history—Zionist and Israeli history, in this case—by an individual who by no means can be described as "great." His influence did not derive, at least not in the first place, from any distinctive personal qualities. Its source lay in the definition of his mission and in the input of that particular mission in a very particular historical situation. Assigned a different task, even in similar historical circumstances, the same figure might not have exerted meaningful influence of a "historic" nature. This certainly also would be the case in a situation in which the same individual held the identical position but in a different historical reality.

General Sir Alan Gordon Cunningham was the last British high commissioner in Palestine, serving from November 1945 until May 1948. It was a chance assignment, bestowed on a relative unknown—and he remained largely an anonymous figure after the Mandate expired and his mission concluded. No glory was heaped upon him for his performance in Government House in Jerusalem, nor for his decades of service in the British Imperial Army. On the contrary, if he is remembered at all, even today, it is because of the episode in which he was relieved of command of the British Eighth Army in November 1941, at the height of the campaign against the German and Italian forces in the Western Desert, at the approaches to Egypt.

To understand Cunningham's place in the history of the State of Israel —and, unavoidably, in Palestinian history as well—a historical perspective is essential.

Perhaps the first question that springs to mind is: What, exactly, was he commissioned to do? From the outset, from the moment that the League of Nations gave Britain the Mandate over the region from the Mediterranean Sea to the Persian Gulf, the high commissioner's task was vague. To begin with, the British had to divide the Mandate area into a number of subunits bearing, in each case, a reasonable connection between the identity of the population and the territory it inhabited. The first high commissioner in Jerusalem, Herbert Samuel (1920–1925), arrived when the Mandate had been divided into two territories: Iraq in the east and Transjordan/Palestine in the west. Samuel, who was given responsibility for the western Mandate, early on reached the conclusion that it would be useful to divide his "kingdom" into two parts. This remained the situation until, with time, the high commissioner's influence over Transjordan increasingly waned until finally it vanished altogether. The bulk of his power resided in Palestine. Samuel chose the loftiest possible title from the selection of those that were available in the contemporary British imperial registry: high commissioner. Only "viceroy," which was reserved for India, outranked it. Samuel had his reasons: the high commissioner's elevated status reflected Palestine's importance and at the same time infused the country with prestige. A knighthood was conferred on the new high commissioner on the eve of his departure for the Holy Land.

If Samuel held sway at the start of his term, his influence subsequently waned, a trend that continued with ever-greater force during the terms of the five high commissioners who followed him, from 1925 until 1945. The position, as Samuel defined it in the period of the formulation of the "Mandate document" (which was ratified by the League of Nations in July 1922), in conjunction with the colonial secretary, Winston Churchill, seemed to carry considerable power. In addition to being the head of the Mandatory administration, the high commissioner was the commander-in-chief of the armed forces in the country and the final arbiter on almost every matter. The growing weakness of the League of Nations (until its effective disappearance) in the interwar period, together with the inability of the Jews and Arabs to establish mutually agreed-upon institutions that would receive the Mandatory inheritance, left the high commissioner alone at the top in Palestine. Effectively, he answered exclusively to the Colonial Office. That ministry, for its part, which generally did not intervene in the ongoing administration of Palestine, was attentive to what the high commissioner had to say—he was the best-informed official about developments in the country, and his task was to implement British policy in practice. If the high commissioner's status was challenged, it was primarily by the British Army during crises, notably during the Arab Revolt (1936–1939) and the Second World War.

Nevertheless, the status of the high commissioner became increasingly attenuated in the quarter of a century that elapsed between Samuel's term and the brief tenure of Field Marshall John Gort (1944–1945). Over and above the crises of the 1930s and 1940s mentioned above (revolt and war), which diluted the high commissioner's authority as the armed forces assumed a more dominant role, the ebbing of his power was principally a function of the accelerating disintegration of the British Empire. The cracks that were already visible in the empire on the eve of the First World War widened considerably during that conflict and afterward, and led to its collapse in the aftermath of the Second World War. Consequently, the Colonial Office became increasingly weak, while other ministries became more influential. Initially, these were the War Office, the Air Ministry, and the Admiralty (and subsequently the Ministry of Defense, which sub-sumed all the others). At a somewhat later stage, in particular following the end of the Second World War and the advent of the cold war, the Foreign Office became a dominant player, as effectively it was in charge of dismantling the empire. These developments had an obvious effect on the status of the British high commissioners and other ruling officials throughout the empire, including Palestine.

Nothing seemingly had changed in this situation when Cunningham was appointed high commissioner in Palestine at two weeks' notice to replace the ailing Gort. But only seemingly. It soon became clear that the character of the high commissioner's office during Cunningham's tenure bore certain resemblances to Samuel's early tenure, 1920–1922. At that time, both London and the nascent administration in Palestine operated in something of a fog of inexperience in the new situation in the Holy Land. Much, therefore, depended on the assessments and actions of the official in charge: the high commissioner. Similarly, at the other end, in the twilight period of the British Empire and of British rule in Palestine, London again was desperately dependent on the assessments and actions of "our man in Jerusalem." This time it was Alan Cunningham.

This hypothesis merits an explanation, however brief. After the Second World War, the Palestine question became a more tangled affair: both at the macro—the international—level of the Cold War, which affected Britain's relations with the United States, and at the micro—the local—level, in the context of the Jews' relations with the Arabs and the relations of both of those national groups with the Mandate administration and the British government.

At the macro level, the British were caught between the hammer and the anvil. They wanted to leave any decision over Palestine's ultimate status to the end of the war. However, the Americans refused to delay a satisfactory political solution to avert the danger of a vacuum into which the Soviet Union or one of its satellites would enter and undermine West-ern dominance in the region. Domestically, Britain was reeling under an economic crisis of unprecedented scope and had lost interest in overseas missions (a tendency that was heightened by Labor's ascension to power in the general election of July 1945). This concatenation of circumstances had a deleterious effect on Britain's relations with the United States. After the war, then, the situation in Palestine fomented Anglo-American friction that went far beyond the local issue.

Similar friction was generated elsewhere. But it was more acute in Palestine, where the two powers were unable to reach agreement between themselves, or with the Jews and the Arabs, about a suitable alternative to British Mandatory rule. In this situation, the only recourse of both the British and the Americans was to rely on the ability of the high commissioner to stand firm in a period which, though temporarily limited, was likely to be volatile. Furthermore, a conflagration in Palestine could set in motion a chain reaction that would have the effect of ousting the West from that country and from other regional strongholds.

Half a year in office was enough time for Cunningham to grasp the crucial importance of his role in the extraordinary situation that had developed in Palestine. He was aided by his resolute motivation to use his new post as a lever to rehabilitate his reputation, which had been severely damaged during the Western Desert campaign of November 1941. As such, he was determined not to back down — that is, not to allow chaos to overwhelm the country — even in an increasingly tangled state of affairs. From the summer of 1946 to the summer of 1947, Cunningham succeeded in quelling Jewish terrorism and preventing Arab violence. Afterward, from September 1947 until May 1948, the high commissioner removed the administration and the army from Palestine "on their feet." This, in turn, exercised a historic influence on the ability of the Jewish community to stand firm and even improve its position during the "Palestine Civil War" until the middle of May 1948, and afterward to establish the State of Israel and overcome the four invading armies.

The results of Cunningham's activity did not disappear with him on May 14, 1948. His contribution to the Palestine question from 1945 to 1947 was meaningful in connection with several fraught issues: the political solution, Jewish immigration, the Yishuv and Zionist struggle against British policy, and the terrorism perpetrated by Etzel and Lehi. He was the most outstanding of the senior British officials who dealt with the Palestine question when it came to promoting the partition idea. In 1946 the Palestine partition plan (conceived in 1937) was not a popular notion in London, to put it mildly. From late 1947, Britain sought to advance the idea in Palestine, albeit not necessarily according to the United Nations plan. Even if supporters of partition, such as Colonial Secretary George Hall and his successor, Arthur Creech-Jones, and of course Cunningham, lost the battle at the time, the powerful foreign secretary, Ernest Bevin, ultimately made use of the concept in order to promote a division of the country between Transjordan and Israel. This succeeded and held fast until 1967. (Indeed, de jure the situation has not changed, as long as Israel does not annex the territories it conquered from Jordan in the Six-Day War.) The post-1948 "Green Line" certainly is a possible (some would say a leading) framework for the country's partition, this time between Israel and the Palestinians. In a certain sense Cunningham was present at the birth of the State of Israel, when he grasped, in the winter-spring of 1946, that partition was the only solution to the Jewish-Arab conflict between the Jordan River and the Mediterranean.

On immigration, the last high commissioner thought that a large influx of refugees would engender a horrific bloodbath and most certainly would make British rule in the country impossible. At the same time, he was sensitive to the moral aspect, which in this case was bolstered by his basic sympathy for the Jewish cause. Concurrently, he understood that the Arabs could not accept an open-borders policy with regard to Jewish immigration. This was another reason, from his point of view, to persist in promoting the partition idea: partition would resolve the immigration issue, which in his view was second to that of a political solution. It was not only the British who viewed immigration as a political matter, he believed; the Jews, and certainly the Arabs, also thought so. Cunningham found it highly problematic that when it came to immigration, the Zionist leaders rejected the legality of the Mandate. For the Arabs, every action concerning immigration done in the spirit of the Balfour Declaration represented a breach of Britain's commitment to them, and vice versa. The proponents of Jewish activism were unwilling to talk to the Arabs about this issue and thereby reach what Cunningham believed was a possible compromise to allow limited immigration on a humanitarian basis.

Cunningham's involvement in the "Cyprus episode"[2] significantly stabilized the situation in Palestine in a period that was difficult for both Britain and for the two communities that inhabited the country. His policy in this connection bore a clear implication for his success in withdrawing from the country with at least a semblance of control, a crucial matter for Britain at that time on the world stage. That semblance also reduced significantly the clashes between Jews and Arabs, at least until late in April 1948.

His influence on the handling of the Jewish terrorism of the time is seen mainly in regard to the question of how to combat it. When it came to the practical decision of fighting terrorism in Palestine, Cunningham was more significant than the commanders-in-chief in Palestine during his tenure — D'Arcy, Barker, and MacMillan — as well as the commanders of the Middle East arena and even the Chiefs of the Imperial General Staff, Alanbrooke and Montgomery. The civilian administration maintained its supremacy over the army on this issue to the last. Closures, searches, arrests, rampaging through the streets, not to mention an antisemitic remark such as the one uttered by Barker in July 1946, may be "catchier," but Cunningham, by means of persistent, dogged effort retained control over the army and the police under particularly difficult conditions. It was because of Cunningham's firm stand in the face of his opponents — in the government above him, in the army that operated parallel to him, and among his subordinates in the administration — that restraint was forced on the security forces and martial law was imposed partially for only two weeks in March 1947. As a result, he was able to maintain the administration's deterrent capability and bring about the eventual moderation of the Yishuv's response to British policy, which did not change quickly enough or take the right direction from the Zionist point of view.

The thrust of Cunningham's policy was that there was no point in seeking a military solution to terrorism. He prevented the army from dealing with the Yishuv in the same way it had dealt with the Arab Revolt of 1936–1939. Of course, external factors came to his aid: the spirit of the time and Britain's grim postwar situation. Still, in the spring of 1946 and again a year later, when conditions were ripe for martial law, Cunningham blocked it. He insisted on a dialogue with the Jewish Agency — and not only about terrorism. He played a major role in thwarting the intention to liquidate the Jewish Agency. His ill-fated intention to replace Ben-Gurion with Weizmann — a hopeless idea from the start — was because of his misreading of the organization's democratic dynamics and the basic sympathy for Britain harbored by the strongman of the time, Ben-Gurion. After grasping the true situation in the final months of the Mandate, he made no more approaches to Weizmann. He turned instead to Ben-Gurion, whom he viewed as his chief interlocutor, notwithstanding his disgust with him. But this was a case of too little and, above all, too late.

Cunningham had a strong appreciation for the Yishuv's organizational, political, and military ability. The Zionist cause benefited from the policy laid down by the last high commissioner. He heightened the administration's cooperation with the Jewish Agency, which had been broken off in 1938, at the conclusion of Wauchope's tenure, and renewed in 1944, under Gort. Cunningham sought cooperation with the Jewish Agency even in the face of its rejection, until the summer of 1946, of the partition idea and its refusal to work together against terrorism until the summer of 1947; this was equally striking in light of the agency's view that he was not the right interlocutor.[3] Nevertheless, he never abandoned his attempt to harness the Jewish Agency to the British cause. Nor was this a merely utilitarian approach. As time passed, Cunningham believed, truly and sincerely, that Britain, its administration in Palestine, and he himself had congruent, even common interests with the Zionist movement and the Yishuv. This was not a popular viewpoint at a time when Britain's imperial policy was set by Attlee, Bevin, and Foreign Office officials who viewed support for the Zionist cause as an obstacle to Britain's postwar policy.

The Arabs' disappointment in Cunningham was warranted. He failed to understand the position of the Palestinian Arabs at the most basic level. Unlike many veterans of the colonial service, he was not impressed by the Arab society in Palestine and made no effort to familiarize himself with it, for good or for ill. The Yishuv's mode of operation was clearer to him. His lack of interest in the Palestinian Arabs was blatant. As a result, he misread their lack of cooperation and was taken aback by their apparently surprising outburst in the autumn of 1947. As far as he was concerned, it would suffice if the Jews were assured a state that would absorb Jewish immigration to keep the Arabs quiescent, even if displeased.

Like his superiors, Cunningham still believed in 1946 that it was possible to decide for another national group who its leaders would be. In the summer of that year, he did not argue with his government, which ruled out David Ben-Gurion and Hajj Amin al-Husseini as interlocutors. Cunningham learned the lesson in the Zionist case, but not where the Arabs were concerned. He was not alone. The British-Jordan connection kept the development of the Arab side in Palestine hidden from London. Cunningham was a partner to his government, the Jewish Agency, the Arab League, and the Palestinian Arabs—who incessantly undermined their own interests—in excluding the Arabs in Palestine from the political process.

At the end of the day, Cunningham devoted more time and energy to internecine struggles within the British bureaucracy than to the Palestine conflict. In addition to the fact that contacts with the Jews and with the Arabs were highly unproductive, leaving him no choice but to take action where he thought he could exert influence—i.e., within the British establishment—this situation was compounded by additional causes (some mentioned above): the personal motivation he brought to Jerusalem; the methods and character of Montgomery, who headed the army from June 1946; the weakness of the Colonial Office; and the rising power of the Foreign Office.

Over and above these more immediate conditions, his tenure as high commissioner, with both its achievements and its difficulties, was a saliently microreflection of a macrohistorical reality. In short, he was a high commissioner who operated within a collapsing imperial structure.

Britain, which had lost control of its empire, was in the process of an inward turn, and a battle raged between the die-hard imperialists and those who insisted that the focus must now be on Britain itself and the severe social and economic crisis it was undergoing. These developments very much hampered the ability of Britain and its "man in Jerusalem" to take the initiative and cope with the deteriorating situation in Palestine. Yet at the same time, and for the same reasons, British public opinion was increasingly less willing to pay the price in human life and material damage that Palestine exacted. It was the same elsewhere in the crumbling empire, whether Crown Colony or Mandatory regime.

Under Cunningham, Mandatory Palestine in its waning days reflected both the general historical situation and the local paralysis caused by Jewish-Arab nonagreement. Nevertheless, the Mandatory regime functioned with impressive efficiency until the end of 1947. Afterward, from October 1947, as an increasingly ferocious civil war raged and the withdrawal process continued, Cunningham's ability to take action was so severely curtailed that he barely could look after his own staff. But despite it all, he was able to preserve a veneer of honorable effort until May 14, 1948.

His success in this regard averted greater bloodshed, kept the administration from having to depart under fire, and actually slowed the West's withdrawal from the Middle East. It is no exaggeration to say that the nonconfrontation between Britain and the Yishuv—which, in contrast to the Arabs, was capable of engaging the British in local warfare—prevented possible deeper Soviet encroachment, made possible Israel's establishment, strengthened Britain's stronghold in Jordan, and allowed both Israel and Jordan to lean on the Free World and also on each other for support in a quiet coalition that bolstered mutual security. Cunningham, in his own way, was a partner to the British tendency whose roots lie in the First World War and is discernible afterward as well: the inauguration of the Zionist and Hashemite project in Palestine, both west and east of the Jordan River. From this perspective, his approach was even more traditional than that of the Foreign Office, which underscored the Arab side of the equation and ignored the Jewish side with hostile intent.

Cunningham suffered from a problem that was particularly acute in Palestine but was characteristic of every colonial situation in which two or more national groups competed for the future of the country the moment the colonial power departed. He was well aware of this. To his amazement, he noted, in every meeting with representatives of the two parties to the conflict, they ignored one another and were unwilling to listen to the other side's problems, not even to further their own cause. He saw no difference between the Jews and the Arabs in this regard. It is very easy to be "black" or "white," he explained, but very difficult to be "grey." We in Palestine, he maintained, stuck closely to the British tradition in this regard. We safeguarded the "grey," no matter the personal opinion of any particular official in the service. He knew that every decision he made or action he took would prompt Jews, Arabs, and others to complain that he was taking one side or the other. In the drama—or tragedy—of Palestine this was a flagrantly impractical position. Cunningham was compelled to take a stand, a situation that worked clearly in favor of the Yishuv.

The last British high commissioner protected the Jewish community from those in London who wished to do it harm. He held that it was out of the question "to throw the Jews into the sea" and that a solution could be found by which Jews and Arabs could live in Palestine. Britain's departure advanced the partition solution, which Cunningham supported.

The Yishuv, which remained intact after Britain blocked the attempt by the Germans and their allies to reach Palestine in the Second World War and treated the Yishuv's struggle against its policy after the war with considerable patience (not least at the behest of the last high commissioner), could now implement the partition principle and establish a state in part of the country.

Let history judge, Cunningham liked to say—a remark actually aimed less at history than at memory. It is unlikely that history judges, but, to paraphrase a popular Hebrew song, what people did not see from there, we certainly can see from here and from now. The way in which this particular individual, Alan Cunningham, perceived his mission as high commissioner amid the tangled history of 1945–1948, makes him, in the historical reckoning, one of the begetters of the State of Israel.

NOTES

1. Isaiah Berlin, "Chaim Weizmann," in *Personal Impressions*, ed. Henry Hardy (Princeton: Princeton University Press, 2001), 34–35.

2. Beginning in mid-August 1946, the British sent the Jewish refugees to Cyprus. Then, in accordance with the immigration quotas, all of them arrived in Palestine.

3. The fact that the Jewish Agency supported partition beginning in the summer of 1937 and also fought against the breakaways' terrorism during the Second World War was no longer relevant when Cunningham arrived in November 1945. At the time, Zionist policy was (as it had been since 1942) to claim all of Palestine, while the Anglo-Zionist struggle against the breakaways' terrorism had been curbed some time before.

13

Bold Decisions

Three Israeli Prime Ministers
Who Went against the Grain

ITAMAR RABINOVICH

Israel's short and turbulent political history is punctuated by critical decisions both taken and not taken by its leaders. In 1948, David Ben-Gurion
carried his associates with him to declare statehood and independence,
disregarding the uncertain odds and Secretary George Marshall's dire
admonition. In the aftermath of the June 1967 War, Levy Eshkol's government, coping with a complex new reality, failed to make a decision regarding the disposition of the territories captured in the Sinai, the Golan
Heights, the West Bank, and the Gaza Strip. Israel thus drifted into a new
reality and is still grappling with its ramifications.

Israel has had nine prime ministers since Eshkol's death in 1969, and all
had to deal with what became the governing issue of Israeli politics and
policies. Of the nine, three sought to perpetuate the status quo (Golda
Meir, Yitzhak Shamir, and Benjamin Netanyahu, at least thus far); two
tried in vain to change it radically (Ehud Barak and Ehud Olmert); and
three (Menachem Begin, Yitzhak Rabin, and Ariel Sharon) managed to
effect significant breakthroughs.

Our interest in the decisions and actions of Begin, Rabin, and Sharon
—the 1979 Peace Treaty with Egypt, the 1993 Oslo Accords, and the 2005
unilateral withdrawal from the Gaza Strip—is twofold. They all took bold
decisions and were able to get them through the Israeli political system
and through the regional and international environment. And all three

went against the grain of their own record, image, and perceived ideological core. A closer look at each of those episodes should offer fresh
insights into the nature of leadership in modern and contemporary Israel
as well as into the relationship between the leaders and those they led in
the Israeli context.

Menachem Begin and the Peace with Egypt

In the aftermath of the 1967 War, Menachem Begin and his party (Gahal
—the block composed of the Herut and Liberal parties) were staunch
supporters of preserving the territorial status quo. The Land of Israel
Movement, newly formed by individuals who represented the full spectrum of Israeli politics and intellectual life, advocated the view that Israel was entitled and, indeed, had a duty to keep the territorial gains of
the Six-Day War. The argument was twofold. Ideologically, it was argued
that this was the Land of Israel, the homeland of the Jewish people, and
the State of Israel was entitled to occupy the full territory of the ancient
homeland. Others made a national security argument stating that the crisis of May 1967 proved that the armistice lines of 1949 were not defensible
and that Israel deserved the defensible borders created by the outcome
of the Six-Day War. Menachem Begin and his party were not part of this
movement, but they subscribed to the same ideology and national security arguments. They laid claim to all territory captured in 1967, but their
more forceful claim was laid to the Land of Israel or, to use the term they
actually disliked, Palestine.

On the eve of the Six-Day War, Menachem Begin and his party joined
the national unity government that was formed in order to enable Prime
Minister Eshkol to steer the country through the crisis on the basis of a
broad national consensus. They stayed in Eshkol's coalition in the aftermath of the war, contributing significantly to the government's failure to
take any bold action regarding the future of the territories captured in the
course of the war. It should be mentioned in this context that on June 19,
1967, in the war's immediate aftermath, Eshkol's cabinet passed a resolution inviting Egypt and Syria to sign peace agreements "on the basis of
the international boundary and Israel's security needs." Menachem Begin
voted for this resolution, which drew a sharp distinction between the ter-

ritories captured from Egypt and Syria and the territories of Mandatory Palestine, and in fact offered Egypt and Syria less than full withdrawal. This position was eroded over time as the post-1967 reality settled in. When in August 1970 Golda Meir's government accepted Secretary of State William Rogers's "initiative" (as distinct from his 1969 "plan"), which ended the "war of attrition" with Egypt in the Sinai, Begin and his party withdrew from the government.

They stayed out of power for the next seven years until the elections of May 1977, when for the first time in Israel's history and after several successive failures, Menachem Begin won the parliamentary elections, thus ending a long period of the Labor movement hegemony in Israel's pre-state and postindependence politics. The immediate background to this transfer of power was the debacle of the 1973 war and the series of scandals that marked the decline of the Labor party. The October war of 1973 also marked the beginning of a peace process that led to the signing of disengagement agreements with Egypt and Syria and the interim agreement over the Sinai (September 1975). Begin was critical of the concessions made by Golda Meir's and Yitzhak Rabin's governments in these initial phases of the peace process. That process was orchestrated by the American secretary of state, Henry Kissinger. Kissinger believed that a comprehensive Arab-Israeli settlement could not be achieved, at least at that time, and pursued instead a "piecemeal diplomacy," negotiating a series of partial agreements. When Jimmy Carter defeated Gerald Ford in the November 1976 presidential elections, he and his administration reversed Kissinger's policy and adopted a policy seeking a comprehensive solution to the Arab-Israeli conflict. Carter believed in practically full Israeli withdrawal from the territories captured in 1967 and in the formation of a Palestinian state as an essential component of such a settlement. This policy led to a clash between Carter and Rabin in the spring of 1977, but the clash did not last long since Rabin had to resign from office for personal reasons, and his successor, Shimon Peres, lost the May elections to Menachem Begin.[1]

It was broadly assumed that Begin was on a collision course with the Carter administration and with large parts of the international community. If Carter's policies were not acceptable to the pragmatic Rabin, they were bound to be rejected by the ideological Begin. In parts of the world, particularly in Great Britain, Begin was still tainted by what was seen as the terrorist legacy of the Irgun, which he had commanded before Israel's independence. It was assumed, and in many quarters feared, that he would radicalize Israeli policies, particularly in the West Bank and the Gaza Strip, where a modest settlement project had already begun.

But these assumptions were proven wrong, at least in part. Begin appointed Moshe Dayan, who defected from the Labor party, as his foreign minister in order to mitigate international opposition and take advantage of Dayan's prestige and international standing.[2] Furthermore, he came to the conclusion that the only way out of the circumstances created by Carter's policies was to seek a separate peace with Egypt. Begin could assume, and then found out in practice, that Egypt might be interested in making a separate peace with Israel in return for a full withdrawal from the Sinai. A message to this effect was transmitted to Begin by the Romanian dictator, Nicolae Ceauşescu. Later, in meetings held by Moshe Dayan in Morocco with Egypt's deputy prime minister, Hassan Tuhami, messages were conveyed that indicated that such a deal was feasible and that Egypt was willing to give Israel at least a degree of latitude with regard to the West Bank and the Palestinian issue. In other words, Begin could assume that he could sacrifice the Sinai in order to obtain peace with Egypt and Egyptian acquiescence with continued Israel control of the West Bank (Begin was willing to offer the Gaza Strip to Egypt, but Egypt's president Anwar Sadat declined). In strategic terms, Begin was within reach of achieving the first major breakthrough in the Arab-Israeli conflict by achieving a peace treaty with the most important Arab state and removing the danger of war with the most powerful Arab army. In ideological terms, he could justify this radical change in his earlier position by arguing that he was giving away the Sinai in order to protect Israel's control of the Land of Israel.[3]

This policy became feasible by the availability of an Egyptian partner. Anwar Sadat, who succeeded the great Abdel Nasser in 1970, was determined to regain the Sinai lost by his predecessor as well as to transform Egypt's domestic and foreign policies. The policy of shifting from a Soviet to an American orientation had been initiated prior to the 1973 war and was reinforced by Kissinger's diplomacy in the war's aftermath. Like Rabin and Begin, but for different reasons, Sadat was horrified by Carter's policies. In order to achieve a comprehensive solution to the Arab-Israeli conflict, Carter collaborated with the Soviet Union and was courting Syria and the Palestine Liberation Organization (PLO). This provided the immediate backdrop to Sadat's decision to proceed with Menachem Begin, travel to Jerusalem, and enter into negotiations that culminated in the Camp David Accords of September 1978 and the peace treaty of March 1979.

The Carter's administration's initial reaction to this Egyptian-Israeli venture was chilly. It realized that this was bound to pull the rug from under its own preferred policy. But in short order the president and his associates understood that if Egypt and Israel decided to make peace, the United States could not be critical or indifferent. The Carter administration thus decided to take charge of the Egyptian-Israeli peace process and to its credit played a significant role in bringing it to a successful conclusion. Washington's assistance was crucial since the actual give and take between Egypt and Israel proved to be difficult. The two main bones of contention were the issue of full withdrawal (Sadat insisted that withdrawal from the whole of the Sinai "to the last inch" was a sine qua non) and the Palestinian issue. This latter issue was of particular significance and complexity. While Sadat was willing in practice to make a separate deal with Israel, he needed cover. Initially, he wanted certain language introduced to a text of any agreement that would mention "the full legitimate rights of the Palestinians." To this Begin objected. In his legalistic frame of mind, "full legitimate rights" included national rights, or in other words, the right to self-determination and statehood. Needless to say, this was unacceptable to Begin. He then came up with the idea of autonomy for the Palestinians. The notion of autonomy was rooted in his familiarity with the Eastern and Central European reality of the interwar period. This was less than independence, but in the end, a formula was found that both Sadat and Begin could live with. Begin's team, three members in particular (Foreign Minister Moshe Dayan, Defense Minister Ezer Weizman, and legal advisor Aharon Barak) played a crucial role in leading the prime minister through the minefield of these difficulties.

While Begin was willing to make the trade "the Sinai for the West Bank," a significant bloc within his own party and movement refused to support his change of heart. In order to get parliamentary approval for his policy and the agreement, Begin had to rely on the support of the Labor party and other members of the opposition. There was a larger issue than straightforward support or opposition in the political system. The Israeli public had been told for a decade that the Sinai was essential for the country's defense, that it made a huge difference whether Egyptian jets would have to fly toward Israel from the Egyptian mainland or from the Sinai. Settlements were built and so was the town of Yamit in order to block Egypt's access to the Gaza Strip. Foreign Minister Moshe Dayan had famously stated that he preferred Sharm a-Sheikh without peace to peace without Sharm a-Sheikh. How was the Israeli public to be swayed? Begin's task in this regard was facilitated by Sadat. Sadat understood the importance of affecting Israeli public opinion, and this is why he chose to begin the process by making his historic visit to Jerusalem, addressing the Israeli public by saying that war should come to an end. Clearly, in order to break the impasse between Egypt and Israel, it was essential to have two leaders who could see the larger historical picture, make bold decisions, and carry their publics with them.

It was not long before Menachem Begin realized that at least part of his calculus was wrong. Sadat was fully committed to keeping the full peace with Israel, but he was not willing to comply with continued Israeli control of the West Bank and its Palestinian population. Shortly after the conclusion of the peace treaty between Egypt and Israel, Begin found himself in a dual difficulty. The Autonomy Plan for the Palestinians was not going anywhere and it strained his relationships with both the United States and Egypt, and the PLO kept attacking Israel from its base in Southern Lebanon. It was against this backdrop that Ariel Sharon persuaded Begin to launch the 1982 war in Lebanon. This war, Sharon explained to the prime minister, would deal a mortal blow to the PLO and help realize his plan to turn Jordan into Palestine. Begin was drawn into the catastrophe of the Lebanon War. A leader who was credited with the historic achievement of peace with Egypt, and was given the Nobel Prize for it, marred his record by the failed war in Lebanon. Begin never overcame this tragedy that led him to resign from office and to seclude himself in his home.

Yitzhak Rabin and the Oslo Accords

During his first term as prime minister (1974–1977), Yitzhak Rabin shared Henry Kissinger's view of the Arab-Israeli conflict and the diplomatic strategy for trying to address it. He did not believe that a comprehensive solution to the Arab-Israeli conflict was available, nor did he believe in dealing with the Arab collective or with the Palestinian national movement. Rather, Rabin believed that Israel should move gradually in phases in mitigating its conflict with such Arab states as Egypt, Jordan, and Syria. As defense minister in the national unity government of the late 1980s, Rabin dealt harshly with the First Intifada. In the election campaign of 1992, Rabin ran on a platform that promised to negotiate an autonomy agreement with the Palestinians within nine months of forming a government. Rabin also spoke clearly in the campaign against withdrawal from the Golan Heights. Rabin inherited the Madrid Process from the Shamir government. While Shamir was reluctant to proceed in the process, Rabin was determined to use it in order to effect a change in Israel's order of priorities. He wanted an end to massive investments in the settlement project in the West Bank, to rebuild the close relationship with the United States, and to invest Israel's resources in building an infrastructure for the twenty-first century.[4]

After being elected, Rabin was told by Secretary of State Howard Baker that Syria's ruler, Hafez al-Assad, was willing to sign an agreement with Israel similar to the one signed by Sadat and that the (George H. W.) Bush administration was willing to underwrite such a peace agreement. Rabin was impressed, and he adopted a dual strategy: he continued the negotiations with the Palestinian delegation to the Washington talks that emanated from the Madrid Process with a view to signing the autonomy agreement that he had promised, but at the same time he tried to find out whether the prospect of signing a full-fledged peace agreement with Syria was realistic.

In the course of 1993, Rabin realized that the Israeli-Palestinian negotiating track in Washington was stale. It was based on the pretense that Israeli was negotiating with a delegation representing the Palestinian population in the West Bank and in Gaza, and not the PLO, but in reality the delegation to the Washington talks was acting on instructions from Tunis. Rabin gradually came to the conclusion that he had no choice but to negotiate with the PLO itself. On March 1, 1993, he formally adopted the Oslo track created by two independent Israeli academics, working under the supervision of Deputy Foreign Minister Yossi Beilin. Beilin eventually briefed Foreign Minister Peres on the Oslo track, and Peres in turn eventually briefed Rabin. In March, Rabin agreed that the director general of the Israeli Foreign Ministry, Uri Savir, would head the negotiations. This was a radical departure from Rabin's earlier attitude toward the PLO. The Oslo track was kept confidential, and by August 1993 it produced a draft agreement. In August 1993, Rabin made two bold decisions. In order to find out whether Syria was a real partner for a peace treaty, he deposited with the secretary of state, Warren Christopher, a hypothetical conditional willingness to withdraw from the Golan Heights in return for a package of peace and security comparable to the one offered to Menachem Begin by Anwar Sadat. When he was disappointed by Assad's response, Rabin endorsed the draft agreement in Oslo. In so doing, Rabin agreed to recognize the PLO as the legitimate representative of Palestinian nationalism, to the establishment of a Palestinian Authority controlled by the PLO and Yasser Arafat in parts of the West Bank and in the Gaza Strip, as well as to enter negotiations for a final status agreement that could lead to the establishment of a Palestinian state.[5]

Both decisions, the deposit made to Warren Christopher conveying the willingness to withdraw fully from the Golan Heights and the Oslo Accords, were bold decisions that represented a radical departure from Rabin's earlier policies. Rabin was a former general commanding officer of the Northern Command and a former chief of staff of the Israel Defense Forces (IDF), and for him withdrawal from the Golan Heights was a painful decision. As mentioned above, he spoke against it during the election campaign of 1992. Likewise, recognizing the PLO and accepting the main features of the Oslo Accords were measures that just a year earlier would have seemed inconceivable for Yitzhak Rabin. In the event, the decision on the Golan Heights remained a dead letter, did not lead to an agreement, and did not have to be implemented. But Rabin did shake Yasser Arafat's hand on the White House lawn in September 1993, and he did sign the first and second Oslo Accords. This was a controversial policy that generated bitter opposition among the Israeli right wing and eventually led to Rabin's assassination in November 1995.

Rabin made these two decisions when he realized that no progress in the peace process was possible without a radical departure from the cautious policy with which he began his tenure. Rabin made a decision with regard to Syria on his own. His policy on the Palestinian issue was carried out in close cooperation with Shimon Peres. In this case, Rabin endorsed a policy formulated originally by his foreign minister and the latter's deputy. But while Rabin was not the original architect of the Oslo Accords, his leadership was essential for their implementation. The Israeli public, or at least a large part of it, was willing to go along with the Oslo process only because a centrist leader such as Rabin became associated with it. Rabin projected a certain ambivalence toward the Oslo process even when endorsing it. This, too, turned out to be an important element in making it acceptable to the Israeli public.

Ariel Sharon and the Withdrawal from the Gaza Strip

During most of his career as an army officer and a politician, Ariel Sharon was identified with the activist and then the right wing of Israeli politics. After ending his military career and becoming involved in politics, he became the most effective leader of the Israeli right wing. As minister of defense in 1982, he was the architect of the First Lebanon War. As minister of housing and minister of agriculture and an important member of Likud governments, he was the primary force behind the construction of the Israeli settlements in the West Bank and the Gaza Strip. The Ariel Sharon of those years was identified with the view that there was no prospect of Arab acceptance of Israel and/or of Arab-Israel peace, and hence, that Israel should hold on to the West Bank and the Gaza Strip. Many of the settlements that Sharon promoted were situated so as to preempt the option of an eventual partition or a peace settlement in the West Bank.

In 2001, Sharon finally realized his long-standing ambition and became Israel's prime minister. He defeated Ehud Barak in the February 2001 elections that were held against the backdrop of the collapse of the Camp David Summit in July 2000 and the outbreak of the Second Intifada. As prime minister, Sharon had to deal with the most severe crisis faced by the Israeli state since the 1950s. Sharon's handling of the crisis indicated that Sharon the prime minister was different from the ambitious, restless general and politician of earlier decades. Sharon defeated the Intifada and resorted to some radical measures in so doing, but he proved to be much more careful and pragmatic than his image had led people to expect. He built a good working relationship with George W. Bush's White House and refrained from crossing red lines. He also proved to be a very skillful politician. Sharon's skillful management of the crisis and his ability to defeat the Second Intifada endowed him with an unusual stature in Israeli politics that enabled him to initiate and carry out radical changes in policy.[6]

Discussion of Sharon's change of heart and departure from his traditional policies focuses as a rule on his decision to withdraw unilaterally from the Gaza Strip and to dismantle all Israeli settlements in that region. This was indeed a radical departure for a leader who for years was the chief architect of Israeli settlement construction in the West Bank and the Gaza Strip. Not long before his decision in 2005 to withdraw from Gaza, he famously said that "the fate of Netzarim [an isolated settlement in the Gaza Strip] is the fate of Tel Aviv."[7] The Gaza and West Bank settlers, who for years saw him as their patron, and the Israeli public at large were shocked by this radical decision. This decision, however, should be seen in a larger context. Sharon was in his second tenure as prime minister. He was in his seventies and looked at political decisions in their historical context. He definitely thought about his legacy and place in history. Sharon continued to believe that a final status agreement with the Palestinians was not possible and that the PLO was not the partner for peace making. He preferred unilateralism and saw his mission as consolidating Israel's existence within secure though not necessarily recognized boundaries. He saw the withdrawal from Gaza as a first step and was determined to continue with a unilateral, though not full, withdrawal in the West Bank. Sharon did not have the support of his own party (the Likud) for this policy, and in order to implement it, he broke away from the party and founded Kadima as a centrist party built upon his own persona, in cooperation with Shimon Peres and a motley collection of Likud, Labor, and other politicians and new recruits. In so doing, Sharon built successfully on his stature. Indeed, at the end of 2005, as he was preparing for elections, the polls gave Kadima 40 seats out of 120 in the Knesset, which would have enabled Sharon to build a stable effective government. Tragically, Sharon was defeated by the failure of his own body incapacitated by illness, and replaced by Ehud Olmert, whose performance in the polls was less successful and launched him on a different course.

Sharon's change of policy was accompanied by a change in ideology and outlook. Prior to his announcement of the unilateral withdraw from Gaza, Sharon began to speak about the ills of occupation and Israel's inability to pay the cost of occupying the Palestinians. This was a harbinger of the policy change. The leader who was identified for decades with a policy of relying on force and as an advocate of preserving the territorial achievements of 1967 now argued against the ills of occupying another people.

It should be mentioned that Sharon's critics have argued all along that his change of heart was not genuine, that given the investigation of himself and his family for corruption, he cynically catered to the liberal media and legal establishment.[8] Sharon may not have been free of personal and political calculus, but upon weighing the evidence it seems that these were subordinate considerations and his change of policy reflected a genuine change of heart. Sharon did see through the unilateral withdrawal from Gaza, but his illness prevented him from either winning subsequent elections or pursuing his policy in the West Bank.

Conclusion

The bold decisions made by Begin, Rabin, and Sharon and their conversion into actual policies warrant some comparison.

Begin came to power in 1977 after nearly thirty years of failing to win power in parliamentary elections. He was clearly surprised by his victory in May 1977 and assumed power unprepared. He had little time to decide on an overall strategy for dealing with the major issues confronting him as a newly elected leader, and he was not accepted by a large part of the Israeli public and of the international community. The circumstances facing Begin as a fresh prime minister were daunting. Jimmy Carter, the us president, was determined to push forward a comprehensive solution of the Arab-Israeli conflict whose contours were totally unacceptable to Begin. Begin's way of dealing with this challenge was to turn the tables and adopt a revolutionary approach to Israel's major policy dilemma.[9]

In 1992–1993, Rabin faced a different situation. Unlike Begin, he enjoyed broad support in the country and a good relationship with the Bush-Baker administration. Rabin had to resign his position at the end of a difficult first term in 1977, but by 1992 he had completely rehabilitated his standing. As minister of defense in two national unity governments (1984–1990) he built a reputation as "Mr. National Security." His problem was policy. He inherited the Madrid process, parts of which were not to his liking. He was determined to change Israel's order of priorities and to divert the large investment of national resources from the settlement project in the West Bank to Israel proper. He did not believe in the prospect of achieving a comprehensive settlement to the Arab-Israeli conflict, but did believe in a gradual process in the quest for a settlement. But finding partners for the implementation of this policy was difficult. Syria's ruler, Hafez al-Assad, refused to engage in a serious discussion of peace with Israel without receiving an initial commitment of full Israeli withdrawal from the Golan Heights. In the Palestinian arena, it became clear that Yasser Arafat completely dominated the delegation to the Washington peace talks and that he was the only effective address for serious negotiation. Arafat was willing to negotiate with Israel, but would not settle on an autonomy plan. In the face of this complex reality, Rabin gradually came to make two bold decisions: positing a hypothetical willingness to withdraw from the Golan Heights in order to open up negotiations with Syria, and negotiating with the PLO. In August 1993, it was time to make a choice between the two options. Assad's disappointing response made it easier for Rabin to opt for the Palestinian track. There were no easy decisions to be made, but in a way his decision to sign the Oslo Accords was easier than moving ahead with Syria. Progress with Syria would mean an immediate formal agreement to withdraw from the Golan Heights and the evacuation of eighteen thousand Israeli settlers. The Oslo Accords were not a final status agreement. There were many painful concessions that Rabin had to make. Bringing Yasser Arafat and his troops from Tunis to Gaza and parts of the West Bank was not an easy matter; but the Oslo Accords were an interim agreement for five years, and the really painful decisions, such as recognizing Palestinian statehood and withdrawing from much of the West Bank and Gaza, were postponed.

Sharon's tough decisions of 2005 were made after four years of an impressive tenure as prime minister. The controversial bully of earlier decades became the authoritative and admired prime minister who defeated the Second Intifada, built a successful relationship with Washington, and masterminded the Israeli political system. It was this mature, successful leader who made the far-reaching decisions of 2005 with a view to consolidating Israel's existence and to securing his place in history not just as a great military leader but as a statesman. It is significant that Sharon's first biography was titled "Warrior"[10] and a more recent one was titled "The Shepherd."[11]

The three leaders and their bold decisions met with varying degrees of success. Begin accomplished a durable peace with Egypt. He was less successful in his dealing with the Palestinian problem, and his achievement was marred by the First Lebanon War. The Oslo Accords are seen in contemporary Israel as controversial. The Israeli right wing that had objected to them in the first place argues that the Second Intifada and the various waves of terrorism are clear proof of the flaws of the Oslo Accords and of their failure. Others argue that while the Oslo process did collapse, some of its positive outcomes and by-products are still valid: the mutual recognition between Israeli and Palestinian nationalists, Israel's acceptance in large parts of the Arab world, and the fact that Israel does not have to control the urban parts of the West Bank that are managed by the Palestinian Authority. Sharon's withdrawal from Gaza is equally controversial. The right wing in Israel argues that Hamas's takeover in Gaza and the rocket launchings from Gaza into Israel that have led to two major military campaigns are clear proof of the weakness of Sharon's plan and the failure of its execution. Others, while admitting that the implementation of Sharon's plan was far from perfect, point to the advantage of Israel and Israelis being out of the Gaza Strip.

Clearly, having the right partners is a key factor in the success or failure of such policies. Begin was lucky to have as a partner Anwar Sadat, who was willing to make bold decisions and was not interested in details. Sadat fully understood the role of public opinion and media in democratic societies, though he himself was a leader of an authoritarian one. He was willing to make a large investment in persuading the Israeli public that the era of war between Egypt and Israel was over and that Israel could give up the Sinai without jeopardizing its national security. Unfortunately, Rabin had the problematic Hafez al-Assad as his partner for the Syrian negotiations and Yasser Arafat for the Palestinian ones. Assad was a tough negotiator and, unlike Sadat, was not willing to make any public gesture in order to help Rabin win over the Israeli public for a peace deal with Syria that would entail full withdrawal from the Golan Heights. When Assad agreed reluctantly, and under American pressure, to make a minor investment in public diplomacy, he did it with such apparent distaste that it ended up having a negative impact on Rabin's efforts. Arafat had the authority to sign the Oslo Accords on behalf of the Palestinian people, but his commitment to a genuine two-state solution remained questionable. He deliberately refrained from taking on Hamas and other terrorist groups, keeping them in reserve as potential allies in the event of another conflict with Israel, and built a corrupt administration in the territories under his control. Sharon chose not to have a Palestinian partner. He agreed to some coordination with Abu Mazen in implementing the withdrawal from Gaza, but his insistence on an essentially unilateral approach to the issue proved to be a mistake. Sharon's investment in preparing Israeli public opinion for the radical move in Gaza was minimal.

Both Rabin and Sharon had excellent personal and working relations with the US presidents and their administrations. Begin never built a comfortable relationship with Carter, and ended his term and life with his relationship with Carter riddled with negative elements. Ironically, in July 2013 in a speech in London, Jimmy Carter offered an optimistic perspective on the current Israeli-Palestinian negotiations and used Begin's example in order to argue that one could expect Benjamin Netanyahu to make a deal with Abu Mazen. Carter justified his optimism by saying that in his day he dealt with Menachem Begin, "a former right-wing terrorist and the last person you would expect to make peace."[12]

Indeed, several of the issues raised above figure prominently in the current discourse on the prospect of an Israeli-Palestinian agreement. The issue of the Israeli-Syrian agreement seems currently irrelevant. Syria is in the throes of a civil war that may last for some time. The discussion of an Israeli-Syrian agreement would have to wait for the end of the civil war and for the emergence of a stable regime that would be both interested in and capable of making an agreement with Israel. Discussion of further progress in Arab-Israeli relations is strictly limited to the Palestinian issue. The Palestinian leadership under Abu Mazen is at least formally committed to a two-state solution and insists that a final status agreement must be predicated on terms similar to the ones discussed with Ehud Barak in 2000 and Ehud Olmert in 2008. It flatly rejects the idea of an interim agreement or any other agreement that falls short of a final status accord. Benjamin Netanyahu is formally committed to the notion of a two-state solution, but his concept of a final status agreement and of the Palestinian state that would emerge from it is quite distant from those of his predecessor, Ehud Olmert. The main question on the Israeli political agenda is whether Netanyahu would be willing to seek an agreement on terms acceptable to the Palestinians, to the United States, and to the rest of the international community. If he does that, he probably would be required to follow the course taken by Sharon in 2005: impose it on his own party, risk the prospect of splitting the Likud and having to form a new political entity, and break away from his personal and family legacy. Many observers doubt that Netanyahu can take the ideological and personal leap that would be required for this to happen. Others argue that as he approaches the end of his third term, he, too, is thinking about his legacy and takes a serious view of the dangers presented to Israel by a perpetuation of the status quo. Whether Netanyahu will join Begin, Rabin, and Sharon in making a bold historic decision and implementing it, or whether he will remain in the group of Israeli prime ministers who chose to perpetuate the status quo, remains an open question.

NOTES

1. William B. Quandt, *Peace Process: American Diplomacy and the Arab-Israeli Conflict since 1967* (Berkeley: University of California Press, 2005).

2. For biographies of Begin see Eitan Haber, *Menahem Begin: The Legend and the Man* (New York: Delacorte Press, 1978); Arye Naor, *Begin bashilton: Edut ishit* (Tel Aviv: Yedioth Aharonot, 1993) (Hebrew). For a powerful criticism of Begin's deviation from his original ideology, see Shmuel Katz, *Lo 'oz velo hadar* (Tel Aviv: Dvir, 1981) [Hebrew].

3. For two accounts of Begin's negotiations with Egypt by his senior ministers, see Moshe Dayan, *Breakthrough: A Personal Account of the Egypt-Israel Peace Negotiations* (New York: Random House, 1981); Ezer Weizman, *Hakrav 'al hashalom: Tatspit ishit* (Jerusalem: Edanim Publishers, 1981) (Hebrew).

4. On Rabin's strategy in the peace process, see Itamar Rabinovich, *The Lingering Conflict: Israel, the Arabs, and the Middle East, 1948–2011* (Washington, DC: Brookings Institution Press, 2011); Itamar Rabinovich, *The Brink of Peace: The Israeli-Syrian Negotiations* (Princeton: Princeton University Press, 1999).

5. Ibid. See also Uri Savir, *1,100 Days That Changed the Middle East: An Insider's Account of the Israeli-Palestinian Peace Accords by Israel's Chief Negotiator* (New York: Random House, 1998).

6. Dov Weissglas, *Arik Sharon — rosh memshalah: Mabat ishi* (Tel Aviv: Miskal, 2012) (Hebrew); Elliott Abrams, *Tested by Zion: The Bush Administration and the Israeli-Palestinian Conflict* (Cambridge: Cambridge University Press, 2013)

7. In a meeting of the Knesset's Foreign Affairs and Defense Committee. See *Ha'aretz*, April 24, 2002.

8. See, for instance, Moshe Yaalon, *Derekh 'arukah ktsarah* (Tel Aviv: Yedioth Aharonot, 2008) (Hebrew).

9. See Haber, *Menachem Begin*, and Naor, *Begin bashilton*.

10. Ariel Sharon with David Chanoff, *Warrior: The Autobiography of Ariel Sharon* (New York: Simon and Schuster, 1989).

11. Nir Hefez and Gadi Bloom, *Haro'eh: Sipur hayav shel Ariel Sharon* (Tel Aviv: Miskal, 2005) (Hebrew).

12. Quoted in Roger Cohen, "Netanyahu the Peacemaker," *New York Times*, July 29, 2013.

14

Leadership in the Arab-Israeli Conflict

SHAI FELDMAN

Jehuda Reinharz's magnum opus—his political biography of Chaim
Weizmann—invites the broader question of the role of individual leaders
in the history of Zionism, Israel, and the Middle East at large. How important were key individuals in determining the fate of the Zionist enterprise relative to other historical factors at play: global developments and
events such as the two World Wars, the Holocaust, and the Cold War;
regional factors such as the rivalry between the Jordanian and the Egyptian monarchies in the late 1940s, or what has come to be known as the
Arab Cold War—the division of the Middle East in the 1950s and 1960s
between the conservative monarchies led by Saudi Arabia and Jordan and
the revolutionary republics led by Egypt, Syria, and Iraq; domestic developments such as the rise of nationalism, first in Europe and then in
the Middle East in the nineteenth century, and the rise of political Islam
toward the end of the twentieth century; or the debates within the Zionist movement between "political Zionism" and "practical Zionism" in the
beginning of the twentieth century, between the Social Democrats and
the Revisionists in the 1930s and the 1940s, and within the Labor movement, between the "diplomats" and the "activists" in the 1950s? Relative to
these other factors and important developments, what role did individual
leaders play in affecting the fate of the Zionist project? How significantly
did these individuals influence the successes and failures of the project's
primary offspring—the State of Israel?

This essay seeks to shed light on this broad issue by focusing on a subset
of the aforementioned questions: the role of individual leaders in affecting

developments in the conflict between Israel and its Arab neighbors. It will evaluate the effect of Israeli and Arab leaders on the evolution of the conflict and on the attempts to resolve it.[1] Without invading the turf of psychiatrists and psychologists, it will also seek to ascertain the extent to which particular personality traits of individual leaders made a difference in determining developments in the conflict. Inevitably, judgments in this realm involve conjectures bordering on counterfactuals as we ask: Would such a development have taken place if the individual leader involved was replaced by someone else? Or, was there something about the particular leader that explains what happened—something without which the development would not have occurred? Addressing the latter requires that we identify the specific personality traits that proved most consequential in determining an individual's influence over the course and history of the conflict.

What, indeed, were the leadership qualities that made a difference in the history of Zionism and the Arab-Israeli conflict? One important quality was the ability to read major changes in the international and regional arenas. Theodore Herzl, the founder of modern Zionism, ascertained the rising tide of nationalism in nineteenth-century Europe—a precursor to the rise of fascism first in Central and Eastern Europe and then in Western Europe—and recognized its ugliest form in the rise of antisemitism and the resulting failure of assimilation as a possible solution to the Jewish Question in Europe.

Another dimension of Herzl's quality, without which Zionism may not have come about, was his unique ability to articulate a compelling narrative. With personal charisma and a capacity to promote his ideas as a political platform ("The Jews' State") as well as in fictional form (*Altneuland*), Herzl was able to appeal to Jews from near and far and to create the nucleus of a political movement that would reach maturity only years after his death. Thus, while he did not invent the idea of Jewish statehood, Herzl rode the waves of nationalism and transformed them into a marketable narrative—an achievement that proved critically important in establishing the basis and path for the embryonic movement's ultimate success.

David Ben-Gurion, a founding father of the State of Israel, was at least as, if not more so, impressive a reader of tectonic changes. As early as 1941, Ben-Gurion recognized the decline of the old colonial powers and became convinced that the United States would emerge as a superpower in the aftermath of the Second World War. Moving forward, he helped shift the center of gravity of the Zionist movement's diplomatic efforts from garnering support in Britain to winning the sympathy of America's political elites. It was, therefore, not accidental that the movement's first official proclamation in May 1942 that its goal was independent statehood was announced at the Biltmore Hotel in New York City.

In the years prior to the Second World War, which brought about the demise of the British Empire, Ben-Gurion assigned utmost importance to placing the Yishuv on Britain's better side. Understanding Britain's imperative of securing stability in the Middle East while rejecting and combatting London's efforts to achieve this by limiting Jewish immigration to Palestine, when the 1936–39 Arab Revolt broke out, Ben-Gurion became convinced that Britain's support could be gained only by adhering to two imperatives. First, the Yishuv must avoid measures that would be perceived as contributing to the escalation of violence. He argued, therefore, for a policy of restraint (*havlaga*) in the face of Arab attacks, even at the expense of some erosion of the Yishuv's deterrence.

Second, the Yishuv needed to be seen as pragmatic by demonstrating a willingness to compromise on what it nevertheless insisted was within its historical rights — settling the entire Land of Israel. Accordingly, Ben-Gurion worked tirelessly to garner internal support for accepting the ministate offered by the 1937 Peel Commission report. In both cases Ben-Gurion insisted on differentiating between what he regarded as a legitimate right — to take measures of self-defense and to settle the entire Land of Israel — and what he considered a sensible and wise policy, arguing that the Yishuv need not insist on actualizing every right it had, if circumstances and other considerations made such insistence counterproductive.

Later, Ben-Gurion proved equally astute in ascertaining how regional changes would affect the character of the struggle for the establishment of the Jewish state and in identifying the requirements that such changes imposed on the Yishuv's security sector. Having conducted a "seminar" to examine this question soon after he assumed responsibility for the defense portfolio of the Jewish Agency in 1946, Ben-Gurion concluded that the primary challenge to the creation of a Jewish state would not be the irregular bands of local Palestinian Arabs, but instead, the conventional military forces of the neighboring Arab states. As a result, he ordered a shift in the doctrine and structure of the Haganah, from a force primarily prepared for conducting counterinsurgency operations (COIN)—such as those carried out during the 1936–39 Arab Revolt—to one prepared for an attack by the Arab states' conventional armies. This, in turn, required the gradual replacement at the top echelons of the Yishuv's security sector of officers who were trained (primarily in the Palmach) for COIN operations by individuals who—in the framework of their service in the British Army during the Second World War—had acquired experience in conducting large-scale operations and in the moving of large military formations.

Finally, the force of Ben-Gurion's personality played a key role in orchestrating the Yishuv's decision to announce the establishment of the State of Israel on May 15, 1948. In retrospect it is easy to forget how closely divided the Yishuv's leadership was between those who supported such a declaration and those who feared its consequences. While radiating confidence in the Yishuv's ability to overcome the expected onslaught of the surrounding Arab states, Ben-Gurion, ever the pessimist, was uncertain about the prospects for the Yishuv's success. Instead, his insistence was propelled by a sense that the movement faced a "window of opportunity" —a "moment" of international goodwill that the horrors of the Holocaust had created—and that it was absolutely essential to act quickly, before this "moment" passed and the resulting "window" closed, as it was far from certain that such an opportunity ever would present itself again.

Ben-Gurion's unique talent in reading large historical trajectories contrasted sharply with his primary adversary on the Palestinian side—Hajj Amin al-Husseini, the grand mufti of Jerusalem. Betting on a German victory in the Second World War, al-Husseini met with Hitler in November 1941, signaling that the Palestinian national movement had allied with Nazi Germany. This proved to be a political disaster for the Palestinians, as it tarnished their reputation in all quarters that really mattered in the aftermath of Germany's surrender and diminished the willingness to hear them out and empathize with their plight.

At least as disastrous was al-Husseini's failure in the second half of the 1940s to read the international and regional balance of power as well as that between the Jews and Arabs in Palestine. Most astonishing was his inability to comprehend that continuing to adhere to an "all or nothing" approach was untenable in the face of the post-Holocaust international support for the creation of a Jewish state—with Harry Truman and Joseph Stalin both favoring the Zionist project—and given the deep suspicions and antipathy that the leaders of Egypt, Transjordan, Syria, Iraq, and Saudi Arabia harbored against one another and, consequently, their unwillingness to fully commit their armies to the fighting in Palestine. Thus he condemned his people, who were themselves fragmented since the 1936–39 Revolt, to a losing battle—losing not only to Israel but also to the neighboring Arab states, who "took over'" the conflict with Israel on May 15, 1948, depriving the Palestinians of any freedom of choice—a freedom they would not regain even partially until the early 1970s.

Decades later, Saddam Hussein proved as disastrous as Hajj Amin al-Husseini at reading the strategic map. With roughly a 1:3 disadvantage in territory and manpower, Saddam's Iraq invaded Iran in 1980 in the hope of a quick victory. Making the same mistake that Napoleon and Hitler did when they invaded Russia, Saddam failed to understand the advantage that strategic depth provides—the ability to lose many battles but ultimately win the war. Then, ten years later, he invaded Kuwait and threatened Saudi Arabia, estimating that the United States was self-deterred by the so-called "Vietnam Syndrome" and that it would not react by undertaking the huge military commitment required to dislodge Iraq's forces from Kuwait. Neither did he seem to comprehend that by invading another sovereign Arab state he would propel key Arab countries such as Egypt and Syria to turn against him and join a us-led coalition.

Finally, on the eve of the us invasion in 2003, Saddam seemed to be ignoring all the signs that the United States was serious and that if he did not comply with the relevant UN resolutions, there would be war. Even more paradoxical was the fact that by early 2003 Saddam no longer possessed the weapons of mass destruction that were the focus of these resolutions. His refusal to accept the transparency measures that these resolutions demanded seems to have been intended merely to preserve the deterrent effect that the residual ambiguity surrounding Iraq's real capabilities provided. Would a more careful and risk-averse leader have taken the gambles that Saddam had undertaken, embroiling his country in three wars at horrendous costs that eventually included his own political and physical demise?

The force of a leader's personality is most apparent when such an individual succeeds in extending his country's influence much beyond what other measures of its relative power would lead one to expect. In the epitaphs of the Arab-Israeli conflict, the best example of this was Egypt's President Gamal Abdel Nasser. With his gift for inspiring rhetoric and the defiant message he effectively communicated to every corner of the Arab world, between the mid-1950s and the mid-1960s, Nasser showed how a leader single-handedly can multiply the weight his country carries in affecting the direction of regional and global affairs. Standing up to the world's great powers, Nasser became the voice of the Arab street that yearned to end what was seen as the centuries-long humiliation suffered at the hands of imperial powers, be they Ottoman, British, or French.

The consequences of what may be called Nasser's "multiplier effect" can be discerned in a number of important junctions during this period. Without the admiration and following that Nasserism had garnered in Syria, it is difficult to see how and why Syrian-Egyptian unity in the framework of the United Arab Republic (UAR) could have been forged in 1958. Similarly, without the resonance of Nasser's rhetoric in the streets of Beirut and his perceived meddling in Lebanon, and as a result, the fears that Lebanon's stability was in jeopardy, it was unlikely that the United States would activate the Eisenhower Doctrine and intervene in Lebanon militarily that year. And if it were not for King Hussein's fear that Nasser would portray him convincingly as a traitor to the Arab cause—and that such a portrayal effectively might threaten his throne—the King likely would not have placed his military forces under Egypt's command on the eve of the 1967 War, thus condemning his country to join a war that it was destined to lose.

Yet Nasser's remarkable success also may have contributed to his eventual undoing. In the aftermath of the 1956 Suez-Sinai War, his ability to emerge politically victorious from what, at least on the Israeli front, could be judged as a military defeat seems to have made him overly confident. And it is this overconfidence—bordering on a sense of invincibility—that at least partly explains the series of colossal mistakes he made on the eve of the 1967 War, with results that also may have contributed to the rapid deterioration of his health some three years later.

Nasser's successor as Egypt's president, Anwar Sadat, provides a different example of the role of personality in making history, in war as well as in peace. Like Ben-Gurion, Sadat read broad historical trends—in his case, the decline of the USSR. A decade and a half before the Soviet Union's ultimate demise, Sadat already had ascertained the limits of Soviet support—that is, that in the era of détente the Soviets would not provide Egypt with the means to defeat Israel militarily and that, given its own limitations, Moscow was incapable of helping to address Egypt's economic problems. In turn, Sadat saw the United States as the key to modernizing Egypt's economy and to extracting from Israel the territory Egypt lost in the 1967 War.

For both reasons, Sadat sought a complete reorientation of Egypt's foreign relations—from the East to the West. Yet neither the global nor the regional conditions seemed conducive to making Egypt's prospective about-face rewarding. As Sadat was much underrated before he became Egypt's president, neither the United States nor Israel took him seriously. Moreover, the Nixon administration's attention was focused elsewhere—on the effort to wind down the war in Vietnam and to extract the United States from its commitments in Southeast Asia. For her part, failing to understand the 1969–70 War of Attrition as a signal of Egypt's willingness to sustain heavy costs in order to restore its sovereignty over the Sinai, Israeli Prime Minister Golda Meir could not be convinced that Israel needed to make some concessions to Egypt, thus providing it with an alternative to war.

Absent such an alternative, Sadat concluded that he had no choice but to create a drama that was sure to draw Washington's attention and convince Israel that what it regarded as an acceptable stalemate could not be sustained except at unacceptable costs. But Sadat also understood that, given the Soviets' stance and America's commitment to Israel, regaining the lost Sinai by purely military means was impossible. Hence, creating a drama was not enough—the drama had to be quickly supplemented by US-orchestrated diplomacy.

Thus, Sadat's unique understanding of the relations and interplay between force and diplomacy dominated the 1973–1979 period in Egyptian-Israeli relations. Guided by this grasp, Sadat transformed Egypt's approach to war with Israel from unlimited to limited aims—hoping for just enough military success to unlock the deadlocked political process and to draw the United States away from indifference and toward deep involvement in Egyptian-Israeli diplomacy. To achieve this, Sadat was willing to follow up such use of force by engaging Israel in direct talks: from the immediate postwar discussions at Kilometer 101 between Egypt's Field Marshal Abdul Ghani el-Gamassy and Israel's General Aharon (Aha'rle) Yariv; to negotiating the two sets of disengagement agreements with Israel in 1974 and 1975; and finally, in the boldest of all moves—by traveling to Jerusalem in November 1977, leading to the 1978 Camp David Accords and the April 1979 Egypt-Israel peace treaty.

Given that Sadat was an Arab autocrat who found himself forced to send hundreds of thousands of Egypt's sons to battle—a battle from which thousands would not return—the two most surprising personal attributes that contributed to the success of his masterstroke were his intuitive understanding of how democracy works and his willingness to demonstrate sensitivity to Israel's security concerns. Thus, his historic trip to Israel was premised on his confidence that, by appealing directly to the Israeli public, he could mobilize it to support Egypt's demands. And by abandoning the Arab disposition to regard Israel's security demands as mere pretexts in the service of the effort to expand the country's boundaries—instead acknowledging that Israel has legitimate security concerns, while insisting that these concerns must be addressed by means other than conquering and holding on to Arab lands—he won over a majority of the Israeli public.

Yet Sadat's great gambit—his willingness to travel to Jerusalem, to recognize Israel, and to acknowledge its security concerns without a firm Israeli commitment to reciprocate by accepting Egypt's territorial demands—could not have succeeded without the cooperation of his Israeli counterpart, Prime Minister Menachem Begin. Had Begin responded to Sadat's initiative by entering negotiations with a "tit for tat" approach, the effects of Sadat's trip may have drowned in a sea of details. Instead, Begin —with a personality that combined a proclivity toward legalism with big "historic" gestures—responded with a gamble of his own: that Sadat's insistence that peace must be comprehensive and that the Palestinian issue must be addressed was mere "lip service" designed to placate the broader Arab audience and not a real commitment to the Palestinians. Thus, Begin finally gambled that by fully meeting Egypt's territorial demands Israel could buy quiet on the Palestinian front.

The significant contribution of Sadat's and Begin's personality traits to the conclusion of Egyptian-Israeli peace—primarily their propensity to engage in great gambles—becomes clearer when compared to the results of the interaction between another pair of Israeli-Arab leaders: Yitzhak Rabin and Hafez al-Assad. Ever suspicious, neither could bring himself to take a game-changing step that might unlock the door to a comprehensive Israeli-Syrian peace. Rabin would not promise Assad that Israel would withdraw from the Golan Heights except as a message delivered indirectly—that is, as a message "deposited" with US Secretary of State Warren Christopher—and Assad refused to engage in any significant act of public diplomacy or to commit Syria to a peace that would exceed the boundaries of a government-to-government nonbelligerence agreement. Instead, each waited for the other to "go first" by accepting what mattered to them most, and they both were unwilling to take steps or offer meaningful gestures that might have significantly improved the negotiations environment. While these personality traits were by no means the only reason that the Rabin-Assad negotiations in 1992–1995 failed, they most certainly contributed to this failure.

A fascinating phenomenon associated with the roles that different leaders have played in the history of the Arab-Israeli conflict are cases in which individuals have demonstrated remarkable judgment and impressive leadership capacities, only to lose their edge at a certain point in their peoples' history, making huge errors and misjudgments thereafter. An excellent example already noted was Nasser's errors on the eve of the 1967 War, ending a long period of remarkable political successes. But Nasser was not the only leader in the region to experience a loss of personal judgment. Another example was PLO Chairman Yassir Arafat. Similar to Nasser and despite some earlier setbacks, until 1990 Arafat was on a winning streak, gaining for the Palestinians a level of salience and international standing much beyond what their small numbers and nonstate status might lead one to expect. Beginning in the 1968 Battle of Karame—which the PLO would not have been able to survive without the intervention of the Jordanian Army—and despite the PLO's expulsion first from Jordan in 1970 and then from Lebanon in 1983, Arafat demonstrated an impressive capacity to articulate the Palestinian national cause. Leading a people who were scattered throughout North Africa and the

Middle East—and without a proximate territorial base from which it could launch ground operations against Israel—by 1974 Arafat addressed the UN General Assembly as if he were a head of state. Then, in 1988, beginning with the Palestinian "declaration of independence," Arafat orchestrated a series of steps that earned his movement the opening of a direct US-PLO dialogue.

Arafat's last successful move before he began to fall was the 1993 Oslo Accords. His acceptance of Oslo was a Sadat-like gambit in many respects. As with Sadat's cashing in of Egypt's relative success in the 1973 War for meaningful political gains by engaging Israel in direct diplomacy, Arafat understood that the message the Israelis had received through the First Palestinian Intifada—that the indefinite occupation of Palestinian lands was unsustainable—would be wasted if he did not convert the Palestinians' relative success in the Intifada to meaningful gains by engaging Israel diplomatically. Moreover, the Declaration of Principles that Arafat eventually accepted in Oslo and signed on the White House lawn on September 13, 1993, involved a Sadat-like monumental gamble: while not promising the creation of an independent Palestinian state, the open-ended process launched in Oslo ultimately would result in Palestinian independent statehood. Indeed, Oslo returned Arafat to center stage after he made a horribly bad gamble by backing Saddam Hussein's invasion of Kuwait only two years earlier.

Yet because the Palestinians' situation was far more precarious than Egypt's, Arafat could not gamble all the way. Far less certain that Israel ultimately would deliver, Arafat hedged in Oslo's aftermath; unwilling to confront Hamas and other opponents of his move, he refrained from taking the steps required to prevent them from launching a reign of terror that contradicted the Palestinians' commitment at Oslo to end the "armed struggle." In turn, this failure allowed the Israeli side to refrain from fully complying with the commitments that it had undertaken in the framework of the same agreement, especially with regard to the pace of Israeli withdrawals.

In the final chapter of his life, Arafat abdicated responsibilities when, beginning in late 2000, he permitted violence to rage in the form of the Second Palestinian Intifada. Equally consequential, in December of that year he refrained from quickly grabbing the Clinton Parameters—the contours of a solution to the Palestinian-Israeli conflict offered by the forty-second president of the United States. This was unfortunate even from a personal standpoint because Arafat's embracing of the Clinton Parameters could have launched a process that immediately would have returned him to center stage. Instead, he allowed the opportunity to slip away, condemning him to isolation in Ramallah, political irrelevance, and eventually, deteriorating health.

Ultimately, Arafat's demise may have been as much a failure of character as it was the result of bad political choices. Indeed, the latter may have informed the former: possibly, Arafat never was built for state building. Unlike Ben-Gurion, who reinvented himself from a pre-state revolutionary leader to a state builder, Arafat seemed as if he could not be bothered by the difficult tasks of state building—such as sewage, road construction, and education—in the territories, which were now for the first time under partial or complete Palestinian control. Instead, the Second Intifada provided Arafat with an opportunity to return to his youth as an armed militant. The result was a monumental setback from which at this writing the Palestinians have yet to fully recover.

While the final chapter of the life of Hezbollah leader Hassan Nasrallah is yet to be written, and it is far from certain that his demise is imminent, there are at least some indications that he has begun to follow Arafat's trajectory—a meteoric rise followed by a series of strategic mistakes. Until the summer of 2006, Nasrallah's rise was nothing short of stunning. Combining strategic thinking with an impressive command of details, Nasrallah demonstrated an admirable gift for reading and exploiting his adversaries' weaknesses. He also proved a charismatic speaker, utilizing a sarcastic sense of humor to taunt Hezbollah's enemies, with Israel leading the pack. Inspiring his followers to sacrifice their lives, between 1983 and 2000 he led many tens of suicide bombers and hundreds of other fighters to attack Israeli targets in a successful campaign to dislodge the Israeli Defense Forces from Southern Lebanon. The result was a humiliating Israeli defeat, propelling it to withdraw unilaterally from every square inch of Lebanese territory in May 2000.

Nasrallah's series of mistakes began six years later. Under pressure to disarm in the aftermath of Israel's withdrawal in 2000 and of Syria's withdrawal from Lebanon in 2005, and fearing that Hezbollah's relative inaction following Israel's withdrawal would be compared unfavorably to Hamas' ongoing war with Israel—and especially its successful operation on June 26, 2006, resulting in the abduction of Israeli soldier Gilad Shalit —Nasrallah ordered a cross-border attack on July 12, 2006. Tactically even more successful than Hamas' earlier attack, Hezbollah's operation led to a thirty-four-day war with Israel, resulting in considerable damage to Lebanon's infrastructure and much suffering to its population. Equally important, the war eroded Hezbollah's legitimacy, as its right to embroil the country in war by unilaterally deciding to attack Israel—while its representatives in government never bothered to invite a decision to do so —was questioned.

Almost two years later, in May 2008, Nasrallah ordered the deployment of Hezbollah fighters in the Sunni neighborhoods of Beirut. The decision seems to have been spurred by the fear of the consequences of Hezbollah's expected indictment by a UN tribunal for its involvement in the assassination of former Lebanese Prime Minister Rafik Hariri three years earlier. But the deployment only exacerbated the antagonism against Hezbollah in Lebanon, as it was seen by many to comprise a violation of the 1989 Taif Accords. While the Accords stipulated the disarmament of all Lebanese militias, it granted Hezbollah an exemption, justified by its role in the "resistance" to Israel. In exchange, Hezbollah promised never to turn its arms against any Arab "brothers." Not surprisingly, the deployment of its forces in western Beirut was seen as a clear violation of this promise.

Then, in April 2009, Egypt's Directorate of General Security, commonly referred to as the Mukhabarat, uncovered a number of Hezbollah terror cells. What led Nasrallah to risk earning the ire of the security establishment of the largest, if not the most influential, of the Arab states remains a mystery to this day.

Finally, in the clearest violation of the Taif Accords to date, in mid-2013 Nasrallah, in an effort to save the Assad regime, committed thousands of Hezbollah fighters to join the civil war in Syria. In at least one battle, in May 2013 in the town of al-Qusayr, four thousand Hezbollah fighters seem to have had a decisive effect, turning the tide in Assad's favor. This ultimately may prove to have been a wise gamble since Assad's survival will mean the survival of the Iran-Syria-Hezbollah axis. But the result was associated not only with hundreds of Hezbollah casualties, but also with even more questioning of the movement's legitimacy, now focused on Nasrallah's right to embroil Lebanon in its neighbor's civil war. Thus Nasrallah provides a third example of a leader whose extraordinary talents resulted in impressive gains for their country or movement, but who after a certain point began to err, sometimes leading to personal misfortunes.

The examples provided in this essay for the role of leaders in impacting the history of the Arab-Israeli conflict are not intended to demonstrate that these individuals affected the course of the conflict more than did other factors, such as changes in the international and regional systems and in the domestic politics of Israel and its Arab neighbors. For example, while the defense credentials of individual Israeli leaders proved helpful to peacemaking, they were not always essential or sufficient to achieve such breakthroughs. Thus it is difficult to see how Rabin could have broken a three-decade taboo to recognize the PLO and sign the Oslo Accords in 1993, how Ehud Barak could have withdrawn the IDF unilaterally from South Lebanon in 2000, and how Ariel Sharon could have disengaged Israel unilaterally from Gaza in 2005 if it were not for their impeccable defense credentials. Yet Begin led Israel into the first and most dramatic peace breakthrough with no defense credentials, while at other points such credentials proved insufficient; they were not enough for Rabin or Barak to overcome the domestic difficulties entailed in a possible deal with Syria, nor were they sufficient to allow Barak to overcome his fears at the 2000 Camp David summit.

The history of conflict and peacemaking in the Middle East demonstrates that strong leaders can overcome difficulties in international and regional arenas as well as in the domestic politics of their countries and in that of their neighbors. Thus, Egypt's President Sadat leaped over the US-Soviet Cold War divide to compel the United States to take an active and productive role in helping resolve the Arab-Israeli conflict. He also leaped over the Arab-Israeli divide to appeal directly to the Israeli people, thus molding Israeli public preferences to create an Israeli domestic environment more conducive to peace. And his counterpart, Israel's Prime Minister Begin, overcame opposition to concessions within his own party by leaping over the Israeli Knesset's Coalition-Opposition divide to recruit a large part of the Opposition to support the concessions he made at Camp David.

These examples demonstrate not only that strong leadership can prove more consequential at times than international, regional, and domestic circumstances, but also that if equipped with sufficient courage and creativity, strong leaders can change these circumstances in a manner that advances the cause of peace. The tragedy, however, is that such leaders have been in short supply. More often than not, Arab and Israeli leaders, even when realizing what course they should follow, are rendered helpless in the face of adverse regional and domestic circumstances.

Leaders who possess the combination of skills and character required to make a positive difference are rare. This is not the only reason why after almost a millennium the Arab-Israeli conflict has yet to be resolved. But surely it is one of the explanations for this conflict's remarkable resilience.

NOTES

1. This essay draws on much of the thinking developed in the framework of writing Abdel Monem Said Aly, Shai Feldman, and Khalil Shikaki, *Arabs and Israelis: Conflict and Peacemaking in the Middle East* (London: Palgrave Macmillan, 2013). I am indebted to my two coauthors for helping to develop many of the thoughts presented in this chapter.

15

At the Crossroads

Ben-Gurion at War

SHLOMO AVINERI

Clausewitz's dictum that war is nothing but the continuation of state policy with other means is only partly true. The main reason is that war maximizes uncertainty, while diplomacy and statecraft try to reach their goals through means that are meant to be predictable. This is the reason why few wars end the way that those who planned them had intended or predicted. As numerous cases show, by abruptly changing power relations, wars can empower the powerless while also proving the powerful to be sometimes hopelessly powerless when the fortunes of war turn in unexpected ways.

The following will try to extricate three discrete episodes from David Ben-Gurion's rich biography, spanning more than half a century of political activity, when, first as a young socialist-Zionist activist and later as a political leader of the Jewish community in Palestine and prime minister of Israel, he was confronted with the unexpected challenge of how to navigate his own—and his movement's and later country's—fortunes when faced with the inscrutability of war. The first two cases involved situations in which under difficult conditions Ben-Gurion succeeded in turning what was a major crisis into a political opportunity, while the third case refers to his ability to turn an ambivalent outcome of a war, which had been to a large extent initiated by Israel under his leadership, into a major political and diplomatic victory by quickly realizing the limits of Israel's power and adjusting his policies to what would have appeared to others as a failure if not a political defeat.

The three cases deal with the outbreak of World War I, the eve of World War II, and Israel's policies in the wake of the Suez-Sinai War of 1956.

World War I

The outbreak of World War I, and the Ottoman Empire's entry on the side of Germany and Austro-Hungary, caught the small Jewish community in Palestine by total surprise. This became particularly crucial for the immigrants of the Second Aliyah from Russia, most of whom kept their Russian citizenship after immigration so as not to be exposed to the arbitrariness of the Ottoman authorities and to enjoy the privileged position, and foreign consular protection, of the Russian Empire as stipulated by the capitulations system imposed by the European powers on the Ottoman Empire. The capitulations gave the foreign consular representatives extraterritorial rights in protecting their nationals and insulated them from the Turkish jurisdiction both in civil as well as criminal matters. That Zionist immigrants to Palestine, who had left Russia because of tsarist policies and persecution, continued to prefer Russian protection in Palestine to being subjected to the Ottoman law of the land suggests one of the many paradoxes of modern Jewish and Zionist history.

For activists of the small socialist-Zionist party Po'alei Zion ("Workers of Zion") in Palestine such as David Ben-Gurion and Yitzhak Ben-Zvi (later Israel's second president), the outbreak of the war also interfered with their study plans in Constantinople. Both went to study law in the Ottoman capital as part of their rather original plan to participate in the emerging quasi-parliamentary life opened up by the 1908 revolution of the "Young Turks," and the war put an end to these plans. But the war had more far-reaching consequences for them and their colleagues.

When the Ottoman Empire joined the war, Ben-Gurion and his colleagues who had kept their Russian citizenship became enemy aliens, and they found themselves in a totally new and unprecedented situation. As the Ottoman authorities threatened to expel all enemy nationals, the Po'alei Zion leadership decided to call upon its members to apply for Ottoman citizenship, so as to be able to remain in Palestine. But acquiring Ottoman citizenship also implied the possibility of being drafted into the Turkish army.

This call for "Ottomanization" advocated by Ben-Gurion and his colleagues was utterly incomprehensible to most of the Jews in Palestine who were Russian subjects. Given the nature of the Ottoman army and the conditions prevailing among its draftees, conscription amounted to an almost certain death sentence, or at least being exposed to dangerous illnesses and "Asiatic conditions"; but for Ben-Gurion the stark options were clear. The Turkish authorities' threat to expel all Russian subjects from their realm meant a serious diminution of the Jewish community in Palestine, and especially its Zionist component, given the fact that most members of the ultra-Orthodox Old Yishuv were, for historical reasons, Austro-Hungarian and German subjects, as they or their ancestors had hailed from these countries. On the one hand, Ben-Gurion and his colleagues argued that those who would join the powers-that-be who ruled the land and stay there, even under difficult conditions, would find themselves in the country at the end of the war and might even be in a position to have an impact on its future, having served the ruling power. On the other hand, those who would be expelled would not be there anymore and probably might not be able to return. At this stage, like many others, Ben-Gurion did not entertain the possibility of the Ottoman Empire losing the war and consequently losing its four-hundred-year old continued rule of the Levant. Few people in the summer of 1914 contemplated such a possibility.

Unsurprisingly, the Ottoman authorities were far from enthusiastic about the "Ottomanization" drive of the "Russian" socialist-Zionists, viewing them with understandable suspicion as being Russians, Jews, and socialists. According to an unverified account, Ben-Gurion and Ben-Zvi personally approached the Turkish military commander Jamal Pasha at his headquarters in the German Augusta Victoria Hospital on the Mount of Olives, but to no avail. Eventually, both of them were expelled, with thousands of others, to Egypt, then under British control. Yet unlike all the other expellees, who were trying to gain some foothold in their new Egyptian exile, Ben-Gurion and Ben-Zvi managed within a few days to find a berth on a boat sailing for America, with the aim of starting a drive there to recruit Jewish volunteers to fight in Palestine alongside the Ottoman army.

Some of the more official biographies of Ben-Gurion, as well as his own autobiographical sketches, try to minimize the fact that initially Ben-Gurion's intention was to recruit volunteers to fight on the side of the Turks not only against Russia but also against Britain. As one can imagine, the drive, supported by the American branch of Po'alei Zion, was not a success: Ben-Gurion's and Ben-Zvi's colleagues lionized the two refugees ("Our Palestinian Heroes"), but the idea of young American Jews volunteering for a foreign army (and the Turkish army at that!) did not find much support, even if the message of fighting against the oppressive and hated tsarist regime did have some appeal. Ben-Gurion's call to bring to Palestine ten thousand young Jewish volunteers to replace the ten thousand Jews expelled by the Ottomans was received with sympathy—but no volunteers came forth. Consequently, Ben-Gurion found himself being drawn into socialist-Zionist American politics, commissioned to write pamphlets and sociological tracts about Eretz Israel—and courting the young New York nurse Pauline (Paula) Moonvess, a fellow member of Po'alei Zion, whom he eventually married in 1917.

And then toward the end of 1917 the wheel of fortune changed: a revolution broke out in Russia, Britain issued the Balfour Declaration—and the United States joined the war. From Egypt, the British Expeditionary Force under General Allenby invaded and occupied Palestine, and it appeared it would be Britain, not Turkey, that would rule Palestine once the war was over. Not only would Turkey be on the losing side, it would also lose control of the Levant—and of Eretz Israel.

Ben-Gurion changed course: he launched a new campaign in the United States to draft American Jewish volunteers—this time to join the British, not the Turkish, army. Under the changed circumstances, this new drive was more successful, and together with a few hundred volunteers, Ben-Gurion (leaving behind a very pregnant Paula) joined the Thirty-Ninth Royal Fusiliers in Canada in May 1918 and, after being shipped to Egypt, reached Palestine as a sergeant in British uniform.

Anyone looking for such a turnabout during World War I naturally would find similarities with Piłsudski, Masaryk, and even Lenin: the parallels are not as outlandish as they may seem. Ben-Gurion and the socialist-Zionists were at home in the world of Eastern European national movements, including the complex relations between socialism and the various and contending national movements in the region: this intellectual ambience, with its surprising alliances, was not foreign to Ben-Gurion and his colleagues.

The arguments in favor of joining the British Army were almost identical to those Ben-Gurion initially had used in favor of volunteering to fight on the side of the Ottoman Empire—only the political and historical situation had changed: one should remain, or be present, in the country; one should be on the side of the ruling or victorious power; it would be helpful if one could have access to arms and military training; only those who are in place can be partners in influencing the future of the country. Being on the side of the victor, and being part of his armed forces, also could compensate for the minority status of the Jewish community vis-à-vis the Arab majority in Palestine and the whole region.

And indeed, with Ben-Gurion's return to Palestine with the Thirty-Ninth Royal Fusiliers, made up mainly of American Jews and erstwhile Palestinian Jewish expellees to Egypt, a new political reorganization of the socialist-Zionist camp in Palestine took place with the founding of the Achdut Ha'avoda (Unity of Labor) movement. The launching point of Ben-Gurion and his political movement in postwar Palestine was imprinted with his ability to change course during the war, to gain access to the new power in the land—all done with a combination of strategic foresight and willingness to change tactics, and allies, during the war. Piłsudski, Masaryk, and Lenin, each in his own way, achieved their national or social aims and rode to power on the back of their ability to shift alliances; Ben-Gurion's tour de force had more limited results, but showed similar dexterity and ability to react swiftly to the dramatic changes in the winds of war so as not to fall victim to its ruthless unpredictability.

On the Eve of World War II

In the mid-1930s the British government realized that it had to think ahead about the future of its mandated territory of Palestine, confronted by the relatively massive post-1933 Jewish immigration to the country and the outbreak of the Arab Revolt in 1936. The Royal Commission on Palestine (the Peel Commission), appointed by the British government to look into this, suggested for the first time the termination of the British Mandate and the partition of the territory into two states, a Jewish and an

Arab one. This was totally rejected by the Palestinian Arab leadership and caused deep division within the Jewish community and the Zionist movement. Faced with this, the British government convened the St. James Conference in London, to which Arab and Jewish representatives were invited, but as expected it led nowhere.

In the course of the February 1939 conference, the Zionist leadership was confronted with the realization that because of the pressures of international developments, the British government was about to shift from its traditional, though sometimes restrained, support of Zionism. As the Colonial Secretary Malcolm MacDonald confided privately to some of the Zionist leaders, Britain intended that after setting a final ceiling for Jewish immigration, no more Jews would be allowed to enter Palestine, and the Jewish community thus would be condemned to a perpetual minority status: Palestine would be turned into an Arab-majority sovereign country, with guarantees for the Jewish minority. By giving up the Mandate, Britain finally was disengaging herself from its historical commitments implied in the Balfour Declaration and integrated into the League of Nations Mandate.

Paradoxically, the reasons leading Britain to adopt a radical pro-Arab policy at the time of a violent anti-British Arab revolt in Palestine lay outside the Middle East. Nazi Germany's moves in early 1939 toward the annexation of rump-Czechoslovakia to the Reich as the Protectorate of Bohemia and Moravia were a blatant violation of the Munich agreements and virtually put an end not only to the British policy of appeasement but also to its political logic—avoiding war and trying to maintain "peace in our time." Toward the end of 1938 the British government came to the conclusion that under these circumstances it had better prepare for war, and an overall reassessment of its foreign and defense policies ensued.

Consequently, a number of initiatives were taken. Conscription, which had been abolished after World War I, was reintroduced; civil defense steps, especially against air attacks, were vigorously undertaken; mass production of combat aircraft and tanks was accelerated, with parallel purchases of planes from the United States; and the development of radar for military use was enhanced—all steps which eventually made Britain in September 1939, and later during the Blitz, much more prepared for war. Slightly later, Britain, together with France, also gave Poland a guarantee against a possible German invasion, signaling that what had failed in the case of Czechoslovakia would not be repeated in the case of Poland—as indeed became clear on September 3, 1939, when both countries declared war on Germany after its invasion of Poland two days earlier.

In this context, Britain also revisited its Middle Eastern commitments and policies. A number of policy reviews concluded that in a case of war against Germany, if Britain would continue to be perceived as sticking to its Balfour Declaration pro-Zionist policies, not only Arabs in Palestine and the region, but also Muslims everywhere, especially in India, might tilt toward Nazi Germany. The Arab Revolt in Palestine, triggered by the massive post-1933 Jewish immigration to the country, signaled clearly to Britain that its position in the Arab world was being eroded and the latent pro-Nazi sympathies of Arab leaders would be strengthened. The fate of the British military presence in Egypt and Iraq, and the lifeline to India via the Suez Canal, would be seriously threatened.

It was precisely at the moment when the Chamberlain government realized that its appeasement policy vis-à-vis Hitler had failed, that it embarked on a policy of appeasing Arab opposition to Zionism. The realpolitik logic was unassailable: the Arab world straddled Britain's route to India, its major imperial possession; there were obviously more Arabs than Jews; the Jews would naturally side with Britain in its war against Nazi Germany, while the Arabs would have the option of supporting Hitler (indeed, as eventually happened not only with the mufti of Jerusalem, but also during the Rashid Ali al-Khailani revolt in Iraq in 1941 and with Egyptian sympathies for Germany during Rommel's advance from Libya into Egypt in 1941–42).

Neither antisemitism nor Orientalist pro-Arabism were at the root of Britain's volte-face in 1939, but sober and strategic considerations. For the Zionist movement it signified the terrible weakness of the Jews in the worst hours of modern Jewish history, compounded by the fact that this happened at the precise moment when Britain realized that it might have to go to war against Hitler's Germany. It is not the case, as sometimes claimed by Zionist leaders, that it was those who appeased Hitler who were now appeasing the mufti: it was the failure of the appeasement of Hitler and a vigorous anti-Nazi policy that now led to courting the Arabs and appeasing them despite—and in a way, because of—the meaning of the Arab Revolt in Palestine, which until then Britain had been brutally and bloodily trying to suppress, in many cases with the help of Jewish paramilitary units.

With the failure of the St. James Conference (the Arab delegation refused even to meet in the same room with the Jewish representatives), Britain proceeded to implement its proposed policies unilaterally and in May 1939 published the White Paper on Palestine. In it Britain disengaged itself from its League of Nations Mandate and was about to prepare Palestine for independence as an Arab-majority country. In the meantime, Jewish immigration would be limited to an absolute ceiling of 75,000 over five years, with no further immigration allowed; and Jewish land purchases would be prohibited in more than 90 percent of the country. The Jews were condemned to a perpetual status of a minority, and for the Zionists this meant the end of the dream of a Jewish commonwealth in Eretz Israel.

At that time Ben-Gurion, who attended the St. James Conference, was already the chairman of the Jewish Agency for Palestine, second only to Weizmann in the Zionist leadership and the most prominent and influential leader of the Yishuv. For him, as for all the Zionist leadership, what transpired at St. James and then became official policy, with the promulgation of the White Paper and its approval by Parliament, was a terrible shock. Britain might have been a sometimes-reluctant ally of Zionism, but as the ruling power in Palestine it was the mainstay of Zionist policies. For Weizmann, this meant the collapse of his patient sustaining of the link to Britain, which despite all its recurring difficulties and disappointments, enabled Jewish immigration and the gradual buildup and expansion of the Yishuv; Jabotinsky, whose pro-British approach was much more radical in seeing Zionism as an ally of British imperial policies in the region, never really recovered from the shock of "Perfidious Albion" changing its policies. Some radical circles in the Revisionist camp, especially those identified with the Stern Group, started to look for allies in their desperation, even after the outbreak of World War II, not only in fascist Italy but also in Nazi Germany, assuming that one could imagine an alliance with the Nazi "persecutor" (*tzorer*) against the British enemy (*oyev*), who is the ruling power in the country and appeases the Arabs.

Like other Zionist leaders, Ben-Gurion realized that the Zionist movement was at a crossroads, a condition that would be further exacerbated in a war situation. He did understand the cruel and inner logic in the new British policy, and he realized more starkly than others that a double vise was threatening Zionism: in case of war, the Jewish people would find itself persecuted by Nazi Germany and at the same time abandoned by Britain. But while Weizmann, still under the spell of his historical achievements in World War I and not fully realizing the changing international context, never gave up his hope of convincing the British government to revert to its initial support of Zionism, Ben-Gurion realized that this would be a futile effort.

Hence, Ben-Gurion launched a novel initiative. Clearly envisaging the fact that a major war was about to break out, this initiative—like his efforts during World War I—also was focused on the United States, but under totally different circumstances, which now included his standing as one of the major Zionist leaders and the premier Palestinian Jewish statesman.

Immediately following the inconclusive outcome of the St James Conference, Ben-Gurion traveled to the United States; and later, during the war itself, he spent long months across the Atlantic, while his colleagues questioned his judgment and looked askance at his lengthy absence from London and Jerusalem—the two obvious centers of Zionist political activity. With his harsh realism, he understood that it would be futile to quarrel with the new British policy which preferred the Arabs as part of the United Kingdom's strategic preparation for a war against Hitler. But just as Britain had launched a new strategy in preparing for war, so should the Zionist movement. Even as it was obvious to him that the Jews would have no choice but to support the British war effort, it was clear to him that a British victory in the war would depend (as it had depended in World War I) on American support. Assuming that Britain would win the war—a crucial outcome, of course, for the Jewish people—it would be the United States that would emerge as the postwar global power; hence, it would be crucial for the Zionist movement to garner its support, as it would be America, not England, that would be the ultimate arbiter of world politics after the victory over Nazi Germany. That's why he traveled to the United States and spent so much time there, even before America's entry into the war. Unlike other Zionist leaders who still saw Britain as a Great Power, he understood that the fate of the world (and hence of Zionism) had now crossed the Atlantic.

Ben-Gurion's lengthy stays in the United States had a double aim: first of all, to unite the disparate and sometimes contentious leadership of American Jewry and focus its aims on one political goal—Palestine, transcending the mere humanitarian efforts on behalf of Europe's besieged and threatened Jewry. Second, by creating the institutional structure for this unified leadership, Ben-Gurion aimed at turning the American Jewish community—which until then had hardly had any impact on US government policies—into an effective vehicle for promoting, through Congress and public opinion, Jewish statehood. It is significant that the most explicit Zionist policy decision aimed at Jewish statehood, under conditions of partition, was articulated by Ben-Gurion in New York in the Biltmore Declaration of May 1942, which for the first time defined the aims of Zionism explicitly as "establishing a Jewish Commonwealth integrated into the structure of the new democratic world."

It was this two-pronged strategy of Ben-Gurion that for the first time turned the organized American Jewish community into a major asset in the Zionist struggle and realized that official American support for these aims would be the mainstay of the future Jewish state.

This foresight proved itself indispensable in the years 1946–1948, when the United States supplanted Britain as the major international player in deciding the future of Palestine: in the establishment of the joint Anglo-American Commission on Palestine and later in the debates at the UN that led to the 1947 Partition Plan. Had the American Jewish community continued to function in the traditional modes of the 1930s, such American support for the Jewish state never would have become possible. Many persons and organizations contributed to this outcome, but it was the forging of a united Jewish structure, encompassing practically all Jewish organizations and not only the various Zionist groups, that made this possible. And the emergence of this political and financial force—also including the United Jewish Appeal—was to a large extent the outcome of Ben-Gurion's extended stay in America just before and then during the war. What initially had appeared as a somewhat rushed, if not bizarre, trip to America after the failure of the St. James Conference and the promulgation of the White Paper proved itself to be a prescient reading of the hieroglyph of political reason.

This activity went hand in hand with a sustained effort to develop and

strengthen the emerging Jewish fighting force during the war, culminating, among other things, in the formation of the Jewish Brigade within
the British Army. The more than thirty thousand Jews from Palestine who
joined the British Army during the war eventually became the nucleus
of the future Israel Defense Force (IDF). While Weizmann was sidelined
during the war, given his almost uncritical support of Britain, and the
Revisionists oscillated between dramatic but structurally irrelevant cooperation with the British (e.g., David Raziel in Iraq) and more than questionable attempts to reach out to fascist Italy and even Nazi Germany
—as well as Begin's call for revolt against Britain while the war was still
ongoing—Ben-Gurion opted for the difficult route of "fighting Hitler as if
there was no British White Paper, and fighting against the White Paper as
if there was no war against Hitler." It was a complex formula, full of internal tensions and contradictions, occasionally leading to faulty decisions:
but it tried to extricate the Zionist movement from the terrible vise in
which it found itself facing Nazi Germany while its only historical ally—
Britain—was virtually willing to sell the Jews down the river—justifiably,
from its point of view—in order to secure the goodwill of the Arabs in
Palestine and the region. Out of this grew the steadfastness, sometimes
verging on moral cruelty, of viewing the war and the catastrophe it visited
upon the Jews as a historical opportunity: if World War I gave Zionism
the Balfour Declaration, so Ben-Gurion said in a closed session in September 1939, the new war had to lead to a Jewish state. While most Jewish leaders were naturally preoccupied with the fate of European Jewry,
Ben-Gurion—while never losing sight of any opportunity to try to help
them—realized that securing the future of the Jews in Palestine had to
take precedence. What would it help if even one hundred thousand more
Jews could be saved in Europe if, after the war, the Yishuv would be unable
to defend itself against a possible Arab onslaught or be condemned to
be a perpetual minority in an Arab-majority Palestine? Ben-Gurion had
no doubt that whatever the outcome of the war, British rule in Palestine
would come to an end, and the real challenge to the survival of Zionism
would depend on its ability to maintain itself in a postwar Middle East,
when it would be Arab enmity, and not British policy, which would be
the major danger. It was a harsh judgment, not that different from the
decision of a military leader knowing that he may have to sacrifice untold

numbers of soldiers in order to save the fort. While all the humane and
Jewish sentiments were focused unsuccessfully on saving the remnants of
European Jewry, Ben-Gurion decided on a future-oriented goal of achieving statehood and giving priority to defending the emerging Jewish commonwealth. He may be justly criticized for the harshness of his decision,
but it was this strategy—which included gaining US support for a Jewish
state in a partitioned Palestine—that made possible the emergence of Israel out of the terrible destruction of European Jewry.

Few political leaders in modern times have been confronted with
such cruel and stark choices; and the ability to withstand both the political pressures, and the moral ambiguities involved, would have put any
statesman to a difficult test. Whatever criticism one could direct at Ben-
Gurion's way of setting national priorities, the fact is that he did correctly
read the signs of the times, and took refuge neither in mere jeremiads nor
irresponsible desperate acts.

The 1956 Suez-Sinai War

The aim of the triple Franco-British-Israeli alliance that led to the Suez-
Sinai War was to bring down President Gamal Abdel Nasser's government in Egypt and replace him with a less radical, pro-Western regime.
Both Britain and France saw in Nasser, who had nationalized the Suez
Canal, a strategic and economic threat to their interests and standing in
the region, and France was particularly interested in toppling Nasser because of his support for the FLN (Front de Libération Nationale) rebellion
against French rule in Algeria. Israel's motivation mainly was fueled by
the support Nasser's regime gave to the Palestinian *fedayeen* (guerillas)
who, crossing over from Gaza, terrorized Israeli towns and villages in the
south of the country; this was accompanied by the continuing Egyptian
blockage of Israel's access to the Gulf of Aqaba and to the Israeli port city
of Eilat at its head. Beyond this, Israel was worried by the ascending power
of Nasser's pan-Arab policies, which threatened to engulf Israel from the
north and east by radical Arab regimes. The British and the French even
had prepared lists of members of a future, pro-Western Egyptian government to be installed in Cairo after Nasser's fall.

In the first days following the campaign, Ben-Gurion saw the consequences of Israel's victory over the Egyptian army in Sinai in such overall terms. In his victory speech in the Knesset, he called the 1949 Israeli-Egyptian Armistice Agreement "dead and buried" and envisaged drawing a new border between the two countries. In a rare flight of imagination —rather uncharacteristic of his realistic approach to international relations and Zionism—Ben-Gurion waxed poetic about a "Third Jewish Commonwealth" (*malkhut Yisrael ha-shelishit*), and renamed the Gulf of Sharm el-Sheikh as Mifratz Shlomo (Solomon's Gulf) and the island of Tiran at its mouth as Yotvat. Showing off his knowledge of classical Greek, he quoted to a bemused Knesset the original passage from the sixth-century Byzantine historian Procopius of Caesarea, who had maintained that there used to be a "Jewish kingdom" on an island in the Gulf. Ben-Gurion went on to identify it with Tiran, while it is obvious that Procopius must have had in mind the island now called Jezzirat el-Pharaun, closer to Eilat, and not Tiran, since the latter was not fit for human habitation because it lacked any water sources. Further quoting biblical stories about King Solomon's ships, which sailed from Eilat to the gold mines of Ophir, Ben-Gurion's grandiloquent statements did not elicit any serious objections from the Israeli public, which was stunned by the enormity of Israel's military victory. At that early stage, the consequences of the fact that the Franco-British invasion was a failure and that the joint expeditionary force had failed to capture even Port Said, at the northern entrance to the Suez Canal, had not yet sunk into public consciousness, nor did it appear that Ben-Gurion himself recognized its implications. That the Soviet Union was busy suppressing the Hungarian Revolution and the United States was in the midst of a presidential election campaign also contributed to the fact that international reaction to the joint attack on Egypt was slow to evolve.

But when the international response gathered force, it changed the political equation almost overnight. A tough message to Israel from the Soviet leadership ("Bulganin's letter") and a clear message from Washington that the United States would not grant Israel a defensive umbrella against Soviet threats were a harsh wake-up call. Now it also became clear that Nasser's regime was not going to collapse, nor would an Anglo-French protectorate be established in Egypt. Moreover, the Suez campaign turned out to be the swan song of British and French imperial dreams from which the Eisenhower administration now distanced itself forcefully. This also implied that no changes in the Israeli border with Egypt would take place, and Israel would have to withdraw sooner or later from Sinai: the military victory would not lead to a political redrawing of the regional map.

For all the success of Israel's feat of arms, it now transpired that the Sinai campaign was not going to achieve the political aims that were at the root of the three countries going to war. But paradoxically, it turned out to be one of Ben-Gurion's finest hours. In a radio speech to the nation, Ben-Gurion totally reversed his claims to a new border; the "Third Commonwealth" and the references to the supposed "Jewish kingdom" on Tiran were not repeated. Few statesmen have shown similar courage in reversing themselves so dramatically in less than a week—and clawing victory out of the jaws of a strategic defeat that could have had dire political and diplomatic consequences.

While using somewhat disparaging and aggressive language about "Gospodin Bulganin," Ben-Gurion maintained that Israel did not have, nor does it have, any territorial claims on Egyptian territory; that its sole aim in launching the Sinai campaign was to put an end to *fedayeen* incursions into its territory and guarantee freedom of navigation, according to international law, to Israeli shipping in the Gulf of Eilat.

After this statement, which retroactively denied Israel's war aims so eloquently put forward in Ben-Gurion's Knesset speech, Israel launched a series of tough negotiations for five months with the United States—and the UN—to ensure that in return for a full Israeli withdrawal from Sinai (and Gaza), the fragile prewar status quo ante along the border with Egypt would not return. While Britain and France retreated shamefully from their minimal beachhead in Port Said, Israel was able to achieve a UN (and US) guarantee of freedom of navigation in the Gulf of Eilat and a demilitarization of the Sinai, with a UN force (UNEF) as a buffer between Israel and Egypt. These undertakings became the basis for the ten formative years in Israel's economic and political development: between March 1957 and May 1967 Israel enjoyed the most peaceful borders with its neighbors, even absent a formal peace agreement.

Giving up the aims of the initial Grand Design that led to the Triple Alliance, Ben-Gurion was able to navigate Israel successfully out of the debacle caused by the Franco-British military failure. For these two powers, Suez was the swan song of their imperial history, and both Anthony Eden and Guy Mollet had to step down. Israel and Ben-Gurion, however, came out strengthened.

Israel's achievement cannot be attributed solely to the fact that the IDF won its military campaign, while the French and the British armies failed. This is, of course, part of the picture; but without Ben-Gurion's flexibility and his astute ability—and political willingness—to change course and redefine the aims of the war while the crisis was still ongoing and taking off in new, ominous directions, Israel could have been thrown into the company of the losers. It is true—and it caused chagrin to many Israelis —that Nasser was able to leverage a humiliating military defeat into a political victory; but Israel, too, was able to turn a strategic defeat—albeit coupled with a military success—into a major political achievement, buttressing its security and geopolitical standing. Leaders less tough—and less flexible at the same time—than Ben-Gurion might have gone down the drain, as did Eden and Mollet (and in 1982, Menachem Begin after the Lebanon War). Once again, despite his uncritical initial triumphalism, Ben-Gurion was quick to read the changing political map and pull his government—and his public—with him. Once again the realization that wars play havoc with states and nations, even if Israel appeared to be winning, gave Ben-Gurion an insight into developments that many of his colleagues—and successors—sometimes dismally lacked, to the great detriment of their people and their own political fate.

Ben-Gurion's patterns of behavior in 1914, 1939, and 1956 are but chapters in a complex career that turned a minor socialist-Zionist activist into the political leader of Israel and a statesman of international stature. They are but one example of his ability to combine sticking to strategic goals with adapting, quickly and ruthlessly, to the tricky changing shoals of events, so dramatically challenged by wars and their outcome. This ability to integrate far-reaching changes in tactical and practical shifts into the wider horizons of overall historical aims is surely one of the marks of statesmanship. Those who lack this unique quality are usually thrown to the wayside of history.

Bibliographical Note

The narrative base for the episodes described here generally follows the friendly, though occasionally critical, biography of Ben-Gurion by Shabtai Teveth, *The Burning Ground* (Tel Aviv: Schocken, 1997) and the more extensive Hebrew edition: *Qin'at David: Hayei Ben-Gurion*, 4 vols. (Tel Aviv: Schocken, 1977.). On the Suez-Sinai War, see S. I. Troen and M. Shemesh, eds., *The Suez-Sinai Crisis 1956—Retrospective and Reappraisal* (London: Cass, 1990), esp. Yitzhak Rabin and Shlomo Avineri, "The Limits of Power" (pp. 239–50).

16

Roosevelt, American Jews, and Rescue Attempts

YEHUDA BAUER

The policies of the Roosevelt administration toward Europe's Jews, and the attempts by American Jews and their organizations to seek aid and influence the government between 1933 and 1945, have been the subject, from the 1960s, of a great deal of historical and other research, mostly written in the United States. The trend began with Arthur D. Morse's *While Six Million Died*,[1] and continued with important contributions, among others, by Saul Friedman, Henry Feingold, Deborah Lipstadt, Richard Breitman, and especially, David S. Wyman, almost the only non-Jew dealing with the subject,[2] whose two major books, *Paper Walls*, dealing with the 1930s, and *Abandonment of the Jews*,[3] discussing the war years, contributed greatly to our understanding of the inner workings of the US government and its president in relation to the fate of the Jews of Europe. Controversies continue to center around a number of issues: first, the reluctance of the administration, in the 1930s, to permit full use of the immigration quotas for Germany and Austria (in theory, over 27,000 a year), with the exception of fiscal year 1938–39, when the quota was over-fulfilled; second, the lack of effective diplomatic (or economic) American intervention between 1933 and 1941 in favor of Central European Jews; third, the lack of effective American intervention in the short period between the start of the mass murder with the German invasion of the USSR on June, 22, 1941, and Pearl Harbor on December 7 of that year; fourth, the effective closing of the doors to Jewish immigration after 1939, and until 1948–1950, and the perceived lack of any policies to rescue European

Jewry; fifth, the lack of any public expressions of sympathy for the fate of the Jews by Roosevelt, and his reluctance to oppose the restrictionist and antisemitic polices of the State Department; sixth, the perceived weakness of any effective response by the leaders of mainstream American Jewish organizations, the various Zionist-controlled groups headed by Rabbi Stephen S. Wise, and the elitist, assimilationist, American Jewish Committee, and their perceived collaboration with an indifferent and sometimes hostile administration; seventh, the lack of recognition and full appreciation by mainstream historians for the work of the radical group of Irgun members from Palestine, headed by Peter Bergson (aka Hillel Kook) who, it is argued, in January 1944 almost single-handedly fought for, and achieved, the establishment of the War Refugee Board, tasked with the rescue of victims of Nazism, and that rescued, it is said, hundreds of thousands of Jews before the war's end; and eighth, the fact that the gas chambers of Birkenau were not bombed, an action that could have saved, it is said, hundreds of thousands of lives, especially those of Hungarian Jews. Generally speaking, accusations were leveled against the Roosevelt administration, and especially the president himself, for being co-responsible for the failure to rescue the Jews of Europe.

This is not just another matter of historical analysis, but has clear contemporary political implications. Liberal figures of the thirties and forties who opposed the administration's policies regarding the Jews are prominently mentioned, but the purpose largely seems to be to say that even liberals opposed Roosevelt. It was, however, primarily the right-wing politicians and intellectuals, non-Jewish and Jewish, whose entreaties were ignored. Prime Minister Netanyahu in 2013 is presented—and indeed, sees himself—as the direct political descendant of Peter Bergson (see the following section), and Roosevelt's policies are being continued by a contemporary wishy-washy Democratic government that presents itself as a supporter of Israel, but actually does little to identify with its interests; when it does, it is largely the result, it is claimed, of pressure by right-wing American Jewish organizations.

It is essential to free oneself from these misuses of history for contemporary political purposes and (re-)examine the record, as far as possible, *sine ira et studio*. Archives have been combed, oral testimonies have been collected, and it is not likely that new documents will be found that will change the picture in a radical way, though some details, unknown so far, may still emerge. What is needed is another, critical, look at the existing secondary literature.

In recent years, several new books have contributed to our understanding. Richard Breitman followed up his *Official Secrets*[4] with a book coauthored with Allan J. Lichtman on *FDR and the Jews*,[5] and Rafael Medoff published his contribution two years ago.[6] An older book, by Ariel Hurwitz, finally was published as well.[7]

Two characteristics of these works (not those of Breitman and Hurwitz) are worth noticing: first, a tendency to concentrate on the United States only, as though America were an isolated island in the war. Not only do the Soviets barely figure in the narrative, but there is little context to explain the difficult relations between the great powers, and between them and the neutrals and the smaller Allies. It seems possible to analyze in great detail the workings and contradictions of governmental policies and completely miss the general picture. Second, war is hardly mentioned in the writings of Medoff, for instance, as is also the case in those of his mentor, Wyman. Even those who sometimes assume the mantle of quasi-military historians, like Alexander J. Groth,[8] seem to miss the realities of the war completely. Were there possibilities of rescue? There is a constant repetition of the failure of the Anglo-Americans (Stalin lived elsewhere) to do what they indeed could have done: they could have asked the neutrals to accept the Jews who managed to reach their borders, temporarily, at the Allies' expense, promising to take them off the neutrals' shoulders after the war—because no one wanted Jews. However, they refused to do so, in April 1943 at Bermuda, and afterward. They could have eased immigration to Palestine, first of all within the quota of 75,000 Jews who the British White Paper of May 1939 allowed to enter—but the British refused to permit entry even to Jews who could have come within that restricted quota. They could have permitted the smuggling of money into Nazi Europe, because the Jewish mainstream organizations who repeatedly begged for funds knew that money would save lives. In one major instance, in June–July 1944, when the Germans were seeking an opportunity for negotiations that they hoped might lead to a separate peace with the West (the famous Brand offer to rescue Hungarian Jews), the Jewish Agency asked for negotiations, which would not lead to anything actually being given to the Germans, but might save lives because the Germans might possibly have ceased the murder, at least temporarily, in order to advance such negotiations. This was opposed, partly because of the justified fear that it might seriously endanger the alliance with the Soviets and partly, connected with that, because of the principle espoused by the Anglo-Americans not to negotiate with Nazi Germany (the Casablanca Declaration of 1943). Yet in fact, after August 1944 such negotiations did take place on the Swiss border and in Zurich, in one case—November 4, 1944—in the presence of an American diplomat, Roswell McClelland. This perhaps could have been broadened, and it was not. Thousands of lives could have been saved and were not. Could the millions have been rescued?

For the Anglo-Americans, the rescue of Jews was a very low priority, because they feared that the Germans would use this to say that the Allies were pursuing the war because of the Jews. Western antisemitism obviously lay behind that. Then, there was the problem of what to do with Jews who possibly might reach Allied shores, a consideration not unconnected to the first one. There was a rising tide of antisemitism in the United States; who were the antisemites in government, apart from obvious cases such as Breckinridge Long, the State Department agent responsible for visas and immigration? How strong was antisemitism in Congress? Has anyone done research on individual representatives and senators? How close was Roosevelt himself—if at all—to antisemitism? We know that Eleanor had clear anti-Jewish views early in her life. Was this position shared by her husband? The famous apocryphal story attributed to an official in the British Foreign Office says that when asked to define what antisemitism was, he replied that antisemitism was to dislike Jews more than was normal. Roosevelt was a normal person.

The story of the thirties, as presented, for instance, by David S. Wyman, appears to be based implicitly on two assumptions: first, that the Jews of Central Europe were threatened by genocide, before the United States entered the war. There were many who realized that a genocide was imminent; such a conclusion could be derived from reading the papers. Second, filling the quotas for Germany and Austria was possible, and Roosevelt could have achieved that goal if only he had wanted to do so. Both of these assumptions are mistaken. As to the first, no one predicted the Holocaust—not Weizmann, not Jabotinsky, and not even great writers and poets, such as Uri Zvi Greenberg or Shmuel Yosef Agnon. Yes, there was a feeling of pessimism, even of doom, but when in August 1939 Weizmann talked about six million Jews who would suffer, he meant refugees from economic and political disasters, such as Eastern European Jews had experienced after World War I. At that same time, Jabotinsky thought that a war was unlikely, and when he talked about the Diaspora that would destroy the Jewish people unless the Jews did away with the Diaspora, he meant the same—major persecutions and economic disaster. No one could have predicted what actually happened. Not only did the Jews fail to predict the Holocaust: the Germans themselves did not foresee it, until Hitler's speech to the Reichstag in January 1939. Hitler then stated that if the Jewish financiers inside and outside Europe would again (*sic!* i.e., because they supposedly had done so in 1914) cause a world war, the result would not be the victory of Bolshevism and thereby the victory of Jewry, but the annihilation (*Vernichtung*) of the Jewish race in Europe. This came as a total surprise to the assembled, cheering Nazis in the Reichstag, because no preparations and no planning had taken place, and none would until 1941.

In the thirties, increased Jewish immigration to the United States might have been a way to help people subject to persecution, not people facing mass annihilation. Roosevelt did not know more than the Nazis. He did try to find refuge for Central European Jews by convening the Evian Conference in July 1938, the year that the United States did fill the immigration quota. This was not out of benevolence or love for the Jews, but because they were part of his liberal coalition, and he had to do something for them—congressional elections were in the offing. Being a liberal and a fierce opponent of the Nazis, he also wanted to help in a refugee crisis. This picture does not fit into the framework proposed by some historians. Even if Roosevelt wanted to help, he confronted significant obstacles at home: an economic crisis of gigantic proportions, and a Congress that overwhelmingly was opposed to the immigration of Jews in an atmosphere of rising antisemitism. Wyman himself brought this out very clearly in the first part of his *Abandonment*: "The anti-immigration forces wielded substantial political power . . . a large number of congressmen were staunchly restrictionist. . . . During the war, hundreds of bills

were introduced in Congress to decrease immigration . . . the tendency
in Congress was clear." Supporters of immigration "were convinced by
fall 1943 that a rising tide of public opinion, along with the anti-refugee
mood in Congress, endangered the entire quota system."[9] This was after
the arrival of the information about the mass murder of the Jews. Before
that, in the thirties, it was even stronger. As for antisemitism, Wyman is
equally clear: "The plain truth is that many Americans were prejudiced
against Jews and were unlikely to support measures to help them. Antisemitism had been a significant determinant of America's ungenerous
response to the refugee plight before Pearl Harbor. During the war years,
it became an important factor in the nation's reaction to the Holocaust.
American antisemitism which had climbed to very high levels in the late
1930s, continued to rise in the first part of the 1940s. It reached a historic
peak in 1944."[10] In the view of Roosevelt's critics, then, the administration should have gone against public opinion and demanded more Jewish
immigration, thus confronting a basically hostile Congress in a period of
economic crisis and rising antisemitism. It is surprising that such views
are expressed by people who claim they are writing history.

But the main points in this controversy relate to the war years. Medoff
and others claim that any intelligent American could have known about
the mass murder of Jews simply by reading the newspapers. When? From
the invasion of the USSR in June 1941 on. Deborah Lipstadt,[11] Walter Laqueur,[12] Richard Breitman, and others have shown that this was not the
case at all. Before Pearl Harbor, there were scattered and unconfirmed
reports of larger and smaller massacres, the major ones being the one in
Kamenets Podolsk in August, and the Babi Yar massacre in Kiev in September, 1941. In both cases the information came late and the figures were
wrong, but that is not the issue: the issue is that these seemed to be unconfirmed reports of mass pogroms. In his *Official Secrets*, Breitman has
shown that for a brief period of time, between July and September 1941,
British decoders read German police reports from the occupied areas of
the USSR that reported massacres, and in a number of cases mentioned
Jews specifically. These decoded reports reached Churchill — but not the
British Foreign Office or the Americans — and the former used them in an
address over the BBC in August. But this is exactly the point: not only did
Churchill not refer to Jews, but the decoders were so shocked by his use

of this material (they thought the Germans might deduce that their codes had been broken), that they did not send such decoded reports after that, not even to their own prime minister. The United States did not receive a word; it was still neutral, Congress was controlled by isolationists, and the Americans had no means to intervene, even had the government concluded that mass annihilation of a people was being conducted. Jewish organizations were unsure how to deal with the reports, the AJC regarding it as rumors, and the Zionists waiting for more information.

Behind this was something that is well understood by some historians (e.g., Feingold, Breitman, and Hurwitz) but totally misunderstood by others and by the general public: the difference between information and knowledge. One does not need a degree in philosophy to realize that information by itself is only the first, though essential, step that can lead to its acceptance as true; the next step requires understanding its importance (or unimportance) and then accepting the need for action (or inaction). It is only when information becomes accepted and understood that action can follow. This process is especially difficult when the information, as in this case, is "unbelievable," as the title of Deborah Lipstadt's book indicates. The killing of astounding numbers of people just because they were Jews, by authorities acting in the name of a supposedly civilized nation, was without precedent. Not only non-Jews, but Jews as well, were unprepared for this kind of a situation. To accuse the Roosevelt administration, or the mainstream Jewish organizations, for not acting on scattered and unconfirmed information in the midst of a war in which their country was not (yet) involved, appears to be a typical case of ahistoric pseudoanalysis.

As indicated above, the historical argument presented by some commentators actually is a reflection of current Jewish-Israeli and Jewish-American politics. Roosevelt is the grandfather of Obama, and Bergson is Netanyahu's ancestor. Facts are then twisted to accommodate political and ideological preconceptions. This becomes clear when one (re)considers the story of the Bergson group. The Bergsonites, as they came to be called, were sent to the United States by the right-wing (Revisionist) Irgun Tzvai Leumi (National Military Organization), which had split off from the mainstream Haganah underground in Palestine in the 1930s. They were to establish a base for Irgun fund-raising and support, but they quarreled with their home base when the Irgun commanders in Palestine,

David Raziel (who was killed while fighting for the British in Iraq in 1941) and his successor, Ya'akov Meridor, followed a policy of supporting Britain in its efforts to fight Nazi Germany. In 1941–1942 Bergson created an organization that sought to establish a Jewish Army, recruited from stateless Jews in the United States and elsewhere, which would fight alongside the Allies against Germany. These would-be soldiers were to have gone to Canada to train there in a British imperial framework. Clearly, this was a fantasy, not only because there simply were not enough stateless Jews to establish such a unit (an earlier version of recruiting US citizens was abandoned), but Canada was governed by the anti-Jewish Mackenzie King. The British had rejected a much more sensible proposal by the Jewish Agency in 1940, to establish a Jewish armed force in the British Army recruited from Palestinian and other Jews. The last thing they wanted was a Jewish Army.

It was not until the end of 1942 that Bergson began acting, and quite successfully, to mobilize American public opinion—based on that half of the population that was not antisemitic—to do something about rescuing the Jews of Europe. If he was indeed the knight in shining armor, and everyone could have known what was happening, why then did he wait until the end of 1942?

A crucial element in this sad saga is the lack of the general context —a grievous mistake for any historian of World War II. The information about what we now know as the Holocaust came, essentially, from June through August of 1942. In June, the report by the socialist Jewish Bund Party, which asserted that seven hundred thousand Polish Jews had been murdered already, was published in British newspapers (from June 25 on) and publicly acknowledged by the British government. In the United States, it was reported largely on the inside pages and sometimes (as in the Labor Zionist *Jewish Frontier*) on the back page. No one knew about the million Jews in the occupied USSR who had been murdered by then. Additional reports came in, and on August 8, as is well known, Gerhart Riegner, the young secretary of the World Jewish Congress office in Geneva, sent his cable to the London and New York offices of his organization reporting that a usually reliable source (Walter Laqueur later found out that it was the German anti-Nazi Eduard Schulte) had heard that 3–4 million Jews would be killed in the coming fall with the aid of prussic acid (the chemical from which the gas Zyklon B, used in the gas chambers of Birkenau, was made). The State Department forbade Stephen S. Wise to publicize the cable, until the Americans could verify its contents—after all, the cable itself contained a sentence stating that the facts could not be confirmed. Contrary to some later historians' views, Wise had no choice. Without State Department approval, no American newspaper would have published such news or, if it had, it would have been construed as just more alarming Jewish rumors. But Wise did inform other Jewish organizations and contacts at the White House. This was at a time when German U-boats were sinking more ships than the Allies were building, the Germans were advancing to Stalingrad, and a thin line of British soldiers was holding El Alamein in the Egyptian desert. The Americans had won their first battle against the Japanese at Midway in June, but the Japanese Navy still controlled the Pacific. The first Allied landing in North Africa would take place in October. An unconfirmed, seemingly crazy, report about mass gassings to take place in the future (though by the late fall of 1942, most of the victims of the Holocaust already had been murdered) would have been rejected.

The Americans took their time, but in the end, in early November, they received confirmation of the Riegner cable from their outpost in Switzerland. Wise was permitted to publish the facts. He did so at a press conference on November 24. This was reported in the *New York Times* on page ten! Elsewhere, the fact that the State Department had confirmed the report generally was not mentioned: this was just another Jew wailing about murder. The information was published, but not believed, as Lipstadt, Breitman, and others have clearly shown: yes, Auschwitz was a horrible concentration camp, in Poland, one of many. Tadeusz Chciuk-Celt, a Polish journalist, reported in the fall of 1942 about mass executions there, but this was in a small Polish paper. It was not until November 27, 1942, that the Polish government-in-exile publicly distributed the information that tens of thousands of Jews and Soviet POWs had been shipped to Auschwitz for the sole purpose of their immediate extermination in gas chambers. It is unclear whether this information previously had been made available to the British Foreign Office.[13] In both Britain and the United States, the Foreign Office and the State Department expressed their disbelief in the correctness of these "rumors." Despite additional information arriving and being published in 1943, it was only in 1944 that the reports about the gas chambers were given credence. It was then, in July, that Washington received a summary of the report of two (and later another two) Jewish escapees from Auschwitz,[14] who had reached Slovakia on April 21, and their report had been received on June 11, accidentally on the same day, in Budapest and in Geneva. The full report was received in Washington as late as November.

Had the US government decided to do something toward the rescue of Jews beyond the relatively minor steps they could have taken — and did not — what exactly could they have done, between the first arrival of reliable information in August 1942 and the summary of the Wetzler-Vrba report (also known as the Auschwitz Protocols) in July 1944? There were no US ground forces on the European continent until the landings in Sicily in July 1943, and there were no Jews in Sicily and very few in Southern Italy, where the Allies landed in September. There were no US forces anywhere else until D-Day, June 6, 1944, and then it took the Western Allies over two months to liberate France and Belgium. They could not liberate what was left of Eastern and Southeast European Jewry, or intervene there. Could they have bombed the places of destruction in Poland and the occupied USSR? Had they done so, what exactly should they have bombed? They had no clear idea where the extermination camps were, because they could not get there before 1944. Lancaster bombers had the necessary range from Britain, but there were no fighter aircraft that could accompany them, until the P-51 Mustang, with its British Rolls-Royce engine and American body, came into service in the winter of 1943. By that time, the Treblinka, Belzec, Sobibor, and Chelmno extermination camps were no longer active, and Auschwitz-Birkenau was a mystery until July 1944. The conclusion is inescapable that even had the US government decided to go all out to rescue the Jews of Europe, they had no means to do so until the summer of 1944. By then, Hungarian Jewry already had been decimated (the deportations to Auschwitz stopped on July 9), and probably some five million Jews already had been murdered. The inter-Jewish controversy about rescuing Jews by putting pressure on the American government is shadow boxing, no more. It is as relevant as the question about how many letter "r's" you need to spell the name Cohen. There was no way that the Anglo-Americans could have rescued the millions, even had they wanted to do so.

What happened in the spring of 1944 that made Anglo-American intervention more feasible? The Western air forces now could target sites in Poland from their base in Foggia in Italy, which effectively became available in November 1943; however, their primary task was to bomb the Romanian oil fields in Ploesti and to provide tactical support for the slowly advancing Anglo-Polish-American forces in Italy. Attacking railroads in Poland would have been ineffective, as experience had shown that the Germans repaired any damage to tracks and bridges within forty-eight hours at most. The only target that might have affected the murder of Jews was Auschwitz-Birkenau, which could be attacked only from July 1944 on, for the reasons stated above. Precision bombing usually did not succeed, which is why Allied air forces in Germany resorted to carpet bombing of cities and major industrial sites. To hit all four gas-chamber-*cum*-crematoria buildings in Birkenau was an almost-impossible task, so that carpet bombing would have been required. The inmates yearned for this to happen, despite the acute danger to their own survival this would have entailed, but the Allies of course did not know that. But even had the Allies bombed Birkenau and destroyed all four structures, it is quite clear that the murder would not have stopped. For the Germans, killing Jews was a priority; for the Allies, their rescue was no priority. After the gas chambers stopped operating at the end of October 1944, the Germans murdered hundreds of thousands of Jews in the death marches, until the end of the war.

Should the Allies have bombed Birkenau nevertheless? From the early summer of 1944 on they certainly could have done it—and they refused, because these were "civilian" targets, and a decision of the Combined Chiefs of Staff in Washington, in January 1944—not connected to Jews— said that force should be invested in attacking only military targets. Had they bombed Birkenau, they would not have saved Jews, but they would have shown that they cared for the lives of a people targeted for extinction. It was a moral issue, and they failed miserably.

Some historians point to the establishment by Roosevelt, in January 1944, of the War Refugee Board (WRB), which was tasked to rescue victims of Nazism—in effect, Jews—as proof that rescue was possible. In fact, the opposite is the case. Directed by a very good man, John Pehle, formerly of the Treasury, the WRB made tremendous efforts to rescue victims. It was one of the factors behind the presidential declaration of March 24, 1944, five days after the German occupation of Hungary, warning the Hungarians not to persecute Jews and threatening to punish those who did. Two weeks later, the Hungarians started to ghettoize Jews, and between May and July they deported 437,000 to Auschwitz. The WRB, and the United States, had no impact at all. The WRB indeed served as a front for the Office of Strategic Services (OSS), the American espionage agency, in recruiting Raoul Wallenberg to go to Budapest, where he was active in the rescue of Jews. The Swedes wanted to send someone in any case, and Wallenberg had little if any contact with the WRB during his work in Hungary—not because the WRB did not try, but because the situation did not permit it. The WRB later claimed that it had intervened in Romania to cause the return from exile in Transnistria (Southern Ukraine) of 48,000 Jews in 1944. The WRB was in fact one of the agencies that were involved, alongside the Jewish Agency for Palestine, the Romanian Jewish community, and the Red Cross. But it was chiefly the desire of the Antonescu dictatorship to find a way out of the war that caused them to permit that return.

After the war, Pehle tried, understandably, to profile the WRB's work, and he claimed that it had rescued hundreds of thousands of Jewish lives. It is true that some lives were saved and that the WRB was involved in rescue and made heroic efforts to help. Its claims are nonsense. It simply tried its very best and could hardly have done more. American historians now present it as a showcase for what could have been done. In fact, it is a showcase for what was done, and how little could be achieved, in the face of the German determination to murder Jews.

The conclusion is, it seems, that the self-accusation especially of American Jews of not having rescued European Jewry, which is deeply rooted in the typically Jewish historical attitude that accuses Jews of being responsible for everything that happens to them (*mipnei hatta'einu* [on account of our sins]), is wrong. The Roosevelt government could have done much more, but it could not have saved European Jewry.

NOTES

1. Arthur D. Morse, *While Six Million Died* (New York: Random House, 1967).
2. Robert W. Ross, *So It Was True* (Minneapolis: University of Minnesota Press, 1998) is another case, and there are a few more.

3. David S. Wyman, *Paper Walls* (Amherst: University of Massachusetts Press, 1968); David S. Wyman, *The Abandonment of the Jews* (New York: Pantheon Books, 1984).

4. Richard Breitman, *Official Secrets: What the Nazis Planned, What the British and Americans Knew* (New York: Hill and Wang, 1998).

5. Richard Breitman and Allan J. Lichtman, *FDR and the Jews* (Cambridge: Harvard University Press, 2013).

6. Rafael Medoff, *FDR and the Holocaust: A Breach of Faith* (Washington, DC: David S. Wyman Institute, 2013).

7. Ariel Hurwitz, *Jews without Power* (New Rochelle, NY: MultiEducator, 2011).

8. Alexander J. Groth, "Accomplices: Churchill, Roosevelt and the Holocaust," in *Studies in Modern European History*, ed. Frank J. Coppa, vol. 67 (New York: Peter Lang, 2011).

9. David S. Wyman, *The Abandonment of the Jews* (New York: Pantheon Books, 1984), 7–8.

10. Ibid., 8–9.

11. Deborah Lipstadt, *Beyond Belief* (New York: Free Press, 1986).

12. Walter Laqueur, *Terrible Secrets* (London: Weidenfeld and Nicholson, 1980).

13. Krystyna Marczewska, ed., *Oboz koncentracyjnyj Oświęcim w Swietle Akt Delegatury RP na Kraj* (Oświęcim, PL: Wladyslaw Waznienski, Muzeum Panstwowe, 1968).

14. Alfred Wetzler, Rudolf Vrba (Walter Rosenberg), and later Czeslaw Mordowicz and Arnošt Rosin.

17

Wasfi al-Tall

An Iconic Incarnation of Jordanianism

ASHER SUSSER

History and biography often have been at odds. The writing of modern history has tended to shy away from the biography of the "great man" as historical inquiry shifted from the elite to the masses and from politics to society. Some were inclined even to argue that the emphasis on society meant that biography was not really history at all. This rather extreme approach eventually gave way to a revaluation of biography in the works of historians and a "new willingness . . . to see whether biography can produce a fuller and richer representation of the past."[1] It was in one of his many brilliant encapsulations that E. H. Carr defined a middle ground on the role of outstanding individuals in history. They were "at once a product and an agent of the historical process, at once the representative and the creator of social forces which change the shape of the world and the thoughts of men."[2] Wasfi al-Tall was one such outstanding individual, albeit on the more modest and parochial level of Jordanian society, "at once the representative and the creator" of the Jordanian national identity, as it emerged in the latter half of the twentieth century.

Wasfi al-Tall was a true Jordanian patriot. He was "not a man of ambiguity, irresolution or half-solutions, but unswervingly frank, with one face, one color and one word."[3] Such was the image of Wasfi al-Tall as he was known in his lifetime, and as he came to be revered by generations of Jordanians since his assassination by Palestinian gunmen in 1971.

Wasfi al-Tall, born in 1919, was the scion of a notable Jordanian family from the northern town of Irbid. His father, Mustafa Wahba al-Tall, was a poet and political activist known throughout all of Greater Syria.[4] The Talls were one of the most distinguished Transjordanian families, even in Ottoman times, having migrated to northern Jordan and southern Syria from the Najd region of Arabia in the mid-eighteenth century. Tall completed high school in the Jordanian town of Salt (the only high school in the country in those days) in 1938 and went on to graduate from the American University of Beirut (AUB) in 1941. At the AUB he was exposed to some of the luminaries of modern Arab nationalism, such as the renowned historian Constantine Zurayq, fittingly described by Albert Hourani as a "consulting don to a whole generation of nationalists."[5]

But Tall never was quite the ordinary exemplar of his generation. He served as an officer in the British Army in World War II, rather exceptional in the Arab world of those days, when the German war effort was initially very popular. In his mind, service in the British Army, just as the Jews of Palestine were doing at the time, was the essential preparation for the inevitable confrontation with the Zionists. In Palestine in 1948 he fought as a volunteer with the Arab Liberation Army. It was an unsettling experience, and he returned disillusioned after the defeat, critical and distrustful of his Arab brethren.[6]

Tall's life and political career were in many ways an embodiment of the Jordanian historical experience, in Jordan's controversial relationship with Abdel Nasser's Egypt and others of the more radical Arab states in the 1950s and 1960s, and in the antagonistic interface with Palestine and the Palestinians. It was this often acrimonious and hostile relationship with the Palestinians that became the crucible in which the Jordanian identity was formed, largely in contradistinction to the Palestinian ultimate "other." Tall's career and the emergence of Jordanianism were intricately interwoven as Tall's image was eventually transformed into an iconic centerpiece of the Jordanian nationalist narrative. As described by one of his countrymen: "Wasfi's biography blended with the history of the entire homeland to the point that in every home [in Jordan] there was a story, a memoir, or a recollection associated with him."[7]

Tall was an extraordinary individual, charismatic, self-assured, pugnacious, provocative, and more often than not, disdainful and disrespectful of his rivals. He always spoke his mind, to all and sundry, King Husayn included. He was one of the very few who would risk arousing the king's disapproval in going to great lengths to impress his views upon him. Husayn appreciated Tall's sincerity and found in him a true partner with whom to share the onus of government, even if on occasion Tall's style and temperament created tensions between the two men. Tall often was brazen and rash, like a bull in a china shop, forcing the king into the uncomfortable position of having to make amends and cover up for his excesses. But Tall had great influence, and as prime minister he was the only non-Hashemite to participate in the regular family councils held by the king.[8]

The Stalwart Defender of Jordan

Wasfi al-Tall was a stalwart defender of the Hashemite kingdom from an early stage of his career. In the late 1950s as director of Jordanian Radio (there was no TV in Jordan then) he waged the no-holds-barred counter-attack in the propaganda war with Abdel Nasser's United Arab Republic (the union between Egypt and Syria from 1958 to 1961), earning himself the reputation both as a staunch anti-Nasserist and as one of the "strong-men" of the Jordanian political scene. As prime minister for the first time in 1962–1963, he continued the vitriolic war of words with Abdel Nasser, never missing an opportunity to reply in kind to Egypt's unabated anti-Jordanian policies and rhetoric.

In his second term as prime minister (1965–1967) he resumed the on-going battle with Abdel Nasser from where he had left off, but now the confrontation with Egypt was coupled with Jordan's struggle against the newly established PLO under the leadership of its first chairman, Ahmad al-Shuqayri. In the eyes of many, at the time, Shuqayri was seen, somewhat unfairly, as no more than a pawn of Abdel Nasser. But allies they certainly were, in common cause against Jordan. Their objective was to coerce the Jordanians to allow the PLO to operate freely among Jordan's large Palestinian population, which was no less than two-thirds of the total, when Jordan controlled the West Bank. The Jordanians, naturally, refused. They were deeply concerned that such a concession would seriously undermine Jordan's stability and might even subvert its long-term survivability.

Wasfi al-Tall was a hard-nosed realist, almost always rational and instinctively opposed to the sloganeering that was so often employed "to deceive the Arab masses."[9] In the summer of 1967 he was no longer prime minister, but as chief of the Royal Court he was still a member of that small coterie of intimate advisors to the king. When the crisis between Egypt and Israel broke in May, he desperately tried to convince Husayn not to join Abdel Nasser's bandwagon. He begged Husayn to stay out of the war. Egypt could not be trusted, he argued, and Jordan had everything to lose. Tall, a man of his convictions, even suggested to Husayn that he be returned to the premiership to bear full responsibility for this momentous decision, whatever the consequences. But Tall was entirely alone, a voice in the wilderness.[10] Husayn decided otherwise. After the calamitous defeat it was not Husayn, of course, but Abdel Nasser whom Tall blamed for the downfall of the Arabs.

The Architect of Black September

In the aftermath of the 1967 debacle, in Jordan's hour of weakness, the PLO and its armed factions established a kind of "state within a state" in Jordan as part of their strategy of armed struggle against Israel. Slowly but surely, they whittled away at the sovereignty of the state, which began to look like an empty shell. Husayn, seeking to avoid a head-on collision with the guerrillas, constantly gave in to their demands, in a rather feeble display of royal infirmity.[11] Husayn was not standing up for his own. In June 1970 he acceded to PLO demands to remove senior officers, whom the Palestinians distrusted, from the army, even though some of the men in question were the king's own relatives.[12] Not for the first time in the kingdom's history, many from within the country, and more from without, began to treat the monarchy as if its days were numbered. The regime seemed to be losing its will to fight.

Impressions notwithstanding, Husayn's indecision did have sound reasoning. He fully realized that a war with the PLO, which was what a collision meant, could spell the loss of the last vestige of legitimacy for Jordan's historical role in the Palestine question. For Husayn this was not just a matter of dynastic ambition or prestige, but the long-term security of the Hashemite Kingdom, which always would be deeply affected by whatever happened across the river in Palestine.

The problem now, however, was more immediate. It was not about what might happen across the river in the future, but about what was already happening in Amman. Husayn's concessions to the PLO were crippling the East Bank establishment as they eroded Jordanian sovereignty. The very existence of the political order in Jordan seemed to be hanging in the balance. Key figures in the royal family, such as Husayn's mother Zayn, his younger brother Hasan, his uncle Sharif Nasir bin Jamil, his cousin Zayd bin Shakir, and others across the entire spectrum of the East Bank elite, most notably none other than Wasfi al-Tall, rallied behind Husayn.

But they also constantly pressured the king, explaining in no uncertain terms that they thought he had gone too far to avoid confrontation and that he was endangering the existence of the regime. As the political elite pressed the king, there were instances when combat units of the armed forces threatened to move against PLO forces, in defiance of standing orders. It required Husayn's personal intervention to bring his mutinous troops under control, to the dismay of his men, who received him with open hostility. Senior commanders were said to have been considering a coup: "If the Hashemite family would not protect them, they hinted darkly, then it was time for native Transjordanians to rule themselves."[13]

Any more concessions to the PLO to avoid conflict would have left the monarchy without a leg to stand on. The choice was clear. The PLO had to be brought to heel. The state within a state, or as the PLO tended to call it, the "dual power" structure (*izdiwajiyyat al-sulta*) had become intolerable. On September 16, 1970, Husayn announced the formation of a military government that was instructed to restore law and order throughout the country. The prime minister was a virtually unknown brigadier of Palestinian origin by the name of Muhammad Da'ud. There could, however, be no mistake. Da'ud was no more than a figurehead, in office but not in power. It was the king and his most intimate advisors from the royal family and from the East Bank elite (Wasfi al-Tall yet again even though he held no position at the time) who really called the shots.[14] Tall was the only East Banker in this informal inner cabinet who was not a member of the royal family, and it actually was he who was seen by many, Jordanians and Palestinians alike, as the real architect of what became known in the Palestinian national narrative as "Black September." The first round of the civil war in September 1970 culminated in a resounding PLO defeat, and by July 1971 they were forced out of Jordan completely.

Halfway through the fighting in September, Muhammad Da'ud resigned, embarrassed by his association with the merciless suppression of the PLO fighting forces. He was replaced on September 26 by another Palestinian, Ahmed Tuqan, who headed a civilian rather than a military government. Tuqan, like his predecessor, was not really in control. Husayn was maneuvering for appearances, and the new appointments were no more than a provisional stopgap measure to placate Arab public opinion in preparation for the next round. On October 28, Tuqan, who had been stridently denounced by his family in Nablus for cooperating with a regime that was "destroying the Palestinian people,"[15] was replaced by Wasfi al-Tall.

Tall, the archetypal representative of the East Bank elite, had acquired notorious anti-PLO credentials since his earlier confrontation with the fledgling organization when he was prime minister in the mid-1960s. At last there was a complete correlation between the men in office and the men in power.

The death of Abdel Nasser on September 28, 1970, just the day after the signing of the Cairo agreement that had been brokered by the Arab League to put an end to the fighting, made it considerably easier for Husayn to ignore pan-Arab censure. The gloves were off, and Tall's appointment by the king signaled that the Jordanians intended to wage a relentless onslaught against the PLO forces, until the removal of the very last of their positions in Jordan. After September, the guerrillas were no longer capable of offering effective resistance, and an Arab world in disarray after Abdel Nasser's passing was less inclined to interfere.[16]

Though determined to oust the guerrillas, Husayn's approach still remained ambivalent even after the civil war. On the one hand, he was critical of, and no doubt concerned by, the extreme tension between his subjects of Jordanian and Palestinian origin. He decried the "voice of regional clamor," which, he said, "should be smothered forever" in favor of the "unity of our [Jordanian-Palestinian] family" on both banks of the Jordan River.[17] On the other hand, he sought to avoid further alienation of his Palestinian subjects. After all, he still hoped to preserve at least a measure of legitimacy and influence in regard to the ultimate determination of the Palestinians' political destiny. But, at the same time, he himself promoted a concerted effort to reinforce the particular Jordanian loyalty, identity, and sense of belonging.

Tall, as opposed to Husayn, was anything but ambiguous and was determined to see the last of the PLO forces in Jordan forthwith. Tall and many of the generals never liked the Cairo agreement in the first place. While Husayn was still willing to parry with the PLO if only for tactical reasons, the generals were champing at the bit and complaining that they had not been allowed "to finish [the PLO forces] off once and for all." As for Tall, like the generals, he "did not believe in half measures."[18]

Though united in their vision of the endgame, Husayn and Tall had their differences. They differed in style and temperament. Tall, with his outspoken resolve, acerbic tongue, and disdain for his critics, seemed at times to be overshadowing Husayn. The king usually was more inclined toward moderation and compromise. Husayn could see no value in unnecessary provocation. But Tall did not care for appearances, and as he once said of his critics, as far as he was concerned they could go ahead and "pave the sea."[19]

The guerrillas were driven out, stage by stage, town by town, until they were confined to their last stronghold in the wooded hills between the towns of Jarash and Ajlun, north of Amman. In early June, Husayn ordered Tall "to take bold and tough action against the guerrillas." By mid-July 1971, "outnumbered, outgunned and outfought," they finally were defeated, and their Jordanian sanctuary was finished.[20]

The expulsion was ruthlessly executed. As much as Tall was revered by Jordanians for his leadership and determination as a national hero, he was detested by the PLO as the architect of their demise in Jordan. They were bound to exact revenge. In November 1971, while attending an Arab League meeting in Cairo, Tall was gunned down by assassins of the "Black September" secret arm of Fatah. The assassination (which the Jordanians suspected the Egyptian authorities had not done their best to prevent) triggered a wave of anger in Jordan, where Tall was glorified by nationalists as the epitome of Jordanian nationalism. The day of Tall's burial "was a day of bleeding grief in the lives of the Jordanians."[21]

State-Promoted Jordanianism

Jordan's conflict with the Palestinians, and the civil war of 1970–71 in particular, was more than just a struggle for political supremacy. It was a traumatic, formative experience that accelerated the coalescence and consolidation of the divergent group identities of Jordanians and Palestinians alike. It widened the distinctive divide between the communities and endowed both Jordanians and Palestinians with an added sense of national consciousness, fueled by mutual mistrust and acrimony. Jordanianism now was defined more explicitly in contradistinction to the Palestinian ultimate "other."[22] The unification of the East and West Banks in 1950, and the continuous migration of Palestinians to the East Bank that followed, failed to produce the assimilation initially desired by the Jordanians. As a result, the Palestinians were eventually perceived by many Jordanians as a threat to their own political patrimony.

The establishment of the PLO in Jordan after 1967 made the threat more palpable. Thousands of young Palestinian men in Jordan rallied to the PLO cause, swaggering with their guns in public, flouting Jordanian sovereignty, and humiliating ordinary Jordanian men and women in the process. Militant Palestinianism was increasingly perceived by Jordanians as more than just another form of affront to their national esteem. It challenged the political order in which they were masters.

After the defeat of the PLO, in which Tall had played such a key role, the Jordanians "seemed delighted to be back in control of [their] country." A strong sentiment of "defiant East Bank Jordanian nationalism was apparent in government circles."[23] As for the Jordanians at the grassroots level, their gut feeling was that the civil war against the PLO had been their victory over the Palestinians. The army that had routed the PLO forces was the army not only of their country, but also of their siblings, who were its officers and men. They had restored the people's dignity that had been trampled underfoot by the PLO forces until law and order were restored.

A trend emerged among East Bankers agitating for a greater say in the affairs of the homeland that they had so valiantly defended against the PLO. They urged the king to abandon his long-held policy of seeking to represent the Palestinians and actually supported independent Palestinian nationalism, which they surmised would only reinforce the separate Jordanian identity. Thus the gulf between Jordanians and Palestinians on the East Bank "grew wider in the wake of the September showdown," ushering in a "new era in Jordan's nation-building process."[24]

In the wake of the civil war, at the initiative of the Wasfi al-Tall government, many Palestinians were removed from the bureaucracy and the military, thus further reducing their representation in the machinery of state, in a process that became known as Ardanna, or "Jordanization."[25] Leftist Palestinian sources began to refer to a vertical division of the Jordanian-Palestinian body politic, as the regime sought to construct a cohesive Jordanian social power base in contradistinction to Palestinian society in order to fully reassert undeniable East Bank political supremacy.[26] In this process Wasfi al-Tall was at once a key agent and instigator of the Jordanization process and a heroic icon lionized by the national narrative. In the eyes of his compatriots, he represented the "spirit of the people" (*ruh al-sha'b*) as the "devoted son of his country, the true representative of the interests of his fellow-citizens." Tall was a "martyr" (*shahid*), who had made the supreme sacrifice (*istishhad*) for his people.[27]

In later years after Tall's death, the "de-Palestinization process" continued as Palestinians were removed from the public sector, especially from the Foreign Ministry. In the universities, Transjordanians were preferred for faculty appointments as well as for student admissions and scholarships. In the late 1980s and early 1990s, Jordanian nationalist student organizations or clubs were founded by nationalists with government support. They competed with Palestinian student groups on the campuses, nurturing the sense of division among the younger generation.[28] Generally speaking, the spread of literacy and print culture served the dissemination of nationalist sentiment among the expanding circles of educated Jordanian men and women,[29] graduates of the schools and ever-increasing number of universities and colleges, whether from urban, rural, or tribal backgrounds.

The "East Bank First" School: Adherents and Adversaries

For Jordan, as for the PLO, the civil war was the end of an era. The kingdom of the East Bank had been saved from chaos and destruction, thanks in no small measure to the likes of Wasfi al-Tall, and Jordan as a state had given its doubters a lesson to remember on Jordanian staying power and survivability. The "Black September" of the Palestinians was for many Jordanian nationalists the "White September" of their revived political independence.[30]

The securing of the East Bank patrimony, the process of Jordanization, and the development of a coherent Jordanian nationalist sentiment led to the emergence of a so-called "East Bank First" school. Though subdivided into a variety of nuanced trends[31] that cut across all strata of Jordanian East Bank society, the people were united by their sense of Jordanian identity. Yet they differed somewhat on the precise role of the monarchy in the state and the role of the Hashemites in the Jordanian national narrative. The most influential were the so-called "extreme monarchists" (*malikiyyin mutahammisin*), for whom the Hashemite monarchy was an indispensable component of the Jordanian identity.[32]

There were others, especially among the clans and tribes of the East Bank, who similarly professed that the Hashemite monarchy was an essential ingredient of the Transjordanian identity; but their loyalty was not unconditional, nor were their positions on the Palestinians at all congruent with those of the monarchy. In their view, there was an unwritten contract (*bay'a*) between the monarchy and the tribes, who had given their loyalty to the crown in exchange for economic security. The Palestinians in Jordan were foreigners and basically disloyal. After all, Jordanians were Jordanians and Palestinians were Palestinians, and identity was all about blood and tribe.[33]

Then there were those who explicitly placed their loyalty to the Jordanian state above their loyalty to the monarchy and developed a historical narrative accordingly. Their political and intellectual roots were in the ideological left—pan-Arabists, Ba'this, and communists—but in transforming into Jordanian nationalists, they developed a historical narrative according to which a cohesive Transjordanian society had already existed in Ottoman times, in the mid-nineteenth century. They argued that Jordan was ripe for statehood before the arrival of the Hashemites from the Hijaz in the 1920s. Its existence, therefore, was independent of the Hashemites or their regime.

Needless to say, King Husayn and his successor Abdallah II did not share these views, neither on the place of the Hashemites nor on the Palestinians. In their thinking on Jordanianness, which of course they did not oppose, it was imperative to uphold a more inclusive integrationist formula of national unity between original Jordanians and Jordanians of Palestinian origin to avoid domestic tension and to offset possibly destabilizing Palestinian irredentism. The king's efforts to keep the Palestinians of the East Bank within the Jordanian fold gave the Palestinians in Jordan much satisfaction, but they further aggravated the more radical segments of the nationalist East Bank constituency, who firmly believed that integrationist policies would in the end encourage the irredentism that the king and they both sought to prevent.

Therefore, there was a palpable tension between some of the more radical nationalists and the monarchy. Among indigenous Jordanians who sought to generate a tribal, lineage-based nationalism, the Hashemites did not really belong, as they were neither indigenous nor of the tribes. The passions of the more radical nationalists often were inflamed by steps by the government that seemed to them to be too conciliatory to Jordan's citizens of Palestinian extraction. After one such occasion in the mid-1990s, Husayn denounced the "rats [who had] come out of their holes," espousing this "ugly chauvinistic view which [was] very different from what [was] in our hearts and minds." Some writers, again, had gone so far as to suggest that the monarchy itself was in fact foreign to Jordan. Husayn retorted with undisguised contempt and a fair measure of historical justification that Jordan would not have come to much had it not been for the Hashemites.[34]

These more coherent nationalist trends came to fruition in the last quarter of the twentieth century, well after Tall's assassination. One can only surmise what exactly his place would have been among them. His brother Muraywid and Muraywid's son, Tariq, are perhaps an indication of sorts. They both subscribed to a position that placed their loyalty to the state above their loyalty to the crown. Not antimonarchist or anti-Hashemite by any means, Muraywid's attitude toward the monarchy was instrumental. The monarchy was an essential unifying symbol of the Jordanian state, for which there was no substitute. But it was the state to which he owed his ultimate allegiance.[35] The measure of tension that existed between Tall and Husayn, such as about the conduct of the war against the PLO, was a perfect example of this apparent ambiguity. What was important for the state's survival, as understood by Tall and Jordanians like him, could in certain extraordinary circumstances mean that they may be at loggerheads with the king in defense of their political patrimony. But it was not the monarchy that they opposed in principle; on the contrary, it played a crucial role in their scheme of things too.

Regardless of the finer distinctions between the various nationalist trends in Jordan, they all deeply distrusted their Palestinian compatriots. For the nationalists of the East Bank, Transjordan, as the name of the land suggested, was their exclusive patrimony. They were the real *abna' al-balad*, the sons of the country—so much so that in popular Jordanian nationalist parlance, Palestinians were referred to disparagingly as "Belgians" as a way of denoting their complete foreignness.[36]

Latent Jordanian-Palestinian tensions erupted every now and then. In the summer of 1997, a government project to improve living conditions in refugee camps was denounced by the more radical nationalists as permanent refugee resettlement (*tawtin*), which in their minds meant the gradual Palestinization of Jordan, threatening the sovereignty of the Jordanians in their own country.[37] The government explained that the project had nothing to do with the final status of the refugees. Once an agreement with Israel was achieved on the refugee question, it would be up to the refugees in Jordan to freely choose whether they wished to alter their status. But until such time, since they were Jordanian citizens, they were entitled just like their compatriots to enjoy decent living conditions as a civil right.[38] King Abdallah II was compelled to dismiss similar charges in the summer of 2009 when some of the more radical nationalists spread rumors in Amman that Jordan was giving up on the "right of return" of Palestinian refugees.[39]

The strident tones of discord between Jordanians and Palestinians represented the deep divisions between the communities. Soccer matches between Jordan's two major clubs, al-Faysali (East Bank Jordanian) and al-Wahdat (Palestinian) have been for decades the scene of brawls between the Jordanian and Palestinian fans of the two, who have come to personify the two conflicting national sentiments.

But all of that did not mean that Jordanians and Palestinians had no common ground. Tensions aside, the great majority of Jordanians and Palestinians were Arabic-speaking Sunni Muslims, with a small minority of Arab Christians (mainly Orthodox) on both sides. They had much more in common in terms of religion, language, and culture than the divisions implied by their relatively recent territorial identities. Jordanians and Palestinians frequently "intermarried," Muslims with Muslims and Christians with Christians. Religion was a more significant social fault line for many of the common folk than their newly acquired national identity, which tended to fire the imagination of certain segments of the intelligentsia far more than it did for many of the lesser-educated classes. Opinion surveys conducted in the mid-1990s showed that elite opinion leaders were more resolute Jordanian or Palestinian territorial nationalists than was the general public. All the same, almost two-thirds of opinion makers and more than two-thirds of the general public were open to various ideas for Jordanian-Palestinian unity (merger, federation, or confederation) in the future.[40]

The radical nature and the vocal public prominence of the Jordanian nationalists guaranteed that the question of national identity would remain one of the more potentially explosive issues in Jordanian politics. Jordanianism and Palestinianness or Jordanianness and Palestinianism are relatively recent twentieth-century creations. But as the life and times of Wasfi al-Tall should teach us, they are not artificial. On the contrary, they are very real indeed.

NOTES

1. Martin Kramer, ed., *Middle Eastern Lives: The Practice of Biography and Self-Narrative* (Syracuse, NY: Syracuse University Press, 1991), 4–17.

2. E. H. Carr, *What Is History?* (New York: Knopf, 1962), 68.

3. Sulayman Musa, *Ta'rikh al-Urdunn fi al-qarn al-ashrin* [The History of Jordan in the Twentieth Century], vol. 2 (Amman, Jordan: Maktabat al-Muhtassib, 1996), 374.

4. Ali Muhafza, "The Political Thought of Wasfi al-Tall," in *Wasfi al-Tall: Fikruhu wamawakifuhu* [The Thinking and Positions of Wasfi al-Tall], proceedings of a symposium held in Amman in Wasfi al-Tall's memory, Al-markaz al-Urdunni wal-Islami lil-dirasat wal-ma'lumat, Amman, Jordan, 1996, 142.

5. Albert Hourani, *Arabic Thought in the Liberal Age, 1798–1939* (Cambridge: Cambridge University Press, 1984), 309.

6. Asher Susser, *On Both Banks of the Jordan: A Political Biography of Wasfi al-Tall* (London: Frank Cass, 1994), 13, 15–22.

7. Bilal Hasan al-Tall, remarks in *Wasfi al-Tall*, 15.

8. Susser, *On Both Banks of the Jordan*, 36–37, 172–74.

9. Kamal al-Sha'ir, "Wasfi al-Tall: Features of His Personality, Thinking and Positions," in *Wasfi al-Tall*, 102.

10. Nadhir Rashid, "Wasfi al-Tall as I Knew Him," and Hazim Nusayba, "Wasfi al-Tall: The Statesman," in *Wasfi al-Tall*, 71 and 120–21.

11. Yezid Sayigh, *Armed Struggle and the Search for State: The Palestinian Na-*

tional Movement, 1949–1993 (Oxford: Clarendon Press, 1997), 247; James Lunt, *Hussein of Jordan; A Political Biography* (London: Macmillan, 1989), 123–124.

12. Susser, *On Both Banks of the Jordan*, 136.

13. Sayigh, *Armed Struggle and the Search for State*, 260.

14. Ibid., 251–61.

15. Daniel Dishon, ed., *Middle East Record, 1969–70* (Jerusalem: Israel Universities Press, 1977), 868.

16. Susser, *On Both Banks of the Jordan*, 141.

17. Husayn's letter of designation to Ahmad Tuqan as prime minister, Radio Amman, September 26, 1970; Foreign Broadcasting and Information Service, September 28, 1970.

18. Lunt, *Hussein of Jordan*, 147.

19. These were the words he used in answering the domestic critics of his anti-Egyptian policies as prime minister in early 1963. See Sulayman Musa, *A'lam min al-Urdunn: Safahat min ta'rikh al-Arab al-hadith* [Leading Personalities from Jordan: Pages from Modern Arab History] (Amman, Jordan: Matabi' dar al-sha'b, 1986), 128.

20. Lunt, *Hussein of Jordan*, 149.

21. Rashid, "Wasfi al-Tall as I Knew Him," 79.

22. Adnan Abu-Odeh, *Jordanians, Palestinians, and the Hashemite Kingdom in the Middle East Peace Process* (Washington, DC.: US Institute of Peace, 1999), 189.

23. William Quandt, Fuad Jabber, and Ann Mosley Lesch, *The Politics of Palestinian Nationalism* (Berkeley: University of California Press, 1973), 140.

24. Abu-Odeh, *Jordanians, Palestinians*, 191–92, 199.

25. Susser, *On Both Banks of the Jordan*, 156–57.

26. *Al-Hadaf*, December 26, 1970 and *al-Hurriyya*, March 15, 1971, as quoted in Yehoshafat Harkabi, ed., *Arav ve-Yisrael* [The Arabs and Israel], nos. 3–4 (Tel Aviv: Am Oved and the Truman Center, 1975), 166.

27. Samir al-Habashna and Ahmad al-Lawzi, remarks in *Wasfi al-Tall*, 19–21, 25, 28.

28. Abu-Odeh, *Jordanians, Palestinians*, 215.

29. Yoav Alon, *The Making of Jordan: Tribes, Colonialism and the Modern State* (London: Tauris, 2007), 156.

30. Joseph Nevo, "Changing Identities in Jordan," in *Israel, the Hashemites and the Palestinians: The Fateful Triangle*, ed. Efraim Karsh and P. R. Kumaraswamy (London: Frank Cass, 2003), 200.

31. This segment is based largely on Tariq al-Tall, "*Al-Ustura wa-siwa al-fahm fi al-'alaqat al-Urduniyya-al-Filastiniyya*" [Myth and Misunderstanding in Jordanian-Palestinian Relations], *al-Siyasa al-Filastiniyya* 3, no. 12 (fall 1996), 152–65; Abu-Odeh, *Jordanians, Palestinians*, 241–48; Sulayman Nusayrat, *Al-Shakhsiyya al-Urdunniyya: Bayn al-bu'd al-watani wal-bu'd al-qawmi* [Jordanian Identity: Between the National and Pan-Arab Dimensions] (Amman, Jordan: Ministry of Culture, 1996), 408–11.

32. Ahmad 'Ubaydat, comments in "Al-Malaf: Al-'alaqat al-Urdunniyya al-

Filastiniyya: Madiyan wa-hadiran wa-mustaqbalan," *Majallat al-Dirasat al-Filastiniyya*, no. 24 (spring 1995): 93, as quoted in Hillel Frisch, "Fuzzy Nationalism: The Case of Jordan," *Nationalism and Ethnic Politics* 8 (winter 2002): 97.

33. Marc Lynch, *State Interests and Public Spheres: The International Politics of Jordan's Identity* (New York: Columbia University Press, 1999), 111.

34. *Jordan Times*, October 19–20, October 23, November 4, 1995; *Jordan* TV, November 9, 1995; *al-Hayat*, November 11, 1995.

35. Muraywid al-Tall, conversation with the author, Amman, Jordan, June 5, 1997.

36. Abu-Odeh, *Jordanians, Palestinians*, 228, 255, 257.

37. *Jordan Times*, May 17, June 8, June 28, 1997; Lynch, *State Interests and Public Spheres*, 112, 118–19.

38. *Radio Amman*, June 8, December 4, 1997.

39. Asher Susser, *Israel, Jordan and Palestine: The Two-State Imperative* (Waltham, MA: Brandeis University Press), 192.

40. Asher Susser, "The Palestinians in Jordan: Demographic Majority, Political Minority," in *Minorities and the State in the Arab World*, ed. Ofra Bengio and Gabriel Ben-Dor (Boulder, CO: Lynne Rienner, 1999), 105–7; Lynch, *State Interests and Public Spheres*, 129–30, 137.

PART III

Intellectual, Social, and Cultural Spheres

18

Particularism, Exclusivity, and Monopoly

The History of a Talmudic Statement

MOSHE HALBERTAL

In the midst of its discussion on the "Noahite Laws," which prescribe the commandments for non-Jews in Jewish law, the Talmud introduces a bold and disturbing statement: "Reish Lakish also said: A Gentile who keeps a day of rest deserves death, for it is written, 'And a day and a night shall not rest,' and Mar has said: Their prohibition is their death sentence. Rabina said: Even if he rested on a Monday" (Babylonian Talmud, Sanhedrin 58b). Non-Jews, according to Reish Lakish, the sage of the third-century Land of Israel, are prohibited from having a day of rest, and Rabina, the Babylonian sage of the fifth century, explicated the statement in such a way that the prohibition applies to any day of the week, not only Sunday or the Sabbath itself. What could be the rationale for such a ruling, and what does it entail in terms of the possible religious life of gentiles as imagined by these Talmudic authorities? How do we understand the way in which the prohibition was extended from Reish Lakish's statement to that of Rabina, and in what possible context were such statements embedded? This ruling, which appears only once in the Babylonian Talmud, reflects a capsule of time within a long and complex history that preceded it and followed it. Analyzing the past textual and historical background of this short statement and its subsequent interpretation among the greatest medieval scholars — Rashi and Maimonides — will shed light on a complex and troubled history of rabbinic attitudes toward non-Jews and their religious life, and the ways in which such attitudes responded to internal developments within Christianity and Islam.

A diametrically opposite view of gentiles who observe the Sabbath appears in one of the biblical visions of Judaism as an all-inclusive religion articulated in the prophetic words of second Isaiah:

> Thus said the Lord: Observe what is right and do what is just; for soon My salvation shall come, and My deliverance be revealed. Happy is the man who does this, the man who holds fast to it: who keeps the Sabbath and does not profane it, and stays his hand from doing any evil. Let not the foreigner say, who has attached himself to the Lord, "The Lord will keep me apart from His people" . . . As for the foreigners who attach themselves to the Lord, to minister to Him, and to love the name of the Lord, to be His servants—all who keep the Sabbath and do not profane it, and who hold fast to My covenant—I will bring them to My sacred mount and let them rejoice in My house of prayer. Their burnt offerings and sacrifices shall be welcome on My altar; for My house shall be called a house of prayer for all peoples. (Isaiah 56, 1–7)

The call to keep the Sabbath is addressed to humanity at large in these verses, and the Prophet warns against a false exclusivist understanding of God's word as if it were directed only to Israel, His people, which might discourage the foreigner. It is important to stress that the Prophet does not call for a full conversion to Judaism, as at this stage a formal process of conversion is not a recognized institution.[1] The foreigners who are not part of the people of Israel should not perceive themselves as separated and thus incapable of an intimate bond with God; they are called upon to keep the Sabbath and do what is right, since they, like Israel, are desired and received by God.

The verses serve as witness that indeed such a phenomenon of non-Jews who kept the Sabbath had occurred as a result of the encounter with the exilic community in Babylon,[2] and we have rather solid and extensive evidence of the continuity of Sabbath observance among gentile sympathizers of Judaism all through the Second Temple period.[3] An inclusive understanding of Torah, which resisted the idea that non-Jews form a separate spiritual entity deprived of sharing in the life of Torah unless they become full-fledged Jews, continued to exist within rabbinic sources following the spirit expressed by second Isaiah.[4]

The countervoice concerning gentiles and the Sabbath, which I think is the earlier source of the statement in the Babylonian Talmud, is quoted in the Midrash:

> Rabbi Yossi son of Hanina said: A heathen who observes the Shabbat, before he accepted upon himself to circumcise, deserves death, since they are not commanded upon it. And what made you say that a heathen who keeps the Sabbath deserves death? Rabbi Hiyya the son of Aba said: it is the way of the world that when a king and his maiden sit and talk with one another whoever comes and inserts himself between them would he not deserve death? This is the case with the Sabbath between Israel and God, since it is said "It [the Sabbath] shall be a sign of all time between Me and the children of Israel," therefore every heathen who comes and inserts himself between them before accepting to circumcise deserves death. (Deuteronomy Rabba 1, 21)

According to this text, the gentile who observes Shabbat challenges the exclusive covenantal bond between God and Israel that is expressed in the monopoly of Israel over the Sabbath. He is like the man who tries to seduce the king's lover, and he deserves death. The harsh stress on exclusivity seems to be grounded in a polemic directed against the early Christian community that observed the Sabbath while its members rejected circumcision and a full-fledged conversion to Judaism. With the emergence of Christianity, the attitude toward gentiles who observe the Sabbath was transformed, since such an observance meant that God had deserted the old covenant, and replaced Israel with the Church. The early Christian community thus had inserted itself between Israel and God. The past sympathizers became competitors, and some rabbinic voices responded in line with this change.[5] Paradoxically, this same group of Christians who kept the Sabbath were denounced as "Judaizers" by the Church when it established Sunday rather than the Sabbath as its sacred day.

This polemic assertion of exclusivity in the Midrash seems to be the source of the statement in the Babylonian Talmud, and the manner in which it is restated in the Talmud can teach us a great deal about the ways traditions are changed and transformed when they are planted in different contexts and acquire a radically different meaning.[6] A close reading of the statement in the Midrash in comparison with its parallel in the Talmud is worth pursuing; it reveals what seem to be three minor changes, yet collectively they radically impact the meaning of the prohibition and its scope.

The first change relates to the use of the term "Shabbat" in both sources. In the Midrash the prohibition is formulated in the following manner: "Rabbi Yossi bar Hanina, A heathen who observes the Shabbat, before he accepted upon himself to circumcise, deserves death." In this statement the Hebrew word "Shabbat" designates a noun; it refers to the day of Shabbat שומר את השבת. Whereas, in the statement of Reish Lakish in the Babylonian Talmud, the noun "Shabbat" turns into a verb גוי ששבת, and it means a non-Jew who rested or had a day of rest. This slight change in formulation, from a noun to a verb, allows for the extension made by Rabina, that the prohibition as formulated by Reish Lakish also refers to resting on any day of the week such as Monday and not only to the day of Shabbat.

The second difference between the two sources relates to the biblical proof text that is quoted to support the prohibition. In the Midrash the proof text is the verse in Exodus 32.17 — "It [the Sabbath] shall be a sign of all time between Me and the children of Israel" — which proclaims the day of Sabbath as a unique covenantal sign between Israel and God. In the Babylonian Talmud the proof text is from a completely different source — Genesis 8.22: "So long as the earth endures, seed time and harvest, cold and heat, summer and winter, day and night shall not cease." This verse articulates God's promise after the flood that the world will endure forever. The verse's application to the prohibition of a day of rest to gentiles in the Talmud is a creative stretch of its meaning, since it refers to the continuity of nature and the cosmos rather than the obligation of ongoing human work.[7]

The change of the proof text in the Talmud is in line with Rabina's extension of the prohibition of the gentile on keeping the day of Shabbat to the general prohibition on having a day of rest.[8] In the Midrash the concern is focused on the fact that gentiles are proclaiming the day of Shabbat to themselves, thus taking it away from the exclusive ownership of Israel and replacing the old Israel with the new Church. The verse from Genesis shifts the concern to the very idea of allowing rest altogether, which seems to be threatening, since it fosters idleness which is socially dangerous.

The third difference between the statement in the Midrash and its Talmudic rephrasing is in the shift from the concrete way in which the gentile is described in the Midrash, "A heathen who observes the Shabbat, before he accepted upon himself to circumcise," to the generalized term in the Babylonian Talmud, "a gentile." The more nuanced description in the Midrash is targeted against the emerging early Christian community, which rejected circumcision as the external sign of the covenant in the flesh and replaced it with a different covenantal structure. According to the Midrash, a non-Jew who has committed himself to circumcision is allowed to observe the Sabbath while in the process of converting, even before circumcision, because in such a case he is observing the Sabbath as part of Israel rather than as a substitute for Israel.

The three differences between the Midrashic source and its restatement in the Babylonian Talmud serve as a classic example of the ways in which traditions are transformed and radically reinterpreted when they travel across time to a different context. In the Midrash the emerging prohibition on a gentile's keeping of the day of Shabbat is attached to an anti-Christian polemic. This polemic is manifested clearly in the fact that the gentile is the one who resists circumcision, and that his proclaiming the day of Sabbath without circumcision is a way of expressing a direct challenge to the particular bond between Israel and God as manifested in the proof text from the verse in Exodus. The possible inclusive attitude expressed in Isaiah is undermined by the trauma of competition that occurred with the emergence of Christianity and the polemic entanglement that shifted to closure and exclusivity.[9] In fifth-century Babylon that polemical background lost its edge, since the challenging presence of Christianity felt in the third-century Land of Israel didn't exist in Babylon. The prohibition was subtly restated and has taken on a different range and meaning altogether.[10] It is no longer directed toward a community that observes the day of Shabbat. The word "shabbat" comes to mean a verb rather than a noun, and the proof text is brought from Genesis rather than Exodus, which shifts the concern from polemical anxiety directed toward Christianity to a worry about the possibility of idleness and its impact.[11]

Rashi, in his commentary on the passage in the Talmud, captured the full meaning of Rabina's reformulation:

> "Rabina said even if he rested on a Monday": You should not say that
> the rest that Reish Lakish has prohibited is for the sake of religious
> obligation, in which the gentile intends to [religiously] observe, such
> as during the day of Shabbat which is a day of rest for Israel or Sun-
> day which is [for the Christians] a day of rest. But rather, Reish Lak-
> ish has prohibited rest in general, meaning that gentiles should not
> avoid work even on a day which is not religiously observed. Rabina
> mentioned Monday because it is the first day during the week which
> is not religiously observed. He could have mentioned as well Tuesday
> and Wednesday. (Rashi, Sanhedrin 58b)

According to Rashi, the extension of the prohibition to Monday and the
rest of the week in Rabina's statement meant more than merely casting the
net to include all the days of the week. Rabina's statement had redirected
the meaning of the practice of rest as such, making it independent of a
religious and communal ritual of rest. Following Rabina, rest is prohibited
to any individual non-Jew on any day. Rashi unraveled correctly that Rabina did not aim to prohibit a religious expression that is structured in a
similar way to the Jewish Shabbat, but rather he aimed at prohibiting rest
as such. Rashi's reading seems to capture the full depth of the implications
of Rabina's statement and it follows the proof text from Genesis well, as
understood by the Talmud.

Maimonides offered a totally different reading for this Talmudic passage than Rashi, which shifts dramatically the nature of the prohibition
and its meaning:

> Similarly, a gentile who rests, even on a weekday, observing that day
> as a Sabbath, is obligated to die. Needless to say, he is obligated for
> that punishment if he creates a festival for himself.
>
> The general principle governing these matters is: They are not
> to be allowed to innovate a religion and create *mitzvot* (command-
> ments) for themselves based on their own decisions. They either
> may become righteous converts and accept all the *mitzvot*, or they
> may retain their commandments without adding or detracting from
> them.
>
> If a gentile studies the Torah, makes a Sabbath, or innovates any
> religious practice, a [Jewish court] should beat him, punish him,

and inform him that he is obligated to die. However, he is not to be executed.

We should not prevent a gentile who desires to perform one of the Torah's commandments in order to receive a reward for doing so, provided he performs it as required. If he brings an animal to be sacrificed as a burnt offering, we should receive it. If he gives charity, we should accept it from him. (Laws of Kings Wars 10.9–10)

From the Talmudic statement of prohibiting rest, Maimonides derives a general principle that dramatically transforms its meaning. The prohibition on rest is read by Maimonides as an example of a larger principle that prohibits a non-Jew from having a separate religion and an independent religious life. A gentile, according to Maimonides, can either observe the Noahite Commandments as ascribed to him by Jewish Law, or he can become a full-fledged convert to Judaism; he cannot establish his own religious rituals and way of life. His religious life ought to be exclusively defined by the terms of Judaism.

Needless to say, this reading is not a straightforward restatement of the Talmud. The Talmud seems to focus particularly on the problem of rest and Sabbath. Its proof text shows a concern with ceasing ongoing work. In that respect Rashi has captured the focus of the Talmud in a deep way by claiming that Rabina's statement—that the prohibition applies to any day in the week—extracted the prohibition from the question of religious life altogether. What is prohibited is rest or idleness with no religious intention. Maimonides, in contrast to Rashi, claimed that resting in general was not prohibited, and unlike Rashi he ruled that a gentile is not prohibited from having a day of rest as such; what was prohibited is a new form of religion.

Maimonides' ruling is unprecedented in understanding the Talmudic text, and it has far-reaching implications on the status of the gentile's religious life. According to Maimonides, in the Jewish polis under Jewish control, no other religion including Islam and Christianity is allowed to exist. Non-Jews are prohibited from having their own religion, and a Jewish court, if it has power, is obligated to enforce it. Their religious life is completely defined by the Jewish framework. They can stay as Noahites keeping the commandments that non-Jews have to observe according to

Jewish law or can become converts; they also can voluntarily adopt Jewish commandments and practice them even if they do not convert.[12] In fulfilling such commandments voluntarily, they might be rewarded, but such practices are allowed as long as they are performed properly within the context of practices of Torah rather than as part of an independent other religion. What is crucial is that the Jewish polis according to Maimonides does not tolerate any other claim of religious authority and established religious practices other than Judaism.

Given that Maimonides' reading has no precedent in the tradition, and given that it diverts dramatically from the straightforward meaning of the Talmud, which, as Rashi explained it, concentrated only on rest rather than on newly formed religious practices, Maimonides' reading calls for an explanation. In its implications on the question of religious pluralism it is troubling. Maimonides not only rejected the pluralist idea that other forms of religious life have intrinsic value, but according to him their very existence is prohibited. Not only is Judaism a particularistic religion, it is the exclusive religion. It does not only monopolize the Shabbat as a unique covenantal sign, the way the Midrash wished to ascertain in its version of the prohibition, but rather it monopolizes the whole field of religious life altogether. It is true that this idea of monopolizing only the day of Shabbat was rejected by Rabina's extension of the prohibition to include all days, but Maimonides had two other alternatives to follow: either that the Talmud prohibited resting in general the way Rashi understood it, or that Rabina prohibited a particular form of worship which resembles Shabbat even when it is done on any other day.[13] Instead of these two more plausible readings, Maimonides opted for the largest possible extension in which the Talmud aims at prohibiting religious life in general, and the Sabbath served as a mere example.

The background of Maimonides' unique ruling was the complex and paradoxical impact of Islam on him as a philosopher and a legal authority. Maimonides owed a great deal to Islamic philosophers, a fact that he openly and happily mentioned in his own writings. In his letter addressed to Samuel ibn Tibbon, the translator of the *Guide of the Perplexed* to Hebrew, that deals with the recommended curriculum, Maimonides described the importance of Aristotle and his Islamic interpreters in the following manner:

Generally, I would advise you to study only the works of logic composed by the scholar Abu Nasr al-Farabi, for everything he has written, especially the *Principle of Existing Things*, is like fine flour. . . . Similarly, Ibn Bajja (Abu Bakr ibn-Sa'igh) was a great philosopher. All his writings are lucid to one who understands, and correct to those that find knowledge.

The works of Aristotle are the basis of all these philosophical books. . . . For Aristotle reached the highest level of knowledge to which man can ascend, with the exception of one who experiences the emanation of the Divine Spirit, who can retain the degree of prophecy above which there is no higher stage. (*Letters of Maimonides*, 136)

Besides his words of praise for al-Farabi and ibn Bajja and his admiration for Aristotle, in that same letter Maimonides recommended his great contemporary Ibn Rushd (Averroës), the qadi of Cordoba, Maimonides' own birthplace. The core of Maimonides' philosophical endeavor concentrated on the encounter between this Greco-Islamic philosophical tradition, which he had internalized, and the Jewish tradition. This immense creative effort also had a deep impact on his legal writings and rulings.

Yet Maimonides' encounter with Islam was not only that of a fruitful and inspiring philosophical dialogue. In his youth Maimonides' family was forced to leave Andalusia and Cordoba as a result of the conquest of Andalusia by a radical Islamic movement, the Almohads. The Almohad conquests led by Abd al-Mu'min destroyed the Jewish communities of Andalusia and the Maghreb. Some Jews died while resisting forced conversion; some accepted Islam under compulsion, continuing to live as Jews in secret; and some fled beyond the reach of the Almohad regime. The Almohad dynasty sought to create a Muslim expanse with no Jews or Christians, rejecting the traditional Muslim view that the "people of the book"—Jews and Christians—were *dhimmi*—entitled to protection. There is a possibility, as some historians maintain, that Maimonides and his family suffered a similar fate in the Maghreb and that Maimonides was required to pretend to have become Muslim; only after moving to Egypt was he again able to be openly Jewish.

Yet with all the harsh experience of Maimonides under the rule of the Almohads, the Almohad movement had a deep impact on Maimonides'

concept of Judaism. Sara Stroumsa, who introduced an important development in the recent study of Maimonides, has shown convincingly that
Maimonides' rulings that anthropomorphic conceptions of God should
be prohibited by law among the masses, insisting on the creation of a
community that adheres to the strict metaphysical conception of divine
unity, had been influenced by the Almohad movement.[14] The Almohads,
unlike all other previous Islamic trends, insisted on turning the philosophical concept of unity, which had been the belief of the elite, into a
dogma that must be upheld by the masses. In the sphere of law, the Almohads also engaged in an unprecedented attempt to codify and unify all the
diverse legal traditions of Islam, an attempt that Maimonides followed in
the Jewish sphere with his great code *Mishneh Torah*.

Maimonides' ruling concerning the status of the religious life of non-
Jews was yet another surprising example of the impact that the Almohads
had on his legal rulings and his concept of political and religious authority. Maimonides' political theory was deeply influenced by al-Farabi and
other Islamic thinkers. His diverse rulings in the *Mishneh Torah* show the
signs of such influence. Maimonides perceived the role of the Jewish ideal
monarch as someone who aims to enforce the seven Noahite commandments on all the inhabitants of the world. Such a universal mission is very
much in line with the Islamic concept of the political universal obligation
of the Muslim ruler. Yet within the Islamic universal aspiration of enforc-
ing monotheism, there was always a place for the independent Jewish
community that is protected under Islamic rule. The only movement in
Islam which denied such a status was that of the Almohads. The Almohads therefore engaged in an attempt at forced conversions of Christians
and Jews that diverted from the common policy of Islam. Maimonides'
unprecedented extension of the prohibition on rest to include a general
prohibition on the existence of any religion outside Judaism follows the
ruling of the Almohads. In the independent Jewish region, according to
Maimonides, all religious life will be governed exclusively by Judaism, and
the non-Jews cannot establish any religion of their own. No other halakhic authority ever made such a statement before Maimonides, and as
we saw, it is rather an improbable reading of the Talmudic source itself.
This creative and troubling ruling had its source in Maimonides' political
theory, which in this case was inspired by the Almohads. The paradoxical

nature of this particular process is that according to Maimonides' view, shaped by Islamic influence, Islam as an independent religion cannot exist within a Jewish polis.

Maimonides therefore accepted the Almohad position that one religion must be the exclusive source of authority within a political structure and it cannot tolerate another independent religion. In the case of the Almohads, it had to be Islam, and in Maimonides' view, the exclusive role should be relegated to Judaism. The exclusivity of Islam and the exclusivity of Judaism might take a different form, since Islam as a universal religion does not recognize a basic legal structure that obligates everyone to adhere to its tenets apart from becoming full-fledged Muslims. This fact meant that if no other independent religion was allowed within the Muslim sovereign sphere, everyone must be forced to convert to Islam. In the case of Judaism, full-fledged conversion is not necessary, and according to Maimonides, non-Jews can maintain the basic structure of observing the Noahite commandments or convert to Judaism.

Such an intolerant ruling, drawn from the Almohad experience and influence, which is completely uncalled for by the authoritative background of the Talmudic sources, manifests a deep and paradoxical element in Maimonides' thought, which blends an open-mindedness with political authoritarianism and conservativism. In terms of Maimonides' own philosophical commitments, Judaism does not monopolize the possibilities of attaining spiritual and religious perfection. The opening line of his treatment of prophecy in the *Mishneh Torah* starts with the claim of the universal possibility of achieving prophecy: "It is one of the basic principles of religion that God causes human beings to prophesize." Unlike Judah Ha-Levi, who made the claim that prophecy can be achieved only by Jews, Maimonides was careful in insisting that all human beings can achieve prophecy, the highest form of religious and human perfection. According to Maimonides, the achievement of prophecy is an outcome of adopting a way of life devoted to spiritual quest:

But the spirit of prophecy only rests upon the wise man who is distinguished by great wisdom and strong moral character, whose passions never overcome him in anything whatsoever, but who by his rational faculty always has his passions under control, and possesses a broad

and sedate mind. When one, abundantly endowed with these qualities and physically sound, enters the Pardes, and continuously dwells
upon those great and abstruse themes—having the right mind capable of comprehending and grasping them; sanctifying himself,
withdrawing from the ways of the ordinary run of men who walk in
the obscurities of the times, zealously training himself not to have a
single thought of the vanities of the age and its intrigues, but keeping his mind disengaged, concentrated on higher things as though
bound beneath the Celestial Throne, so as to comprehend the pure
and holy forms and contemplating the wisdom of God as displayed
in His creatures, from the first form to the very center of the Earth,
learning thence to realize His greatness—on such a man the Holy
Spirit will immediately descend. And when the spirit rests upon him,
his soul will mingle with the angels called *Ishim*. He will be changed
into another man and will realize that he is not the same as he had
been, and has been exalted above other wise men.

In Maimonides' description, the spiritual path leading to the highest
religious achievement does not involve anything that is particular to the
Jewish way of life and its commandments; it rather elaborately described
the path to prophecy in general human terms that are in line with philosophical religious conceptions of perfection. This same conviction that
the road to religious perfection is open to all human beings also was articulated in Maimonides' last rulings of laws of the Sabbatical year:

Not only the tribe of Levi, but any one of the inhabitants of the world
whose spirit generously motivates him and he understands with his
wisdom to set himself aside and stand before God to serve Him and
minister to Him and to know God, proceeding justly as God made
him, removing from his neck the yoke of the many reckonings which
people seek, he is sanctified as holy of holies. God will be his portion
and heritage forever and will provide what is sufficient for him in
this world like He provides for the priests and the Levites. And thus
David declared: "God is the lot of my portion; You are my cup, You
support my lot." (Psalms 16.5)

Like his description of prophetic achievement, the total devotion to
God—and becoming God's portion and heritage in terminology that is

reminiscent of Isaiah's words—is independent of any particular elements of Jewish law and practice and open to all the inhabitants of the world. Thus, Maimonides' ruling that under Jewish sovereignty no other religion should be tolerated was not based on the principled claim that religious meaning can be found only through and within Torah. Rather, it was grounded in the political assumption that in the sovereign Jewish state the authority of Torah among the people could survive only when it was not challenged by any other recognized religions.[15] The prohibition on the existence of other religious life was based on political considerations rather than on a metaphysical assertion.

In one of the most important moments in the history of religious toleration, Moses Mendelssohn, in his defense of Judaism, introduced the advantage of particularism over universalism. A universal religion such as Christianity, though it addresses itself to the whole of humanity, is liable to deprive all other religions of significance. Christianity's claim that it is the only road to salvation also prepared the ground for a paternalistic and brutal enforcement of its own creed on non-Christians. The lofty idea of universalism easily can turn into a monstrous, coercive tool. Particularism is freed of that problem, and Judaism, being a particularistic religion, allows for the free and tolerant expression of other forms of religious life, each endowed with its own significance and value. In its universal dimension, according to Mendelssohn, Judaism demands what can be gained by human reason without obligation to a particular form of life as a condition for salvation. Mendelssohn's great innovative philosophical contribution was to uncover the problems that are inherent in the universal claim and the advantages of particularism. As an interpreter of Judaism he has cast it in a most tolerant light, an interpretation that appeals to the modern Jew who seeks loyalty to the particular Jewish form of life and adheres to the basic values of pluralism and toleration.

The study of the history of the Talmudic statement prohibiting a non-Jew from a day of rest, its prior origins in the Midrash, and its subsequent medieval interpretation by Maimonides, shows the complex ways in which a statement travels through time, transformed and reinterpreted when it is planted in different historical and cultural contexts. The disturbing history of that statement also reveals two structural dangers that are inherent to the idea of particularism, that of monopoly and exclusivity.

A particularist way of life turns into monopoly when it prohibits others from sharing its values and achievements in order to signify uniqueness; such a turn was at the heart of the midrashic reading constituting the monopoly of Jews over the day of Sabbath. A particularist tradition also can turn into an intolerant exclusivity when it demands that others define themselves solely in its terms, as Maimonides developed the meaning of the Talmudic statement. In the case of Jewish particularism, these two inherent dangers developed in ways that are inextricable from the response at different moments of the interpretive chain to the cultural and political context in which the tradition was embedded. The Midrash shifted from the inclusive picture of second Isaiah to monopoly in response to Christianity, and Maimonides internalized the exclusivist approach of his oppressors—the Almohads—into his own political authoritarian worldview.

NOTES

1. See Y. Kaufman, *From the Furnace of Biblical Innovation* (in Hebrew) (Tel Aviv: 1966), 126, and J. Levenson, "The Universal Horizon of Biblical Particularism" in *Ethnicity in the Bible* ed. M. Brett (Leiden: Brill, 1996), 162–63.

2. See M. Weinfeld, "The Universalist Trend and the Separatist Trend in the Epoch of the Return to Zion" (in Hebrew), *Tarbitz* 3 (1964): 228–42.

3. Regarding gentiles observing the Sabbath, see Flavius Josephus, *Against Apion*, trans. and comm. by John M. G. Barclay, vol. 2 (Leiden: Brill, 2006), 282, and the citations mentioned there by Barclay from Eusebius, *Preparation of the Gospel* 13.12.11–16; Philo, *Life of Moses* 2.21–22; Philo, *On the Creation* 90–127. For a discussion of this phenomenon, see as well L. H. Feldman, *Jew and Gentile in the Ancient World*, (Princeton: Princeton University Press, 1996), 352, 356, 375.

4. M. Hirshman, *Torah for the Whole World: The Universalist Trend in Rabbinic Literature* (in Hebrew) (Tel-Aviv: Ha-Kibbutz ha-Me'uchad, 1999).

5. On the theme of the exclusive relation of the Sabbath to Israel, see Mekhilta de-Rabi Ishmael, Massekhta de-Shabbeta 1, "[B]etween Me and Israel and not between me and the nations of the world."

6. Deuteronomy Rabbah was edited in the sixth century, thus not earlier than the Babylonian Talmud, but it contains earlier materials. From the literary analysis that follows, it seems that it was the source of the statement in the Babylonian Talmud in Sanhedrin. Rabbi Yossi bar Hanina, who is the author of the statement in the Midrash, was of the same generation as Reish Lakish, who is the author of the statement in the Babylonian Talmud.

7. The imaginative reading uses the fact that the verse in Genesis employs the verb לא ישבותו to designate that the world's continuity will not cease, which associates with the verb of rest. The proof text also reveals the tendency to correlate the distinction between the group and the others with the distinction between civilization and nature. The others in essence are part of the natural world and not fully capable of transcending it.

8. The Midrash Exodus Rabbah, which was edited much later than the Babylonian Talmud and Deuteronomy Rabbah, presents an artificial combination of both sources and presents both proof texts side by side; see Shemot Rabbah, 25, 11.

9. In the liturgy of the Sabbath, the unique relationship between Israel and the Sabbath is articulated as well: "And You did not give it, Lord our God, unto the nations of other lands, nor did You, our King, make it the heritage of worshipers of idols, nor do the uncircumcised dwell in its rest; but to your people Israel You gave it in love, unto the seed of Jacob whom You choose." This passage follows the Midrash rather than the Talmud, and it originated in the liturgy of the Land of Israel. On the early evidence of its source in the Land of Israel, see E. Fleisher, *Kovetz al-Yad* 13 (1966): 152.

10. The difference between the meaning of the prohibition in the Midrash and the Talmud was pointed out without reference to the historical background and transformation by E. Adler, "The Sabbath Observing Gentile," *Tradition* 36, no. 2 (Fall 2002): 15–19.

11. Later medieval interpreters of the Talmud had to struggle with the fact that the rabbinic prohibition on gentiles observing the Shabbat as articulated both in the Midrash and the Talmud is in contradiction to the biblical commandment that the Sabbath also is aimed for allowing rest for the slave and the resident alien in the midst of the people of Israel, as stated in Deuteronomy 5:13. See, for example, Nahmanides' comment in *Hidushei ha-Ramban*, Yevamot 48b and the Rashba there as well.

12. On Maimonides' position, see also J. Blidstein, "On the Legitimacy of Non-Jewish Ritual in Maimonides and Meiri" (in Hebrew), *Da'at* 61 (2007): 41–47.

13. This interpretation of the Talmud was offered by Meiri in his commentary on Sanhedrin. On Meiri's position, see Blidstein's analysis in footnote 12.

14. On the Almohad's impact on Maimonides, see S. Stroumsa, *Maimonides in His World: Portrait of a Mediterranean Thinker* (Princeton: Princeton University Press, 2009), 53–83.

15. As pointed out by Jacob Blidstein, Maimonides' prohibition on non-Jews adding religious practices outside of Torah is structurally similar to his understanding of the prohibition on Jews to add or subtract any commandment. This prohibition also is grounded upon a political consideration concerning the necessary conditions for the authority of the law, rather than on metaphysical assumptions concerning the eternity of the stable law. See my discussion of Maimonides' concept of the stability and eternity of Torah in "The Book of Commandments and Maimonides' Architecture of Halakhah" (in Hebrew), *Tarbitz* 59 (1990): 457–80.

19

"The Individual in Jewish History"

A Feminist Perspective

SHULAMIT REINHARZ

In this essay, I begin with the proposition that the *Festschrift*'s title, "The Individual in History," is likely to conjure an image of a man,[1] even though the editors may have chosen the word "individual" deliberately in order to adopt a gender-neutral stance. While the phrase "The Individual in History" successfully avoids using a specifically male pronoun, the choice of the generic word "individual" hides the fact that we might be talking about a woman. To indicate both females and males, one cannot use generics. One needs to use "women and men" or something similar.

Feminist linguists have demonstrated that "man" is understood as "man" and not as "all people." To the listener or reader, "man" does not conjure up "man and woman." "Man" is not a gender-neutral word. Thus, the Great Man Theory of History is understood as meaning the Great *Male* Theory of History. As sociologist Sherryl Kleinman wrote, "Male-based generics are an indicator—and more important, a reinforcer—of a system in which 'man' in the abstract and men in the flesh are privileged over women."[2] At this stage in human history with patriarchy still a dominant cultural force, we must use the word "women" if we want to be certain that the reader or listener realizes we are including them.

It is understandable, given women's experience and their own perceptions of their lives, that only a small number of Jewish women have risen to a level of such perceived significance that they would be studied within the context of "The Individual in Jewish History." "The Great Woman Theory of Jewish History," or even "The Individual Woman in Jewish

History," is a project worth undertaking and not yet fully begun although Moshe Shalvi published a CD-ROM encyclopedia on the topic of Jewish women. Other (usually coffee-table) books exist that highlight a selection of such women.[3] Many historical studies have been written about a particular issue related to Jewish women. And yet, those Jewish women who have been made great by historians and by virtue of their position are not numerous.

Relatively few women are mentioned in the Bible by name, and when they do appear, their story frequently focuses on their reproductive role,[4] suggesting that most were rarely in the forefront of public life. There are obvious exceptions to this generalization, including the Matriarchs Sarah, Rebecca, Rachel, and Leah.[5] Other women with public roles include Miriam the prophetess, Deborah the judge, Zipporah the circumciser, Yael, Esther, Ruth, and Naomi. In later periods we have Bruriah, the Talmudic scholar who was humiliated; Doña Beatriz de Luna, or Gracia Nasi, the wealthy merchant; Glückel of Hameln, the German merchant and diarist; the American educator Rebecca Gratz; the American Henrietta Szold, who founded Hadassah, the Women's Zionist Organization of America; Bertha Pappenheim, the European social reformer; the American poet Emma Lazarus; and a few women from Israel, particularly the parachutist Hannah Senesh, the poet Rachel, and Prime Minister Golda Meir. Writings about these women focus less on their impact on Jewish history and more on what Judaism has meant to them, or why they became prominent in contrast to the vast majority of women.

Writing about the "individual in Jewish history" provides an opportunity to think about why the list of women we could consider is short and what names should be added. This topic is immense. In order to keep it manageable, I have chosen three foci taken from feminist theory: the problem of archives; the problem of greatness; and the problem of periodization.

The Problem of Archives

Clearly, if we are to try to build an understanding of a historical time period and focus on the individual male or female, we need to have archival material. Herein lie some initial conundrums. In order to have archival material about individuals, there needs to be an understanding at the time of an individual's life that she is sufficiently important for someone to collect her archives and deposit them somewhere for safekeeping. These materials need to be accepted, catalogued, protected, and preserved. Furthermore, the woman in question needs to engage in activities that lend themselves to becoming archival materials. She needs to understand herself as being an important individual in history, an archive-able person.

In religious Jewish history, women's voices were muted if not silenced altogether. In the synagogues, if they went at all, women were pushed to the back of the hall or to an upstairs balcony where they were screened off from the view of men. Women's skimpy religious education did not include the study of Talmud, and thus they had little to contribute to the evolution of *Halacha*, the foundation of Jewish existence. We do learn about Jewish women from newspapers in which they place pleas, which sometimes they wrote themselves, asking for help in finding their absconding husbands so that the women can obtain a *get*. We also learn about women from responsa, written by rabbis, commenting on their questions.[6] And from their marriage contracts, birth and death certificates, and court records we can glean some information.

But these kinds of materials usually tell us about the woman in a limited context. The materials do not constitute the makings of a biography, for example. There is a paucity of archival materials about women in general, not only Jewish women, in the pre-modern and modern periods. The history of women is a relatively new field, with professorships being established only in the 1970s in the United States and even later in Israel. In fact, the 1988 conference in Jerusalem, "We Were There Too: Jewish Women and the Foundation of the Jewish State," was hailed as a breakthrough topic and novelty.[7]

Only occasionally do historians endeavor to sketch an "individual in Jewish history" (or any history) without materials being available. Archives and archival policies are critical tools in the profession of historians. And yet, a historian dedicated to the study of a Jewish woman sometimes can and typically must do the painstaking work with no direct archival material. An example is Hilde Spiel's recently published *Fanny von Arnstein: Daughter of the Enlightenment*.[8] "[Fanny] was a social phenomenon which operated by its emanations alone. It is not without reason that we have no letter of hers, and very few documents from her own hand. Her ephemeral figure, her intangible charm, has been preserved only in the mirror of her contemporaries. But the outward form that was hers became her image. It was neither a Prophet nor a wise woman, but a great lady, who became *a symbol of the liberation of women and the emancipation of the Jews* [emphasis added]." How many historians would take on such a task —writing the biography of an individual who left no letters and very few documents—and without this essential material, nevertheless conclude that the subject was important enough to warrant being called "a symbol of the liberation of women and the emancipation of the Jews"? It comes as no surprise that in this case the intrepid biographer was a woman—Hilde Spiel—as was the translator from German to English—Spiel's daughter Christine Shuttleworth.

Not only are there countless cases in which the archival material simply does not exist, but there may also be an incorrect perception that such archives do not exist, thereby cutting off research before it even has begun. For example, when Jehuda Reinharz and I sought documents about the life of Manya Wilbushewitz Shohat, many people actually laughed, telling us that she left no documents and that our pursuit was fruitless. Those who had heard of her said, "She was a wild woman, not a thinker or writer." Two years later, we had gathered so many documents written by or to Manya that the quantity was staggering. We enlisted the help of Israeli Professor Motti Golani to compile a large, one-volume book of selected documents, which did not even include a large group that detailed her life in Russia before she came to Palestine[9] in 1904 at the age of twenty-four.

The problem of women's underrepresentation in archival collections has received some attention. In the United States, the Schlesinger Library, a component of the Radcliffe Institute of Advanced Studies, a nonlending library and archive of material related to American women's lives, has made an important contribution. The Schlesinger Library was created in 1943, a full 167 years after the founding of the United States of America. Thus, for more than a century and a half, there was no specific place to deposit works by women. The Schlesinger Library was established as a consequence of Maud Wood Park donating to Radcliffe her papers relating to her own suffrage activism. Thus, the Schlesinger's opening ceremonies were held on the twenty-third anniversary of the granting of suffrage to the women of the United States through the Nineteenth Amendment. Although the unique holdings of the Schlesinger Library make it possible to begin a study of *American* Jewish women, it does not function this way for European or Israeli women. Moreover, its focus is not on *Jewish* women.[10]

Recently, Israeli television producer and author Yael Nitzan has taken it upon herself to create a "Museum of Israeli Women," which will be located in a building already donated by the Municipality of Haifa. As her promotional materials state, "Although in other countries there are museums documenting the accomplishments of women, Israel, with the world's highest ratio of museums per person, has none dedicated to the women who contributed to the founding of the State of Israel and to its development."[11] The proposed name of the museum is instructive. It is not intended as an Israeli Women's Hall of Fame, but rather, it seems, as a museum of Israeli women in general. Thus, the promotional article mentions Golda Meir, but also the four thousand women in the Jewish Brigade of the British Army, the female physicians in the Yishuv (representing 20 percent of all physicians), and the female dentists who outnumbered male dentists. And much more. Although archival materials about women must be integrated into all the national archives, having a special focused institution is likely to raise consciousness about the holdings of *all* the archives within Israel and about the necessity for contemporary women to deposit their own papers.

A final problem related to archives is that some phenomena of particular relevance to women are not recorded at all, or if they are recorded, they are not noticed. An example is the rape of Jewish women during the Holocaust, the Nazi war against the Jews. Although rape is a tool of almost all wars, there was a common belief that Nazi men did not rape Jewish women because they had incorporated the belief that Jewish women were despicable, and because they were forbidden to have sex with Jews. As early as 1935, the Nuremberg Laws criminalized sexual intercourse between people of different racial backgrounds (Jews were considered a race). Germans found guilty could face incarceration in a concentration camp, while non-Aryans could face the death penalty. The overall theory underlying these laws was *Rassenschande* (racial pollution), or the desire not to damage the purity of the so-called Aryan people. Nevertheless, there is evidence that rapes did take place both in Western and

Eastern Europe, in concentration camp brothels and elsewhere. Women who gave videotaped testimony as part of various projects testified to that effect, but viewers of the tapes overlooked it. Despite protests that the phenomenon did not exist, the Hadassah-Brandeis Institute published Sonja M. Hedgepeth and Rochelle G. Saidel's *Sexual Violence against Jewish Women during the Holocaust*.[12] The evidence the contributors turned to was right before their eyes, but they did not see it because the material did not exist in conventional archival form but rather in oral testimony.

The Problem of Greatness

Contemporary art historian Linda Nochlin made a splash in the field of art history when she posed a biting question, "Why have there been no great women artists?" Her famous 1988 essay—with this question as its title—proposed an answer: "Art is not a free, autonomous activity of a super-endowed individual, 'influenced' by previous artists, and, more vaguely and superficially, by 'social forces,' but rather, the total situation of art making, both in terms of the development of the art maker and in the nature and quality of the work of art itself, occur in a social situation, are integral elements of this social structure, and are mediated and determined by specific and definable social institutions, be they art academies, systems of patronage, mythologies of the divine creator, artist as he-man or social outcast."[13] Nochlin was asserting that a wide array of social forces kept women from becoming recognized artists, and then kept them from being considered "great." If museums did not consider the art produced by women to be "great," then women's art would not be collected, exhibited, and studied, and the women would be written out of history.

Another concern in art history and many other fields is the phenomenon of attributing a woman's work to someone else. Perhaps the most famous example is the Italian Baroque painter Artemisia Gentileschi (1593–1656), today considered "one of the most accomplished painters in the generation after Caravaggio." The description of Artemisia Gentileschi in her Wikipedia entry states, "In an era when female painters were not easily accepted by the artistic community or patrons, she was the first female painter to become a member of the Accademia di Arte del Disegno in Florence. She painted many pictures of strong and suffering women from myth and the Bible—victims, suicides, warriors—and made a speciality of the Judith story." Before extensive research had been completed on Artemisia Gentileschi, many of her paintings were attributed to her father, Orazio Lomi Gentileschi. The uniqueness of her role as a woman painter in the seventeenth century, the fact that her painting instructor raped her, and the lurid details of her (successfully) prosecuting the rapist took a toll on her role as an artist. Feminist art historians have provided evidence that Artemisia was one of the most progressive and expressionist painters of her generation.

An important example of misattribution in *Jewish* history and the history of the Yishuv is the implicit decision by historians to consider the Kibbutz Degania, founded in 1909, to be the first kibbutz. In extensive research about Manya née Wilbushewitz (later Shohat), it is clear that through library and observational research, she conceived the idea that in developing societies, collective structures can provide a solution to the problem of insufficient resources. With this idea in mind, she entered into a contract in 1907 with an individual who could loan her the land on which she could implement her hypothesis. She also recruited a group of women and men to carry out her idea. Per her original agreement with the leader of the men, the "collective" would be disbanded after one year so that the group could take on a different challenge—guarding property. Manya's fellow pioneers understood her ideas and learned that her collective had made a profit (unlike most enterprises at the time) and created a similar collective (with no attention to gender) that has become known as the first kibbutz.[14]

A striking *contemporary* example of misattribution is the case of Jewish woman Rosalind Franklin, who was denied credit for her role in discovering the double-helix structure of DNA. The missing contribution of Dr. Franklin in the book by Nobel Prize winner James Watson, *The Double Helix: A Personal Account of the Discovery of the Structure of DNA* (1968), became a cause célèbre. In 2012, forty-four years after the publication of his previously labeled "painstakingly honest" book, Watson apologized for writing Rosalind Franklin out of history. Franklin did not live to read the apology, having died in 1958. Many people tried to bring her back into history in symbolic ways, including the renaming of a Chicago medical school, which had been a haven for Jewish students barred from other schools by quotas against Jews. The new name is the Rosalind Franklin University of Medicine and Science.

In 1974, when contemporary Jewish American artist Judy Chicago confronted her own ignorance about the existence and accomplishments of individual women in history, she launched an extraordinary project, called *The Dinner Party*, which involved four hundred artists, researchers, and laypeople. Their intention was to present, in an artistic manner, the great women of history. Judy Chicago documented the process of creating *The Dinner Party* in the film *Right Out of History*. The fact that she did not know anything about most of these women distressed her enormously. For many years after this complex and massive work was completed, *The Dinner Party* was warehoused. Very few people were able to view it, review it, or learn from it. It took a feminist philanthropist, Elizabeth A. Sackler, to change this situation by funding the Elizabeth A. Sackler Center for Feminist Art, at the Brooklyn Museum of Art, where *The Dinner Party* is on permanent and respectful display. Without donors committed to underwriting the work of individual women, the work of many talented women remains unknown. In such cases, the individual is simply "written out of history." The record of individual *women* in Jewish history is a long litany of "were it not for." Were it not for Elizabeth Sackler, Judy Chicago's singular work would be a rumor rather than a reality.

The question Linda Nochlin posed regarding great women artists can be asked of women in other fields. Have there been any great women scientists (other than Marie Curie)? Have there been any great musicians or composers? Have women written any operas? Have there been great women athletes? The answers are in: yes, yes, yes, yes, and yes. And yet, because only a few scholars know this answer, the incorrect stereotype of women's limited talent sticks. This stereotype was made painfully public in a statement by the then-president of Harvard University, Larry Summers, who asserted that one reason there are relatively few women in top positions in science may be "issues of intrinsic aptitude."[15] Summers's remark ignited a firestorm because it revealed a self-fulfilling prophecy —women are less talented than men, therefore we should not invest in them and should not expect much from them. Their underrepresentation is justified. Nowadays the public will not tolerate overtly sexist or racist remarks such as those that attribute limitations to race, sex, or ethnicity.

And yet, the intolerance of prejudice may be attributed only to "political correctness" and not to sincere belief. It takes a long time to overturn the sexist history of civilization.

I contend that we must apply Linda Nochlin's question to the concerns of this *Festschrift*. One must underscore that the title implies women and men and then ask, have there been great Jewish women, women who have changed Jewish history? Sometimes the problem is not with women being excluded from the historical records, but rather that those women who *are* included are not identified as Jews. In one small, unpublished research project, I examined books that explain how the contemporary women's movement was founded and developed. I began this project knowing that starting with Betty Friedan, author of *The Feminine Mystique* (1963), and ending with Sheryl Sandberg, the author fifty years later of *Lean In: Women, Work and the Will to Lead*, Jewish women were and are highly overrepresented in the women's movement as theorists and activists. And yet, this fact often is not mentioned.

So too, Jews are overrepresented among the meta-theorists of women's lives, people such as Linda Nochlin, née Weinberg, the woman whose question is addressed in this section, as well as Judy Chicago (née Cohen) and Elizabeth Sackler. The overall contribution of all of these *Jewish* individuals and countless others to the women's movement is not a topic of study. Their *Jewishness* is written out of history. So we have a case of double jeopardy. Individual Jewish women have difficulty being theorized as shapers of Jewish history because writers either do not work to include women and/or because writers do not know or do not see the necessity of not only mentioning that they were Jews, but exploring what impact being Jewish had on their lives and accomplishments.

The Problem of Periodization

Like Linda Nochlin, the late Joan Kelly-Gadol, a prominent historian of the Renaissance (fourteenth to seventeenth century in Europe), similarly asked a question that galvanized feminist scholars' imaginations. Her 1977 essay "Did Women Have a Renaissance?"[16] became famous. Her essay asked if the period generally known as "the Renaissance" had qualities that applied to men and women, or only to men? Was the Renaissance a renaissance in women's lives, or only in men's? If the Renaissance did *not* apply to women, should it be considered to have existed in a general way and should we consider it to be a taken-for-granted period of history? To answer her provocative question, Kelly-Gadol examined women's roles in society during the 1350s to 1530s. Careful study enabled Kelly-Gadol to comment on females' economic and political activities, their sexuality and cultural production, and the gendered division of labor in the Renaissance more broadly. As has been found in many other studies, including Hilde Spiel's biography of Fanny von Arnstein, mentioned previously, social class was a factor in differentiating women — but not completely. "Wives of the nobility during this time were granted more power than peasant wives in regard to economic and political functions, although both classes of woman were still imprisoned (in their own homes) during the Renaissance."[17] Moreover, a woman's physical beauty (with which Fanny von Arnstein was blessed in addition to her wealth) or lack thereof was a sine qua non for access to high society.

We think of the Renaissance as the period when new artistic and literary work flourished. But, as Kelly-Gadol points out, the works of art and literature created during this time "to celebrate life also emphasized female dependency and male domination." Kelly-Gadol shows that bourgeois literature denied female independence of thought and action. She concludes that the Renaissance "set the norm of female dependency on the male figure. Men had to perform productive labor, while women stayed at home to perform reproductive labor such as household duties and the care of children."[18]

We can conclude from Kelly-Gadol's famous essay that not only did women *not* have a Renaissance, but that the liberating influence of the Renaissance on men was paired with an imprisoning influence on the women. The effect of Kelly-Gadol's widely read essay has been an effort to challenge conventional periodization of history and to create new categories that fit women's experience.[19] I predict that this reperiodization will take a long time, given the absence in 2013 of any major commemoration in the United States of the fiftieth anniversary of the birth of the Women's movement in 1963 — in contrast, perhaps, to the extensive and extended commemoration of the fiftieth anniversary of the Civil Rights movement during the same year, the arrival of the Beatles on the American scene, and much more.

If Jewish history takes women seriously, then we have to ask if we need to launch a study of the reperiodization of the past and present. A period must be identified that begins with the ordination of Rabbi Regina Jonas in Germany right before the Nazi rise to power which ultimately took her life in Auschwitz; and the rebirth of women's ordination in 1972, when the American woman, Sally Priesand, became a female rabbi. To be accurate, however, we need to look for examples of Jewish women who took the role of rabbi without being ordained.[20] We have to consider carefully "who is a rabbi?" when setting parameters for the study. This whole effort of renaming needs to be applied to all aspects of history and Jewish history, including the relabeling of the chapters of the Bible. My initial efforts in this domain show how powerful a project this can be. Changing "In the Beginning" (*Bereshit*) to "The Life of Chava," for example, followed by transforming all Biblical chapter titles to include the name of a woman, shifts the male-centric paradigm rooted in the Torah.

Toward a Feminist Theory of History

The writing of history has a history of its own. Types of historical writing as well as topics of study have been popular and unpopular at different times. In the United States, for example, only since the 1970s have "social history" and "women's history" been a respected modality for investigating the past. Before then, the lives of the poor or the disenfranchised were more likely to become the stuff of literature than of serious historical analysis.

It is also the case that history is written within various frameworks — explicit or not — that help explain the historical phenomenon being examined. For example, Marxist-inspired history places little emphasis on the individual and focuses more on economic factors and the conflict between social classes. Other models, such as that inherent in the work of sociologist Max Weber, emphasize important ideas, for example, the impact of religious ideas on economic behavior, as he discussed famously in *The Protestant Ethic and the Spirit of Capitalism* (1905). Of course, neither of these two models addresses or resolves the chicken or the egg conundrum, that is, religious ideas such as Protestantism can in fact be understood as a consequence of economic ideas, not just their origin.

Thomas Carlyle, *On Heroes, Hero-Worship, and the Heroic in History* (1840), is credited with the least-complex theory of history, that of the "great man" or hero. It was his contention that in any age, a great man arises who shapes events, so that the world could not have evolved as it did were it not for that individual. This theory is embedded in the Bible, both in terms of the anthropomorphic depiction of God, who is considered responsible for the creation of the world and just about everything that came after. Implicitly, the Bible gives the message that after creating the world, the great God chose a few men to be great themselves. Man is thought to be created in God's image—making God and Man very similar. Because God typically is depicted as male, the saying that women are created in God's image has not been emphasized.

Not all "great men" are benevolent, of course. The tyranny of rulers throughout history obviously has had an enormous impact on history and the writing of history. Oppressive rulers expect and compel historians to attribute positive historical change to them. These rulers reinforce this expectation by not allowing other interpretations to be published or taught. As the common phrase goes, "History is written by the victors." Michel Foucault, a proponent of this framework that rests on a model of history as social struggle, wrote in his series of lectures, "Society Must Be Defended" (1975–1976), that victors "use their political dominance to suppress a defeated adversary's version of historical events in favor of their own propaganda," which then justifies the inevitability and appropriateness of their victories. The philosopher Paul Ricoeur defined Nazism and other totalitarian regimes as committing violence to history (*History and Truth*, 1965). Historical writing reflects the concerns and power relations of the time in which it is written. Conflicting historical narratives fuel military engagements around the world as much today as in the past, perhaps the most famous current example being the Israeli-Palestinian struggle. It is fair to say that competing narratives frame all conflict—that the narrative competition is the conflict. In the case of women not being included or not being included correctly in the historical record, the oppressive forces are not as clearly visible as are the forces of war, making it more difficult—but perhaps more imperative—to use the paradigm of conflict in writing the history of women.

As is well known, George Orwell's terrifying *1984* depicts a society where the historical record is manipulated for nationalist aims and the accumulation of power. His clever aphorisms, "He who controls the present, controls the past. He who controls the past, controls the future" may not be as stark nowadays as it was in fiction when Orwell penned his masterpiece in 1949. The reason is that by 2014, people have become attuned to the notion of "narrative," which indicates clearly that there always are multiple histories of events, each one supporting the interests of a particular group. The word "propaganda" has fallen out of favor, perhaps because it suggests deliberate distortion. And yet, narrative accounts of history that privilege a certain point of view or the vested interests of a group are difficult to differentiate from propaganda or hagiography.

Until recently, the "feminist theory of history," itself considered a radical and perhaps unscientific and ideological approach by many historians, has used a *gendered lens* when examining documents and a *theoretical framework* that is grounded in understanding stereotypes of gender and the unequal power of the sexes. The product of this work has been a large outpouring of studies about individual women, as well as groups of women in various historical periods, reperiodized or not.[21] In her 1992 article that helped launch the new journal *Women's History Review*, Antoinette Burton raised the bar higher than utilizing a gendered lens and a feminist theoretical framework. She stated that "if feminist reconceptualizations of history are to be taken seriously—if, in other words, history is the production of knowledges [plural intended] about the past and is itself contingent on the conditions of the present—feminist theorists must begin to reference the imperial legacies of Anglo-European feminisms and the multiplicity of feminist movements around the world."[22]

Burton's article reminds me of a course I taught at Brandeis in 1985 titled "Women's Intellectual Work: The History of Women's Contributions to the Discipline of Sociology." I do not believe that such a course was offered in any other university, and I was excited to work with my students, first to locate and then to study the women I knew we would discover.[23] The course exceeded my expectations in terms of engaged learning. Because I knew I would want to teach the course again, I asked the students to give me feedback during the last session. After expressing much appreciation for what we had encountered and achieved together, one student said, "But all the women were white." To which I responded,

"Next time the course will integrate women of color into the syllabus." I made this promise without knowing how I would fulfill it, but promising that I would do so. The second time I offered the course, I was able to integrate extraordinary women of color. This time, during the last session, a student said, "But all the women were heterosexual." And I made the promise to integrate lesbian founders and contributors to sociology. I now realize I should develop a course on Jewish women founders of sociology. And I wonder where, when, and if this process will end. I do know that this course is getting closer to enacting its title, "Women and Intellectual Work." Not some women but all women.

Burton's challenge in terms of Jewish history is not only the imperative to write women into history, but to be inclusive internationally. In the Jewish context, this means that we must carefully examine and define who is a Jew. She suggests implicitly that to make statements about Jews, we must include people who call themselves Jews wherever they exist, whatever class they occupy, whatever sexual status they embody, and more. These definitions are not stable. Yet, they form the basis of understanding "The Individual in Jewish History."[24]

NOTES

1. My informal survey of what people think when they hear the phrase, "The Individual in Jewish History," elicited the following names: Herzl, Ben-Gurion, Rashi, Rambam, and Hillel.

2. Sherryl Kleinman, "Why Sexist Language Matters," AlterNet, March 11, 2007. http://www.alternet.org/authors/sherryl-kleinman.

3. See, for example, Elinor and Robert Slater, *Great Jewish Women* (New York: Jonathan David, 2006).

4. For an explanation of this focus, see Elinor W. Gadon, *The Once and Future Goddess* (New York: HarperCollins, 1989).

5. To whom should be added Zilpah and Bilha, mothers of the tribes of Gad and Asher, and of Dan and Naphtali, respectively.

6. *Agunot beItonut haYehudit, 1857–1896*, no. 40, 2010.

7. The conference was created by the Hadassah-Brandeis Institute at Brandeis University, the Lafer Center for Women and Gender Studies at the Hebrew University, and the Tauber Institute for the Study of European Jewry at Brandeis University. The proceedings were published as Ruth Kark, Margalit Shilo, and Galit Hasan-Rokem, eds., *Jewish Women in Pre-State Israel*, foreword by Shulamit Reinharz (Waltham, MA: Brandeis University Press, 2008).

8. Hilde Spiel, *Fanny von Arnstein: Daughter of the Enlightenment* (New York: New Vessel Press, 2013).

9. Jehuda Reinharz, Shulamit Reinharz, and Motti Golani, eds., *The Fearless Visionary in the Land of Israel: The Letters of Manya Shohat, 1906–1960* (Hebrew). (Jerusalem: Yad Ben Zvi, 2005).

10. A few feminist archives have been established recently, including two in England (Feminist Archives North and Feminist Archives South) and in the United States. See Alexis Pauline Gumbs, "Feminist Archives: Seek the Roots: An Immersive and Interactive Archive of Black Feminist Practice," *Feminist Collections* 32, no. 1 (November 2011). These new archives are more likely to be online than older archives. See also the Feminist Theory Archives, Pembroke Center for Teaching and Research on Women, Brown University, Providence, RI.

11. Livia Bitton-Jackson, "Yael Nitzan: The Museum of Israeli Women," Jewish-Press.com, August 23, 2012 and May 3, 2013.

12. Hadassah-Brandeis Institute, HBI Series on Jewish Women (Waltham, MA: Brandeis University Press, 2010).

13. Linda Nochlin, *Women, Art and Power and Other Essays* (Boulder, CO: Westview Press, 1988), 147–58.

14. See Shulamit Reinharz, "Toward a Model of Female Political Action: The Case of Manya Shohat, Founder of the First Kibbutz," *Women's Studies International Forum* 7, no. 4 (1984): 275–87; Shulamit Reinharz, "Manya Wilbushewitz-Shohat and the Winding Road to Sejera," in *Pioneers and Homemakers: Jewish Women in Pre-State Israel*, ed. Deborah S. Bernstein (Albany, NY: SUNY Press, 1992); Reinharz, Reinharz, and Golani, *Fearless Visionary*.

15. *Inside Higher Ed*, http://www.insidehighered.com/news/2005/02/18/summers2_18#ixzz2fZNjIDSN.

16. By the 1970s, Kelly-Gadol had become well-known for her publications on feminist history. Her article "Did Women Have a Renaissance?" in *Becoming Visible: Women in European History*, ed. Renate Bridenthal and Claudia Koonz, was considered groundbreaking in the area of historical scholarship.

17. "Joan Kelly," Wikipedia.

18. Ibid.

19. See Paula Hyman, "Feminist Studies and Modern Jewish History," in *Feminist Perspectives on Jewish Studies*, ed. Lynn Davidman and Shelly Tenenbaum (New Haven: Yale University Press, 1994).

20. Ana Lebl, "Jewish Women in the Former Yugoslavia," working paper series, Hadassah International Research Institute on Jewish Women (now Hadassah-Brandeis Institute), Brandeis University, Waltham, MA, November 1, 1999. http://www.bjpa.org/Publications/details.cfm?PublicationID=2151.

21. See Shulamit Reinharz, *Feminist Methods in Social Research* (New York: Oxford University Press, 1992), esp. chap. 7, "Feminist Oral History."

22. Antoinette Burton, "History Is Now: Feminist Theory and the Production of Historical Feminism," *Women's History Review* 1, no. 1 (1992): 25–39.

23. Shulamit Reinharz, "Teaching the History of Women in Sociology: or Dorothy Swaine Thomas, Wasn't She the Woman Married to William I?" *American Sociologist* 20, no. 1 (spring 1989): 87–94.

24. The Hadassah-Brandeis Institute, established in 1997 at Brandeis University, has taken up this challenge and published more than fifty books and supported hundreds of research projects within the framework of "Jews and gender worldwide." See www.brandeis.edu/hbi.

BIBLIOGRAPHY

Bitton-Jackson, L. "Yael Nitzan: The Museum of Israeli Women." *The Jewish Press*, August 23, 2012 (updated May 3, 2013). http://www.jewishpress.com/sections /jewess-press/impact-women-history/yael-nitzan-the-museum-of-israeli -women/2012/08/23/.

Burton, A. "'History' Is Now: Feminist Theory and the Production of Historical Feminisms." *Women's History Review* 1, no. 1 (1992): 25–39.

Gadon, E. W. *The Once and Future Goddess*. New York: HarperCollins, 1989.

Golani, M., J. Reinharz, and S. Reinharz, eds. *A Fearless Visionary in the Land of Israel: The Letters of Manya Shohat, 1906–1960*. Jerusalem, Israel: Yad Ben Zvi, 2005. [Hebrew]

Gumbs, A. P. "Feminist Archives: Seek the Roots: An Immersive and Interactive Archive of Black Feminist Practice." *Feminist Collections* 32, no. 1 (2011): 17–20.

Hasan-Rokem, G., R. Kark, and M. Shilo, eds. *Jewish Women in Pre-State Israel: Life History, Politics, and Culture*. Foreword by S. Reinharz. Waltham, MA: Brandeis University Press, 2008.

Hedgepeth, S. M., and R. G. Saidel, eds. *Sexual Violence against Jewish Women during the Holocaust*. Waltham, MA: Brandeis University Press, 2010.

Hyman, P. "Feminist Studies and Modern Jewish History." In *Feminist Perspectives on Jewish Studies*, L. Davidman and S. Tenenbaum, eds., 120–39. New Haven, CT: Yale University Press, 1994.

Jaschik, S. "What Larry Summers Said." *Inside Higher Ed*, February 18, 2005. http://www.insidehighered.com/news/2005/02/18/summers2_18 #ixzz2fZNjIDSN.

"Joan Kelly." In Wikipedia, July 10, 2014. http://en.wikipedia.org/wiki/Joan_Kelly.

Kelly-Gadol, J. "Did Women Have a Renaissance?" In *Becoming Visible: Women in European History*, R. Bridenthal and C. Koonz, eds., 175–201. Boston: Houghton Mifflin, 1977.

Kleinman, S. "Why Sexist Language Matters." *AlterNet*, March 11, 2001. http:// www.alternet.org/story/48856/why_sexist_language_matters.

Lebl, A. "Jewish Women in the Former Yugoslavia." *Working Paper Series*. Waltham, MA: Hadassah International Research Institute on Jewish Women (now Hadassah-Brandeis Institute), 1999.

Nochlin, L. *Women, Art, and Power: And Other Essays*. Boulder, CO: Westview Press, 1988.

Reinharz, S. *Feminist Methods in Social Research*. New York: Oxford University Press, 1992.

———. "Manya Wilbushewitz-Shohat and the Winding Road to Sejera." In *Pioneers and Homemakers: Jewish Women in Pre-State Israel*, D. S. Bernstein, ed., 95–118. Albany: State University of New York Press, 1992.

———. "Teaching the History of Women in Sociology: Or Dorothy Swaine Thomas, Wasn't She the Woman Married to William I?" *American Sociologist* 20, no. 1 (1989): 87–94.

———. "Toward a Model of Female Political Action: The Case of Manya Shohat, Founder of the First Kibbutz." *Women's Studies International Forum* 7, no. 4 (1984): 275–87.

Slater, E., and R. Slater. *Great Jewish Women*. New York: Jonathan David, 2006.

Sperber, H. "The Agunot Phenomenon in Eastern European Jewish Society during 1857–1896 as Reflected in the Jewish Press." *Kesher: Journal of Media and Communications History in Israel and the Jewish World* 40 (2010): 102–108.

Spiel, H. *Fanny von Arnstein: Daughter of the Enlightenment*. New York: New Vessel Press, 2013.

20

Thomas Carlyle versus Henry Thomas Buckle

"Great Man" versus
"Historical Laws"

YAACOV SHAVIT

The historian and essayist Thomas Carlyle (1795–1881) accused his contemporary, the Victorian historian Henry Thomas Buckle (1821–1862), author of *Introduction to the History of Civilization in England, France, Spain and Scotland* (1857), of shallow dogmatism, inordinate conceit, and of forcing the facts to fit his theory. However, when asked if he had read Buckle's book, Carlyle replied that he had not, but that he had read extracts from it in the papers.[1] It is only fair to Carlyle, writes St. Aubyn, one of Buckle's biographers and admirers, to state that his opinion was privately expressed, and that he did not voice his criticism publicly, as many others did. They too, in St. Aubyn's view, did not properly read Buckle's book, or they read it and did not understand it. St. Aubyn also gave Carlyle credit, stating that if he had reviewed the work, he presumably would have taken more trouble to discover what it contained. Nevertheless, a devoted admirer who shared Buckle's view of it, St. Aubyn also was generous enough to write that "Ignorant as was Carlyle's comment on Buckle, it contained a germ of truth . . . in the nature of things no historian can avoid imposing a priori upon the past certain ideas which his study of history may verify but which it has not in the first place suggested."[2]

It appears that this biographer-disciple of Buckle was deluding himself. Even if Carlyle had taken the time to read the two volumes of Buckle's hefty work, he would not have changed his negative a priori opinion about it. Carlyle was unaware of the great impact that Buckle's historical-sociological theory had or how popular Buckle was outside the borders of England, including in tsarist Russia. Consequently, he would not have known that Buckle's critics often referred to the collection of his own lectures, *On Heroes, Hero-Worship and the Heroic in History* (1841),[3] and found support in it for their opposition to Buckle's theory, according to which the historical development of the various civilizations was determined by "objective" not subjective laws, namely, not by great men.

At the beginning of the first lecture, Carlyle wrote: "Universal History, the history of what man has accomplished in this world, is at bottom the History of the Great Men who have worked here. They were the leaders of men, these great ones; the modellers, patterns, and in a wide sense creators, of whatsoever the general mass of men contrived to do or to attain; all things that we see standing accomplished in the world are properly the outer material result, the practical realization and embodiment, of Thoughts that dwelt in the Great Men sent into the world: the soul of the whole world's history, it may justly be considered, were the history of these."

In the view of his critics, Carlyle did indeed exaggerate in the exclusivity he granted to "great men" as the force that creates and leads historical processes; nonetheless, his opinion was regarded as a reaction to Buckle's "historical determinism" and his tendency to ignore the role played by a genius personality in human history and the weight that a historian ought to attribute to human actions motivated by free choice, desires, plans, imagination, character traits, and the like.[4]

Buckle described his historical view as the absolute opposite of Carlyle's, which placed the great personality at the center of historical development. "In the long run," Buckle wrote, "or on the general average of affairs individuals count for nothing . . . such men, useful as they were, are only tools by which that work was done which the force and accumulation of preceding circumstances had determined should be done. . . . They are like meteors which dazzle the vulgar by their brilliancy, and then pass away, leaving no mark behind."[5]

The fundamental clash between these two British writers of the Victorian period — one of whom (Buckle) is a forgotten historian — is a clash between two totally disparate approaches to the writing of history. Carlyle believed that historical writing was an art, while Buckle thought it was a science. He did not believe in universal historical laws, and "spoke with great contempt," asserts Ernst Cassirer, "of all logical methods."[6] He thought as a transcendentalist, believing that the "great man" is an emissary of God, and his appearance is a "revelation," not subject to any law or system. At the same time, the two men advocated two completely different political views, regarding the mutual relations between the public and the leader, or between the personality and his generation. In Carlyle's eyes, as I noted, the "great man" is the creator and shaper of "history," among other things, owing to his power to lead the masses on a new path, while Buckle did not attribute any importance to the individual and his biography. For him, the main driving power of progress was the activity of the intellectual class and the diffusion of knowledge.

The tension between these two approaches also appeared in the context of Jewish historiography in general and modern Jewish historiography, namely of the nineteenth and twentieth centuries, in particular.[7] In the first context, a time when Jews began writing general histories, historians discussed at length whether Jewish history is subject to universal "historical laws" or follows its own laws, and also what roles are played by different individuals in that history. In the second context, a time when the Jewish public underwent a process of "politicization," or in other words, when Jews joined non-Jewish political movements or organized into Jewish political movements and parties, the essence of the interrelationships between a public organized in a political ideological movement with common interests, on the one hand, and a charismatic leader, on the other, became not only a theoretical, historical question but a practical, topical one as well.

I do not intend to argue that Buckle and Carlyle were authorities on these questions, or that others found a source of inspiration in their works. I do mean to depict them as two historians who present two alternatives, or even two extremes, which emerged in Jewish historical and political thought from the second half of the nineteenth century.

In the chapter "Henry Thomas Buckle, Prince of the Sages: Environment, Culture, Civilization and Progress" in *Darwin and Some of His Kind*, Jehuda Reinharz and I reviewed Buckle's theory and described its influence on the historical view of several Jewish historians and men of letters, in particular in Eastern Europe.[8] I will cite only one example. Simon Dubnov (1860–1941) wrote that in his youth he read the first chapters of Buckle's book (in a Russian translation) "on the advantage of intellectual over moral elements in the dynamics of history."[9] Thomas Carlyle is mentioned only incidentally in that chapter as one of the British intellectuals and men of letters who influenced the Eastern European intelligentsia in general, and the Jewish intelligentsia in particular. The author only hints at the fact that he appears as Buckle's antithesis. Now I have the opportunity to complete the picture by a brief discussion of the subject, which certainly is not unfamiliar to the celebrant of the jubilee, who, in his biography of Chaim Weizmann, dealt with the nature of Weizmann's greatness as a leader, as well as with the interrelationship between him and the Zionist movement and the Jewish public.

By 1928, the book *On Heroes, Hero-Worship, and the Heroic in History* (1841) had been printed in twenty-eight editions in England, in twenty-five in the United States, in six translations into German (the first in 1853), into Polish in 1892, and into many other languages.[10] Parts of the book were translated into Russian in 1856 and appeared in the periodical *Sovremennik* (The Contemporary), and the entire book was translated by the economist Valentin Ivanovich Yakovenko in 1891. Prior to the translation he published an article on Carlyle and his influence in Europe. Editions of this translation were printed in 1898 and 1908. The translation was censored in order to delete excerpts that "were offensive to religion." However, apparently Carlyle's book made far less of an impression on the Jewish intelligentsia in Eastern Europe, including Jewish historians, than Buckle's seminal work. I did not find many mentions of Carlyle in Jewish publications on current events, but he sometimes is referred to as the "great [English] author and scholar." I found quotations of his words, for example, in relation to the Dreyfus Affair: "How great is the force of the voices of people when they are united—said the English scholar Carlyle—this is the acknowledgement of their emotions, which have more power than an acknowledgement of their opinions."[11] However, the fact that Carlyle's name was not on the reading list of Jewish men of letters does not mean (as I will show later) that they did not read his *On Heroes*, and certainly does not prove they were not influenced by him, either directly or indirectly.

In studies on modern Jewish historiography, Carlyle and his book hardly are mentioned as having influenced contemporary historians or the writers of Jewish history. Possibly this is because writing about remarkable men in Jewish history and the role played by various people in that history did not need Carlyle's inspiration, since hagiography was not foreign to the Jewish tradition of historical writing.[12] Nevertheless, Carlyle's book enhanced the tendency to discuss the role of the "great man" in shaping Jewry and the history of the Jews, and in the modern age, drew attention to the status and role of the "personality" in political movements in general, and in the Zionist movement in particular.

I do not intend to describe here the development of Carlyle's historical view and attitude toward the historical character, which were given expression not only in his *On Heroes*,[13] but even more so in his biographies of Frederick the Great (1858–1865) and Oliver Cromwell (1845), in his book on the French Revolution (1837), and in many other biographies. I also am not interested here in surveying the various—and contradictory —interpretations of Carlyle in several works by historians and men of letters[14] as a moralist, a mystic,[15] a conservative who hoped to introduce order into chaos,[16] even as a protofascist enemy of democracy, "the father of British Imperialism," or an admirer of the power (*Kraft, Tatkraft*) of "heroes." I am interested here in his reception by the Jews.

As I noted, Carlyle's book gained "unparalleled success in stimulating countless readers,"[17] and many who had read none of his books "came to associate him exclusively with dictatorial views"[18]—that is how they understood the book.[19] However, it was Carlyle's didactic, subjective, and emotional approach,[20] and the dramatization of the lives of the people he wrote about, that brought him so many admiring followers (needless to say, similar to the popularity that quite a few contemporary biographies enjoy). And perhaps the book was popular because people crave "heroes" on whom they can pin their hopes and by whom they can expect to be led and guided. The "adoration of heroes" did not vanish after Napoleon— the last political "hero" that Carlyle wrote about. On the contrary, Napoleon heralded the appearance of new "heroes" as well as the phenomenon of "hero worship" in the generations after him.

I found the first mention of *On Heroes* in the writings of Heinrich Graetz, when he dealt with the question of why humans need a cult of heroes. In 1883 he wrote in the fourth letter in *The Correspondence of an English Lady on Judaism and Semitism* that "The gifted Thomas Carlyle has struck a powerful chord of the human keyboard: man's need for hero-worship. He accounts for the great achievements of world history on the basis of this human inclination according to which men are readily amazed by and willing to submit to a figure who towers over the ordinary and mediocre. When such a figure appears it naturally exerts an attractive force and the duly rendered homage transforms him into a historical world hero. His admirers overlook his faults and exaggerate still more his outstanding qualities. This inclination to hero-worship is rooted in the clearly noble side of human nature, in the need to wonder." However, Graetz wrote, there always is skeptical criticism, which examines whether the figure is imbued with true, or rather false, greatness.[21]

Mentions of *On Heroes* begin to appear in Jewish literature from the last quarter of the nineteenth century, namely, nearly half a century after the publication of Carlyle's book. They are dispersed here and there in the literature of the period and demonstrate that the book was known to the Jewish-Russian intelligentsia. Thus, for example, in the 1904 article "Moses," Ahad Ha'am wrote: "It has been well said by Carlyle that every man can attain to the elevation of the Prophet by seeking truth; but whereas the ordinary man is able to reach that plane by strength of will and enormous effort, the Prophet can stand on no other by reason of his very nature."[22] Ahad Ha'am did not acknowledge that he was quoting from Carlyle's lecture on Muhammad. About three years later, the author, editor, and Orthodox public figure Rabbi Benjamin (Joshua Radler-Feldman, 1880–1957) published two articles on Carlyle in Y. H. Brenner's periodical, *Hame'orer* (The Awakener). Brenner was enthused about the first part of the essay, "Idol Worshippers: Man as Divinity (from Carlyle's theory),"[23] and wrote to R. Benjamin: "Blessed was the hour when I received your theory—Carlyle's theory." He added that he himself had translated, "with the help of a man who knows English," the first chapter of *On Heroes*, and urged R. Benjamin: "Your lecture is so wonderful! Write the second chapter, write the second chapter."[24] However, after he read and printed the second half of the essay,[25] he was far from enthusiastic about the mystification of the leader as a divinity. Although it is true, Brenner wrote to R. Benjamin, that "in the Jewish street . . . sacrifices are offered to the masses and sacrificial lambs are brought to the proletariat," and the term *heroism* is attributed to those adhering to "bourgeois ideologies," how is it possible to describe the "murderer" Bismarck as a "hero"?[26] Like Graetz, Brenner, too, was apprehensive about the admiration of heroes, because those so-called heroes often are negative characters.

About eighty years after it appeared in 1919, *On Heroes* was translated into Hebrew by Isser Joseph Einhorn (1886–1925), an agronomist and writer on the natural sciences, and was published by the Steibel publishing house in Warsaw (with notes and a picture of the author and his biography, along with an introduction by Fischel Lachover [1883–1947]). It later was printed in two more editions (the third in 1922). An improved version of the introduction was printed in Lachover's book *Betehum umihutz letehum: Masot uma'amarim al sofrei eiropah* (1953).[27] In his introduction, Lachover quoted from the book *Histoire de la littérature anglaise* by Hippolyte Taine (1828–1893) in which he wrote that if an Englishman, particularly one who had not reached the age of forty, was asked who was the most outstanding British thinker, he first would cite Carlyle, but immediately would suggest that he was not worth reading, because "you won't understand any of it."

Jewish intellectuals in Eastern Europe began to refer to Carlyle's theories as Russian thinkers and men of letters from the 1860s on began to show interest. We may find it quite ironic that a conservative thinker such as Carlyle was a source of inspiration for both the radical and the conservative Jewish intelligentsia; however, that was also the case as far as the Russian intelligentsia was concerned. For example, the Russian Jewish literary critic and intellectual historian Mikhail Osipovich Gershenzon (1869–1925) wrote to his brother in February 1892: "I am writing to you under the impression left on me by the best of all books which I am now reading. From now on, this book is my gospel."[28] And the religious thinker and Slavophile Nikolai Alexandrovich Berdyaev (1874–1948), who was exiled from Russia in 1922, called *On Heroes* "a fascinating work from both the literary and ethical standpoint. . . . We should acknowledge him as one of the greatest artists-thinkers of our time." Berdyaev wrote that one would have to be narrow-minded to criticize Carlyle as a "shallow author" because he does not meet the criteria of those who speak in the name of "economic materialism."[29] Toward the end of his life, Berdyaev again related what a powerful effect his reading of Carlyle had on him.[30] In his last words, Berdyaev referred to Nikolai Mikhailovsky (1842–1904), who wrote several essays on the mutual relations between a leader and the masses: "Heroes and Crowd" (*Geroi i tolpa*, 1882), "More on Heroes" (*Eshche o geroiakh*, 1891), "More on the Crowd" (*Eshche o tolpe*, 1893), and "Scientific Letters—On the Question of Heroes and the Crowd" (*K voprosu o geroiakh i tolpe*, 1884). Mikhailovsky was of the opinion that "a hero cannot pave a new path in history, but he can dam up or augment its deep streams which exist in any case by virtue of the objective circumstances. There are moments in history when an individual—not necessarily a hero —can give substantial strength to a crowd, and thus imbue a certain event with more force.[31] "Mikhailovsky," Billington wrote, "had expressed admiration for many of Carlyle's observations, but had refused to accept 'the positive side of his program,' which can be expressed literally in two words: 'find a hero.' Mikhailovsky sought only to describe dispassionately the behavior of demagogues and the general laws of mob psychology."[32] The radical *narodnik* ("populist") and revolutionary Pyotr Lazarevich Lavrov (1823–1900) wrote a book about Carlyle and was influenced by his views, but reduced them in order to adapt them to the theories and practices of the Russian populist terrorists (*narodniki*). I should also mention a book by the Marxist theoretician Georgi V. Plekhanov (1856–1918), author of *On the Question of the Individual's Role in History* (1898),[33] which tried to present the "middle road" between the dynamic, inevitable force of the masses and the adoration of the (political and military) leader. He defined someone as a great leader not because he left an individual stamp on great historical events, but because his special traits made him an instrument that serves social needs. To support this definition, he uses Carlyle and writes that Carlyle called "great men" "beginners," an extremely apt definition, since they see farther and have a stronger will than others. The great man carries out scientific tasks, which the prior development of society has placed on the agenda; he discovers new needs; he initiates the way to satisfy those needs. He is a hero, not, Heaven forbid, because he possesses the power to delay or change the course of events, but rather is a hero because his activity serves as a free, conscious expression of that vital, subconscious course. In other words, he is an instrument of the "natural ('objective') course of events." Not even a great personality, Plekhanov wrote, can impose on the society moves or relations that are not appropriate to the "objective" state of the social and economic forces.

These Russian thinkers, and others whom I have not mentioned, believed that no progress can be made without the conscious intervention of a historical personality in the course of events. Moreover, their opposition to historical determinism was based, among other things, on the view that the "historical personality" has the power (this also can be the active intervention of a group of people) to break down "determinism" or a "static situation" and move "history" in a new direction. In actual fact, they saw no contradiction between Carlyle and Buckle; in the latter they found not only a historical-scientific method that introduced order into historical processes, but also a view that regards intellect, free thought, and science as the forces that foster progress and lead to the creation of democratic institutions. At the same time, since leaders, who were such driving forces, did appear in reality, they were unable to ignore the role that Carlyle assigned to the individual leader. Against this background, Nahman Syrkin (1868–1924) was able to reject theories that suggested an all-inclusive and one-dimensional history and to view the historical personality as an important active and dynamic element. Jonathan Frankel writes that for Syrkin, "Thomas Carlyle, despite his many exaggerations, was nearer the truth than Herbert Spencer. The view that the great personalities are merely children of the time is false, for [such] personalities and geniuses stand in contradiction to their own time."[34]

In his autobiography, the historian Joseph Klausner (1874–1958) writes that in preparation for the entrance examinations to the *gymnasium* in 1889, he learned to read Greek and Latin, French and English, and among other works, read Buckle. "And afterwards I remained attached to Carlyle, who influenced my entire world-view."[35] In fact, in his historiographical writings, Klausner wavered between Buckle and Carlyle. On the one hand, he stressed the influence of the national environment in shaping the character and culture of peoples; while on the other hand, he noted the role of the "one genius in a thousand, a prominent figure who stands above his time, and is free of the 'tyranny of the environment.'" In other words, man is the one who creates history and the great man leads it:

The greater a man is, the greater is the action of his mind, the more he excels in his spirit . . . consequently the greatest man helps the extraordinary events, the only ones we call history, to unfold. Thomas Carlyle says in his book, *On Heroes*, that the great man in history is in relation to the mediocre members of his generation like lightning that falls from the heavens and kindles a fire in the dry trees. According to this view, the great man is a sort of solitary spectacle, who has no connection with the lives around him nor does his own life depend on them or derive from them. It is difficult to accept such a view. The historical "hero" is also a product of his place and time. . . . However, we should not go from one extreme to the other. . . . The great man does not create something from total nothingness; the new idea or the need for a new deed are hovering in the air even before the great man's birth, but they are not sufficiently clear to the "mediocre" masses. The "hero" properly clarifies them for himself, and he also has enough courage to express — clearly and explicitly — what the majority only senses, more or less. Such a man, if he has supporters, can do great things and create things that others regard as "beyond the boundary of historical possibility," as violations of the "laws of history."[36]

In other words, Carlyle was perceived as the great protector of faith in the role of the "great man" in history, as the opponent of the trend of "reducing" his role, or showing him as "he really is," a "small man." He calls for the revival of faith in the "great man" and his mission: "I am well aware that in these days hero-worship, the thing I call hero-worship, professes to have gone out, and finally ceased. This, for reasons which it will be worth while some time to inquire into, is an age that as it were denies the existence of great men . . . not to worship him," and regards him as a "creature of the Time," not as the "indispensable savior of this epoch."[37]

At least in this regard, Carlyle was not a Prophet. The craving for a hero and worship of him did not vanish in the second half of the nineteenth century. On the contrary, it grew stronger. In the context of Zionist history, this yearning was given clear expression in the attitude toward Theodor Herzl and the various reactions to the "hero worship" of him.

One example that illustrates Carlyle's influence, although his name is not mentioned, is a piece published by Vladimir (Zeev) Jabotinsky in the *Odesskie novosti* periodical on June 15, 1912, entitled "The Instigator" (*Podzhigatel'*). The narrator is in the company of a young twenty-five-year-old man who is praising terror and harshly attacking those who claim that "the role of the personality in history is nil" and "history supposedly occurs of its own volition." The truth is, he said, "that history is created by the genius" and without a leader, there is no progress. The young man goes on to say that there are two types of ideological leaders. One type gives the movement an idea or ideas, but in order to fulfill them a leader of the second type is required: an "igniter," namely someone in whom an inner fire is burning, with which he ignites the members of his generation. They do not notice his errors, contradictions, or faults: "They only feel his fire, *pantōn genetōr*, a divine fire, and from that fire a revolution begins, that fire makes history—and not those 'wise men' who with such a sharp eye knew how to read the needs of the society and so precisely embodied them in their social and political ideals. It is not those needs, not those ideas that drive history, but the personality of the leader. He is the fly-wheel of the social machine, without which that machine cannot move from the freezing point."[38]

These words clearly echo Carlyle's, which he repeats again and again in his lecture: "The Great Man was always as lightning out of Heaven; the rest of the men waited for him like fuel, and then they too would flame,"[39] and elsewhere in the book he writes that great men are "the lightning, without which the fuel never would have burnt."[40]

In this story, Jabotinsky is referring to Herzl, but it can be read as a "prophecy" of the status he ultimately gained in the movement he founded and led, a movement he came to personify—this notwithstanding the fact that in personal letters, Jabotinsky rejected Carlyle's version of the "myth of the leader." For example, he wrote in August 1930 (in German): "I have an organic hatred for personality worship, and I am repulsed by it. Fascism has some good ideas, but I am simply physically unable to discuss them serenely and directly. I am repelled by the worship of the Duce, as I am by any public dishonesty. When something similar happens among us, I see it as a real danger."[41]

And it is impossible not to say something about the fate of the two books—Buckle's and Carlyle's. As I said earlier, Buckle's book was nearly forgotten, and in the generations after its publication, it was mentioned only in works dealing with the development of writing about "universal history." In contrast, the Jewish-German philosopher, Ernest Cassirer (1873–1945), whom I mentioned previously, attributed a far-reaching influence to *On Heroes*. He wrote that Carlyle's lectures "created a sort of sensation; but nobody could have foreseen that this social event was pregnant with great political consequences . . . none of the hearers could think for a moment that the ideas expressed in these lectures contained a dangerous explosive . . . his lectures were also the beginning of a new revolution. A hundred years later these ideas had been turned into the most efficient weapon in the political struggle."[42]

I already have mentioned that Buckle regarded historical writing as a "science," while Carlyle viewed it as art. In his view, the true historian ought to be the artist or the poet. Hence, he believed his fellow countryman Walter Scott was a consummate example of such a historian. In Scott's novels, life "is actually filled by living men, not by protocols, state papers, controversies and abstractions of men. . . . History will henceforth have to take thought of it."[43] As I noted, the turn to biographical writing in modern Jewish historiography did not begin with Carlyle's influence or inspiration, and biographies were not written solely about "great men." However, these biographies, without a word being said about them as art, namely, as "literature," were consistent with Carlyle's view that historical writing is not only writing about processes, discussions, decisions, or even events, but also about human beings, without which history lacks any human dimension. The biography—and perhaps only the biography—can give history that dimension.

The prominent Swiss historian Jakob Burckhardt (1818–1897) wrote, for example, that *Die historische Grösse* is a relative and ambiguous concept, and hence "we cannot hope to arrive at an absolute definition" or to propose a "scientific system." "Real greatness," he wrote, "is a mystery" (*Die wirkliche Grösse ist ein Mysterium*).[44] Nonetheless, Burckhardt too tried to make a typology of "greatness," and to cite typical examples of great men, who are one of a kind: "Thus greatness has probably always been rare, and will be rare." Those are the men who hold the fate of peoples and states in their hands, and at times history takes shape in them: "The great men are necessary to our life in order that the movement of history may periodically wrest itself free from antiquated forms of life and empty argument."[45] Carlyle is behind this essay, evidence that the attempt to decipher the conundrum of "greatness" and its influence on the masses continued even after him, actually expanding. In 1881 Nietzsche wrote in *Dawn* (*Morgenröte*) some rather harsh words about Carlyle's "hero cult": "It was the old muddled and surly-headed Carlyle, who spent a long life trying to make reason romantic for his fellow Englishmen, to no avail, and who supplied the nineteenth century with the formulas of the 'hero cult.'"[46]

Nietzsche, like Burckhardt, understood that a "personality cult" was an inseparable part of the "climate of the time" in the nineteenth century, and so it was impossible to avoid trying to clarify how "great men" appear, what the "signs of greatness" are, how they operate on the "masses," and how and where they turn the wheels of history. It is possible that in the context of the British political culture, Nietzsche is right, and not only in the context of other European political cultures, including the one in which Nietzsche contributed his part with the myth of the *Übermensch*.

In actual fact, the total antithesis between Buckle and Carlyle does not do justice to Buckle. His interest was in the history of progress, and he believed that progress is not produced by one man, or by a group of men, but rather by society. A very exceptional individual can intervene in the operation of the general laws in special circumstances, but his success always depends on objective circumstances.

One could say that Jewish historiography in general and that of Zionist history in particular followed both Carlyle and Buckle. Quite a few biographies were written, not only of "heroes" of the stature that Carlyle referred to, and studies were written on mass movements and historical processes, sometimes with an apersonal approach. Weizmann is an example of a "hero" who earned his place in Zionist history because of the role he played in a formative historical event (the Balfour Declaration), but the "hero worship" of him was attended throughout his political life with criticism, even hostility. In any event, in contrast to Carlyle's "heroes," none of the Zionist leaders (except, perhaps, for Jabotinsky) was the subject of total, ongoing "hero worship."

Even after having read Carlyle, and quite a few biographies of great leaders, we do not seem to have an answer to the question of how a leader is created and why he gains that position. It is only possible to describe how he became a leader and how he rose to the position of leadership. Since we cannot transfer a "hero" who changed the face of "history" from one time period and one place to another, we never can know whether in that new place and time he would have been a "hero" and the subject of "hero worship."

NOTES

1. Quoted from Sir Charles Gavan Duffy, *Conversations with Carlyle* (London: Sampson, Low, 1892), 107 in Giles Saint Aubyn, *A Victorian Eminence: The Life and Works of Henry Thomas Buckle* (Westford, Hertfordshire, UK: Barrie, 1958), 165.

2. Saint Aubyn, *A Victorian Eminence*, 169.

3. On the history of the various editions, see Carl Niemeyer's introduction to the 1966 edition, University of Nebraska Press, Lincoln.

4. See, for example, Johann Gostav Droysen, *Grundriss der Historik* (Outline of the Principles of History), trans. E. Benjamin Andrews (Boston: Ginn, 1893).

5. Quoted in Saint Aubyn, *A Victorian Eminence*, 168–69.

6. Ernst Cassirer, *The Myth of the State* (New Haven: Yale University Press, 1963), 193. For Carlyle, Cassirer writes, "[H]ero worship was the oldest and firmest element in man's social and cultural life," 189.

7. For another comparison between a British Victorian philosopher, who proposed a "systematic method," and Carlyle, see A. Shpayer, "Tsvei veltanshoyungen: a paralel tsvishn Carlyle un Spencer," *Di tsukunft* 2 (Feb. 1911): 82–84 and 3 (March 1911): 140–48.

8. Yaacov Shavit and Jehuda Reinharz, *Darvin vekama mibene mino: evoluzia, geza, seviva vetarbut—yehudim korim et darvin, spencer, buckle verenan* (Darwin and Some of His Kind: Evolution, Race, Environment and Culture—Jews Read Darwin, Spencer, Buckle and Renan) (Tel Aviv: HaKibbutz Hameuchad, 2009), 153–90. In the meantime, a new study on the subject has been published: Ian Hesketh, *The Science of History in Victorian Britain: Making the Past Speak* (London: Pickering and Chatto, 2001). Hesketh discusses Buckle's theory in the first chapter: "The Enlarging Horizon: Henry Thomas Buckle's Science of History."

9. S. Dubnov, *Sefer haha'im*, trans. into Hebrew, M. Ben-Eliezer (Tel Aviv: Dvir, 1936), 86.

10. See Niemeyer's introduction, xxi fn. 3.

11. "Divrei hayamim, mi'afela le'or gadol," *Hazefira*, May, 14, 1899. Earlier he was mentioned as a man with anti-Jewish views, and there he is called "one of the great scholars of the previous generation." *Hazefira*, August 9, 1889.

12. In regard to historical writing in ancient times, there is the biography of Herod in Josephus's books, *Jewish Antiquities* and *Wars of the Jews*, which also includes a psychological analysis of his personality and motivations. On biographical novels in Jewish literature in nineteenth-century Germany, see Nitsa Ben-Ari,

Roman im ha'avar (Tel Aviv: Dvir/Makhon Leo Baeck, 1997). She mentions the German author Luise Mülbach, who wrote hundreds of historical biographical novels and explained that her objective was to remove the great characters and their great deeds from the silence of the den into the market of life and to introduce them to the public at large (ibid., 32).

13. B. H. Lehman, *Carlyle's Theory of the Hero: Its Sources, Development, History, and Influence on Carlyle's Work: A Study of a Nineteenth Century Idea* (Durham, NC: Duke University Press, 1928).

14. Gustav G. Cohen (1830–1906) of Hamburg, a merchant and Zionist activist and the father-in-law of Otto Warburg, wrote a philosophical work entitled *Über Thomas Carlyle*, which I was unable to obtain.

15. When Walicki compares the conservative romantic messianism of the Polish poet Adam Mickiewicz and that of Carlyle, he writes that "the English author made some concessions to rationalism. He stated, for instance, that the 'hero as a prophet,' as a direct messenger of God, was a product of an earlier age, who would not recur in the new age of scientific progress." Andrzej Walicki, *Philosophy and Romantic Nationalism: The Case of Poland* (Oxford: Clarendon Press, 1982), 263. However, it is possible, of course, to attribute to the "leader" traits of a prophet in the "scientific" and "rationalist" age too.

16. See Eugen Oswald, *Thomas Carlyle: Ein Lebensbild und Goldkörner aus seinen Werken, dargestellt, ausgewählt, übergetragen durch Eugen Oswald Werken* (Leipzig: W. Friedrich, 1882), 8.

17. See Malcolm Harden, *Six Victorian Thinkers* (Manchester, UK: Manchester University Press, 1991), 15–41.

18. Ibid., 35.

19. Crane Brinton, *English Political Thought in the 19th Century* (New York: Harper, 1962), 164–77.

20. David Newsome, *The Victorian World Picture: Perceptions and Introspections in an Age of Change* (London: J. Murray, 1997), 158–59.

21. Heinrich Graetz, *The Structure of Jewish History and Other Essays*, trans., ed., and intro. Ismar Schorsch (New York: Jewish Theological Society of America, 1975), 201.

22. Ahad Ha'am, "Moses," in *Selected Essays by Ahad Ha'am*, trans. Leon Simon (Philadelphia: Jewish Publication Society of America, 1917).

23. *Hame'orer* 2, no. 1 (January 1907), 42–49.

24. Y. H. Brenner letter, January 10, 1907, in Y. H. Brenner, *Kol kitvei Y. H. Brenner*, vol. 3 (Tel Aviv: Dvir, 1957), 294.

25. Y. H. Brenner, February 1907, in Brenner, *Kol kitvei Y. H. Brenner*, 49–54.

26. Brenner, *Kol kitvei Y. H. Brenner*, 3:447.

27. Paul Philip Levertoff (1878–1954), a yeshiva graduate who converted to Christianity, published a pamphlet in Hebrew in London in 1907 entitled "Tomas karleil: haskafotav vede'otav, hashkafot bikorti'ot." He also wrote in praise of Carlyle that he was innovative in every subject he wrote about and that his historical writing was

"history of the heart," namely, of the man "possessed of a living soul," and that he was opposed to any method that tried to rationalize human history. Fischel Lachover, *Betehum umihutz letehum: Masot umea'amarim al sofrei eiropah* (Jerusalem: Mossad Bialik, 1953), 125–39.

28. Mikhail Osipovich Gershenzon, *Pis'ma k bratu: Izbrannye mesta* (Moscow: M. i S. Sabashnikovy, 1927), 13.

29. Nikolai Berdyaev, "Sub'ektivizm i individualizm v obshchestvennoi filosofii. Kriticheskii eti'ud o N. K. Mikhailovskom" (St. Petersburg: Izd-vo O. N. Popovoi, 1901), 205.

30. Nikolai Berdyaev, *Samopoznanie: opyt filosofskoi avtobiografii* (Moscow: DEN, 1990).

31. See N. K. Mikhailovsky, 2 vols. (Russian) (St. Petersburg: Aleteya, 1998).

32. James H. Billington, *Mikhailovsky and Russian Populism* (Oxford: Oxford University Press, 1958), 169.

33. *K voprosu o roli lichnosti v istorii* (Russian). (Consulted the Hebrew translation published by Sifri'at Hapoalim in 1944.)

34. Quoted from Nachman Syrkin's *Geschichtsphilosophische Betrachtungen* (Thoughts on the Philosophy of History) 118, in Jonathan Frankel, *Prophecy and Politics: Socialism, Nationalism, and the Russian Jews, 1862–1917* (Cambridge: Cambridge University Press, 1981), 295–96. And see there Syrkin's words at a meeting in New York in 1921, that Weizmann is "the greatest, emptiest good-for-nothing that I have ever met [but] . . . All great leaders and men who created ideas and movements have to be *batlonim* . . . Practical. . . . men do not do those things," 296.

35. Joseph Klausner, *Darki likrat hatehi'ah vehage'ulah: Otobiografia, 1944–1974* (Tel Aviv: Masada, 1946), 26.

36. Joseph Klausner, "Hamateri'alismus hahistori betenuah hale'umit-hatzionit," in *Yahadut ve'enoshut, kovetz ma'amarim* (Warsaw, 1910), 148–70.

37. Thomas Carlyle, *On Heroes, Hero-Worship, and the Heroic in History* (London: Fraser, 1841), 16–17.

38. Trans. into Hebrew in a volume of stories (Tel Aviv, n.d.), 13–17.

39. Carlyle, *On Heroes*, 90.

40. Ibid., 17.

41. Letter to Mrs. Miriam Lang, August 27, 1930, in *Haskalah-Umma* 3/4, no. 61/62 (September 1980): 332–37.

42. Cassirer, *The Myth of the State*, 189–90.

43. Quoted in A. Dwight Culler, *The Victorian Mirror of History* (New Haven: Yale University Press, 1985), 44.

44. Jakob Burckhardt, *Reflections on History* (*Weltgeschichtliche Betrachtungen*), trans. by M.D.H. (London: Allan and Unwin, 1950), 172–203.

45. Burckhardt, "The Great Men in History," in *Reflections on History*, 203.

46. Friedrich Nietzsche, *Dawn: Thoughts on the Presumptions of Morality*, trans. Keith Ansell-Pearson (Stanford, CA: Stanford University Press, 2011), 187–88.

21

The Evolution of
Roza Georgievna Vinaver

*The Making of a Jewish Liberal Politician's
Wife in Imperial Russia*

CHAERAN Y. FREEZE

The euphoria generated by the February Revolution of 1917 quickly turned into disillusionment and anger toward the new Provisional Government, which proved incapable of dealing with calamitous inflation, peasant and labor unrest, and opposition to the war and the regime's aggressive war aims. In the midst of the April crisis, Roza Vinaver (1872–1951) received a phone call from Mariia Filipova Kokoshkin:[1] "Roza Georgievna, hurry and get the Kadet flag and come to the Kazan Cathedral. They are organizing a [pro]government demonstration." Roza, whose husband Maksim Moiseevich Vinaver (1862–1926) was serving as a senator in the Civil Cessation Department of the Senate, hastily grabbed the green flag and rushed to meet her friend. She found that a massive crowd already had assembled to support the Provincial Government. Marching arm in arm to the Mariinskii Palace with the Kadet (Constitutional Democrat) activists were the "simple people," including one woman who screamed hysterically, "My husband is in the mad house! There are seven children at home, and I'll kill him—Lenin!" As they approached the square, they encountered a different crowd, ridiculing the "capitalist ministers." Roza proudly declared that her husband's Kadet party had organized a more "impressive" demonstration that supported the Provisional Government, which simply required more time to establish itself to succeed.[2]

In her memoirs (completed in 1944), Roza describes how she was re-socialized to fit into the public world of her husband, a famous lawyer, founding member of the Kadet party, and Jewish deputy from St. Peters-burg elected to the First Duma.[3] Her narrative focuses on Maksim's activities and his influence on her life—from her reading habits to the upbringing of their children, from her leisure activities to the hosting of political events in her home. While downplaying her own achievements, Roza reveals how she successfully performed the role of a liberal politi-cian's wife. The heart of her narrative is an unwavering affirmation of her husband's liberal Kadet values and ethos: the rule of law, basic civil liber-ties, constitutional democracy, and above all, *vsenarodnost'* or a broad, su-praethnic national identity that affirmed patriotism without chauvinism and narrow sectarianism.[4] Her desire to emphasize this latter ideal and commitment to *Rossiia* (the Russian Empire) may explain the marginal (though not absent) discussion of her husband's struggle for Jewish legal rights. As the memoir progresses, Roza's individuality and voice gradually fade, cast in the shadow of her husband's towering figure and his life and career that she valorized.

Born in Moscow in 1872, Roza depicted her childhood as carefree and one in which she felt completely at home in Russia. That was a great improvement over the previous decade: her father, Gendel' Simkhovich Khishina (a merchant who later acquired the venerable status of "hon-orary citizen" [*pochetnyi grazhdanin*]) recalled how, in the early 1860s, Jews were restricted to residing in one house at the Glebov Monastery. By contrast, Roza averred that she grew up when "Jews lived freely in Mos-cow."[5] She attended a Russian elementary school, where she was content to play pranks, and later enrolled in a German gymnasium "renowned for its strictness," where she failed a grade because of her inattentiveness. At home, her mother Khane Evseevna Khishin (who had received a superb German education and "loved to recite Schiller") ran a strict Orthodox household: "All religious rituals were strictly observed, and we children knew them well. We were fearful of the Jewish God and knew perfectly what kind of punishment awaited us for each kind of sin. I dare say that if you eat a piece of bread [during Passover], God will punish this sin by reducing the days of your close relatives. God forbid that you should drop the Bible; when you pick it up, you need to kiss it. We observed all the fasts very strictly."[6] Roza wrote that she "punctiliously observed all the religious rituals" until she was about sixteen or seventeen years old. The question of religious observance became a contentious issue with her mother when Roza decided to marry Maksim, who, as we shall see, was not at all religious.

In contrast to a very Jewish life at home, on the outside Roza led a "purely Russian" life. Her life in Moscow meant non-Jewish friends, the theater, social gatherings, and above all full immersion in Russian culture. As she put it, "Our language was purely Russian, and even in our family, this Russian culture deeply pervaded our soul beginning from the earliest age." She claimed that never did she experience any form of antisemitism for "we lived a common life with our Russian Orthodox friends, with our [Russian] nannies who took us to church, and with our [Russian] teachers."[7] For her, there was no contradiction between the two identities; rather, a natural and compatible duality embodied the very ideal of *vsenarodnost'*—a unity with Russian culture and society that was supraethnic and free from prejudice or boundaries. She argued that the creation of a Russian-Jewish soul—that is, "a synthesis of two cultures"—existed only in Russia. Even during the pogroms, Roza insisted, "Our Russian friends were ashamed and grieved for us."[8] Echoing the Kadet party's hatred of autocracy, her memoirs blame the government for instigating antisemitism and pogroms. In the same vein, she castigated the Moscow governor-general, Grand Duke Sergei Aleksandrovich, for the expulsion of Jews from Moscow in 1891 as "morose, harsh, and antisemitic."[9] Au fond, she drew a sharp distinction between the innocent Russian people and a capricious autocracy that issued the order to drive the Jews out of Moscow: "There was never a pogrom in Moscow but I experienced this bloodless pogrom. All these sufferings instilled bitterness deeply in the soul but, strange as it might seem, this grievance did not affect my attitude toward the Russian people (as I already mentioned earlier). The love for this people, the intimate connection with everything Russian—Russian history, literature—remained strong, unshakeable."[10] To emphasize this point, she reiterated: "It was not the Russian people (*narod*) that gave the orders [for the expulsion]—this we always felt, and for that reason there was no animosity in the relationship to the surrounding Russian milieu."[11] Viktor Kelner and Oleg Korostelev suggest that this illusion of synthesis and unwavering faith in the assimilation project—widely shared by members of the liberal intelligentsia in an age of rising nationalism—was "simultaneously a strength and weakness."[12]

Meeting Maksim, born in Warsaw in 1862, radically transformed Roza's carefree life: differences in age, family backgrounds, and worldviews led to dramatic changes to accommodate her husband's way of life. Their first meeting took place at the home of her cousin Semën Vladimirovich Lur'e in Moscow when Roza was just an adolescent. Although she paid no attention to the assistant barrister from St. Petersburg who was ten years her senior, he confessed later that he had "noticed her." When they met again soon after her graduation from gymnasium, Roza was still a "very merry," giggly young girl (khokhotushka) "carried away with her lessons on literature and philosophy with one of the gymnasium teachers" whom she adored. To her dismay, her new acquaintance criticized her beloved teacher and tried to persuade her that "he, M[aksim] M[oiseevich] could supervise her studies better." Initially wary because, as she put it, "I was then an extremely frivolous girl," the young woman soon acceded.[13] So began Roza's reeducation under the guidance of the older, brilliant assistant barrister. Separated by several hundred miles, they had to rely on correspondence to conduct their discussion of literature.

Directed to read Goethe's Die Wahlverwandtschaften (Elective Affinities [1808]), Roza felt intimidated by Maksim's instructions to evaluate the book: "This was difficult for me; I was very fearful of not having understood it properly, and it was awkward for me to express my own thoughts." She also confessed that she did not always engage in her studies in the way he expected because "I loved to dance and enjoy myself with students who were not so serious."[14] Her suitor's selection of Goethe's Die Wahlverwandtschaften clearly was no accident, not least because he himself was "enamored" with Romanticism and had devoured the works of such Polish writers as Adam Mickiewicz and Juliusz Słowacki in Warsaw. Goethe's novella employed the discourse of chemistry to explore the relationship between the legal and social dimensions of marriage and the irrepressible forces of attraction that transcended class, social, and even moral boundaries.[15] As one character in the novel observes, human "elective affinities" always pulled together: "With the alkalis and acids, for instance, the affinities are strikingly marked. They are of opposite natures;

very likely their being of the opposite nature is the secret to their effect on one another—they seek one another eagerly out, lay hold of each other, modify each other's character, and form in connection an entirely new substance."[16] In all likelihood, the young lawyer cleverly was seeking to highlight the romance between the older Eduard and young, orphaned Ottilie as well as the magnetic attraction of opposites. In Roza's mind, the latter clearly stood out: "It was clear that my endless gaiety attracted this serious person."[17]

Although Roza portrayed herself as a naïve and frivolous girl in need of intellectual supervision, she also demonstrated an independent streak when she continued to pursue higher education during their courtship. Her father had opposed sending her to university, not out of hostility to female education but rather for fear that she would end up in Siberia like the radical children of other prominent Jewish families in Moscow. The arrest of three Narodnavoltsy (members of the People's Will),[18] who were students at Moscow University, had sent shock waves throughout the Jewish community: Osip Solomonovich Minor (the son of the state rabbi of Moscow, Zelik Minor), Mikhail Rafailovich Gots (the grandson of the "tea king," Kalonimos Zeev Vysotskii), and Matvei Isidorovich Fundaminskii (the son of the merchant Isidor Fundaminskii).

Following her father's death, her mother no longer could rein in her daughter's ambitions, and Roza enrolled in "collective courses" organized by the students themselves. The government had closed down the Vladimir Guerrier Higher Women's Courses (established in 1872) for fears of sedition in 1888.[19] According to Roza, her cohort of students "studied to quench their insatiable thirst for knowledge, not for the sake of a degree." Each believed that she had to develop her own Weltanschauung through the study of philosophy, but first she had to complete the prerequisite courses on natural history. Roza described her superb education with "the best scientific forces in Moscow": the renowned professors Ivan Mikhailovich Sechenov on physiology, Karl Eduardovich Lindeman on comparative anatomy, and Kliment Arked'evich Timiriazev on plant physiology. Mutual respect developed between the students who "absorbed everything greedily" and the professors who "empathized with us and always responded to our inquiries and doubts." As a result, Roza came to the marriage with a higher education that later helped her to interact with her husband's intellectual and political circles in St. Petersburg. She also acquired experience in socializing with elite Russian women and developed intimate friendships with them. For instance, she befriended Mar'ia L'vovna Tolstaia (daughter of the famous writer), who also attended the courses and spent time with Roza outside of the lecture halls.[20] She clearly felt at ease in high society, especially among her circle of Kadet families: "We often gathered in the Kadet club for amiable conversations, sometimes for cordial dinners, and even banquets with speeches."[21]

In some respects, Roza had more in common with her husband's colleagues than with his family: Maksim's family was as thoroughly Polish as Roza's was Russian—"Poles of the Mosaic faith" as she described them. Their Polish credentials were outstanding: her father-in-law, for instance, allegedly participated in the Polish Uprisings of 1863 and nearly was exiled to Siberia. Her husband won a gold medal for writing a brilliant piece about Polish customary law in the juridical faculty of Warsaw University. Following the suppression of the uprisings, Maksim became immersed in Polish literature and culture, especially the Romantic writers who shaped their generation. Roza recalled that even in St. Petersburg "he often read Mickiewicz's *Pan Tadeusz* with me." When the young bride first traveled to Warsaw to visit her husband's family, she encountered a language barrier: "No one wanted to speak with me in Russian. I did not understand the Polish language, and so I spoke French in Warsaw." She attempted to study Polish, but quickly forgot the language as her father-in-law began to understand Russian because of his frequent trips to St. Petersburg. The cultural barrier proved limited to Maksim's extended family, for he became very Russified, devoting himself to the reading and discussion of the Russian classics—Pushkin, Lermontov, and Gogol—with friends.[22]

Class differences were more challenging—notwithstanding Roza's declaration that she willingly accepted their modest station in life. In describing Maksim's grandfather, she permitted herself a slight jab at the irresponsibility of his children: "He [Avraham Vinaver] was a very well-to-do individual; however, as it often happens in well-to-do Jewish families, the children grew up greatly disposed to laziness and did not know anything apart from leading the good life."[23] By the time Roza became acquainted with her future husband, she claimed that his father and siblings all had lost their fortune. She mentioned one uncle who was a renowned chess player in Paris, but glibly observed, "Apart from chess, he was not occupied with anything else in life."[24] In contrast to these ne'er-do-well relatives, her husband worked his way into Warsaw University to study law in the juridical department. Given the dire financial position of his family, she noted that Maksim began to give lessons from the age of fourteen to support his family and siblings. With hardly any prospects in Warsaw unless he converted to Christianity, Maksim moved to St. Petersburg without a penny to his name. In this foreign city, Roza explained, he was forced to give lessons in secret "because it was unbecoming of a lawyer, even a young one, to be engaged with lessons."[25] She praised him for being the dutiful son who never went a day without sending assistance to his family.

Not surprisingly, Khane Khishina reacted with horror when her daughter announced her intention to marry this impecunious assistant barrister, even if he was working for the famous criminal lawyer Vladimir Danilovich Spasovich (1829–1906).[26] Roza ventured that her mother's shock (which caused her to fall seriously ill) was partly because of her impropriety: "At that time, matchmakers still existed, especially in wealthy, bourgeois families. It was considered a sign of licentious behavior for a girl to choose her own partner for life."[27] In her own defense, Roza pointed out that the young people already had rejected traditional matchmaking and insisted on the right to make their own romantic choices. The new initiatives, however, led to huge scandals. Her mother's opposition to the match probably was based more on economic considerations, as Roza openly admitted: "My impending marriage alarmed my mother greatly. The liberal professions were not very respected among the prominent Moscow bourgeoisie."[28] Her mother was sorely disappointed that Maksim refused to abandon his law career and take over the family business. Roza's father had passed away in 1891 (the fateful year of Jewish expulsion from Moscow), leaving his wife to oversee his commercial firm. If that were not enough, the groom insisted that his bride leave "this [bourgeois] environment" as soon as possible. The desperate mother only acceded out of fear that her daughter might commit suicide—a familiar scene (or so she thought) in Moscow when parents opposed their daughters' marriages.

Life in St. Petersburg was very different from the affluence to which Roza had been accustomed in Moscow. "The circumstances of our lives were extremely modest," she recalled, "not at all commensurate with my husband's [large] salary."[29] This discrepancy, she explained, was because of her husband's principled opposition to "any kind of *embourgeoisement*" and his boundless generosity to his family and friends. In the first instance, she observed that in contrast to Moscow, where the intelligentsia lived "side by side" with the bourgeoisie, in St. Petersburg, the former "shunned capital" and socialized with people who shared a common mind-set and aspirations, not with those from their own social estate. This mentalité shaped her husband's attitude toward the education of their children. In contrast to her family's concerns about economic utility, he "was guided exclusively by [the children's] abilities and not by their prospects of establishing a good life when choosing a profession for them."[30]

As for his generosity, Roza remarked that her husband's pocket was always open to his friends without any regard for his own budget. In fact, she remembered "two or three people who had the right to withdraw money directly from Makskim Moiseevich's bank account." To make light of their circumstances, she jested that their nearly empty bank account allowed her to evade household responsibilities: "The modesty of our needs personally made it possible for me to be free of any petty calculations and not occupy myself with managing the house." Besides, her husband was convinced that any concerns such as organizing a household "lowered [a woman's] spiritual standards and did not allow her to develop her intellectual abilities."[31] Later in her memoir, however, Roza acknowledged how difficult these lean years were for her, especially when Maksim's closest friend, the philosopher Leopol'd Aleksandrovich Sev (who eventually married her sister) came to live in their cramped space: "This intimate life was sometimes tortuous because he [Sev] demanded great intellectual and moral support from his friends. [. . .] Having arrived from my completely bourgeois Moscow environment, the perpetual presence of this strict censor of life during the first years of marriage was somehow unpleasant for me."[32] Looking back, she acknowledged Sev's contributions to their family, including his introduction to the famous Russian philosopher Vladimir Solov'ev, with whom he enjoyed a close relationship.

Rather than adhere to her husband's negative attitude toward "capital," Roza clearly induced him to adopt a more bourgeois lifestyle. Maksim's rapid advancement in his legal career culminating in his confirmation as a full-fledged lawyer by the minister of justice in 1904 may have eased their finances. The couple traveled often to the mountains or locales where they found a rich array of art. "We greedily took in everything valuable that a country could offer," she wrote. "From Italy, we brought back a great quantity of reproductions, sculptures, photographs, and based on them, M. M. gave a lecture to an intimate circle, providing a vivid picture of what he had seen."[33] They also purchased a summer cottage (*dacha*) in Tver province and spent the summers there with their children. Some time before the outbreak of World War I, they even purchased a summer house in France that would provide them refuge after the Bolshevik Revolution of 1917 and the failure of the Kadet-organized Crimean regional government during the Civil War.[34] The hardships during the war years and travel through Athens made them appreciate their home all the more: "The *dacha* was in complete order. . . . All our belongings had been preserved. We found everything there that we especially needed. We arrived in France in lamentable attire: shabby dresses and boots all in patches. . . . And there at our *dacha* we found dresses, undergarments, boots, and even hats! There were also books—books for children and a small juridical library that my husband had brought here before the war and which proved very useful subsequently for his legal work in Paris." With relief, Roza recalled thinking that they had "returned to the bourgeois comfort which we had been deprived of in the Crimea and in Athens."[35]

If class initially divided the couple, their relationship to Judaism and the Jewish community also required some negotiation. Both had grown up in households run by strictly observant mothers; however, whereas Maksim's mother had all but given up on her "freethinking" husband and children, Roza's mother refused to capitulate. She made her daughter promise to fulfill all the religious rites after she married. Although Roza claimed that she had already "moved away" from religion, a letter in the archives suggests that she may have kept her word, at least on Passover (a common practice among acculturated Russian Jews). In an invitation to the editor of *Russkoe bogatstvo*, Arkadii Georgievich Gornfel'd, for Passover (dated sometime between 1906 and 1914),[36] she wrote with an ironic tone:

Most esteemed Arkadii Georgievich,

I hasten to remind you that, as a loyal and pious Jew, you are called
upon to fulfill your duty, which we will try to make as pleasant
as possible. It is all happening on the 21st of March at 9 P.M., and
incidentally I suggest that on that day you eat only lightly (I'm sure
that this "lightly" will have to be examined under a microscope).

Your devoted Roza Vinaver

According to Roza, her husband was not particularly interested in Jewish matters in Warsaw, but his move to St. Petersburg fostered a desire
for greater involvement in the cultural and legal activities of the Jews.
Viktor Kelner and Oleg Korostelev correctly observe that her memoirs
only mention his "Jewish work" from time to time and instead tend to
focus on his political activities in the Duma and the Kadet party.[37] One
reason for the marginalization of the "Jewish narrative" may have been
Roza's own lack of interest or her critical opinion of the organizations in
which her husband was involved. Regarding the Society for the Spread of
Enlightenment among the Jews of Russia (OPE),[38] she observed that this
organization achieved very little in the 1890s and that its methods were
ineffective: "And here a group of the young Jewish intelligentsia wanted
to use this legal institution to replenish old wineskins with new content."
Her description of its head, Baron Goratsii Osipovich Gintsburg, was at
once political and sarcastic: "This was the dearest and kindest person who
autocratically (*samoderzhavno*) controlled this institution and tolerated
neither interference nor criticisms. Gatherings of this society were not
called very often. The baron conducted the general meetings very autocratically." She also mocked Gintsburg's unprofessional and rude interac-
tions with members of the society.[39]

The other Jewish institution that merited space in Roza's memoirs
was the Historic-Ethnographic Commission, founded by her husband
and historian Simon Dubnow in 1892. Full of admiration for the zeal of
this group, which consisted of lawyers, doctors, engineers, and other
white-collar professionals, she valued the significance of their research
for contemporary life. In particular, Roza highlighted the commission's
discovery of a stone in the Crimea "with an inscription that attested to
the presence of Jews who were already there eighty years after the birth

of Christ." Given the debates on the status of Jews in Russia, in her view this finding demonstrated both to the government and to Russian society "that Jews in Russia are not a newly-arrived element, but can be counted among the most native population in Russia."[40] The fact that she felt a need for scientific proof (even a stone in the Crimea) that Jews belonged organically to Russia suggests some insecurity about the liberal assimilation project to which she clung so fiercely; if Jews did indeed belong to Russia, why did they require justification for their inclusion?

Roza's narrative changes abruptly about one-third of the way through the memoirs, thereafter focusing almost exclusively on her husband's public activities after the Revolution of 1905, especially his leadership in the State Duma, Kadet party, Provisional Government, and Crimean Regional Government. However, these sections are neither firsthand accounts nor original; most of the information can be found in a collection of articles written in Vinaver's memory.[41] Still, this part of the memoir offers two important insights. First, Roza's discussion of her husband's struggle for equal rights for Jews reflected her internalization of the Kadet value of *vsenarodnost'*. She always was careful to minimize any parochial, ethnic interests: "The struggle for Jewish equal rights by no means introduced dissonance in the general Russian [Kadet] Party. My husband was convinced that equal rights for Jews was for the good of all of Russia."[42] Perhaps to downplay the "Jewish" story, she excluded any real discussion about her husband's role in the Union for the Attainment of Full Rights for the Jewish People in Russia, making only brief mention of the organization.[43] She did include a quote from her husband's speech following the pogrom in Belostok that reiterated the universal consequence of hatred: "It is not the Russian people who are hostile toward us but this clique, which seeks to instigate the people against us for its own purposes. Being criminally blind, they do not observe that they undermine not only us, but the healthy body of the enormous mass of the Russian population; they are subverting the entire state organism."[44]

The post-1905 segments of the memoirs also illuminate the challenges of being the wife of a prominent public figure and a mother to his children. First, it meant constantly being in the public eye and being available to assist the spouse at any moment. Roza recalled how some women found this role extremely onerous, especially the first wife of Pavel Miliukov,[45]

Anna Sergeevna, the daughter of an illustrious history professor. "Anna Sergeevna very much disliked it when they showered attention on her as the wife of Miliukov," she observed. "In general, she did not like the bustle that always surrounded famous people. It was embarrassing for her to be in the public eye." As an accomplished historian herself, Anna Sergeevna had published a few articles in the journal *Russkoe bogatstvo* (Russian wealth); however, Roza remarked, "As it often happens, the life of such a prominent person as Miliukov so filled her time that she completely abandoned her own work."[46] Roza knew very well the need to be on call at all times. One morning, for instance, she received a phone call from her husband informing her that the first All-Russian Lawyer's Congress with 150 attendees was going to take place at their home that very day.[47] "I quickly began to free three of the largest rooms of furniture; in one I set up a buffet (without hors d'oeuvres), I put the borrowed chairs in the other rooms, and in three hours everything was ready."[48]

Despite occasional unexpected incidents like the lawyers' congress, Roza clearly appreciated the regular schedule that her husband sought to maintain. She recollected his routine after the dissolution of the First Duma: he always began his day very early. After breakfast, he usually accepted visitors who came to discuss various issues with him, mainly of a legal or public nature. At noon, her husband went to court or to the Senate to deal with legal work. When he returned home around 5:00 or 6:00 in the evenings, he would rest and then spend time with the children. Around midnight, he began working on his court cases until 3:00 or 4:00 in the morning when he finally went to bed. While Roza could organize her day around his schedule, she often expressed great regret about the impact of his rigorous work habits on his health, especially after his heart attack in 1911.[49]

Maksim's busy life did not hinder him from making all the important decisions about the upbringing of their four children: Valentine (1895–1983), Evgenii (1899–1979), Sofiia (1904–1964), and Mishel' or Mikhail (1906–1920).[50] Compared to their mother's carefree, spoiled childhood full of games and pranks, the Vinaver children's daily lives were strictly regimented. They had to rise early every morning and were not permitted any comforts: "Their beds were hard; not one soft chair was supposed to be in their rooms." In terms of dress, Roza recalled that "we dressed them more than modestly for we greatly feared that the children, especially the girls, would begin to pay attention to their external appearance." Her husband ensured that even summer vacations included learning opportunities, and he set up a contest among the children to see who could cultivate the land most efficiently at their summer house.[51] Looking back wistfully at her own blissful childhood, so different from theirs, Roza recollected the joy of "free time" when she and her sister happily were left to themselves: "The unfortunate children who grew up under the supervision of any governess never played such delightful games."[52]

The strict father also insisted that the children receive a home education until the age of fourteen to avoid the harmful influence of the gymnasium, reminiscent of the justification that Roza's father gave for restricting her enrollment in the higher women's courses. As an admirer of classical education, Maksim set aside time in the evenings to read Greek and Roman history and literature to the children, especially Greek tragedies such as Sophocles. Their mother was responsible for teaching them mathematics and hired other teachers to teach them gymnastics, drawing, and choral singing. Whenever complex questions arose about their upbringing, the father consulted with his best friend Sev (the house guest about whom Roza complained earlier), who apparently had a significant influence on their oldest son.[53] Quite apart from the routine anxieties of raising children during the most tumultuous time in Russian history, Roza also worried incessantly about the safety of her family.

The possibility of arrest and violence against her husband as a prominent politician or her family represented a real threat for Roza. Fearing violence in St. Petersburg following the October Manifesto in 1905, Maksim sent her away to Finland with the children while he remained behind in St. Petersburg to complete his work. "How difficult it was for me to depart and leave my husband," Roza recollected. She was especially worried because the ultranationalist and antisemitic Black Hundreds had sent threatening letters to her husband. They already had murdered a Jewish member of the First Duma, the lawyer Grigorii Borisovich Iollos. Her anxieties had escalated when he kept receiving more letters: "I worried every time he had to leave the house; I went out on the street in advance to see whether there were suspicious figures at our entrance and was happy when he returned safe and sound."[54]

The next test of Roza's strength came on the heels of the dissolution of the First Duma on July 7, 1906. In response, deputies from the Kadet, Trudovik, and Social Democratic parties decided to sign the Vyborg Manifesto calling for passive resistance against the state, including "the refusal to pay taxes or furnish recruits to the government."[55] This "empty gesture" (it achieved nothing) resulted in considerable damage to the Kadet party, for the state decided to prosecute all those who had signed this "revolutionary" act. The trial of the Vyborg Manifesto signatories brought all the wives of the Duma deputies together — women who never had seen the inside of a courtroom before, let alone witnessed their spouses being treated like political criminals. Roza recalled the media circus after the court convicted the deputies and sentenced them to three months' imprisonment and the loss of their civil rights: "All the condemned deputies from St. Petersburg, with family and friends, gathered in the courtyard of the St. Petersburg District Court. A crowd of reporters and photographers surrounded them. Even a cinematographer appeared to capture their procession to the prison [on film]." For three long months, the wives of the Duma deputies gathered together "without distinction by party" in the Kadet club to support each other.[56] The humiliation of this period soon dissipated with the February Revolution of 1917, when top Kadet leaders formed the core of the new Provincial Government. That celebration, however, would prove short-lived.

The Bolshevik seizure of power in October 1917 forced the Vinavers into hiding to evade arrest, and they moved to Moscow, where fewer people would recognize them. In Moscow, Roza, who usually had been deferential to her husband's decisions, insisted on a different course of action that saved his life. A young man sent by the Socialist Revolutionary leader Boris Savinkov invited her husband to attend a meeting to discuss important matters. As was his custom, her husband consulted with his colleagues; however, in this case, his wife "personally protested very much and did not let him go."[57] Everyone who attended the meeting was arrested, including the young man who had invited Maksim. A few days later, the family fled to the Crimea, but traveled separately so that no one would recognize them; they later moved to France, where Maksim Vinaver passed away in 1926.[58]

The death of Maksim Vinaver, whose life had been so intimately tied to hers, left Roza completely bereft of meaning. In the conclusion of her memoirs, she mourned the loss of the "foundation" on which she had built her life. "There is a legend sketching the position of a woman in past times," she explained. "The woman—this is a zero alongside a number. Her whole life depends on the significance of this number: a large number meant a high position. And when the number disappears, the woman is left a zero. And so I was left a zero." There is no doubt that Maksim Vinaver was a larger-than-life figure, admired by Jews and Russians alike. As Simon Dubnow described him, Vinaver was an accomplished politician: "It became clear to me why he occupied a distinguished position next to Miliukov in the new Russian Constitutional Democratic Party, the chief moving force in the opposition of 1905."[59] He also was "a complicated person," whom everyone regarded as "very stern and demanding." People were "intimidated by his intellect and merciless criticisms."[60] His wife admitted that he always expressed disgust for vain people, which garnered him many enemies.[61] As her Passover invitation to Gornfel'd illuminates, Roza had a unique ability to use her tongue-in-cheek charm—an invaluable skill—to survive among the giant personalities of her husband's circles. She enjoyed warm friendships on her own terms with leading Kadet politicians such as Ivan Petrunkevich, Fedor Kokoshkin, Feodor Rodichev, Sergei Muromtsev, Pavel Miliukov, and Vasilii Maklakov, not just with their wives.[62]

Although Roza sought to portray herself as the "zero" alongside a large and brilliant number, her memoir tells of a far more engaged, and engaging, woman who played a major role in her husband's career. The memoir, for all of its self-effacing modesty, also reveals much about the lives, values, and roles of Russian Jews in late Imperial Russia and in the revolutions of 1917 and their aftermath. Perhaps most important, even the memoir of a self-conscious "Russian Jewish" intellectual shows that assimilation meant at once a combination of discrete cultures—hybridity, not the effacement of one by the other. Jewishness did not become a "zero" but remained a distinct number alongside the new Russian number, enhanced rather than diminished by the combination of cultures and identities.

NOTES

1. Mariia Filipova Kokoshkin was the wife of the prominent jurist Fedor Fedorovich Kokoshkin (1871–1918), one of the founders of the Kadet Party. He served on the Juridical Council of the Provincial Government in 1917.

2. Roza Georgievna Vinaver, "Vospominaniia Rozy Georgievna Vinaver, zheny chlena 1-oi gosudarstvennoi dumy Maksima Moiseevicha Vinavera," Collection of V. Maklakov, box 15, folder 3 (January 1944), 94–95, Hoover Institute Archives, Stanford, California. The memoir has also been published in Russian with notes and commentary by Viktor E. Kelner and Oleg A. Korostelev, "Vospominaniia Rozy Georgievnoi Vinaver, zheny chlena Gosudarvennoi Dumy Maksima Moiseevicha Vinavera," Arkhiv evreiskoi istorii 7 (2012): 11–134. For the sake of clarity, the text here uses the couple's first names.

3. On Maksim Vinaver, see P. N. Miliukov, M. M. Vinaver i russkaia obshchestvennost' nachala XX veka (Paris: Imp. coopérative Étoile, 1937).

4. On the Kadets (their program, organization, and politics), see William G. Rosenberg, Liberals in the Russian Revolution (Princeton: Princeton University Press, 1974), 11–46.

5. Vinaver, "Vospominaniia Rozy Georgievna Vinaver," 5.

6. Ibid., 5–6.

7. Ibid., 7.

8. Ibid., 8.

9. Ibid., 9.

10. Ibid., 11.

11. Ibid.

12. Kelner and Korostelev, "Vospominaniia Rozy Georgievnoi Vinaver," 12.

13. Vinaver, "Vospominaniia Rozy Georgievna Vinaver," 20–21.

14. Ibid. The book as was translated as Srodstvo dush in Russian.

15. On marriage in Goethe's Die Wahlverwandtschaften, see Peter J. Schwartz, After Jena: Goethe's 'Elective Affinities' and the End of the Old Regime (Lewisburg, PA: Bucknell University Press, 2010); Karl Keydecker, "The Avoidance of Divorce in Goethe's Die Wahlverwantschaften," Modern Language Review 106, no. 4 (October 2011): 1054–72.

16. Johann Wolfgang von Goethe, Elective Affinities (New York: Collier, 1900), 55.

17. Vinaver, "Vospominaniia Rozy Georgievna Vinaver," 21.

18. On Jewish involvement in the Party of the People's Will (Narodnaia Voia), the terrorist group that carried out the assassination of Alexander II, see Erich E. Harberer, Jews and Revolution in Nineteenth-Century Russia (Cambridge: Cambridge University Press, 1995), 186–229.

19. Christine Johanson, Women's Struggle for Higher Education in Russia, 1855–1900 (Montreal, Québec: McGill-Queens University, 1987), 48–50.

20. Vinaver, "Vospominaniia Rozy Georgievna Vinaver," 11–12

21. Ibid., 62.

22. Ibid., 19.

23. Ibid., 14.

24. Ibid.

25. Ibid., 16.

26. Spasovich, who described himself as a liberal, reform-minded lawyer, supported ethnic restrictions in the legal profession. He justified discrimination against Jews for the sake of "preserving professional independence from the state." Flooding the bar with Jews, he argued, would lead to intolerance by the state, which "may abolish . . . the [lawyers' corporate] council." However, Spasovich had defended Jews on many occasions, most notably serving as the lead defense lawyer in the David Blondes ritual murder trial. Jewish lawyers such as Vinaver, Genrikh Sliozberg, and others did not see his role in the debate as motivated by antisemitism but rather by his fear for the future of the profession. See Benjamin Nathans, *Beyond the Pale: Jewish Encounter with Late Imperial Russia* (Berkeley: University of California Press, 2002), 346–66.

27. Vinaver, "Vospominaniia Rozy Georgievna Vinaver," 22.

28. Ibid., 23.

29. Ibid., 17.

30. Ibid., 18.

31. Ibid., 17–18.

32. Ibid., 31–32.

33. Ibid., 19.

34. On the Crimean episode, see Rosenberg, *Liberals in the Russian Revolution*, 357–81.

35. Ibid., 124.

36. *Rossiiskaia natsional'naia biblioteka*, fond 211, opis' 1, delo 410, list 11, as cited in Nathans, *Beyond the Pale*, 147.

37. Kelner and Korostelev, "Vospominaniia Rozy Georgievnoi Vinaver," 12–13. In a collection of essays dedicated to Maksim Vinaver on the tenth anniversary of his death, his Kadet colleagues highlighted his devotion to the "Jewish question in Russia" as being central to his life. Miliukov, *M. M. Vinvaver i russkaia obshchestvennost' nachala XX veka*, 14.

38. For more on the OPE, see Brian Horowitz, *Jewish Philanthropy and Enlightenment in Late Tsarist Russia* (Seattle: University of Washington Press, 2009).

39. Vinaver, "Vospominaniia Rozy Georgievna Vinaver," 25.

40. Ibid., 26–27.

41. Kelner and Korostelev, "Vospominaniia Rozy Georgievnoi Vinaver," 12; see Miliukov, *M. M. Vinaver i russkaia nachala XX veka*.

42. Vinaver, "Vospominaniia Rozy Georgievna Vinaver," 49.

43. For more on the *Soiuz dlia dostizheniia polnopraviia evreiskogo naroda v Rossii*, see Christoph Gassenschmidt, *Jewish Liberal Politics in Tsarist Russia, 1900–1914: The Modernization of Russian Jewry* (New York: New York University Press, 1995).

44. Vinaver, "Vospominaniia Rozy Georgievna Vinaver," 51.

45. Pavel Miliukov (1859–1943) was the founder of the Kadet party and the key theoretician of Russian liberalism. See Melissa Kirschke Stockdale, *Paul Miliukov and the Quest for a Liberal Russia, 1880–1918* (Ithaca, NY: Cornell University Press, 1996).

46. Vinaver, "Vospominaniia Rozy Georgievna Vinaver," 77.

47. Kelner and Korostelev note that she must have confused the event or date because the first All-Russian Congress of Lawyers took place in St. Petersburg on March 28–30, 1905, under the leadership of N. V. Teslenko. They suggest that she may have been referring to the second congress, which began in Moscow but was broken up by the police. As a result, meetings took place in private apartments. See Kelner and Korostelev, "Vospominaniia Rozy Georgievnoi Vinaver," 116.

48. Vinaver, "Vospominaniia Rozy Georgievna Vinaver," 39–40.

49. Ibid., 85.

50. Kelner and Korostelev, "Vospominaniia Rozy Georgievnoi Vinaver," 115.

51. Vinaver, "Vospominaniia Rozy Georgievna Vinaver," 34–35.

52. Ibid., 4.

53. Ibid., 34–35.

54. Ibid., 57.

55. Stockdale, *Paul Miliukov and the Quest for a Liberal Russia*, 162.

56. Vinaver, "Vospominaniia Rozy Georgievna Vinaver," 58–59.

57. Ibid., 84.

58. Maksim Vinaver served in the Kadet-led government of the Crimean Regional Government during the Civil War and cooperated with Anton Denikin and his Volunteer Army against the Bolsheviks. See Vinaver, "Vospominaniia Rozy Georgievna Vinaver," 85–95; Rosenberg, *Liberalism in the Russian Revolution*, 357–81.

59. Lucy S. Dawidowicz, *The Golden Tradition: Jewish Life and Thought in Eastern Europe* (Syracuse, NY: Syracuse University Press, 1996), 463.

60. Vinaver, "Vospominaniia Rozy Georgievna Vinaver," 17.

61. Ibid., 18.

62. For descriptions of those friendships, see ibid., 61–84.

22

Spatial Coherence as Sovereignty

ARNOLD J. BAND

The history of modern Hebrew literature is so peculiar that historians have struggled to find adequate models with which to comprehend this complicated phenomenon. They were faced with a bewildering set of anomalies: writers who often did not speak the language in which they wrote, who were alien to the general societies in which they lived, who often did not live together with their readers in coherent communities, but were, in fact, spread over several European imperial states in which they were, at best, subjects. To cope with this phenomenon, historians have resorted to two concepts that have been rejected in the past generation. At times they (Joseph Klausner and Y. F. Lachower) would refer to the centers (*merkazim*) of literature moving from Berlin, to Galicia, to Vilna, to Odessa, and finally to Tel Aviv. These centers housed writers of significant talent, but even in Odessa and Warsaw, they hardly formed a coherent community—and as centers they did not last very long. The audience they attracted was sparse and fleeting compared to the masses which, by the end of the nineteenth century, preferred to read Yiddish, or a bit later, several European languages. A second model, "the republic of letters," introduced into the discourse by Simon Halkin, was significantly expanded, but ultimately rejected by Dan Miron. Neither of these models, it should be noted, copes with the sociopolitical status of the Jews in Europe in the modern period, a lacuna that is perfectly understandable given the powerless status of the Jews in Europe.

The creation of the State of Israel, however, immediately changed this powerless status and therefore enables us to introduce considerations of political sovereignty. While there are a variety of definitions of sovereignty, the oft-quoted brief definition offered by Max Weber is still serviceable. Weber defines the state as "the form of human community that (successfully) lays claim to the monopoly on legitimate physical violence within a given territory."[1] This monopoly of legitimate force within a territory we call *sovereignty*. In the modern period, the monopoly of force involves considerations of subject populations, their demands for rights, economic opportunities, and social expression. Territory is not only a piece of land, but involves its inhabitance by a coherent community of individuals who interact socially and culturally. It is a network of public and private spaces. Sovereignty, furthermore, is rarely absolute, but is constrained and compromised by all sorts of forces. Sovereignty, therefore, in our definition, does not always include the existence of a recognized state. Arguably, the notion of sovereignty is useful even when we are studying a situation in which most of these features are absent, as they were for European Jews. In that case, absence of power becomes a defining presence. Sovereignty, furthermore, can be partial or shared, nascent or declining. Moreover, it is rare for sovereign states to exist in isolation; they impinge upon each other, often violently. And when we speak of sovereignty, we might be referring to concrete political facts such as governments, armies, and laws, or imagined units, somewhat like Benedict Anderson's "imagined communities." However complicated, as a dynamic geopolitical concept it is eminently useful.

In this essay we will use the notions of sovereignty as a heuristic device to examine cultural developments, in this case literary works, in their geopolitical contexts, to enhance our understanding of one of the most remarkable aspects of modern Jewish history: the crystallization of a dynamic center of Hebrew literary activity in Palestine in the later years of the 1920s. Note that in this case we can use the term "center" with confidence since we discover that spatial coherence led to a type of cultural sovereignty (hence the title of this paper). We hope this method will help us avoid reading history backward, to interpret works of the 1920s, for instance, in the light of subsequent developments: the Shoah and the establishment of the State of Israel. Rather, we should attempt to read works written in Tel Aviv of the 1920s or 1930s in light of the specific geopolitical forces that impinged so relentlessly upon this community of writers. Since this group of writers and editors was one of the cluster of voluntary social structures that cohered to form the basis of the state that came into existence in 1948, it is both interesting in itself and for the light it sheds on the nature of the society that created and maintained the state after 1948. While much work has been done to document the achievements of the period (one thinks of the significant work of Zohar Shavit, in particular), our understanding of certain features of this development will be enhanced by placing them in the sovereignty calculus.

To render the development of the late 1920s intelligible, we must introduce two crucial historical developments that precede them, one internal, the other external. In the Yishuv, after some twenty-five years of minor achievements and pervasive setbacks, the community began to exhibit clear signs of cohesion and development between 1906 and 1910. This growth took many forms and has been well detailed in Arieh Saposnik's *Becoming Hebrew*.[2] The creation of institutions such as the Herzliyah Gymnasium, Bezalel School of Arts and Crafts, the Gymnasia Ivrit in Jerusalem; the teaching of Hebrew speech and texts in at least twenty schools throughout the Yishuv; the publication of *Ha'omer* and *Hapoel Hatzair*; the arrival of such young literary figures as Y. H. Brenner, S. Y. Agnon, Devorah Baron, Asher Barash, David Shimonovits, and Rachel Bluvstein were sure signs that a new coherent community had taken shape, dedicated to the basic principles of national renewal in the ancestral Hebrew homeland where Hebrew would—in the future—be the dominant language. Clearly, despite the continuation of Ottoman rule even after the Young Turks Revolution of 1908, the Jewish community of the Yishuv had the organizational resources to create a network of coherent institutions and, in many senses, began to form a coherent cultural society that exhibited many aspects of a sovereign society. Even though many Jewish communal activities were shut down during World War I and almost half the population of the Yishuv had to leave Palestine, many institutions were operational again by 1918 and plans for immigration resumed, clear signs of the strength of basic sovereign institutions. In that year, the cornerstone of the Hebrew University was laid in Jerusalem.

More important than the growth of the Yishuv was the clash of sovereign empires during World War I: by the time the war was over, four great empires were gone. The Russian Empire where most Jews lived collapsed during the war and was destroyed in the revolutions of 1917. Imperial Germany lost territories and was impoverished. Germany's ally, the Austro-Hungarian Empire, was dismembered; and Turkey, the former Ottoman Empire, lost Palestine to the British in 1917–18. The creation of the League of Nations brought about the emergence of new sovereign, democratic states such as Austria, Hungary, Poland, Czechoslovakia, and the Baltic states. The Mandate system introduced new, semi-independent states into the Middle East, among them the British Mandate of Palestine, which was accompanied by the Balfour Declaration and the idea of a Jewish National Home. The years after World War I witnessed many border wars and pogroms. The negotiations surrounding the Versailles Treaty raised many thorny questions regarding sovereignty and the rights of minorities, including the Jews. All of these tumultuous events, in addition to the great expectations regarding Mandatory Palestine, impelled and colored the Third Aliyah that brought to the Yishuv those writers and readers who comprised the viable literary community of the late 1920s.

The growth and development of the Hebrew literary community in the Yishuv was, to a great extent, the result of the rapid deterioration or destruction of the Hebrew literary communities in the Diaspora, and all writers were keenly aware of this fact. Within about a decade, between 1914 and 1924, the world that produced Mendele Mokher Seforim, H. N. Bialik, Shaul Tchernichowski, and Ahad Ha'am was gone. There were, to be sure, "enclaves" (cf. Shachar Pinsker) here and there, but these were often transitory. The Russian Revolution of October 1917 offered temporary relief from tsarist oppression, but within a few years proved to be even more hostile to Hebrew creativity. A significant group of Hebrew writers resided in Weimar Germany between 1922 and 1924, but none of them had been born in Germany and many of them left Berlin for Palestine in 1924. Their audience, furthermore, was rarely in Germany. New York had its cluster of Hebrew writers and readers, but it was overshadowed by the massive Yiddish world and the rapid Americanization of the huge Jewish population that had migrated from Eastern Europe after 1870.

While the brevity of the dynamic period of the Weimar Hebrew group is easy to understand, the rapid disintegration of the Hebrew community in Poland requires more analysis. Poland, after all, was the center of vibrant, though turbulent, Jewish life between the wars. With three million Jews

— 350,000 in Warsaw alone—and the success of the Tarbut schools, one of the most noble experiments in Hebrew education from kindergarten through gymnasium, one might expect a burgeoning Hebrew public. But Polish Jewry, including Vilna (then part of Poland), could not maintain a Hebrew daily newspaper throughout this period, and by the 1930s few modern Hebrew books were published annually. By the mid-1930s few Hebrew writers or editors were left in the country. One usually attributes this decline to the harsh economic boycotts and political discrimination, and these were certainly a factor; but they could not be the only explanation because the interwar period, for all its dark moments, was a period of astounding social and cultural activity of Polish Jewry as a whole, particularly in the Yiddish press. There are two other, less famous reasons that might explain this decline. First, despite the increasing hostility of the Polish Christian population and government to the Jews, Polonization of Jews proceeded at a dizzying rate. Shmeruk (citing Paul Glickson) states that one hundred thousand copies of Polish language newspapers published by Jews for Jews were sold daily in Warsaw in the 1930s. He concluded, as does Ezra Mendelsohn, that given the rapid Polonization of the Jews of Poland, the future of the community was in doubt even if there had been no Shoah. Second, the Hebrew language Tarbut schools were not designed to perpetuate the Jewish community of Poland; their curricula and teachers, consciously or unconsciously, were preparing their students for life in a Hebrew-speaking society that implied *aliyah* to Eretz Israel. Certainly, more than a few of the 67,000 *olim* in the Fourth (Grabski) Aliyah and of the 94,000 Polish Jews among the Fifth Aliyah had been educated in the Tarbut schools or the various Zionist youth movements. The very success of this education spelled its ultimate doom since the implicit goal of the Hebrew/Zionist-oriented schools and youth movements was to remove the Jews from Poland. By doing so, they precluded the possibility of a Hebrew-reading audience in that country.

The basic outlines of the actual institutionalization of the Tel Aviv community in the 1920s have been formulated, and I do not intend to rehearse them here. A simple comparison of publication figures will set the parameters of the change. In the four years from 1920 through 1923, the total number of Hebrew books published annually in Eretz Israel in each year respectively were: 48, 56, 63, and 75. In the years from 1925 through

1928, the numbers rose even more dramatically: 152, 254, 316, and 321. (These numbers and those for Warsaw are taken from the Harvard On-Line Library Information System [HOLLIS].) The number of books sold rose from 4,000 in 1918 and 6,900 in 1919 to 150,000 in 1928. While the Jewish population in the Eretz Israel almost tripled in that period from about 60,000 to about 175,000, the number of books sold multiplies by a factor of twenty. By 1925 when the Histadrut began to publish *Davar* under the editorship of Berl Katznelson, there were three Hebrew dailies in Tel Aviv, and the schools in Eretz Israel were beginning to turn out successive classes of Hebrew-speaking youngsters. In that same year, the Hebrew University formally was opened in Jerusalem, and while the early classes were very small, the symbolism of a Hebrew university in Jerusalem was overwhelming.

In Poland the trend of publication of Hebrew books moves in the opposite direction and by 1930 reaches the disastrous number of eighteen per annum. This does not mean that the Yishuv was an independent cultural center by the late 1920s. The economy was fragile and underwent two depressing recessions in that decade, in 1922 and from 1928 through 1930. Editors and publishers constantly were seeking financial subsidies from both America and Europe. But by 1929 when the Agudat Hasofrim was formally organized in Tel Aviv, it was clear to most involved parties that the center of the Hebrew world was there, not in Berlin or Warsaw or New York.

One can enumerate a variety of reasons contributing to this success. First, as suggested above, the Yishuv showed remarkable talents for self-organization and for establishing institutional structures, especially through the Labor movement, particularly after 1906 but even before then. While public life was often chaotic and contentious, the Jews of Eretz Israel could work together, especially when led by such charismatic figures as Brenner and Katznelson. Foremost among the institutions contributing to the crystallization of a coherent cultural center was the Histadrut, founded in 1920. The labor-oriented society that the Histadrut was intent on creating was going to be Hebrew speaking. The three ideological goals (*kibushim*—"conquests") were of labor, of the soil, and of the language, and these slogans were taken seriously. These were all components of sovereignty. Second, the conquest of Palestine by the British Army in 1917 rid the Yishuv of Ottoman control that was repressive and certainly not conducive to the realization of Jewish aspirations. While the Mandatory powers were an extension of British colonialist goals and Albion could be perfidious, the Balfour Declaration, the recognition of Hebrew as an official language (together with English and Arabic), the lack of interference in the internal affairs of the Jewish settlers, and the introduction of many Western norms of public behavior all contributed to the strengthening of the Yishuv. Third, the disastrous political events in Europe and the restriction of immigration to the United States, both diverted immigration waves toward Eretz Israel and induced many to draw certain conclusions about the destiny of the Jews in the modern world with its intensified sovereign nationalisms. Last but by no means least, the ideology that animated much of Hebrew literature from the 1880s on, first as Hibbat Zion, then as Zionism, offered a coherent interpretation of history and the political events of the times. In the whirl of upheavals after 1914—the wars, the disintegration of mighty sovereign empires, the creation of new sovereign states, the intensification of antisemitism—the generation of a Hebrew-speaking national homeland (state?) in Eretz Israel made sense. While the leadership of the Zionist movement was not always interested in the development of a Hebrew culture—Bialik himself was not an eager settler, and neither Berdiczewski nor Frischmann ever considered *aliyah* —the basic Ahad Ha'amic formulation of cultural Zionism was compelling for many people. The Yishuv could, indeed, be a cultural center for the Jews of the Diaspora. It also was a refuge which still accepted Jews after the Johnson Act (1921) that began to restrict immigration to the United States. This key act of American national sovereignty was crucial in the formation of a sovereign Jewish community in Eretz Israel.

What we witness in the 1920s is a fascinating contrast between the awareness of the chaos and homelessness engendered by the geopolitical churning of sovereign states in Europe and the possible sense of nascent sovereignty and stability in the Yishuv. The contrast was always in the mind of the Hebrew writers. The passing of hegemony to Eretz Israel was not regarded with a sense of triumphalism by the more sensitive writers. When one reads the correspondence generated by the independent literary journal *Hedim* in its early years, 1922–1923, one cannot escape the note of desperation among writers such as Yaakov Rabinovitz, Asher

Barash, Avraham Shlonsky, and Yitzhak Lamdan, who realized that they now had the responsibility to keep Hebrew literature alive and vital. A careful reading of several of the great imaginative works of the period will demonstrate how Hebrew writers embodied in their writing the preoccupations of sensitive Jews of the chaotic period. (This reading should strive to avoid unintentional foreshadowing, i.e., reading a work of literature in the light of subsequent historical developments.)

The apocalyptic mood of the period was captured most forcefully in Yitzhak Lamdan's epic poem *Masada*, published in Tel Aviv in 1927, an expressionistic evocation of the inescapable terrors and false options facing Jews after World War I, all leading to the desperate, absurdist conclusion that the only solution lies in "Masada," the author's mythical name for Eretz Israel. This *poema* gives expression to the desperate flight from broken homes and traditions in the *golah* and the agonized trials of return to Zion, here heroically called "Masada," echoing both the cataclysmic historical event in Josephus and the desire to create a new foundation, a *masad* for the new Jewish sovereignty. The poetic voice expresses a mélange of desires: for revenge, for utopian fulfillment, for a radical revolt against Jewish history. The hero strives to mount the wall of the city and calls out to God for aid. He vows that Masada will never fall again: *"shenit Masada lo tipol,"* later one of the key phrases of the Zionist youth movements. Sovereignty implies security.

Even more affected by the upheavals of the period and the transfer from Europe to Eretz Israel and all that it implies is the massive life oeuvre of Uri Zvi Greenberg. Greenberg experienced first the savage fighting of World War I, then the pogrom of Lemberg in 1918. These bitter personal experiences convinced him by the early 1920s that Jews had no future in Europe, that Christian Europe would rid itself of its Jews. Writing first in Yiddish, then, after 1923, in Hebrew, he adopted many of the modernist idioms of the period that allowed him to express his apocalyptic visions. His constant relocations between the wars brought him to Warsaw (1918–1923), Berlin (1923), Tel Aviv (1923–1930), Warsaw (1930–1939), and finally Tel Aviv (1939–1981). His *Eimah gedolah ve-yareah* ("Great Fright and the Moon") (Tel Aviv: Hedim, 1925) injected into Hebrew poetry the intense reaction of a powerful poet to the violent disruption of traditional modes of behavior, to the carnage of his personal experiences. While his poetry expressed both his personal anxieties and his agonized sorrow over the murder of Jews in the Shoah (*Rehovot Hanahar* [Streets of the River]) (Tel Aviv: Schocken, 1951), his essays and some of his poems profoundly articulate a vision of Jewish sovereignty in the ancestral homeland shaped by traditional Jewish messianic imagery. After the massacre in Hebron of 1929, Greenberg left the Labor party and became one of the most forceful spokesmen for Revisionist Zionism. He spent most of the 1930s in Poland editing and organizing for that movement.

As the political situation worsened in Europe in the 1930s, the stream of Jews seeking refuge in Eretz Israel widened and, as is well known, some 250,000 *olim* arrived between 1930 and 1939. This *aliyah*, usually called the "German Aliyah," actually included 94,000 Polish Jews, in addition to significant numbers from the Baltic nations and Romania, many of whom had excellent Hebrew training in a variety of schools, thus adding measurably to the potential reading audience for both Hebrew books and journals. The hegemony of Tel Aviv, already well established by 1929, was corroborated. It is significant to note, however, that of the 137 Hebrew writers listed by Agudat Hasofrim as residing in Eretz Israel between the wars, only twenty-eight arrived in the 1930s precisely when the population doubled. The happy result of this massive Hebrew *aliyah* was not only the strengthening of the new creative center in Eretz Israel, but the saving of this group from the slaughter of the Nazi period. For while hundreds of Yiddish writers were killed in the Shoah, significantly fewer Hebrew writers suffered this fate. In a study published anonymously in 1973, Yisrael Cohen lists sixty-five Hebrew writers killed in the Shoah.[3] The impact of the differing fates of these two groups of writers, the Hebraists and the Yiddishists, has had the obvious consequence. After World War II, Yiddish literature could have no real future: most of its writers and many of its readers were killed in the Shoah.

While Greenberg's articulation of the dialectic between the lack of Jewish sovereignty in the Diaspora and the renewed sovereignty in Zion is the most forceful we have in Hebrew poetry of the period, the prose articulation probably is most profound and influential in Agnon's *Oreah nata lalun* (A Wayfarer Who Stayed for a Night), which was published serially in *Ha'aretz* in 1938 and 1939. In that novel, the narrator, a resident of Jerusalem, relates the story of his yearlong visit to his hometown in

Galicia several years earlier. He finds his town devastated by the ravages of World War I: much of the Jewish population has fled, and those who have remained are crippled or impoverished. (Often, this book is called by critics: "sefer hashoah lifne hashoah [a book about the Shoah before the Shoah].") The town's Jewish institutions are barely operative, and the narrator is given the key of the town *bet midrash* for his own use and safe-keeping. In a final episode that is not too subtle, when he returns home to Jerusalem, he finds the key to the *bet midrash* in his suitcase, actualizing the midrashic saying: "In the future, the synagogues and study halls of the Diaspora will be transferred to Eretz Israel."

The three writers we have discussed were not political scientists or historians, but it is certain that their imaginative writing, either in poetry or prose, was informed acutely by the issues of their times that were generated and shaped by the various aspects of sovereignty we have discussed. Our argument is not based on a teleology that reads imaginative works of the 1920s or the 1930s in the light of subsequent developments, the Shoah and the establishment of the State of Israel, but rather on a careful reading of these works against the background of the geopolitical forces that shaped them. Without them, there would have been no Lamdan's *Masada*, no *Eimah gedolah veyare'ah* or *Rehovot hanahar*, and no *Ore'ah nata lalun*.

Our argument that spatial coherence enables sovereignty requires that we consider the impact of the creation of the sovereign State of Israel in May 1948; the shift in both life and literature was profound, though not always detected at the time. Stateless sovereignty, after all, does not have the compelling power of state force. During the Mandatory period, state force, policing, was in the hands of the British government, which had to mediate, for instance, in the bitter struggle between Jews and Arabs in the years 1936–1939. Questions of morality in such instances were conditioned by the absence of or limits on one's power. But once the state was established and endowed with sovereign power, with force over a population in a certain territory, questions of state morality became paramount. Having achieved political sovereignty, the Jewish population of the State of Israel was confronted with moral issues, particularly in relation to its Arab minorities, which it had never known before and about which much has been written over the years. The shift in power underlies the discussions in a recent issue of *Jewish Social Studies* that presents fifteen essays from a conference: "History and Responsibility: Hebrew Literature and 1948," held at Stanford University in June 2011.[4] In the introduction (2), the editors state: "As we were preparing the conference, we deliberately chose the neutral '1948' over loaded terms such as 'The War of Independence' (*milhemet ha'atzmaut*), 'War of Sovereignty' (*milhemet hakomemiut*), or 'The War of Liberation' (*milhemet hashihrur*)." The editors also avoided using in the title the Arab term for the events of 1948, "Nakba"—the Catastrophe. The fifteen authors of this volume, however, mostly Israelis, are keenly aware of the fact that Israeli literature has paid little attention to the suffering of the Arabs displaced by the war in 1948–1949, and this is the overriding theme of this entire volume.

Ironically, the Israeli literary composition most cited in this volume of essays is S. Yizhar's novella *Hirbet Hiz'ah*, the oft-cited story originally published in 1948 during the war, a pained description of the evacuation of Arabs from their village by Israeli soldiers. The essays by Hasak-Lowy (27–37), Setter (38–54), and Hochberg (55–69) deal with this central novella. Setter, in a most persuasive essay on this novella, notes that throughout his writing, Yizhar returns repeatedly to the events of 1948 as if Israeliness itself implies a postponement of responsibility for the Nakba. What these essays on this novella seem to overlook is the basic fact that the story was written and published in the very period of the war of 1948 when the fate of the nascent State of Israel was severely threatened and Jewish casualties were many. That Yizhar did write this story in those days was an act of high moral significance.

A second cultural phenomenon generated by the transition from statelessness to statehood is eloquently presented by Michael Gluzman in his article "Sovereignty and Melancholy: Israeli Poetry after 1948" (164–79). The editors sum up Gluzman's article succinctly: "From the Haskalah onward, Hebrew writers perceived themselves as 'watchmen unto the House of Israel,' prophets bearing a responsibility for giving voice to the national aspirations and concerns of the Jewish people. . . . The establishment of the State of Israel in 1948 provoked a profound shift in this self-perception and in the dynamics of Hebrew poetry's relation to readers and the project of statehood. After the establishment of state sovereignty . . . the writers' national role became superfluous" (7).

These two crucial phenomena, the displacement of the Arabs and the diminution of the historic role of the Hebrew author are two of the most eloquent markers of the transition from stateless sovereignty to state sovereignty in 1948.

NOTES

1. Max Weber, "Politics as a Vocation," in *From Max Weber: Essays in Sociology*, ed. H. H. Gerthand and C. Wright Mills (New York: Oxford University Press, 1958), 78.

2. Arieh Saposnik, *Becoming Hebrew* (New York: Oxford University Press, 2008).

3. *Yediot Genazim* 5, no. 81 (Nissan, yr. 10).

4. *Jewish Social Studies*, n.s., 18, no. 3 (spring/summer 2012). (This number actually was published in spring 2013.)

23

Exemplary Leaders

Martin Buber and Franz Rosenzweig

PAUL MENDES-FLOHR

[Die] Sehnsucht nach Führerschaft allüberall lebendig—
so groß und mächtig, daß sie auch die verkehrtesten, windigsten
und groteskesten Ausdrucksformen nicht verschmäht.
—Max Scheler

A pervasive longing for leadership—a "savior, prophet, or *Weltverbesse-rer*" who would save "our world"[1]—gained intensity in the wake of the First World War and Germany's humiliating defeat. Alarmed by what he deemed to be "most objectionable, erroneous and grotesque expressions" of the quest for a leader (*Führer*), the philosopher Max Scheler (1874–1928) deemed it of utmost urgency to clarify what constituted genuine leadership.[2] Even before the war, he was exercised by the cult of leadership associated with the likes of the poet Stefan George and the educator Gustav Wyneken of the German youth movement.[3] But he first addressed the issue publicly of "how and whom we should elect as our leaders" in a lecture he delivered in the summer of 1921 at the University of Cologne. In "Vorbilder und Führer,"[4] he advanced a typological delineation of leadership, broadly distinguishing between *Vorbilder*, exemplars of ethical and intellectual values, and *Führer*, executive or organizational leaders. The latter type represents administrative leadership, whose authority in a given organization—such as a military unit, a business, or a research institution—is acknowledged by the members of that organization. One need not identify with the values and worldview of the *Führer*, or even

like him or her. It is otherwise with a *Vorbild*, who embodies and person-
ifies the values and ideals to which one subscribes and aspires to realize.
In contrast to administrative and organizational leaders (*Führer*), the exemplary individual reaches into "the depths of the soul of every person
and every human group."[5] Hence, whereas leaders address one's will,
Vorbilder (the plural of *Vorbild*) appeal to the fundamental axiological
disposition (*Gesinnung*) "beneath" one's will.[6] *Vorbilder* project ideal images of the self, as "the old saying of the renown mystic,"[7] cited by Scheler,
attests: "Vor jedem schwebt ein Bild des, der er werden soll; bevor er das
nicht ist, ist nicht sein Friede voll"[8] (Above everyone hovers an image of
what he should be. Until he is not that, he will not be at full peace with
himself).

In contradistinction to *Führer*, *Vorbilder* need not be our contemporaries; indeed, they often are drawn from the past, such as Moses, Jesus, and
Buddha. And they also may be fictional figures drawn from myth, legends,
and literature. Be they real historical figures or imaginative constructs,
Vorbilder, according to Scheler, may be classified according to five basic
types: Saint, Genius, Hero, a Leading Mind, and a Master of the Art of
Living.[9] The type of *Vorbild* with whom an individual or a society identifies reflects their governing values and ideals.

Without an explicit reference to Scheler, Gershom Scholem notes three
Vorbilder—"types of piety"—characteristic of traditional Jewish society:
the *talmid hakham*, the *tsaddik*, and the *hasid*—the rabbinic scholar, the
just man, and the individual of exacting, supererogatory piety.[10] These
"ideal human types" denote the "basic attitudes" that shape the spiritual
and axiological landscape of rabbinic Judaism. They are not static modal-
ities of a fixed content, however. As Scheler underscores, *Vorbilder* are
refracted through the experience and imaginative reflexes of each individual and group, and thereby may be transformed with regard to how
one understands their conative precepts. Hence, while the value structure
of specific *Vorbilder* endures, the conception of the content and norms
that are in accord with those values may differ. Context inflects the cultural and normative horizons of *Vorbilder*. Within the context of early
twentieth-century German Jewry, this axionormative dialectic animates
what was celebrated as the Jewish Renaissance, and in particular the revalorization of the *talmid hakham*.

Martin Buber and Franz Rosenzweig represent differing, albeit comple-
mentary conceptions of the *talmid hakham* as the guiding *Vorbild* of Jewish spiritual renewal. In one crucial respect, however, they both challenge
Scheler's dichotomous opposition between *Führer* and *Vorbild*:[11] while
embodying the renewed ideal of the *talmid hakham*, they also assumed
the responsibility of administrative leadership.

   With their entrance into Western secular culture, the Jews ceased to
be a text-centered culture. As Moshe Halbertal observes, "Loyalty to a
shared text no longer marks the boundaries of the modern Jewish community, for the assumption that the values and norms of the community
should be justified by reference to a shared text lost its validity."[12] Or as
Rosenzweig put it in more dramatic terms:

> Then came the Emancipation. At one blow it vastly enlarged the in-
> tellectual horizons of thought and soon, very soon afterwards, of
> actual living. Jewish "studying" or [rather] "learning" [of sacred, ca-
> nonical texts] could not keep pace with this rapid extension. What
> is new is not so much the collapse of the outer barriers; even pre-
> viously, while the ghetto had certainly sheltered the Jew, it had not
> shut him off. He moved beyond its bounds, and what the ghetto gave
> him was only peace, home, a home for his spirit. What is new, is not
> that the Jew's feet could take him farther than ever before [. . .] The
> new feature is that the wanderer no longer returns at dusk, allowing
> him to spend the night in solitary learning. To abandon the figure of
> speech—he [now] finds his spiritual and intellectual home outside
> the Jewish world. The old style of learning is helpless before his spir-
> itual emigration.[13]

The displacement of the canonical texts of traditional Judaism by alternative curricula led to the eclipse of the *talmid hakham* as Jewry's *Vorbild*.
Buber's and Rosenzweig's revalorization of the *talmid hakham* thus would
entail the re-centering of Jewish community in shared canonical texts,
thereby rendering the Jews once again a "people of the book." Buber and
Rosenzweig subscribed, however, to radically contrasting conceptions of
what constitutes the restored canon and its normative function. Accordingly, their image of the renascent *talmid hakham* differs fundamentally.

   For Rosenzweig, the canon in which he sought to re-center Judaism ultimately had a normative function; the texts of the canon were to be read and interpreted in order to determine the meaning of Jewish religious practice.[14] Buber would read the canon as providing the Jews with a shared vocabulary and a metanarrative in support of "the life of dialogue," which as a universal principle is by definition not culturally specific. The canon is instructive but not sacred. Hence, Buber not only read canonical texts with different "commitments and expectations"[15] than did Rosenzweig, but he also was decidedly more selective with regard to which texts he would honor as belonging to the canon.

Consonant with ascribing to the canonical texts of Jewish tradition a normative horizon, Rosenzweig located the study of these texts — *Talmud Torah* — in a *Lehrhaus*, the German rendering of the traditional *bet midrash*, which is usually attached to a synagogue and often coextensive with a synagogue, as is suggested by the Yiddish designation of the latter simply as a *shul* (school). Although Rosenzweig's *Lehrhaus* occupied no permanent quarters and was held in various public institutions, it was regarded as a possible "passage way" to the synagogue and traditional Jewish religious practice.[16] At Rosenzweig's *Lehrhaus* one studied the texts of Jewish tradition with a dialogical openness to the possibility that the texts would exact a normative claim on one's self, leading to the synagogue and ritual observance, to a life of "Torah and *mitzvot*." As an "old-new"[17] *talmid hakham*, Rosenzweig was as a *Vorbild* of this process.

Buber, whom Rosenzweig would with affectionate irony cast as a quintessential *epikorus*,[18] projected an entirely new image of the *talmid hakham* and removed him (and her) from the synagogue. For Buber the *bet midrash* was the antechamber not to the synagogue and *mitzvot* but to what in hasidic parlance is called the "marketplace": God is to be served in the secular sphere of everyday life. Buber's severance of "Jewish teachings" from "Jewish Law" was the great divide between him and Rosenzweig, who found the division not simply arbitrary but a fundamental misunderstanding of what constitutes "Jewish knowledge." In an open letter to Buber, he chided him for failing to realize that all "that can and should be known is not really knowledge!" All that "can and should be taught is not teaching!" For "teaching begins where the subject matter ceases to be subject matter and changes into inner power."[19] He commended Buber for advocating a renewal of Jewish learning and including within its ambit the

entire literature of the traditional Jewish library, without any a priori win-
nowing of essential from unessential teachings, typical of the apologetics
of bourgeois, postemancipation Jewry. He thus finds it incomprehensible
and flagrantly inconsistent that Buber leaves the Law "in the shackles put
on it . . . by the nineteenth century."[20] Buber's response to this critique was
a terse reaffirmation of his fundamental belief that "revelation is never a
formulation of law."[21]

What Buber and Rosenzweig did share was a firm conviction that Jewish literacy is not simply a fount of knowledge but rather is the wellspring
of Jewish spiritual and ethical values. As representatives of the restoration
of Judaism as a text-centered culture, they were *talmidei hakhamim*, students of the sages, who placed themselves in the "chain" of the Jewish
tradition of passing on its foundational texts by reading them and inter-
preting their meaning anew. For, as Rosenzweig aptly observed in citing a
rabbinic *midrash*, the *talmidei hakhamim* are not mere sounding boxes of
what their teachers taught them. Through a paradoxical twofold move of
humbling themselves to the teachings of their predecessors, they reveren-
tially comment on those teachings, while drawing out of them new meaning and even instruction. They are, as a *midrash* on Isaiah 54:13 explains,
"builders": "'And all thy children shall be taught of the Lord, and great
shall be the peace of thy children!' Do not read 'banayikh', thy children,
but 'bonayikh', thy builders."[22]

Though both Buber and Rosenzweig conceived of the renaissance of
Jewish learning as embracing in principle the traditional canon in its entirety, in practice Buber's view of the canon was, as already noted, far more
circumscribed than Rosenzweig's. While he valued the Hebrew Bible as
the founding text of the canon, in his writings and teaching he largely ignored postbiblical literature other than some *midrashim* and hasidic lore.
Rosenzweig's "canon" was far more inclusive: in addition to the Hebrew
Bible, he referenced in his writings and included within the curriculum of
the *Lehrhaus* the traditional prayer book, Talmud, medieval philosophers,
and poets.[23]

In his role as the *Vorbild* of a posttraditional *talmid hakham*,[24] Rosenzweig also assumed the responsibilities of leadership as the founding director of the Freies Jüdisches Lehrhaus in 1920 in Frankfurt am Main. Even
after he was afflicted with a neurodegenerative disease (ALS) that rendered

him physically disabled, he continued to oversee the intellectual content of the *Lehrhaus* and also sustained fastidious attention to the most technical administrative details.[25] Although the organized Jewish community of Frankfurt undertook to finance the activities of the *Lehrhaus*, its fiscal stability was severely weakened by the runaway inflation of the 1920s. The challenge of balancing the budget under those uncertain financial circumstances also threatened one of the cardinal principles of the *Lehrhaus* set by Rosenzweig. From the outset, he insisted that in order to ensure that those attending the *Lehrhaus* took their studies seriously, they should pay tuition, and a substantial one at that.[26] For the *Lehrhaus* was not an institute for adult education in which one came for "cultural entertainment." Rather, the "learning" that took place at the *Lehrhaus* demanded intensive spiritual and intellectual engagement in the study of texts, in *Talmud Torah*. Rosenzweig was not prepared, then, to forgo tuition, even in the most trying financial times. He would not compromise, even if it meant a decline in enrollment. From the small attic apartment in which his illness confined him, Rosenzweig kept a keen eye on virtually all aspects of the *Lehrhaus*: from its finances to the structure of its course schedule and the design of its announcements and programs, down to the size and color of the paper (he chose a different color for each semester's program).[27]

Buber was by disposition a more private person than Rosenzweig. He preferred his study to the public sphere. He assumed the mantle of teacher and leader with great reluctance, at least initially. He delivered his famous *Drei Reden* in Prague from 1909 to 1911, only after Leo Hermann, the leader (*Obmann*) of the Prague *Bar Kochba* Jewish university students' association, who had invited him to address his circle, agreed on special arrangements to spare him any possible embarrassment. In his reply to the invitation, Buber explained that he had little experience in public speaking and thus feared he would not be an effective speaker. To ease Buber's anxiety, Hermann told him that his lecture would be held in a theater in which someone would be assigned to sit in the director's pit and signal to Buber if his lecture was not going over well, whereupon he would bring it to a quick close and depart, returning directly to his home in Berlin. To Buber's surprise and the delight of *Obmann* Hermann and his colleagues, the lecture was well received.[28] Thus Buber's career was launched as a public speaker.[29]

Buber's career as a teacher also began hesitantly, and indeed, somewhat fortuitously. In December 1921—just two months prior to the first signs of the illness that would soon leave him nigh totally paralyzed—Rosenzweig and his wife paid Buber a visit. In the course of their conversation, they suddenly broached the possibility of Buber conducting a seminar in reading hasidic texts. As Rosenzweig later related, "But I had to know how he would go about it so I could tell people. When he said he couldn't tell exactly, I suggested that since he and two of his disciples were there, he might give us a trial lesson." Buber thereupon retrieved a few hasidic texts from his study and began to read them together with Rosenzweig, his wife, and the two disciples. Although Buber "proved a rather awkward teacher," Rosenzweig nonetheless decided to invite him to teach at the *Lehrhaus*. Buber "replied that, to his own surprise, *though refusing had been second nature to him for many years*, he had immediately felt disposed to accept my proposal."[30] So at the age of forty-four Buber began to teach. And a year later, he would accept a lectureship at the University of Frankfurt—also without forethought and by force of circumstance. It was Rosenzweig who originally received and accepted the lectureship, which bore the title "Jewish Religious Philosophy and Ethics," but before he could begin, it became increasingly clear that his illness, which also affected his speech, would prevent him from doing so. He then turned to Buber and urged him to accept the lectureship in his stead.[31] Reluctantly, Buber yielded to Rosenzweig's appeal and in the summer semester of 1923 commenced what would be an illustrious professorial career.[32] As illustrious as it may have been, he nonetheless remained uncomfortable in the position. In a letter to a Jerusalem colleague, he candidly noted, "Ich bin kein Universitätsmensch."[33]

Prior to his friendship with Rosenzweig, which occasioned a decisive shift in his intellectual and vocational trajectory, Buber regarded himself as an independent scholar (*Privatgelehrter*) whose leadership role as a public intellectual, aside from a brief but intense period of Zionist political and cultural activism,[34] was confined to occasional lectures and most significantly various editorial projects. While still active in the World Zionist movement, on the eve of the Fifth Zionist Congress in December 1901, he founded the Jüdischer Verlag, together with members of the Democratic Faction (Chaim Weizmann, Ephraim Moses Lilien, Berthold Feiwel, and Davis Trietsch).[35]

Soon after he ceased to be active in Zionist affairs, he began to lay the groundwork for *Die Gesellschaft*, a series of social-psychological monographs on modern urban society and culture. Between 1906 and 1912, he edited forty volumes, written by some of the leading scholars and intellectuals of Europe.[36] Concurrently, he edited very well received volumes on Celtic, Chinese, Finnish, and hasidic myths and folklore. His 1909 collection of *Ecstatic Confessions*—theistic and "pagan," European and Asian[37]—was to play a seminal role in the crystallization of literary expressionism.[38] In 1916, in the midst of the World War, he founded the monthly *Der Jude*, realizing a project already adumbrated in a pamphlet of 1903 issued together with Chaim Weizmann (as publisher) and Berthold Feiwel (as co-editor) to create a *Revue der jüdischen Moderne*.[39] Published between 1916 and 1928, *Der Jude* under Buber's editorial leadership became not only the preeminent cultural and political organ of German-speaking Jewry, but also arguably one of the most engaging intellectual forums of the Weimar Republic.[40] At the twilight of the ill-fated republic, Buber participated in an ecumenical—better, transconfessional—journal,[41] *Die Kreatur*, as the Jewish editor together with a Protestant editor (Viktor von Weizsäcker) and a Roman Catholic editor (Josef Wittig). Appearing between 1926 and 1930, the journal highlighted the promise and ultimately the tragedy of the Weimar Republic.[42]

Perhaps more than any other Jew, Buber embodied the irenic promise of Weimar and the wounds of its brutal betrayal in the wake of the dark turn in the course of German history: he was both prominent in Jewish affairs and a respected voice within the social and cultural life of post–World War I Germany, particularly in the movement for the reform of adult education[43] and that of religious socialism.[44] With Hitler's seizure of power in January 1933, Buber immediately surrendered his professorial appointment at the University of Frankfurt and assumed a central role in the "spiritual and intellectual resistance" to National Socialism and its program to disenfranchise and to humiliate the German Jewish population through legislation incrementally denying them not only their civil rights but, above all, their dignity.[45] It was at this fateful juncture in German Jewish life that Buber truly emerged as both a leader and a *Vorbild*.

To counter the Nazi assault on Jewish dignity and self-respect, Buber set out in Frankfurt to renew the program of Rosenzweig's *Lehrhaus*, which had effectively ceased to function in 1927.[46] At the same time, he initiated the establishment of the *Mittelstelle für jüdische Erwachsenen-bildung* (Jewish Center for Adult Education), which under Buber's directorship was active throughout the German Reich from 1934 until 1938, when the Nazi regime forbade it to continue its activities.[47] The principal focus of the *Mittlelstelle's* educational program was seminars, or as Buber called them *Lernzeit* (periods of learning), sometimes lasting a few days, devoted to the study of traditional Jewish texts. Geared both to the Jewish community at large and to specific constituencies, such as youth leaders and teachers, the texts studied most often were from the Hebrew Bible, with an emphasis on indicating its abiding existential relevance.[48] In an article published less than nine months after Hitler's appointment as chancellor, Buber spoke of the challenge to renew what he called a "biblical humanism": "A Hebrew humanism can rise only from a sensitive selection that out of the totality of Judaism discerns the Hebrew person in his purest state. Thus our humanism is directed to the Bible. To be sure, a Hebrew man is not a biblical man. The 'return' that is meant here cannot in the nature of things mean a striving for the recurrence or continuation of something long past, but only a striving for its renewal in a genuinely contemporary manifestation."[49]

Buber traveled the length and breadth of Germany to conduct seminars on select biblical texts. Under his leadership and example, the *Mittelstelle* largely addressed assimilated and acculturated Jews who were eager to give content to an identity imposed on them by Nazi legislation. The guiding principle of the *Mittelstelle* was that a *Trotzjudentum*, a defiant affirmation of one's identity as a Jew in the face of antisemitism, is not sufficient to restore and sustain Jewish self-esteem.[50] Rather, a genuine pride in one's primordial identity is to be borne by knowledge of one's distinctive cultural and religious patrimony.[51]

Buber's authority as a communal leader and teacher, one may surmise, rested in the type of Jewish sensibility he represented for a beleaguered Jewish community. In an essay on "Biblical Leadership" (*Biblisches Führertum*), significantly published shortly after the Nazi *Führer* seized the helm of Germany, he reflected on what constitutes leadership from the perspective of the Hebrew Bible. In terms that obliquely touched upon the contemporary political situation, but which also may be read as a statement on the calling of Jewish leadership at that dire hour, he observes that the Bible defines leadership as a response to a given situation. The authors of the Bible were, therefore, "not concerned with the difference between [leaders and their character], but the difference between the situations in which the person, the creaturely person, the appointed person . . . stands his test or fails."[52]

But success, Buber underscored, was not an "intrinsic value" for the writers of the Bible. Indeed, the biblical leader must perforce fail, for he is commissioned by the situation in which he finds himself "to fight, and not to conquer."[53] Thrust by providence into situations not of their choosing, biblical leaders are not primed by a quest for power, but are themselves "led, that is, insofar as they accept what is offered to them, insofar as they take upon themselves the responsibility for that which they have been entrusted with, insofar as they make real what has been laid upon them from outside of themselves."[54] In words reminiscent of Walter Benjamin's oft-cited critique of historians and their wont to record the feats of the victorious, while their true task should be "to brush history against the grain" and to retrieve the memory of those defeated by the imperious march of history,[55] Buber spoke of the "way" of true leaders as leading "through the work that history does not write down and cannot write down."[56]

Of the five types of biblical leadership Buber discerned,[57] it was the Prophet "who above all other types is 'contrary to history.'" He "is appointed to oppose the king, and even more history."[58] It would be an errant "overinterpretation" to read this aperçu on prophetic leadership as reflecting Buber's self-understanding of his leadership.[59] Nonetheless, in pointing to a type of leadership (*Führertum*) that, while it may be administrative and even political in nature, is primed by a sense of calling in the face of a dire, indeed hopeless situation, it offered a perspective to suggest—contra Scheler's typological dichotomy[60]—a possible continuum between a *Vorbild* and a *Führer*, a typological overlapping that applies, mutatis mutandis, equally to Rosenzweig. Indeed, one may argue that the authority of the leadership assumed by Buber and Rosenzweig was a function of their role as a *Vorbild* appropriate to the situation to which they respectively responded.

NOTES

Epigraph: Max Scheler, "Führer und Vorbilder," in *Schriften aus dem Nachlass*, vol. 1: *Zur Ethik und Erkenntnislehre*, ed. Maria Scheler (Bern: Francke Verlag, 1957), 257.

1. Ibid.

2. Cf. "Darum ist die Lehre von den Vorbildern [genuine, exemplary leaders] viel wichtiger, fundamentaler als die heute einseitig bevorzugte Führefrage." Ibid., 263.

3. Ibid, fn. 1.

4. Editor's note to Scheler, "Führer und Vorbilder," 514.

5. Ibid., 258f.

6. Ibid., 267. Thus Scheler also speaks of the *Gesinnung* as *Wert-Bewußtsein*, which ontologically is prior to one's will and as such constitutes the center of one's personhood (*Personzentrum*). Ibid.

7. This "renowned mystic," whom Scheler does not identify, is the German poet and Orientalist Friedrich Rückert (1788–1868). I wish to thank my colleague Willimien Otten for identifying this unnamed mystic.

8. The citation is from Friedrich Rückert's poem "Angereihte Perlen," in *Werke*, vol. 2: *Leipzig und Wien* (Leipzig: Bibliographisches Institut, 1897), 42–46.

9. Ibid., 269.

10. Gershom Scholem, "Three Types of Jewish Piety," in Gershom Scholem, *On the Possibiity of Jewish Mysticism in Our Time, and Other Essays*, ed. Avraham Shapira, trans. J. Chipman (Philadelphia: Jewish Publication Society, 1997), 176–90.

11. Noting that a *Führer* can be a leader of a "moral alliance or a gang of bandits," Scheler insists on a phenomenological distinction between leadership and exemplary agency. It is the attitudinal "attachment" (*Bindung*) that one has to the *Führer* and *Vorbild* (Exemplars and Leaders) respectively, and that thereby distinguishes them. Hence, while attachment to a leader is not based on "a communication of knowledge" (*Wissensmitteilung*) and "is never merely based on instruction," the *Vorbild* instructs one, if but subliminally. "*Führersein and Lehrersein* [sind] *ganz verschiedene Dinge*." Max Scheler, "Vorbilder und Führer," 261, 258. In his discussion of religious *Vorbilder*, Scheler acknowledges that they also may be leaders, but ascribes their leadership to the charismatic power they exercise on a given community. Cf. "*Vorbild* und *Führer* fallen aus diesem [religiösen] Gebiete (in den höheren Rangarten) *zusammen*. D.h. die religiösen Vorbilder bilden die Hauptart aller 'charismatischen' Herrschaft. . . ." Ibid., p. 277 (italics in original). Limiting his purview to a phenomenological analysis, Scheler does not consider whether *Vorbilder* also can assume an executive and organizational *function*. Nor does he, of course, then consider whether there is a relation between the phenomenological and functional dimensions of the *Vorbild*-cum-*Führer*, that is, whether there can be an intrinsic relationship between exemplary and executive leadership. Cf. note 59 following.

12. M. Halbertal, *People of the Book: Canon, Meaning, and Authority* (Cambridge: Harvard University Press, 1997), 130.

13. Rosenzweig, "Upon Opening of the *Jüdisches Lehrhaus*," in Franz Rosenzweig, *On Jewish Learning*, ed. Nahum N. Glatzer (1955; reprint, Madison: University of Wisconsin Press, 2002), 96. With respect to the distinction between "studying" and "learning," see Scholem: In traditional "European Jewry, the highest praise you could pay to somebody was the deceptively simple sentence, '*Er kann lernen*' (He knows *how* to learn). No more modest formula could be found to express the highest valuation. The little verb *lernen* (to learn) has an enormous implication. *Lernen* does not only mean studying; it means complete mastery of the intellectual tradition of the Talmudist's world. . . ." Scholem, "Three Types of Jewish Piety," 180 (emphasis added). In establishing the *Lehrhaus*, Rosenzweig had hoped to renew the "how" of *lernen*—as opposed to the "how" of academic study.

14. In accord with their sacrality, as Halbertal notes, "[C]anonical texts are read with special commitments and expectations. In other words, canonization affects not only the status of a text but the way it is perceived and read." Ibid., 11. For an extensive phenomenology of religious reading practices, see Paul J. Griffith, *Religious Reading: The Place of Reading in the Practice of Religion* (New York: Oxford University Press, 1999).

15. See the citation from Halbertal in note 14.

16. In an open letter to Hermann Cohen on the reorganization of Jewish education in Germany, Rosenzweig insisted that the "transmission of literary documents will never suffice; the classroom must remain an ante-room to the synagogue and participation in its religious service." Rosenzweig, "It Is Time: Concerning the Study of Judaism," in Rosenzweig, *On Jewish Learning*, 30.

17. This is a play on the title of Theodor Herzl's utopian novel *Altneuland*, outlining his vision of renewal of the Land of Israel as the home of the Jewish people. A more accurate description of Rosenzweig's approach to Jewish learning would be a "post-traditional" approach, namely, that his adoption of the traditional canon and reading practice was not based on traditional rabbinic authority but validated by a philosophy of religion developed independently of the tradition.

18. Rosenzweig to Buber, December 12, 1923, in Martin Buber, *Briefwechsel aus sieben Jahrzehnten*, ed. Grete Schaeder, vol. 2 (Heidelberg: Verlag Lambert Schneider, 1973), 149.

19. Rosenzweig, "The Builders: Concerning the Law," in Rosenzweig, *On Jewish Learning*, 74.

20. Ibid., 77

21. Buber to Rosenzweig, June 24, 1924, in Rosenzweig, *On Jewish Learning*, 111.

22. Cited by Rosenzweig as the epigraph to his open letter to Buber, "The Builders," in *On Jewish Learning*. See previous note 18. As Scholem notes, the paradox is built into the very term *talmid hakham*: "[T]he real sage, who so unpretentiously is called a pupil of the sages, is the teacher of his community. . . . The *talmid hakham*, as I have described him, had a central social function in the Jewish community, he

had authority in the world of tradition but did not evade his responsibility for the application of the Old Torah in his own time." Scholem, "Three Types of Jewish Piety," 179.

23. See Benjamin E. Sax, *Language and Jewish Renewal: Franz Rosenzweig's Hermeneutics of Citation* (PhD diss., University of Chicago, 2008); Nahum N. Glatzer, "The Frankfurt Lehrhaus," in *Leo Baeck Institute Year Book*, vol. 1 (London: East and West Library, 1956): 105–22.

24. See previous note 17 for the explanation of this locution.

25. When it became clear that because of illness it would be necessary for him to relinquish the directorship of the *Lehrhaus*, Rosenzweig penned a letter to his mother in which he acknowledged that he would seek to appoint a "successor," someone "through" whom he could continue to "speak and act." Franz Rosenzweig to Adele Rosenzweig, end of August 1922, cited in Glatzer, *Franz Rosenzweig*, 117.

26. The term "free" that modified "Jewish" in the name of the *Lehrhaus* was not meant to suggest that participation in its courses and lectures would be without cost. Rather, it denoted that it would be open to all questions and perspectives. The "new learning" is "a learning that no longer starts from the Torah and leads into life, but the other way round: from life, from a world that knows nothing of the Law . . . back to the Torah. . . . There is no one today who is not alienated. . . . [Hence] from the periphery back to the center; from the outside in. This is a new sort of learning." Rosenzweig, "On the Opening of the *Jüdisches Lehrhaus*," in *On Jewish Learning*, 98f.

27. When Jehuda Reinharz and I were students at Brandeis University in the late 1960s, these details were related to us by Nahum N. Glatzer, who was on the faculty of the *Lehrhaus* and was Rosenzweig's research assistant. In a twenty-page letter to Rudolf Hallo, his successor as director of the *Lehrhaus*, Rosenzweig described in exacting detail the history of the *Lehrhaus*, its conception, curriculum, lectures, administration, and finances. See Franz Rosenzweig, *Briefe*, ed. Edith Rosenzweig in collab. with Ernst Simon (Berlin: Schocken Verlag, 1935), 448–65.

28. Leo Hermann, "Erinnerungen an Bubers 'Drei Reden' in Prag," *Mittelungsblatt der Hitachduth Olej Germania* (Tel Aviv), no. 48 (November 26, 1971): 4–5.

29. While still a university student himself, he gave occasional lectures — such as a *Referat* (an academic paper) on Ferdinand Lassalle at a socialist club in Leipzig and several addresses at committee meetings of the World Zionist Organization. But when invited to address a large audience in Prague, he explained to his hosts that he feared that in the absence of "eye contact" he would falter. See Hermann, "Erinnerungen an Bubers 'Drei Reden' in Prag," 4.

30. Nahum N. Glatzer, ed., *Franz Rosenzweig: His Life and Thought*, 3rd ed. (Indianapolis: Hackett Publishers, 1995), 105f. (Emphasis added.)

31. Rosenzweig to Buber, January 12, 1923, cited in Glatzer, *Franz Rosenzweig*, 125–28.

32. Buber to Rosenzweig, n.d. (presumably between January 12–18, 1923), in Buber, *Briefwechsel*, vol. 2, 150–52.

33. Buber to Shmuel Hugo Bergmann, April 16, 1935, in Buber, *Briefwechsel aus sieben Jahrzehnten,* 589.

34. See previous note 29. Also see Martin Buber, *The First Buber: Youthful Zionist Writings of Martin Buber,* ed. and trans. Gilya G. Schmidt (Syracuse, NY: Syracuse University Press, 1999).

35. In 1920 Buber relinquished the position as the business director of the *Jüdischer Verlag* to Siegmund Katznelson, while retaining the position of its literary director.

36. Georg Simmel, *Die Gesellschaft: Sammlung sozialpsychologischer Monographien,* series ed. Martin Buber (Frankfurt am Main: Rütten and Loening, 1906–1912).

37. Martin Buber, *Ekstatische Konfessionen: Gesammelt* (Jena, DE: Eugen Diederichs Verlag, 1909).

38. The significance of *Ekstatische Konfessionen* for German Expressionist authors is explored in detail in Dietmar Gotschnigg, *Mystische Tradition im Roman Robert Musils: Martin Buber's 'Ekstatische Konfessionen' im 'Mann ohne Eigenschaften'* (Heidelberg: Lothar Stiehm Verlag, 1974).

39. As announced in this prospectus, the journal was to appear monthly starting in May 1903. It was not, however, realized until April 1916, with Buber as the sole editor.

40. See Elenore Lappin, *Der Jude 1916–1928: Jüdische Moderne zwischen Universalismus und Partikularismus* (Tübingen: Mohr Siebeck, 2000).

41. The journal did not engage in theological debate or confessional disquisitions; as the title of the journal signaled, its contributors tacitly endorsed the premise that as "creatures" of the divine order, all human beings — Jew, Catholic, and Protestant — share a responsibility for it. In this respect, *Die Kreatur* was transconfessional.

42. Among the contributors to *Die Kreatur* were the likes of Walter Benjamin, Nikolai Berdyaev, Hans Ehrenberg, Rudolf Ehrenberg, Florens Christian Rang, Eugen Rosenstock-Huessy, Franz Rosenzweig, Dolf Sternberger, and Margarete Susman.

43. See Martin Buber, *Schriften zu Jugend: Erziehung und Bildung,* vol. 8: *Martin Buber Werkausgabe,* ed. Juliane Jacobi (Gütersloh, DE: Gütersloher Verlagshaus, 2005).

44. See the protocol of the conference of religious socialists that Buber organized: Walter Cyliax, *Sozialismus aus dem Glauben: Verhandlungen der Sozialistischen Tagung in Heppenheim a.d. B., Pfingstwoche 1928* (Zürich: Rotapfel, 1929). Buber's socialism was decisively informed by the anarchism of Gustav Landauer, whose posthumous writings he edited.

45. See Ernst A. Simon, *Aufbau im Untergang: Jüdische Erwachsenenbildung im nationalsozialistischen Deutschland als geistiger Widerstand* (Tübingen: Mohr/Siebeck, 1959). Nahum N. Glatzer, "Reflections on Buber's Impact on German Jewry," *Leo Baeck Institute Year Book,* vol. 25 (1980): 105–22.

46. On the reopening of the Lehrhaus, see Buber, "Ein Jüdisches Lehrhaus," *Frankfurter Israelitisches Gemeindeblatt* 12, no. 3 (November 1933): 95.

47. See *Mittelstelle für jüdische Erwachsenenbildung bei der Reichsvertretung der Juden in Deutschland* (Frankfurt am Main), Rundbrief, nos. 1–4 (1934–1937). Buber appears on the masthead of this and all other publications as the director of the *Mittelstelle*.

48. See Martin Buber, "Ein Hinweis für Bibelkurse," *Mittelstelle für jüdische Erwachsenenbildung bei der Reichsvertretung der Juden in Deutschland*, Rundbrief, no. 3 (January 1936): 1–2.

49. Martin Buber, "Biblical Humanism," in *The Martin Buber Reader: Essential Writings*, ed. Asher D. Biemann (New York: Palgrave Macmillan, 2002), 47. Cf. Martin Buber, "Biblischer Humanismus," *Der Morgen* 9, no. 4 (October 1933).

50. For a discussion of the origins and significance of the concept of *Trotzjudentum*, see Jehuda Reinharz, *Fatherland or Promised Land: The Dilemma of the German Jew, 1893–1914* (Ann Arbor: University of Michigan Press, 1975), 79.

51. As the editor of *Der Jude*, whose maiden issue was published at the height of the antisemitic campaign orchestrated by the German Army in the midst of the World War, Buber became a *Vorbild* of Jewish pride, but one who transcended the limits of *Trotzjudentum*. See Arthur A. Cohen's perceptive comments on the significance of calling a journal *Der Jude* (The Jew) in a cultural and political milieu in which the very term "Jew" was a mark of derision: Arthur A. Cohen, "Introduction," *The Jew: Essays from Martin Buber's Journal Der Jude, 1916–1928*, ed. Arthur A. Cohen and trans. Joachim Neugroschel (Tuscaloosa, AL: University of Alabama Press, 1980).

52. Martin Buber, "Biblical Leadership," in Biemann, *The Martin Buber Reader*, 33. "Biblisches Führertum," in Martin Buber, *Kampf um Israel* (Berlin: Schocken Verlag, 1933).

53. Ibid., 37.

54. Ibid., 41

55. Walter Benjamin, "Theses on the Philosophy of History," in Walter Benjamin, *Illuminations: Essays and Reflections*, ed. Hannah Arendt (New York: Schocken Books, 1969), 257.

56. Ibid., 48. Cf. "The truth to which biblical leaders give witness through their words and actions is hidden in obscurity and yet does it work, though indeed in a way far different from what is known and lauded as effective by world history." Ibid., 37.

57. Pursuant to his thesis that leadership is situational, he contends that each of the five types of biblical leaders (the Patriarch, the Political Leader, the Judge, the King, and the Prophet) "constitute different forms of leadership in accordance with different situations." Ibid., 38.

58. Ibid., 40.

59. During the initial years of the Third Reich, when Jews still were allowed to publish journals and books but under severe restrictions, they often refracted their critique of the regime through scholarship. See Martina Urban, "Persecution and the Art of Representation: Schocken's Maimonides Anthologies of the 1930s," in

Maimonides and His Heritage, eds. Idit Dobbs-Weinstein et. al (Albany: State University of New York, 2009), 153–80.

60. See previous note 11. Scheler does, in fact, consider the relationship between *Vorbilder* and *Führer*, but regards it as preeminently dialectical: the *Vorbilder* honored by a society will determine the type of leadership it will seek. "Es sind die wirksamen *Vorbilder*, die auch für Führerauslese, Führerwahl, und vor allem für die Qualitäten der Führerschaften selber kausal bestimmend oder doch wesentlich mitbestimmend sind." Scheler, "Vorbilder und Führer," 263. In this context, he pertinently refers to the analysis of the relation between *Vorbild* and ethos in his *Der Formalismus und die materiale Wertethik: Formalism in Ethics and Non-formal Ethics of Values*, 5th rev. ed., trans. Manfred A. Fringe and Roger Funk (Evanston, IL: Northwestern University Press, 1973), ch. 6, sect. B4 and 6. Scheler does acknowledge that *Vorbilder* in some cases, especially with respect to religious teachers and educators, and even occasionally in politics, may be leaders, but only when there is a "charismatic-affective bonding" with their followers (ibid.). Otherwise, a relationship between exemplary individuals and leaders is at most dialectical. By limiting the relationship between *Vorbilder* and *Führer* to a charismatic-emotional effect, Scheler eo ipso vitiates the cultural significance of *Vorbilder* as exemplifying the values and ideals of a society. Apparently following Max Weber in associating leadership with charisma, he obfuscates possible alternative explanations of a *Vorbild* serving as a *Führer*. Rather than positing that the leadership exercised by an exemplary individual on her followers is a function of her *affective* charisma, one may ask whether a *Vorbild* who is not charismatic can serve effectively as a leader. And if so, what would be the source of her authority on matters administrative and organizational? On one level, of course, her authority would rest in her acknowledged skills essential to the executive tasks she has assumed. But if her embodiment as a *Vorbild* is also a factor, one may *ex hypothesi* assume that *respect* also may be a factor in establishing her authority as a leader—and as a cognitive and axiological posture, respect need neither be engendered nor accompanied by an emotive effect. Moreover, one must remain cognizant—as Scheler undoubtedly was—that charisma may override one's values.

PART IV

Witnessing History

24

Inside Kishinev's Pogrom

Hayyim Nahman Bialik, Michael Davitt, and the Burdens of Truth

STEVEN J. ZIPPERSTEIN

Chaim Weizmann's *Trial and Error*, his grand, lyrical autobiography of the late 1940s, returns repeatedly to lessons learned from the 1903 Kishinev pogrom. It offered him, he writes, the first glimpse of what the new century might have in store for Jews in Europe and also Palestine: "I had some experience with the atmosphere that precedes pogroms," he recalls telling Palestine High Commissioner Herbert Samuel in 1920. It forever would remind Weizmann of how inconceivable it was for him, despite his desire to pursue chemistry research, to avoid the political fray. Describing himself in the wake of the Palestinian riots of 1929: "I found it impossible . . . as in fact I had found it impossible in an earlier crisis, that which followed the Kishinev pogrom and other pogroms thirty years before—to abstract myself . . . from Jewish life."[1]

He writes that his move in 1904 to England, which altered the course of the remainder of his life and had a considerable impact on the course of Zionism's history, too, was a direct by-product of the miasma set in motion by the Kishinev massacre and Theodor Herzl's effort soon afterward, loathed by most of those closest to Weizmann, to secure a slice of East Africa as a Jewish haven. Kishinev also taught him to recognize the imprint of mendacious officialdom: "Just before the [1937 Palestinian] riots broke out I had an intimate talk with the High Commissioner. He asked me whether I thought troubles were to be expected. I replied that in Czarist Russia I knew that if the Government did not wish for troubles, they never happened."[2]

Kishinev, in short, is one of the book's lodestones, and yet nearly everything he says about the massacre's details, its historical lessons, even its immediate impact on him (except, perhaps, for the reason for his Manchester move) is easily proven inaccurate. Weizmann's letters to his fiancée at the time of the pogrom hardly mention the event, the claim in the autobiography that its outbreak caused him to return to Russia immediately to help organize self-defense groups is without foundation, and his insistence that Kishinev and massacres like it were concocted by the tsar's highest officials has long been disproven, or at least qualified. Still, the certainty Weizmann brings to his depiction of the massacre, an event whose details, mangled or not, would come to occupy a central role in the memory of Jews at the time, is likely sincere and also illustrative. More than any event of its time, including the Dreyfus Affair (in 1903, the two were reported on side by side in the Jewish press) the Kishinev pogrom would define the contour of contemporary Jewish life for countless Jews and others, providing the rationale for so much including unfettered Jewish mass migration to the United States, Russian Jewry's embrace of the Left, its still-starker repudiation of the Right.

Widely recognized as the first instance when Russian Jewry captured sustained attention in the Western world, the pogrom—the term itself widely embraced only in Kishinev's wake to depict anti-Jewish riots—would dominate headlines in newspapers in the United States and elsewhere for weeks (it would dominate the Jewish press for months). It would inspire a spate of instant books—several finished in a matter of weeks—plays, poems, and the like, and would make Kishinev into a synonym for Jewish calamity.[3] Vladimir Korolenko would transmute the horrors enacted at just one of its addresses, 13 Asia Street, into one of the era's most widely cited depictions of horror; it provided the first instance for Tolstoy to speak out in defense of Jews who denounced the Russian government as culpable in the massacre's wake.[4]

Amid this torrent of reportage, relief efforts, public meetings, and gruesome imagery—Kishinev's outrages were among the first of its kind captured promiscuously in newspaper photography—the two most influential sources on it were, arguably, Hebrew poet Hayyim Nahman Bialik and Irish radical and journalist Michael Davitt. Both were dispatched to Kishinev to amass data, which they did with diligence; both produced work, while drastically different in form and substance, that managed to distill the catastrophe in ways all the more enduring because they were so concrete, so detailed. And both came away from the city with the same anguished impressions of the behavior of the town's Jewish males—substantial numbers of whom, or so they claimed, proved unable or unwilling to protect the city's women from rape. For both, this behavior indelibly defined its terrors.[5]

In the din of accusations and counteraccusations following the pogrom —at the time, among the more persistent leveled by Jews against their coreligionists was that the city's wealthiest protected themselves, their neighborhoods, and their property at the expense of the poor—the charge that Jewish men hid themselves when rapists ravaged Kishinev's girls and women took precedence over so many other travesties including, astonishingly, the horrors experienced by the women themselves. Such impressions fed, of course, on regnant stereotypes of feminized Jewish males, whose passivity was said to be the by-product of Diaspora (as argued by Zionists) or the superstitions of traditional religiosity (as argued by Jewish socialists and others). In the immediate aftermath, the desecration of synagogues and Torah scrolls, the shattered glass of store windows, the down feathers blanketing the city's streets, and of course, the rows of dead bodies whose photographs were reproduced in countless newspapers— these were among the more vivid images linked to Kishinev. But soon no image could compete with that of rape as the most horrific focal point of the pogrom with the moral failings of Kishinev's men overshadowing all else in this regard, this shorthand for the abject vulnerability of the Jewish people under tsarism, its devastation of soul and body alike.

In this essay I argue that the writings of both Bialik (despite the density of his majestically dark Kishinev poem) and Davitt enjoy a certain transparency, an immediacy, that sheds light not only on how the pogrom would be perceived but also on what it is that transpired amid its horrors. Davitt's account of his time in Kishinev was published first in the *New York American*, then reprinted in a spate of newspapers in the United States and elsewhere, and soon afterward in expanded form in the best-selling book, *Within the Pale: The True Story of Anti-Semitic Persecutions in*

Russia. Immediately on his book's publication, Davitt emerged as a folk hero among Jews—he already was a much-celebrated Irish political figure —with plays and poems written about his time in Kishinev in English and Yiddish. Lightly disguised in the script "Kishineff," which was written but never produced for New York's resplendent New Star Theater, its protagonist, the swashbuckling Dave Michels, journalist from the United States, all-but-single-handedly saves the city's Jewish maidens and is told at the play's end that he is "the truest, dearest friend our people ever had." In Bialik's case, his best-known, fullest distillation of his reactions to Kishinev went into his "Be-'ir ha-haregah" ("In the City of Killing," originally published under another title for censorship reasons) appearing in its original Hebrew version in November/December 1903. Its almost immediate impact on Jewish literature, on politics, eventually on Israeli pedagogy (it would remain a mainstay of the educational curriculum for decades), and even on military affairs (it is widely credited with influencing the formation of the Haganah, the kernel of Israel's armed forces) is well known.[6]

Never have Davitt and Bialik been examined side by side. This despite the fact that, though apparently they never met, their stays in Kishinev investigating the riot's aftermath overlapped: Bialik was there for some five weeks starting in early May, Davitt for eleven days, with both in the city at the month's end. While there, they relied on the same assistant, the teacher and Hebrew-language newspaper contributor Pesakh Averbach. Bialik sat together with him in the homes of victims and had him collate and translate their testimonies into Hebrew from their original Yiddish; for Davitt, Averbach served as part of a small team of translators since the Irish journalist was not familiar with Russian or Yiddish. Tel Aviv's future founding-mayor Meir Dizengoff stepped in to translate for Davitt, too.[7]

Both, in addition to their published accounts of the massacre and its aftermath, left behind extensive notes on what they witnessed. Bialik's, in the form of transcripts of victim testimonies contained in several notebooks accompanied by photographs, were almost entirely sequestered from view for more than eighty years among his archival papers in Tel Aviv before they finally were edited (superbly so, by Yaakov Goren) and published. Davitt's remain in Trinity College, Dublin, where I reviewed them recently, the first Jewish studies scholar to have drawn on them. (Contained in his archive are treasures, including the only copies of the notorious Kishinev-based newspaper *Bessarabets* outside the former Soviet Union.)[8]

In Bialik's case, much scholarship has been devoted to the discrepancy between his poem's scathing condemnation of Jewish passivity and the description in his notebooks of Jewish self-defense—the most significant concerted, if foiled, attempt in the early morning of the massacre's second day. The episode, in fact, was extensively documented at the time with pogromists' lawyers making the argument—in a series of consecutive trials lasting well into December—that the defendants merely were protecting themselves from Jewish assailants, who were the ones who initiated the assault on Kishinev's gentiles. Why Bialik shunted this episode aside has been explained, on the whole, as a by-product of his effort in his poem to merge nationalist outrage and personal anguish, a meshing strikingly original yet also consistent with the poet's Zionist commitments. Just before his departure for Kishinev, Bialik signed a letter, widely circulated by Odessa's Jewish intellectuals and mostly composed by Bialik's ideological mentor, the influential essayist Ahad Ha'am (pen name for Asher Ginsberg), that took for granted the passivity of Kishinev's Jews; and some argue that Bialik cleaved to such assumptions despite evidence to the contrary.[9]

No doubt there is truth in this. Yet reading Davitt's Kishinev notes together with Bialik's invites a reassessment of what it meant to make sense of the pogrom and its confounding, often contradictory details. The fact that Davitt, too, albeit in his unpublished notes and not in his articles or book, levels precisely the same criticisms of the behavior of Jews as does Bialik indicates that the latter's observations might well have been grounded in more than ideological commitment. That Davitt, a scrupulous journalist who certainly did not shun controversy (as a Irish radical, he had spent years in English jails) chose for reasons never explained to sequester his criticisms raises intriguing questions, not only with regard to Davitt's motivations, but also about how it is that complex, unsettling stories tend to be narrated, reproduced, and also, at times, obliterated.

The fact that Bialik and Davitt shared the same translator in Kishinev perhaps offers something of an explanation, but Davitt was a painstakingly honest, hardworking journalist—his book remains to this day one of the most authoritative on the pogrom in large measure because of its meticulous, on-site research—and he shared, of course, none of Bialik's

Ahad Ha'amist, Odessa-bred cultural influences. Davitt states in his notes that his impressions were the by-product of numerous conversations with Jewish men who, he insists, acknowledged to him that they witnessed their wives, and other relatives, raped and they watched helplessly.

This essay, then, is an effort to make sense of how the two of them made sense of their time in Kishinev. Fortunately, the evidence at hand is rich and varied: Kishinev's pogrom may well have been among the most comprehensively covered events in Russian Jewish history. Obviously, neither Bialik nor Davitt had the time or inclination, or for that matter the opportunity, to wade through all but a fraction of this material, but both immersed themselves in much of it; they spoke with its victims extensively, and both, it seems clear, strained hard to tell the truth as they saw it. Looking closely at them as they struggled to tell this truth reveals something crucial, as I see it, about the various, conflicting ways in which a moment in time might be fixed in history, what it is that history manages best to record and what falls between its grates, and also how it is that a poem might contain a historicity, a kernel of essential information too unwieldy, too raw or indelicate, too slippery for expressly historical or journalistic sources to take hold of. Bialik's poem has been termed a "poetic chronicle" or, as literary historian Dan Miron has put it, " studded with details, accurate pictures, and a factual tone." This may well be truer than could previously have been imagined.[10]

Henry Hyndman, the British businessman-turned-Marxist-politician and author of the first introduction to Marx in the English language, tells in his reminiscences of an encounter with Davitt on a Parisian Budapest-bound train as Davitt made his way to Kishinev. Hyndman, who had been active in pro-Irish causes, relates how as he entered his sleeping car he noticed the name "M. Davitt" on the seat opposite his. He was so pleased to discover Michael Davitt walking in a few minutes later that "our fellow passengers were astonished to see two elderly and apparently sane travellers suddenly set to work to dance a fandango of jubilation in the corridor of the sleeping-car." The first words out of Davitt's mouth were: "There is not a police bureau in Europe [that] would believe that this was an accidental meeting."[11]

They talked much of the way about the boon of small landownership

(Davitt's keenest preoccupation as an Irish nationalist), about the beauty of the Bavarian and Austrian countryside, about socialism, and also about Jews. Hyndman was in touch with Davitt after his Kishinev stay, too. The gist of what Hyndman took away was that while Davitt felt great antipathy for those responsible for the massacre, he also saw Jews themselves as fanning discontent, or worse. "Undoubtedly, Davitt in private while not excusing the Russian authorities felt that Russia would be much better off if she had no Jews at all within her boundaries." Sitting together on the train, Hyndman related to him the story of one ragged Jew who, within a few years of stumbling into a Russian village, had "to use Marx's phrase, . . . eaten up the pores of this simple society. Everything had become his, and the peasants themselves, with their families, were little better than his slaves." The impression Hyndman gave was that Davitt agreed that the story captured something essential, if also unfortunate, about the role of Jews in economic life.[12]

Davitt's views on Jews were complex, born of sympathy and also unassailable assumptions regarding inbred racial characteristics that caused Jews to exploit those weak, ignorant, or naïve. In his bloated, six-hundred-page tome published the year before, *The Boer War for Freedom*, he singled out as the prime exploiters of the region a clutch of no fewer than forty "Anglicized German Jews," who were, as he put it, along with Cecil Rhodes the "capitalist kings" most responsible for the oppression of the Boers. In the preface to *Within the Pale*, he states, "Where anti-Semitism stands in fair political combat . . . or against the engineers of a sordid war in South Africa . . . I am resolutely in line with its spirit and programme." And, as he argues later in the book, "If the race generally are exploiters and extortionists, who made them so?" True, he would soon defend Irish Jews against the infamous Limerick boycott of 1904 and, in the wake of his Kishinev dispatches and his popular book, would loom large in Jewish life as a beloved protector. But he shared a set of emphatic viewpoints on the essential characteristics of the races—English motivations he would forever distrust, African "savages" he sidelined in his book on South Africa, Moldavians were overwhelmingly responsible for the worst of Kishinev's outrages because they were the descendants of Roman slaves, and Jews—while harmless in those places where there were gentiles clever enough to compete with them such as in the United States—were justly feared in backward Russia. Certainly, this did not justify their oppression, but it did constitute a sufficient argument for Jews to consider seriously mass migration, preferably to Palestine.[13]

Still, he was a highly professional journalist. Born without money (in contrast to his erstwhile comrade, later his rival, the towering Irish radical leader Parnell), Davitt made his living from journalism and accepted the Kishinev assignment because he needed the cash. (Bialik agreed to take on the task of collecting data on the pogrom, in no small measure, for the same reason.) The Hearst newspaper chain that hired Davitt for the assignment soon would adopt Kishinev as little less than a crusade. "In my various newspapers," wrote Hearst in a letter to the editor printed in his own *New York American* on May 20, 1903, "in New York, Chicago, and San Francisco I have published the fullest obtainable details of the Kishineff crimes." Hearst led his own relief campaign — side by side with many others in New York and elsewhere — to which he gave its largest single donation. Davitt's photograph appeared on the paper's front page immediately after he agreed to take the job with the announcement that he was its "agent" or "commissioner" in Kishinev. Crowds of Jews now gathered daily outside the offices of the *New York American* and other papers seeking news of the riot, especially of relatives who might have been harmed. In a contemporaneous summation of the pogrom and its aftermath, the characteristically understated Columbia University scholar, Zionist leader Richard Gottheil, declared, "Few events in modern history have called forth the indignation of the civilized world as have the riots at Kishineff."[14]

In the midst of this frenzy Davitt was instructed to ascertain whether there was truth to the reports of multiple rapes, the murder of infants, and the likelihood that another pogrom was in the offing. (Initial reports indicated that as many as a hundred, perhaps more, were killed; the actual number was forty-four, with five dying of wounds afterward.) Rumors that the horrific photographs from Kishinev were doctored or that all that had really happened was the antics of a few local ruffians were circulated by the Russian government, and this, too, Davitt sought to investigate. And at the same time, rife was the widespread "fear that even yet [readers] had not learned the worst" as the *New York American* stated on May 13.[15]

Davitt's notes show him to be exceedingly cautious — so cautious that his London-based editor soon was badgering him for copy that Davitt insisted was not ready because he was still immersed in fact checking. On his arrival in Odessa, via a ship from Constantinople, on May 20 (according to Russia's Julian calendar, May 7) he sat for some seven hours with the Kishinev Jewish communal leader and Zionist Jacob Bernstein-Kogan, who filled him in with the help of translator Dizengoff. Soon in Kishinev, one hundred miles to Odessa's west and linked by rail, he interviewed large numbers in his hotel room—which was besieged by Jews hoping to obtain his help to emigrate—and spoke with those who could provide him with information at local Jewish and Russian hospitals, in the homes of pogrom victims, in local government offices, and elsewhere.[16]

"To arrive at definite conclusions as to the immediate and the contributory causes of the sanguinary outrages perpetrated upon the Jews of Kishineff on the 19th and 20th of April, was a tedious and painful process, beset with innumerable difficulties."[17] This is how Davitt begins the narrative on the pogrom in his book. His notes reveal that he weighed all matters with due skepticism: that the windows of some Christian homes may well have been shattered by pogromists, too, as reported in a Russian newspaper, could well mean that the attack was not exclusively an anti-Jewish one but, as he asks himself, the "organization of workingmen animated by a political & economical animus against the bourgeoisie." If buildings near General Governor S. S. von Raaben's home and that of the city mayor Karl Schmidt were also damaged, the allegation that local officials were complicit would seem fallacious. Surely such authorities would not "allow a prearranged fire to blaze near their official residences."[18]

He attempts to discover how many pogromists were there. (Told that there were only about three hundred, the bulk of them "imported hirelings," he asks in his notations, "What were the 30,000 Jews doing?") He identifies the weapons used by the attackers (mostly clubs) and what they did at night ("violating women"). He quantifies how many of the city's liquor stores and brothels are owned by Jews, how many Jewish prostitutes work in Kishinev, were there a disproportionate number of masons amid the pogromists, and how many women participated in the attacks alongside men? He attempts to find out whether the rumor that a five-year-old girl was raped is true, and after interviewing no fewer than ten doctors at the Jewish hospital and two at the Russian institution, he is unable to confirm the report. The youngest victim, aged twelve months, died, he discovers, because the mother dropped the infant while in flight.[19]

He counts the number of fresh graves at the cemetery, interviews local rabbis to learn how many husbands have divorced their wives because they were raped (eleven is the number he jots down), and confirms that at least in one instance nails were, as rumored, driven into the head of a Jewish victim. He produces a list with the names of thirteen girls and women between the ages of seventeen and forty-eight who were raped, with another six unnamed but identified; he notes that some forty were said to have been raped. The Russian doctors with whom Davitt speaks tell him that the magnitude of the pogrom, as reported by Jews and in the press abroad, was not exaggerated.[20]

His analysis of how and why the pogrom broke out is remarkably clear-headed, quite similar to how historians with access to sources inaccessible to Davitt would later reconstruct it. He argues that its root cause was the exasperating and confounding nature of anti-Jewish legislation in Russia; the recent expulsion of the Jews from the countryside, which was, especially in a rather remote, border region like that of Kishinev's Bessarabia, readily contravened by bribery; and the abiding uncertainty about whether Jews enjoyed any protection at all under the law. This was coupled with the highly combustible charge of Jewish ritual murder—leveled after the killing of a Christian boy in a town near Kishinev right before the pogrom's outbreak—which unleashed passions unchecked because of the ineptitude of the local administrators, the indifference of the police, and the hostility of the city's Orthodox clergymen. Perhaps the most crucial indigenous factor was Russia's fiercest antisemitic newspaper, the Kishinev-based *Bessarabets*, with some twenty thousand readers and the region's only daily. Davitt placed blame for the pogrom's organization squarely on the shoulders of its editor Pavel Krushevan, together with a small entourage of fanatics close to him, including local seminarians (Kishinev sported the largest seminary in the region, a hotbed of both left-wing and right-wing politics, with some one thousand students) who, as reported by many sources at the time, helped guide pogromists to Jewish homes. Most historians today concur that Krushevan exerted a critical, if mysterious, and hard-to-pin-down influence on the riot. And, as it happens, there is ample proof that it was Krushevan, perhaps along with one or two others, who was the author of the original version of what would eventually be entitled *The Protocols of the Elders of Zion*; he certainly was its first publisher.[21]

By far, the lengthiest description in Davitt's notations is of a girl who was raped and then murdered in an outlying, impoverished neighborhood on the first night of the pogrom. Only passing, sparse reference found its way into his newspaper reports (these were constrained by Russian censorship, nearly all either spirited across the border while he was in Kishinev or forwarded from Berlin after he left) or his book. I quote only a brief selection:

> The house where the girl was ravished & murdered. . . . The entire place littered with fragments of the furniture, glass, feathers, a scene of the most complete wreckage possible. It was in the inner room (in carpenter's shed) where . . . the young girl of 12 was outraged & liter-ally torn asunder. . . . About a hundred feet from this house there is a long wooden shed. . . . In this shed 23 persons sought refuge after learning of the approach of the rioters. . . . The young girl . . . by some accident or chance was left in her house, the house nearest the gate-way entrance to the yard. . . . The shrieks of the girl were heard by the terrified crowd in the shed for a short while & and then all was silent.

He then added, "Correct above: The young girl & the wife of the man who told me the tale (he being present) were taken out of the shed, and carried into the house & violated."[22]

On his return from Kishinev, Davitt admitted to a friend that, "In their naked horror" what he saw surpassed "almost anything which the imag-ination could invent."[23] Invention was something he assiduously avoided —his notations are interspersed with lists of "facts" painfully accumu-lated. Hence the following comments cannot be dismissed, it seems to me, either as invention or as passing impression:

> Note: Jewish men appear except in rare instances, to have acted as contemptible cowards. In no instance have I heard from women of any courageous stand being made by either their husbands or sons. . . . Several of these miserable poltroons came to my hotel to recount their marvelous escapes but not one had a story of courage or of counter attack to relate.[24]

Davitt knew, of course, of various efforts of Jews to resist and described how early on the second morning of the pogrom at the city's wine mar-ket, a large group of mostly laborers and shopkeepers, numbering at least

250, battled rioters before being stopped by police with several arrested. Nowhere either in his dispatches or in his book did he mention the confessions made by Jewish men in his hotel room: the nearest he came is the observation in the book of how striking it is that the mayhem caused by rioters numbering no more than two thousand could have transpired in a city with tens of thousands of Jews. "Ninety per cent of [the Jews] hid themselves, or fled to safer parts in and out of the city for refuge."[25] Davitt's decision not to include these reactions—among the fiercest, certainly the most critical of Jewish behavior in the very extensive notes he took—brings us to Hayyim Nahman Bialik's altogether different choice to situate much the same observations into what generations of readers would come to see as the incendiary core of his epochal poem.

Several of those close to Bialik in Odessa, where he had lived on and off since the early 1890s, most recently as a teacher at one or another of its modern Jewish schools, admitted years later that they were surprised at his sudden rise, almost immediately after the publication of his Kishinev poem (in fact, his second on the pogrom, by far the most famous) as the literary conscience of their generation. Bialik's fame would move rapidly well beyond the confines of Hebrew literary devotees, especially once Vladimir Jabotinsky's brilliant Russian translation of the poem—the flamboyant young activist, a superb orator, would recite it whenever given a platform—appeared. (No better analysis exists of the transmutation of Bialik's poem into Jabotinsky's Russian than Michael Stanislawski's.)[26] In the pogrom's wake, Bialik's was but one of many dozens of poems in Russian, Yiddish, and Hebrew about the massacre, with several already blended into synagogue services, especially in the United States, by fall 1903 and the onset of the High Holy Days. Once Bialik's poem was published late that year, all others essentially were shunted aside.[27]

The prophetlike figure Bialik would now rapidly become in the Jewish imagination—in his Kishinev poem, he echoed, no doubt intentionally, Alexander Pushkin's "The Prophet," the brief, powerful work consigned to memory by countless Russian readers—was vastly different from the convivial, somewhat coarse, often slovenly, largely self-taught young man (in 1903, he was twenty-nine) his Odessa friends knew so well. Chaim Tchernowitz, an Odessa-based writer and educator then quite close to Bialik—he also was among the kindest, least carping figures in this circle of relentlessly lacerating intellectuals—admits in his memoirs that the Bialik whose reputation so soared in these years bore little resemblance to the rough-and-tumble man with whom he spent so much time. His vaulted reputation as a Talmud scholar, a *matmid* or Talmudic devotee, itself the title of one of his most beloved poems, Tchernowitz says was inconceivable, for example, since the poet was so hungrily in need of company that he was rarely ever alone.[28]

What it is that Bialik made of his time in Kishinev was what consolidated this reputation, one that has remained sturdy ever since—its ongoing potency confirmed by how entire schools of Hebrew poetry have, over the years, erupted in reaction to its grip. Those five weeks in Kishinev would leave a profound imprint on his life, and not only because of his great poem, and yet because some details associated with his stay were deemed at variance with his reputation by those now ever-watchful over him, they were, with his own connivance, sidelined or silenced. Silence, particularly shamed silence, is one of Bialik's most abiding, poetic themes, and Tel Aviv University's Michael Gluzman has astutely shown how his earliest revelatory piece of prose writing—the lengthy autobiographical letter he composed while still in Kishinev for Joseph Klausner, then at work on what would be the first biographical sketch of the poet—was studded with elisions, major and minor. These included Bialik's transmutation of a shameful childhood experience that now, having heard so much from Kishinev's raped Jewish women, he conflated with an episode from his own past. And in keeping with this keen self-protection, he would lock away the extensive notes he took while in Kishinev, much to the surprise of his loyal assistant Pesakh Averbach, who admitted in print some years later that he had no idea why they had never seen the light of day.[29]

Greatest of all the elisions was the removal from his official biography—until the open secret, known in literary circles but kept under wraps long after the poet's death, was revealed after the demise of his widow, Manya—that Bialik had fallen in love in Kishinev with a painter, Ira Jan, or Esfir Yeselevitch, four years his senior and married with a child, for whom he almost certainly composed the most passionate of his poems. It is likely that he seriously considered joining her in Palestine; she left her husband and daughter soon after they met, started laboriously to teach herself Hebrew—she came from a Russian-speaking family; her father, a doctor, was one of the Jewish notables who hosted Bialik during his Kishinev stay—

and then left for Palestine, where she would be its first professional female Jewish painter. At the time Bialik tentatively had agreed to teach at a new school in Palestine slated for orphans of the Kishinev massacre. Even the size of his salary was negotiated.[30]

Only a handful of letters of what was an extensive correspondence survive—all hers, none his—and these, too, were hidden away for many years by Bialik's archivists; assiduous literary historians Ziva Shamir, Nurit Govrin, and others have poured over them gleaning whatever nuggets they might contain. All agree that Jan's love for Bialik was deep and longstanding; few disagree that Bialik loved her too, although he resisted the Palestine venture and chose Warsaw instead, where he would edit the journal *Ha-Shiloach* together with Klausner. His love poetry, while fiercely erotic, also suggests a certain revulsion at sexual passion, at least the act of sexuality, that may well have intruded on this, perhaps the one, truly deep romantic relationship he would enjoy with a woman.[31]

The best known of all Bialik's editorial excisions in the wake of his Kishinev stay was his exclusion of all mention of Jewish self-defense in "Be-'ir ha-haregah" despite the description of such efforts in his notes. Historian Dubnow, who dispatched Bialik to Kishinev—with a patronizingly lengthy list of assignments he expected him to perform while there —wrote years later in his autobiography that he never was disappointed by the decision not to release Bialik's notations or, for that matter, to use them in any way: his poem, stated Dubnow, told more of the truth and exerted a far greater impact than the information culled from his transcript ever could.[32]

Whether or not it told more of the truth was much debated at the time of its appearance. Critic and short story writer David Frischman, a great admirer of Bialik's, lacerated him in print on this score. Bialik's mentor, Mendele Mocher Seforim (the Yiddish and Hebrew writer S. Y. Abramovitch), recalling the 1881 Odessa pogrom with great anger several decades later, loathed Bialik's poem, which he construed as a personal affront. Many of Kishinev's Jews would continue to see the poem as a bruising insult, penning replies to it at nearly every one of the community's commemorative moments before and after the Second World War.[33]

Bialik's words about Jewish male cowardice stung, as they were meant to do:

And see, oh see, in the shade of that same corner
under the bench and behind that barrel
lay husbands, fiancés, brothers, peeping out of holes
at the flutter of holy bodies under the flesh of donkeys
choking in their corruption and gagging on their own throats' blood
as like slices of meat a loathsome gentile spread their flesh—
they lay in their shame and saw—and didn't move and didn't budge,
and they didn't pluck out their eyes or go out of their heads—
and perhaps each in his soul then prayed in his heart:
master of the universe, make a miracle—and let me not be
    harmed.[34]

Nowhere in his notebooks did Bialik record anything nearly as un-
reservedly critical of Jewish behavior as Davitt. In the longest, most
heart-wrenching account of multiple rape in his notes, the narrative of
Rivka Schiff, he has the victim exonerate her husband from blame: she
recounts how he sought to bribe the pogromists, how they threatened his
life, and then how he hid while they fell upon his wife, one after the other
raping her. Once the horrors ended, her immediate fear was that he might
have been killed. Still, it seems likely that as in Davitt's case, Bialik too heard
accounts similar to those that so unsettled the Irish radical. Davitt claimed
that no fewer than one hundred Jews sought him in his hotel room, with
many of them sharing with him such tales, which may have been linked to
an effort to persuade him to help with their emigration since their lives and
that of their families in Kishinev had been rendered unbearable.[35]

No less likely is it that what both wrote down and what it is that Bialik
—whose poem is packed with journalistic-like observations, accurate depictions of Kishinev's topography, and a keenly precise account of the massacre's pacing—decided to publish was then all-but-common knowledge,
albeit just the sort of indelicacy that falls between the cracks, especially
when a beleaguered people, such as Jews, is its target. Kishinev's canonic
story would be consolidated rapidly—for Jews across the political spectrum, for the bulk of Russian liberals and radicals, and for numerous sympathizers abroad, too. What would emerge would be a strikingly seamless,
consensual account much like the one found in Weizmann's autobiography, shorn of carping about the rush to safety of Kishinev's wealthier Jews,

with Krushevan cut down to size consistent with the belief that the massacre was the work of the government. Now the Kishinev pogrom would be described as set in motion, plotted not by random pogromists but by governmental authorities at the highest levels, above all Minister of Interior Vlacheslav Plehve, assassinated one year later after several attempts on his life and largely because of his role in fomenting Kishinev's pogrom. (Few, if any, historians now believe Plehve to have been responsible for the massacre.) Krushevan himself now would be dismissed as a pawn, "a typical *pogromshchik*" in the words of Norman Cohn's influential study; the seminarians, reported widely at the time as playing a major role, disappeared from view almost entirely. Kishinev would become, above all, the most conclusive of all evidence that the Russian state was in the midst of little less than war with its Jews.[36]

Hence the lines separating advocacy from journalism, polemics from history were casually traversed: Dubnow's was a "historical commission" that, as he tells it, had its work superseded by the proliferation of pogrom press accounts and polemical literature with their resounding denunciations of Russia. While still in Kishinev, Bialik already had started transmuting his witness testimonies into poetry. Davitt arrived in Kishinev with a large relief donation in hand from newspaper titan William Randolph Hearst. The *Yiddish Daily Forward* launched the first in a series of major relief campaigns for Kishinev's Jews that did much to transform the paper, then little more than a publicity sheet for the Socialist party, into the indispensible fixture it would now become.

Bialik's poem would have been read and recited against this backdrop, this veritable landslide; some later commenting, wryly, on the sparse reportage of Nazi atrocities in the early 1940s, insisted that in its time Kishinev garnered immeasurably more attention from the world than did Hitler's catastrophe.[37] The appropriation of some details of the massacre by Bialik, not others, and his decision to spotlight the failings of some of Kishinev's men while sidelining the resistance shown especially on the pogrom's second morning was, no doubt, tinged with his own deeply felt cultural Zionist inclinations. But now, with the surfacing of Davitt's notations written at more or less the same time as Bialik's stay, it seems likely that this, too, was a part of Bialik's endeavor at piecing together the pogrom's raw data, his culling of reportage unmediated, certainly devoid of contextualization or countervailing evidence. Like nearly all else in the poem, traversing in astonishing detail every quarter of the city and its suburbs, this, too, can be said to have been done with the intention to tell the truth, an expression of the poet's desire to capture the pogrom's terrors as meaningfully as he knew how.

The veritable mountain of factual accounts of the Kishinev pogrom produced at the time, nearly all in its immediate wake and often later, too, larded with polemics, were frequently little less imaginative—if, undoubtedly, less artful—than Bialik's. His poem was designed to co-exist, intimately, in tandem with this textual onslaught, to complement it while at the same time, he hoped, superseding it in resonance and impact. (Bialik was never more ambitious than in this, the most fertile of all periods of his life.) History is best extracted, perhaps, from just this sort of muddle, this multitude of sources with straightforward accounts such as Davitt's *Within the Pale* less sturdily transparent at times than a prophetic-like eruption such as Bialik's. In his splendid memoir, among the best of its kind, erstwhile anarchist Victor Serge observes that having attempted the writing of history in the 1920s, "Historical work did not satisfy me entirely. . . . It does not allow enough space for showing men as they really are, dismantling their inner workings and penetrating deep into their souls."[38] Serge then poured himself into fiction, eventually producing his now-classic, posthumously published autobiography *Memoirs of a Revolutionary* late in his life, by then an obscure and impoverished Soviet exile living in Mexico. Yet it is this book that remains his greatest historical monument and, in its own way, a far more valuable documentary source than his attempts at straightforward historical investigation. Disciplinary boundaries separating history and fiction, reportage and poetry and memoir are crucial, of course, but historical excavation may well be done best when all these, and others too, are ransacked promiscuously in an effort—rigorous, self-critical, as well as imaginative—to extract the fullest sense of the inner workings deep in the souls of the past.

NOTES

Hasia Diner of New York University was the first to alert me to the richness of the Michael Davitt Papers housed at Trinity College, Dublin. Davitt specialist Carla King, of St. Patrick's College, Drumcondra, Dublin, helped facilitate my use of this material. Now, as so often in the past, this essay too has benefited from a critical reading by my Stanford colleague and friend Aron Rodrigue.

1. Chaim Weizmann, *Trial and Error: The Autobiography of Chaim Weizmann*, vol. 1 (Lexington, MA: Plunkett Lake Press, 2013), 254, 343; Jehuda Reinharz, *Chaim Weizmann: The Making of a Zionist Leader* (Oxford: Oxford University Press, 1985), 149–52, 157–66.

2. Weizmann, *Trial and Error*, 91, 392.

3. Cyrus Adler, ed., *The Voice of America in Kishineff* (Philadelphia: Jewish Publication Society of America, 1903), ix–xxvi; Sam Johnson, "Use and Abuses: 'Pogrom' in the Anglo-American Imagination," *Jews in the East European Borderlands*, ed. Eugene M. Avrutin and Harriet Murav (Boston: Academic Studies Press, 2012), 158–66.

4. Vladimir Korolenko, *Dom no. 13* (London: Vseobshch. evr. rab. soiuz v Litve, Polshe, i Rossii, 1903); Michael Davitt, *Within the Pale: The True Story of Anti-Semitic Persecution in Russia* (Philadelphia: Jewish Publication Society, 1903), 268–72; Edward H. Judge, *Easter in Kishinev: Anatomy of a Pogrom* (New York: New York University Press, 1992), 89.

5. On Bialik, see Avner Holtzman, *Hayyim Nahman Bialik* (Jerusalem: Merkaz Shazar, 2009), 17–21; and Ya'akov Goren, *'Eduyot nifge'e Kishinov, 1903* (Tel Aviv: Hakibutz Hameuhad, 1991), 9–49. His poem, "Be'ir ha-haregah" (originally published as "Masa Nemirov") has been reprinted numerous times; his entire poetic corpus can be found in *Kol shirei Kh. N. Bialik* (Tel Aviv, 1967–68). On Michael Davitt see Carla King, "Michael Davitt and the Kishinev Pogrom, 1903," *Irish Slavonic Studies* 17 (1996): 19–43.

6. "Kishineff," New York Public Library for the Performing Arts, NCOF+p.v.344; A. R. Malachi, "Pera'ot Kishinev be-aspaklariat ha-shirah be-ivrit ve-yidish," *Al admat Bes'arabyah* 3 (Tel Aviv, 1963–64): esp. 64–98; Monty Noam Penkower, "The Kishinev Pogrom of 1903: A Turning Point in Jewish History," *Modern Judaism* 24, no. 3 (October 2004): 187–225.

7. *Sefer Bernstein-Kogan* (Tel Aviv, 1946–47), 135–36.

8. On Bialik's notebooks, see Goren, *'Eduyot*, 48–49. On Davitt's papers, see Carla King, *Michael Davitt* (Dundalk, IE: Dundalgan Press 1999).

9. See Yeruham Fishel Lachower, *Bialik*, vol. 2 (Tel Aviv, 1934/35), 424–26; David G. Roskies, *Against the Apocalypse* (Cambridge: Harvard University Press, 1984), 89–92; Steven J. Zipperstein, *Elusive Prophet* (Berkeley: University of California Press, 1993), 202–209.

10. Malachi, "Pera'ot Kishinev," 67; Dan Miron, "Introduction," *Songs from Bialik*, ed. and trans. Atar Hadari (Syracuse, NY: Syracuse University Press, 2000), xxxviii.

11. H. M. Hyndman, *Further Reminiscences* (London: Macmillan, 1912), 52.

12. Ibid., 55.

13. Michael Davitt, *The Boer Fight for Freedom* (New York: Funk and Wagnalls, 1902), p. 28; Davitt, *Within the Pale*, ix, 89; Dermott Keogh, *Jews in Twentieth-Century Ireland* (Cork, IE: Cork University Press, 1998), 27–32; Lawrence Marley, *Michael Davitt* (Dublin: Four Courts Press, 2007), 256–59.

14. King, "Michael Davitt and the Kishinev Pogrom," 20–24; Richard Gottheil, "Kishineff," *The Forum* 35 (July/September 1903): 159.

15. Davitt Papers, Trinity College, Dublin, MS 9577/5.

16. *Sefer Bernstein-Kogan*, 135–36; Davitt Papers, Trinity College, Dublin, MS 9578, MS 9501/5301; Davitt, *Within the Pale*, 17–27. Also see King, "Michael Davitt and the Kishinev Pogrom," 29–30.

17. Ibid., 101.

18. Davitt Papers, Trinity College, Dublin, MS 9577/5.

19. Ibid.

20. Ibid.

21. Davitt, *Within the Pale*, 121–40; M. B. Slutskii, *V skorbnye dni* (Kishinev, 1930); A. Beilin, *Der kishinyever pogrom* (Warsaw, 1932). The most authoritative description can be found in Judge, *Easter in Kishinev*.

22. Davitt Papers, Trinity College, Dublin, MS 9578.

23. Davitt to Sidney Webb, Davitt Papers, Trinity College, Dublin, MS 9400/4970.

24. Davitt Papers, Trinity College, Dublin, MS 9577; King, "Michael Davitt and the Kishinev Pogrom," 30.

25. Davitt, *Within the Pale*, 170.

26. Michael Stanislawski, *Zionism and the Fin-de-Siecle: Cosmopolitanism and Nationalism from Nordau to Jabotinsky* (Berkeley: University of California Press, 2001).

27. Ibid., 178–202; Chaim Tchernowitz [Rav Tsa'ir], *Masekhet zikhronot* (New York: Va'ad Ha-Yovel, 1945), 116–125; Malachi, "Pera'ot Kishinev," 1–64.

28. Tchernowitz, *Masekhet*, 119–120.

29. Michael Gluzman, et. al., eds., *Be-'ir ha-haregah* (Tel Aviv: Resling, 2005), 13–36; Michael Gluzman, "Pogrom and Gender: On Bialik's Unheimlich," *Prooftexts* 25, nos. 1–2 (winter/spring 2005): 39–59; Pesakh Averbakh, "Kh. N. Bialik ve-'ir ha-haregah," in *Ha-pogrom be-kishinev bi-melot 60 shanah*, ed. Chaim Shorer (Tel Aviv: Haigud haolami shel yehudei besarabyah, 1963), 28.

30. Ziva Shamir, *Lintivah ha-ne'elam* (Tel Aviv: Hakibbutz Hameuhad, 2000), esp. 7–50; Lachower, *Bialik*, 442–43.

31. Ariel Hirschfeld, *Kinor 'arukh* (Tel Aviv: Am Oved, 2011).

32. Simon Dubnov, *Kniga zhizni* (Book of My Life) (St. Petersburg, reprint 1998), 240–43.

33. See, for instance, Shlomo Dubinsky's article on self-defense during the Kishinev pogrom in *Ha-Aretz*, August 10, 1928.

34. Hadari, *Songs from Bialik*, 3.

35. Davitt Papers, Trinity College, Dubin, MS 9577.

36. Norman Cohn, *Warrant for Genocide* (London: Eyre and Spottiswoode, 1967), 108.

37. Getzel Kressel, "Ha-pogrom be-Kishinev ba-aspaklariat ha-Velt," *Al admat*, 100.

38. Victor Serge, *Memoirs of a Revolutionary*, trans. Peter Sedgwick (New York: New York Review of Books Classics, 2012), 304.

25

Julian Tuwim

Confronting Antisemitism in Poland

ANTONY POLONSKY

The Polish parliament designated 2013 as the "Year of Julian Tuwim," commemorating the sixtieth anniversary of the poet's death. Yet Tuwim, one of the most accomplished writers of Jewish origin who established themselves on the Polish literary scene in the period between the two world wars, a man described as the "Polish Heine,"[1] is still virtually unknown in the Jewish world outside Poland. He was a key figure in the Skamander group,[2] which emerged as the dominant literary clique in Poland in the optimistic years of the 1920s. As the first generation of writers to come to maturity in an independent Poland, they were eager to throw off the heavy burden of commitment to the Polish cause that had weighed down literature in the nineteenth century. In the words of one of their members, Jan Lechoń: "And in the spring let me see spring, not Poland."[3]

Tuwim himself put it more sharply. "I don't want tombs, I don't want a sad Orthodox chapel, the lamentations of crows, owls, and other night birds."[4]

The group included a number of poets and writers, most notably Lechoń himself, Kazimierz Wierzyński, and Jarosław Iwaszkiewicz, who were not Jewish. Writers of Jewish background also were important in its ranks, including Antoni Słonimski who, though the son of a socialist and baptized in infancy, had many distinguished Jewish forebears and regarded himself as a "Jew of antisemitic antecedents"; Mieczysław Grydzewski, who, as editor of the influential literary weekly *Wiadomości Literackie*, was a key figure in propagating the group's works; and Tuwim himself. Indeed, with his cult of the modern city and its crowds of anonymous people seeking both a living and new diversions, which made him seem most akin to the American poet Walt Whitman, Tuwim embodied the Skamander aesthetic more than any of his contemporaries.

He was born into a middle-class Jewish family in the textile town of Łódź and had a remarkable gift for verse, writing not only serious poetry but also verse for cabarets and for children. He was obsessed with verbal coinages and innovative rhymes and expressed in his poetry a sensual love of life and nature. In the poetry that he wrote in the 1920s, he explored a large number of different themes, most of which reflected the artistic views of the Skamander group, which combined a fairly conventional aesthetic with the exploration of different aspects of the urban experience.

Jewish themes were a central part of Tuwim's oeuvre. He was very conscious of his double identity as a Pole and a Jew, and he expressed this in a number of his early poems. In "Under the Impetus of the Ages," he wrote:

> There flows in me semitic blood
> Hot blood, passionate blood
> From somewhere beyond the Nile I draw my heritage
> From the tropics I am!
> Perhaps my ancestor, the father of Jews,
> A Nubian dancer took to bed
> And by the mysterious glow of the stars
> Found desirous frenzy in his arms!
> From the tropics I am,
> Where the pallor of the sun bakes the sands
> And now, when ages have passed, my song resounds:
> Aj, lado-lado-luli-lel!
> Oh Aria! how I love you!
> Oh sun-Poland! My land!
> The eternal mighty giant, time, has brought me,
> From the desert, where the lascivious toil
> Of supple tigresses blazes the blood
> To You, Poland . . . And into your myth
> I weave marvelous Slavic song:
> Aj, lado-lado-luli-did!
> Although I draw my birthright from beyond the Nile

The hop of Slavs froths in me
And through it I sing the People of the Piasts
Aj, lado-lado-luli-lel[5]

He believed that antisemitism was one of the many ridiculous superstitions of the petite bourgeoisie that could be destroyed by mockery. Thus, in his poem "The Anonymous Power," he provided a grotesque interpretation of the antisemitic view of the world:

Already large stores of gold have been accumulated in synagogue
     basements.
Black smugglers have brought ammunition
Berlin bankers are conferring in secret
A hidden telephone rings in a Warsaw temple

In London, in the great lodge, all is already decided
The masons place seven seals on the decree.
Yellow candles shed light on a blood-spattered Talmud
Everything is wrapped up in canvas and the secret is sworn

And suddenly the jews in the Kremlin receive a telegram
The lines crackle! The editorial offices boil!
The Paris Rothschild rubs his hands with pleasure
Shares are bought in Amsterdam and Rome.

A huge dragon flies in the heavens
At night it is seen by the boldest aviators
It flaps its wings darkly over the cities and spreads panic
As a signal, a rocket is fired from over the Prussian border

And in our small towns, on a stiflingly hot holiday
Whispered rumours come forth from halls in which people are
     gasping for breath
"A Kike with peyes stole into a Church
And has butchered a young girl in a brickyard to make matzoh."[6]

At the same time, he attacked what he described as the "materialism" and "philistinism" of the Jewish bourgeoisie. His poems on this topic, although intended ironically, have a hollow ring today after the Holocaust. Thus in "Bank" he wrote:

Like black hairy balls
Sruleks roll around the bank

They jump, jump onto the counters
One Srulek bargains with another

One Srulek submits to another
A Srulek runs to the cash box

He counts with trembling fingers
And then runs away from the other Sruleks

In armchairs far from the cash box
Sit the corpulent big Sruls

A Srulek with a fawning smile
Bows to the fat Sruls

And in the depths — in a quiet place — great like a king
Ponders
    alone
       the head
        Srul.[7]

Yet his sense of identification with the Jews was strong. In 1924 he wrote: "With me the Jewish question lies in my blood, it is a fundamental element in my psyche. It is like a powerful wedge cutting into my view of the world, affecting my deepest personal experiences. . . . For me the 'Jewish problem' is a tragedy, in which I myself am one of the anonymous actors. What will be the end of this tragedy and when it will occur, I cannot at present predict."[8]

He expressed his Jewish feelings even more clearly in his poem "Jewboy" (Żydek).

He sings in the courtyard, clad in rags
A small, poor chap, a crazed Jew.

People drive him away, God has muddled his wits
Ages and exile have confused his tongue.

He wails and he dances, weeps and laments
That he is lost, is dependent on alms.

The gent on the first floor looks down on the madman.
Look my poor brother at your sad brother.

How did we come to this? How did we lose ourselves
In this vast world, strange and hostile to us?

You on the first floor, your unhinged brother
With his burning head dances through the world

The first floor gent fancies himself a poet
He wraps up his heart, like a coin, in paper

And throws it out from the window, so that it will break
And be trampled and cease to be

And we will both go on our way
A path sad and crazed

And we will never find peace or rest
Singing Jews, lost Jews.[9]

It has often been observed that one of the most characteristic tropes of modern antisemitism, and one which distinguished it from traditional Christian anti-Judaism, was its hostility to Jewish integration and to acculturated and integrated Jews. According to the antisemites, although a small number of Jews had kept to the "assimilationist bargain" and had adopted the culture and way of life of the country to whose citizenship they aspired, most saw this acculturation purely in terms of the advantages it brought to them as individuals or as a group. Thus they constituted an unassimilable mass, all the more dangerous because they understood the language and customs of the host country and could use this knowledge to advance specific Jewish interests. This disillusionment with the politics of Jewish integration was first articulated in Germany, in the wake of the economic crisis of the 1870s, and was set out by Heinrich von Treitschke in his well-known essay "A Word about Our Jewry," written in 1880. One particular aspect of this hostility was the allegedly negative impact Jewish writers were having on the national culture. Thus, according to Richard Wagner, the central problem was the "Judaization of modern art." Disillusioned by the failure of the Revolutions of 1848, he argued in his 1850 essay, "Judaism in Music,"[10] that this had been caused by the degeneration of German society, the product of Jewish cultural influence. The Jews were unable to be a genuine part of the European community or participate in its culture. "Alien and apathetic stands the educated Jew in midst of a society he does not understand, with whose tastes and aspirations he does not sympathize, whose history and evolution have always been indifferent to him."

Given the much slower pace of Jewish acculturation in the Polish lands, it is not surprising that these motifs surfaced here a generation later than in Germany. Tuwim was bitterly attacked by Polish cultural conservatives and antisemites, who denounced him for "debasing" the Polish language and for his "semitic" sensuality. Józef Mackiewicz, the Vilna journalist, asserted bluntly that Tuwim was not a Polish poet, while the Kraków writer and critic Karol Hubert Rostworowski described him as a "Jewish poet writing in Polish." The right-wing journalist Adolf Nowaczyński referred to him as "Jozue" Tuwim. When a Yiddish translation of a Tuwim poem appeared, *Gazeta Literacka* crowed that Tuwim finally had decided to write in Yiddish. The right-wing literary weekly *Prosto z mostu* abounded in headlines such as "Tuwim and Słonimski are one hundred percent Jews," "A new center of Masonry has been established in Warsaw," "The Literary Ghetto," and "Jewish Poetry in the Polish Language."[11]

Tuwim responded vigorously to the attacks on him, seeing himself as the scourge of the nationalist right, and turning his scorn on his detractors in a series of deadly ripostes. This is one of his responses to the nationalist critic Stanisław Pieńkowski:

> Spitting poison and froth from his mouth
> He spits, snorts and splutters
> And writes that I am a butcher
> A yid and bolshevik
> Jewboy, bacillus
> A baboon and a Skamandrite
> That I sell out the Fatherland
> That I deform the Polish language
> That I provoke and profane
> And the Devil knows what else.

And to think that from all
The fine activity
Of this gentleman — from the spittle
Wheezing, screaming, scribbling,
Spewing, kicking and wailing
On which he has lost half his life
From the books and articles
From the words, sentences and titles
From the reviews, from the sneering paragraphs
In a word from that whole
Journalistic mess
Will remain . . . one poem
And that will be — mine, not his.
Indeed *this* very poem . . . O stern revenge
Inspired by a Jewish God.
Here is a phrase, a few words with which I toy
To immortalize my enemy.[12]

The Right also was shocked by his open exaltation of physicality and sexuality. In addition, while the aesthetic of the Skamander was not particularly radical, the group was regarded by the exponents of modern poetry in Poland as excessively conservative. But what marked it above all was its desire to appeal to a wider audience, "to bring poetry to the street." Tuwim in particular wrote extensively for the cabaret, and his desire to bridge the gap between high and popular culture was deeply suspect to the Right, brought up on the concept of the poet as Prophet (*Wieszcz*), expounding weighty truths to the nation.

Finally, the Right saw him as a blasphemer. They were incensed by his attempt to appropriate Jesus and by his use of religious and Christian language in a new and deliberately shocking way as in the first section of his poem "The Word and the Flesh":

And the Word was made flesh
And it has dwelt among us,
I feed the starving body
With words as if they were fruit . . .[13]

Tuwim seemed to the Right to embody everything they hated about the intellectual culture of the big city. In opposition to the literary aesthetic of the Skamander group and also of the Modernists in Poland, the Right's literary ideologues called for an art that would stress national, Catholic, and rural values and would sustain group solidarity. They admired in an uncritical way the great Polish Romantic poets, whose work effectively was bowdlerized by them. Among more recent writers, they favoured Sienkiewicz and to a lesser extent Reymont. Above all, they admired the poetry of Jan Kasprowicz, a metaphysical and nature poet of peasant origins, whose later work had a strongly Catholic character.

Tuwim's mood darkened in the 1930s with Nazism and Stalinism on Poland's borders and intensifying antisemitism in Poland. He identified strongly with the ordinary urban man, yet in Poland this petty bourgeois element for whom he wished to produce was strongly affected by antisemitism. "I am going down, it is very difficult, it is awful for me in this country," he wrote in the 1930s.[14] On another occasion he wrote, "It is difficult to be a stepson with a stepmother."[15]

He responded by writing *Bal w Operze* (A Ball at the Opera), one of the most remarkable of the apocalyptic visions that were produced in the doom-laden years prior to the outbreak of the Second World War, which, because of its strongly antigovernment and possibly blasphemous character, could not be published in full until after the war. "A Ball at the Opera," is a savage description of a corrupt fascist dictatorship written by an individual in despair. Unlike some other Polish "catastrophist" writers of the 1930s, such as Konstanty Ildefons Galczyński and Stanisław Ignacy Witkiewicz, Tuwim clearly situates this fascist dystopia in Poland.

When Tuwim began to write "A Ball at the Opera," the optimism that had characterized the 1920s had long been dissipated. Hitler had come to power in Germany; Stalin ruled in the Soviet Union. The death of Piłsudski had unleashed a struggle for power within the government camp (the *Sanacja*) in which one of the participating groups hoped to establish its power by coming to terms with the nationalist Right by adopting nationalist, corporatist, and antisemitic policies. The establishment by Adam Koc in 1936 of the Camp of National Unity (Obóz Zjednoczenia Narodowego — OZON) marked an important stage in this process.

The worsening political climate was particularly painful to Tuwim. In the first place, he was extraordinarily sensitive to the surrounding atmosphere. In addition, as someone who considered himself both Polish and Jewish, the pervasive climate of antisemitism, stimulated as it was by Hitler's coming to power in Germany; the persistence of the depression; and the willingness of a section of the government camp to adopt an antisemitic platform was extremely painful to experience.

The poem is an apocalyptic vision in which Tuwim's horror of a corrupt society's filthy doings fuses with a foreboding of the destruction of that society. The poem starts and ends with a series of quotations from the Revelation of Saint John and is, in fact, a description of the end of the world. For these quotations Tuwim uses the Protestant translation of the Bible produced in 1632 (the so-called Biblia Gdańska), rather than the late sixteenth-century Catholic translation of the Bible of Jan Wujek. The quotations at the beginning of the poem read as follows (using the King James version):

> And the great dragon was cast out, that old serpent, called the Devil, and Satan, which deceiveth the whole world: he was cast out into the earth, and his angels were cast out with him. (Rev. 12:9)
>
> Come hither; I will shew unto thee the judgement of the great whore that sitteth upon many waters: With whom the kings of the earth have committed fornication, and the inhabitants of the earth have been made drunk with the wine of her fornication. So he carried me away in the spirit into the wilderness; and I saw a woman sit upon a scarlet coloured beast, full of names of blasphemy. . . . And the woman was arrayed in purple and scarlet colour, and decked with gold and precious stones and pearls, having a golden cup in her hand full of abominations and filthiness of her fornications. . . . And I saw the woman drunken with the blood of the saints and with the blood of the martyrs of Jesus; and when I saw her I wondered with great admiration. (Rev. 17:1–6)
>
> And after these things I heard a loud voice of much people in heaven saying, Alleluia; Salvation and glory and honour and power unto the Lord our God; For true and righteous *are* his judgements; for he hath judged the great whore, which did corrupt the earth with

her fornication, and hath avenged the blood of his servants at her hand. (Rev. 19:1–2)

The poem ends with the penultimate verse of the Revelation (22:20). In Tuwim's Polish version, the verse is given (all in capitals) as:

TAK MÓWI TEN, KTÓRY ŚWIADECTWO DAJE O TYCH
RZECZACH:
ZAISTE, PRZYDĘ RYCHŁO, AMEN
I OWSZEM, PRZYDŹ, PANIE JESUSIE

This is rendered by the King James Version as "He which testifieth these things saith, Surely I come quickly. Amen. Even so, come Lord Jesus" and in the Revised Standard Version as "He who testifies to these things says, 'Surely I am coming soon.' Amen. Come, Lord Jesus."

The use of "owszem" in the translation, which does not seem to be justified by the original Greek and which may be what led Tuwim to use the Gdańsk version rather than that of Wujek, modifies the meaning of the verse in complex and ambiguous ways that are central to the meaning of the poem and that will be discussed later.

As its title implies, the poem is a description of a ball held in honor of the fascist dictator Pantokrator (Ruler of All) at the Opera in Warsaw. It culminates in an overwhelming and brilliant climax in which "the great dragon . . . that old serpent" appears with the Whore of Babylon on its back.

> And while the fizz of the champagne hit the ceiling
> And the metallic flourish of the band continued
> The secret policeman winking to the secret policeman
> Did not see or perceive from the large chandelier
> How in a lightning flash
> A photo-flash, a blaze of light
> All are taken by all the devils
>   taken by all the devils
>   taken by all the devils
> So that the apes, overtaken by laughter, fell
> From the heavenly carousel.

This nightmarish vision is followed by the penultimate verse of Revelation, with which the poem concludes. The version quoted by Tuwim diverges from the original Greek and is highly ambiguous. I would suggest that the meaning intended by Tuwim should be rendered in English as follows:

> Thus says He who has given testimony of these things:
> Indeed, I will come quickly. Amen!
> And if you *do* indeed have the power to bring an end to these
> abominations, come Lord Jesus!

Explicitly Jewish motifs seem almost completely absent from the poem. One exception might be the quotations from Revelation. These should be seen as part of the attempt by some Jews in the modern period to appropriate Jesus and his early followers. They have, however, a more complex character, since the apocalyptic character of Revelation is very similar to the apocalyptic books of the Hebrew Bible, in particular the Book of Daniel and the writings of the exilic Prophet Ezekiel, which clearly struck a deep chord with Tuwim. One also might speculate that the belief that Jesus was a well-meaning and noble but ultimately unsuccessful Prophet, whose claim that his revelation would lead to universal brotherhood had clearly failed, has a long history in Jewish understandings of both Jesus and Christianity. The use of the term "Owszem" also echoes the notorious statement by the Polish prime minister Felicjan Sławoj Składkowski in parliament in 1936. After a series of violent anti-Jewish incidents in June 1936, he asserted "My government considers that nobody in Poland should be injured. An honest host does not allow anybody to be harmed in his house. An economic struggle? That's different (*Owszem*)."[16]

"The Ball at the Opera" was the last significant poem that Tuwim wrote before the outbreak of the war. In September 1939, he made his way with his wife through Romania and France and from there, after the fall of France, via Portugal to Brazil and ultimately to the United States, where he spent the bulk of the war. After his arrival in Brazil in August 1940, Tuwim's poetic inspiration returned, in spite of his sense of guilt at being in such an idyllic spot at such a tragic time. In response to a request to write about his childhood memories from the editor of *Wiadomości Literackie*, which had reestablished itself in exile in London, he began a long narrative poem entitled *Kwiaty Polskie* (Polish Flowers). He wrote to his sister explaining the end of his creative block: "How do I explain, dear Irena, that in Poland in the past five years I was able to write practically nothing whereas here I have been writing nonstop. I think that 1) the atmosphere in Poland was so unbearable that it seeped into my subconscious and blocked my 'poetic orifices' 2) that here—I feel compelled to rebuild in some measure that unbearable, but, above all, most beloved Poland."[17]

In exile he sought to evoke his beloved but remote Poland in his long poem *Kwiaty polskie* (Polish Flowers). He described his goal as follows:

> My song born in defeat and anguish,
> Huge serpent reared beyond the seas,
> You rose from flowers, motley, twisted,
> You will turn into flowers again.

In a section of the first part of the poem, he addresses a former fascist whom he encounters in Rio and who has now become a democrat, even conceding that "Jews are also human," launching into a savage denunciation of the Poland of the late 1930s, which makes explicit all that is implied between the lines in "The Ball at the Opera":

> Do you remember . . . but a few short years ago
> When the Iron Wolf[18] disintegrated
> Into hundreds of little dogs of the Hitler breed
> When like leprosy or black smallpox
> Poland was covered by savage student corporations
> Of stormtroopers, readers of *Der Stürmer*, "intellectuals"
> When Generals from drinking too much coffee
> Caught the fascist infection:
> The First Cohort and the Falanga
> Of the last dregs and scum;
> When a milksop leader, a whipper-snapper "enlightened"
> By a mystic mission straight from Munich
> Wrote upon the walls
> The epitaph of frightened ministers
> When the street was ruled by petty middle-class scoundrels

Excellent "Catholics"
Except that they had not yet become Christian . . .
When the rampant braggarts so beat the Jews
That I felt more shame for my fatherland
Than pity for my beaten brethren . . .
When in the worm-like press
There was nothing but roars and flashes:
The Jew, Jews, Jews, Jews, Jews
Mangy and scabby Kikes
The Jew is our greatest enemy
The Jew waits with a knife at your threshold
The Jew causes hunger, the Jew causes misery
The Jew steals, the Jew insults the priest
The Jew tramples on the White Eagle
The Jew laps up the blood of infants
The Jew poisons, violates, betrays, denounces
The Jew bestializes, defiles, corrupts
And again; the Jew, the Jew, the Jew . . .[19]

The attentive reader will notice that Tuwim does seem to have some guilt over his failure to confront antisemitism directly in "The Ball at the Opera." He was convinced that the new Poland would be free of the vices of the past, purged by the wartime experience:

We are modest men, we're simple men,
No supermen, nor any giants.
We ask our God for a different might,
For another road to greatness:

Kindle the clouds into a glare, and
Strike at our hearts with a bell of gold,
Open our Poland as with a bolt
You clear up the overcast heavens.
Allow us to rid our fathers' home
Of our cinders, and holy ruins:
Let our house be poor but also clean,
Our house, raised from the cemetery.

At the same time, he felt enormous guilt that he was living comfortably in Buenos Aires:

> When we approach O Necropolis
> Your suburbs, in a quarantine we
> Will kneel in the field, full of hope and
> Anguish: hope—that friends shall come to meet
> Us from the City of the Crosses,
> Bearing forgiveness in their eyes and
> Tears of happiness not a reproach.
> Anguish—that these tears, this kindness and
> These greetings shall be of no avail . . .
> THE SILENT THING between us shall rise—
> A dreadful phantom.

He increasingly was preoccupied with the fate of Polish Jewry and of his beloved mother, who had had a nervous breakdown during the war and had withdrawn to a sanatorium in Otwock near Warsaw. In 1941 he moved to New York, where he became convinced that only the Soviet Union could defeat the Nazis. This led to a breach with another Skamander poet, Jan Lechoń, who also had made his way to New York and who wrote to him in May 1942 severing all relations because of Tuwim's "blind love for the Bolsheviks."[20]

He became much more conscious of his Jewish identity, writing to his mother in Poland, "So with pride, with mournful pride we will bear that rank, eclipsing all others—the rank of the Polish Jew—we, who miraculously and arbitrarily have remained alive. With pride? Let us say rather: with contrite and biting shame. Because it fell to us for your suffering, for your glory."[21]

He now produced his last great work, the prose-poem "We, Polish Jews. . . ." Suspecting the fate of his mother, who already had been murdered by the Germans, he dedicated it "To My Mother in Poland / or to her beloved Shadow." He began by explaining why he now identified with the Jews of Poland:

And immediately I can hear the question: "What do you mean— WE?" The question, I grant you, is natural enough. Jews to whom I

am wont to explain that I am a Pole have asked it. So will the Poles
to the overwhelming majority of whom I am and shall remain a Jew.
Here is my answer to both.

I am a Pole because I want to be. It's nobody's business but my
own. I certainly have not the slightest intention of rendering account, explaining, or justifying it to anyone. I do not divide Poles into
pure-stock Poles and alien-stock Poles. I leave such classification to
pure and alien-stock advocates of racialism, to domestic and foreign
Nazis. I divide Poles just as I divide Jews and all other nations into
the intelligent and the fools, the honest and the dishonest, the brilliant and the dull-witted, the exploited and the exploiters, gentlemen
and cads. I also divide Poles into fascists and antifascists. Neither of
these groups is of course homogeneous; each shimmers with a variety of hues and shades. But a dividing line certainly does exist, and
soon will become quite apparent. Shades may remain, but the color
of the dividing line itself will both brighten and deepen to a marked
degree.

I can say that in the realm of politics I divide Poles into antisemites
and antifascists. For fascism means always antisemitism. Antisemitism is the international language of fascism.

He went on:

If, however, it comes to explaining my nationality, or rather my sense
of national belonging, then I am a Pole for the most simple, almost
primitive reasons. Mostly rational, partly irrational, but devoid of
any "mystical" flourishes. To be a Pole is neither an honor nor a glory
nor a privilege. It is like breathing. I have not yet met a man who is
proud of breathing.

I am a Pole because it was in Poland that I was born and bred, that
I grew up and learned; because it was in Poland that I was happy and
unhappy; because from exile it is to Poland that I want to return,
even though I were promised the joys of paradise elsewhere . . .

Above all a Pole—because I want to be.

He then went on to explain his Jewish allegiance:

"All right," someone will say, "granted you are a Pole. But in that case, why 'we JEWS'?" To which I answer: BECAUSE OF BLOOD "Then racialism again?" No, not racialism at all. Quite the contrary.

There are two kinds of blood: that inside of veins, and that which spurts from them. The first is the sap of the body, and as such comes under the realm of physiologists. Whoever attributes to this blood any other than biological characteristics and powers will in consequence, as we have seen, turn towns into smoking ruins, will slaughter millions of people, and at last, as we shall yet see, bring carnage upon his own kin.

The other kind of blood is the same blood but spilled by this gang leader of international Fascism to testify to the triumph of his gore over mine, the blood of millions of murdered innocents, a blood not hidden in arteries but revealed to the world. Never since the dawn of mankind has there been such a flood of martyr blood, and the blood of Jews (not Jewish blood, mind you) flows in widest and deepest streams. Already its blackening rivulets are flowing together into a tempestuous river. AND IT IS IN THIS NEW JORDAN THAT I BEG TO RECEIVE THE BAPTISM OF BAPTISMS; THE BLOODY, BURNING, MARTYRED BROTHERHOOD OF JEWS.[22]

The new Poland to which Tuwim returned and pledged his complete support must have been a terrible disappointment to him. Antisemitism persisted, and in the aftermath of the war, perhaps fifteen hundred Jews died in anti-Jewish violence, the worst incident being in Kielce. He was determined to ally himself with the new order, writing in 1950 to the poet Mieczysław Jastrun that they needed to talk about "the unimportance of lyricism in the project of the socialization of minds and in general about the exceedingly limited influence of poetry on transformations of historical significance in humanity's history."[23] Yet he must have found the new political orthodoxy suffocating, although he did compose a sterile "Ode to Stalin" in which he spoke of the Revolution as an eternal beauty and of Stalin as an immortal hero.[24] His muse dried up, and he devoted himself to translation, editing and writing children's stories. He wrote one poem in which he described the death of his mother:

I

At the cemetery in Łódź
The Jewish cemetery, stands
The Polish grave of my mother,
My Jewish mother's tomb.

The grave of my Mother, the Pole,
Of my Mother the Jewess;
I brought her from land over Vistula
To the bank of industrial Łódź.

A rock fell on the tombstone,
Upon the face of the pale rock
A few laurel leaves
Shed by a birch tree.

And when a sunny breeze
Plays with them a golden game,
The leaves are patterned into
The Order of Polonia.

II

A fascist shot my mother
When she was thinking of me;
A fascist shot my mother
When she was longing for me.

He loaded — killed the longing,
Again began to load,
So that later . . . but later
There was nothing left to kill.

He shot through my mother's world:
Two tender syllables;
Threw the corpse out the window
Upon the holy pavement.

Remember well, little daughter!
Recall this, future grandson!

The word has come true:
"The ideal reached the pavement"[25]

I took her from the field of glory,
Returned to mother-earth . . .
But the corpse of my name
Still lies buried there.

He died in December 1953 aged fifty-nine. On the day following his death, his former friend Jan Lechoń wrote in his diary: "Tuwim has died. . . . And now I cannot forget about these past seven years—but I remember still twenty more years—the gallivanting about, the silences, the jokes, but above all his poems. . . . Everyone who came after him and many of his contemporaries should say now: 'We are all from him.'"[26] Tuwim's poetry is almost unknown in the Jewish world. Yet his work can be compared to that of Heine, with its irony, sense of the fragility of love, and complex view of his Jewish roots. He deserves to be better known. His last words are reported to have been, "On grounds of economy, please extinguish the eternal light that once illuminated me."[27] That light is still there for us, if we would only seek it out.

NOTES

1. J. Ratajczyk, *Julian Tuwim* (Poznań: PLRebis, 1995), 111.

2. The name of the group was a reference to the river that flowed past Troy, which in Stanisław Wyśpiański's play *Acropolis* was described as glittering "with a Vistula wave."

3. Jan Lechoń, "Hierostrates," in *Poezje*, selected and introduced by Matylda Wełna (Lublin: Wydawnictwo Lubelskie, 1989), 30.

4. Quoted in Ratajczyk, *Julian Tuwim*, 87.

5. "Pod bodźcem wieków," quoted in Janusz Dunin, "Tuwim jako Żyd, Polak, Człowiek," *Praca Polonistyczne* 51 (1996): 88.

6. *Jarmark rymu*, 54.

7. Ibid., 53.

8. Ibid., 105–106.

9. Julian Tuwim, *Words in the Blood* (Warsaw, 1926); *Dzieła* 1 (Łódź: Wyd. Łódźkie): 283.

10. *Neue Zeitschrift für Musik* 33, nos. 19 and 20 (September 3 and 6, 1850).

11. For these and other attacks on Tuwim, see Ratajczyk, *Julian Tuwim*, 102–103.

402   WITNESSING HISTORY

12. *Jarmark rymu*, 68.

13. Pisma Zbiorowe, ed., *Słowa we krwi*, vol. 1 (Warsaw, 1926), 266.

14. Quoted in Ratajczyk, *Julian Tuwim*, 95.

15. Ibid., 96.

16. *Sprawozdanie Stenograficzne Sejm Rzeczypospolitej*, June 4, 1936, col. 7.

17. Ratajczyk, *Julian Tuwim*, 115.

18. A reference to Vilna (an iron wolf appeared in a dream to its founder Gedymin), where the fascist offshoots of the Endecja were particularly strong.

19. Julian Tuwim, *Kwiaty Polskie* (Warsaw: Philip Wilson Warsaw, 1993), 109–112.

20. Lechoń to Tuwim, May 29, 1942, New York, in Julian Tuwim, *Listy do przyjaciół-pisarzy*, 43n.

21. Julian Tuwim, *My, Żydzi polscy*, 6.

22. Translated by Mrs. Langer; first published in *Free World*, New York, July 1944.

23. Julian Tuwim to Mieczyław Jastrun, March 30, 1950, in Tuwim, *Listy do przyjaciół-pisarzy*, 421–22.

24. Julian Tuwim, "Do narodu radzieckiego," in *Wiersze 2*, ed. Alina Kowalczykowa (Warsaw: Czytelnik, 1986), 344.

25. A reference to a poem by the nineteenth-century Polish poet Cyprian Kamil Norwid in which the poet describes the sacking by Russian soldiers during the 1830–31 Uprising of Chopin's piano in Warsaw. In the course of this, Chopin's piano was thrown out of a window and smashed.

26. Tuwim, *Listy do przyjaciół-pisarzy*, 62.

27. Ibid., 147.

26

The Terrible Secret

Some Afterthoughts

WALTER LAQUEUR

When and how did authentic information about the Shoah first become known? The question has been discussed in detail in my book *The Terrible Secret* and in *Breaking the Silence* (Laqueur and Richard Breitman).[1] In the thirty years that have passed, additional information has become known. News about Hitler's decision to destroy European Jewry and its implementation percolated out of the Nazi-occupied countries in various ways. The information came from individuals and groups including the Bund and Orthodox Jewish organizations. The central document was Gerhart Riegner's cable sent to Washington on August 10, 1942. The general picture as presented in the 1980s need not be revised; specific issues have been clarified, others, on the contrary, are now less clear than before. My intention in the following essay is to point to some aspects that deserve further investigation.

Riegner, a native of Berlin and a lawyer by profession who was thirty years of age at the time, represented the World Jewish Congress (WJC) in Geneva. He had received the information through two intermediaries (Benno Sagalowitz, the press officer of the Swiss Jewish community, and Isidor Koppelmann, a businessman) from a German industrialist whose name he had sworn never to reveal. Riegner did in fact have to reveal it to the American diplomats in Switzerland, who made it a condition for transmitting his cable to Washington. However, these Americans were the exception. In a letter to me dated Geneva, September 21, 1984, he writes, "May I remind you, however, of our gentleman's agreement. Somewhere you will have to say that up to this date I refused to identify the German source." Riegner subsequently mentioned the name in his 2001 autobiography—once. He also mentioned it in a long interview with the German weekly *Der Spiegel* in October 2001.

Breitman and I had written that there were not many interesting jobs for young émigré lawyers at the time in connection with Riegner being offered the position of representing the WJC at the League of Nations. Riegner in his letter says, "It was not that I was looking for a job. I had still a fellowship (in Geneva) which had just been renewed for another year. The real reason: I felt I could not refuse to cooperate in the fight against Hitler with the only Jewish group which tried to fight him."

Riegner mentions in that same document that news about mass killings of Jews had reached him well before the summer of 1942. He specifically mentions reports on several thousand Jews being killed in Westpreussen (broadly speaking, the region south of Danzig), tens of thousands killed in various Polish towns, and killings by injections and in mobile gas vans. When Riegner and Lichtheim met Bernardini, the papal nuncio in mid-March 1942, they reported inter alia on eighteen thousand Jews shot in eastern Galicia and of massacres in Romania (Jassy?) and elsewhere.

Riegner died in 2001 at age ninety. A few years earlier he had written his autobiography, entitled *Niemals Verzweifeln: Sechzig Jahre für das jüdische Volk und die Menschenrechte,*[2] which dealt with the events of summer 1942 in only a few pages, however. He continued to work for the World Jewish Congress after the war. He was active in relations with the Catholic Church, but also with the emigration of Jews from various North African countries.

In view of the paucity of information published by Riegner in later years, his 1984 four-page letter to me mentioned earlier is of particular interest. Some of his corrections are indeed minor—the authors had described him as a bespectacled young man, whereas Riegner says he came to need glasses only later in life. We had written that Lewandowski, the most eminent composer of synagogue music in Germany, was Riegner's maternal grandfather, whereas in actual fact he was the brother of his great grandfather—but he, too, was a cantor.

Other information is of considerable historical interest. Riegner reported, for instance, that there were two versions of his cable. The longer one, which was not dispatched, contained the following:

Furthermore known here that from Paris 28,000 Jews were to be arrested and deported on 16/7 stop several thousands succeeded escape so that arrestations concerned about 14,000 stop equally several thousand Jews arrested in province especially Tours Poitiers stop at same time general terror started leading among others to plundering biggest Paris synagogue rue Victoire stop from non occupied zone Jews ten thousand foreign Jews will be delivered to Germany transports of first three thousand Jews taking place from six to ten August stop simultaneously large razzias Lyon Marseille Toulouse stop since 16/7 daily big deportations transports Dutch Jews starting from Holland stop Berlin Vienna announce equally increased deportations :stop middle July only 15,000 Jews remained Prague 33,000 whole protectorate stop 40.0000 [sic] Jews aged 65 to 85 already concentrated Theresienstadt stop from Slovakia 56,000 Jews deported already

The longer version, obviously composed hastily, is rendered here typos and all. Most of the details contained were accurate; to give but one example: The roundup of Paris Jews at Vel d'Hiv (*Opération vent printanier* —Operation Spring Breeze) had taken place two weeks before Riegner's meeting with the American diplomatic representatives. The deportation of Jews from Westerbork in Holland began in June 1942. The destination of the deportations was not clarified. In Holland, the official version was that those deported were to be used for work in Germany. But since those deported included small children and others clearly incapable of participating in war work, the official version often was met with disbelief even at this early stage.

Riegner had received the information that led to his cable from Isidor Koppelmann, the Basel businessman who had been the liaison with the German industrialist Eduard Schulte, whom he had met on several occasions earlier on. While some details were inaccurate, it was essentially (in Christopher Browning's words) an astonishingly accurate piece of wartime information. The basic difference between the Riegner cable and the various other reports was briefly this: The former maintained for the first time that there had been a decision at the highest level of the Third Reich to annihilate European Jewry. The others reported local cases of murder, deportation, and other forms of persecution.

Where did Schulte's information originate? In all probability the infor-
mant was production manager Otto Fitzner, his number two at Giesche,
the mining company of which he was the director. Fitzner was a veteran
Nazi and close to Karl Hanke, the supreme Nazi leader in Silesia (Fitzner's
role is now being investigated by scholars in Germany). The issue of the
killing of the Jews and Auschwitz came up at the very time of Himmler's
inspection tour in Auschwitz in July 1942. The Giesche office was very
close to Oświęcim-Birkenau; its very name has been preserved to this
day—Giszowiec, a suburb of Katowice. It was founded as a working-class
community. The history of this community, which was meant to be patterned after British garden cities, and the history of the Giesche Corporation has recently been studied in detail by well-known Polish journalist
Malgorzata Szejnert.[3] Szejnert mentions in some detail Schulte's initiative in summer 1942, basing her information not only on the Laqueur-
Breitman book, but also on documents in Warsaw archives. Her main
topic, however, is the Black Garden; and while she deals with the politics intruding on industrial activities, it could be that further searches in
Warsaw archives might lead to new information concerning Fitzner and
Schulte.

Schulte died in Zurich in 1966 and left no written records about his
activities. What we know about him is based on Breitman's research in
Washington archives and my interviews in Zurich and elsewhere with
some of those who had been in contact with the industrialist at the time.
Dora, Schulte's second wife, was unwilling to discuss the activities of
her husband, about which she apparently knew little. Schulte's older son
Rupprecht, a classmate and friend of mine, cooperated willingly; we met
repeatedly in San Diego, where the younger Schulte had settled, and in
London. The information that emerged was integrated into *Breaking the
Silence*. The following generation—one of Schulte's grandchildren became a professor at the University of Alaska, another an FBI agent, a third
went into farming in Britain—expressed much interest in the activities of
their grandfather, but they had no information that had not been revealed
hitherto.

If it had not been for the Fitzner-Schulte channel, the information
about the intention to exterminate European Jewry probably would have
become known outside Germany within a number of months, because,

as Peter Longrich and others have shown, the knowledge was widespread among the Nazi leadership and a secret so widely known was no longer a secret and could not be hidden.

What of those in the West who were in a position to know at least some of the truth and who had heard about the Riegner report? In the preparation of my work I interviewed a fair number of those who had been in intelligence during World War II or had access to information because of their position in government. I encountered a defensive attitude in many cases. George Kennan, who had been in Germany until early 1942, wanted to know exactly what was meant by the term "Holocaust." William Hayter, a British diplomat located in New York at the time (later ambassador in Moscow and still later warden of New College Oxford) suggested that I should ask Isaiah Berlin, who also had been on a mission in New York at the time. Berlin was not amused when I related this to him. His mission to New York had been on very different lines. I interviewed Walter Eitan (Ettinghausen) in Jerusalem, an Oxford don, later the first secretary general of the Israeli foreign ministry. He had worked in Bletchley during the war, the intelligence center in which the intercepted German communications were decoded—the British having broken most of the German codes. But Eitan refused to cooperate, stressing that he had been sworn to secrecy. I pointed out that several of his former bosses had published books about their work in the meantime—but to no avail.

The old school tie helped in a few instances: Gideon Rafael (Ruffer) had been a fellow kibbutz member; during the war he headed a small institute near Haifa, which debriefed arrivals from Nazi-occupied Europe. There were a few hundred such cases, Palestinian citizens who happened to be in Germany when the war broke out and were subsequently exchanged. But the information from these sources was, as a rule, of a local character. They could not know about decisions by the Nazi leadership. In later years the *mukhtar* of Kibbutz Hazorea became Israeli ambassador to the Court of St. James and the United Nations.

Arthur Schlesinger, who had been in the Office of Strategic Services (oss), was one of the few who expressed amazement in later years that he and his German Jewish colleagues in the oss had paid so little attention at the time to the fate of the Jews. So did Raymond Aron, who also was privy to that information except concerning France.

There was, I believe, no conspiracy of silence, but there was a great deal of ignorance concerning the character of Nazism and its intentions. Those looking for prophetic (and correct) estimates of the objectives of the Third Reich are better advised to consult the long valedictory cable (April 25, 1933) of Sir Horace Rumboldt, British ambassador in Berlin, than the estimates of Herbert Marcuse, Franz Neumann, Otto Kirchheimer, and other members of the Frankfurt School who had joined the oss.[4]

Franz Neumann wrote *Behemoth* at the time, the "definitive analysis of the Third Reich" in the words of C. Wright Mills, who reviewed it. It dealt with profit motives and the general economic structure of the system, the relations between industrial and banking capital, and other important issues. But it was hardly likely to shed light on the fate of the Jews or other victims of the regime, for there was no obvious connection between profit motives, the economic structure of the regime, industrial capital, and Auschwitz. According to Neumann, racism and antisemitism were substitutes for the class struggle. The Jews were extremely valuable as scapegoats for all the "evils" in Germany, and therefore, the Nazis would not embark on a policy of "total extermination of all the Jews."

How to explain that a paleoconservative such as Rumboldt, wholly unaffected by modern social theory let alone neomarxism, was a better guide to Nazi policy, not only with regard to the Jews? Was it mainly because this was an unprecedented phenomenon? Why was Nazi Germany and its intentions widely, and for so long, misunderstood? This is yet another issue that deserves more careful consideration than it has been given so far.

Richard Lichtheim represented the Jewish Agency in Switzerland during the war and closely collaborated with Riegner. He was a highly educated man, but deeply pessimistic with regard to Nazi designs in general and the fate of the Jews in Nazi-occupied Europe in particular.

This was very much in contrast to most of the Germany experts in the foreign ministries and the intelligence services in London and Washington. When the Riegner cable reached Washington and London, these experts rejected it: Undersecretary Sumner Welles, who tended to take it a little more seriously, was in a minority. In the view of the experts, it did not make sense. If Jews were deported to the East, surely it was the Nazi intention to make them work for the war effort rather than to kill them.

In some cases open antisemitism may have been involved. Breitman and Lichtman report that Morgenthau called Breckinridge Long (a Kentucky horse breeder and assistant secretary of state) an antisemite to his face. But ignorance was probably a more important factor than antagonism toward Jews.

Furthermore, intelligence had been tasked, and among their assignments the fate of the Jews figured low. The main task was to gather information that would lead to the defeat of the enemy. But with all of this, how can one defend the order by the State Department no longer to transmit cables from abroad by private individuals or nongovernmental organizations, an instruction that clearly was intended to suppress information such as that conveyed by the Riegner cable, which had been a distraction as far as the State Department was concerned.

The British, it will be recalled, did not exercise such censorship; the Riegner cable was handed to Sidney Silverman, member of parliament, whereas Stephen Wise, who was the addressee in the United States, was never informed. It would be interesting to know exactly who gave the order to withhold information, both in the case of the Riegner cable and the general order a few months later not to transmit such information in the future.

Internal censorship in the case of some of the media has been explored. It would be unfair to single out the *New York Times* for almost suppressing the Riegner-Wise report (it carried a brief story in the middle of the paper); other American media did the same, except for the *New York Herald Tribune*, which carried it on page one. True, the owners of the *New York Times* were more than a little self-conscious about the Jewish ownership of the paper and acted accordingly.

Naturally, the Jewish media in Palestine acted differently. But it would be a gross exaggeration to claim that the public and the leadership of the Yishuv understood the full meaning and implications of the information from Europe and did all that could be done to save human lives.

In the transmittal of information on the Shoah, Carl Jacob Burckhardt is another personality whose important role has not been sufficiently investigated. Burckhardt hailed from an old Basel patrician family; he was a history professor who wrote a three-volume Richelieu biography. He was a friend of Hofmannsthal, Rilke, and other leading contemporary writers.[5]

Burckhardt also served as a diplomat during the Second World War and thereafter. He met Hitler as well as many other leading Nazis, including those such as Himmler and Heydrich directly connected with the murder of European Jewry. On two occasions, Burckhardt played an important role in the present context. He was well-informed about events inside Nazi-occupied Europe, but refrained from informing his fellow members on the executive board of the International Committee of the Red Cross (ICRC). And he was strictly opposed to taking any action designed to save Jewish lives. The official excuse was that those killed by the Nazis were civilians, whereas the Red Cross was dealing only with military personnel. From a purely legalistic point of view, the argument was correct; to its honor it should be added that the Red Cross has not always acted in accordance with purely legal considerations. Burckhardt shared the social antisemitism of the upper-class Swiss; it did not prevent him from being on friendly terms with individuals of Jewish origin such as Hugo von Hofmannsthal or Leopold Baron von Adrian (an Austrian diplomat and grandson of Meyerbeer)—provided they were leading cultural or aristocratic figures. All in all, his anti-Jewish feelings were less pronounced than those of his famous ancestor (the Renaissance historian) who had written that he refused to go to the theater because of the presence of the Jewish riffraff. In a letter to his friend, Adrian Burckhardt wrote that he had known some "pure Jews with the highest moral standards." But he still found it difficult to generate any sympathy, let alone help for the German Jews (this was written in 1933) because the German Jews had produced a degenerate Berlin culture that was deeply amoral. There had been, perhaps, some minor transgressions committed by the Nazis. But if German Jews needed help, the rich Jews could take care of them—those who arrived in their fine cars and stayed in the best hotels in Switzerland. "Fine cars," "best hotels"—this was hardly an accurate description of the living conditions of those escaping Nazism that year.

Burckhardt, who was vice chairman of the ICRC during the war (he became chairman in 1944), did virtually nothing to help Jews in Europe. He was well informed through various contacts, but did not bring up the issue in the meetings of the ICRC executive board, even though some of its members would have supported such a move. This is on the authority of Prof. Favez, the official historian of the ICRC in wartime.[6]

There was one interesting exception when Riegner and Lichtheim handed over their cable to Leland Harrison, the chief US envoy in the Swiss capital. He insisted on confirmation by a trustworthy outside source, and since Burckhardt's German contacts were well known, he was particularly eager to hear from him. The Jewish representatives contacted Burckhardt through an academic colleague, Prof. Paul Guggenheim, and surprisingly, while asking for the strictest secrecy, Burckhardt confirmed Schulte's message; he had heard from a contact in the German Foreign Ministry and one in the War Ministry (and also from a German diplomat in Switzerland) that there had been a decision on the highest level "to make Nazi-occupied Europe 'judenrein.'" This was the official term used at the time for the deportation and the murder of the Jews.

A few weeks later Burckhardt was contacted by Paul Squire, the American consul in Geneva, who sought his confirmation once again. But on this occasion he was noncommittal; perhaps he was afraid that he had gone too far at the earlier meeting. In any case, it was remarkable that on at least one occasion he was willing to share information with foreigners that he had refused to give to his own colleagues. One can only speculate what his motives were.

Switzerland was in a precarious situation in 1942; the Swiss could not know that Hitler had no intention of invading their country. Clearly there was no wish to provoke Nazi Germany. But it also is obvious that for whatever reason Burckhardt, the Red Cross, and some Swiss leaders went well beyond what prudence and caution demanded. Burckhardt tried to intervene in some individual cases; he tried to help Jochen Klepper, a non-Jewish German actor married to a Jewish woman. But he gave up when he was told that this was futile. Klepper, his wife, and his daughter committed suicide in 1942.

After the war the ICRC came under much criticism for its unwillingness to make public, however cautiously, the known facts about the murder of the Jews. In response, Swiss professor Jean Claude Favez was appointed by the Red Cross to write a report. Favez criticized me for inaccuracies in *The Terrible Secret*, which was adding insult to injury because the Red Cross archives had refused me access. But the Favez version, in turn, came under attack from the ICRC executive board—he had not sufficiently considered the pressures and threats from Nazi Germany that

Switzerland faced during the war. Eventually, more than fifty years after the event, the ICRC through the head of its archive (not the president of the International Red Cross) admitted that the activities of the organization (or rather their absence) had been less than honorable.

Burckhardt's attitude did not change in later years. He made the Jews largely responsible for the outbreak of the war; had the Allies only listened to him, the war could have been prevented. Committing atrocities was not a German monopoly; they had been committed by both sides. He was not aware of any misjudgment or misconduct on his part and therefore was very annoyed when contemporaries blamed him for his excessive Germanophilia and lack of true neutrality. For instance, he attacked Elizabeth Wiskemann, who had worked for the British embassy in Bern during the war, calling her a "German-Jewish refugee" (and therefore hopelessly prejudiced) even though she was neither German nor Jewish nor a refugee.

Favez called Burckhardt a complex, even contradictory, personality: arrogant, charming, easygoing, a worrier, at bottom a pessimist. Like many other Swiss politicians, he thought that Germany would win the war. But the full facts about Burckhardt's activities became known only after his death in 1974. Paul Stauffer (1930–2008), a Swiss historian and diplomat (he served as ambassador in Pakistan, Iran, and Poland), devoted two massive studies to Burckhardt's activities before and during the war.[7] These were careful books, in no way tending toward extreme statements nor was their intention to denounce or denigrate Burckhardt. Yet now it appeared beyond any shadow of a doubt that Burckhardt largely had invented events and even fabricated documents concerning his activities, particularly during the war. He had taken liberties (to put it mildly) that he would not have committed in his biography of Richelieu. Not to mince words, it was a matter of forgery. And since Burckhardt also helped others to reinvent their record during the Nazi era, it led to bitter exchanges and scandals over a number of years. Perhaps the most widespread scandal concerned Marion Gräfin Dönhoff (1909–2002), a German aristocrat from East Prussia, who became the influential publisher and editor of the weekly *Die Zeit*. She was by no means an ardent Nazi, and no one made her responsible for the fact that her brother, a lawyer, had worked for the Gestapo in Paris. But Countess Dönhoff, who moved in the same upper-class circles as Burckhardt, was more ambitious and concocted a resistance record for herself.[8] According to her version, she had been involved with the conspiracy of July 20, 1944; and only owing to her native modesty, her name had not appeared in the documents that fell into the hands of the Gestapo—and this had saved her life. She claimed to have been close to the Stauffenberg brothers, who tried to assassinate Hitler in 1944, but no evidence of this ever was found.

When Stauffer, in his books on Burckhardt, revealed the truth, Countess Dönhoff called him a forger. But he was anything but a forger, and perhaps it is even an exaggeration to call Dönhoff a forger; for all one knows, she did not deliberately falsify her resistance record. It was quite fashionable in certain circles in Germany after the war to acquire an anti-Nazi record, and it is possible that she persuaded herself that she had been a genuine, if not card-carrying, member of the Resistance.

The Burckhardt/Dönhoff rewriting of their record during the Second World War proved to be quite successful. While the Nobel Peace Prize escaped Burckhardt, he received countless other honors. He won several Goethe Prizes, the prestigious German literary award; was presented with the French *Légion d'honneur*; was made an honorary citizen of Lübeck; and received several honorary doctorates. He even was made an honorary fellow of the Weizmann Institute in Rehovot, Israel. Countess Dönhoff, with her doubtful resistance record, received honorary doctorates from Columbia University as well as from Georgetown University and Smith College. The German government issued a special ten-euro coin in her honor, as well as a postage stamp. She also received the Peace Prize of the German Book Trade (with the German president providing the *laudatio*) as well as other honorary citizenships and other awards. The entries "Burckhardt" and "Dönhoff" in Wikipedia are models of hagiography.

Further investigation is needed concerning the various channels by which the information of the Shoah was sent to London and Washington —those that were successful and those that were not.

The Dönhoff case leads to another interesting connection. She had acquired a doctorate before 1933, supervised by Edgar Salin, a professor in Basel who also supervised the dissertation of the famous sociologist Talcott Parsons. Salin hailed from a well-known Frankfurt Jewish family (his mother was née Schiff). He was as much interested in ancient Greek civilization as in political economy and belonged to the highly esoteric Stefan George circle. Like other Jewish members of this circle (such as Ernst Morwitz, Ernst Kantorowicz, and Friedrich Gundolf), Salin had no interest in things Jewish, did not identify with his coreligionists, and did not belong to any Jewish organizations. But it was claimed after the war that Salin had been informed early on by a friend, a fellow economist named Arthur Sommer, about the decision to exterminate European Jewry. (Sommer served in the war ministry with the rank of colonel.) This version is based on claims by Haim Pazner, a student of Salin, who was loosely connected with the work of Jewish organizations in Switzerland. Haim Pazner, who later migrated to Israel, was the father of the Israeli ambassador to France and Italy. Breitman and I mistakenly had stated in *Breaking the Silence* that Salin and Sommer knew each other from the Stefan George circle. In fact, they had cooperated in the Friedrich List society. George Friedrich List was a major German economist unjustly forgotten for a long time; both Salin and Sommer had belonged to the group before 1933. According to these reports, the information about the mass murder was to be conveyed to Washington by way of the Bank for International Settlements, founded in 1930 in Basel and headed by Thomas McKitterick, an American. It is possible that such an initiative existed, but no trace of this back channel has ever been found.

After the war, Salin, assisted by Countess Dönhoff, took a leading part in a campaign to gather support for von Weizsaecker, the man accused in the Nuremberg foreign ministry trial (the Wilhelmstrasse trial). As Kempner, the deputy head of the American team in Nuremberg, put it in a letter to Salin: he had provided comfort to former Nazis and neo-Nazis by his defense of a person who not only had known about the Holocaust, but as his signature on documents showed, had collaborated in the deportations to Auschwitz.[9] In 1961 Salin became an honorary fellow of the Weizmann Institute.

More attention should be given to the efforts to suppress this information and the lack of action; who precisely were those mainly responsible? But the question also arises—what if the information had been widely broadcast, what if those responsible for the mass murder (many of whose names were known) had been threatened with punishment as war criminals —what impact would it have had on the Nazi campaign of annihilation?

The timetable of the destruction of European Jewry has to be read side by side with the chronology of the war. During the summer of 1942, when most of the Polish Jews as well as those from the Baltic countries, Germany, and so on, were killed, the war went well from a German point of view. The great change in the fortunes of the Third Reich came only with Stalingrad and the invasion of North Africa and Italy during the winter of 1942–43. It is very unlikely that Hitler would have desisted from his campaign or that his orders would have been disobeyed by his underlings even if maximum publicity had been given to the mass murder. According to estimates, 80–85 percent of the Jews under Nazi rule already had been killed by February/March 1943. True, the Nazi leadership tried to prevent information on the murder from reaching the outside world. Thus, the police general Daluege gave an order that the figures on those killed should no longer be transmitted even in coded form. The Nazi leadership would have been annoyed if the facts of the mass murder had been widely broadcast; they would have taken stricter measures to maintain secrecy, but Auschwitz and the other death factories would not have been dismantled.

After the spring of 1943, the situation changed; Mussolini was overthrown, the German Army in the east was retreating all along the front. The Battle of Kursk was lost, the Ukraine reoccupied by the Red Army; the Soviets had reached the old border with Poland and Romania. The Germans were in constant retreat in Italy; massive air attacks on German cities undermined German morale, and the belief in a final victory was rapidly vanishing. There was growing pessimism even among the military leadership.

At this very time hundreds of thousands of Eastern European Jews were still alive—the Łódź ghetto was still in existence, as was the Kovno ghetto, and half a million Hungarian Jews were still alive. If a somewhat higher priority had been given to saving these remnants, tens, perhaps hundreds of thousands of Jews could have been saved. A week before the events described here, there had been a military coup against Hitler that almost succeeded. The destruction of the Jews had been very high on the Nazi list of priorities, but from 1943 on this changed; they were fighting for their survival.

Elsewhere I have described two extreme cases of missed opportunities in which human lives could have been saved with a minimum of effort.

This refers to the deportation of Jewish children from Paris on July 31, 1944, less than a month prior to the liberation of the city. More bizarre (and tragic) was the deportation of the Jews from the islands of Rhodes and Kos. Kos is very close to neutral Turkey, 2.5 miles to be precise, half of it in Turkish territorial waters. It could be reached by a good swimmer and, of course, by a rowboat, however small. Rhodes is not much farther away from the Turkish mainland. And yet a few German soldiers rounded up some 1800 Jews (of which 160 returned) and began their deportation to Auschwitz.

For the Germans this was a logistical nightmare—Rome was in Allied hands. The Balkans were in flames, and the Allies had absolute sea and air superiority in the Mediterranean. It would have taken about one hour to reach the Turkish mainland by rowboat; it took the convoy twenty-four days to reach the death camp. No massive Allied operation would have been needed to intercept the convoy, no substantial diversion of resources from the war effort of the Allies. Two motorboats and a handful of soldiers with a few Bren guns probably could have done it. The German captain might have been persuaded to surrender without a fight. But no such attempt was made. It seems unlikely that the German garrison would have made a tremendous effort to chase the Jews of Rhodes and Kos had they disappeared overnight. The Germans knew that the days of their stay were numbered—in weeks, perhaps days. The convoy had to pass through Yugoslavia; it might not have been difficult to persuade the local partisans to disable the railway lines. Perhaps it was not all the fault of the politicians and diplomats who sabotaged rescue attempts; there was no Jewish organization or leadership.

Was it just a matter of a few isolated cases? In 1944 hundreds of thousands of Hungarian Jews were still alive. It has been suggested that the idea that Auschwitz could have been bombed is tantamount to Monday morning quarterbacking, that the difficulties were great, that many of the inmates of the camps would have been killed. However, the transports to Auschwitz would have stopped for a certain period of time, perhaps a long period if the attacks had been repeated.[10]

Opinions are divided, and the technical issues involved are outside the framework of this essay. The same is true with regard to the bombing of railway lines leading to the camps, and above all, tunnels and bridges.

They too could have been repaired, but it would have slowed down the transports—by days and weeks, perhaps even months, and this at a time when the Allies from East and West were advancing rapidly.

If no such attacks were made, it was not because it was deemed technically impossible, but because the fate of those concerned had very low priority. The issue of bombing quite apart, yet another aspect of this situation was seldom discussed. The victims of the deportations were not quite aware of their fate, which was certain death in the gas chambers. Had they known this, it is almost certain that at least some would have tried to hide or escape.

At the same time, many of those engaged in conducting the transports would almost certainly have done their work with less eagerness had they been warned that they might be held personally responsible—and this at a time when the outcome of the war was no longer in doubt.

Could such warnings have been issued to victims and perpetrators alike? Allied radio stations had a near monopoly in many of the regions affected. In the case of Rhodes, there were powerful Allied radio stations in Egypt, Cyprus, Palestine, and Southern Italy. Broadcasting was not the only means of issuing warnings. But no such warnings were given. No one can say how many lives would have been saved; all we know is that the attempt was not made.

NOTES

1. *The Terrible Secret* was first published by Little, Brown in Boston in 1980. Paperback editions were issued by Penguin (1982) and Holt Rinehart (1998). A new edition with a new preface written by me appeared in 2012 under the imprint of Transaction. A new edition of the French translation with a new preface was issued by Gallimard, Paris, in 2011. *Breaking the Silence* originally was published by Simon and Schuster, New York, in 1986. It was reissued by Touchstone Books and Brandeis University Press, 1994.

2. Gerhart Riegner, *Niemals Verzweifeln: Sechzig Jahre für das jüdische Volk und die Menschenrechte* (Gerlingen, DE: Bleicher Verlag, 2001).

3. Malgorzata Szejnert, *Czarny Ogrod* (Black Garden) (Cracow: Znak, 2007).

4. On the Rumboldt cable, see most recently Abraham Ascher, *Was Hitler a Riddle?* (Stanford: Stanford University Press, 2012).

5. A brief biographical sketch appears in Walter Laqueur, *Harvest of a Decade* (New Brunswick, NJ: Transaction, 2012).

6. Jean Claude Favez, *Une mission impossible? Le CICR, les déportations et les camps de concentration nazis* (Lausanne: Editions Payot, 1988).

7. *Sechs furchtbare Jahre: Auf den Spuren Carl Burckhardts durch den zweiten Weltkrieg* (1998) and *Zwischen Hofmannsthal und Hitler*. Carl Burckhardt, *Facetten einer aussergewöhnlichen Existenz* (Zurich: Verlag Neue Zürcher Zeitung, 1991).

8. Klaus Harpprecht, *Die Gräfin: Marion Dönhoff: Eine Biographie* (Reinbek near Hamburg: Rowohlt Verlag, 2008).

9. Quoted in Ulrich Rauff, *Kreis ohne Meister* (Munich: C. H. Beck, 2010), 402.

10. Michael Neufeld and Michael Berenbaum, eds., *The Bombing of Auschwitz: Should the Allies Have Attempted It?* (New York: St. Martin's Press, 2000).

27

A Testimony to the World of German Orthodox Judaism

A Translation of the Rabbi Jehiel Jacob Weinberg's Introduction to His Seridei Eish

DAVID ELLENSON

Jehuda Reinharz has served as both a teacher and a role model for me throughout his career. As president of Brandeis University, Jehuda provided an example of how a great scholar and intellectual could simultaneously be an innovative and fabulously successful university president. I marveled at the way in which he combined these roles throughout his sixteen-year presidential tenure at Brandeis, and I tried to emulate his example during my own service as president of Hebrew Union College–Jewish Institute of Religion (HUC-JIR). I am proud that we developed a friendship during this period, and I am grateful that our relationship has continued and grown even closer these past few years as he has served as president of the Mandel Foundation.

However, it was as a graduate student at HUC-JIR and Columbia University during the 1970s, working on the German Jewish religious and cultural experience, that I first encountered Jehuda—through the written page. His book *Fatherland or Promised Land: The Dilemma of the German Jew, 1893–1914*,[1] taught me so very much. His description of the struggles and dilemmas of the Jews in Germany resonated with me: how they sought to navigate the tensions and dilemmas brought on by a German world, where "vituperative German political and radical anti-Semitism" collided with the "idealistic principle of emancipation." His observation in the preface to that book, where Jehuda stated, "Each German Jew sought to resolve his own inner conflict between the equally compelling ideological concepts of *Deutschtum* and *Judentum*" and that each one accordingly "was forced to examine his loyalties to German nationality on the one hand and to Jewishness on the other,"[2] presented a hermeneutic of tension from which I learned.

Indeed, the insight Jehuda offered regarding this conflict intrigued me and two years later helped lead me to focus my own PhD dissertation on Rabbi Esriel Hildesheimer (1820–1899) of Berlin. To be sure, *Fatherland or Promised Land* dealt with a "Burgfrieden" between two major German Jewish organizations of that period—the anti-Zionist Centralverein deutscher Staatsbürger jüdischen Glaubens (Central Association of German Citizens of Jewish Faith) and the pro-Zionist Zionistische Vereinigung für Deutschland (Zionist Federation of Germany).

While the ideological conflict between them did not focus on religion, the arguments their struggles evoked were hauntingly mirrored in the themes of Rabbi Hildesheimer and his life. As I learned more about the life of Rabbi Hildesheimer, it was clear to me that he, no less than the leaders Jehuda studied, navigated between the two poles of *Deutschtum* and *Judentum* as he established his modern Orthodox Berlin Rabbinerseminar in 1874. As a nineteenth-century German Jew immersed in both German and traditional Jewish religious culture, Hildesheimer sought a synthesis between these elements through the education of modern German Orthodox rabbis who would strive to embrace both of these poles. When, in the final sentence of *Fatherland or Promised Land*, Jehuda observed, "The question of the primacy of *Deutschtum* or *Judentum* dominated the intellectual milieu of the German Jews until the Nazis decided the issue in 1933,"[3] the frank accuracy of this unadorned sentence evoked powerful emotions in me as I considered the grievous fate the Rabbinerseminar and the German Jewish community ultimately suffered at the hands of the Nazis.

In light of the themes explored in *Fatherland or Promised Land* and the influence this book had on my own scholarship, I am grateful to express my gratitude and offer tribute to Jehuda by translating the introduction that Rabbi Jehiel Jacob Weinberg (1884–1966), the last director of the Rabbinerseminar prior to its closure by the Nazis in 1939, wrote to his prominent collection of rabbinic writings, *Seridei Eish*, after World War II. Written in Hebrew, the introduction offers a moving description of the torments Rabbi Weinberg and his students suffered at the hands of the Nazis, the "miraculous" preservation of his writings by his student Rabbi Eliezer Berkovits, a capsule history of the leadership of the Rabbinerseminar during its sixty-five years of existence, and a moving monument to the religious ideology and legacy of *Deutschtum* and *Judentum* that defined the aspirations and character of its faculty and graduates. As such, the Weinberg introduction provides a powerful testimony to the cultural-religious spirit that informed the religious leadership of modern German Orthodox Judaism and serves as a reminder of its enduring legacy despite its physical destruction by the Nazis.

Rabbi Weinberg himself was forged in the crucible of two disparate worlds—the rabbinical yeshivas of Lithuania and the modern German university. Born in Poland, during his childhood and adolescent years he studied in the talmudic academies of Mir and Slobodka. A student of Rabbi Nathan Zvi Finkel (1847–1927), he served as a rabbi in the Lithuanian town of Pil'vishki from 1907 to 1914. Weinberg journeyed to Berlin in 1914 for medical treatment. While the outbreak of World War I initially prevented his return to Russia, Weinberg apparently found the intellectual and cultural life of the German capital very much to his liking, and he elected to stay there even when the opportunity to return to Pil'vishki presented itself in 1916. As his biographer Marc Shapiro has phrased it, "Despite all his nostalgia for the east, he was now under the spell of the west."[4]

Indeed, several years later, Weinberg chose to expose himself to the rigors of formal academic study. In 1920, after a semester at the University of Berlin, he moved to Giessen, where he enrolled at the university under the tutelage of "the great Semitic and masoretic scholar Paul Kahle (1875–1965), a pious Christian and a vigilant defender of Jewish literature against anti-Semitic attacks."[5] There, Weinberg also studied Old Testament with Professor Hans Schmidt and philosophy under Ernst von Astor. During the summer of 1923, he completed examinations for the doctorate and wrote a dissertation on the Peshitta, the Syriac translation of the Bible. In addition, Weinberg taught courses at Giessen on a variety of subjects

—Bible, Mishnah, and Talmud—for both beginning and advanced university students.

After the untimely death of Rabbi Abraham Elijah Kaplan (1890–1924), an Eastern European Jew who was the successor to Rabbi David Zvi Hoffmann (1844–1921) as rector and as the senior lecturer in Talmud and codes at the Rabbinerseminar, Weinberg was the ideal choice to succeed Kaplan. Schooled in both *Wissenschaft* and Talmud, Weinberg was appointed to the staff of the Orthodox seminary in October 1924, and became the supreme rabbinical authority for all the Orthodox rabbis who were educated there as well as head of the Rabbinerseminar. He remained head of the seminary until the Nazis closed it on November 9, 1938— Kristallnacht. It was never to be reopened.

Rabbi Weinberg had been unprepared for this development and was in Warsaw when this tragedy occurred. In ill health, he was trapped in the Warsaw Ghetto, where he witnessed untold horrors until his transfer in 1941 to a German detention camp for Soviet prisoners in Wuelzburg. Though incarcerated and subjected to harsh treatment and conditions, Weinberg, as a Soviet citizen, avoided being sent as a Jew to a concentration camp. Precisely why this occurred is not completely clear; however, it was surely a stroke of good fortune. While he remained imprisoned in Wuelzburg until April 1945, Rabbi Weinberg did manage to survive.

In shock after the Shoah, Weinberg stayed for nine months in a hospital in Nuremburg. Then in 1946 Weinberg's student Rabbi Saul Weingrot of Montreux, Switzerland, brought him to that peaceful Swiss city. There he continued his work as a talmudic scholar and *decisor* of Jewish law, and upon his death in 1966, Weinberg was universally recognized as one of the foremost students of Jewish law in history.

His responsa collection, *Seridei Eish* (Remnants of the Fire), was first published in four volumes in Jerusalem (1961, 1962, and 1966) by Mossad Harav Kook and was republished in 1999. Classics in the world of halakhic literature, the writings in *Seridei Eish* unquestionably display the immense talmudic erudition and wisdom of Rabbi Weinberg. Just as surely, they offer substantial and moving eyewitness testimony to the sorrow and hope that Rabbi Weinberg witnessed throughout his lifetime—especially during the dark years of the Holocaust. I am privileged to offer the introduction of this Central European Orthodox leader to his work in English translation in honor of my teacher and friend Jehuda Reinharz.

A Translation of the Introduction to
the *Seridei Eish: At the Gateway to the Book*

At the outset of my book my hands are extended in prayer toward heaven in a prayer of thanksgiving to God, May His eternal Name be blessed. In His mercy and His kindness, He brought me forth in His time from Germany, the land of blood, and from the city of Berlin, which was transformed during the days of the evil and cruel régime into the capital of wickedness worldwide. Even though I was in captivity in the Warsaw Ghetto and in a prison camp in Germany, He rescued me in His great mercy from the hands of the murderers, the killers of our people and the destroyers of virtually every Jewish institution in the Exile—May His great Name be blessed.

I am the man who watched in anguish the rod of His wrath. I passed through every level of the Nazi Hell,[6] may their names be blotted out, and countless afflictions and punishments befell me. I suffered and was subjected to untold torments. With my own eyes I witnessed deeds of murder, violence, and destruction committed by the infinitely cursed evil ones, deeds of cruelty, capricious and deceitful acts inside the walls of the ghetto, and abominable and perverted deeds in concentration camps and prisons, the likes of which had never been witnessed from the day that God created heaven and earth. In the ghetto the German beast revealed himself in all his perversion and malice. We saw the vileness of men without human conscience whose cruelty exceeded by untold measures that of a wild beast. How God afflicted me—to see the untold affliction of hundreds of thousands of my brothers in the household of Israel before they were released from their suffering by being thrown into the fiery furnaces and gas chambers, or being killed by flames, by murder, by strangulation! And it was not given me to die! Only a few were rescued from this Nazi Inferno through the miracle of miracles.

In the face of this horrible destruction, unparalleled in human history, in which virtually all the Jewish communities of Central, Northern, and Southern Europe were obliterated, destroyed, and wiped off the face of the earth; in consideration of the slaughter of six million Jewish souls; in view of the great, horrible, and menacing conflagration in which the lives of the great leaders of the nation, her scholars, her holy and righteous ones, her rabbis, and heads of *yeshivot* were destroyed by fire—in light of all this, trembling seizes and shame covers my face to come and tell of the miracles that were done for a small hyssop like me. I do not know to what to ascribe the miracle of my rescue, certainly not from additional merit, but from my lack of merit, I was not counted among the martyrs to His great and awesome Name.

Nevertheless, the rule of Jewish law is explicit and clear that an obligation of thanksgiving must be expressed—I am obligated to thank God who kept me in life, sustained me, and allowed me to see my book see the light of day.

I have entitled it, "*Seridei Eish*—Remnants of the Fire," for it is just as its name suggests—a small remnant from the inferno whereby God scorched the city of destruction and wickedness. And a great miracle occurred to this, my book. Six months before World War II, the evil Gestapo ordered me to leave Berlin. I was not given permission to take a book, or clothing, or any other item with me. I left the city only with the clothes on my back in the company of one of my students. All of my many writings—among them responsa, novellae on Torah, explanations of talmudic passages, and studies on a variety of Torah subjects—were lost.

Only one bundle of writings was rescued by my precious student, HaRav HaGaon, a giant in Torah and secular knowledge, Dr. Eliezer Berkovits, who was a rabbi in the greater Berlin community and later in several cities in England and in America, and who now serves as a rabbi and teacher at the Beit Midrash Gadol in Chicago (the Skokie yeshiva). He guarded these writings like they were the apple of his eye. And during the time that he waited in London and the city was bombed by the Nazis, may their names be blotted out, and he needed to take cover in a hiding place, he took these letters with him and would not leave them until the end of the war. When he then discovered where I lived, he returned them to me with joy. May God remember him for good!

The rescued letters were all mixed up and in complete disarray, and I labored and worked many hours to organize and arrange them and unite them into a book. These writings were placed in my book in two sections. They include responsa to questions and doubts that rabbis, householders (*balebatim*), and community leaders posed on matters of Jewish law and on issues of repair of ritual baths, the building of synagogues, the repair of cemeteries, and the like. In my book, scattered novellae and explanations on talmudic passages, commentaries on the Rambam and early rabbinic authorities that had already been published in different collections and journals were also brought together. Most of these words were recited orally in set lessons I delivered every day at the Rabbinerseminar in Berlin before attentive and discerning students.

Needless to say, the contents of my book represent only a small part of the many responsa I wrote during the time I served as a teacher of Talmud and Jewish law in our great *bet midrash*.

The Rabbinerseminar, first founded by Rabbeinu Hagadol, HaGaon Rabbi Esriel Hildesheimer, may the memory of the righteous serve as a blessing, succeeded in the education, growth, and formation of those preparing for the rabbinate, for halakhic decision making and leadership in Israel. It succeeded and grew to become the central institution of higher education for matters of Jewish law and matters of communal-public conduct and administration in Germany and Central Europe. From the day that Rabbi Hildesheimer, a native of Halberstadt in Germany, returned from his first rabbinical position in Eisenstadt, Hungary, to his homeland and to the city of Berlin its capital, a new period began for Jewish life in Germany, which had already been flooded by the stream of European assimilation. When he first came to Berlin as the founding rabbi of the Orthodox congregation Adass Jisroel,[7] his community, together with the magnificent community in Frankfurt,[8] stood together at the head of a resurrected Orthodox religious movement whose purpose was to restore the crown of Judaism and the beauty of a life guided by our holy tradition to their glory. Later, he established (1874) the Rabbinerseminar for Torah and the conferral of rabbinic ordination, and he remained at its head until his death [in 1899]. Rabbi Hildesheimer was a talmudic genius, a student of the 'Aruch la-Ner, Rabbi Jacob Ettlinger of Altona,[9] who also possessed an all-encompassing secular academic education. He felt that the surest guarantor for returning the prestige of Judaism to its ancient state lay in the precise study and learning of the sources of Judaism—Talmud, responsa, geonic, and rabbinic literature. The shining light of pristine Judaism would keep the external brilliance of the new European culture at bay. However, he demanded that his students not abandon engagement in the field of academic Jewish study that was built on the foundations of the *Messorah* (Jewish tradition). He claimed that it was not enough in our days that rabbis know those parts of the tradition dealing with *issur* (prohibition) and *heter* (permission) in areas of Jewish dietary law and family purity, albeit without a doubt they serve as the incontrovertible foundations of a Jewish life. Rather, rabbis were needed who could stand before the entire world and demonstrate the righteousness of Judaism and her eternal truths in a secular academic idiom. It was incumbent upon the rabbis, as the bearers of God's word, to provide the Jewish people and the world the insights of Judaism on every problem of ethics, of justice, and social repair that the new generation would attempt to solve and confront. They were obligated to teach that Judaism is not a collection of laws and religious customs alone, but an indispensable spiritual force in human life. It was also understood, they should not fail to provide a proper and appropriate response to any problem or attack lodged against Judaism from the perspective of contemporary secular knowledge and culture. Rabbi Hildesheimer placed special emphasis upon the import demanded of synagogues and on the propriety of public appearance in this modern setting. In a cultural context where scurrilous misinformation was rampant, sermon and speech could render a salutary impact. It is impossible for a rabbi in our days to evade and shrink into an isolated corner in his study. He needs to stand at the gate and discover a path to the hearts of the youths who grow up and are educated in secular schools in order to draw them near and cause them to enter the spiritual world of Torah Judaism. He needs to know what is happening around him in the world of science and literature, the spiritual streams that flow and are renewed from era to era. A rabbi lacking such basic education and knowledge of modern thought will not be able to uncover the path required to make contact with and provide entry to the inner world of youth and the souls of the current generation.

The truth of the matter is that despite its official name, Rabbi Hildesheimer did not want simply to create an institution for rabbis and religious clergy. Rather, he intended above all to create an institution for the growth of a religious intelligentsia. The failure of Judaism in his generation was caused primarily because there was a lack of such a religious intelligentsia. All the intellectual elite of that era were without religion, and they defamed the religiously pious and slandered them as opponents of enlightenment and condemned them as bereft of culture. The most prominent and learned rabbis of that time, who occupied their posts in large cities, isolated themselves within the four ells of Jewish law alone. While they truly did accomplish wonders and miracles in the field of Torah, they insulated themselves and lost connection with most of their fellow Jews. There were not among them persons like Rabbi Saadia Gaon, Ibn Ezra, Maimonides, Nachmanides, or Crescas, who knew how to penetrate the fortresses of secular knowledge and expose its barrenness in broad daylight.

This intelligentsia that was educated in the Rabbinerseminar of Rabbi Hildesheimer understood that it was necessary that rabbis go forth prepared for this mission—to illuminate Judaism and to preserve and safeguard our Torah, our faith, and the holy distinctiveness of our nation. At the Rabbinerseminar they were educated to do this in a systematic and profound manner.

During this period the Rabbinerseminar burst beyond its narrow confines, and its rabbis were appointed in virtually every major city and provincial town in Germany. These graduates maintained their loyalty and love for the school that forged their spiritual, Jewish, and ethical culture and commitments. Rabbi Hildesheimer was for the Judaism of the West what Rabbi Meir, the Light of the Exile, was for medieval Europe. No important matter or practical halakhic question was decided and no great action was undertaken without consulting the "Rabbi" (the Orthodox Jews of Germany identified Rabbi Esriel as "Rabbi" alone). He illuminated the West with his Torah, his righteousness, and his wisdom; and he was privileged to raise up many great disciples and outstanding sages, and they sat on the seats of judgment in major cities (among them were Rabbi Marcus Horovitz in Frankfurt on Main, Rabbi Dr. Lerner in Altona, Rabbi Nehemiah Nobel in Frankfurt, Dr. Eduard Baneth, Rabbi Dr. Jakob Freimann, Professor E. Mittwoch, Professor Dr. Freimann, etc.). A number of them earned high office as heads of institutions for higher Jewish learning (*Hochmat Yisrael*) and as professors in European universities. All of them sanctified and glorified the name of Heaven and the name of Israel on the highest spiritual levels and through the examples of their personal lives. In so doing, they sanctified and elevated the name of their great rabbi. When the old "Rabbi" died, may his memory be for a blessing, his great student and colleague, our Master, the outstanding and remarkable Gaon, Rabbi

David Tzvi Hoffmann, may the memory of the righteous be for a blessing, assumed the post as head of the Rabbinerseminar. There is no need to say a great deal about Rabbi Hoffmann. His book of responsa, *Melammed Le-ho'il*, is recognized throughout the rabbinic world as a legal work of the first order. And his academic works in every field of Torah and *Wissenschaft* are foundational works for academic investigation. Rabbi E. M. Lipschütz wrote an enthusiastic assessment full of admiration for Rabbi Hoffmann as an introduction to his Hebrew translation of Hoffmann's work, *Die wichtigsten Instanzen gegen die Graf-Wellhausensche Hypothese* [The Most Important Arguments Against the Graf-Wellhausen Hypothesis]. Anyone who had the privilege of knowing Rabbi Hoffmann knows that there is not the slightest hint of exaggeration or hyperbole in his words. I will only add, because I knew him, that there is no one left in Israel like him.

In his old age, when his powers began to wane, Rabbi Hoffmann requested that he receive new assistance in fulfillment of the great tasks of the Rabbinerseminar. The administrators of the Rabbinerseminar then appointed Rabbi Abraham Elijah Kaplan, a unique personage among the young rabbis of Lithuania, and he was selected to succeed Rabbi Hoffmann. To the sorrow and distress of his students and his many admirers, his days of service at the Rabbinerseminar were not long. After four years of fruitful and blessed service, Rabbi Kaplan died on the 16th of Iyyar 5684 (May 20, 1924). He was only thirty-four years old when he died.

When I was called to come and stand in the place of these giants as director of the Rabbinerseminar, to sit on the exalted seat of the Geonim and Lights of Israel, I realized how deficient my merit was — that I was not fit to express an opinion and to decide Jewish law for the many. Nevertheless, I was not able to avoid accepting this profound yoke on myself. This mission of responsibility was thrust upon me by the faculty of the Rabbinerseminar and the board of the Rabbinerseminar (*Curatorium*), which was composed of great rabbis and prominent men. I labored with all my might and engaged in extensive and comprehensive research to articulate Jewish law clearly. On difficult questions I sought the agreement of the great scholars of the generation, who responded and almost always agreed with me.

This book is divided into two parts. It is the fruit of my exhaustive labor in Torah and practical decision making. The first section includes responsa on the stunning of animals prior to their slaughter and, in regard to poultry, immediately severing their neck. These are responses to questions that in their time roiled the entire Jewish world. The lives of thousands of souls relied on them in cursed Germany. At the beginning of their Nazi regime, these filthy enemies of the Jews, may their names and memory be blotted out, outlawed kosher and accepted ways of Jewish ritual slaughter. In their wickedness, they plotted to prevent Jews from eating meat. Thank God these responsa stopped being of any practical value whatsoever to them.[10] For already during the days of this evil decree our brothers in the Household of Israel in all the lands of their dispersion resolved not to accept even the slightest change in the manner that ritual slaughter (*shechitah*) had been conducted in Israel throughout the generations. The people of Israel are holy and God forbid that they alter even a hairsbreadth of the holy tradition for whose sake they were slaughtered and for which our father and our father's fathers sacrificed their lives during all the years of our Exile. However, because of their historical importance, I did not refrain from publishing them. They serve as a reminder of the bitter despair that assaulted countless Jews in the household of Israel and the great care and piety with which the rabbis of Israel made every effort to find whatever rescue and salvation they could for the lives of myriads of Jews. They also provide a reminder of the heroic bravery with which the *g'dolei yisrael* (great leaders of the Jewish people) stood their ground and would not bow to the evil decrees of the antisemites who, on account of their burning hatred, spewed out evil libels against the people of God and His holy Torah.

In the second section of the book I placed responsa I wrote to questioners in Germany and other lands, most of which were composed when I served as *rav u'moreh* at the Rabbinerseminar in Berlin. A smaller number [of the legal writings contained in this volume] were written after my liberation, with God's help, from my imprisonment and my captivity in the detention camp and after I found rest in the comfortable city of Montreux. I included everything that came into my possession, what was found in the package of letters mentioned above that was rescued by my student, and what I wrote based on abbreviated notes that my former students provided me at my request. To my sorrow, not all responded to my request, but I still hope that they will do this in the future; and may it be God's will to keep me in life and sustain me and I will attempt, *b'li neder* (without making a vow), to produce a third volume of responsa and halakhic novellae.

My book also includes letters that are neither brilliant nor even innovative or insightful. However, they point to a memory of days past, days of comfort and growth, days of distress and depression. During them, I was privileged to occupy the position that great leaders of Israel had held, and perhaps these writings can be held up as a type of mirror through which to view the religious-communal life of German Jewish communities, which to our great sadness were destroyed and passed from the earth. From them, the children of coming generations will see the spiritual situation of Jewish leaders and rabbis in Germany who, in their integrity and the holy awe of God that rang in their souls, courageously attempted with all their strength to preserve the Jewish heritage so that it would not, God forbid, be snuffed out in the distress of the time.

An additional notion strikes my heart—the students of the Rabbinerseminar were scattered to the four winds and to every corner of the world. Perhaps my book will serve as a type of connection and as a bond of memory to those early days when they were tied and connected so strongly to the Rabbinerseminar and the spiritual inspiration that was so precious in their eyes.

The Rabbinerseminar was destroyed on account of our many sins. But its holy memory has not ceased from the heart of its students. Many of them have achieved greatness and serve brilliantly in major cities in all parts of the world. They sanctify and glorify the name of Israel and the reputation of our Torah and our faith. Others made *aliyah* to our Holy Land and work as rabbis, as teachers, and stand at the head of religious education. Others stand at the head of government, and all of them strengthen the Torah of Israel in the Land of Israel. May His great Name be blessed!

May my book stand as a humble monument to the small sanctuary that for eighty years disseminated Torah and light to the scattered of Israel.

NOTES

1. Jehuda Reinharz, *Fatherland or Promised Land: The Dilemma of the German Jew, 1893–1914* (Ann Arbor: University of Michigan Press, 1975).
2. Ibid., vii.

3. Ibid., 234.

4. Biographical details about the life of Rabbi Weinberg are taken from Marc B. Shapiro, in his masterful and definitive biography, *Between the Yeshiva World and Modern Orthodoxy: The Life and Works of Rabbi Jehiel Jacob Weinberg, 1884–1966* (London: Littmann Library of Jewish Civilization, 1999), 65.

5. Ibid., p. 84.

6. The Hebrew word that I have translated alternatively in this paragraph as "Hell" or "Inferno" is *tophet*. Rendering it into a single English word that captures all its resonances is virtually impossible. To be precise, in the Bible, *Tophet* is the name given to the location in Jerusalem in the Valley of Hinnom, where pagan worshippers burned children alive before their gods Moloch and Baal. While *Tophet* appears in several places in the Bible, its usage in Jeremiah 7:31–32 will give the reader a full sense of its meaning. There it states (JPS Translation), "And they have built the shrines of Topheth in the Valley of Ben-hinnom, to burn their sons and their daughters in fire . . . Assuredly, a time is coming . . . when men shall no longer speak of Topheth or the Valley of Ben-hinnom, but of the Valley of Slaughter and they shall bury in Topheth until no room is left." In using this term in the context of the Holocaust to describe the Nazi Inferno, where millions of children and adults were burned to death in gas ovens, Rabbi Weinberg employed the most horrific and evil image available to him to describe the depravity and cruelty of the Nazis and the world they created. "Hell" or "Inferno" does not fully convey all of the meaning of the term.

7. Rabbi Hildesheimer returned to Berlin in 1869.

8. The *Israelitische Religionsgesellschaft*—the congregation of Rabbi Samson Raphael Hirsch.

9. Rabbi Ettlinger also ordained Samson Raphael Hirsch.

10. Marc B. Shapiro, *Between the Yeshiva World and Modern Orthodoxy* (Oxford: Littman, 2002), 117–129, provides the background required for an understanding of the points Weinberg is making in this sentence and in this entire paragraph. Shapiro reports that on April 21, 1933, shortly after assuming office as chancellor of Germany, Hitler issued a decree forbidding Jewish ritual slaughter throughout Germany unless the animal—in opposition to preferred Jewish practice—had been stunned prior to being slaughtered. He also decreed that poultry—again in opposition to dominant Jewish practice—"had to be killed by the head being instantly severed from the body" (p. 117). Weinberg issued lenient responsa on both of these matters of *shehitah*, responsa that would have permitted meat and poultry slaughtered in accord with the demands Hitler sought to impose so that observant German Jews could be provided with kosher meat and poultry. While there were certainly halakhic grounds for the Weinberg positions, a number of prominent rabbis opposed such leniencies for a variety of political and other considerations that Shapiro explains. As a result, none of the views Weinberg expressed were acted on, and the traditional Jews of Germany did not have easy access to kosher meat. This is the context in which Rabbi Weinberg offers his account in this introduction.

28

Authors/Survivors/Witnesses — Aharon Appelfeld, Abba Kovner, Primo Levi, and Elie Wiesel between Literature and Testimony

DINA PORAT

"Surviving is a privilege that is accompanied with a duty . . . we, the survivors, have an obligation not only towards the dead: we have to open the eyes of the next generations as well, tell them about all our experiences, so that they serve as a lesson. Knowledge means self-defense . . . survivors must assume the role of a seismograph. They should be, more than others, aware of a looming danger . . . and pinpoint it."[1]

Simon Wiesenthal here presents a widely accepted view, according to which every survivor must bear testimony, and must relate it as fully and as accurately as possible, so that it serves a purpose: to commemorate the dead and be a basis for study and lessons for the future.

This essay examines how four survivors who became famous authors — Aharon Appelfeld, Abba Kovner, Primo Levi, and Elie Wiesel — challenge this common view, each in his own way, and comment on literary endeavor as testimony. They are troubled by similar questions and use similar terms, as if debating the following issues among themselves: What is the purpose of testifying? Is a full and accurate testimony indeed a possibility? Did they survive in order to testify, and hence — is this their life mission? Is there a possible connection between a failure to bear witness and taking one's life?

"I am interested in the past, not for the past's sake, but rather as material for the building of future Jewish life and collective consciousness," declared the partisan and poet Abba Kovner in a ceremony held at the residence of the president of the State of Israel marking the twentieth anniversary of *Yalkut Moreshet*—a journal dedicated to the collection of testimonies and primary materials and the publication of documentation and research.[2] He said so publicly, perhaps in order to be quoted, and to highlight the contradiction between the declared mission of *Moreshet* —"heritage" in Hebrew, a significant title in this context (and it was he who came up with this title when *Moreshet* was founded in the early 1960s)—and his wish that the past be described in a manner that present and future generations may be able to live with.

This was Kovner's view already at the time he was an inmate of the Vilna ghetto. When approached by Yitzhak Rudashevski, a boy writing a diary, who hesitated whether to include a description of a crying baby's fate in a *melina* (a hiding place) crowded with dozens of terrified Jews, Kovner answered emphatically not to include it, because no one would be able to understand this intense moment in the *melina*, and the judgment and verdict of later generations might be unfair.[3] For the same reasons, Kovner tried to convince poet Avraham Sutzkever to soften his wording in poems he wrote during the days of the ghetto and with the partisans in the forests, and also suggested burning files collected after the war about Jews who collaborated with the Germans—and again, he was the one who initiated the collection of these files to begin with.[4] His reasoning was that if the inability to understand—not to identify with or feel empathy for—the experiences of the survivors is a given, then why invest the enormous effort needed to make other people understand. Moreover, if in any case the full truth cannot—or even should not—be openly exposed, because it goes against the needs of future Jewish society, should it not then be openly admitted and accepted that a survivor cannot and perhaps should not be requested to say, write, or even remember everything. And one may add that if the exact description of the past is an impossible goal to reach, then how can it serve as a source of lessons for the future, and how can a testimony be a fulfillment of the debt to the dead and to the reality in which the dead perished.

Wiesel is no less explicit than Kovner in pinpointing the direction he deliberately chose: "And I do love them, the Jews of my town, the Jews of the ghetto," writes Wiesel about his community. "That is why I glorify them and I make no secret of it. To me the Jews of Sighet are neither ugly nor repulsive. There was generosity and mutual aid; no quarrels or recrimination, no thefts or petty jealousy in the ghetto."[5] And the same goes for Auschwitz and the terrible reality that he endured for nine long months: "I prefer to emphasize the kindness and compassion of my brothers in misfortune. These qualities were found in the Kingdom of darkest night, as I can testify—indeed, as I must" (87). His goal is clear-cut: "I should act not as their detractor, but as a *melitz yosher*, their intercessor" (68). It is beyond a goal—it is a must that amounts to a duty.

Wiesel, born and raised in Orthodox surroundings, and still a believer and a practicing Jew in his own way, subscribes to an overarching view that originates in Jewish sources: The "enemy"' as he always biblically defines the Nazis, is the ultimate evil personified, and the Jews are the ultimate good and innocent incarnate. They cannot be blamed nor put to shame or even criticized, for they are the sons of light.

Kovner is similarly adamant: to him the Jews of Europe are "innocent of crime and unashamed."[6] "There are tools for self-defense," he said in an eye-opening testimony: "we defend our existence . . . our heritage . . . our best years. We repress painful events. Painful failures . . . we are first of all Jews. So, we are careful not to write or say what might be seen as a total Jewish failure, and most rightly so. Being a Jew, one loves his people. You cannot love and be objective."[7] Wiesel, as we recall, did not even try.

Primo Levi, also using the term "defense," agrees that for purposes of defense, or perhaps more for "self-defense," reality is sometimes distorted by witnesses, yet he strongly rejects the glorification of the dead. In his preface to *The Drowned and the Saved*, he points at what he calls "a stylization [for which] we are ourselves responsible, we survivors, or, more precisely those among us who have decided to live our condition as survivors in the simplest and least critical way," meaning less critical of the dead and the use of their memory. "Every victim is to be mourned, and every survivor is to be helped and pitied, but not all their acts should be set forth as examples."[8] Levi, an individualist, secular leftist Italian Jew, who first started identifying as a Jew in Auschwitz,[9] was not engaged in constructing the future-oriented Jewish or Zionist tropes pursued by Kovner and Wiesel. For him a testimony is "an act of war against Fascism"

(p. 18), namely, an act of a more universal nature. Having refused to glorify the Jews, he could have glorified the antifascists with whom he was imprisoned in the camps or with whom he fought in the mountains in Italy, but he refuses, in his skeptical way, to do either.

Can and should a survivor regard himself as destined to survive in order to bear witness? Should he hold this view all the more if his testimony has a future-oriented purpose? "Did I survive in order to combat forgetting?" asks Wiesel. "I must confess that at the time such questions did not occur to me. I did not feel invested with any mission" (80). It was only later that such a sense of mission evolved, until he knew it was his duty to testify, in order "to stop the dead from dying . . . to plead for the dead and defend their memory and honor . . . to justify my survival" (239, 380).

Levi, again, strongly disagrees. An Orthodox friend told him that he, Primo, survived not just by chance, or because of his good fortune, as Levi himself preferred to think, thereby pushing off the doubt that constantly tormented him that he might have survived at the expense of someone else, perhaps even a better, worthier person than he. The doubt continued to gnaw at him though he knew he had wronged no one. He was chosen to survive, said the friend, by providence, so that he could bear witness. "Such an opinion seemed monstrous to me," says Levi. "It pained me as when one touches an exposed nerve, and kindled the doubt I spoke of before: I might be alive in the place of another. . . . I felt innocent, yes, but enrolled among the saved, and therefore in permanent search of justification in my own eyes and those of others . . . the thought that this testifying of mine could by itself gain for me the privilege of surviving. . . . troubles me because I cannot see any proportion between the privilege and its outcome" (82–83). He apparently did not think so highly about himself as a witness. Levi, doubting the connection between survival and testimony, certainly testimony as a tool for future goals, magnifies the role of luck, pure hazard, and chance in the survival of the inmates, because those who perished, he insists, were the good and virtuous ones and still were not worthy enough to be chosen for life. In other words, no process of choice was involved, and a person was just a feather in the wind. Why do we testify, asks Levi, and answers candidly: either to fulfill a moral obligation owed to the dead, or "to free ourselves of their memory" (84).

Can and should a survivor indeed struggle to convey a complete testi-

mony, a full account of past events, as Wiesenthal claims? "Not to forget
a detail, not to erase anything, this is the survivor's obsession," says Wiesel
(380), an obsession and a commitment. But is it, he asks, possible to fulfill
it? Testifying in the Eichmann trial in Jerusalem in 1961, Abba Kovner
refused to take the oath in its usual wording—the truth, all the truth, and
nothing but the truth. He could not tell "all the truth" and could not swear
to abide by that oath because the true full picture of the Holocaust is not
transmittable. Later that morning, when asked to describe in court a painful and complicated incident that took place in the Vilna ghetto, he tried
to avoid answering because: "The greatest difficulty is for me to speak
out and not for someone else to hear."[10] Kovner could not cast doubt on
the court's capacity to understand the witnesses, otherwise there was no
point in hearing the testimonies of 106 witnesses during the trial, so he
put the blame on himself—it was his difficulty to speak out. But doesn't
the transmission of a testimony indeed depend on the understanding and
compassion of the listener? Therefore, though the bench must hear and
understand, the judges would not understand fully. Kovner, who gave
twenty-five testimonies, none similar to the other, said point blank: "Every
morning I get up and have another memory and another view of what
happened." He published "An Epilogue to the Historians," concluding that
whoever reads the testimonies and the documentation, and assumes he
caught the truth in the palm of his hand, simply does not understand what
the Holocaust was.[11]

As if they had convened in order to decide on the best way to articulate
the dilemma, our protagonists offer very similar wording. Remembering
everything might bring one to the brink of madness, said Kovner time and
again to his public, yet to forget—is impossible. "To be silent is impossible," said Wiesel, "to speak—forbidden" (89). "Remembering all means
casting a merciless light on faces and events," he goes on. "How can you
hope to transmit truths that you yourself have said lie beyond human understanding and always will." The words are, anyhow and in any case, too
poor to convey the events, because there is an abyss between the word
and the content that same word conveyed in the past, prior to the event it
now tries to describe (139), and no new words have been invented.

"It is impossible not to tell, but living in this while telling—is impossible as well," said Appelfeld.[12] He is the most adamant among the four

regarding the impossibility of giving a full account and the lack of tools to do so: "All we could say," he says, referring to the group of youngsters with whom he reached the Land of Israel, "was but stammering . . . words from the old vocabulary. And, in any event, a forgery. Only later did we understand that without new words and a new tone, nothing would ever be said" (15). They had no language fit for the experiences they underwent. Appelfeld points, as if with a sharp needle, at the survivors. "The Horror and the Commitment" is the title of his chapter on testimonies, using the term "commitment" much as Wiesel did. It is a chapter in his collection of essays titled *Essays in the First Person Singular*, yet he speaks almost exclusively in the first person plural and explains why: "To come forth and speak about yourself is not only a disproportion, but a sin . . . the survivors' 'I,' apparently seemed unfit for testimony; not merely unfit —but grossly pretentious. Who would dare to be a spokesperson for so much death" (95).

The survivors, Appelfeld writes, usually revealed not more than the external shell, the cover, of the horrors. The inside, which was ugly and deformed, was not told (21). Please recall: "To me," said Wiesel, "the Jews of my community were not ugly nor repulsive," or was he saying that perhaps they were to some extent, but he was determined not to mention that. Appelfeld says that they were what ugly circumstances and conditions during the Holocaust made them become, and this is why the survivors hid the real testimony, keeping it away from even themselves. They know that the facts, even reliable credible ones—a place, a date, a name—are but a camouflage of the essence, which, says Appelfeld, we fear so much. Levi agrees, speaking in a broader sense about the many survivors of traumatic experiences, who, subconsciously, tend to filter their memory, avoiding the parts that include the personal humiliation or the personal involvement in occurrences, dwelling, when they meet, on "moments of respite, on grotesque, strange or relaxed intermezzos, and skimming over the most painful episodes, which are not called up willingly from the reservoir of memory" (24, 32).

Appelfeld masterfully describes a perpetual circle in which the survivors are caught: they want, sorely want, to forget (49), because they feel guilty (43), and so they try to keep silent as the best solution (36). Statistically speaking, Appelfeld is right: out of the 360,000 survivors who came to Israel and stayed, only about 40,000 gave testimony—that is, no more than 11 percent—and about 9,000 memoirs have been published, sometimes by the same survivors who testified.[13] The choice the vast majority of the survivors made is clear indeed: to keep silent, even up to the recent decades when society has matured and is open to listen to them with empathy. But as Appelfeld goes on to articulate, they also wish, sorely wish, to testify quickly and unburden their hearts. And then they discover they could not possibly go on testifying, because it made them live constantly in the midst of horror, and because those who heard them could not stand it either: "Writing or Life" (*L'Ecriture ou la vie*) is the title of Jorge Semprún's memoirs on his experiences in Buchenwald, first published in 1994, fifty years after liberation.[14] What is the essence of testimony, asks Appelfeld, and answers: it is a secret agreement between the survivors and their listeners—an agreement of silence and misunderstanding. The survivors actually live in a perpetual circle, drawn to their testimony and repelled by it, escaping and returning, never free (49). Thus, the commitment has not been, and will not be, fulfilled, because of the fear of the abyss, of the inability to deliver a full testimony, because of the inner pain that cannot be exposed to the eye and ear of a stranger (26).

Appelfeld is quite clear about the value of testimonies. So many have been recorded, but they should be read very cautiously—they are but a weak frame (26–27). So many have been recorded, but there is still more hidden than known, kept under the veil of silence. Appelfeld assumes that the reader of testimonies will immediately notice that they are an attempt to impose chronological order on that time; they are neither introspection nor the equivalent of introspection—they are, rather, a cautious wrapping made of superficial facts designed to prevent the revelation of what lies within. And the listeners, or readers, adopt these chronologies, these generalizations, as an irrefutable testimony. Only here and there a few sparkling words escape the seven seals, as evidence of the experiences the heart does not even reveal to the mouth, says Appelfeld, using an ancient Hebrew expression (95–96).

And since the testimony was not integrated into the flow of life, and found no soil to live on, it gradually was pushed into the archive, the monument, the sterile space of scientific research. The issue of meaning became just a historical question—in other words, it ceased being a personal one. Seemingly, this is as it should have been, says Appelfeld sarcastically: the survivors testify; the files are on the shelves, numbered and catalogued; the archive functions; the researcher has his documentation. And there is satisfaction too, because we are alive after all, and the destruction was followed by revival, so there is a clear lesson also. But anyone can feel that these are all crusts, plaster put on the horror (20–21). "What we had to do, we have not done," we the survivors (113), not because the commitment was forgotten or put aside with an easy heart. It just could not be fulfilled.

Levi adds one more dimension to the issue of presenting a full picture, and actually joins Appelfeld: "I must repeat: we, the survivors, are not the true witnesses. . . . We survivors are not only an exiguous but also an anomalous minority" (83). The vast majority of the camp prisoners, called by Levi "the complete witnesses," the ones whose deposition could have had a significance of general value, because they saw the gorgon and fathomed the depths—they are mostly gone. And the few who were left alive were in no position to evaluate the extent or the significance of what was happening around them in the camps, because they lived more and more from one minute to the next, concentrating on surviving (17). More numerous, in proportion, among the survivors are those who enjoyed some sort of privilege, which enabled their survival. It gave them a better point of observation from which to watch the camps, and at the same time it distorted and falsified what they saw. Most of those privileged left us, if at all, a conditioned testimony, conditioned by the compromises they bowed to. The result is that very few testimonies were left untainted by privilege and can reveal the true complexity. This analysis enhances the feeling that Levi did not think too highly of his own testimony, even after becoming a known and internationally read and admired author. Working as a chemist in the camp's lab, he was in fact one of the privileged ones.

In his analysis of testimonies, Saul Friedlander reaches the conclusion that "each individual testimony remains a story unresolved," that no mythical framework or redemptive stance is evident, neither in testimonies nor even in the best of literature and art.[15] Let us see whether this is indeed the case with the authors/survivors' testimonies and literary work discussed here. Perhaps in their case one should take into account not just the individual story, but rather the needs of the society they lived in:

a society that was as badly wronged and mutilated as could be and would like not only to hear the full account of how and why this happened, but also to believe in a myth that bridges between past and future.

Wiesel found his redemptive stance in the deliberate idealization of a lost world, and in the compassion for the moral and personal stature of the Jews who formed that world. In order to keep the dead from dying, he has become, in addition to his prolific writing and teaching, a moral voice, an international figure who reminds, warns, reproaches, demands, travels around. He started out doubting his mission and talent and only later developed into a torch bearer. Faith offers consolation, and "to write is an act of faith" because it maintains the generations-old tradition of "telling" — *vehigadta* (you should tell your sons) — as it always has; and if there is no proper language to describe a certain experience, one should invent it (307). Bearing witness is part of the telling, and therefore is an integral part of one's life, and makes him a part of the long national chain. "Precisely because death awaits us in the end, we must live fully [was he thinking about Levi, or about a long line of other poets and authors who took their lives during or following the Holocaust?]. Precisely because an event seems devoid of meaning, we must give it one. Precisely because the future eludes us, we must create it" (17).

Kovner found his redemptive stance in his literary output, in the enormous work he did in order to instill the Jewish culture and tradition he loved and cherished into the life of a left-wing socialist atheist kibbutz, in order to create a new reality — Judaism and Zionism combined. The permanent exhibition of the Diaspora Museum, displaying Jewish life and creativity in exile — at the time quite contrary to Zionism distancing itself from any traits of the exile — is his intellectual contribution to preventing the dead and their memory from fading away. At some moments of crisis during the Holocaust, and even shortly after, Kovner contemplated suicide. Such thoughts did not recur once he immersed himself in creativity and became a public figure whose voice often was heard throughout the country.

Most of the literary works of Kovner and Wiesel do not address the Holocaust directly, though publicly they are regarded as "Holocaust authors." Appelfeld devoted no less than forty books to describing life mainly before and after the Holocaust. Only recently, at an elderly age, did he turn to writing on that period itself, and he explained the reason: whoever tried to testify, made an effort to rescue his image of man and carried a secret mission to mankind (25). Tried, not necessarily succeeded. And Appelfeld himself? "Since I cannot find God within me or outside of me, and because I cannot bear this notion of the rule of chance and accept it with equanimity, I therefore see myself as responsible, and lovingly accept the attributes of the Creator of the universe. I will be compassionate, I will love. As long as there is a soul in me, I will feel compassion for human beings" (71). Appelfeld was not raised in a religious Jewish environment, yet his recent work glorifies the spiritual quest of Jews even in the darkest days, and the love and compassion among members of Jewish families and among friends and acquaintances. The Holocaust is not about horror; it is about love, he declared on his eightieth birthday. His most recent book is titled simply and significantly *My Father My Mother.*[16] Thus he actually joins Wiesel and Kovner, though taking another route in both his writing and way of life—the intimate, the personal, the familial, the private.

So, despite all the shortcomings of testimony and of themselves as witnesses, three of these writers did find consolation: consolation in building a future—a national, Jewish, Zionist, or a personal future. Levi apparently did not: the few testimonies that are valid and reliable are still an act of an anti-fascist struggle, for a world based on the political and universal values he and his comrades held. His writing is restrained, in a minor key, sober, eschewing rhetoric and phraseology and lessons for the future, and facing naked truth. He does not spare himself as an author and as a witness. Perhaps he lacked the warmth that a sense of belonging offers—the Jewish faith and uniqueness to Wiesel, Zionism and his kibbutz to Kovner, parental love and compassion for fellow survivors to Appelfeld. The antifascist quest for human rights is certainly a lofty goal, yet one needs a close human group to be part of. He must have been deeply disappointed in mankind, whom he saw morally deteriorating, and the memory of this deterioration did not leave him. According to a friend, Alvin Rosenfeld, who maintained a correspondence with Levi, he was deeply disappointed in what he regarded as his failure to reach out to the German public. He wished to have an impact, through his writing, on the process leading to awareness by the Germans of their past, which started after decades of postwar attempts to evade it. Proper German recognition of his suffering could serve as a drop of belated justice, but it did not come.[17] Appelfeld, Wiesel, and Kovner did not address the Germans at all; they spoke and wrote to Jewish audiences, because for them the most important soul-searching account is the inner Jewish one, as it is for the vast majority of survivors, who mention the Germans but briefly in their memoirs and testimonies because they do not belong to human society anymore.

Let us end with Kovner, who, broadening the concept of the survivor as the conveyor of testimony, describing him as a kind of Jewish historian, is convinced that every Jew is an actor on the stage of Jewish history, and a writer and researcher, charged with a national mission: "To keep silent and let the horror fade away with the yesterday, let legend come out of the fog, and let illusion turn into consolation."[18] This mission is quite the opposite of the one suggested by Wiesenthal with which we started. Indeed, our protagonists all agree—and did not change their mind over time and in spite of the processes that took place around them—that a full and accurate testimony, either literary or prosaic, is not a possibility, and yet they all agree that testifying is an urge and a must. Thus the question at the heart of our discussion is how each of the four found his own way to testify and to write, between the yes and the no; how he channeled—or not—his testimony in order to find consolation in a goal he undertook to fulfill, for himself, his surrounding, his nation, and mankind in general, so as to find a reason to go on living.

NOTES

1. Simon Wiesenthal, *Justice—Not Revenge* (Hebrew) (Tel-Aviv: Sifriat Ma'ariv, 1991), 367, 369.

2. See his speech in D.2.598, the Givat Haviva Archive.

3. Abba Kovner, *Scrolls of Testimony* (Philadelphia: Jewish Publication Society of America, 2001), 100–101

4. A conversation with Sutzkever on May 3, 1994, and with Josef (Yulek) Harmatz, who first collected the material in the files and then destroyed them, on June 3, 2000.

5. Elie Wiesel, *All Rivers Go to the Sea* (New York: Knopf, 1996), 66–67. Further page references to Wiesel in parentheses refer to this book.

6. Kovner, *Scrolls of Testimony*, xv.

7. His testimony to Shlomo Kless, on December 17, 1982, Institute for Contemporary Judaism, 36 (170).

8. Primo Levi, *The Drowned and the Saved* (New York: Summit Books, 1986), 20. Further page references to Levi in parentheses refer to this book.

9. Ferdinando Camon, *Conversations avec Primo Levi* (Paris: Gallimar, 1991).

10. *The Eichmann Trial, Testimonies*, vol. 2 (Hebrew) (Jerusalem: Publications Service, Ministry of Information, 1974), 349.

11. His testimony to Kless (see note 7). See Abba Kovner, "Epilogue," in *On the Narrow Bridge: Essays* (Hebrew) (Tel Aviv: Sifriat Poalim, 1980), 223–24.

12. Aharon Appelfeld, *Essays in the First Person Singular*, (in Hebrew) (Jerusalem: Hasifria Hazionit [Zionist Library], 1979), 19. Further page references to Appelfeld in parentheses refer to this book.

13. Data is from the Yad Vashem website.

14. Jorge Semprún, *L'Ecriture ou la vie* (Paris: Gallimard, 1994).

15. Saul Friedlander, *Memory, History, and the Extermination of the Jews of Europe* (Bloomington: Indiana University Press, 1993), 121–22.

16. Aharon Appelfeld, *Avi Imi* (My Father and My Mother) (Tel Aviv: Kineret-Zmora-Bitan, 2013).

17. Alvin H. Rosenfeld, "Primo Levi—The Survivor as Victim," in *The End of the Holocaust* (Bloomington: Indiana University Press, 2011), 185–212.

18. Ruzka Korczak and Yehuda Tubin, eds., *Abba Kovner—Seventy Years* (Tel Aviv: Moreshet and Sifriat Poalim, 1988), 60.

PART V

In the Academy

29

On a Desperate Postdoc and the Emergence of Modern German Antisemitism

DANIEL R. SCHWARTZ

The impact of individuals—as opposed to larger historical processes—on history can be analyzed in various ways. One way is by applying two parameters, intentionality and directness, that create a matrix. Thus, in some cases an individual's impact is intended and direct: for example, a rebel or conqueror or reformer sets out to accomplish something, and does so. In other cases an individual's action might be unintended but its impact nevertheless is direct. Thus, for example, in 1862 the hapless Confederate officer who lost some cigars along with a copy of Robert E. Lee's Special Order 191 for invading the North certainly did not mean to do so. Nonetheless, once Union soldiers chanced upon the order in a Maryland cloverfield and passed it up the line (without the cigars), the result was no less direct and no less critical than it would have been had a Union spy ferreted out the same document.[1] And then, to complete the matrix, there are the cases in which an individual's impact was indirect—cases in which the action was intended but touched off a causal chain that led indirectly to an uncontemplated result, or cases in which the action was unintended and the result was similarly indirect and uncontemplated. The present study, offered in honor of a respected colleague and biographer and appearing in a volume that addresses the individual's impact on Jewish history, addresses a case of the third type: an individual's action that was fully deliberate but began an indirect chain of causation that led to a result that was completely uncontemplated by the agent, but of quite massive and catastrophic significance for Jewish history.

In a recent study I pointed to a previously unnoticed element in the background of the episode known as the Berlin Antisemitism Debate (*Berliner Antisemitismusstreit*) of 1879–1881.[2] That debate generally is recognized as a major turning point in the history of modern German antisemitism, because it raised antisemitism from a gutter phenomenon to one that was respectable: for more than a year, antisemitic sentiments and arguments were voiced, debated, and defended by professors, politicians, and others in first-class newspapers and other respectable forums.[3] The debate began in November 1879 with the publication of an attack on the Jews of Germany in general, and on the Jewish historian Heinrich Graetz in particular, by Professor Heinrich von Treitschke of the University of Berlin,[4] and its proximate roots usually are traced back to earlier trends of the 1870s. Namely, scholars trace its genesis to the burgeoning of nationalist feeling in the wake of the foundation of the empire in 1871, and especially to the growth of anti-Jewish sentiment in the wake of the stock market crash of 1873, which many blamed on Jewish entrepreneurs.[5]

Without detracting from the importance of those general factors, in my study I showed that an earlier and totally unrelated episode, viz., a protracted and acerbic controversy between two Berlin medievalists in the 1860s, which focused on the editing and historical study of medieval Latin texts, made a significant and necessary contribution to the genesis of the debate. Namely, I showed that one of the results of the medievalists' feud was that a young medievalist, Max Lehmann (1845–1929), was forced to leave the field, and his move into his new field, modern German history, soon brought him to establish a relationship with von Treitschke. That relationship would have serious direct and beneficial implications for Lehmann's own career, but that is not our concern here. What is important for us is that, while an impoverished postdoc, Lehmann had supplemented his income by writing scores of book reviews, and among them one happened to be on the eleventh volume of Graetz's *Geschichte der Juden* (1870). That meant that when, in 1879, in the course of preparing the second volume of his *Deutsche Geschichte im neunzehnten Jahrhundert*,[6] von Treitschke wanted to read the Graetz volume (which deals with the century from the mid-eighteenth to the mid-nineteenth century),

Lehmann had a copy available to lend him, along with his own review of it. Since, as von Treitschke himself wrote, when he read the volume in the summer of 1879 it infuriated and disgusted him;[7] and since that reaction explains his attack on the Jews in general and Graetz in particular a few months later;[8] and since the contents and formulations of his attack on Graetz correspond entirely with those of Lehmann's critique of the volume published more than eight years earlier (see appendix I), it follows that without the medievalists' feud the *Antisemitismusstreit* might not have happened.

In the present study, I will now add, on the basis of newly discovered material, that Lehmann's relationship with von Treitschke, which constituted the link between the medievalists' feud and the *Antisemitismusstreit*, did not come to be merely by chance. Rather, the relationship was deliberately and calculatingly sought out by Lehmann, although his motivation had nothing to do with the result that interests us. This will fill out the picture presented in my first study and also contribute a case study concerning the general issue addressed by the present volume.

The two main antagonists in the medievalists' feud were Dr. Georg Heinrich Pertz (1795–1876), who directed the Monumenta Germaniae Historica publication project in Berlin, and Prof. Philipp Jaffé (1819–1870) of the University of Berlin. Jaffé had been one of the star workers in Pertz's project until 1863, when he quit in a huff[9] and set up his own publication project with an equally ponderous name (Bibliotheca Rerum Germanicarum). Jaffé was a Jew, until his baptism in 1868, but that appears to have had only a marginal role in his feud with Pertz and its aftermath—beginning with Jaffé's suicide in April 1870.

Rather, what linked the feud to the *Antisemitismusstreit*, which broke out nearly a decade after Jaffé's death, was the career of Jaffé's student Max Lehmann, who was not Jewish.[10] After completing his 1867 doctorate on a Cologne chronicle of the twelfth-thirteenth centuries under Jaffé's supervision, Lehmann stayed on to work on the Bibliotheca, proofreading and indexing and also loyally taking his *Doktorvater*'s part in his feud with Pertz. Thus, already in his dissertation and in some later publications as well, Lehmann published some scornful and nasty comments about the work of both Pertz and his son, whom Pertz had been grooming to succeed him.[11] Accordingly, when Jaffé committed suicide in April 1870, apparently because of the strain of the feud, Lehmann was left an orphan from a professional point of view. That was because Jaffé's Bibliotheca and Pertz's Monumenta were the only two projects in town (and practically, in the world) in Lehmann's field, which was the editing and historical study of medieval Latin texts from Germany, but the Bibliotheca folded on Jaffé's death and the Monumenta was not an option, given all that Lehmann had written about Pertz. Lehmann, left out in the cold, changed his profession, turning from medieval history and Latin texts to a hobby from his youth in which he also had dabbled as a scholar: modern German history, especially military history. He would remain in that field throughout the rest of his career, which was to culminate in a Göttingen professorship.[12]

Lehmann's move from medieval German history and Latin philology into modern German history was to blossom, within a few years, into a close relationship with a new patron: Heinrich von Treitschke. Their friendship was mutually beneficial, with Lehmann functioning as something of a research assistant for von Treitschke, supplying him with materials, especially in the field of military history,[13] and von Treitschke recommending Lehmann to various colleagues, which eventually paid off in getting Lehmann started on his own career.[14]

For the *Antisemitismusstreit*, however, the import of Lehmann's move was very specific. Beginning in the late 1860s, Lehmann supplemented his income by writing numerous book reviews,[15] and among the works he happened to receive for review in the summer or autumn of 1870 was the eleventh volume of Graetz's *Geschichte der Juden* (1870). The January 14, 1871, issue of the *Literarisches Centralblatt für Deutschland* (henceforth *LCD*) includes Lehmann's angry review of the volume, in which he takes umbrage (in the midst of the Franco-Prussian War!) at Graetz's enthusiasm for the French and criticism of the Germans, complains that the Jews of Germany demanded all the rights of German citizenship without consenting to become Germans in any essential way, and protests against Graetz's claim that Jews had "educated" the Germans and that is what fostered the highest achievements of German culture. Lehmann also had specific complaints about some of Graetz's claims concerning the Jews' participation in the Prussian army. Given that von Treitschke not only read Lehmann's copy of the Graetz volume, but also that his rage and disgust led him to write "Unsere Aussichten" and that his complaints about

Graetz in that essay echo Lehmann's review quite closely (see appendix I), the question arises: Would the *Antisemitismusstreit* have occurred had Lehmann not been in touch with von Treitschke? That is, of course, an instance of the question addressed by the present volume, about the relative importance of individuals as opposed to larger historical trends—an instance that, given the post-1879 trajectory and results of modern German antisemitism, has quite a lot riding on it.

When I wrote my original article, I did not know, or even ask, whether Lehmann himself turned to von Treitschke, actively seeking him out, or rather just happened to meet him. That question did not matter much in that context, and I was content to point to (a) Lehmann's statement, in his autobiographical memoir, that he came to von Treitschke's notice because of an article he had written in the *Historische Zeitschrift* of 1869,[16] and (b) flattering statements by Lehmann about von Treitschke in various publications between 1869 and 1873.[17] The latter showed that Lehmann had a high opinion of von Treitschke, but did not necessarily mean that he actively was seeking to establish a relationship with him. Indeed, in 1869 he was still working with Jaffé and writing on the tenth century[18] and had no need to cultivate a new patron, especially an historian who worked on a much later period of history. But from the point of view of the present volume, the question—whether Lehmann actively sought out von Treitschke's patronage and found his way to him, or rather circumstances just happened to sweep him into von Treitschke's circle—is of cardinal importance.

As it happens, since my original article was finalized, my dossier on Jaffé and Lehmann has been enriched by various documents that turned up here and there, and among them two are quite relevant. The first, found in a Leipzig archive and transcribed in appendix II, is a very revealing letter by Lehmann, and it identifies him as the author of a flattering but anonymous review of a volume of von Treitschke's collected studies; that review is, accordingly, the second new document in the Lehmann file. The review is interesting enough, but in the present context the letter is even more important, for it shows that, within four months of Jaffé's death, Lehmann was self-consciously and actively seeking to cultivate von Treitschke. In the letter, which Lehmann sent to the editor of the *LCD* shortly after the appearance of (what his letter now identifies as) his review of von Treitschke's studies,[19] Lehmann voiced his chagrin that his initials ("Chiffre"), M. L., had been omitted from the review as published; he asked the editor to clarify retrospectively, in the next issue of the journal, the fact that he was the author of the review. As Lehmann explains, that would be "a very great favor" for him, for "the matter is of extraordinarily great importance for me, [since] I would like to circulate the contents of my review all around."

   This pathetic request shows that Lehmann, who must have been desperate after Jaffé's death,[20] consciously was cultivating von Treitschke and pinning his hopes on him.[21] Indeed, his review (as we now know it was) of von Treitschke's collected studies is extremely flattering to von Treitschke: it begins with a long opening paragraph that showers all sorts of praise *ad personam* on von Treitschke, portraying him as the paragon of all virtues, and it ends with the statement that "centuries from now, he will still be counted among the first of his people."[22] We may, therefore, conclude not only what I concluded in my first study, namely, that the particular way the Berlin *Antisemitismusstreit* began, as a result of von Treitschke's furious and disgusted reaction to reading the eleventh volume of Graetz's *Geschichte*, happened because of von Treitschke's relationship with Lehmann, but also that the establishment of that relationship was a project pursued quite calculatingly by Lehmann.

   If we now turn to the basic question addressed by the present volume, and ask whether we should understand the *Antisemitismusstreit* as a result of general trends or, rather, as the result of an individual's (Lehmann's) initiative, it seems to me that the latter alternative is clearly to be preferred. To see this, we must realize that (a) the *Antisemitismusstreit* was very much a debate among academicians, especially historians, but (b) there seems to have been virtually nothing, in academe in general or among historians in particular, that may be viewed, even in retrospect, as having laid the groundwork for it in that context.

   (ad a) That the *Antisemitismusstreit* was a dispute among academicians and historians is clear: it began, as noted, as the direct result of one modern historian's (von Treitschke's) reaction to a work about modern history by another historian (Graetz); the latter is the only specific object of the former's anger in his opening salvo of the *Antisemitismusstreit*; historians were prominent among those who took part in the debate; von

Treitschke's main opponent was another prominent Berlin historian, Theodor Mommsen; and the debates between von Treitschke and Graetz, and between von Treitschke and Mommsen, are frequently academic debates about the proper interpretation of historical texts and data. Thus, for example, there is frequent discussion of the question whether von Treitschke was justified in assuming that in Tacitus's days Christians were considered a type of Jew and that, therefore, Tacitus's statement that the Christians were accused of *odium generis humani* ("hatred of the human race"—*Annals* 15.44) shows that the Jews were too.[23] Similarly, the exchanges between von Treitschke, Mommsen, and others devoted considerable attention to debating what precisely Mommsen meant in a passage in his *Römische Geschichte* in which he says that the Jews, "in the ancient world as well" (!), were "an effective ferment that fostered cosmopolitanism and national decomposition."[24]

(*ad b*) Although, as noted above, antisemitism had been growing in Germany during the 1870s, scholarly literature on the antecedents of the *Antisemitismusstreit* does not point to anything that indicates that antisemitism's path to respectability should have been expected to be routed via professors in general or historians in particular. Histories of antisemitism in German universities begin only in the wake of the *Antisemitismusstreit*,[25] and it is very difficult to find any reason to expect that its spokesman would be von Treitschke. True, scholars who have searched his pre-1879 writings for adumbrations of his attack on Jews in "Unsere Aussichten" have come up with enough to show that the attitude it bespeaks was not an unprecedented surprise; but they have found nothing that suggests that he would come to harp upon the theme or, much less, to be its flag bearer.[26] If, nevertheless, he did, it is likely that there was some special impetus, something extrasystemic; and since we can see that he used Lehmann's copy of Graetz and echoed his review of it, we should recognize that Lehmann's role was crucial.

True, even without his relationship with Lehmann, von Treitschke might have come to Graetz's volume some other way and might have reacted to it the same way. The way things happened, however, was via Lehmann. Without their relationship, who knows if von Treitschke ever would have thought of reading Graetz or have found a copy of his work —a copy that, moreover, he could take with him on a Swiss vacation and read at his leisure?[27] And who knows what his reaction would have been, had not Lehmann's review of the volume, and marginalia within it, directed him to those aspects of it that had angered Lehmann? Thus, it is the case that it was von Treitschke's relationship with Lehmann that made things happen the way they did, and we now see that the relationship was one that Lehmann deliberately sought out and cultivated, in the context of his reorienting of his career in the summer of 1870.

As noted above, the *Antisemitismusstreit* is considered a major watershed in the history of modern German antisemitism. It granted respectability to attitudes that would go on to beget unthinkably catastrophic results; suffice it to say that the slogan that von Treitschke's "Unsere Aussichten" popularized, "Die Juden sind unser Unglück," would come to grace the front page of every issue of *Der Stürmer*. Thus, the case we have studied presents a striking instance of how a single individual's decision to embark on a certain course of action, because of his own narrow personal circumstances in the wake of a feud about something as recondite as medieval Latin philology, can have far-reaching results, in the real world, quite unrelated to anything he himself contemplated.

NOTES

1. On this case see J. M. McPherson, "If the Lost Order Hadn't Been Lost," in *What If? Military Historians Imagine What Might Have Been*, ed. R. Cowley (London: Pan Books, 2001), 223–38.

2. D. R. Schwartz, "From Feuding Medievalists to the Berlin Antisemitismusstreit of 1879–1881," *Jahrbuch für Antisemitismusforschung* 21 (2012): 239–67.

3. For a monograph on the debate, see M. Stoetzler, *The State, the Nation, and the Jews: Liberalism and the Antisemitism Dispute in Bismarck's Germany* (Lincoln: University of Nebraska Press, 2008). For a collection of 121 documents, see K. Krieger ed., *Der "Berliner Antisemitismusstreit," 1879–1881: Eine Kontroverse um die Zugehörigkeit der deutschen Juden zur Nation—Kommentierte Quellenedition*, 2 vols. (Munich: Saur, 2003).

4. H. von Treitschke, "Unsere Aussichten," in Krieger, *Der "Berliner Antisemitismusstreit," 1879–1881*, 1:2:6–16. Appeared originally in *Preußische Jahrbücher* 44 (1879): 559–76; pp. 572–76 deal with Jews. For an English version of those final pages, see Stoetzler, *The State, the Nation, and the Jews*, 311–16.

5. See, especially, N. Kampe, "Von der 'Gründerkrise' zum 'Berliner Antisemitismusstreit': Die Entstehung des modernen Antisemitismus in Berlin, 1875–1881," in *Jüdische Geschichte in Berlin*, ed. R. Rürup (Berlin: Hentrich, 1995), 85–100; J. Katz,

"The Preparatory Stage of the Modern Antisemitic Movement (1873–1879)," *Antisemitism through the Ages*, ed. S. Almog (Oxford: Pergamon Press, 1988), 279–89; and Krieger, *"Berliner Antisemitismusstreit,"* 1:x–xi.

6. We know that his work on the first volume had ended already in February of 1879 and that by the summer of that year he was working on the next volume (which eventually appeared in 1882). See U. Wyrwa, "Genese und Entfaltung antisemitischer Motive in Heinrich von Treitschke's 'Deutscher Geschichte im 19. Jahrhundert,'" in *Antisemitische Geschichtsbilder* (Antisemitismus: Geschichte und Strukturen, 5; ed. W. Bergmann and U. Sieg; Essen: Klartext, 2009), 86–87.

7. See von Treitschke's letter in Krieger, *"Berliner Antisemitismusstreit,"* 1:4.

8. See Schwartz, "From Feuding Medievalists," 242.

9. For what occasioned this, and other details, see ibid., 252–53.

10. Although some have thought he was, because of an understandable mistake; see ibid., 249.

11. For details, see ibid., 262–63. Here is just one striking example of Lehmann's enthusiastic participation in the feud: Less than a month before Jaffé shot himself, Lehmann published a review of a work by Pertz, opening with the bald statement that "this volume too fails to belie the well-known shortcomings of Pertz's historical writing" (*Literarisches Centralblatt für Deutschland*, March 19, 1870, col. 332 [my translation]). It is difficult to know whether it is more amazing that a whippersnapper of twenty-five could write—and be allowed to publish—such abuse about a scholar born half a century before him, or that he could, a few months later, produce the kind of tasteless flattery quoted in appendix III. A study of the history of book reviewing and its norms seems to be a pressing desideratum.

12. On Lehmann's career, see especially his autobiographical memoir, "Max Lehmann," in *Die Geschichtswissenschaft der Gegenwart in Selbstdarstellungen*, vol. 1, ed. S. Steinberg (Leipzig: Meiner, 1925), 207–32. For his publications, see ibid., 226–31, and especially his posthumous *Bismarck: Eine Charakteristik*, ed. G. Lehmann (Berlin: Arnold, 1948). Further literature is cited in Schwartz, "From Feuding Medievalists," 244, n. 21.

13. Ibid., 246, n. 36.

14. Ibid., 244, n. 31; see also Lehmann, "Max Lehmann," 219, concerning his 1879 appointment as lecturer at the military academy in Berlin: "Ich verdankte diese wichtigste aller Vorbereitungen auf die Universität sicher der Fürsprache von Treitschke."

15. In the pages of the *Literarisches Centralblatt für Deutschland* alone, I found around sixty reviews by Lehmann ("M.L."—see my n. 21) from 1869 through 1873, almost all of them pertaining to modern German history, and most to military history.

16. See Lehmann, "Max Lehmann," 215, referring to his "Der Krieg in West-Deutschland und die vorangehenden Unterhandlungen des Jahres 1866, " *HZ* 22 (1869): 80–147.

17. See Schwartz, "From Feuding Medievalists," 246, n. 30.

18. M. Lehmann, "Das Aufgebot zur Heerfahrt Ottos II. nach Italian," *Forschungen zur deutschen Geschichte* 9 (1869): 435–44. In 1869 Lehmann also produced the twenty-page index to the fifth volume of Jaffé's Bibliotheca.

19. *LCD*, August 6, 1870, cols. 908–911, on von Treitschke, *Historische und politische Aufsätze*, n. F. II (Leipzig: Hirzel, 1870). See appendix III. The *LCD* is currently (April 2013) accessible via HOLLIS (Harvard OnLine Library Information System).

20. In this connection, note that a check of subsequent issues of *LCD* shows no notice clarifying that Lehmann was the author of the review. That probably shows that the editor, Friedrich Zarncke, thought that Lehmann was ascribing too much weight to the matter — which corresponds to my assessment of Lehmann's mood as desperate and his request as pathetic.

21. It also confirms, incidentally, that "M. L." was Max Lehmann — a point I established in the original study on the basis of various indirect arguments (Schwartz, "From Feuding Medievalists," 244–45).

22. ". . . den man noch nach Jahrhunderten unter die Ersten seines Volkes zählen wird" (col. 911). For my translation of the long opening paragraph, which portrays von Treitschke as excelling in everything in which a German gentleman should aspire to excel, see appendix III.

23. See Krieger, "*Berliner Antisemitismusstreit*," 15 (von Treitschke), 34, 97 (Graetz), 113, 119 (von Treitschke), 165, 183–184, 187 (Graetz), 263. For a summary, see Stoetzler, *The State, the Nation, and the Jews* 126–29.

24. T. Mommsen, *Römische Geschichte*, vol. 3, 2nd ed. (Berlin: Weidmann, 1857), 530 ("auch in der alten Welt war das Judenthum ein wirksames Ferment des Kosmopolitismus and der nationalen Decomposition"). For the debate, see Krieger, "*Berliner Antisemitismusstreit*," 19, 616–17 (von Treitschke), 702–703 (Mommsen), 723, 783; see also C. Hoffmann, *Juden und Judentum im Werk deutscher Althistoriker des 19. und 20. Jahrhunderts* (Studies in Judaism in Modern Times 9; Leiden: Brill, 1988): 87–103.

25. For the rise of academic antisemitism in the wake of the *Antisemitismusstreit*, see N. Kampe, "Jews and Antisemites at Universities in Imperial Germany (II): The Friedrich-Wilhelms-Universität of Berlin: A Case-Study on the Students' 'Jewish Question,'" *Year Book of the Leo Baeck Institute* 32 (1987): 43–101, and N. Kampe, *Studenten und "Judenfrage," im Deutschen Kaiserreich: Die Entstehung einer akademischen Trägerschicht des Antisemitismus* (Kritische Studien zur Geschichtswissenschaft 76; Göttingen: Vandenhoeck and Ruprecht, 1988).

26. Note, especially, Wyrwa, "Genese und Entfaltung," 86–87. Antisemitism appeared in von Treitschke's *Deutsche Geschichte* beginning with only the second volume, which appeared after the *Antisemitismusstreit*. For some precedents, see Schwartz, "From Feuding Medievalists," 264 n. 117.

27. See his letter cited in note 7.

APPENDIX I

Comparison of Heinrich von Treitschke and Max Lehmann
on H. Graetz, *Geschichte der Juden*, XI

von Treitschke, 1879	Lehmann, 1871
Man lese die Geschichte von Graetz: welche **fanatische** Wuth gegen den "Erbfeind," das **Christenthum**, welcher Todhaß grade wider die reinsten und mächtigsten Vertreter germanischen Wesens, von **Luther** bis herab auf **Goethe** und **Fichte**! Und welche hohle, beleidigende Seltbs**überschätzung**! Da wird unter beständigen hämischen Schimpfreden bewiesen, daß die Nation Kants eigentlich erst durch die Juden zur Humanität **erzogen**, daß die Sprache **Lessings** und **Goethes** erst durch **Börne** und **Heine** für Schönheit, Geist und Witz empfänglich geworden ist! Welcher englische Jude würde sich je unterstehen, in solcher Weise das Land, das ihn schützt und schirmt, zu verleumden? Und diese verstockte Verachtung gegen die deutschen Gojim ist keineswegs blos die Gesinnung eines vereinzelten **Fanatikers** . . .	[opening:] Daß der Verf[asser] als eifriger, um nicht zu sagen **fanatischer** Jude aller Orten einen erbitterten **Haß** gegen das **Christenthum** zur Schau trägt, ist begreiflich . . . . In einer maßlosen Weise werden ihre bedeutenden Männer **überschätzt**, namentlich Mendelssohn, **Börne**, **Heine**. Ersterer wird geradezu mit **Lessing** auf eine Linie gestellt . . . "den geläuterten Geschmack, steht wörtlich auf S. 369, das lebhafte, rücksichtslose Wahrheitsgefühl und den Freiheitsdrang verdanken die Deutschen größten Theils diesen beiden Juden;" **Börne** war "mehr als **Lessing**" (S. 378), er "unternahm nichts weniger als das deutsche Volk zu **erziehen**" (S. 277) . . . Links **Luther**, S. 318 sehr treffend mit Pfefferkorn auf eine Linie gestellt, und Friedrich der Große, **Göthe** und **Fichte** . . .

Left: H. von Treitschke, "Unsere Aussichten," *Preußische Jahrbücher* 44 (1879): 573–74 = Krieger, "*Berliner Antisemitismusstreit*," 1:2:12. For an English translation, see note 4. Right: M. Lehmann, *Literarisches Centralblatt für Deutschland*, January 14, 1871, cols. 29–30—a review of H. Graetz, *Geschichte der Juden* 11 (1870). The review is signed M. L.; see note 21. In this table, bold letters show verbatim agreement. The table includes all von Treitschke's comments on Graetz, but only the parallel passages in Lehmann's review.

APPENDIX II

Transcription of Letter from Max Lehmann to Friedrich Zarncke,
the editor of the *Literarisches Centralblatt für Deutschland*

Berlin, 17. August 1870
Karlstr. 28

Hochgeehrter Herr Professor,
So eben sehe ich, daß unter der Anzeige von Treitschkes h. und p. Aufsätzen in
der Nummer vom 6. August Ihres geschätzten Blattes meine Chiffre M.L., welche
ausdrücklich im Manuscript stand, ausgefallen ist. Sie würden mir einen großen
Gefallen erweisen, wenn Sie in der nächsten Nummer Ihre Leser darauf aufmerk-
sam machten; es liegt mir außerordentlich viel daran, ich wünsche den Inhalt
meiner Anzeige nach allen Seiten hin zu vertreten.
Zugleich spreche ich die Bitte um ein Exemplar der Nummer vom 6. August
aus, welche mir bisher noch nicht zugegangen ist.*

> Mit der Versicherung ausgezeichneter Hochachtung
> Er. Hochwohlgeboren
> ganz ergebenster
> Max Lehmann

*The letter is found in the Zarncke *Nachlass* in the special collections department of the
Leipzig University Library. My thanks to Steffen Hoffmann, of that department, who
supplied me with this and other materials, and to Pierre Meinig, who transcribed it. On
Zarncke and his journal, see T. Lick, *Friedrich Zarncke und das "Literarische Centralblatt
für Deutschland": Eine buchgeschichtliche Untersuchung* (Buchwissenschaftliche Beiträge aus
dem Deutschen Bucharchiv München 43; Wiesbaden: Harrasowitz, 1993).

APPENDIX III

Opening Paragraph of a Review by Max Lehmann
of H. von Treitschke's *Collected Studies*, August 1870

True, it is no longer the case that what many of our scholars know about Heinrich von Treitschke is only that he is a Prussian-leaning and not untalented publicist. The rise of his reputation is best demonstrated by the flood of hatred with which he is persecuted wherever, between the Bodensee and Königsau, the German state, which is seeking to assert itself, has enemies. But only in the future will it be possible to appreciate his worth fully. Only when the project of national unification is completed will even the most stubborn radical, who today makes the sign of the cross whenever he hears von Treitschke's name, join us in the conviction that since the days of Ulrich von Hutten such a voice has not been sounded in Germany. Heinrich von Treitschke surpasses E. M. Arndt in the extent of his knowledge, Gentz in the nobility of his disposition, Fichte in his art of description. That which most reminds us of Hutten is his pure truthfulness and unflinching bravery, which allow him to castigate even his own party, harshly, for its failures and his own nation for its weaknesses, and even more—the deep flame of his passion, his love of the fatherland, which—blazing up toward heaven—warms even the coldest hearts. And although usually such passion is the privilege of people in their natural state, here it comes together with an incisive and sharp logic and a comprehensive scholarly education in history, political science, and literature. How could such resources not be capable of creating a commensurate form?! We can hardly imagine anything more exciting than this back-and-forth between scientific proof and charming description, between serious and incisive preaching and a bright and playful mood—writing that is totally individual, but always with proper tact and respect for the boundary between style and mannerism, the result being that his writing also contributes to the development of our language.*

LCD, August 6, 1870, cols. 908–909 (my translation [D.R.S.]). The review was published without the author's name, but Lehmann's authorship is demonstrated by his letter presented in appendix II. For a passage from the end of this review, see note 22.

30

Lawrence H. Fuchs

The Scholar as Citizen

STEPHEN J. WHITFIELD

Jehuda Reinharz was the last president of Brandeis University with whom Lawrence H. Fuchs (1927–2013) worked—and with all of these educational leaders, beginning with founding president Abram L. Sachar, Fuchs worked closely. He was a member of the faculty for exactly half a century, from 1952 until 2002. He began teaching at Brandeis only three months after its first class graduated; and when he retired, he received an honorary degree from the institution that he had served with such devotion and such diligence. On that occasion Reinharz explained that "Larry Fuchs has been an articulate voice for fulfillment of the American dream, of an ethnically and racially diverse democratic land of immigrants within a vibrant civic culture. For half a century, he has really been an incredible statesman on our campus as a faculty member, scholar, and dean."[1] The university turned fifty on Reinharz's watch; and, shrewdly as well as predictably, he turned to Fuchs to chair the anniversary committee that would highlight a unique niche in the history of American higher education.

Brandeis constituted the core of Fuchs's professional life, and he exerted an impact on virtually every unit of the campus. Less than a decade after joining the faculty, he had become chairperson of the Department of Politics, and then served as dean of the faculty as well. He was elected to three terms as a faculty representative to the board of trustees. As a political scientist, Fuchs started out as something of a behaviorist. But from the beginning, he also was interested in culture, which led to a change of disciplines and to his pivotal role in the creation of the Department of

American Studies in 1970. For the next three decades or so, he remained its chairperson, except when he took leaves of absence. He pioneered in adding the study of the black experience in the United States to the Brandeis curriculum.[2] And well before he retired, he adapted to social change by offering the first course on the Asian-American experience. Under his auspices, American studies became the first home for the education program, the film studies program, the journalism program, the legal studies program, the environmental studies program, the women's studies program, and even an early version of health studies.

Fuchs reviewed and reimagined virtually every element of the institution, from athletics to admissions to the library. He was a prodigious fund-raiser and a genial goodwill ambassador. He spoke to every chapter of the Brandeis University National Women's Committee (now called the Brandeis National Committee), the nation's largest volunteer organization dedicated to the support of a library. To provide intellectual heft, Fuchs devised the idea of study guides to disseminate academic knowledge throughout the chapters, which numbered well over a hundred. Across most of the historical span of the university, no faculty member matched him in the breadth and depth of his contributions. It would be hard to identify a significant feature of the university that does not bear the imprint of his initiative, imagination, energy, and dedication. He not only came up with ideas; he also made them operational. He was, in the best sense of the appellation, Citizen Fuchs.

This essay seeks to connect his academic life to his broader political commitments and to demonstrate his flair for drawing upon his own expertise and values to help change American history. As a Jew, Fuchs felt a special need to enlarge the design of democracy and to further the realization of the nation's ideals. From an institutional base in the world's only nonsectarian, Jewish-sponsored university, he sought to evaluate and also to extend the scope of civic inclusion. His career showed how smoothly biography could blend into history.

Born in the Bronx to Jewish immigrants from Austria and Poland, Fuchs spent his boyhood most memorably in the bleachers at Yankee Stadium, and served as a Navy medic as World War II entered its final phase. Thanks to the G.I. Bill, he earned a bachelor's degree in political science at NYU. After obtaining a doctorate at Harvard, Fuchs became an instructor in Harvard's Department of Government. But in 1952 President Sachar offered him $3,200 a year to teach four courses a semester at Brandeis. Fuchs accepted the invitation, even though Professor Louis Hartz stopped him in Harvard Yard to tell him: "You are crazy." Provost Paul H. Buck, Fuchs recalled, "was actually quite furious at me, very angry [at me] for doing it." But Brandeis gave him a chance to enjoy "enormous flexibility to be in politics" and the freedom to engage "in civic work." There were no regrets.[3] And he seized a chance to entangle his public life quite inextricably with the Kennedy family. That family, more than any other, smashed the Protestant hegemony that had marked the colonial era and which had endured until the presidential election of 1960.

Three years later, the assassination of John F. Kennedy produced an outpouring of grief, mourning, and instant nostalgia for Camelot. Within two weeks of the shock of Dallas, 65 percent of those polled claimed to have voted for him in 1960 (compared to only 30 percent for Richard M. Nixon), in rather sharp contrast to the dead-heat election itself. Martyrdom suddenly inspired so many admiring volumes, by authors claiming to have known Kennedy well, that a political satirist conjectured that a book would soon appear by the cabbie who drove Jack and Jackie on their very first date, a volume entitled *Taxi to Greatness*.[4] Fuchs himself was too modest to have trumpeted his friendship with the president; and yet the personal connection to the most celebrated of political dynasties was historically important. A famously voracious reader, the junior senator from Massachusetts was undergoing hospitalization in 1956 and 1957 when he studied at least parts of Fuchs's first book, *The Political Behavior of American Jews* (1956). That volume, which inaugurated the field of American Jewish political studies, produced spin-offs, which Kennedy also read. They included articles that tracked the persistence of ethnic voting, such as "American Jews and the Presidential Vote," which appeared in the *American Political Science Review* (1955). Fuchs's research highlighted the tenacity of the Jewish dedication to liberalism, which he defined as support for civil liberties, civil rights, labor unions, government welfare programs, the United Nations, and the regulation of business.[5]

But even if Kennedy had never read the article that appeared in the *New England Quarterly*, that 1957 piece would have made its author's reputation anyway. "Presidential Politics in Boston: The Irish Response to

Stevenson" may have marked the first time (or very close to the first time) that a scholar had used in print the indispensable term "wasp" in a non-entomological sense. Fuchs noted that "some local politicians" were designating White Anglo-Saxon Protestants with the acronym of "WASPS."[6] Along with an article that Andrew Hacker published in the same month in the *American Political Science Review*, no scholar can invoke a prior claim in introducing that inescapable term in print. Senator Kennedy's own interest was hardly etymological, however. Because of the political need for outreach to the Jewish community, he and his chief aide and speechwriter, Theodore Sorensen, contacted Fuchs, who provided basic drafts of two speeches for Kennedy. "The first" that he delivered, Fuchs recalled, "was on ethnic loyalties and foreign policy, and it included a Justice Brandeis-like statement on the compatibility of Zionism with Americanism; the second was on immigration, written for delivery to the American Jewish Committee and the American Jewish Congress."[7] (The latter agency had tapped Fuchs to join its advisory board of the Commission on Law and Social Action.)

Even more salient, however, was an article that Fuchs published in the Jesuit weekly *America*. In that magazine he argued that, were Kennedy to secure the Democratic Party nomination, his religion would be an electoral plus, with more votes gained than lost because of his Catholicism.[8] The author thus helped confirm Senator Kennedy's ambition—and hope —that Roman Catholicism might be brandished as a political advantage in 1960, instead of a humiliating repeat of Al Smith's defeat in 1928. Though the assistant professor at Brandeis and the junior senator from Massachusetts shared the belief that diversity need not mean divisiveness, and that the postwar atmosphere of tolerance was gaining momentum, Kennedy's quest for the nomination was problematic. Liberals were suspicious of the bona fides of a senator who had egregiously failed to vote to censure Senator Joseph R. McCarthy in 1954. That stance of neutrality shed an odd light on the putative author of a book entitled *Profiles in Courage*.

Making matters worse was the identity of one noteworthy McCarthy-ite: Kennedy's own father. The prejudices of Joseph P. Kennedy, and his support of appeasement prior to the Second World War, imposed a special burden on a candidate who needed to win over not only liberals but Jewish liberals in particular. In a candid private meeting in Hawaii in the spring of 1959, Senator Kennedy admitted to Fuchs: "My father is an anti-semite."[9] In helping to mount John F. Kennedy's charm offensive among liberals and Jews, Fuchs demonstrated how an individual can affect, however modestly, the course of history.

One advantage was a formidable gift for networking, even as the Rolodex was first coming to market. He seemed to know just about everyone —and that included the unofficial leader of the liberal wing of the Democratic Party, Eleanor Roosevelt. Fuchs knew her from their shared service on the Brandeis board of trustees, and then as the coteacher of a two-hour seminar (1959–1961) on international organizations that he and the former First Lady offered on Monday mornings.[10] "Mrs. Roosevelt and I were good friends," he recalled. "We didn't have a long time in our relationship, but we had a close relationship." The pair also cohosted a television program, *Prospects of Mankind*, which WGBH taped on the Brandeis campus in 1959 and 1960. She resisted Kennedy's appeal not only because of his failure to oppose McCarthy, or even his failure to be much older, but primarily because Adlai Stevenson seemed to be the worthiest incarnation of her husband's legacy. Fuchs did not share her enchantment; he regarded two Democratic Party defeats as enough. Kennedy himself was more caustic, telling Fuchs: "The only way that Adlai Stevenson will get into the White House will be when I am president and invite him there."[11]

To alleviate her concerns and to neutralize her opposition to Kennedy, Fuchs brought them together on the Brandeis campus, where *Prospects of Mankind* was being filmed in Slosberg Auditorium, with the senator as guest and with Mrs. Roosevelt as host. Before the show the trio had lunch together for an hour. Her infatuation with Stevenson did not entirely evaporate; her "I'm Madly for Adlai" button was presumably not trashed. But the former First Lady did not thereafter try to torpedo Kennedy's pursuit of the nomination.[12]

Even before it was secured, Fuchs was urging his fellow Jews, both in the academy and in the media, to share his enthusiasm for Kennedy's candidacy. In Hawaii the senator had told Fuchs of the value of enlisting the support of Max Lerner, a syndicated columnist for the *New York Post* and the founding visionary of the social sciences at Brandeis. In that capacity Lerner had recruited Fuchs in 1952, and Fuchs pressed Lerner to discover for himself how reassuringly liberal Kennedy actually was. Mostly in New

England, Fuchs addressed Jewish groups and argued that the Democratic candidate should not be penalized for his father's bigotry. The patriarch was not running for the presidency. "My pro-Kennedy letters to liberals, mainly Jews, and speeches to largely Jewish audiences were beginning to elicit a positive response," Fuchs later noted. "Kennedy made all the right noises in speeches about Israel, immigration and separation of church and state."[13]

As the author of *The Political Behavior of American Jews*, Fuchs enjoyed matchless authority to tap into the concerns and proclivities that this minority group exhibited. His book offered a powerful explanation for the formation and persistence of a commitment to liberalism — as well as a heritage of loyalty to the left wing of the Democratic Party — that exceeded the attachment of other blocs of voters. Modern Judaism, he asserted, represented a worldly faith, a religion that had renounced asceticism in favor of challenging social injustice. The influence of Judaic ethical demands therefore accounted for the willingness of most Jews to pull the Democratic Party lever, even as they enjoyed the comforts of suburbanization and an ascent into embourgeoisement. Fuchs could certify that John F. Kennedy would honor the traditions of the New Deal and the Fair Deal that had won the support of most Jewish voters.

During the campaign Senator Hubert H. Humphrey chaired the Civil Rights Advisory Committee; and Fuchs joined a future Brandeis president, Morris B. Abram, in serving on that committee. Fuchs also belonged to the board of the Massachusetts chapter of the Congress of Racial Equality; the strategy that CORE adopted "of direct nonviolent action appealed to me," he recalled. By the mid-1950s, he was also conducting a local "radio news interview broadcast, and I had the privilege of interviewing Dr. [Martin Luther] King on one of his trips to Boston to raise money and gather support."[14] In 1960 King was sentenced to jail in Georgia. Senator Kennedy phoned Coretta Scott King to convey his concern, and his brother Robert Kennedy called a judge to ensure that there would be no mistreatment of the civil rights tribune. King's father was so thrilled by this palpable show of support that he announced that he would not vote for the GOP nominee. "Daddy" King, a Baptist minister, initially had rejected Kennedy's candidacy because of his Catholicism. Upon learning of that religious objection, the Democratic nominee remarked: "Imagine

Martin Luther King having a bigot for a father. Well, we all have fathers, don't we?"[15] That November Kennedy got the ballots of seven out of ten blacks.

But Fuchs had overestimated the electoral benefits of Roman Catholicism. Kennedy did eke out a white-knuckle victory in the popular vote. But in getting elected, he failed to win a majority of Protestants—for the first time in American history. Kennedy received 49.8 percent of the popular vote, even as his party's candidates for Congress were securing 54.7 percent of the vote, which meant that the standard-bearer had run behind them by an embarrassing 5 percent. Two University of Michigan political scientists concluded that "the religious issue was the strongest single factor overlaid on basic partisan loyalties in the 1960 election." Their study "calculated that JFK had lost 6.5 percent of the national vote of Protestant Democrats and independents and 17.2 percent of the Southern vote because he was a Catholic." Kennedy's plurality allows interpreters to attribute the margin of his victory to any number of factors. One of them might be the support of Jewish voters in greater numbers than expected, perhaps because of the evident anti-Catholic bias that some Protestant ministers expressed. For example, the *New York Times* detected "a backfire of sympathy for Mr. Kennedy" in New York, despite the views of his father; the November 3, 1960, headline announced a "Shift to Kennedy by Jews."[16]

In the aftermath of that election, Fuchs sought to put the evolving status of Catholicism in historical context by publishing *John F. Kennedy and American Catholicism*. Conversations with Kennedy had reinforced Fuchs's intention to write such a book, though JFK by no means dominates the text itself. The publisher, however, had insisted on putting Kennedy's name in the title; the year was 1967. When William F. Buckley, Jr., reviewed the volume (quite favorably, incidentally), he observed that Fuchs's own evidence suggested that, by September 1960, the candidate's Catholicism was forfeiting him as many votes as he was gaining, which is why Kennedy hoped to bury the religious issue for good by delivering an exceptionally eloquent speech to the mostly Baptist clergymen of Houston. Nor had Fuchs foreseen the tepid support that Kennedy elicited from most of the leading prelates of the Church. The hierarchy may have feared that he was stirring up bigotry, and perhaps a Democratic victory in November would doom the status of Francis Cardinal Spellman as the nation's leading Catholic.[17] So lukewarm was the Church itself that, according to two family loyalists, Joe Kennedy "said that he was thinking of joining the Jewish religion. 'The Jews are giving us more help than we're getting from the Catholics,'" he complained.[18] He did not actually pursue the option of conversion. But because a higher proportion of Jews backed the Democratic ticket (about 80 percent) than did Catholics,[19] Fuchs could have taken satisfaction in thinking that his own impact among Jews might have mattered.

Soon after the election, Mrs. Roosevelt told the incoming secretary of state, Dean Rusk, that Fuchs deserved to become assistant secretary of state for international organization affairs. That post would have put him in close contact with the new US ambassador to the United Nations, Adlai Stevenson. But in Washington, Rusk told Fuchs that Harlan Cleveland would be chosen instead.[20] Fuchs immediately went over to the office of the newly formed Peace Corps. Its director was the president's brother-in-law, Sargent Shriver, who quickly appointed Fuchs as the first director of the Peace Corps in the Philippines. In the spring of 1961, before Fuchs could get to the islands, Shriver invited him to the family compound at Hyannis Port, where they were joined by Ethel Kennedy and two of her children in commandeering a small boat off Cape Cod. Sailing nearby on the yacht the *Honey Fitz* was President Kennedy, who was smoking what Fuchs suspected was a contraband Cuban cigar. (Had Fuchs teased him about the legitimation of a tyrant such as Fidel Castro, the presidential rebuttal should have been the later rationale offered by General Alexander Haig in similarly hypocritical circumstances: "I prefer to say that I'm burning his crops.") But although Fuchs had served in the US Navy, the boat that he and Shriver were steering suddenly capsized; and a laughing President yelled out to them: "There goes the Peace Corps!"[21] They all managed to reach dry land, and the Philippines soon would host the largest initial contingent of volunteers assigned to any single country (128 at the outset, 630 when Fuchs left two years later). In the agency's first year, a third of all Peace Corps volunteers were assigned to the Philippines. Fuchs also was given the unusual rank of ambassador.[22]

From across the Pacific, Fuchs managed to involve himself in American foreign policy. Perhaps most important, he helped write the speech that the president delivered in September 1961 at the United Nations, where he pleaded for greater control of the weaponry of mass destruction. Kennedy warned of the threat to everyone of a nuclear "sword of Damocles." In Jewish tradition peace and justice are deemed inseparable. Soon after the assassination in Dallas, Fuchs returned home and was decisive in creating the Commonwealth Service Corps, a domestic version of the Peace Corps, in Massachusetts. By gubernatorial appointment, he became the first chairperson of the organization, which was designed to increase and promote volunteer activity to meet family and other needs. What he nicknamed "a baby Peace Corps" soon became a model for the federal Volunteers in Service to America (VISTA).[23]

During this decade, racial issues became especially urgent, and in 1965 Fuchs also became the principal author of the plan to promote the desegregation of Boston's schools.[24] That spring he joined those who marched from Selma to Montgomery to jump-start the passage of the Voting Rights Act, the law that helped reduce the discrimination that Fuchs would spend a lifetime combatting. The act mandated that within a decade the requirements for English literacy that states earlier had adopted be banned. Such laws long had been used in Southern states to keep blacks from the polls, but representatives of another beleaguered minority also came to condemn literacy tests as discriminatory. In 1975 Fuchs therefore joined the national board of directors of the Mexican American Legal and Education Defense Fund (MALDEF) and served for four years. He also became vice chairperson of the Facing History and Ourselves Foundation. Fuchs saw no conflict between his own sense of peoplehood and his feeling of solidarity with others. He professed to "like people who are united by a love of their ethnic ancestry," and as he once wrote to the sociologist David Riesman, "Of course, there are more explosive dangers in that kind of passion, which so easily turns against other people in vicious ways. But I have never found that love of one's ethnic ancestry was incompatible with humane values, including an appreciation of and respect for others, in my own life or in those of close friends and associates."[25]

Whatever the historical assessment of Fuchs's role in reinforcing the influence of the Kennedy family, he was no mere factotum. Once, John F. Kennedy asked him to undertake an assignment (the details of which are lost to history). Fuchs demurred, claiming that he would have to think

about it. Kennedy turned to his brother Bobby, and both of them chuck-
led, as though such hesitation demonstrated a gesture of disloyalty at
odds with the reputation of the famously frictionless Kennedy machine.
The brothers sardonically repeated to one another: "I'll have to think
about it!" But among the three brothers, Fuchs may have been closest to
Senator Edward M. Kennedy, who consulted with Fuchs over the longest
span. On the July 4, 1976, weekend, the youngest Kennedy brother celebrated the bicentennial by inviting Larry and Betty Fuchs to a clambake
in Hyannis Port. The bicentennial guest list was eclectic and very small
(and therefore a measure of the senator's esteem for Fuchs). The list consisted of the senator's mother, Rose Fitzgerald Kennedy; the Senator's
sister-in-law, Jacqueline Onassis; Sargent Shriver; the Soviet specialist at
Harvard Adam Ulam; the playwright Lillian Hellman; and the journalist
Bob Woodward and his then-girlfriend.[26] And though the full historical
record of Fuchs's relationship with the Kennedy family is elusive, a final
item should be mentioned, as a measure of his citizenship. In the immediate aftermath of the 9/11 terrorist attacks, he was asked by Senator Kennedy to help craft legislation that would achieve greater national security
while still somehow protecting the core of civil liberties.

Fuchs thus remained faithful to the progressive idealism that has remained an ethos integral to American Jewry. The erosion of privilege
and the expansion of democratic rights have continued to be the kinds of
aims that have animated most Jewish voters, and the revised dissertation
that he published in 1956 not only analyzed the sources of such liberalism
but remains the most influential text by a single author on this subject.
Nevertheless, *The Political Behavior of American Jews* has been sharply
criticized for ascribing the enduring liberalism of this "model minority"
to what the author called "Torah-based values."[27]

Sociologist Werner Cohn, for example, described the Jews' liberalism
not as a consequence of their religious heritage, but instead as "primarily
an extension of the European Jewish response to emancipation[,] which
came from the left and was opposed by the right." Cohn denied that *zeda-
kah* or other Judaic values made Jews liberal, but insisted that their historic
insecurity and their overriding anxieties about survival were decisive. Sociologist Charles Liebman also doubted that Judaic values could help explain the group's proclivities for political liberalism, because "those Jews

who were most religious . . . were not as liberal in American politics as the moderately religious or secular-ethnic Jews." Instead Liebman, much like Cohn, interpreted liberalism as emanating from "feelings of marginality, the psychological insecurity which prompted them to strive for a comfortable universalistic ethic which would also allow them to identify as Jews."[28] Fuchs rebutted such skeptics, however, by emphasizing the divergence of the United States from the rest of the Diaspora. From the beginning, he declared, the republic promised more than mere indulgence. George Washington, for instance, "explicitly repudiated the enlightenment concept of tolerating Jews by insisting that in the United States, 'all possess alike liberty of conscience and immunities of citizenship.'" So long as Jews obeyed the law as good citizens, the rights to which this minority was entitled were presumed to be the same as everyone else's.[29] American Jews therefore harbored fewer fears of marginality and insecurity than did their coreligionists elsewhere in the Diaspora. But a religious patrimony continued to separate Jews from their American neighbors. Hence, *The Political Behavior of American Jews* has remained the basis for further discussion and diagnosis of its subject. Its author managed to explain why Jews have remained more liberal than other well-to-do Americans, because Judaism itself makes this particular minority singular.

All of Fuchs's writings on ethnicity, religion, and race showed an arc toward the conclusion that, properly managed, diversity was valuable. It is, in any case, irrepressible. The capstone of his appreciation of *e pluribus unum* was *The American Kaleidoscope* (1990), a mammoth volume that won the John Hope Franklin Prize of the American Studies Association for the most important book published in the field that year, as well as the Theodore Saloutos Memorial Book Award for the best volume on American immigration history. *The American Kaleidoscope* is truly synoptic. It decodes the mysteries of how so disparate a people can somehow be held together without the imposition of state power and without the fissures of balkanization. His elucidation of what in 1965 two political scientists, Gabriel Almond and Sidney Verba, first called the "civic culture" shows how ancestral and religious differences came to be respected and legitimatized, without undermining the process of absorption and what was once called Americanization. Fuchs was not the sort of multiculturalist who conceptualized the republic as merely a collection of minorities, nor did he exalt diversity unthinkingly. Instead he argued that everybody, whatever their skin color or their historic bloodlines and customs, and whatever their own memories of discrimination and bigotry, depended on the political and legal framework of the civic culture. The conclusion to *The American Kaleidoscope* is as lapidary as it is patriotic. "No nation in history has proved as successful in managing ethnic diversity. No nation before had ever made diversity itself a source of national identity and unity." He insisted that " no nation in history has so eroded the distinction between natural and native-born citizens or made it so easy for aliens from vastly different cultures to become citizens."[30]

In the struggle to make the republic more welcoming to immigrants and refugees, in honoring the promise that is enshrined in Emma Lazarus's poem at the base of the Statue of Liberty, Citizen Fuchs was entrusted with one more mission. President Jimmy Carter appointed him executive director of the Select Commission on Immigration and Refugee Policy. He moved to Washington in 1979 and served for two years, producing an eleven-volume final report that became the basis for the Immigration Reform and Control Act of 1986. This law was hailed as the first significant overhaul of immigration policy since 1965. Fuchs then became vice chairman of the US Commission on Immigration Reform. (Chairing it was Congresswoman Barbara Jordan.) When Congress passed the Legal Immigration Reform Act of 1990, the year that *The American Kaleidoscope* was published, he was appointed to a seven-year term on the commission that the law established. The mandate of the commission was to evaluate the effectiveness of the policy and to recommend changes to the Congress and the president. The political and legal dilemmas that Fuchs faced stemmed from illegal immigration. The Select Commission established "the principle that it was wrong to invite illegal aliens through the back door," so that "the front door" could be "open[ed] more widely in 1986 and 1990."[31]

He went to Washington, he said, because of a yearning to shape immigration and refugee policy, and to better the lives of the vulnerable. He returned to Waltham, he added, because the experience of crafting social policy "makes me a better teacher and a better scholar."[32] When *People* did a profile of him, he was quoted as expressing his faith in the capacity of the democratic system to defeat "xenophobia" and "ethnic hostility" and to reinforce the ideal of "civic unity."[33] Fuchs had come to personify not only the liberalism that has characterized the Jewish political profile, but also a liberality of spirit that made the nation more hospitable to newcomers and more protective of minorities. *People* therefore aptly photographed him in contemplation, sitting on a bench in the Great Hall on Ellis Island.

NOTES

1. Quoted in Emily Sweeney, "The Voice of the American Dream," *Boston Sunday Globe*, May 26, 2002, 1.

2. Lawrence H. Fuchs, "The Changing Meaning of Civil Rights, 1954–1994," in *Civil Rights and Social Wrongs: Black-White Relations since World War II*, ed. John Higham (University Park, PA: Pennsylvania State University Press, 1997), 60–61.

3. Arnie Reisman and Ann Carol Grossman, "Interview with Larry Fuchs," in *Brandeis at 50: Minds That Matter* (1998), 1, 2, Robert D. Farber University Archives and Special Collections, Brandeis University, Waltham, MA (transcript in possession of author).

4. "Kennedy Assassination Survey," National Opinion Research Center, accessed July 15, 2013, http://www.ropercenter.uconn.edu.resources.library.brandeis.edu/data_access/ipoll/poll.html; Victor S. Navasky, "It's Not the Book, It's the Subject," *New York Times Book Review*, December 5, 1965, 8.

5. Lawrence H. Fuchs, "JFK and the Jews," *Moment* 8 (1983): 22, and "Introduction," *American Jewish Historical Quarterly* 56 (1976): 187–88.

6. Lawrence H. Fuchs, "Presidential Politics in Boston: The Irish Response to Stevenson," *New England Quarterly* 30 (1957): 435.

7. Fuchs, "JFK and the Jews," 22.

8. Ibid., 24.

9. John F. Stewart, "Recorded Interview with Lawrence H. Fuchs," November 28, 1966, 5, John F. Kennedy Library Oral History Program, John F. Kennedy Presidential Library and Museum, Boston (transcript in possession of author).

10. Fuchs, "JFK and the Jews," 25; Reisman and Grossman, "Interview with Fuchs," 11.

11. Quoted in Sweeney, "Voice," 1, and in Fuchs, "JFK and the Jews," 24, 25; Lawrence H. Fuchs, "The Senator and the Lady, " *American Heritage* 25 (1974): 57–61, 81–83.

12. Stewart, "Interview with Fuchs," 19, 24, 28.

13. Ibid., 18, 24, 25, 26.

14. Fuchs, "The Changing Meaning of Civil Rights," 60–61.

15. Quoted in Taylor Branch, *Parting the Waters: America in the King Years, 1954–63* (New York: Simon and Schuster, 1988), 366, 370.

16. Lawrence H. Fuchs, *John F. Kennedy and American Catholicism* (New York: Meredith Press, 1967), 186–87; David Nasaw, *The Patriarch: The Remarkable Life*

and Turbulent Times of Joseph P. Kennedy (New York: Penguin Press, 2012), 742, 748, 751–52; Homer Bigart, "Shift to Kennedy by Jews," *New York Times*, November 3, 1960, 28.

17. Stewart, "Interview with Fuchs," 54; William F. Buckley Jr., "A Long Way from Rome," *New York Times Book Review*, May 14, 1967, 8; John Cooney, *The American Pope: The Life and Times of Francis Cardinal Spellman* (New York: Times Books, 1984), 272.

18. Quoted in Nasaw, *Patriarch*, 748; Kenneth P. O'Donnell and David F. Powers, *"Johnny, We Hardly Knew Ye": Memories of John Fitzgerald Kennedy* (Boston: Little, Brown, 1972), 217.

19. Fuchs, "JFK and the Jews," 26.

20. Matthew Fisher, "Keeping Peace Alive: Local Man Was First Peace Corps Director," *Waltham Daily News Tribune*, February 23, 2001, A7; Stewart, "Interview with Fuchs," 47.

21. Lawrence H. Fuchs, "Peace Corps Philippines: Big Ideals and Big Adjustments," in *Answering Kennedy's Call: Pioneering the Peace Corps in the Philippines*, eds. Parker W. Borg and Maureen J. Carroll et al. (Oakland, CA: Peace Corps Writers, 2011), 11, 446–47; Fisher, "Keeping Peace Alive," A7; Hannah Agran, "Just a Year Short of Half a Century," *Justice*, April 16, 2002, 11.

22. Fuchs, "Peace Corps Philippines," in Borg and Carroll, *Answering Kennedy's Call*, 11, 446–47; Fisher, "Keeping Peace Alive," A7; Stewart, "Interview with Fuchs," 49–50; Agran, "Just a Year Short," 11.

23. Quoted in Sweeney, "Voice," 5; Stewart, "Interview with Fuchs," 51–52.

24. Ibid., 5.

25. Fuchs, "The Changing Meaning of Civil Rights," 62, 66; Lawrence H. Fuchs to David Riesman, May 31, 1985, in *Civil Rights and Social Wrongs*, ed. John Higham (State College: Pennsylvania State University Press, 1997).

26. Fuchs, "JFK and the Jews," 23; Lawrence H. Fuchs, e-mail to author, April 4, 2011.

27. Fuchs, "Introduction," 182.

28. Ibid.; Werner Cohn, "The Politics of American Jews," in *The Jews: Social Patterns of an American Group*, ed. Marshall Sklare (Glencoe, IL: Free Press, 1958), 625–26; Charles Liebman, *The Ambivalent American Jew* (Philadelphia: Jewish Publication Society of America, 1973), 139–44.

29. Quoted in Fuchs, "Introduction," 183.

30. Lawrence H. Fuchs, *The American Kaleidoscope: Race, Ethnicity, and the Civic Culture* (Middletown, CT: Wesleyan University Press, 1990), 492.

31. Lawrence H. Fuchs, "Immigration History and Immigration Policy: It Is Easier to See from a Distance," *Journal of American Ethnic History* 11 (1992): 72.

32. Quoted in Barbara Eisman, "Fuchs Returns after Government Service," *Justice*, October 27, 1981, 3.

33. Quoted in John Stickney, "To Open the Door or Close It: An Expert Evaluates the Explosive Issues of Immigration," *People* 18 (1982): 104, 108.

31

Three Brandeis Presidents

Open Leadership in an American University

DAVID HACKETT FISCHER

Every university is a challenge to its leaders—some more so than others. Among the most challenging is Brandeis. This private university was founded in 1948, with large purposes and small resources. Its prospects for success were not what a gambler would call a betting proposition. From 1636 to 1860, approximately 900 colleges and universities were founded in what is now the United States. Of that number about 720 failed—a mortality rate of 80 percent. In the next century, from 1860 to 1960, the numbers were larger, but life chances were not much better.[1]

Brandeis struggled against these odds and survived. More than that, it flourished. In two decades, it moved into the upper strata of American research universities—a rare achievement. Always its progress was unsteady. Surges of growth alternated with stagnation and sharp decline. In one dark period (1969–1973) Brandeis came dangerously close to failure. But even in hard times this extraordinary institution kept advancing. One might ask how and why.[2]

None of the easy explanations work. Brandeis did not succeed because of an abundance of material resources—quite the contrary. It did not move ahead because the stars somehow were aligned for its success, or because it was lucky in its time and place. The dangerous early years, from 1948 to 1957, were a period of painful contraction in American higher education, between the postwar surge of the G.I. Bill (1945–1948) and the bigger increase circa 1962 when the children of the Baby Boom went to college. Brandeis was born in the intervening period when a small cohort of Depression babies came of age and American colleges struggled with reduced demand. In the early and mid-1950s, the number of colleges and universities actually fell in the United States — one of the few such declines in American history. College enrollments also contracted in those years, in absolute numbers and as a proportion of the college-age population.[3]

The timing of Brandeis was problematic in other ways. Its founding coincided with the birth of Israel as a modern state. Zionist leader Chaim Weizmann, soon to be the first president of Israel, said in 1947, "I was astonished to hear a few months ago that someone wants to establish a Jewish university in America. I raise my voice in warning. Do not waste the strength of the Jewish people. There is no substitute for Zion."[4] Crises of support for Brandeis coincided with wars in the Middle East, when the American Jewish community rallied to the support of Israel.

The location of Brandeis also was a mixed blessing. The gift of a campus in Waltham, Massachusetts, was a vital asset, but it constrained growth. The Boston area was a great advantage, but Brandeis faced formidable competition from stronger neighbors. In short, no simple determinant or contingency model can explain how this university got ahead.

In my experience, Brandeis succeeded mainly in another way. Its greatest assets were the strengths of its many leaders (hundreds of leaders) and the critical choices that they made. Altogether, from 1948 to 2014, the university was led by nine presidents and acting presidents. As a long-serving member of the faculty, I worked with them all and held each of them in high esteem.[5] What follows is a personal account of the challenges they confronted, the decisions they made, and the actions they took.

Three presidents in particular had the greatest impact on the institution. Abram Sachar (1948–1968), Marver Bernstein (1972–1983), and Jehuda Reinharz (1994–2010) were the longest-serving presidents in the history of the university. Together they led Brandeis through forty-eight of its first sixty-six years. They also were memorable for the quality of their leadership. Each of them had a clear vision of Brandeis and a driving purpose. All of them were open leaders. They excelled in recruiting other leaders of high ability and engaging them in a common effort. They created a community of leadership that was remarkably broad and deep in so small a university. It is instructive to ask how they went about it, all the more so as they did it in different ways.

Abram Sachar was the first president for twenty years, from 1948 to 1968, and he is universally recognized as the founder of Brandeis. More to the point, he was the man who mobilized many founding leaders in the first Brandeis generation.

Marver Bernstein served eleven years from 1972 to 1983 as the steward of Brandeis. He became president in a difficult time, when the university almost went under. Marver Bernstein gathered a group of gifted leaders who were not only the stewards of Brandeis, but also its saviors in a critical moment. They rallied others to that common effort.

Jehuda Reinharz was president for seventeen years from 1994 to 2010, and a great transformative leader. In a turbulent era of economic boom and three busts (1994, 2001, and 2007–2009), he revived the university, renewed its founding vision, reformed the structure of the institution, raised more money than all the other presidents combined, recruited a new generation of leaders, and led Brandeis to new levels of achievement.

What follows is a personal history of these three men. It makes no claim to objectivity. They were my employers, my colleagues, and my friends. We worked in similar fields of scholarship. Abram Sachar and Jehuda Reinharz were historians, as am I. Marver Bernstein toiled in adjacent fields of politics and government, often with historical approaches. All three were scholar-presidents who continued to write and publish very actively through their presidential terms. I formed high respect for their stamina and strength of purpose, even when we disagreed.

The essay that follows is a testament of friendship. At the same time, it is a serious inquiry into the character of their leadership and a search for the sources of their success. All of these men made mistakes, sometimes big ones. Each of them was criticized relentlessly by members of the faculty, sometimes with reason. But we have more to learn from the many things they did right.

The example of their success reaches beyond Brandeis, and beyond universities in general. Open leadership of free and cantankerous people is not an easy role. As open institutions are spreading through the world, it is instructive to study the history of leaders who were able to make these challenging systems work. Universities in general are interesting that way, for their complexity and creativity. The short history of Brandeis University in particular has much to teach us.

Abram Sachar, Founder of Brandeis, 1948–1968

We might meet Abram Sachar through the eyes of a bright young chemist who was a candidate for a job at Brandeis. The year was 1950. Half a century later, Saul Cohen vividly remembered that first impression. He found Sachar sitting in his office, "a young fifty, ruddy, sturdy, his hands were clenched on the desk as though holding reins or about to leap." The two men exchanged the customary courtesies. Sachar went straight to the point and offered a job. Saul Cohen said he was interested, but he wanted to keep his lab going, and Brandeis lacked the facilities. Perhaps he could come part-time. Sachar "half rose from his chair, his face turning red, and waved his arm above his head and said, 'No! You must come full-time. This is going to be a great university.'"

Cohen thought to himself, "Was he a visionary or a fantasist? A castle builder?" He went home and talked it over with his wife, Doris. They knew many people at Brandeis and were related to more than a few of them in the small world of Boston's Jewish community. "Let's do it," said Doris, "they'll be a good group. . . . It will be fun." They did, and it was. Much of it was about Sachar.[6]

Inventing the Brandeis Idea: Sachar among the Founders

Abram Sachar did many things for Brandeis, but three things most of all. First, he took the lead in creating an idea of Brandeis and framing a vision of what it became. This idea did not arise from his thinking alone. Brandeis had many founders. In the years after World War II, they were drawn to the idea of a new American university of Jewish sponsorship, but they had different models in mind.

One important group of founders were refugee intellectuals who dreamed of a "European university in America." Some were thinking of a university without fraternities or football. They wanted a university that was devoted more to higher learning than to higher education, and firmly in the hands of first-rate scholars and scientists. Several found their models in Oxford and Cambridge. Many remembered the great German universities before 1932, with their twin traditions of *Lehrfreiheit* and *Lernfreiheit*, freedom to teach and freedom to learn. A leader from the start was Albert Einstein, who had been urging the establishment of such a university in America since 1935. After the war he became the titular head of a new Foundation for Higher Learning.[7]

Other prominent founders of Brandeis were religious leaders who had a different dream, of a new Jewish university, centered on the study of Jewish values and on the training of Jewish leaders in America and the world. This group also was diverse. One of their leaders was Conservative Rabbi Israel Goldstein; another was Liberal Reform Rabbi Stephen Wise, head of the Jewish Institute of Religion.[8]

Another vital group of founders were Jewish businessmen, mostly in New England and New York. Some of them wanted a small American college of high quality, like Amherst or Swarthmore but of Jewish sponsorship, and open to all without discrimination.[9]

Some of the most influential founders were American Jewish scholars and scientists such as Saul Cohen, who had in mind a private American research university, small in size but very strong in achievement. Their models were Princeton, Johns Hopkins, and Chicago.[10]

Yet another model was that of David Niles, a personal assistant to Franklin Roosevelt and Harry Truman. He dreamed of a first-class Jewish-sponsored American university, dedicated to the nation's service in law, government, and public affairs.

Other founders of Brandeis believed that the university should be linked to ideas of social justice. An inspiration was the Progressive leader Louis Brandeis, who was celebrated as "a great Jew and a great American."[11]

These founding groups shared much in common, but as discussions continued, they grew more conscious of their differences. Albert Einstein, Israel Goldstein, Stephen Wise, and several New York philanthropists withdrew for various reasons. New England businessmen and lawyers became more prominent, and their leading choice for president was Abram Sachar.

Sachar brought to the job a unique breadth of academic experience in strong universities. He had been an undergraduate at Washington University in St. Louis and at Harvard, a doctoral student in history at Cambridge University, a charismatic lecturer and productive scholar at the University of Illinois, and head of the Hillel Foundation, working with many institutions. Sachar deeply understood the diversity of American universities. He knew them from the inside, as complicated places where people did profoundly different things — and did them differently. He was comfortable with that diversity.

Sachar was himself a very complicated man. A recent writer has described him as an academic autocrat, a word that recurred among faculty critics. It is true that sometimes he could be cruel and even tyrannical.[12] But these moments were aberrations. The central pattern in his career and the source of his success was the opposite of autocracy. Sachar worked within an American tradition of open leadership. In the early republic, one of its inventors was George Washington, who summarized its central idea in a sentence: "A people unused to restraint must be led; they will not be drove." A large part of this style of open leadership is the ability to listen and learn from strong-willed, contrary-minded people, and then to engage them in a common cause. Washington learned to lead that way by trial and error when he ran the Continental Army. He did it again as president when he brought Alexander Hamilton, Thomas Jefferson, and John Adams together in the same room and kept them working together. Abraham Lincoln and Franklin Roosevelt developed other methods of open leadership. Our most successful leaders have excelled in that way.[13]

Sachar was adept at using those open methods when he worked with the founders of Brandeis. He surrounded himself with strong-minded, high-spirited, independent people, and was comfortable in their company — not the way of an autocrat. Sachar had strong views and a formidable manner, but he was good at listening and learning from others, and even better at building a collective effort from a construction of their creative differences. Sachar's memoirs might be read as a running record of that open process, in great detail. He consulted very actively with individuals and small groups, and he was able to learn from the knowledge and judgment of people whose thinking was different from his own. If one were to ask which of the founders' many visions and dreams were adopted in the creation of Brandeis, the short answer is, approximately all of them, in a free and open exchange that Sachar designed and kept going for many years.[14]

An example might illustrate the point. At the start, most founding trustees of Brandeis were thinking in terms of a small undergraduate college. Sachar listened and responded by inviting Saul Cohen, then a new faculty member, to attend a board meeting — much to Cohen's surprise.

Cohen listened as trustees "talked of Williams, Wellesley, Haverford, and Amherst as models." He wrote, "I thought this would be a great mistake and surprised myself by taking the floor in quiet, determined disagreement." He argued that Brandeis should be "from the start, a small research university, comprising both a college and a graduate school," on the model of "Johns Hopkins, Chicago, and Princeton which were . . . not beyond our projected scale." As he spoke, the trustees began to listen in their turn, and Sachar encouraged this open exchange. Saul Cohen remembered how it happened. "I sensed that Dr. Sachar, who had moved aside as I came forward, approved and was excited by the turn of the discussion." The result was a complex and constructive compromise. It combined the idea of a small research university with a strong commitment to undergraduate teaching. This hybrid model became a central part of the Brandeis Idea.[15]

Other discussions followed. In that process of exchange, Sachar led the founders in framing a complex but clearheaded idea of Brandeis. It is a bundle of paradoxes. My dictionary defines a *paradox* as a "seeming contradiction," that is, not a contradiction.

This paradoxical Brandeis Idea might be summarized in a few sentences. It was, and is, a university that is Jewish in sponsorship, but nonsectarian in the sense of being open to all. It is a small research university, with a strong commitment to undergraduate teaching. It seeks to combine higher learning with higher education, to their mutual gain. It is a university that is young in its American spirit, but old as Moses in its traditions. It is a university devoted to disinterested scholarship and also to social justice; a university with deep roots in the Boston area and a broad reach throughout the world.[16]

As this process of conceptual invention moved forward, a few founders dropped out, but many more joined in. On June 14, 1948, Sachar laid out his Brandeis Idea in the grand ballroom of Boston's Statler Hotel, before a gathering of a thousand people. Most offered strong support. Four months later, on October 8, 1948, Sachar did it again before an even larger and more diverse crowd in Boston's Symphony Hall, which he remembered as "one of the largest university convocations of the twentieth century." It rallied support for what was then one of the smallest universities, with a grand total of 107 students and 13 faculty that first fall.[17]

Sixty-five years later, this Brandeis Idea is still in place, and unique in its

totality among more than four thousand American colleges and universities. In many ways it is stronger than ever. The Brandeis Idea has been
continuously challenged, tested, opposed, and revised. Sachar presided
over that open process through its first twenty years. Many other leaders
weighed in, sometimes in massive collisions. But the more this dynamic
Brandeis Idea changed, the more it retained its fundamental character.

Enacting the Brandeis Idea:
Sachar and the Pursuit of Excellence

Sachar's second major contribution was to make the Brandeis Idea a reality. He went about that task by centering on another theme that was
widely shared among the founders. When they described their purposes,
most of them used words such as "excellence," "highest standards," "first
class," "top rank," "first rate," "a great university."

The founders of Brandeis believed that a small but absolutely first-class
university might be more viable than a mediocre institution. Part of their
reasoning came from an old New England saying, attributed to Daniel
Webster. In 1807 he embarked on a legal career and was warned that he
could not hope to succeed in a crowded bar. Webster is said to have replied,
"There's always room at the top." That saying became an American cliché
in the mid-twentieth century, even as others mocked it. A British cynic
wrote, "There's always room at the top, because so many are pushed off."[18]

The Brandeis founders believed in this American idea. Nearly all of
them agreed on the pursuit of excellence, as a practical way of getting on
with the job. But the difficulty of their task was compounded by the fact
that they also had many different ideas of excellence in a university. Some
understood excellence as the rigorous mastery of a discipline. Others
found it in soaring expressions of creativity. A large number of Brandeis
founders thought of excellence as a moral or an ethical idea, or a largeness
of spirit, or a gift for great teaching, or important writing, or major research. A few wanted the best and toughest college football team in North
America. Here again, Sachar was comfortable with diversity. He pursued
all of these different ideas of excellence and happily embraced them in a
spirit that was extraordinarily open and flexible. This open approach was
fundamental to his success.

Another ingredient was even more important. Sachar sought other people who could function as leaders in the pursuit of excellence, and he delighted in their strength. In the 1950s, Sachar established self-governing departments. Their leaders worked *with* Sachar, more than they worked for him. He was comfortable with those relationships.

To keep the quest for excellence going, he also looked for large-spirited colleagues who were willing to search for others who were better than themselves. That phrase was often repeated. Herman Epstein, a biophysicist who played a major role in building the sciences, wrote that "we should recommend only those we considered more accomplished in their fields than we were in ours." Founders of the history department repeatedly said the same thing in different words: "If we want to get stronger, we must hire people who are better than we are." They also were highly eclectic in their search for excellence. Many Brandeis leaders felt the same way, including Sachar.[19]

The details of this pursuit of excellence at Brandeis are deeply interesting to anyone who might embark on a similar quest. Sachar began by creating a small set of very strong groups and by building multiple centers of excellence. Most of these groups centered on basic disciplines in the arts and sciences. There was a large measure of opportunism in how Sachar went about it — a general goal, rather than a fixed plan. He worked in a very open and interactive way, with many different people, and together they improvised a creative diversity of methods.

In the natural sciences Sachar concentrated on four groups, never twice in the same way. In chemistry he encouraged one man to take the lead. Saul Cohen hired first-class laboratory chemists who were working on important problems. They bonded together, and most remained at Brandeis through their careers, training other first-class chemists.

Biochemistry began in a different way. Sachar consulted Fritz Lipmann, a Nobel laureate who had strongly supported the founding of Brandeis, and talked with many other eminent people. The plan was to found a graduate program and a center for cutting-edge research in a field that had not yet been separately organized in most universities. Lipmann was asked to make a list of the top five biochemists. Sachar went after all of them, and three came to Brandeis: Nathan Kaplan from Johns Hopkins, William Jencks from Harvard, and Martin Kamen from Washington University. They in turn recruited younger biochemists from 1956 to 1963.

Physics was built in a third way. Sachar decided to concentrate on the-oretical physicists—he couldn't afford labs. He persuaded Leo Szilard to accept a visiting appointment at Brandeis in 1954. With advice from him and others, Sachar recruited promising young physicists at the start of their careers, a dozen by his count, mostly in the period from 1954 to 1961. Many came, and were rapidly promoted. Similar methods were used in mathematics, where gifted mathematicians were thought to mature early. This department also achieved a critical mass of first-class mathemati-cians within a few years. These programs were extraordinary for quality and stability.

In the field of American history, yet another method was tried, with Sachar's active participation. A faculty was recruited mainly by Leonard Levy, John Roche, and colleagues they selected, while Sachar watched in-tently. Then he took the lead in another way. He talked with a family of donors in Chicago, Colonel Henry Crown and Irving and Rose Crown. The result was a generous annual gift from the Crown family to fund the largest graduate fellowships in American history. The Crown Fellowships attracted superb students. They were taught by a small core of faculty at Brandeis and by colleagues in universities throughout the Boston area. Each student was encouraged to develop an individual program, but all were expected to do first-class work. The program remained small, but of high quality for many years. Its students and faculty won five Pulitzer prizes.

Yet another path to excellence was used in the Department of English and American Literature. Its leader was Robert Preyer, a wonderful col-league who seemed to know everyone in the field. He recruited such first-class scholars as Aileen Ward, critics, such as Philip Rahv and Irving Howe, and the poets J. V. Cunningham and Allen Grossman. Sachar added a large endowment from Fannie Hurst for two visiting chairs, which brought to Brandeis some of the most distinguished poets and novelists of that gen-eration, not for single lectures, but for a semester of serious teaching.

In music, Sachar made a major effort with a creative proposal to recruit Leonard Bernstein. In 1951 Bernstein was already very busy in New York and Tanglewood. Sachar talked with him for a few minutes before a per-formance and proposed that he come to Brandeis for short visits, teach a course on modern music or whatever subject he pleased, and work with a few good students in small groups, with other faculty helping in his absence. Bernstein agreed in a moment, just before he went onstage. This improvised arrangement worked. Saul Cohen delighted in the memory of "a large bright corner room, Leonard Bernstein at the piano, looking back over his shoulder, talking to a dozen wide-eyed students." Further, Bernstein was asked to help organize an annual Creative Arts Festival. This also was done with his inimitable panache. Festivals bearing his name continue to this day.[20]

Other methods were used with remarkable success in psychology, sociology, anthropology, politics, philosophy, linguistics, theater arts, Mediterranean studies, and Near Eastern and Judaic studies. Within fifteen years, most of these programs were ranked by peers as among the best in American universities.

The open pursuit of excellence became a flexible instrument of great power in Sachar's hands. At the same time, he insisted that nothing less than excellence would do. One faculty member who became a builder of excellence in his own right was Professor Cyrus Gordon. He complained about a quality of ruthlessness in Sachar's presidency. But he did not complain about the result. Gordon wrote that Sachar "performed a feat unmatched in twentieth-century America: he built a research university from scratch."[21]

Sachar and the builders of Brandeis believed that excellence in itself attracted other excellent people, who tended to stimulate each other in an open system. This tendency appeared in unscripted opportunities for creative interplay among lively colleagues who were profoundly different from one another. There was a remarkable flow of camaraderie that expanded across boundaries of departments, programs, ideologies and orthodoxies. I remember learning from many unexpected friendships and associations. In the early 1960s, when walking down the long hill from the academic quadrangle to the faculty center, I would sometimes meet Herbert Marcuse on the path, and we would talk. One day our conversation was about a German scholar whom we both admired and Marcuse knew. Otto Vossler had done some truly remarkable work on Thomas Jefferson, freedom, and tolerance in an age of revolution. Herbert and I had an exchange of views on those subjects, as we walked and talked together, the yang and yin of Brandeis University.[22]

Other spontaneous associations followed when the historians over-flowed their building. I moved with John Roche to the Judaic studies building and got to know many colleagues there. A cherished memory is of long talks with Nahum Sarna on the Book of Genesis, of which he had an unrivaled knowledge. Later I got to know his very able son and now my colleague, Jonathan Sarna, and often talked with Marshall Sklare, a first-class sociologist in the Near Eastern and Judaic studies department, and with Tzvi Abusch, whose mastery of ancient Middle Eastern languages was very helpful to my work on the origins of liberty and freedom. At Brandeis the general level of excellence has been sustained by many colleagues in Jewish studies.

Other friendships formed when Seyom Brown in politics and I in history joined together to found a new program on peace studies. Later we were happy to pass the program on to Gordie Fellman and the sociologists. In that cause we also worked closely with Henry Linschitz, a brilliant chemist and a wonderful colleague. During World War II he had built the explosive triggers in the earliest atomic bombs—and climbed the tower at Los Alamos before the first detonation. Afterward Henry joined and led the peace movement. He and I worked together as co-chairs of United Campuses to Prevent Nuclear War (UCAM).

I remember with particular fondness two cherished friends in physics. Steve Berko's work put him in the front rank of his discipline. At the same time he contributed much of his time and energy to building the university, and we worked on various committees and causes together. Jack Goldstein was another colleague and friend for many years. Jack and I were having lunch one day in the Sherman Center, and I remarked on a problem of physics that appeared in my bowl of onion soup. Why did the melted cheese preserve its heat while the soup cooled so rapidly? Jack taught me about the physics of phase change, and that led to a conceptual conversation about changes of phase in historical processes, which in turn had an impact on my work. That sort of academic cross-connection happened frequently at Brandeis. Sachar intended it, and he participated in it. He and I would run into each other in the library, and two historians would talk shop about books and authors. Later he invited me to his chancellor's office, where we explored a collection of history videos that he had made and discussed visual approaches to history.

Creative people in many fields were happy to be at Brandeis. Cyrus Gordon founded a remarkable Department of Mediterranean Studies, centering mainly on ancient languages and archaeology. He remembered his time at Brandeis from 1956 to 1973 as "my best years in academe," a "time of productive innovation." Pauli Murray wrote that her years at Brandeis were "the most exciting, tormenting, satisfying, embattled, frustrated, and at times triumphant period of my secular career." Lewis Coser wrote something similar about sociology, as did Morton Keller in history. All of it flowed from an institutional environment that Sachar created, in company with other open leaders.[23]

Enlarging the Base: Sachar's Constituencies

Abram Sachar's third major contribution was to broaden the base of Brandeis, which he did in many ways at once, and two in particular. One was to build on the Jewish heritage in a large-spirited way. He created an open environment where Jews and gentiles alike were attracted to Brandeis by qualities of Jewish culture that were strongly supportive of a great university.

One of these qualities was the heritage of the Children of the Book. Another was a depth of traditional respect for serious learning. Both became central to the institution. Most important was a special intensity of striving in Jewish culture. It appeared in the borscht belt joke that Jews are just like everybody else, only more so. On reflection I would say, much more so. Brandeis attracted Christian students who were drawn to that spiritual intensity and shared it in many forms: descendants of New England Puritans, Bible Belt Christian fundamentalists, and students from the large Armenian community in the Boston area who had their own unique Armenian work ethic, as strong and creative as the Protestant and Jewish work ethics, but very different in substance.

I was deeply impressed by the relentless quality of constructive self-criticism that kept driving Brandeis forward. It appeared in passionate meetings in which great scholars debated the details of the undergraduate curriculum. On one occasion, Frank Manuel raged against an imbecile curricular reform. "No! No! No!" he explained, "We are reversing six thousand years of evolution. We are making dumb Jews!" That quality of striving in Jewish culture attracted serious people who were not Jews.

Another way that Sachar broadened the base of Brandeis was to engage the American heritage of a nonsectarian institution. Some thought that these purposes were contradictory, but they were interlocked in the Brandeis Idea. Even as Sachar created strong connections between Brandeis and the Jewish community, he also reached actively across ethnic and religious lines, and built relations between Jews and Christians. In the era after the Second World War, the vibrant intellectual life of American Jewish communities appealed to many gentiles. Some also became active leaders at Brandeis. An example was John Roche, a leader at an early age in political science and constitutional law, and also in liberal democratic politics. He was raised in a working-class Irish community, served in New Guinea during World War II, did his graduate work in an Ivy League university, and taught in an excellent Quaker school, Haverford College. Then he came to Brandeis. He explained, "I was born a Catholic and I'm a practicing Quaker, but I'm going to Brandeis because at heart I'm a Jewish intellectual." He served as dean of faculty, who at that time was the executive officer of Brandeis. On campus he was called "Abie's Irish Roche," after a long-running Broadway comedy called Abie's Irish Rose, about a Jewish boy and Irish girl who found happiness in ways that were loathed by critics and loved by sellout crowds.[24]

Another Christian strongly drawn to Brandeis was Pauli Murray. She hated "intellectual laziness," loved the sharp edge of intellectual rigor, and delighted in the intensity in Jewish culture. Like many Christians, Pauli Murray was a Seeker. And like Cromwell, she believed that a Seeker was the next best thing to a Finder. She joined the faculty of Brandeis and later became an ordained Episcopal minister. After her death this Brandeis professor was elevated to Episcopal sainthood.[25]

I am a third example—catechized as a Presbyterian, confirmed as a Lutheran, married to a Methodist, and raised in Baltimore to an ecumenical idea of American culture. It was a vision of religious liberty and at the same time an idea of community that brought together many religions, races, and ethnicities in peace, equity, and mutual respect. That was the broth in which I was cooked—a spicy Baltimore bouillabaisse. In my youth, three leaders worked together to that end. Walter Sondheim was a successful businessman. Thomas D'Alesandro was mayor of the city. My father, John Henry Fischer, was superintendent of Baltimore's schools.

They were Baltimoreans all, born and bred in a tough town that inspired strength, courage, and loyalty in its native sons. They were Protestant, Catholic, and Jewish, with a common civic consciousness. In the crucial decade after the Second World War, they worked together on a variety of causes. One purpose in the early 1950s was to end Jim Crow in the city of Baltimore—the abolition of formal segregation by law, in which they succeeded. They also opposed discrimination against religious groups in general and antisemitism in particular, and they supported what was then called the "interfaith" movement. Later, after my Lutheran father John Fischer became president of Teachers College at Columbia University, he served on an interfaith commission with Father Theodore Hesburgh of Notre Dame and Abram Sachar of Brandeis.

The founding of Brandeis became a symbol and instrument of that cause. Jews and gentiles rallied to it, and they joined together to broaden the base of the institution, with Sachar leading them on. If some Jews such as Israel Goldstein thought that Brandeis was not Jewish enough, others believed that it was doing something urgently important by building bridges among people of different faiths. That idea had special power and broad appeal in the years after World War II, when the world awakened to the horror that religious and racial hatred had visited upon humanity.

Many gentiles supported Brandeis in that spirit. Some became major donors. The predominantly Christian board of the Ford Foundation was a leading example, with two large gifts that transformed the fiscal condition of the university in 1962 and again in 1964. I delighted in the bonhomie between Sachar and Boston's Cardinal Cushing, who worked happily together and helped each other in unexpected ways. Once, Cardinal Cushing made a cash contribution to some of Sachar's causes. Sachar was surprised. He asked, "Where did you get the money?" Cushing replied in his gravelly voice, "From some of my Jewish friends."

Many Christian and Jewish leaders shared this nonsectarian spirit when Brandeis was young, and still do so today. It was personal. A case in point was an undergraduate in my first course at Brandeis, Myra Hiatt, later Myra Hiatt Kraft. Sometimes Myra would drive out to visit my wife, Judy, and help with two small babies whom she dearly loved. I also got to know her father, Jacob Hiatt, a businessman in Worcester, Massachusetts, trustee of Brandeis, and a serious scholar with a master's degree in

European history and international relations from Clark University. The Hiatt family believed deeply in interfaith understanding. To that end they endowed two chairs: one in Christian studies at Brandeis, and the other in Jewish studies at Holy Cross.

The first incumbent of the Hiatt chair at Brandeis was Krister Stendahl, a wonderful character, who served as chief bishop of the Lutheran Church of Sweden, dean of the Harvard Divinity School, and Hiatt Professor of Christian Studies at Brandeis. We both had our offices in the Judaic studies building. It was always a delight to watch his tall Viking frame emerge from a small Volkswagen in which he whizzed around the campus. All of this broadened the base of Brandeis in many ways at once.

Another factor was the complex interplay of Judaism and American culture in the years before and after the Second World War. The war itself and its purposes created a larger and more open spirit in America. Cultures met and mixed in the lives of many people. Among the most visible were the extraordinary achievements of American Jews in Hollywood and on Broadway. For its American Jewish creators, this popular culture was an affair of the heart. Everyone could see and hear it when Irving Berlin sang his own song, "God Bless America," with a trembling voice and tears in his eyes. Even the most cynical spirits discovered the depth of meaning that America had for him, and for many Jews in his era.

At the same time, Americans who were not Jews awakened to the horror of the Holocaust, the dream of a Jewish homeland (in its early years), and a vision of coexistence for Jews and Palestinians. After 1945, many Protestant leaders embraced those ideas: Eleanor Roosevelt and Harry Truman to name but two—both great friends of Brandeis. Abram Sachar strongly promoted these ways of expanding the base of Brandeis, by reinforcing its Jewish and its American heritage. Both were urgently important to his Brandeis Idea.

Troubles in Sachar's Time: Money and Governance

Toward the end of Sachar's second decade as president, troubles began to grow. He was a brilliant fund-raiser, miraculously so in the early years when he persuaded people to give money to an institution that did not exist. He traveled tirelessly, and raised an estimated $200 million in twenty years. The money came from thousands of donors, much of it in small gifts.[26]

The peak period of Sachar's fund-raising was 1962–1965, when Brandeis received one of the most important gifts in its history. The Ford Foundation gave a set of challenge grants to eight major research universities. Brandeis received one of them, $6 million dollars, on the condition that it raise another $18 million in a three-for-one matching gift. A massive campaign was mounted. In December 1964, Sachar announced that he had achieved this goal. The Ford Foundation followed with a second grant of the same size, and another major campaign was organized. The estimates came to a grand total of $65 million, of which $43 million was to be for the endowment of faculty chairs, scholarships, and fellowships. About $12 million was for the building program, and $10 million was for current spending.

It did not quite work that way. The flow of gifts was large, but much of it was in the form of pledges, and expenses were larger. In early years, I was told that Brandeis had the highest unit cost per student of any American university.[27] Brandeis almost always ran in the red. Some faculty colleagues thought that the annual deficit was a fund-raising device, announced every year just before the Palm Beach meeting, when the trustees were asked under the terms of their original agreement with Sachar to make up the difference. But the shortfall was real, and sometimes it was larger than the official deficit. Rates of inflation, which had been climbing since World War II, suddenly began to accelerate in the mid-1960s. Costs were high and rising, while the endowment was small and shrinking. By the end of 1967, the book value of the endowment was probably about $29 million, maybe less. In the late 1960s, Brandeis was getting itself into deep waters.[28]

Another problem was developing in the governance of Brandeis. It had many ingredients. Abram Sachar was a man of character and contradictions. He believed deeply in his vision of a free and open institution. For many years he strongly defended academic freedom, which was central to the Brandeis Idea. In the late 1940s and 1950s, he also worked to promote an open spirit of academic freedom in American colleges and universities more generally, and in the country as a whole. At that time constitutional rights were under attack in politics, the press, and the universities themselves. Academic freedom was challenged severely in the early years of the Cold War by Senator Joseph McCarthy. Bad things happened in the best universities. Sachar resolved that Brandeis would be different: he made it a bastion of academic freedom.

A case in point was Ray Ginger, a gifted historian, brilliant teacher, and excellent colleague. Ginger was on the faculty of the Harvard Business School, and was fired for refusing to testify about his wife's politics. This was done in an exceptionally cruel and ungentlemanly way by highly placed leaders at Harvard. Ray and his pregnant wife were given a few days to leave town, or suffer immediate forfeiture of the two months' salary remaining on his contract. Sachar offered Ray Ginger a job at Brandeis. Ray rose quickly to tenure, published book after book at Brandeis, and taught some of the largest and most successful courses in the university. His survey of American history was so popular that in one semester it met in the gym.

Sachar was steadfast in support of academic freedom, and not only in that instance. He once told me that the most difficult cases at Brandeis centered not on ideologies of the right and left, but on anti-Zionism. He strongly defended academic freedom in those cases as well.

But there was another problem at Brandeis, and it grew. Sachar rightly believed that strong presidential leadership was fundamental to the success of Brandeis. His British years in a Cambridge college made him very dubious about faculty leadership. My experience of an Oxford college left me with another understanding. Oxford's Queens College in the mid-1980s was exceptionally well run by its dons, in company with a first-class provost, Robert Blake. That combination of good faculty and an able leader was highly effective.

At Brandeis, Sachar clearly understood the need for faculty participation in governance, and he deeply respected expertise in learned disciplines, but he did not trust faculty to lead the university as a whole. Increasingly, that feeling was reciprocated. In general, strong presidents are not loved by faculties; strong, effective presidents are loved least of all. It had happened to Woodrow Wilson at Princeton, Charles Eliot at Harvard, and Abram Sachar at Brandeis.

Another problem developed with the students. In the midst of the Vietnam War, Sachar and many of his age group were appalled by a minority of the younger generation, who turned furiously against American institutions in general and universities in particular. He also was increasingly angry with faculty critics of his presidency and insisted that academic freedom must be accompanied by academic responsibility.

These conflicts exploded in most American universities, and earlier at Brandeis than in other places. In 1961–62, an anthropologist named Kathleen Gough called off a class and led her students in an antiwar rally and peace march to the Watertown Arsenal. She was an English Marxist, hostile to American institutions. In the Cuban missile crisis she was alleged to have said, "*Viva* Fidel, Kennedy to Hell." Sachar summoned her to his office, reprimanded her, and may (or may not) have said that she had no future at Brandeis. Faculty meetings followed and were deeply divided. I had just arrived and was lobbied for my vote by colleagues on both sides of the question. My judgment was in the center, with what turned out to be a plurality of the faculty, who thought that Kathleen Gough was wrong to call off her class and that Sachar was wrong to act without due process. She and her companion and department chairman David Aberle decamped for Oregon and then Simon Fraser University in Canada, where she was suspended for attempting to call a faculty strike and shut down the institution.

At Brandeis some faculty grew increasingly troubled by Sachar's style of governance, and he was deeply angry with them. Even his friends and supporters were worried. Two very able colleagues who had served as his deans of faculty were lunching at the Faculty Center one day when Sachar passed by. One of them, John Roche, said quietly, "There is a serious problem here, and there he is." Saul Cohen agreed and disagreed in a Brandeisian spirit: "True," said Saul, "he is a problem, but also the solution, and solutions usually have problems."[29]

Other views were expressed more strongly. When infuriated faculty members told Sachar how he should run the university, he told them, "You couldn't run a grocery store." Finally, in 1968, Sachar and the board agreed that it was time to resign. A new position was created for him as chancellor of the university. His continued presence brought important gains for the university, and also more tension between the founder and his successors.

Altogether, the history of Abram Sachar's presidency is a history of true greatness. He led a gifted group of leaders in founding a great university, and they built it from nothing but a dream. The genius of Abram Sachar shaped the university in ways that have kept it growing. In the substance of Brandeis University, his spirit survives today.

Crisis and Disaster: The Failed
Presidency of Morris Abram

The years that followed, from 1968 to 1973, were difficult for many American universities. For Brandeis they were very dangerous. After a long boom, the economy stagnated and slipped into steep decline. The impact on many institutions was severe, especially for Brandeis.[30]

Economic troubles were compounded by social strife. Generations were moving apart. Crime and violence increased. Major leaders were assassinated. Violent riots broke out in hundreds of American cities. The conflicts spread widely and in 1968 became a world crisis. In the United States, the Vietnam War divided the country and disrupted many universities — Brandeis more than others. In Washington the failures of the Johnson presidency were followed by the tyranny and corruption of the Nixon administration.

Brandeis suffered not only from these general problems, but also from others that were uniquely its own. When wars broke out in the Middle East, the American Jewish community rallied to the support of Israel, and fund-raising for Brandeis became more difficult. And at the worst possible time, it suffered a major crisis of succession in its own leadership. Sachar retired from the presidency in 1968, after a tenure of twenty years. The board found a replacement in Morris Abram, a man of many talents, with a record of high achievement in law, diplomacy, and civic service. He was very well connected in the United States and through much of the world. I have happy memories of him and his wife in a personal way, and in particular of an afternoon when Abram's friend, the shah of Iran, had sent him a gigantic bowl of caviar, with the largest and palest grey eggs we had ever seen, in vast profusion. Six of us, Morris and Jane Abram, John and Connie Roche, and my wife Judy and I gathered around the caviar in Themis House and talked of people, events, and Brandeis.

Morris Abram was bright, serious, well meaning, and very able, as he had demonstrated in many fields. But he had little experience of academic leadership and was unlucky in his timing. Just as he was getting started, a group of African American students seized a building on campus, allegedly assaulted a student who happened to be working there, barricaded themselves inside, and issued many demands for a black studies department and greater representation in related programs, which the university was already in process of enacting. The faculty was divided by this event. Most opposed the forcible takeover, and also forcible repression. Students also were split, with many in support of the African Americans. Finally, the demonstrators were persuaded to leave the building without violence. But the Brandeis community remained deeply riven.

More violence followed in the protests and "strikes" against the Cambodian invasion in the spring of 1970. A "National Strike Information Center" was founded in the sociology building, which succeeded mainly in infuriating supporters of the university. In another outbreak, radical students tried to burn down the History building, but it stubbornly failed to catch fire.

More serious and much more destructive was a noble experiment that went disastrously wrong. In programs encouraged by Professor John Spiegel, Brandeis undergraduates were recruited to teach in penitentiaries, and convicts on parole were admitted as special students. The results, in September of 1970, were horrific acts of violence that claimed a life. Three male convicts and two female Brandeis students broke into a National Guard armory, seized weapons and hundreds of rounds of ammunition, and set fire to the building. Their avowed purpose was to arm the Black Panthers and overthrow the American government. Three days later they robbed a bank at Brighton, Massachusetts, in the name of revolution, and murdered a policeman in cold blood.

In these brutal acts, a small number of wayward students did grave injury to their cause, and also to Brandeis. Professor John Roche, himself very much to the left of center, observed that campus radicals were "the first revolutionary army in history to begin a war by destroying its own base." Donors, trustees, some faculty, and many friends of Brandeis were horrified. Pledges of financial support were canceled. The university was written out of wills. Annual gifts shrank to low levels. Endowment funds were consumed to pay overdue bills. President Abram had been forced to borrow heavily, and the university's credit rating fell to new lows. The hard times grew into a full-blown fiscal crisis. In 1970 Brandeis came close to collapse.

On top of everything else, President Abram made known that a donor had offered $2.75 million to found a law school, and that he was inclined to accept it. Faculty and trustees reacted with horror. The money was barely enough to fund a single chair. A new set of large unfunded obligations could have completed the financial ruin of the university.

Early in 1970, Morris Abram and the board agreed that he should go. The trustees turned to an experienced administrator, Charles Schottland, an aide to Dwight Eisenhower and former head of the Social Security Administration. He briefly became acting president of Brandeis, while the board looked for a permanent replacement.

Marver Bernstein, Steward of Brandeis, 1972–1983

In this painful moment, the trustees searched for an academic leader of experience, maturity, and wisdom who could restore the health and integrity of a troubled institution. They found their man in Marver Hillel Bernstein, a scholar of high distinction in political science and public administration. He knew his subject intimately, in part from the personal experience of working in Washington during World War II.

After the war, Bernstein joined the faculty of Princeton for twenty-six years, from 1946 to 1972. He published major works in his field. Some of them were on the problem of "agency capture," in which public bodies were controlled by the private industries that they were created to regulate. Bernstein's writings on this subject have grown in importance with the passage of time, and they are still actively in use.

At the same time he developed another expertise in methods of negotiation, which he helped to make a discipline in its own right. In 1967 he earned a national reputation when he succeeded in negotiating an end to extreme partisan gridlock in the New Jersey Legislature. It was a skill with many uses in a university.

At Princeton he also had much experience of academic leadership and became a highly successful dean of the Woodrow Wilson School of Public and International Affairs. With his guidance, it became one of the strongest centers in its field. In 1972 the trustees of Brandeis chose him as their president. His temperament was very different from the men who preceded him. So also was his task.

Marver Bernstein's Team, 1972–1983

At Brandeis, Bernstein began by forming a team of leaders — and to a high standard. He brought in David Steinberg as his executive assistant (1973–1977), and later as vice president and university secretary (1977–1983). The two men worked closely together. Steinberg had a top academic record at Harvard. He was a prize-winning historian of the Philippines and Southeast Asia, and an inspiring teacher with ten years of experience in Michigan's superb history department. David had a gentleman's easy manners and an understated combination of tact and strength. He shared the founding vision of Brandeis as a first-class research university with a strong commitment to undergraduate teaching. Later he would become a highly successful university president in his own right.

Bernstein also found another kindred spirit at Brandeis. Jack Goldstein was an astrophysicist who had been recruited by Sachar in 1956. Goldstein drew upon a broad range of experience that was common to his extraordinary generation. He had served in the Pacific during the Second World War, then did graduate work in physics at Cornell, published important papers in his field, worked for a time in private industry, and then returned to the academy. Along the way he also worked in Africa, where he taught science to young African students while he was writing papers of high importance on theoretical problems in astrophysics.

Jack Goldstein had an extraordinary mind. I was much impressed by his consuming curiosity about the world and have rarely met a colleague who moved so easily in so many of the arts and sciences. He had a deep interest in philosophy and music, and he was widely read in history and literature. One of his many hobbies was photography, in which he was highly creative. Some of his work was exhibited in major galleries throughout the world. He had been serving as dean of the Graduate School, then became dean of faculty, and Bernstein made him provost of the university.

Bernstein, Goldstein, and Steinberg made a strong team. They were men of sterling character and integrity. All three were calm and quiet leaders — highly intelligent, thoughtful, reflective, always soft-spoken and understated. They shared a scholar's respect for the pursuit of truth and a teacher's passion for the inquiring spirit, and they nurtured those ideals at Brandeis.

They also worked well and easily with others. Bernstein made a habit
of bringing small groups of trustees and faculty together for informal dinners in his office. There were no agendas for these gatherings, but only
open conversations that discussed problems of current concern. I greatly
enjoyed their spirit.

All three of these men believed deeply in the founding vision of
Brandeis. They shared its aspiration to great strength in the fundamental
disciplines of the arts and sciences. They also had a very strong commitment to undergraduate and graduate teaching. Their leadership was
marked by an integrity of purpose, method, and result.

Fiscal Stewardship

Marver Bernstein was called to the presidency of Brandeis at the most difficult moment in its history. From his long experience of administration,
he knew that he faced a hard challenge, but had no idea of its magnitude.
In the last years of Sachar's presidency and the agony of Abram's shattered
term, the university had drifted into deep financial trouble, with problems
and obligations that even its own leaders did not fully understand, in part
because the quality of the record keeping was so poor.

The first task was to restore the university to solvency and fiscal stability, which had never been its strength and now became a crushing
weakness. They were amazed to discover that the creative disorder of the
founding had descended into a condition of administrative chaos that was
dangerous to the survival of the institution. Jack Goldstein remembered
the shock of that discovery in the fall of 1972, when Bernstein took his
team on a retreat to Cape Cod. Goldstein wrote, "Perhaps that was when
he received his first inkling of what was really in store; it was certainly
when I received mine. We couldn't even advise each other; no two units
of the University kept their books in the same way, no one could say with
assurance how much money there was or there wasn't. . . . There seemed
to be a deficit, perhaps a large one; no one was sure. How much were we
committed to spend? The bottom line was not quite clear. What income
could we anticipate? Again no one was sure how to count it. Four, nearly
five years had passed under circumstances that left us without stable or
long-term governance or planning."[31]

In the absence of careful accounting, money disappeared. The great majority of people at Brandeis were honest, but a few administrators and faculty members had abused their trust. Endowments of many chairs, never very large, shrank to nearly nothing, or disappeared entirely as capital funds were tapped for current expenses. Before 1973, the university had borrowed many millions in an effort to stay afloat. Many things of value were sold. Land had been sold. Gifts and collections that had cash value quietly vanished. I remember a splendid collection of Old Master etchings that had been given to the university by its loving owners. One day I wanted to use them for a course and was told that they were gone.

Strict economy was necessary. Bernstein set a personal example. His predecessor Morris Abram lived in Themis House, a large country mansion and estate on a high hill in Weston, not far from the campus. Bernstein would have none of that. Themis House was sold, and he moved into a very modest home in Weston, where only a few people could gather and Bernstein himself sometimes did the cooking. On the campus, maintenance was deferred in modern buildings that urgently needed it—and were quick to show the effect of neglect. The perennial operating deficit persisted, and trustees dipped into their pockets to make up the difference.

At first, Bernstein's strength was not in fund-raising. Jack Goldstein remembered that he "had a terrible time asking people for money. Somehow it was painful to him."[32] Many such stories were told. He started slowly, but in the late 1970s he did better at fund-raising. The economy revived, and a peace treaty was signed between Egypt and Israel. Bernstein began to raise some serious money. He was also very frugal, and in this difficult era the endowment experienced much greater growth than it had done under Abram Sachar. In 1968, when Sachar left the presidency, the book value of the endowment was about $29 million. It declined under Morris Abram; by 1973 the value of the endowment was probably below $20 million.

Bernstein succeeded in turning things around. By the end of his presidency in 1983, the book value of the Brandeis endowment was estimated variously at between $90 and $100 million. It was still painfully small by comparison with the needs of the university, and also by the measure of assets in other leading institutions. But the first hundred million is the hardest, and it was Bernstein who reached that goal, quietly quintupling the endowment. He was the first to point out that he did so with the help of a hardworking board of trustees and many others including Sachar, who continued to pitch in as chancellor of the university.[33]

That year, Bernstein wrote in his quiet style that "after ten years of striving," Brandeis was "in the soundest financial position in its 35-year history," with "steady growth in assets, equity, endowment funds, and [annual] fundraising in the range of $15 to $16 million."[34] It was a painfully small sum, a pittance in comparison with needs. But this was a difficult time for the most affluent universities. Together Bernstein and his team and members of the board managed to keep the university afloat, and also on a more or less even keel. More than that, they kept it moving forward and were stewards of continued growth in very hard times.

Somehow Bernstein and Jack Goldstein also did other material things that were not easily done, but fundamental to their purposes. They went to work on raising faculty salaries and struggled to get them up to the level of "Ivy Four," the median level of the eight universities in the Ivy League, which was no small feat for so young and impoverished a university. They also did the unglamorous work of improving fringe benefits. Sachar had raised faculty salaries to remarkably high levels, but not much had been done for other benefits. To move forward on that front was a hard struggle. Yet Bernstein's team managed to do that too.

Faculty Stewards

One of the most important contributions of Bernstein and his team was to strengthen the quality of the Brandeis faculty, after a period of stress when it began to drift into decline. They believed deeply in Sachar's Brandeis Idea of a small research university and were strongly committed to the importance of undergraduate teaching in basic disciplines in the arts and sciences. Like Sachar, they believed that the key was the pursuit of excellence, especially in the individual quality of scholar-teachers.

In 1973 Brandeis was at risk in that way. Many top faculty members had been lost in the years from 1967 to the early 1970s. An example was the history department, where six world-class senior scholar-teachers were hired away in those years. Geoffrey Barraclough became Chichele Professor and Fellow of All Souls at Oxford. Frank Manuel went to New York University. Norman Cantor departed for Binghamton and then NYU as provost. Leonard Levy moved to Claremont. Stephan Thernstrom de-

parted for UCLA and then Harvard. John Roche went to Tufts. A strong
cadre remained in American History, but Morton Keller, then chairman
of the history department, remembered "one dark day when all four senior
members of the American History program shared outside approaches."[35]

Other Brandeis programs suffered in the same way. There is always
much turnover in a first-class faculty. In a university, the only thing worse
than a faculty that everybody is trying to hire away is a faculty that nobody
is trying to hire away. But the losses at Brandeis in these troubled years
(circa 1967–1973) were deeply threatening, both in quality and numbers.

Marver Bernstein, Jack Goldstein, and David Steinberg went to work
on the task of rebuilding the faculty, with goals similar to those of Sachar,
and once again with remarkable success. They concentrated efforts in the
major disciplines of the arts and sciences. They also understood, as Sachar
had done, that the key to excellence in the Brandeis faculty was a balanced
combination of junior and senior appointments. The hardest task on a
severely restricted budget was to attract and keep strong senior scholars.
To that end Bernstein created the rank of university professor, for more
strength and stability among senior colleagues. The first university professor was Saul Cohen in Chemistry, followed by J. V. Cunningham, a poet
much respected in English and American Literature.

The impact of these policies began to be felt throughout the university.
An example once again was the history department. The many history
programs at Brandeis had languished in the crisis years, and now they
began to flourish again with the support of Bernstein, Steinberg, and especially Goldstein. Together they worked closely with historians in another example of open leadership, and studied their opportunities.

Very quickly, they reversed the trends in history appointments by several initiatives. They succeeded in bringing back two first-class senior historians who had left Brandeis. Frank Manuel was persuaded to return as
university professor. Geoffrey Barraclough also came back. He resigned
the Chichele Professorship at Oxford and a much-coveted fellowship at
All Souls and rejoined the Brandeis history department, which had many
attractions for him. Geoffrey was a superb medieval historian who also
had invented a new field that he called "contemporary history"—not the
history of our own era, but rather the historical origins of urgent problems in our time. His approach was brilliantly conceived and broadly

developed. It was much valued in America, Asia, and Africa—more so, perhaps, than at All Souls.

Geoffrey liked Boston and Brandeis very much, and took a genuine interest in the department and the university. For many years Geoffrey and I jointly taught a graduate course together on the history of history. We were joined in sessions on epistemological and ethical questions by Alistair McIntyre, a first-rate scholar-teacher who had just come into the philosophy department and was an excellent colleague in every way. After class the three of us dined together and talked shop, much to my delight.

History began to flourish in other ways. We always had cultivated a broad diversity of subjects and methods, which could work only with strong support from Bernstein and Goldstein, for it required a continuing flow of junior tenure-track appointments. In the 1970s Brandeis became a center of invention in many historical fields. Rudolph Binion and John Demos were world leaders in a new interdisciplinary field of history and psychology. Environmental history began to flourish at Brandeis. Our students took the lead. Brian Donahue got his doctorate in the history program, joined the faculty, and became director of the environmental studies program at Brandeis.

John Demos and I worked together in the new social and demographic history. One fall we returned to discover that we had independently written two monographs, which were among the first to explore the history of aging as a new field.

The new economic history flourished at Brandeis, with help from two Harvard colleagues, Morton Horwitz and Robert Fogel, who were active in teaching graduate students and helping to advise on Brandeis history department dissertations, in which they took a deep interest.

While we introduced these new approaches, we also tried to reinforce our traditional strengths. One of them was the study of history, politics, and law, which Leonard Levy and John Roche had established at Brandeis. Morton Keller took it over and trained a generation of first-class scholars in that field, and they kept that tradition growing.

We also tried to continue a commitment to intellectual history, by supporting the inventive work of Marvin Meyers and also by appointing a young colleague from Stanford, James Kloppenberg, an intellectual historian who continued at Brandeis for twenty years and then became chairman of the history department at Harvard.

Within the American history programs, we tried to think globally in the 1970s. One of the world leaders was a great French scholar, Emanuel Le Roy Ladurie, who was developing new methods in French rural history. We invited him to visit us, which he did, and we redefined our seminar on American history to include Languedoc. Our colleagues in Sociology allowed us to use the beautiful space in Pearlman Lounge, which we filled to overflowing when Le Roy Ladurie joined us.

All of these things happened at the same time among a small community of Brandeis history department faculty and excellent students on Crown Fellowships. It could not have happened without Jack Goldstein, Marver Bernstein, David Steinberg, Abram Sachar, and the Crown family.

Similar activity went on in other disciplines. In this work Bernstein and Goldstein made a team as effective as Sachar and Saul Cohen had been. The sciences did well in these years. Physics and chemistry maintained their high quality. New developments occurred in biology and biochemistry. Steve Berko made another major contribution. He and Jack Goldstein were quick to see the coming importance of neuroscience. In the early 1970s, I remember hearing them talk urgently about possibilities in this field. During the late 1970s, they laid the institutional foundations for neuroscience programs that began to develop in the 1980s and have had a major presence at Brandeis in the twenty-first century.

Yet another example was music. Bernstein took a personal interest and built the music programs in three ways at once: musicology, composition, and performance. Once he told me that no university could claim to be civilized if it lacked a first-class string quartet. He raised the money, and the result was the Lydian Quartet, one of the best in the world. The Lyds, as they are lovingly called, not only were excellent performers; for many years they also have been gifted teachers and good colleagues—very active in the life of the university.

Bernstein also helped support musicology, especially early music. Robert Marshall and his colleagues made Brandeis a leading center for Bach studies and helped lay the foundation for a global revival of early music.[36]

They recruited Margaret Bent from Britain, a leading scholar in the field. She became chair of the department, and later moved to Princeton and then to Oxford. They also kept Brandeis growing in composition, with a talented and diverse group of composers in the prime of their productive careers.

One of the most important areas for Brandeis was Near Eastern and Judaic studies. It was Bernstein who recruited Jehuda Reinharz as a faculty leader. Reinharz remembers that Bernstein invited him into his small home in Weston. To Reinharz's amazement, Bernstein himself went into the kitchen and cooked the meal, while Sheva Bernstein did the interview. It was an odd way to recruit top talent, but it worked. Reinharz left a flourishing program at Michigan and came to Brandeis as the Richard Koret Professor of Modern Jewish History.

Stewards of the Undergraduate College

Bernstein told me that he found one sort of fund-raising easier than all others. Whenever he asked for money to help students directly, "The checkbooks always came out." Part of it was about how he did the asking. When he sought help with scholarships, he did it with passion and conviction, and no embarrassment at all. A major result was continuing strength in the gifted young people who came to Brandeis in those years.

Some colleagues remember the 1970s as a period of decline in the quality of Brandeis students. I did not see it in history courses. My undergraduates and graduate students had been excellent in the 1960s. During the 1970s they were even stronger—among the strongest I have taught in any university. In 1974, for example, a Brandeis undergraduate came to my office. He was a politics major, with a particular interest in political philosophy and public ethics. He asked if he could do an independent readings course on the political and social thought of the American founders, in the era of the American Revolution and the New Republic. We did many independent courses of that sort, numbered History 98, one student and one teacher, meeting once a week to discuss the readings and do some writing.

The student was Michael Sandel. He came to us from Minneapolis and Los Angeles, where he was president of his senior class at Palisades High School. He had extraordinary gifts for working with ideas and people.

There was a quality of contagious optimism about him, and a confidence that the progress of knowledge and truth could make things better, which in turn inspired a passion for teaching and learning. Like so many of my Brandeis undergraduates, he was a student who taught his teacher. I was delighted to learn more from him than he did from me. Sandel became a Rhodes Scholar at Oxford, earned a doctorate with Charles Taylor at Balliol College, and went on to a brilliant career at Harvard. His writings have reshaped the field of moral philosophy. A course called "Justice" became one of the largest at Harvard, with an enrollment of eleven hundred students in 2007. Sandel taught it in Memorial Hall with a roving microphone and an intensity of individual interaction—a remarkable feat. Then he began to teach on an even larger scale, with a TV series called *Justice: What's the Right Thing to Do?* and experiments in podcasts, webcasts, and master classes on ethics for thousands of students in an Asian soccer stadium.

We had many superb students at Brandeis in the 1970s. Bernstein's team gave strong support to special efforts at individual teaching and learning. In the early seventies, I was teaching the new social history at Brandeis, working from large piles of empirical evidence (a primitive form of Big Data) to reconstruct the main lines of change in American history. Five seniors in the class of 1974 became interested, and Jack Goldstein made possible an experiment in teaching. The students, Marc Harris, James Kimenker, Richard Weintraub, Susan Kurland, and JoAnn Early Levin, all wrote senior honors theses on the new social history of the town of Concord, Massachusetts, from 1750 to 1850. In the first semester they reconstituted every family in the town from quantitative data found mostly in manuscripts. They processed the data with the Brandeis mainframe computer, which had less capacity than our cell phones do today, and in the spring each student wrote a separate thesis on the main lines of change in demography, economics, social structure, education, and politics, Later we added another thesis on the environmental history of Concord by Brian Donahue. Jack Goldstein found a few thousand dollars that enabled us to publish the theses in single volume. We did it again for other New England towns.[37]

The quality of these linked projects in teaching and research was strong in the 1970s, perhaps stronger than in the 1960s, because we were learning how to do it. It was an experimental artifact of the Brandeis Idea, and of a unique institution that Bernstein and Goldstein and Steinberg led forward during its most difficult decade.

The hard times took a toll. Buildings were neglected. Roofs leaked. Heating systems failed from time to time, and office furniture fell apart. But all of that mattered very little when students and faculty and the leaders of the university were absolutely first-class.

Stewards of the Institutional Culture

The labor of leading Brandeis was intense and unremitting. Finally, after eleven years of toil, Bernstein reached the age of sixty-five. He and the board agreed that it was time to retire. His services were much in demand, but he wanted to get on with his scholarship and accepted an appointment as university professor at Georgetown University. Bernstein had many years of creative service still ahead when he and his wife Sheva died suddenly in an Egyptian hotel fire, to the shock and horror and sadness of all who knew them.

Jack Goldstein remembered the contributions of Marver and Sheva Bernstein in a graceful speech and essay. On their Brandeis years, he observed that "this university, perhaps more than any other, lives on countless individual acts of faith, large and small. Students perform acts of faith when they decide to come here; faculty perform acts of faith when they decide to stay. . . . donors and supporters give if they trust, or else go elsewhere. Such acts of faith can continue only if at the core of Brandeis there is something—and someone—good and worthwhile and solid and dependable." He added that in the light of his experience, "If the University had not managed, in those difficult years, to maintain its character and its integrity, there would be little point in trying to search for them now."[38]

In that spirit, Marver and Sheva Bernstein, Jack Goldstein, and David Steinberg brought this university through a dangerous era. They did it by rallying others to their cause, by recruiting many open leaders, and by strengthening the material fabric of the institution. They put the finances of the university on a stronger foundation than ever before. For all the complaints about fund-raising, they quietly multiplied the endowment fivefold in hard times. They revived the faculty and recruited outstanding students. But most of all they strengthened Brandeis in another way.

Their greatest contribution was the gift of their integrity. That gift still has an enduring presence in the institution.

Jehuda Reinharz: Transformative President of Brandeis, 1994–2010

Universities find their presidents in many ways. Most appoint search committees of trustees, faculty, and students, with very mixed results. Others hire head hunters at high expense and sometimes dismal consequences. A third method was tried at Brandeis by Samuel Thier, president from 1991 to 1994. Sam, as everyone called him, was a physician and a professor of medicine at Yale and Harvard. He did important research in nephrology, earned many awards for teaching, and had a long history of experience as a leader in complex institutions. Thier also combined two strengths that do not always coexist in academe: intelligence and judgment. He came to the presidency after another difficult period when many universities struggled with external challenges, and Brandeis suffered internal divisions. One was a regrettable and entirely avoidable controversy about how "Jewish" Brandeis should be. The first thing that this physician did was to heal the university. He did it by a quiet example of competence, strength, and decency—an extraordinary success for open leadership.

He also did something else. From the moment of his inauguration, Thier was thinking about his successor. In 1991 he appointed Jehuda Reinharz as provost and senior vice president for academic affairs, and gave him much responsibility in quasi-presidential roles, with excellent results. In 1994 Thier took another job, eventually running Boston's major hospitals, and Reinharz moved easily into the Brandeis presidency. It was the smoothest and most successful presidential transition in the history of the university —a credit to both men.

Reinharz brought to his presidency a strength of character that set him apart from most academic leaders of his generation. He had been born in Haifa in 1944. His formative years were also those of Israel as an independent nation, and he shared the large spirit of that beginning. In 1958 his family moved to Germany, and three years later to the United States, where he graduated from high school in Newark, New Jersey. Reinharz took pride in having started in America as a first-generation immigrant.

In his inaugural address as president of Brandeis, he said, "When my family and I landed in New York City, I had no money, knew no English, and had no immediate relatives who had attended college."[39]

Everywhere he excelled, as an undergraduate at Columbia and valedictorian at the Jewish Theological Seminary; as winner of top fellowships in medieval Jewish history at Harvard and modern Jewish history at Brandeis; and as a teacher and scholar in Michigan's excellent history department, where he founded a new program in Judaic studies and raised money for three positions. Then Marver Bernstein recruited him to join the faculty at Brandeis, and Samuel Thier prepared him for the presidency.

Reinharz's origins and early career gave him a distinctive way of thinking about that job. American university presidents of his generation understood their roles in different ways. After many years of academic stress and strife in the late twentieth century, more than a few presidents thought of themselves as mediators, which many trustees and faculty wanted them to be. In a period of rising costs, shrinking resources, and economic instability, they learned to master the art of small solutions, because large ones were rarely in reach. Reinharz was not like that. He was a driver, a developer, a builder, and an entrepreneur. I have always been struck by his optimism, his large purposes, and his confidence that they could be achieved.

He also had a clear idea of what Brandeis was about. When he came to Brandeis, Abram Sachar was still chancellor, and the two men became friends. Reinharz said that "Sachar was very important to me." From Sachar and his own experience, Reinharz formed a deep respect for the founding vision of Brandeis. One of Reinharz's first and most symbolic acts was to raise money for the construction of the Brandeis Archives. He also funded an endowment for a first-class university archivist. I asked him why. He answered, "A university that forgets its past will not have a future."

Even as he built on the Brandeis Idea, as president Reinharz intended to lead the university in new directions. He did it very much as an open leader. From the start Reinharz made himself highly accessible to faculty and students. He had an open-door policy and took pride in rapid response to e-mails. He genuinely liked to work with people as individuals and small groups, and he listened intently to what they had to say. Always he was an open leader, but most of all Reinharz really meant to lead, with serious goals in mind. More than that, he became something rare in academe at that time: a great transformative leader who changed the structure of the university in fundamental ways.

Transforming the Board of Trustees

Reinharz began to lead in a transformative way even before he took the job. When the trustees asked him to be president, he asked something of them in return. Reinharz explained that the performance of almost everyone at Brandeis was evaluated on a regular basis: students, staff, faculty, and the president all were evaluated at frequent intervals—with one exception. Nobody evaluated the trustees. Reinharz asked that members of the board also agree to be evaluated, and not by the board itself. He observed that if trustees evaluated other trustees, everybody would be found to be a fine person. He proposed another plan—that every trustee would be evaluated individually every year. It would be done by the president and the board chair, on the basis of eight criteria. The central concern was the active engagement of board members in the growth and development of Brandeis, which could be done in many ways. For example, one of the eight criteria was: "How effective is the trustee at opening doors for Brandeis?" Reinharz regarded this function as one of the most important contributions that a trustee could make. Few incoming presidential candidates (none of my acquaintance) would have proposed such a grading system for a board of trustees. Fewer would have succeeded. The Brandeis trustees agreed, for the good of the university.

Then Reinharz went to work enlarging the Brandeis board and broadening its base. He persuaded many prominent leaders to join. A leading example in every sense was D. Ronald "Ron" Daniel, senior partner at McKinsey, member of the Harvard Corporation, treasurer of Harvard University, and chairman of the Harvard Management Company. Another was Vartan Gregorian, Armenian immigrant, historian, and a truly great academic leader. Gregorian and Daniel recruited other board members and opened many a door for Brandeis.

Reinharz brought in Ann Richards, the former governor of Texas, who came to teach a course at Brandeis and was a huge success with students and faculty. Everyone who worked with her was impressed by her intellect, judgment, political skill, and good humor. She became a very active member of the board. Reinharz remembers that Ann Richards was instrumental in meetings, applying Texas methods to concentrate minds on the business at hand. She also opened doors in more ways than one, engaging others to join in, helping with her political connections throughout the country, and enlisting new supporters in Texas.

Another of Reinharz's recruits for the board was Jack Connors, a leading businessman in Boston, prominent Catholic layman, chairman of the board for Boston's largest health care organization, chairman of the board at Boston College, and a trustee of many major institutions, with a web of connections unrivaled in Boston. He became a trusted friend and advisor.

Altogether, forty-eight new members agreed to join the board. As the numbers rose, so also did quality, commitment, and service. The Brandeis board became stronger, more diverse, and more active than ever.

The Transformation of Fund-Raising

The most striking and visible result of Reinharz's presidency was his success in transforming the process of fund-raising. Its growth after his inauguration was unprecedented. Reinharz had a rare gift for fund-raising. Jack Connors had worked with many chief executives, and he said that Reinharz "knows how to raise money." He became the most effective fund-raiser in the history of the university.[40] Altogether, Reinharz raised $1.2 billion for Brandeis, more than all other presidents combined, even when adjusted for inflation.

Reinharz's fund-raising had many strengths. The first was that he genuinely loved to do it, and he had a special way of thinking about what he was doing. He said, "I like to raise money. . . . For me, raising money is about making friends. It's a way of bringing more people into a circle that keeps growing." His purpose was not only to raise money, but also to enlarge that circle and strengthen its base. He also believed deeply in his purposes and goals for Brandeis, and in the vital importance of what he was about. A deep sense of purpose and resolve helped him to reach others and to bring them into the growing circle.

As president and fund-raiser, Reinharz was blessed with many personal strengths. He was, and is, very bright, articulate, energetic, creative, and charismatic. When Ann Richards met him for the first time, she said, "I didn't know you were so handsome." More important, he was deeply informed about his job, about scholarship and teaching, about the way that universities work, and about the many different people who lead these complex institutions. He works well with people because he is genuinely interested in them. And he has an infinite capacity for taking pains.

But the success of his fund-raising was not achieved primarily through the gifts of charisma and personal charm, useful as they may have been. When he came to the presidency, Reinharz built a highly effective system of fund-raising, far beyond the efforts of others who had preceded him. With great difficulty he recruited Nancy Winship to run this system, with the title of senior vice president for institutional advancement. She had held one of the top jobs in Jewish philanthropy, and every effort was made by her colleagues to keep her. Nancy insisted that Reinharz must be interviewed by her family and also by her children, which he remembers as one of his toughest challenges. Afterward she called and said, "You passed." Reinharz worked closely with her and with an able staff. Fund-raising at Brandeis became more professional and more systematic than ever before. It was organized with many specialized subunits, each with its own web of leaders.

One unit centered on corporations and foundations. Earlier presidents had worked effectively with foundations, but not so well with corporations. Reinharz and his team had unprecedented success with them. Together they were able to establish a fully funded professorship in the philosophy department, called the J. P. Morgan Chase Chair in Ethics, after the Wall Street firm that contributed the money. This same fund-raising unit also worked with foundations on major gifts. The Mellon Foundation became very supportive of Brandeis, with graduate research grants, postdoctoral fellowships, junior faculty positions, and much more.

Other units centered on alumni. In the early classes their numbers were small and assets smaller. For many years, most Brandeis alumni did not contribute to their alma mater. Every president tried to build relationships with graduates. Jehuda did it on a new scale and by a new method. A central rule was, "Pay attention." With the open leadership of Allen Alter and Paul Zlotoff, the Brandeis Alumni Association was reconstructed. Reinharz founded new programs for alumni and personally led eight alumni trips. Many participants who had never contributed to the university prior to these trips did so afterward. In Reinharz's presidency, Brandeis alumni even began to approach the extraordinary participation rates of Princeton and Dartmouth, who led the way. Participation is the key. From 1995 to 2010, participation rates rose from low levels to among the highest in American higher education. Altogether, annual giving by alumni multiplied sevenfold in fourteen years, from $3.2 million to $25 million a year. So also did the scale of giving: in those years thirty-seven Brandeis alumni made individual gifts of a million dollars or more, and as large as $16 million.

Three major capital campaigns also gave particular attention to the identity and recruitment of new donors who had no prior connection to the university. One campaign alone added 154 donors who each gave a million dollars. A third of them had never given to Brandeis before.

A vital concern was to keep faith with donors and to respect the purposes of their gifts. Here again Reinharz wrought a revolution in the university's financial practices. In earlier years Sachar had raised money for many specific purposes and created specific endowments for those purposes. In moments of fiscal stress some of these small endowments were integrated into the general funds of the university; others were spent to pay for current expenses. Some of the faculty talked with Reinharz about the problem. He ordered that funds should be transferred back and used for the purpose of the original gift.

Reinharz systematized these practices and extended them through the entire fund-raising operation. Yet another special group was established, called the Donor Relations Unit. Its task was to track individual contributions and to make sure that they were used for the purpose that the donor had intended. Every individual gift was studied meticulously, in a process that carefully followed the movement of money in each individual gift for a particular purpose, whatever it may have been—buildings, student scholarships, graduate fellowships, faculty chairs, and many other things. Reinharz also insisted on close and continuing relations with as many donors as possible. This too was done.

More elaborate efforts were made to improve record keeping, with close audits and detailed accounting. All this ensured much more control and reduced possibilities for error. This infinite capacity for taking pains, and close attention to small questions and large issues, made a huge impact in terms of repeat contributions. The work was done by letters, phone calls, and personal contacts. E-mails were answered quickly. Reinharz himself played a very active role, once again working closely with many others.

The community of donors at Brandeis might be thought of as a complex set of interlocking circles. They are defined not by the size of their contributions but by the nature of their relationship with the university. One circle consists of what is sometimes called the "Brandeis inner family." These are people who donate not only money but time and energy and affection. They are deeply devoted to Brandeis, and together they are in many ways much like a family. From time to time, there are family quarrels, but more often there is family affection, loyalty, and love. This "inner family" grew greatly in Reinharz's presidency.

He formed close friendships with donors such as Morton Mandel, who begins a volume of his memoirs with stories about Jehuda. "In my book," Morton Mandel wrote, "he is a world class educator, a widely respected scholar, a humanitarian, and an undisputed A player."[41] The Mandel Foundation, now larger than the Carnegie Corporation, gave strong support to Brandeis, especially for the humanities. The Mandel family became very active in the "inner family," contributing time and energy to the university. Barbara Mandel, Morton's wife, became a major leader on the board. In all of these ways, Jehuda strengthened the process of fund-raising by making it a family affair in more ways than one.

The Endowment Transformed

Much of the money went into the growth of the endowment—a larger proportion than ever before. Throughout its history the endowment of Brandeis had been painfully small—perhaps about $29 million when Sachar left office, maybe less than $19 million when Morris Abram departed. Marver Bernstein succeeded very quietly in increasing the endowment to between $90 and $100 million, no small feat. When Reinharz took office the total endowment of the university had grown to about $195 million in fiscal 1995. He revolutionized those numbers. In his administration the Brandeis endowment reached a peak of $718 million in 2008. The Great Recession drove it down again to about $620 million, but it climbed back quickly, to more than $700 million by the time that

Reinharz left office in 2010. These numbers were without precedent in the history of the university.

Reinharz also created a new position of chief operating officer and recruited Peter French to fill it. Together they created a "rainy day fund," which increased from $10 million in 1994 to $110 million. This contingency fund made a difference in the downturn of 2001–2003 and helped the university to weather a hard blow in the Great Recession of 2008–2010.

The Transformation of Undergraduate Recruitment

At the top of Reinharz's list was what he regarded as his most urgent task — improving access to affordable higher education for young people. In his inaugural address at Brandeis, he talked of his own beginnings, of coming to America in his teens unable to speak English. He remembered that he could go to college only because he got help from many people. Reinharz believed that this is the sort of sacred debt that we incur to one generation and repay to another. Through his seventeen years at Brandeis that is exactly what he tried to do. He made a major effort to find money for student scholarships, raising $167 million for that purpose alone.

Reinharz also tried to control the surging cost of tuition for undergraduates and their families — a major social problem. The drivers of these rising costs are as broad as the expanding budgets of universities. A major factor is the huge expansion of administration and the growing bureaucratization of many institutions in the United States. Here he had mixed results. Tuition continued to rise at Brandeis during his presidency. But the university did better than most institutions in controlling rates of increase. In fiscal year 2000, by the measure of tuition and fees actually charged to undergraduates, Brandeis was the fifth most costly university in the United States. By fiscal year 2010, costs at Brandeis had fallen to fifty-sixth place. When room and board were added to the computation, Brandeis fell to seventy-sixth place — a remarkable relative improvement that continued through much of his presidency.

Other problems also existed in the recruitment of undergraduates. Here again Reinharz acted decisively at the start of his presidency. He transformed the admissions process by changing the criteria for admission, with more attention to motivation for coming to Brandeis. His object was to recruit students who really wanted to be here. That factor had not been as prominent before. Earlier admissions gave more attention to scores and numbers. Two things changed as a consequence. Admissions statistics improved in such a magnitude as to constitute a revolution in undergraduate recruitment. The number of applicants increased sharply. The proportion of applicants accepted by the university fell, from 68 percent in 1994 to 32 percent in 2010. Board scores and rank in class improved. By 2010, 87 percent of entering students were in the top 10 percent of their graduating classes. At the same time, the student body became more diverse in ethnicity, nationality, and religion. Students of color rose from 11 percent in 1994 to 28 percent in 2010. Overall, on Reinharz's watch, the rank of Brandeis in US News and World Report rose from thirty-four to thirty-one among national research universities.

A second result was an improvement in undergraduate morale. Here again, a major factor was the change that Reinharz introduced in criteria for admission, with more attention to students for whom Brandeis was their first choice. After the new policy took effect, Brandeis began to be ranked in national surveys as among the happiest colleges in the United States.[42]

There were many other elements as well. The dining system was transformed in structure and function, with more attention to the quality of food, healthy diets, and the ambience of dining areas. Ratings by students showed strong patterns of improvement and satisfaction.

Most important, with Reinharz's encouragement, Brandeis students increasingly took an active role in shaping their own institution. An example was Deborah Bial, a Brandeis alumna who was struck by the importance of mutual support among undergraduates. An Hispanic student at Brandeis told her about an informal circle of friends who functioned as her "posse," helping her to cope with the challenges of college life. In 1989 Bial took the lead in founding the Posse Foundation, to encourage the same thing on a larger scale. A primary purpose was to recruit and train leaders in high school, so that they could encourage the formation of "posses" of ten to twelve students, help them to gain admission to strong colleges, succeed in their studies, and function as leaders after college. Funds were raised for scholarships, and thousands of young people applied. The record was stunning. Of those who joined the Posse program, often from disadvantaged high schools, more than 90 percent graduated from college. This system spread rapidly to forty colleges and universities. Deborah Bial received a MacArthur fellowship in 2007 and honorary degrees from many universities, including Brandeis, her alma mater. Her role was a classic example of open leadership among students and recent alumni, which Reinharz greatly encouraged. He did it again with Jonah Seligman, an undergraduate leader who founded a program on leadership and mustered support from trustees, administrators, alumni, and students.[43]

The Transformation of Undergraduate Education

Jehuda Reinharz also presided over a fundamental change in the structure of undergraduate education at Brandeis. From the start, teaching and learning had centered on basic disciplines in the arts and sciences. This vision of the founders had been shared by Abram Sachar, Marver Bernstein, and many Brandesians.

From time to time others had thought about adding professional schools. Sachar received a serious proposal for a medical school, and Abram strongly believed that a university named for Louis Brandeis should have a law school. Every passing year brought talk about these initiatives and others like them. All but one were defeated. The faculty in arts and science was strongly opposed to a scattering of scarce resources, and trustees were keenly aware of the heavy costs of medical schools and law schools. The only major exception was the Heller School, a top-quality postgraduate school, founded for the professional training of administrators in welfare programs and highly regarded in its field.

For undergraduates, many small preprofessional programs were created through the years to help them prepare for careers in teaching, communications, journalism, and other fields. A larger effort was made for premedical preparation. But all of these programs were "minors," without strong material resources, and they were not accepted by the faculty as fields of concentration.

Reinharz broke decisively with this policy. He strongly supported an array of new professional programs for both undergraduate and postgraduate students. He also encouraged synergies with the basic disciplines of the arts and sciences.

In that regard, a major change was introduced at the Heller School.

Here Reinharz led a transformative reform with many interlocking parts. First, he integrated the Heller School more fully into the life of the university. For many years it had operated apart from the undergraduate curriculum and departments in the arts and sciences. A new undergraduate prevocational major was created and called Health, Science, Society and Policy. The leaders were Peter Conrad in Sociology and Stuart Altman, a leading expert on health care systems. The faculty of the program included scholars from the Heller School and many academic departments of the arts and sciences. The new major grew rapidly into one of the most popular concentrations in the university and qualitatively one of the best. Stuart Altman himself taught the introductory course, which became one of the largest in the university.

Reinharz undertook a broad series of reforms to strengthen the Heller School, already one of the best of its kind in the nation. He launched yet another massive fund-raising effort for a large expansion of its plant and programs, and fully endowed three new professorships. He also sought to attract more world-class scholars to the Heller School. It was Reinharz who recruited Robert Reich to move from his job as secretary of labor to Brandeis as a university professor. Reich taught both undergraduate and graduate courses in the Heller School, and he also ran a very active faculty seminar on social justice. My book on fairness and freedom first was presented as a paper to Reich's group, and he helped it along. He contributed in a major way to the life of the university and to linkages between the Heller School and the arts and sciences.

Another major contribution was the appointment of Lisa Lynch as the head of the Heller School. She was a leader in her field of labor economics, was director of research in the Department of Labor, and held senior appointments in the Federal Reserve. She was respected as a prolific scholar of great importance in her field, as a teacher who won prizes at MIT for both undergraduate and graduate courses, and as an able leader and excellent colleague. All of this raised the Heller School to a new standard of excellence. Much of it happened on Reinharz's watch, and he was directly involved.

Something similar happened in another set of new vocational programs that multiplied in business and finance. In 1994, at the beginning of Reinharz's presidency, a new school was founded as the Brandeis

International Business School. Its first dean was Peter Petri, a superb choice. He was a long-serving member of the Brandeis faculty, a scholar highly respected in his field, an excellent leader, a highly effective promoter of his program, and a first-class teacher. A new undergraduate major in business also was founded, with overlapping faculties in economics and international finance. It rapidly became the largest field of concentration at Brandeis.

Yet a third professional major developed from a very small education program, which for many years had been an orphan at Brandeis. Reinharz expanded it to a full-fledged major, gave it a building of its own, and funded endowed professorships in teacher education. The program began to operate on a much larger scale than before, both for undergraduates and graduate students.

A fourth professional program was international and global studies. Its purpose was to prepare undergraduates for global careers in many fields. It was staffed mostly by colleagues in the arts and sciences, and it rapidly became a major field of concentration in its own right. Together, these new programs wrought a major change in the Brandeis curriculum. Here again, Reinharz was the driver.

Increasing Support for Programs in the Arts and Sciences

At the same time Reinharz also expanded support for the traditional arts and sciences. He raised the money for a large and very handsome new building, the Mandel Center for the Humanities. It became a home for programs in philosophy, literature, and other disciplines. Simultaneously he worked to strengthen the history program by establishing its endowment on a firm foundation, and in 2005 he was instrumental in securing another million-dollar gift from the Crown Foundation for graduate fellowships.

In the creative arts, Reinharz built a large addition to the Rose Art Museum. The natural sciences also flourished. His largest building project was a huge expansion of facilities for scientific research. The biological sciences in general, and neuroscience in particular, grew rapidly during his presidency.

Altogether, between 1994 and 2010, Reinharz raised money for seventeen centers and institutes, and thirty-six professorships in nearly all departments of the humanities, social sciences, history, the natural sciences, and the creative arts. He insisted that each of these chairs should be fully funded, which in most cases required an endowment of $3 million or more. He also raised another $5 million for the permanent endowment of postdoctoral Kay Fellows and Mellon Fellows in the humanities and social sciences. These postdoctoral fellows added many lively and pathbreaking courses throughout the university and strengthened their own careers. Here was yet another transformative change in the material base of the Brandeis curriculum.

The Transformation of Undergraduate Education: Multiple Majors

The combined result of these changes was a new way of thinking about the structure of undergraduate education at Brandeis. Since the mid-twentieth century, leading American colleges and universities had organized their curricula around a concept of general education and mastery of a single major.

In the 1990s this model faded rapidly in American higher education, in two ways at once. During Reinharz's presidency, Brandeis undergraduates themselves seized the initiative. They began to adopt multiple fields of concentration on an unprecedented scale. By 2010 only about 20 percent of Brandeis students graduated with a single major. They began to invent their own complex programs in every imaginable combination—and some that were unimaginable. The faculty and administrators did not invent this system and tried to limit it. In 2014 the maximum allowable number was, incredibly, six areas of concentration: no more than three majors and three minors.

The most common number was two or three areas of concentration: a professional major in business, health and human services, global studies, or education (the top four choices), and a nonvocational concentration in various disciplines of the humanities, social sciences, natural sciences, and creative arts. Other concentrations centered on mastery of skills such as languages, or computer science, or programs for personal development.

Many faculty members did not favor this new trend. Registrars and deans complained that it made their lives a living hell. Students did not agree. Multiple majoring allows students to center their education on their own personal combinations of choices and needs. It also creates new ways of combining concentrations with general education. Brandeis students have taken the lead, and they have gone farther and faster than other universities.[44] The trend is now spreading rapidly in most American colleges. Reinharz made it possible by leading a transformation of the traditional curriculum at Brandeis. He added strong preprofessional majors to a very strong and appealing array of concentrations in the arts and sciences.

Transforming the Campus

At the same time, Reinharz led another effort to transform the physical condition of the campus and its many buildings. He did it in a very purposeful way. Early in his presidency, he sent invitations to Brandeis graduates who had made careers in architecture and landscape design. He asked them to visit the university and to study it as an image and an artifact, and to think about its improvement. They observed that the campus was overcrowded with small buildings. Some said that it lacked a center; others, that it needed a spine. Many urged more attention to the preservation of open space. Reinharz went to work on all of those problems in several ways at once. He worked to protect and preserve the open space of Chapel Field and to give it more presence on the campus. He also joined several paths together into a broad landscaped avenue that ran through the academic quadrangle at the top of the campus, then along the east side of the library, and downhill beside Chapel Field. It continued through a broad expanse of flowering trees to another open field between the new student center and the administration buildings, and on to the music building at the south end of the campus.

Then he created a large building program, not only to add more usable space, but also to reduce the clutter of small structures. The result added 486,000 square feet of space (an increase of more than 15 percent) in twenty-nine entirely new or radically renovated buildings. He established a fixed rule: for every new building that went up, an old building had to come down. The result was a reduction in the total number of buildings on campus from one hundred to ninety-seven. Much attention was given to the modernization of infrastructure. Systems for heating and cooling were transformed. Sweeping changes were made in the design and equipment of classrooms and lecture halls. A major program was added for landscaping. Parking lots were moved to the periphery of the campus. When I complained to Reinharz about time and distance, I was told to buy a motor scooter, which Reinharz himself used to get around. Altogether, the result was a sweeping physical transformation of the Brandeis campus, and much the largest and most successful building program since Sachar's presidency.

Transforming the Brandeis Idea:
Judaism and Pluralism Together

Reinharz also worked at reframing the Brandeis Idea. He thought of the university as dedicated to what he called the "four pillars" of excellence: social justice, pluralism, and sponsorship by and service to the Jewish community. All of these ideas had been present at the creation of Brandeis. Reinharz made them stronger and deeper. He began by strengthening the university's commitment to its Jewish heritage and also to pluralism, both at the same time. Like Sachar and Bernstein before him, Reinharz saw no conflict or contradiction in these two goals. He saw an opportunity to enlarge the identity of the institution in two ways at once. Once again he did it in a transformative way, reframing commitments to Judaism and to pluralism in ways that went far beyond the principles and acts of his predecessors.

Throughout his long presidency he founded and funded many programs, dedicated to the study and teaching of Judaism, and also to service to the Jewish community in highly practical and specific ways. He founded the Fisher-Bernstein Institute for Jewish Philanthropy and Leadership, and a master's program for Public Policy and Jewish Professional Leadership. He endowed an Institute for Informal Jewish Learning, the Mandel Center for Studies in Jewish Education, and a new Hadassah-Brandeis Institute. A separate undergraduate major in Hebrew language was created during his tenure as president and he raised endowments for the new Schusterman Chair in Israeli Art, the Edmond J. Safra Chair in Sephardic Studies, and the Karl, Harry and Helen Stoll Chair in Israel Studies.

Reinharz thought of this effort in a very large-spirited way. Jonathan Sarna wrote, "He glories in the university's Jewishness." A California journalist added, "President Reinharz has been able to articulate a vision for the university that makes its ties to the Jewish community central to what the university is about." More than that, he understood this linkage as a global enterprise. "Brandeis is a microcosm of world Jewry," he explained to a journalist. "This imposes special obligations on us."[45]

At the same time Reinharz promoted nonsectarian pluralism, also in highly specific ways. He expanded active recruitment of students and faculty of many different religions, nationalities, and ethnic groups on a global scale. He personally led global trips for the purpose of recruiting students in Argentina, Brazil, Colombia, Mexico, China, Korea, India, Turkey, Jordan, and Israel. By 2010, 12 percent of Brandeis students came from countries other than the United States, and the numbers were rapidly increasing.

He did the same thing in the United States and Canada. By the end of his presidency a majority of all Brandeis students were not Jewish, for the first time in the history of the university. Reinharz created stronger bases of support for Protestant and Catholic chaplains and services, and rehabilitated the three chapels that were central to the Brandeis Idea. He appointed the first imam in the history of the university, provided much support for Islamic observance on campus, and did the same thing for Asian religions.

Reinharz transformed another major part of the Brandeis mission by creating a more open and pluralist approach to Middle Eastern studies. He obtained a large endowment from the Crown family for a new Crown Center in Middle East Studies, and added strong support for Palestinian scholars such as Khalil Shikaki—and fiercely defended him and his academic freedom.

Some people at Brandeis were not happy about all this. In 1998, Hillel director for student activities Elisheva Rovner observed that "Brandeis has a huge identity problem.... on the one hand Brandeis wants to maintain its unique role at the forefront of the Jewish community, while on the other hand it has a desire for diversity."[46] Complaints were made on every side of the question. A small, deeply alienated, and very bitter minority of the faculty complained that Reinharz had made Brandeis "too Jewish." They themselves were often of no religion at all. They became Reinharz's implacable enemies.

Troubles

Reinharz was appointed for a series of five-year terms, beginning in 1994. By the middle of his third term, circa 2006, he was thinking that it was time for the presidency to pass into other hands. When he made his feelings known to the board of trustees, they responded with horror and did all in their considerable power to persuade him to continue for a fourth term. The board offered him a very generous financial contract. He reluctantly agreed.

Then, in 2007–2009, markets crashed throughout the world. Nobody knew how far down they would go. Brandeis was in better fiscal condition than ever before, but it was still vulnerable. The board had authorized heavy borrowing for a large construction project in the sciences. Worse, some of the university's most generous donors had invested heavily with Bernie Madoff. The university itself had not done so, and Brandeis lost a smaller proportion of its endowment than most institutions. But it was still dependent on annual giving to balance its operating budget, and the flow of contributions greatly diminished. Some members of the board of trustees wanted worst-case contingency plans, and they unanimously agreed that the university should make an announcement: if absolutely necessary, it could sell some very valuable paintings in the art museum. Some friends of Reinharz quietly urged him not to do it and warned that it would cause a media storm. But the board was unanimous, and the announcement went out. The result was not a storm but a hurricane of criticism in the media, some of which reported that the paintings actually had been sold. The announcement also explicitly had stated that nothing would be sold without the approval of the attorney general of Massachusetts and the agreement of donor families. In fact, nothing was sold. But the announcement itself was a big mistake. It did real damage to Brandeis, and Reinharz got the blame. He himself had been a strong supporter of the Rose Art Museum, had greatly enlarged it, and had increased its endowment, but he was personally attacked and even vilified outside and inside the university.

Other troubles developed over issues of academic freedom. One was about an exhibition called *Voices of Palestine*, of what some deemed to be intensely antisemitic art allegedly by Palestinian children. It caused an uproar. Reinharz asked the student who had mounted the exhibition to post curatorial materials of the usual kind with the images. She refused. He ordered it to be taken down, which caused another storm. A faculty committee concluded that the exhibition should have been curated, but that Reinharz had been wrong to order its removal without due process.

Another issue was about sanctions against a faculty member who had used the word "wetbacks" in class. When students complained, an angry provost required him to take "sensitivity training" and threatened him with dismissal. Reinharz was not involved until these rulings were reversed. "It never got to me," he said. But again he got the blame. All of these issues were resolved by various means before he left office.

By 2010 the endowment had largely recovered from its losses. Reinharz decided to retire from the presidency and take the job as president of the Mandel Foundation. He continued at Brandeis as the Koret Professor of Jewish History and director of the Tauber Institute for the Study of European Jewry.

After a long and brilliantly successful presidency, Reinharz left in a swirl of controversy. Something very similar had happened to Sachar. The two most successful leaders in the history of the university—Sachar and Reinharz—were also the most grievously abused. That pattern often recurred in other American universities. But these controversies have tended to fade, and the contributions have endured. Many Brandesians believe that we have been fortunate to have had Reinharz as president. He transformed the university, very much for the best, and is cherished and respected by many friends among faculty, alumni, trustees, and donors.

Conclusion

What have we learned from this inquiry? The first is that open institutions exist in great variety, and their leaders have led them successfully in different ways. Even if we confine our subject to one institution and to three of its most effective leaders, we find patterns of striking diversity in their character and purpose, and still more in the problems and opportunities that they faced. No single model of leadership fits them all. To search for a fixed idea is to miss the very nature of open leadership. It is also to lose two of the greatest strengths of open institutions, their flexibility and creativity.

But there are also some common themes. The first is that each open institution has its own distinctive culture, history, and traditions. The most effective leaders are attentive to the character of their institutions, even as they seek to change them in some respects.

A second finding is that open institutions need strong leaders, more so today than ever before, as power and authority have become more broadly distributed and even dispersed among trustees, faculties, students, alumni, administrators, private donors, and public regulators. A key to institutional success is a strong president within a frame of responsibility and accountability. The question is, how might one find and support strong leaders, how might they realize their strength?

First, Find Your Leader. This is the hardest task. With the best of intentions, our selection processes by ad hoc search committees have yielded mixed results. A better solution emerged from bitter experience in World War II. It developed in 1940–1942 within the US Navy's Submarine Service and was called the PCO, or the Prospective Commanding Officer system. As it evolved during the war, candidates for command were sent on a war patrol with an experienced skipper and were carefully observed in action. This way of identifying, teaching, and assessing leaders proved to be highly effective, and it has spread widely in many institutions.

Something similar to this method has been used in universities from time to time. At Brandeis, Samuel Thier used it when he put Jehuda Reinharz in a protopresidential role for three years. Many people watched while Reinharz learned about the job and others learned about him. The result, as we have seen, was the most successful presidential transition in the history of Brandeis.[47]

But often trustees must find a president more quickly. The Brandeis board was taken by surprise in most of its presidential transitions. In those situations, an acting presidency has been used twice, with Charles Schottland and Stuart Altman doing very well in that difficult role, while a search committee looked for a permanent president.

But under heavy pressure of time and circumstance, search committees have not functioned well. A sign of trouble appears in the fact that all but two Brandeis presidents were removed by the boards that appointed them. The only exceptions were Sam Thier and Jehuda Reinharz.

Something like a modified PCO system might be used in a more inven-

tive way, by a concerted effort to employ more people of presidential cal-
iber in the university and to watch them carefully. Whatever the method,
continuing review and careful assessment is critically important.

Assessing Presidential Performance: The Vision Test. Almost as difficult
as the challenge of appointing a president is the task of evaluating performance. One part of that process is clear enough. The three presidents
discussed here shared a vital strength in common. All of them began with
a clear idea of Brandeis, an understanding of its character, a memory of its
history, and a vision of its future.

Today most presidents are instructed to start in a different way, not
with a vision but a strategic plan, which commonly emerges from a set of
committees, or experts on strategic planning in general. The creation of
a strategic plan tends to be a protracted and costly process. I have seen
it continue for many months, even for more than a year. Presidents who
begin that way may gain something in the way of understanding, but they
lose one of the most valuable moments in their administration: the first
hundred days when other people are most supportive, and the institution
is more malleable than it will ever be again.

Our three leaders did not need to wait for the completion of an elaborate strategic plan. They had a vision and a purpose that served them well.
They also clearly understood the character of the university. They worked
with the grain of the institution even as they shaped it in new ways. And
all three were experienced scholars, teachers, and academic administrators. They thought of the university as a whole, set many plans in motion,
and studied their opportunities. It made all the difference.

The Test of Appointments. In many ways this is the most important and
most problematic of presidential roles. Thomas Jefferson wrote that in his
experience the most difficult task of presidential office is the appointment
of other officers. This is a critical problem in open systems. It frequently
appears in colleges and universities, and it is always the acid test of leadership. First-class leaders make first-class appointments. Second-class leaders make third-class appointments. Strong leaders are comfortable with
strength around them. Weak leaders are insecure and feel a need to sur-
round themselves with people who are even weaker. The three presidents
we have studied all made many strong appointments. Failure to do so in
top offices is quickly apparent. It is one of the earliest and most accurate

signs of a failed presidency and appears in two ways: the choice of weak leaders, and the removal of strong ones. When it happens repeatedly and a president is unwilling or unable to put it right, a board should correct its own failed appointment.

The Test of Opportunity. First-rate presidents are principled opportunists. All three of our presidents were very successful at this. They were quick off the mark and made effective use of the critical first period in their presidency. Sachar's early leadership was truly extraordinary in that way. Bernstein was quick to discover the depth of the problems before him and to act upon them. Reinharz seized major opportunities for Brandeis throughout his service.

The Test of Crisis Management. Presidential crises often take us by surprise, but they also are predictable in some ways. Every Brandeis president has dealt with a money crisis and with critical tests of academic freedom, to name but two. A common error of conscientious presidents is to act too quickly and to intervene too directly. Sachar was his own best critic in the Gough-Aberle affair (1962). He wrote, "As I look back upon the episode, I am inclined to agree that it was a mistake to take upon myself the full responsibility for the reprimand of Miss Gough. The issues of academic freedom are so sensitive that, since the times were tense and emotions ran high, I should have protected myself by having the dean of faculty or a faculty committee undertake the responsibility."[48] On these questions, faculty committees can be very helpful, especially when they are very slow to reach a conclusion. Often in moments of crisis a president might begin with a moment of inaction. A wise rule emerges from this experience. For a moment, at least, don't just do something—stand there!

The Test of Teaching and Research. At Princeton, nearly all presidents have continued to teach on a regular basis—sometimes a semester seminar every other year, sometimes less, sometimes more. William Bowen taught the introductory economics course while president. Something similar has happened at Brandeis. Sachar taught regularly, and Bernstein also did so from time to time. Reinharz made a point of visiting a class every week, always with permission. He often did the assigned reading in advance, and afterward wrote a letter of encouragement and support. He sat in on lectures and helped to teach a seminar on the history of leadership. At Brandeis, with its strong teaching traditions, it is vitally important for presidents to continue in a teaching role. Our three presidents all continued to work and publish actively in their scholarly disciplines. That continued engagement helped them to stay in touch, and it also helps others to remember what this institution is all about.

The Test of Excellence. Quality is critically important in every institution, but first-rate research universities must aspire to something more: the pursuit of excellence in teaching and research. The faculty themselves are central to this process, but it is a mistake to believe that faculty alone can achieve this goal. An active and leading role by the president is fundamental here. Sachar worked closely with his faculty, but his driving will to excel was the prime mover. It was the same again with Marver Bernstein and Jack Goldstein, and once more with Jehuda Reinharz.

In some of our strongest research universities, presidents sit on ad hoc committees and participate actively in the promotion to tenure. At Brandeis, President Evelyn Handler sat on ad hoc committees. She rarely spoke, but listened carefully and did not hesitate to overrule a recommendation if it did not meet the test of excellence. Other research universities have a central promotion committee that reviews all cases and reports directly to the president.

Abram Sachar, Marver Bernstein, and Jehuda Reinharz all were proactive in the pursuit of excellence. All three took the initiative in recommending strong appointments and engaging in recruitment, while working closely with faculty and deans. In a strong research university, this presidential role is fundamentally important, and it has a very long reach.

NOTES

The author wishes to thank Sylvia Fuks Fried, Paul Jankowski, Alice Kelikian, Jonathan Krasner, Jehuda Reinharz, Michael Sandel, Jonathan Sarna, Colin Steel, and Stephen Whitfield for their advice and criticism.

1. For the numbers, see Donald G. Tewksbury, *The Founding of American Colleges and Universities before the Civil War* (New York: Teachers College Press, 1932), 28; for discussion, see Frederick Rudolph, *The American College and University* (New York: Knopf, 1962; 2nd ed., Athens: University of Georgia Press, 1990), 47; for detail on individual institutions, see Richard Hofstadter and Wilson Smith, *American Higher Education; A Documentary History*, 2 vols. (Chicago: University of Chicago Press, 1961).

2. For histories of Brandeis see Stephen J. Whitfield, *Brandeis University at the Beginning* (Waltham, MA: Brandeis Office of Communications, 2010); David Hackett Fischer, "The Brandeis Idea: Variations on an American Theme," *Brandeis Review* 19 (fall–winter 1998): 26–30.

3. For data on institutions, enrollments, and degrees in American higher education, see US Office of Education, "Projections of Educational Statistics," in *Historical Statistics of the United States*, series H (Washington, DC: US Government Printing Office, 1970, 1976), 700–715, 731–65, 689–99. The magnitudes of these swings were large: degrees more than trebled from 1944 to 1951, then fell by nearly a third by 1955, and began to surge very rapidly from 1961 on. The number of American colleges actually declined in the early and mid-1950s.

4. Simon Rawidowicz, "Only from Zion: A Chapter in the Prehistory of Brandeis University," in *Israel: The Ever-Dying People and Other Essays*, ed. Benjamin Ravid (Rutherford, NJ: Fairleigh Dickinson University Press, 1986), 241.

5. The presidents and acting presidents of Brandeis have been: Abram Sachar, Charles Schottland, Morris Abram, Charles Schottland, Marver Bernstein, Evelyn Handler, Stuart Altman, Samuel Thier, Jehuda Reinharz, and Fred Lawrence—a total of nine, or ten if we count Charles Schottland twice.

6. Saul Cohen, *Memoirs of Saul G. Cohen: Scientist, Inventor*, Educator (Newton, MA: Montefiore Press, 2008), 211–12.

7. Silvan S. Schweber, *Einstein and Oppenheimer: The Meaning of Genius* (Cambridge: Harvard University Press, 2008), 102–108 passim; Jamie Sayen, *Einstein in America* (New York: Crown Books, 1985); Abram L. Sachar, *Brandeis University: A Host at Last*, ed. Jehuda Reinharz, rev. ed. (Lebanon, NH: University Press of New England; Waltham, MA: Brandeis University Press, 1995) 17–23, 38–39.

8. Israel Goldstein, *Brandeis University: Chapter of Its Founding* (New York: Bloch, 1951); Israel Goldstein, *My World as a Jew: The Memoirs of Israel Goldstein* (New York: Herzl Press, 1984).

9. Sachar, *Brandeis University*, 11–41.

10. Cohen, *Memoirs*, 199–218.

11. Sachar, *Brandeis University*, 29–33, 117.

12. For a mistaken view of Sachar as an "academic autocrat," see Nancy Diamond, "The 'Host at Last': Abram Sachar and the Establishment of Brandeis University," *Perspectives on the History of Higher Education* 28 (2011): 223–52; rpt. in Roger L. Geiger, ed., *Iconic Leaders in Higher Education*, vol. 28 (New Brunswick, ME: Transaction, 2011), 223–52, and also the editor's comments, xii. Sachar had his tyrannical moments, but he worked in a more open way that was vital to his success.

13. George Washington to Lord Stirling, Jan. 10, 1777, *The Papers of George Washington, Revolutionary War Series*, ed. W. W. Abbott et al., vol. 8 (Charlottesville: University of Virginia, 1988), 110–11.

14. Sachar, *Brandeis University*, 29–81, passim.

15. Cohen, *Memoirs*, 218.

16. David Hackett Fischer, "The Brandeis Idea: Variations on an American

Theme," *Brandeis Review* 19 (fall-winter, 1998): 26–29; Stephen J. Whitfield, *Brandeis University at the Beginning* (Waltham, MA: Brandeis University Press, 2010), 115–120; Abram L. Sachar, *Brandeis University*, 29–41, 43–45.

17. Ibid., 33–34, 37.

18. John Simpson and Jennifer Speake, eds., *Oxford Dictionary of Proverbs*, 5th ed. (online version) (Oxford: Oxford University Press, 2009), s.v. "always room."

19. Cohen, *Memoirs*, 230.

20. Ibid., 224. Sheryl Kaskowitz, "All in the Family: Brandeis University and Leonard Bernstein's 'Jewish Boston,'" *Journal of the Society for American Music* 3 (Feb. 2009): 85–100.

21. Cyrus H. Gordon, *A Scholar's Odyssey* (Atlanta: Society of Biblical Literature, 2000), 89.

22. Otto Vossler, *Die amerikanischen Revolutionsideale in ihrem Verhältnis zu den europäischen*, vol. 17 of *Historische Zeitschrift: Beiheft* (Münich and Berlin: R. Oldenbourg, 1929).

23. Gordon, *A Scholar's Odyssey*, 89; Pauli Murray, *The Autobiography of a Black Activist, Feminist, Lawyer, Priest, and Poet* (Knoxville: University of Tennessee Press, 1987), 389; Joyce Antler, "Pauli Murray: The Brandeis Years," *Journal of Women's History* 14 (2002): 1–5; Morton Keller, *My Times and Life* (Stanford: Stanford University Press, 2010), 86–90.

24. Stephen J. Whitfield, *Brandeis University at the Beginning* (Waltham, MA: Brandeis University Press, 2010), 89–90.

25. *Huffington Post*, August 20, 2012.

26. Sachar, *Brandeis University*, 324.

27. Conversation with Dean of the Graduate School Eugene Black.

28. Richard M. Freeland, *Academia's Golden Age: Universities in Massachusetts, 1945–1970* (Oxford: Oxford University Press,1992), 207–33.

29. Cohen, *Memoirs*, 272.

30. David Hackett Fischer, *The Great Wave, Price Revolutions and the Rhythm of History* (Oxford: Oxford University Press, 1996), 179–234.

31. Jack Goldstein, "In Memoriam: Marver and Shiva Bernstein," *Brandeis Review* (summer 1950): 44–47.

32. Ibid.

33. Marver Bernstein, "What the New President Should Know about Brandeis," *Brandeis Review* 2 (1983): 1; Fox Butterfield, "Higher Education: Brandeis Seeks to Restore Its Old Sense of Identity," *New York Times*, Nov. 11, 1984; Joshua Humphreys et al., *Educational Endowments and the Financial Crisis: Social Costs and Systemic Risks in the Shadow Banking System: A Study of Six New England Schools* (Boston: Center for Social Philanthropy, Tellus Institute, June 2010), 24, 32–36, 63.

34. Ibid.

35. Keller, *My Times and Life*, 95.

36. See, for example, the handsome tribute to Marshall's work in John Eliot Gar-

diner, *Bach: Music in the Castle of Heaven* (New York: Knopf, 2014), 210, xxviii, 146n, 194n, 205, 210–11, 213n.

37. Brian Donahue, Marc Harris, James Kimenker, Richard Weintraub, Susan Kurland, and JoAnn Early Levin, *Concord: The Social History of a New England Town* (Waltham, MA: Brandeis University Press, 1974, 1983).

38. Jack S. Goldstein, "In Memoriam," *Brandeis Review* 10, no. 1 (summer 1990): 44–47.

39. Jehuda Reinharz, "Inaugural Remarks as President, Brandeis University," April 9, 1995, Waltham, Massachusetts, typescript, p. 1.

40. *Boston Globe*, November 17, 2013. The best study of Morris Abram's career at Brandeis is Jonathan Krasner, "Seventeen Months in the President's Chair: Morris Abram, Black-Jewish Relations and the Anatomy of a Failed Presidency," paper presented at "Blacks, Jews and Social Justice in America" conference, Brandeis University, Waltham, Massachusetts, June 10–12, 2014. I am grateful to Professor Krasner for allowing me to read his paper and cite it here.

41. Morton L. Mandel, *It's All About Who* (San Francisco: Jossey-Bass/Wiley, 2013), 3.

42. "Top 10 Colleges with the Happiest Students," *Huffington Post*, August 30, 2012; Brandeis ranked sixth in this national survey.

43. For the history, mission statement, and activities of the Posse programs, see http://www.possefoundation.org.

44. For early comparative numbers see Tamar Levin, "For Students Seeking Edge, One Major Just Isn't Enough," *New York Times*, Nov. 17, 2002; Matthew Konjoian, "Students Load Up with Double Majors," *Justice*, January 28, 2003; Ben Sacks, "Are You a Double Major? At Brandeis, That Just Makes You Like Everyone Else," *Brandeis Hoot*, January 25, 2008.

45. Uriel Heilman, "At 50 Brandeis," *jweekly.com*, February 20, 1998.

46. Ibid.

47. Arnold Lotring and Jeff Fowler, "PCO Training: Making the Best Better," *Undersea Warfare* 2 (fall 1999): 1–4, http://navy.mil/navy/data/cno/n87/usw/issue_5/pco_training.html.

48. Sachar, *Brandeis University*, 254.

JEHUDA REINHARZ SELECT BIBLIOGRAPHY

Books

Fatherland or Promised Land? The Dilemma of the German Jew, 1893–1914. Ann Arbor: University of Michigan Press, 1975.

The Letters and Papers of Chaim Weizmann, 1918–1920, ser. A, vol. 9 (Oct. 1918–July 1920). Editor. Jerusalem: Israel Universities Press; New Brunswick, NJ: Rutgers University Press, 1977. Hebrew translation: *Kitvei Chaim Weizmann, Sidra Rishona: Igrot*, vol. 9 (October 1918–July 1920). Jerusalem: Mossad Bialik, 1978.

The Jew in the Modern World—A Documentary History. Coeditor with Paul R. Mendes-Flohr. Oxford: Oxford University Press, hardcover and paperback eds., 1980; 2nd ed., 1995; 3rd ed., 2011.

Dokumente zur Geschichte des deutschen Zionismus, 1882–1933. Editor. *Schriftenreihe Wissenschaftlicher Abhandlungen des Leo Baeck Instituts*, vol. 37. Tübingen: J. C. B. Mohr, 1981.

Mystics, Philosophers and Politicians, Essays in Jewish Intellectual History in Honor of Alexander Altmann. Coeditor with Daniel Swetschinski. Durham, NC: Duke University Press, 1982.

Israel in the Middle East: Documents and Readings on Society, Politics and Foreign Relations, 1882–Present. Coeditor with Itamar Rabinovich. Oxford: Oxford University Press, 1984. 2nd rev. and expanded ed. Waltham, MA: Brandeis University Press, 2008.

Chaim Weizmann: The Making of a Zionist Leader. Oxford: Oxford University Press, 1985. Paperback ed., Oxford University Press, 1987. Hebrew translation: *Chaim Weizmann baderekh el hamanhigut*. Jerusalem: Hasifriyah Hazionit, 1987.

The Jewish Response to German Culture: From the Enlightenment to World War II. Coeditor with Walter Schatzberg. Hanover, NH: University Press of New England, 1985. Paperback ed., 1991.

Living with Antisemitism: Modern Jewish Responses. Editor. Waltham, MA: Brandeis University Press, 1987. Paperback ed., Hanover, NH: University Press of New England, 1988.

Toldot hashomer hatsair begermanyah, 1931–1939. Givat Havivah: Sifriat Poalim, 1989.

The Jews of Poland between Two World Wars. Coeditor with Yisrael Gutman, Ezra Mendelsohn, and Chone Shmeruk. Waltham, MA: Brandeis University Press, 1989. Paperback ed., 1991.

The Impact of Western Nationalisms: Essays Dedicated to Walter Z. Laqueur on the Occasion of His 70th Birthday. Journal of Contemporary History 26, nos. 3–4 (September 1991). Guest editor with George Mosse. Expanded ed., London: SAGE Publications, 1992.

Chaim Weizmann: The Making of a Statesman. Oxford: Oxford University Press, 1993. Hebrew translation: *Chaim Weizmann: Aliyato shel medinai.* Jerusalem: Hasifriyah Hazionit, 1996.

Tsiyonut vedat. Coeditor with Anita Shapira and Shmuel Almog. Jerusalem: Merkaz Zalman Shazar, 1993. English translation: *Zionism and Religion.* Waltham, MA: Brandeis University Press, 1998.

Essential Papers on Zionism. Coeditor with Anita Shapira. New York: New York University Press, 1996.

Leumiyut upolitikah yehudit: Perspektivot hadashot. Coeditor with Yosef Salmon and Gideon Shimoni. Merkaz Zalman Shazar and Tauber Institute, 1996.

Zionism and the Creation of a New Society. Coauthor with Ben Halpern. Oxford: Oxford University Press, 1998. Rev. ed. in paperback, Waltham, MA: Brandeis University Press, 2000. Hebrew translation: *Hatsiyonut: Yetsiratah shel hevrah hadashah.* Jerusalem: Merkaz Zalman Shazar, 2000.

Idan hatsiyonut. Coauthor with Anita Shapira and Jay Harris. Jerusalem: Merkaz Zalman Shazar, 2000.

Im hazerem venegdo: Manyah Shohat, igrot veteudot 1906–1960. Coeditor with Shulamit Reinharz and Motti Golani. Jerusalem: Yad Ben Zvi, 2005.

Eropah hamehulelet vehamekulelet: Masah al yehudim, yisre'elim, eropah vetarbut hamaarav. Coauthor with Yaacov Shavit. Tel Aviv: Am Oved Publishers, 2006. English translation: *Glorious, Accursed Europe: An Essay on Jewish Ambivalence.* Waltham, MA: Brandeis University Press, 2010.

Darvin vekamah mibeney mino: Evolutsyah, geza, sevivah vetarbut: yehudim korim et darvin, spencer, bakel, verenan. Coauthor with Yaacov Shavit. Tel Aviv: Hakibbutz Hameuhad, 2009.

Aktueller Antisemitismus in Deutschland—Ein Phänomen der Mitte. Coeditor with Monika Schwarz-Friesel and Evyatar Friesel. Berlin: De Gruyter, 2010.

Hael hamadai: Mada populari beivrit bemizrah eropah bamahatsit hasheniyah shel hameah ha19.: Ben yeda utemunat yekum hadashah. Coauthor with Yaacov Shavit. Tel Aviv: Hakibbutz Hameuhad, 2011.

Haderekh leseptember 1939: Hayishuv, yehude polin vehatenuah hatsiyonit erev milhemet haolam hasheniyah. Coauthor with Yaacov Shavit. Tel Aviv: Am Oved Publishers, 2013.

Die Sprache der Judenfeindschaft im 21. Jahrhundert. Coauthor with Monika Schwarz-Friesel. Berlin: De Gruyter, 2013.

Hamoriut: Masa be'ikvot hahamor, mitologyah, alegoryah, simliut veklishaah. Coauthor with Yaacov Shavit. Jerusalem: Zalman Shazar, 2014.

"Ignác Goldziher: Renan ke'orientalist." Coedited with Yaacov Shavit. Forthcoming.

Pamphlets

The German Zionist Challenge to the Faith in Emancipation. Spiegel Lectures in European Jewish History, no. 2. Tel Aviv University, 1982.
Statecraft as the Art of the Possible. Annual Chaim Weizmann Lecture in the Humanities. Weizmann Institute of Science, 1992.
Writing the Biography of Chaim Weizmann. Annual Chaim Weizmann Lecture in the Humanities. Weizmann Institute of Science, 1992.
Zionism and the Great Powers: A Century of Foreign Policy. Leo Baeck Memorial Lecture, no. 38. New York: Leo Baeck Institute, 1994.

Articles

"The Lehrhaus in Frankfurt/Main." *Yavneh Review* (summer 1969): 7–29.
"Zionism in the United States: 1897–1972." *Encyclopedia Judaica* 16 (1973): 1141–49. Reprinted in *Zionism.* Israel Pocket Library series. Jerusalem: Keter Publishing House, 1973.
"Ideology and Practice in German Zionism, 1897–1914." In *Conference on Intellectual Policies in American Jewry.* Edited by Herbert A. Strauss, 52–64. New York: American Federation of Jews from Central Europe, 1972.
"The Farband—A Labor Zionist Movement." *Encyclopedia Judaica Year Book* 1 (1973): 201–202. Reprint, *Encyclopedia Judaica Supplementary Volume,* 1980, s.v. "Farband."
"Nahum Glatzer as a Teacher." *Jewish Heritage* 15, no. 1 (1973): 47–49.
"Deutschtum and Judentum in the Ideology of the Centralverein deutscher Staatsbürger jüdischen Glaubens." *Jewish Social Studies* 26, no. 1 (1974): 19–39.
"Consensus and Conflict between Zionists and Liberals in Germany before World War I." In *Texts and Responses: Studies Presented to Nahum N. Glatzer,* edited by Michael A. Fishbane and Paul R. Flohr (Leiden, NL: Brill, 1975).
"From Relativism to Religious Faith: The Testimony of Franz Rosenzweig's Unpublished Diaries." Coauthor with Paul R. Mendes-Flohr. *Leo Baeck Institute Year Book* 22 (1977): 161–74.
"The Origin and Development of the Bund jüdischer Corporationen." *Wiener Library Bulletin* 30, no. 43–44 (1977): 2–7.
"Three Generations of German Zionism." *The Jerusalem Quarterly* 9 (1978): 95–110.
"The Esra Verein and Jewish Colonization in Palestine." *Leo Baeck Institute Year Book* 24 (1979): 261–89.
"Ideology and Structure in German Zionism, 1882–1933." *Jewish Social Studies* 42, no. 2 (1980): 119–46.
"Charisma and Leadership: The Case of Theodor Herzl." Coauthor with Shulamit Reinharz. In *Mystics, Philosophers and Politicians: Essays in Jewish Intellectual*

History in Honor of Alexander Altmann. Edited by Jehuda Reinharz and Daniel Swetschinski, 275–313. Durham, NC: Duke University Press, 1982.

"Chaim Weizmann as Political Strategist: The Initial Years, 1918–1920." In *Essays in Modern Jewish History: A Tribute to Ben Halpern.* Edited by Frances Malino and Phyllis Albert, 271–94. Rutherford, NJ: Fairleigh Dickinson University Press, 1982.

"Achad Haam und der deutsche Zionismus." *Bulletin des Leo Baeck Instituts* 61 (1982): 3–27.

"Martin Buber's Impact on German Zionism before World War I." *Studies in Zionism* 6 (1982): 171–83.

"Chaim Weizmann: The Shaping of a Zionist Leader before the First World War." *Journal of Contemporary History* 18, no. 2 (1983): 205–31.

"Ahad Ha'am, Martin Buber and German Zionism." In *At the Crossroads: Essays on Ahad Ha'am.* Edited by Jacques Kornberg, 142–55. Albany: State University of New York Press, 1983.

"Laying the Foundations for a University in Jerusalem: Chaim Weizmann's Role, 1913–1914." *Modern Judaism* 4, no. 1 (1984): 1–38.

"East European Jews in the Weltanschauung of German Zionists, 1882–1914." *Studies in Contemporary Jewry* 1 (1984): 55–95.

"Chaim Weizmann and the Elusive Manchester Professorship." *AJS Review* 9, no. 2 (1984): 215–46.

"Weizmann and the British General Elections of 1906." *Studies in Zionism* 5, no. 2 (1984): 201–12.

"Science in the Service of Politics: The Case of Chaim Weizmann during the First World War." *English Historical Review* 100, no. 396 (July 1985): 572–603.

"The Zionist Response to Antisemitism in the Weimar Republic." In *The Jewish Response to German Culture: From the Enlightenment to World War II.* Edited by Jehuda Reinharz and Walter Schatzberg, 266–93. Hanover, NH: University Press of New England, 1985.

"Chaim Weizmann: Itsuvo shel manhig tsiyoni lifney milhemet ha'olam harisho-nah." *Yahadut Zmanenu* 2 (1985): 261–84.

"The Zionist Response to Antisemitism in Germany." *Leo Baeck Institute Year Book* 30 (1985): 105–40.

"Chaim Weizmann: Mada besherut hapolitika." *Zmanim* 20 (winter 1986): 5–17.

"Chaim Weizmann: Scientific Marksman and Zionist Leader." *Brandeis Review* 5, no. 3 (spring 1986): 15–19.

"Chaim Weizmann, the East-West Jew." *Jewish Theological Seminary Alumni Association Bulletin* (May 1986): 13–14.

"Hashomer Hatsair in Germany, 1928–1933." *Leo Baeck Institute Year Book* 31 (1986): 173–208.

"Hashomer Hatsair in Nazi Germany, 1933–1938." In *Die Juden im National-Sozialistischen Deutschland, 1933–1943.* Edited by Arnold Paucker, 317–50. Tübingen: J. C. B. Mohr, 1986.

"The Response of the Centralverein deutscher Staatsbürger jüdischen Glaubens to Antisemitism in the Weimar Republic." *Israel and the Nations: Essays Presented in Honor of Shmuel Ettinger*. Edited by Shmuel Almog et al., lxxxv–cx. Jerusalem: Merkaz Zalman Shazar and Historical Society of Israel, 1987.

"Yesod le'universitah ivrit biyerushalayim: Helko shel Chaim Weizmann, 1913–1914." In *Cathedra* 46 (December 1987): 123–46.

"Hashomer Hatsair: Under the Shadow of the Swastika, 1933–1938." *Leo Baeck Institute Year Book* 32 (1987): 183–229.

"The Social Sources of Zionism." Coauthor with Ben Halpern. *Studies in Zionism* 8, no. 2 (autumn 1987): 151–71.

"Liberal and Zionist Leaders in Europe before World War II." In *Jewish Leadership in Modern Times: A Symposium* by Jehuda Reinharz, S. Yizhar, and Yoram Peri, 1–9. Cambridge: Harvard University Library, 1988.

"Advocacy and History: The Case of the Centralverein and the Zionists." *Leo Baeck Institute Year Book* 33 (1988): 113–22.

"Zionism in the United States on the Eve of the Balfour Declaration." *Studies in Zionism* 9, no. 2 (autumn 1988): 131–45.

"Herzl's 'Loyal Opposition' — Chaim Weizmann." In *Vision Confronts Reality, Herzl Yearbook*, no. 9. Edited by Ruth Kozodoy, David Sidorsky, and Kalman Sultanik, 120–70. Rutherford, NJ: Fairleigh Dickinson University Press; London: Associated University Presses, 1989.

"Reflections on the Growth of the Jewish National Home, 1880–1948." *Jewish History: Essays in Honour of Chimen Abramsky*. Edited by Ada Rapoport-Albert and Steven J. Zipperstein, 595–609. London: Peter Halban, 1988.

"Nationalism and Jewish Socialism." Coauthor with Ben Halpern, in *Modern Judaism* 8, no. 3 (October 1988): 217–48.

"The Adjustment of German Jewish Refugees in Palestine, 1932–1939." In *Jewish Solidarity in the Modern Period*. Edited by Binyamin Pinkus and Ilan Troen, 173–94. Beer-Sheva: Ben-Gurion University 1988.

"Weizmann, Acetone and the Balfour Declaration." *Rehovot* 10, no. 4 (1988/89): 3–7.

"Tmurot hevratiyot bamaavar miyishuv lemedinah ribonit." *Skirah hodshit* 35, no. 11 (December 1988): 3–9.

"Chaim Weizmann veyehudei germanyah." *Zion* 44, no. 1 (1989): 73–104.

"Zionisten und Liberale in den Deutschsprachigen Ländern (Deutschland, Österreich und Böhmen)." Coauthor with Benjamin Ben-Baruch. *Bulletin des Leo Baeck Instituts* 82 (1989): 49–63.

"From Yishuv to Sovereign State: Changes in the Social Structure of the Jewish State in the 1940s." In *From Ancient Israel to Modern Judaism: Intellect in Quest of Understanding: Essays in Honor of Marvin Fox*. Edited by Jacob Neusner, Ernest S. Frerichs, and Nahum M. Sarna, vol. 4, 173–87. Atlanta: Scholars Press, 1989.

"Hamaavar miyishuv lemedinah ribonit: Tmurot hevratiyot ve'ideologiyot." *Hatsiyonut* 14 (1989): 253–62.

"Zionism in Germany in the Weimar Period." *Yahadut zmanenu* 5 (1989): 115–26.

"Chaim Weizmann." In *Encyclopedia of the Holocaust*. Edited by Israel Gutman, vol. 4, 1641–43. New York: Macmillan, 1995.

"Hamekorot hahevratiyim shel hatsiyonut." Coauthor with Ben Halpern. *Zmanim* 33 (winter 1990): 73–85.

"Chaim Weizmann." In *Staatslexikon: Recht, Wirtschaft, Gesellschaft*, 5 vols., 7th ed., 919–21. Freiburg: Herder Verlag, 1985–1989.

"Abraham Margaliot: Hahistoryon, ed re'iyah umashkif hasar pniyot." In Avraham Margaliot, *Beyn hatzalah le'avadon: Iyunim betoldot yehudei germanyah (1932–1938)*. Jerusalem: Mekhon Leo Baeck, 1990: 17–21.

"Ahad Ha'Am—In the Eye of the Storm." *Jewish History* 4, no. 2 (fall 1990): 49–58.

"Chaim Weizmann and German Jewry." *Leo Baeck Institute Yearbook* 35 (1990): 189–218.

"Die Ansiedlung deutscher Juden im Palästina der 1930er Jahre." In *Menora: Jahrbuch für deutsch-jüdische Geschichte*. Edited by Julius H. Schoeps, 163–84. Munich, 1991.

"Zionismus und die österreichische Linke vor dem Ersten Weltkrieg." In *Juden in Deutschland. Emanzipation, Integration, Verfolgung und Vernichtung*. Edited by Peter Freimark, Alice Jankowski, and Ina S. Lorenz, 229–51. Hamburg: H. Christians Verlag, 1991.

"The Cultural Background of the Members of the Second Aliyah." Coauthor with Ben Halpern. *Middle Eastern Studies* 27, no. 3 (July 1991): 487–517.

"Building a National Home under the Palestine Mandate." In *Bar Ilan Studies in History*, vol. 3, *Modern History*. Edited by Michael Cohen, 51–66. Ramat Gan: Bar Ilan University Press, 1991.

"The Transition from Yishuv to State, Social and Ideological Issues." In *New Perspectives on Israeli Society: The Early Years of the State*. Edited by Laurence Silberstein, 27–41. New York: New York University Press, 1991.

"His Majesty's Zionist Emissary—Chaim Weizmann's Mission to Gibraltar." *Journal of Contemporary History* 27, no. 2 (April 1992): 259–77.

"Der Aufbau einer Jüdischen Selbstverwaltung und das Parteienspektrum im Palästina der Mandatszeit." In *Deutsch-jüdische Geschichte im 19. und 20. Jahrhundert*. Edited by Ludger Heid and Joachim H. Knoll, 589–611. Bonn and Stuttgart: Burg, 1992.

"European Jewry and the Consolidation of Zionism." In *The Impact of Western Nationalisms*. Edited by Jehuda Reinharz and George L. Mosse, 305–18. London: SAGE Publications, 1992.

"Jewish Nationalism and Jewish Identity in Central Europe." *Leo Baeck Institute Year Book* 27 (1992): 174–67. A shorter version was published in *The Jews in European History*. Edited by Wolfgang Beck. New York: Leo Baeck Institute; Cincinnati: Hebrew Union College Press, 1994.

"The Balfour Declaration and Its Maker: A Reassessment." *Journal of Modern History* 64, no. 3 (September 1992): 455–99.

"Chaim Weizmann: Statesman without a State." *Modern Judaism* 12, no. 3 (October 1992), 225–42.

"The Conflict Between Zionism and Traditionalism before World War I." *Jewish History* 7, no. 2 (fall 1993): 59–78.

"Hanatsig hatsiyoni shel hod malkhuto: Shlihuto shel Chaim Weizmann legibraltar be 1917." *Hatsiyonut* 17 (1993): 99–116.

"Ha'imut beyn tsiyonut umasortiyut lifney milhemet haolam harishonah." *Iyunim* 3 (1993): 366–79.

"Conflits entre sionistes et libéraux en Europe centrale (1880–1920)." In *La société juive à travers l'histoire*. Edited by Shmuel Trigano, 4:425–44. Paris: Fayard, 1993.

"Old and New Yishuv: The Jewish Community in Palestine at the Turn of the Twentieth Century." *Jewish Studies Quarterly* 1, no. 1 (1993/94): 54–71.

"Remarks on Behalf of Participants from Abroad." Eleventh World Congress of Jewish Studies. *Jewish Studies* 34 (1994): 5–7.

"Tsiyonut ve'ortodoksiya: Nisuin shel nohut." In *Tsiyonut vedat*. Edited by Shmuel Almog, Jehuda Reinharz, and Anita Shapira, 141–66. Jerusalem: Merkaz Zalman Shazar, 1994.

"Manhiguto shel Chaim Weizmann: Medina'ut ke'omanut ha'efshari." In *Chaim Weizmann: Hanasi harishon: Mivhar igrot uneumim*, 11–21. Jerusalem: Archive of the State of Israel, 1994.

"Zionism and the Austrian Left before World War I." In *Brücken über dem Abgrund*. Edited by Amy Colin and Elisabeth Strenger, 79–94. Munich: Wilhelm Fink, 1995.

"'Itsuvo shel Chaim Weizmann kemedina'i, 1914–1922." *Kivunim* (December 1994): 99–114.

"Germany, Zionism." In *Encyclopedia of Zionism and Israel*, 2nd ed., 476–84. New York: Herzl Press, 1995.

"United States, Zionism in." In *Encyclopedia of Zionism and Israel*, 2nd ed., 1326–33. New York: Herzl Press, 1995.

"Chaim Weizmann, Acetone and the Balfour Declaration." In *The Interaction of Scientific and Jewish Cultures in Modern Times*. Edited by Yakov Rabkin and Ira Robinson, 183–228. Lewiston, NY: Edwin Mellen Press, 1995.

"Jewish Studies: A Historical Perspective." Forum of the World Union of Jewish Studies. *Jewish Studies* 35 (1995): 5–9.

"Hayishuv be'ikvot milhemet ha'olam harishonah." In *Tmurot yesod ba'am hayehudi be'ikvot hashoah*. Edited by Yisrael Gutman, 383–409. Jerusalem: Yad Vashem, 1996.

"Shorshey hapolitizatsyah shel hatsiyonut batfutsot." In *Leumiyut upolitika yehudit: Perspectivot hadashot*. Edited by Jehuda Reinharz, Yosef Salmon, and Gideon Shimoni, 93–113. Jerusalem: Avraham Harman Institute of Contemporary Jewry, 1996.

"Chaim Weizmann: Statecraft as the Art of the Possible." *Jewish Spectator* 61, no. 4 (spring 1997): 27–35.

"Neumo shel Chaim Weizmann: Divrey parshanut." *Toldot ha'universitah ha'ivrit biyerushalayim.* Edited by Shaul Katz and Michael Hed, 323–26. Jerusalem: Magnes, 1997.

"The Zionist Leadership between the Holocaust and the Creation of the State of Israel." Coauthor with Evyatar Friesel. In *Thinking about the Holocaust after Half a Century.* Edited by Alvin H. Rosenfeld, 83–116. Bloomington: Indiana University Press, 1998.

"Tarbut politit umetsiut baaliyah hashniyah." Coauthor with Ben Halpern. In *Sefer haaliyah hashniyah.* Edited by Israel Bartal, Zeev Zahor, and Yehoshua Kaniel, 11–37. Jerusalem: Yad Ben Zvi, 1998.

"Tguvot ha'agudah hamerkazit vehahitahdut hatsiyonit al ha'antishemiyut biyemey republikat Weimar." In *Toldot hashoah-germanyah.* Edited by Avraham Margaliot and Yehoyahim Kochavi, 13–67. Jerusalem: Yad Vashem, 1998.

"Zionism and Orthodoxy: A Marriage of Convenience." In *Zionism and Religion.* Edited by Shmuel Almog, Jehuda Reinharz, and Anita Shapira, 116–39. Waltham, MA: Brandeis University Press, 1998.

"Ktivat habiografyah shel Chaim Weizmann." In *Ruach Hazman: Leket hartsaot al shem Dr. Chaim Weizmann.* Edited by Merav Segal, 67–91. Jerusalem: Keter, 1999.

"Hatsiyonut kezehut yehudit." In *Idan hatsiyonut.* Edited by Anita Shapira, Jehuda Reinharz, and Jay Harris, 37–44. Jerusalem: Merkaz Zalman Shazar, 2000.

"Zionism and the State of Israel in Historical Perspective." Coauthor with Mark A. Raider. In *Haam hayehudi bameah haesrim.* Edited by Mordecai Naor, 546–51. Jerusalem: Am Oved and Merkaz Zalman Shazar, 2000.

"Hatsiyonut umedinat yisrael beperspektivah historit." Coauthor with Mark A. Raider. In *Haam hayehudi bameah haesrim.* Edited by Mordechai Naor, 546–51. Jerusalem: Am Oved Merkaz Zalman Shazar, 2001.

"Zionism." Coauthor with Mark A. Raider. In *International Encyclopedia of the Social and Behavioral Sciences.* Edited by N. J. Smelser and Paul B. Baltes, 16685–91. Oxford: Pergamon Press, 2001.

"Ha'otonomyah haleumit hayehudit: Hagdarat hathumin ha'ideologiyim." In *Klal yisrael, hashilton ha'atsma'i hayehudi ledorotav,* vol. 3, *The Modern Period.* Edited by Israel Bartal, 251–67. Jerusalem: Merkaz Zalman Shazar, 2004.

"Naftali Halevi kotev leCharles Darvin." Coauthor with Yaacov Shavit. *Haaretz,* November 28, 2008.

"Nahum Goldmann: Jewish and Zionist Statesman." Coauthor with Evyatar Friesel. In *Nahum Goldmann: Statesman without a State.* Edited by Mark A. Raider, 3–59. Albany: State University of New York Press; Tel Aviv: Tel Aviv University Press, 2009.

"Nahum Goldmann and Chaim Weizmann: An Ambivalent Relationship." In *Nahum Goldmann: Statesman without a State.* Edited by Mark A. Raider, 125–38. Albany: State University of New York Press; Tel Aviv: Tel Aviv University Press, 2009.

"Aktuelle Judenfeindschaft: Ein Vergleich zwischen den USA und Deutschland."
    In *Aktueller Antisemitismus in Deutschland—Ein Phänomen der Mitte.*
    Coeditor with Monika Schwarz-Friesel and Evyatar Friesel, 213–24. Berlin:
    De Gruyter, 2010.
"Shifting Sands." *Jewish Review of Books*, Winter 2015.

Reviews

Review of *Chaim Weizmann* by Israel Kolatt and Isaiah Berlin. *American Jewish
    Historical Quarterly* 60, no. 1 (September 1970): 110–13.
Review of *Achdut Ha'avodah, 1919–1930* by Josef Gorni and *Hashomer Hazair
    —From Youth Community to Revolutionary Marxism* (1923–1936) by Elkana
    Margalit. *Societas—A Review of Social History* 5, no. 1 (winter 1975): 81–84.
Review of *Jüdische Selbsthilfe unter dem Nazi Regime, 1933–1939* by S. Adler-Rudel
    and *Island Refuge: Britain and Refugees from the Third Reich, 1933–1939* by A. J.
    Sherman. *Association for Jewish Studies Newsletter* (winter 1975).
Review of *German Jewry*: Part 2, *Additions and Amendments to Catalogue
    no. 3, 1959–1972* (London: Institute of Contemporary History, 1978 [Wiener
    Library Catalogue, ser. no. 6]); *Persecution and Resistance under the Nazis*,
    Part 1: Reprint of Catalogue No. 1, and Part 2: New Material and Amendments
    (London: Institute of Contemporary History, 1978 [Wiener Library Catalogue,
    ser. no. 7]); *Jüdisches Leben in Deutschland, Selbstzeugnisse zur Sozialgeschichte
    im Kaiserreich*, edited by Monika Richarz (Stuttgart: Deutsche Verlags-Anstalt,
    1979); and Isaiah Friedman, *Germany, Turkey, and Zionism, 1897–1918* (New
    York, Oxford University Press, 1977). *American Jewish Society Newsletter*
    (September 1979).
Review of *Stephen S. Wise* by Carl Hermann Voss. *American Historical Quarterly*
    59, no. 4 (June 1970): 534–36.
Review of *Not Free to Desist* by Naomi Cohen. *Midstream: A Monthly Jewish
    Review* (January 1973).
Review of *Israel: A Personal History* by David Ben Gurion. *Jewish Social Studies*
    35, no. 2 (April 1973): 158–60.
Review of *Jewish Reactions to German Anti-Semitism, 1870–1914* by Ismar
    Schorsch. *Jewish Social Studies* 25, no. 3–4 (July-October 1973): 297–99.
Review of *In the Arena* by Emanuel Neumann. *American Jewish Historical
    Quarterly* 67, no. 2 (December 1977): 178–79.
Review of *Society and Religion: The Non-Zionist Orthodox in Eretz-Israel,
    1918–1936* by Menachem Friedman. *AJS Newsletter* 24 (March 1979): 32–33.
Review of *The Letters and Papers of Chaim Weizmann*, Series B: *Papers*. Edited by
    Barnet Litvinoff. *Middle East Studies Association Bulletin* 19, no. 1 (July 1985):
    90–92.
Review of *Berl: The Biography of a Socialist Zionist* by Anita Shapira. *Middle
    Eastern Studies* 22, no. 4 (October 1986): 589–92.

Review of *Arthur Ruppin, Briefe, Tagebücher, Erinnerungen*. Edited by Shlomo
    Krolik. *Studies in Contemporary Jewry* 4 (1987): 400–402.
Review of *The Beginning of the Israeli-Arab Conflict* (Hebrew) by Eliezer Beeri.
    Middle Eastern Studies 23, no. 4 (October 1987): 550–52.
Review of *Ben Gurion: The Burning Ground, 1886–1948* by Shabtai Teveth. *Studies
    in Zionism* 11, no. 1 (spring 1990): 87–90.
Review of *Beterem Puranut* by Hagit Lavsky. *Studies in Zionism* 12, no. 1 (spring
    1991): 93–95.
Review of *Second Chance: Two Centuries of German-Speaking Jews in the United
    Kingdom*. Edited by Werner E. Mosse et al. *Journal of Modern History* 65, no. 4
    (December 1993): 843–45.

EDITORS AND CONTRIBUTORS

Shlomo Avineri is the Herbert Samuel Professor Emeritus of Political Science at the Hebrew University of Jerusalem and a member of the Israel Academy of Sciences and Humanities. He is the author of *Herzl: Theodor Herzl and the Foundation of the Jewish State* (2013).

Arnold J. Band is professor emeritus of Hebrew and comparative literature at the University of California, Los Angeles. He is the author of books and articles on Hebrew literature, both modern and biblical, and has directed thirty doctoral dissertations.

Yehuda Bauer is professor emeritus of history and Holocaust studies at the Avraham Harman Institute of Contemporary Jewry at the Hebrew University of Jerusalem and academic advisor to Yad Vashem. He is the author of *The Death of the Shtetl* (2009).

Michael Brenner is professor of Jewish history and culture at Ludwig Maximilian University in Munich and the Seymour and Lillian Abensohn Chair in Israel Studies at American University, where he directs the university's Center for Israel Studies. He is the author of *A Short History of the Jews* (2010).

Meir Chazan is senior lecturer in the Jewish History Department at Tel Aviv University. He is the author of *Moderation: The Moderate View in Hapo'el hatza'ir and Mapai, 1905–1945* (2009) (Hebrew).

David Ellenson is chancellor emeritus and former president of Hebrew Union College–Jewish Institute of Religion. He is currently a visiting professor at both New York University and Brandeis University. His most recent book is *Jewish Meaning in a World of Choice* (2014).

Immanuel Etkes is professor emeritus of history of the Jewish people at the Hebrew University of Jerusalem. He is the author of *Rabbi Shneur Zalman of Liady: The Origins of Chabad Hasidism* (2014).

Shai Feldman is the Judy and Sidney Swartz Director of the Crown Center for Middle East Studies and professor of politics at Brandeis University. He is the co-author of *Arabs and Israelis: Conflict and Peacemaking in the Middle East* (2013).

David Hackett Fischer is University Professor at Brandeis University. He is the author of *Albion's Seed* (1989) and *Washington's Crossing* (2005).

ChaeRan Y. Freeze is professor of Near Eastern and Judaic studies and women's, gender, and sexuality studies at Brandeis University. Freeze is the coauthor of *Everyday Jewish Life in Imperial Russia: Select Documents, 1772–1914* (2013).

Evyatar Friesel is professor emeritus of Jewish history at the Hebrew University of Jerusalem. He is the coauthor of *Aktueller Antisemitismus—Ein Phänomen der Mitte* (2010) (German).

Sylvia Fuks Fried is executive director of the Tauber Institute. She is associate editor of the Tauber Institute Series, coeditor of the Schusterman Series in Israel Studies, and director of Brandeis University Press.

Motti Golani is professor of Jewish history at Tel Aviv University. He is the author of *Palestine between Politics and Terror, 1945–1947* (2013).

Aviva Halamish is professor of history at the Open University of Israel. She is the author of *Me'ir Ya'ari ha-admor mi-Merhavyah: Shenot ha-medinah* (2013) (Hebrew).

Moshe Halbertal is the Gruss Professor at NYU Law School, professor of Jewish thought and philosophy at Hebrew University, professor of law at the IDC, and a faculty member at the Mandel Leadership Institute in Jerusalem. He is the author of *Maimonides: Life and Thought* (2014).

Eran Kaplan is the Richard and Rhoda Goldman Chair in Israel Studies at San Francisco State University. He is the coauthor of *The Origins of Israel, 1882–1948: A Documentary History* (2011).

Walter Laqueur, a political commentator, historian, and editor, has taught at Brandeis University, Georgetown University, Harvard University, the University of Chicago, Tel Aviv University, and Johns Hopkins University. Most recently he is the author of *Optimism in Politics: Reflections on Contemporary History* (2014).

Frances Malino is the Sophia Moses Robison Professor of Jewish Studies and History and director of Jewish Studies at Wellesley College. She is the coeditor of *Voices of the Diaspora: Jewish Women Writing in the New Europe* (2005).

Paul Mendes-Flohr is professor emeritus of modern Jewish thought at the Hebrew University and the Dorothy Grant Maclear Professor of Modern Jewish History and Thought in the Divinity School at the University of Chicago. He is the coeditor of *The Letters of Martin Buber: A Life of Dialogue* (2013).

Derek J. Penslar is the Stanley Lewis Professor of Israel Studies at the University of Oxford, and the Samuel Zacks Professor of Jewish History at the University of Toronto. He is the author of *Jews and the Military: A History* (2013).

Antony Polonsky is the Albert Abramson Professor of Holocaust Studies at Brandeis University and chief historian at the Museum of the History of Polish Jews. He is the author of *The Jews in Poland and Russia* (2013).

Dina Porat is professor of Jewish history at Tel Aviv University and chief historian at Yad Vashem. She also heads the Kantor Center for the Study of Contemporary Jewry and is the author of *The Fall of the Sparrow: The Life and Times of Abba Kovner* (2010).

Itamar Rabinovich is president of the Israel Institute (DC), professor emeritus of Middle Eastern history at Tel Aviv University, distinguished global professor at New York University, and distinguished fellow at the Brookings Institution. He is the author of *The Lingering Conflict: Israel, the Arabs, and the Middle East, 1948–2012* (2013).

Mark A. Raider is professor of modern Jewish history and a research associate in the Center for Studies in Jewish Education and Culture at the University of Cincinnati. He is also visiting professor of American Jewish history at Hebrew Union College — Jewish Institute of Religion. He is the editor of *Nahum Goldmann: Statesman without a State* (2009).

Shulamit Reinharz is the Jacob Potofsky Professor of Sociology at Brandeis University and founding director of the university's Women's Studies Research Center and of the Hadassah-Brandeis Institute. She is the author of *Observing the Observer: Understanding Our Selves in Field Research* (2010).

Jonathan D. Sarna is the Joseph H. and Belle R. Braun Professor of American Jewish History at Brandeis University and chief historian of the National Museum of American Jewish History. He is the author of *When General Grant Expelled the Jews* (2012).

Daniel R. Schwartz is the Herbst Family Professor of Judaic Studies at the Hebrew University of Jerusalem. He is the author of *Reading the First Century: On Reading Josephus and Studying Jewish History of the First Century* (2013).

Anita Shapira is the founder of the Yitzhak Rabin Center for Israel Studies and professor emerita in Jewish history at Tel Aviv University. She is the author of *Israel: A History* (2012) and *Ben-Gurion: Father of Modern Israel* (2014).

Yaacov Shavit is the Geza Roth Professor of Modern Jewish History at Tel Aviv University. He is the coauthor of *Glorious, Accursed Europe: An Essay on Jewish Ambivalence* (2010).

Eugene R. Sheppard is associate director of the Tauber Institute, associate editor of the Tauber Institute Series, and associate professor of modern Jewish history and thought in the Department of Near Eastern and Judaic Studies at Brandeis University. He is managing coeditor of the Brandeis Library of Modern Jewish Thought and the author of *Leo Strauss and the Politics of Exile: The Making of a Political Philosopher* (2006).

Asher Susser is the Stanley and Ilene Gold Research Fellow at the Moshe Dayan Center for Middle Eastern and African Studies at Tel Aviv University. He is the author of *Israel, Jordan, and Palestine: The Two-State Imperative* (2012).

Stephen J. Whitfield is the Max Richter Professor of American Civilization at Brandeis University. He is the author of *Commerce and Community: A Business History of Jacksonville Jewry* (2010).

Steven Zipperstein is the Daniel E. Koshland Professor in Jewish Culture and History at Stanford University. He is the author of *Elusive Prophet: Ahad Ha'am and the Origins of Zionism* (2012).

INDEX

Abdallah II (king of Jordan), 177, 261, 263

Aberle, David, 493, 527

Abram, Morris, 466, 494–96, 498, 499, 513, 529n5

Agnon, Shai Yosef, 243, 337, 343–44

Ahad Ha'am (Asher Ginsberg): Ben-Gurion and, 171, 175; Brandeis and, 115; on Carlyle, 306; cultural Zionism and, 43, 115, 241; Diaspora Hebrew literary communities, collapse of, 338; on Herzl's *Altneuland*, 30, 43–46, 50–52; on Kishinev pogroms, 369, 370; Weizmann and, 171, 174

aliyah. *See* immigration to Palestine

Almohads and Maimonides, 277–79, 282

Altman, Stuart, 517, 529n5

Altneuland (Herzl, 1902), 28–53; Ahad Ha'am on, 30, 43–46, 50–52; Buber on, 45, 46, 50, 51; David Littwak in, 28, 31, 33–35, 36, 37, 38, 44–45, 48, 49; *Der Judenstaat* and, 28–29, 34, 37, 46, 48; leadership and, 33–35, 210; messianic symbolism in, 66; modern interpretations of, 36–40; Mumford on, 42–43; opera about Shabbetai Zvi in, 25, 30, 31; politics and the New Society in, 28–33; Rosenzweig and, 358n17; utopian genre and, 36–37, 48–50, 51–52

American Jewish Congress, 156–58

American Zionism, 129–39; Brandeis's impact on, 123–25, 129–39; defeat of Brandeis Group by Weizmann forces, 114, 123–24, 130, 158; European Zionists and, 113–14, 116, 118, 119–20; immigrant versus American-born members of, 131–32; Jewish population in America and, 159n1; organizational situation of, 113, 119–23; Szold's impact on, 129–39; views of, 114–19

Anglo-American failure to rescue European Jewry, 239–50; actual ability to do so, 248–50; American Jews and, 239–40, 245–46, 250; antisemitism and, 242, 244, 409; bombing failures, 240, 416–17; historiography of, 239–41; immigration opportunities lost, 239, 241, 242, 243–44; intelligence experts and, 407–9; knowledge of Final Solution, 243, 405–7; possible avenues of rescue, 239–40, 241–42; realization of genocide potential in 1930s, 242–44; Riegner cable and, 246–47, 403–5, 407–9, 411; Roosevelt and, 239–40, 242–45, 249–50; wartime knowledge of Holocaust, 244–50; WRB, 240, 249–50

antisemitism: Brandeis and, 112–13, 117, 118, 123, 126n9; economic impact of Jews, beliefs about, 371–72; failure to rescue European Jewry from Holocaust and, 242, 244, 409, 410; Herzl and, 22–23, 46–51; in Ireland, 102, 107, 109n18; Jewish acculturation, attacks on, 388–89; of Joseph P. Kennedy, 465, 466; Reinharz's experience of, 1, 4, 6, 7–8; Reinharz's study of, 9–10; in Russia, 319, 329; Tuwim and, 386, 388–91; Vilna Gaon